The Ballad of John Latouche

ALSO BY HOWARD POLLACK

Walter Piston

Harvard Composers: Walter Piston and His Students, from Elliott Carter to Frederic Rzewski

John Alden Carpenter: A Chicago Composer

Aaron Copland: The Life and Work of an Uncommon Man

George Gershwin: His Life and Work

Marc Blitzstein: His Life, His Work, His World

The Ballad of John Latouche

An American Lyricist's Life and Work

HOWARD POLLACK

OXFORD
UNIVERSITY PRESS

OXFORD
UNIVERSITY PRESS

Oxford University Press is a department of the University of Oxford. It furthers the University's objective of excellence in research, scholarship, and education by publishing worldwide. Oxford is a registered trade mark of Oxford University Press in the UK and certain other countries.

Published in the United States of America by Oxford University Press
198 Madison Avenue, New York, NY 10016, United States of America.

Library of Congress Cataloging-in-Publication Data

Names: Pollack, Howard.
Title: The ballad of John Latouche / by Howard Pollack.
Description: New York, NY : Oxford University Press, [2017]
Identifiers: LCCN 2016051730| ISBN 9780190458294 (hardcover : alk. paper) | ISBN 9780190458317 (epub)
Subjects: LCSH: Latouche, John, 1914–1956. | Lyricists—United States—Biography. | Librettists—United States—Biography. | LCGFT: Biographies.
Classification: LCC ML423.L2577 P65 2017 | DDC 782.1092
[B]—dc23 LC record available at https://lccn.loc.gov/2016051730

1 3 5 7 9 8 6 4 2
Printed by Sheridan Books, Inc., United States of America

for Erik and Joe

CONTENTS

LIST OF FIGURES

ACKNOWLEDGMENTS

Researching Latouche's life and work presented some distinct challenges. To date, not much has been published about the lyricist, notwithstanding the many brief discussions in memoirs and biographies, and passing references in music and theater studies. The modest Latouche papers at Columbia University, although housing an important, if incomplete, series of diaries, contain little in the way of manuscripts and correspondence. And by the time research for this book began, most of the lyricist's friends and associates were no longer alive.

Fortunately, the papers of, among others, George Balanchine, Leonard Bernstein, Margaret Freeman Cabell, André Cauvin, Maya Deren, David Diamond, Coleman Dowell, Vernon Duke, Duke Ellington, Kenward Elmslie, Lehman Engel, Peggy Glanville-Hicks, Stanton Griffis, Lillian Hellman, Libby Holman, Frederick Kiesler, Leo Lerman, Sam Locke, Eleonora von Mendelssohn, David Merrick, Marta Mierendorff, Douglas Moore, Jerome Moross, Michael Myerberg, Alois M. Nagler, Ruth Page, Dawn Powell, John Powell, Earl Robinson, Lynn Root, Virgil Thomson, Dale Wasserman, Kurt Weill, Ruth Yorck, and most prodigiously, Latouche's agent, Lucy Kroll, filled in many gaps, as did the general collections of the Library of Congress (including recordings held in its Recorded Sound Research Center), New York Public Library (including an important cache of materials that made their way to the library courtesy of Gore Vidal), the National Archives, the FBI, Karamu House, and other institutions.

In addition, I had the good fortune to be able to interview such surviving friends and associates as John Ashbery, Kaye Ballard, Shannon Bolin, Kenward Elmslie, Leyna Gabriele, Ellsworth Kelly, Miles Kreuger, Gerrit Lansing, Norman Lloyd, Robert Miles, Nora Lourie Percival, Willis Pyle, Charlotte Rae, Ned Rorem, Mildred Smith, Harrison Starr, Jerry Stiller, and Susanna Moross Tarjan, as well as some family or family friends, including Libby Green, Burford Latouche Jr., Harold Newman, Vivian Rowsey, and Rose Manning Seigel (with representatives of Latouche's estate kindly permitting me to quote from his unpublished work).

The many librarians and archivists who assisted me on this project included, to name only a few, Richard Boursy and Elizabeth Frengel (Yale University); George

Boziwick, Jeremy Megraw, and Doug Reside (New York Public Library); Anne Causey (University of Virginia); Lynda Claassen (University of California, San Diego); Helen Freeman (Sawyer Free Library); Mark Horowitz and David Sager (Library of Congress); Jennifer Lee (Columbia University); Jill Meissner (Austrian Frederick and Lillian Kiesler Private Foundation); Suzanne Robinson (University of Melbourne); and Ulrich Weber (Swiss National Library). Several of my friends and colleagues provided indispensable aid by researching and photographing archival materials, especially Paul Covey, John Grimmett, Jennifer Kobuskie, and Alex Lawler, but also Grace Edgar, John Gabriel, Johanna Groh, Cory Meals, James Park, Samuel Parler, Anne Searcy, and Alex Winkler. Additional assistance came from, among many others, Edgar Alanis, Dorothy Baker, John Baxindine, Jill Bays-Purtill, Thomas Blubacher, Robert Carsen, Marie Carter, Steven Cassedy, Lucy Dabney, Gordon Davidson, Christina Davis, John Dawson, Shelia Demetriadis, Ellen Donaldson, John Franceschina, Olivia Gay, Hughes Griffis, Eugene Hayworth, Craig Holmes, Michael Holmes, Michael H. Hutchins, David Kanzeg, Nathan Kernan, Marjan Kiepura, Julia Kleinheider, Jane Knox, John Mauceri, Gerald Max, Anne Melville, Catherine Minucci, Darby Moore, Larry Moore, John Moriarty, James O'Leary, Ron Padgett, Tim Page, Rebecca Paller, Maurice Peress, David Perkins, Kenneth Ponche, Kevin Prufer, Phillip Ramey, Tony Root, Max Schmid, Kevin Shannon, Mary Skinner, Stephen Sondheim, Charles Turner, Martha Wasserman, Richard Wilbur, and Gayle Wohlken.

A few debts warrant special acknowledgment. Erik Haagensen, who had conducted enormous research on Latouche in preparation for the 2000 off-Broadway revue about the lyricist, *Taking a Chance on Love*, and his husband, Joseph McConnell, offered extraordinary assistance, including providing me with a wealth of unpublished songs, lyric sheets, scripts, and letters. Furthermore, Haagensen helpfully reviewed this book while still in manuscript, as did Alan Gomberg, Harlan James, Benjamin Sears, and Tony Sessions.

Another windfall came in the form of a rough draft of Andrew Drummond's unpublished monograph on Latouche dating from the 1970s, which the author's widow Maria generously gave me along with accompanying notes and papers. As part of his research, Drummond, a theater professor at New York's Kingsborough Community College, had spoken with numerous people about the lyricist, even traveling abroad to interview writer Paul Bowles, film director André Cauvin, and cabaret singer Spivy LeVoe; his manuscript, as much an omnibus as a biography, not only reported on these conversations but preserved materials, including letters and lyrics, that do not seem to have survived otherwise.

Meanwhile, Alex Lawler, who had assisted me on my previous book, stayed close at hand during this entire project; his extraordinary resourcefulness and unflagging enthusiasm proved a steady boon. And as the book went into production, Thomas Finnegan and Ken Hassman provided the expert copyediting and indexing, respectively.

Finally, a word of thanks to the University of Houston, whose library staff and unstinting support helped make this book possible.

INTRODUCTION

This book stems from the recognition that several eminent American composers, including Earl Robinson, Vernon Duke, Duke Ellington, Jerome Moross, Douglas Moore, and Leonard Bernstein, created some of their most memorable stage work—Robinson's *Ballad for Americans* (1939), Duke's *Cabin in the Sky* (1940), Ellington's *Beggar's Holiday* (1946), Moross's *Ballet Ballads* (1948) and *The Golden Apple* (1954), Moore's *The Ballad of Baby Doe* (1956), and Bernstein's *Candide* (1956)—in collaboration with the Virginia-born lyricist-librettist John Latouche (1914–1956), who died tragically young at the age of forty-one; and that this body of work not only encompasses an impressive variety of styles and genres, ranging from musical comedy and operetta to choral cantata and opera, but also displays a rare standard of skill, wit, and inventiveness.

For Latouche, these milestone achievements formed only part of an astonishingly venturesome and diverse although largely forgotten career, including the creation of such other musical theater pieces as *Banjo Eyes* (1941, music by Vernon Duke); *The Lady Comes Across* (1942, music also by Duke); *Rhapsody* (1944, music by Fritz Kreisler, adapted by Robert Russell Bennett); *Polonaise* (1945, music by Frédéric Chopin, adapted by Bronislaw Kaper); *The Happy Dollar* (1954, music by William Friml, the son of operetta composer Rudolf Friml); and *The Vamp* (1955, music by James Mundy). In addition, Latouche wrote dozens of songs for cabaret acts, theatrical revues, and numerous other uses. Moreover, he translated the poetry of Paul Verlaine and Bertolt Brecht, prepared for American presentation plays by Pierre Beaumarchais, Jean Cocteau, Jura Soyfer, and August Strindberg, and adapted for radio Broadway shows by Sidney Howard and the team of George S. Kaufman and Ring Lardner, all the while writing his own poems, stories, and stage and radio plays.

Latouche also pursued a side career in film, including writing the scenario and narration for the Belgian filmmaker André Cauvin's 1945 documentary *Congo* (and an illustrated travelogue with the same title, also 1945). He further provided songs for two landmark avant-garde feature films by the German-American director Hans

Richter, *Dreams That Money Can Buy* (1947) and *8 x 8: A Chess Sonata in 8 Movements* (1957); authored the script for Herbert Matter's documentary about the sculptor Alexander Calder, *Works of Calder* (1950); and started his own independent film company, Aires Productions, which produced two shorts: the animated *The Peppermint Tree* (1955), based on his poem of the same name, with animation by Willis Pyle, narration by Carol Channing, and music by Donald Fuller; and *The Very Eye of Night* (1956), the last completed film of the notable avant-gardist Maya Deren.

In addition to all this, Latouche undertook numerous aborted and unfinished projects, including some involving composers Kurt Weill, Ernesto Lecuona, Coleman Dowell, and Milton Rosenstock.

In the course of this multifaceted career, Latouche blurred the lines between serious and popular art, and also among different artistic disciplines, as manifested by his varied activities as well as by his interest in creating a lyric theater that would incorporate, in new combinations, music, word, dance, decor, and film. This alone makes his work interesting. Yet at its best, his output further exhibits not only a high level of sophistication, but an enriching humanity, and if only a small portion of his large catalog remains in the repertory, his achievement retains its historical importance as well, especially with respect to cultural life in New York in the mid-twentieth century.

An extraordinary personal life complemented this remarkable professional one. Composer Ned Rorem went so far as to say, paraphrasing Oscar Wilde, that Latouche "put his genius into his life and his talent into his art," although others, including such collaborators as Vernon Duke, Duke Ellington, and Douglas Moore, might have begged to differ, as they considered his work to possess "genius" as well. In any case, he cut a vibrant figure: charismatic, brilliant, querulous, hilariously funny, exuberantly unconventional, extravagantly generous, and to the likes of Rorem and Gore Vidal, surpassingly witty and entertaining company.[1]

Even as a teenager in Richmond, Virginia, the son of a single impoverished mother, herself the daughter of poor Jewish immigrants, Latouche captivated the city's intellectual and artistic elite. Within a short time of his arrival in New York, first to attend Riverdale Country Day School and then Columbia University, he became the admired wunderkind of a circle that included Marc Blitzstein, Paul and Jane Bowles (whom he introduced to each other), Aaron Copland, E. E. Cummings, Edwin Denby, Buffie Johnson, Carson McCullers, Dawn Powell, Virgil Thomson, and Carl Van Vechten. At the same time, he befriended New York's growing refugee artist community, and soon could count among his friends Yul Brynner, Marlene Dietrich, Frederick and Stefanie Kiesler, Erika and Klaus Mann, Eleonora and Francesco von Mendelssohn, Anaïs Nin, and Ruth Yorck. And as a student of psychology and a devotee of the occult and Eastern spirituality, he also developed friendships with such prominent doctors as Max Jacobson, Max Rinkel, and Andrew Salter as well as with the medium Eileen Garrett, ghost hunter Hans Holzer, palmist

Margaret Mamlok, and astrologers Charles Jayne and Natacha Rambova, many of these immigrants as well. Although Latouche never, as he had hoped, made it to Europe, Europe came to him.

By the time of his death, Latouche's Manhattan residence had become one of the city's leading artistic salons, where one could find, in addition to those cited above, such other friends as John Cage, Truman Capote, Ellsworth Kelly, Jack Kerouac, Lena Horne, Frank O'Hara, Sono Osato, Larry Rivers, Orson Welles, Eudora Welty, and Tennessee Williams—a dazzling constellation of diverse artists working in sundry fields, all attracted to Latouche's brilliance and *joie de vivre*, not to mention his support for their work.

Latouche had a similarly elaborate love life. He had affairs, sometimes overlapping, with a number of men, including photographer Harry Dunham, composer Donald Fuller, workman Frank Merlo, dancer Walter Stane, painter Harry Martin, and poet Kenward Elmslie, with whom he purchased a country home in Calais, Vermont, in 1953 as a haven from his hectic city life. But he had romantic involvements with women as well, including in the early 1940s a brief marriage to Theodora Griffis, the mainly lesbian daughter of the prominent businessman and diplomat Stanton Griffis; and in the 1950s an ardent relationship with Alice Bouverie, a scion of New York's baronial Astor family. Suffice to say, Latouche lived a very full forty-one years; commented Ned Rorem, "since he had lived three lives in one, wasn't he really 123 years when he disappeared forever?"[2]

The Ballad of John Latouche

1

John Latouche and His Family

John Treville Latouche was born late in the afternoon of November 13, 1914, at Baltimore's Maryland General Hospital. His parents, Burford and Effie Latouche, only recently had moved to Baltimore from Richmond, Virginia, to which they returned around four months after their son's birth. John—who mostly went by his middle name until about age twenty-one—duly grew up in Richmond, where even to this day, some sixty years after his death, some locals remember him as Treville (pronounced Tre-VILL).

A port city on the James River with a population in the mid-1910s of about 150,000, Richmond had served as Virginia's capital since 1780, when the Commonwealth relocated its government seat there from nearby Williamsburg. Four of the country's first five presidents—George Washington, Thomas Jefferson, James Madison, and James Monroe—had made Richmond their home at one point or another, as did Chief Justice John Marshall. Yet another founding father, Patrick Henry, delivered his legendary "Give me liberty, or give me death!" speech from the pulpit of a Richmond church (as mentioned by Latouche in his popular cantata, *Ballad for Americans*). This rich history helped the Confederate States of America decide to make the city its capital in 1861, and for a few short years Richmond functioned both as the Confederacy's seat under President Jefferson Davis and as its center of military operations under Gen. Robert E. Lee.

However, even before the Civil War, the town had begun to lose prominence compared to other national centers. This relative decline continued after the war, which helped make the city a focal point for the so-called Lost Cause and foster the town's reputation, in historian Virginius Dabney's words, "for stodginess and stuffiness." After visiting Richmond in 1905, writer Henry James commented, "there was something in my whole sense of the South that projected at moments a vivid and painful image—that of a figure somehow blighted or stricken, discomfortably, impossibly seated in an invalid-chair, and yet fixing one with strange eyes that were half a defiance and half a depreciation of one's noticing, and much more of one's referring to, any abnormal sign" (although James at least could recommend "the weird chants of the emancipated blacks"). At the same time, Richmond's tobacco and textile industries and its financial and government services provided a cushion during economic downturns, including the Great Depression (although its segregated black population—who constituted about a third of the city's population during Latouche's boyhood—enjoyed far fewer opportunities than local whites).[1]

Richmond thus developed a dual personality, including close commercial ties with the North even as it sacralized the rural South. "Its head was given to an industrial north," writes Edgar MacDonald, "its heart to an agrarian south. Down the James, it looked eastward to a European homeland; to the west, it felt the lure of the frontier." John Latouche, a man who eventually made New York his home but who retained ties with Richmond, a poet who could pen lyrics of the utmost urbanity alongside verse of folksy charm, would reflect some of these tensions in both his life and work.[2]

Like other provincial capitals of the day, Richmond had its fair share of movie palaces, arts clubs, and nightspots, along with theaters that hosted visiting concert artists and touring companies. And although something of a backwater, early-twentieth-century Richmond could also boast, if no one as exceptional as Edgar Allan Poe (1809–1849), who had spent his early years there, at least three accomplished artists of national repute: writers Ellen Glasgow (1873–1945) and James Branch Cabell (1879–1958) and composer John Powell (1882–1963). In the early 1920s, Richmond even hosted an adventurous little magazine, the *Reviewer*, that during its short tenure published the work not only of Glasgow and Cabell, but of Amy Lowell, Gertrude Stein, Carl Van Vechten, and other advanced authors. Cabell would play a particularly decisive role as a mentor to the young Latouche, but the latter also had some casual contact with Powell and surely would have been familiar with Glasgow and her work as well. In any event, their collective achievement provides something of the background against which Latouche's own work emerged and thus warrants some consideration here.[3]

Although Glasgow, the ironic realist, and Cabell, the allegorical fabulist, appear in some ways opposites, both satirized in their many novels the shibboleths common to their time and place, including lofty sentiments that often disguised vulgar strivings for money, power, and sex. "A Virginian," explained Cabell, tongue in cheek, "must write always about the beauty of chivalry and the peerless moral standards and all the yet other outstanding features of Virginia in fiction." Such mockery made him and Glasgow somewhat heretical locally, even as it won them the admiration of critics of American life like H. L. Mencken. All the same, both Glasgow and Cabell disassociated themselves from some of the more progressive trends of the period and assumed, in general, relatively conservative profiles, their novels maintaining a somewhat acquiescent respect for the ways of life that in many respects repulsed them; "neither could quite give up the idealism and romanticism of the nineteenth century," notes Marie Tyler-McGraw.[4]

Composer Powell cut an even more contradictory figure. Born like Glasgow and Cabell into a privileged Richmond family, he returned to his native city from abroad in 1914 after notable success as a concert pianist. As a composer, he came to widespread attention especially for his symphonic poem *Rhapsodie Nègre* (1918), whose title and style evoked French traditions, but whose distinctive use of black folk idioms anticipated the work of the African-American composer William Grant Still, among others. More characteristically, Powell championed—as composer, lecturer, and promoter—Anglo-American folk music of especially Appalachia, including helping to establish the White Top Music Festival in southwestern Virginia in 1931. This advocacy had its notorious side, as Powell simultaneously promulgated white racial purity through sponsorship of the Anglo-Saxon Clubs of America in 1922 and Virginia's Racial Integrity Law of 1924, although it might be noted that such activities, albeit reviled by many blacks and whites alike, brought Powell and his wife, the playwright and theater director Louise Burleigh (whom he married in 1928), into a cordial alliance with such black Pan-Africanists as Marcus Garvey and his wife, Amy Jacques Garvey.[5]

Latouche's adolescent involvement with community theater in Richmond apparently brought him into some contact with Burleigh, and through her, with Powell; in June 1940, while working for NBC Radio in New York, the twenty-five-year-old Latouche began his only known letter to the composer by saying, "You probably won't remember me—I am the scrubby-kneed boy who used to pop into your house to see your wife every now and then." He now was writing Powell, he explained, to say that through their mutual friend, the folksinger and dulcimer player Andrew Rowan Summers, he had heard about White Top, and to propose that NBC record the festival—which he described to poet Archibald MacLeish as "the most remarkable musical event we have in America"—for national broadcast (a proposal that came to naught, as heavy rains forced White Top to cancel its 1940 and, as it happened, final season). Latouche very likely knew something about Powell's racial politics, which ran counter to his own, but nonetheless recognized some common ground in their interest in American folk balladry, the young writer even assuring Powell that he had been "working in experimental radio and theatre here in New York, basing most of my works on folk sources."[6]

Over time, the titles alone of three of Latouche's most celebrated achievements—*Ballad for Americans*, *Ballet Ballads*, and *The Ballad of Baby Doe*—attested to this shared enthusiasm, as did his general love of traditional ballads. "John was so modest," wrote novelist Carson McCullers in her eulogy for him, "that few people realized he was one of the most profound folk musicians in this country. When he played his little spinit [*sic*] piano I was continually amazed at his repertoire and his astonishing memory. The last time he was in my home in Nyack he was entertaining us all with old English Ballads." Latouche's friend Ruth Yorck similarly recalled him sitting for hours at the piano playing and singing not only American but European folksongs (as well as songs of his own devising, sometimes created on the spot); another friend, Lord Kinross, similarly asserted, "He knew and loved and tried to sing, as he thumped at the piano, all the songs of the English music-hall and the less familiar songs of the English pub." Whether Powell's advocacy and dissemination of folk music directly or indirectly influenced Latouche, their Richmond backgrounds surely helped frame their understanding and appreciation of African-American and Anglo-American folklore.[7]

The connection with Cabell would prove much closer, both personally and artistically, as will be shown. But Latouche fundamentally inhabited a different world from these older Richmonders, not only because he was some thirty years their junior and spent his adult life in New York, but because his irrepressible nonconformity set him apart from their more conventional habits and attitudes. He vehemently decried the treatment of blacks in the South and otherwise distanced himself from many Southern traditions, admitting in a 1935 college profile that he "early acquired a dislike for hominy, Civil War veterans, ginger ale without gin, and the word, 'you-all,' " and telling a journalist in 1940 that he lost a youthful job reviewing books for the *Richmond News Leader* for "panning every book about the South." That said, he retained many aspects of his Southern heritage in his art and his lifestyle, right down to his melodious Virginian accent and the black-eyed peas served at New Year's, not to mention his penchant for walking about barefoot even when fully clothed and talking "white Southern trash" when deep into his cups. "One has only to step into his Greenwich Village apartment," reported the *Richmond Times-Dispatch* in 1949, "to recognize that here is the home of a cosmopolitan artist whose way of life has been tempered by the graciousness and charm of the South."[8]

In 1940, following the great success of *Ballad for Americans*, the newly founded *Current Biography* published an article on the work's little-known librettist; this entry subsequently became a seminal source of information on Latouche, making it all the more regrettable that it contained so many erroneous and misleading statements, most if not all apparently originating with the subject himself.[9]

For a start, the article stated that Latouche was born in 1917, not 1914, a fabrication that the lyricist largely maintained for the rest of his life, to the point that when he died in 1956, not only his obituaries but his death certificate gave 1917 as his year of birth (although adding to the confusion, his gravestone put his birth year as 1915, the year he also provided to the military as his date of birth). Latouche had been shaving off a year or two from his age as early as January 1939, when the press alternately reported him to be twenty-two or twenty-three, not twenty-four; he presumably reasoned that such prevarication could only enhance his reputation as "the boy wonder of Broadway." Along these lines, he told *Current Biography* that while at Columbia he had won the Stephen Vincent Benét Prize for Being Generally Astonishing While Awfully Young—which sounds like a joke at the expense of Benét, but which points nonetheless to some pride in his own precociousness (which in fact needed no exaggeration). More seriously, this preoccupation with youthfulness informed much of his work, including his last major effort, *The Ballad of Baby Doe*, which meaningfully concludes with the words, "ever young."[10]

Current Biography further reported, "Although he looks French (he is dark-complexioned and has light blue eyes) and his name is French, Latouche is actually of Irish descent. The explanation is that at the time of the Edict of Nantes many Frenchmen came to Ireland and settled there; later many came to America. Among those was his great-grandfather, who became a wealthy landowner in Virginia." Latouche similarly had claimed French-Irish lineage some years earlier in a thumbnail profile for Columbia's 1935 Varsity Show program book, and asserted elsewhere to have descended from French Huguenots, and to have been christened John Patrick Diggs Treville Latouche, a name that would suggest some Irish ancestry as well. Privately, he also professed to have descended from a medieval French nobleman from the Poitou region of France, a drawing of whose family crest he apparently received from Pierre de La Nux, the son of André Gide's piano teacher, Max de La Nux. "I dont have to tell you," Latouche added to a friend with respect to this genealogical claim, "how unimportant I consider such things; God knows, the sorry mess his descendents made of themselves would bleach the most azure of bloodstreams."[11]

Aside from the fact that French Protestants would not have left France because of the Edict of Nantes but rather because of its revocation a century later, surviving documents, including censuses, tell a different story. Latouche's great-grandfather John Latouche (1820–1890) was the British-born son of a Frenchman and an Englishwoman, and a possible descendant of the famed late-eighteenth-century French naval commander Louis-René Levassor de Latouche-Tréville, who fought in the American Revolution (perhaps explaining the lyricist's comment to his mother, after joining the navy, "I suppose there's enough seawater left in the Latouches' blood to get me worked up about it"). An accomplished custom tailor, this great-grandfather—who appears to have been the same John Latouche who, as a lieutenant in the Twenty-fifth Virginia Infantry Battalion of the Confederacy, supervised guards at Richmond's infamous Libby Prison—had several children with the Maryland-born Fannie Weeks (or Wicks, c. 1830–1899), including not only the lyricist's grandfather John Santees, but a great-uncle Treville, after whom the lyricist in part would be named, and another great-uncle Louis, after whom his brother would be named. Grandfather John Santees Latouche (c. 1868–1946) in turn married a Virginia native, Neva St. Clair (St. Clare) Duggins (c. 1872–1951), with whom he had six surviving children: the lyricist's father, Archer Louis Burford (known both as "Archie" and "Burford"), along with John St. Clair, Marie Louise (later, Abbott), Victor Burnett, Leon Lafayette, and Neva St. Clair (later, Niewoehner).[12]

Grandfather John continued the family tailoring business, typically operating out of one or another storefront on Main Street, Richmond's principal thoroughfare. His son Burford (1894–1947) worked in his late teens as a clerk, but by his twenties had taken up tailoring and laundering as well. Like most of his family, Burford received little formal education, completing only six grades of school, although he could write tolerably well, as an extant letter documents.[13]

Thus, the oft-made contention, principally derived from *Current Biography*, that Latouche descended paternally from a wealthy landowner of Franco-Irish lineage appears more fantasy than anything else, for he plainly came, on his father's side, from a family of humble tailors of mostly English origin. Given his difficult and impoverished childhood, the lyricist perhaps compensated by identifying with the cachet of Virginian planter aristocracy and the glamor surrounding, say, the French-Irish-American heroine of Margaret Mitchell's novel *Gone with the Wind* and its popular 1939 movie adaptation (although Latouche thought the film, as he wrote to this mother, "bad beyond belief. . . . I am one of the traitors who has a vague idea that the South did lose it [the Civil War]"). No Patricks or Diggses seem to appear in Latouche's family line, although there existed a well-known aristocratic Irish family, Digges Latouche, descended from French Protestants; considering the lyricist's penchant for embellishing the truth, he might have rechristened himself accordingly. At any rate, *Current Biography* compounded its error-riddled account of Latouche by referring to the writer's father as deceased, whereas Burford then was residing, as he had for some time, at a state mental institution.[14]

Latouche further misled *Current Biography* by omitting any mention of his Jewish parentage on his mother's side. Indeed, apart from an early 1932 description of himself, in an anthology of high-school verse, as "the product of a conglomerate ancestry, with Irish, French, and Jewish blood the principal strains," Latouche rarely referred to his Jewish background, about which he felt "conflicted" and "fearful," according to his partner, Kenward Elmslie; he rather presented his ethnicity as Franco-Irish or more simply Irish even to his closest friends. Writer Gore Vidal, for instance, called him "a short chunky Irish wit" (although he knew enough to add, "with the obligatory Jewish mother"), while another friend, the medium Eileen Garrett, wrote in her memoirs, "Although Latouche had not visited Ireland, the land of leprechauns and fairies was in his heritage." Actress Carol Channing described not only Latouche but even his mother, Effie, "with her white Irish lace collar and cuffs," as Irish. Meanwhile, in her memoirs, Ruth Yorck, although herself Jewish, discussed his ancestry exclusively in terms of his French background, even though his bloodline appears to have been only one-sixteenth French.[15]

In fact, both Latouche's maternal grandparents were Jewish immigrants: Morris Seigel (c. 1850–c. 1918) came to America from Germany in 1880, Jennie (c. 1874–1928), from Russia in 1891. Jennie's gravestone identifies her, in Hebrew, as Sheinah Glike, the daughter of Reb Chaim Manush Halevi, that is, Chaim Manush of the tribe of Levi. Family lore holds that this Chaim Manush—Latouche's great-grandfather—was a rabbi (as the honorific "Reb" might suggest), and further contends that Jennie had been a mail-order bride, or that the marriage had been otherwise arranged, a notion supported by the fact that she and Morris married about 1892, shortly after Jennie, still in her teens, arrived in the United States.[16]

Morris appears to have been an itinerant peddler dealing in second-hand clothes, trekking through Illinois, Pennsylvania, Virginia, and Ohio before settling in Richmond at the turn of the century. The Virginia capital had a small but vibrant and tightly knit Jewish community, dating back to the eighteenth century, that over the years had established several institutions that addressed its special needs, including the *Jewish South,* a weekly paper founded in 1893—by which year, the town's approximately three thousand Jews made up around 4 percent of the local population. As a whole, the city seemed to take pride that, as the *Richmond Times-Dispatch* stated in 1905, "A Jew born and reared in Virginia is a Virginian, and is treated as a Virginian," which however left unanswered the question of the treatment of Jews like Morris or Jennie born elsewhere; and indeed, the new wave of poor Eastern-European Jewish immigrants, as opposed to older Sephardic and German-Jewish immigrants, often faced increased discrimination with respect to housing, employment, and education, not to mention hotels and clubs. "You do not have to go a thousand miles from Richmond," stated a local rabbi in 1910 in response to such exclusionary practices in New York, "to find these conditions. We have this same sort of snobocracy in our own fair city."[17]

As they moved from state to state, Morris and Jennie Seigel had a number of children, six of whom survived to adulthood: Mary (later, Bottoms), Essie ("Effie," later Latouche), Rosa ("Rose," later Chandler, then Mimms), Abraham ("Abe"), Joseph, and Emanuel ("Manny"). Effie (1895–1964), the lyricist's mother, was born in Chicago. Her given name appears as Etta or Ethel in some early sources, but as Essie Evelyn or, more commonly, Effie in later ones; at some point, although apparently after her divorce from Burford Latouche, she also assumed "Tupper" as her maiden name, often identifying herself as E. E. Tupper Latouche or Effie Tupper Latouche.

In Richmond, Latouche's maternal grandparents established a used clothing business at 1908 East Main in Shockoe Bottom, an area long central to the town's Jewish community, and not far either from where Edgar Allan Poe had spent his adolescence, indeed, on the same block as the Old Stone House that today serves as the city's Poe Museum. According to family accounts, Morris, who often traveled out of town, was alcoholic, abusive, and possibly a bigamist; a newspaper item reported in 1909 that during a row in which Jennie had attempted to send Morris away after six months' absence, Morris stabbed her in the legs and stomach with an ice pick. The circumstances surrounding Morris's final years remain unknown—he's thought to have died in the mid-1910s—but his much younger widow continued the clothing business at one or another East Main Street address practically to her death in 1928.[18]

Like children from other poor families, the Seigel siblings cut short their schooling to help support their family. Effie worked as a packer in a tobacco factory before, at age fifteen, she and the seventeen-year-old Burford Latouche, still a clerk living at home, took the so-called Cupid's Express train with ten other couples on April 17, 1911, to get married that day in Washington, D.C. (On their marriage application, they gave their ages as nineteen and twenty-one, respectively.) The three Seigel boys, for their part, apparently inherited something of their father's unruly ways: in 1918, the police apprehended Abraham for shooting a black chauffeur in the arm after a traffic accident; and in 1930, Joseph and Emanuel received a four-month jail sentence and a $100 fine for violating Prohibition.[19]

Burford and Effie at first lived with the former's parents, but as mentioned, they moved to Baltimore shortly before John's birth in 1914, and soon after circled back to Richmond, where they attempted to establish themselves as tailors and launderers themselves. In the spring of 1917, they relocated to Penniman, a new ammunitions plant town outside Williamsburg, but soon returned again to Richmond, residing mostly at downtown addresses, although in 1919, about the time they had a second boy, Louis Burford, they moved to East Highland Park, a suburban neighborhood north of the city.[20]

Despite growing up in an historic Jewish neighborhood, and Jennie Seigel's lifelong attachment to Jewish traditions, including attendance at Richmond's historic Orthodox synagogue, Keneseth Beth Israel, Effie and her siblings tended to marry outside their religion and reject their Jewish background as socially stigmatic, with Rosa becoming devoutly Catholic. In Effie's case, she essentially raised her sons as Protestant, providing them with a Christian religious education; John even won an elaborately inscribed Bible when he was about ten years old, as his mother later recalled, for memorizing dozens of verses from Scripture. At the same time, John surely inherited certain aspects of his Jewish heritage, and his swarthy "French" looks and ironic "Gallic wit" with reason could be described as Jewish-American as much as anything else.[21]

As an adult, Latouche identified himself as "Protestant by conviction," even as he contributed gifts in the 1950s to the Abbey of Regina Laudis, a community of nuns in Bethlehem, Connecticut. He further maintained an interest in biblical literature, and spoke respectfully of his Christian faith, although within limits: "Christianity and modern thought have finally taught us to be tolerant of the faults of others, but it is extremely difficult to tolerate the pleasures of others, for even the most civilized of us," he wrote in his journal in 1944. In contrast, he generally made little explicit reference to anything Jewish, although in his diary, he occasionally excoriated anti-semitism, even as he indulged in some stereotyping himself, noting while in the navy, for instance, the "caricature Jew in the next bunk" who "turned out to [be] charming, and a great admirer of [Paul] Bowles' music. Someone literate in camp anyway, thank God." In a transcribed conversation with his doctor, Max Jacobson, in 1949, he also showed deep admiration for the new state of Israel and characteristic fascination with something so fanciful as British Israelism, the belief that the British, including the monarchy, descended from the ancient Israelites. (This same conversation, which occurred during Passover, also documented some fluency in Yiddish; asking Jacobson for some matzo and salami, he requested "a bissel of yontif," that is, "a little bit of the holiday.") However, Latouche's sprawling spiritual interests centered not so much on either Christianity or Judaism as on far-Eastern religions—Hinduism, Confucianism, Taoism, and Zen Buddhism—and on such occult arts as astrology, tarot, and telepathy.[22]

As it turned out, Effie married a man all too much like her father: not only a poor provider, but a violent alcoholic whose blows allegedly caused her to miscarry a child. She finally brought charges against him and the two divorced in early 1923, when son John was eight years old. After spending some time in Western State Hospital in Staunton, marrying one Fannie Price in 1925, working as a barber in Richmond, and once again moving to Baltimore, Burford wrote Effie in 1927 a contrite letter in which he blamed "whisky and bad company" for his past misconduct, and apologized, as a man "starting to live a Christian life," for all "the many years of suffering" he had caused her and her mother (both of whom he described as "good, true, and kind to all friends"). He further assured her that he still cared about her and offered to pay three dollars a week in child support (a paltry sum even then). He even proposed that John, now age twelve, come to Baltimore to study at the Peabody Institute, indicating that music had assumed at this point some central importance in the young lad's life.[23]

The following year, in 1928, Burford and his new wife, Fannie, had a son, Burford Jr., but that family also quickly dissolved; the 1930 census found Fannie at Western State Hospital and Burford living again with his parents in Richmond. Burford Jr. was placed in the care of the boy's maternal grandparents, who raised him. Subsequently, Fannie divorced Burford and remarried, becoming Fannie Nunnally, while Burford was admitted to another mental health institution, Eastern State Hospital, outside Williamsburg. During these later years, even long before Burford's death in 1947, Effie commonly referred to herself as a widow, much as her son John described himself as fatherless (which to all practical purposes he was).[24]

As a single mother still in her twenties, Effie eked out a living as a seamstress. "My father faded out of our lives early," Latouche stated in 1949, "leaving the support and rearing of me and my brother to my mother. As has happened to so many mothers, she had to turn to her needle for our support. I helped when I could and as much as I could, but yet my mother saw to it that I had time for schooling and association with families which made me a part of the culture of the South. She was marvelous." Such assistance on John's part included delivering newspapers with his younger brother, Louis, and finding employment in his early teens as a clerk.[25]

During these hard years, Effie continued the seemingly endless peregrinations that had marked her married life, including living for a while in the mid-1920s with her ex-husband's uncle and aunt, Frederick and Frances ("Fannie") Latimer, who frightened young John with stories about "bloody bones who lived in the closet under the stairs." In the early years of the Depression, with John now in high school, the family's circumstances apparently worsened all the more, forcing them into a series of mostly unpleasant boarding houses. Years later, after chronicling, at John's request, their many addresses during this period, Effie added, "Perhaps you wonder why so much moving around—Well—that is something I cannot bring myself, to write about." But she expressed satisfaction that after he graduated from high school, John was "lucky enough to shake the dust of Richmond, off your shoes."[26]

As Latouche pursued his later education and career in New York, Effie continued her work as a seamstress, eventually securing a position as a tailor for Berry-Burk, a large and well-regarded clothier in downtown Richmond. During these years, John aided his mother financially, and after he moved into a large top-floor apartment on East 67th Street in 1952, she spent considerable time there herself, in part to help with housekeeping chores and otherwise bring some order to her son's chaotic life. After John's death in 1956, Effie stayed in Manhattan until her own death in 1964, living in an apartment on the Upper West Side. Meanwhile, her son Louis, after serving in the army during World War II, remained in the Richmond area with his wife, Ora Lee, he working as a salesman, she, as a seamstress. Louis died in 1962, two years before his mother.[27]

Effie helped nurture John's talent, encouraging his early education and submitting his juvenilia to magazines for publication. She clearly took great delight in her son's accomplishments, hiring a charter bus so that Virginian friends could attend a post-Broadway Washington performance of Latouche's 1954 opera *The Golden Apple,* with the lyricist commenting, after the show won the New York Drama Critics' Circle Award, "Effie is having my swelled head for me. She rides up and down in the apartment elevator asking everyone, 'Did you know we won the Critics Award?'" For his part, Latouche basked in his mother's pride; on the day of the Central City world premiere of *The Ballad of Baby Doe,* he made of point of standing "outside the Teller House all afternoon talking to people and telling each, in turn, that his mother had flown in for the performance too."[28]

A good cook, Effie loved to host parties, and after moving to New York, she enjoyed entertaining many of her son's friends, some of whom she remained close with even after her son's death; in 1958, for instance, she cared for an ailing Jane Bowles, then convalescing in Tennessee Williams's apartment. "Mrs. LaTouche is pert and dynamic and her famous son is the image of her," observed a journalist at the time of the premiere of *The Ballad of Baby Doe.* "Everyone recognizes her without an introduction." Writer Coleman Dowell, who came to loathe Latouche, remained nevertheless inordinately fond of Effie, whose seeming obliviousness regarding the homosexuality of Latouche and his friends he found charming: "She was small, plump, disingenuous, full of appalling, unfunny Southern stories, and was delightful." Latouche's agent, Lucy Kroll, also liked Effie, writing to the latter's sister in 1964, after both Effie and John had died, "You know that Effie was so dear to me and John was like my brother." In contrast, several other of Latouche's friends, such as poets Kenward Elmslie and Gerrit Lansing, thought Effie, whatever "mystical blood understanding" she shared with her son, boorishly provincial and uneducated. "All she ever talked about was food," remarked Paul Bowles.[29]

Latouche's relationship with his mother, as with virtually all those close to him, had its share of emotional volatility. Coleman Dowell—although not the most reliable witness—claimed that the two "would fight fearsomely; he would back her into a corner threatening mayhem." All the same, as evidenced by his postcards and letters to her (sometimes addressed "dearest mother" or "dearest one," but most often "dear Effie," and alternately signed, "John," "J," and "Treville"), Latouche could be an effusively loving and appreciative son, telling Effie in June 1955, for instance,

> the past year especially, I do not know how I could have survived the going without you. At the same time, with all the personal and temperamental difficulties that had to be adjusted, I feel that I have gotten to know you better than I ever did—not only as a "mother," but as a person; and a vital, remarkable person you turn out to be indeed. I become increasingly aware that part of the persistent energy I have, (which offsets my tendency to melancholy and depression) comes from you—an energy which continues plugging away in the face of the most terrible discouragements ... the feeling of your belief in me helps to smooth the rigors of an unpredictable and sometimes appalling world.... You are a bouncing, cheerful angel, and I love you.

A few months later, after the two had decided on a state of "interdependence" rather than "dependence" or "independence," he wrote to her from Vermont, "at a distance, I realize how fortunate I am in having such a dear and loving mother, who at the same time is still young enough to be a companion and friend—and still young enough to grow in depth of understanding." Effie described such correspondence to Coleman Dowell as "love lettahs—jest exactly like a lettah from a lovah."[30]

Latouche maintained only distant relations with other family members. He seems to have been somewhat close to his uncle Leon Latouche, a hospital corpsman "ideally located in the Navy," of whom the lyricist further wrote in 1951, "he still has an emotional quotient of roughly (the adverb is ill-chosen) ten years. A real old fashioned Miss Priss; rather touching, for all that." Regarding his mother's family, he had most contact with Effie's sister Rosa and her large family, but an intriguing connection also emerges with respect to his uncles Abraham and Emanuel: for many years, the former entertained children and adults dressed as Santa Claus, while the latter appeared at Shriner events as a clown—a striking concurrence given Latouche's own reputation as a jester and clown.[31]

As for brother Louis, their relationship deteriorated over the years. Louis apparently became jealous and resentful of his famous older brother, whose middle name, Treville, he seems to have adopted as his own. On his side, John increasingly distanced himself from Louis, whose drunken and violent behavior painfully reminded him of his father, and perhaps of himself as well. Indeed, with an alcoholic and abusive grandfather, father, and brother, Latouche must have been all too aware of this dark legacy on both sides of his family, and, as his diaries make abundantly clear, he worked hard if fitfully—through diet, exercise, yoga, and psychoanalysis—to avoid a similar fate.[32]

Finally, Latouche had some remote contact with his half-brother, Burford Jr., who became a Virginia businessman, and who had only casual relations with the Latouches. Burford Jr.'s two boys—Burford III and Thomas, neither of whom had sons—would appear the last descendants of the lyricist's paternal grandparents to bear the Latouche name.[33]

2

The Young Writer

Latouche had what seems to have been in many ways an unhappy, anxious childhood—hardly surprising given the poverty, rootlessness, abuse, alcoholism, and psychosis that plagued his family. "Last night I lay in bed, awake, petrified with fear that there was someone coming in the unlocked door . . . ," he wrote in his journal in 1938. "I was completely awake, but reality took on the form of a nightmare. When I was a child afraid of the dark I was possessed by such terrors, but I am now a man, and still those doors may be opened, letting out old terrors retained as long, flooding my brain with fears." Such "terrors" haunted Latouche his entire life, including his dread of sleeping in the dark.[1]

The young Treville, as he was then known, at least found that the arts provided some solace. Near the end of his life, he said of his childhood,

> When life became unbearable I would retire to the Bluebird and Isis Theaters [two Richmond movie theaters on Broad Street]. At seven I saw [Alla] Nazimova in "Salome," which was so extraordinary that I wanted to get through the archway surrounding the screen to that glamorous world it framed. The next day I climbed the telegraph pole behind the theater and through a window so that I was behind the screen, with the images reversed. I touched it but couldn't get into that one-dimensional magic.

This little escapade—which had him thrown out of the theater—gave evidence of not only early artistic sensibilities, but also an innate adventurous streak; meanwhile, the specific allure of Nazimova's Salome anticipated the presence of various vamps and sirens in his theatrical work, including an apparently lost revue sketch entitled "How It Feels to Be Mae West."[2]

Latouche showed his emerging artistic proclivities in other ways. According to one of his aunts, during his family's time in Penniman, Virginia, which would put him at about age five, he danced and passed the hat for sailors at the local YMCA. Back in Richmond, he started staging garage theatricals, including one in which he played Dracula, and his friend Jean Clarke Wood, his principal victim. Latouche must have had these early shows in mind, perhaps this very one, when he spoke about his first play at age eleven, *The Gypsy Legend, or The Lover from the Grave*:

> It was a smash hit with the neighborhood children, and netted $.53....
>
> Next followed *Things That Walk in Darkness*, which frightened so many children into hysterics that further productions were banned. The play, though an artistic failure, was a financial success—it brought in $1.84, clear profit, since the scenery and costumes were shamelessly stolen from unfinished houses and unsuspecting mothers. The author has never grown away from this theory.

And at age fourteen, on Halloween night, presumably in 1929, he presented in the basement of a friend's home another show, *Walpurgis Eve*, which so frightened his kiddie audience that they left in "convulsions," according to Jack Woodford (pen name for Josiah Pitts Woodfolk, 1894–1971), the Chicagoan writer who made Richmond his occasional home during these years. "It was a honey," wrote Woodford. "It expressed the Halloween spirit perfectly: sadism." In a similar vein, Latouche arranged a mock funeral for a friend's doll, complete with a burial in the girl's backyard, confirming a youthful taste for what might be called, given his background, Southern Gothic.[3]

However he came by his musical abilities, Latouche also learned enough piano while still in his teens—if Woodford can be believed—to perform Claude Debussy's *Trois Chansons de Bilitis* for voice and piano (from Pierre Louÿs's sapphic collection of poems). Indeed, as mentioned, music became for Latouche something of a focus at about age twelve, to judge from his father's suggestion that he come to Baltimore to study at the Peabody Institute.[4]

Books became another great love. He read widely and voraciously throughout his life, early devouring the Tom Swift and Tarzan adventure novels of Edward Stratemeyer and Edgar Rice Burroughs as well as, soon enough, the writings of Freud and the Swiss Renaissance scientist Paracelsus. In his autobiography, Woodford—who remembered meeting the hungry and tattered Treville at about age thirteen, and whose petite blond daughter, Louella Woolfolk, became the lad's close friend—claimed that by the time Latouche reached his midteens, "he had read all of the world's literature, some of it in French, and he had picked up a smattering of other languages from [James Branch] Cabell and his own study." Discovering that Latouche could absorb books with lightning speed—a trait substantiated by later observers such as filmmaker André Cauvin, who marveled at the lyricist's astonishing memory—Woodford even had writer and editor Edward Aswell, on a visit to Richmond, put the young man to the test by having him quickly read a book "on some esoteric subject" and exhaustively questioning him afterward about its contents: "Aswell agreed then with all the local illuminati that Virginia had another Poe to snub on its hands, except that this one appeared to be a thousand times more brilliant." Woodford further mentioned that Latouche, who reminded him of a modern François Villon, would neglect to return certain books checked out from the public library on the grounds that local Richmonders would have no interest in them. "This sort of thing was constantly leading to explosive situations involving the police and everybody who knew him [Latouche]," recalled Woodford. "But he knew so many influential people that somebody always squared the beef somehow."[5]

Latouche's digesting of books assumed a weirdly literal dimension, as revealed years later in one of his diary entries. Allegedly, as early as six years old he became fascinated with certain words, among them, the word "fatigued." On one occasion, eager to use the word, he told his nursery school teacher, "Oh, Miss Rhine, I'm just so fatigooed," which elicited laughter from a visiting adult and in turn the children in the class, and which prompted his teacher to admonish, "Little boys shouldn't try to swallow the dictionary." Recalled Latouche, "The boy who swallowed the dictionary—for months this terrible phrase haunted my dreams, and I could see it happening in a literal sense. Even today, I still absently tear off the corners of books and chew them, partly due to a habit arising out of a vitamin deficiency, no doubt, but also due to some animistic motivation that somewhat by eating the books, I would absorb the wisdom in them."[6]

Latouche made his first real mark as a writer while at Richmond's John Marshall High School, which he attended from the fall of 1928 through the spring of 1932. Named for the famous chief justice on whose former property it then stood, John Marshall functioned as one of the region's leading educational institutions, from its opening in 1909 until its demolition in 1961. A large, three-story stone building, with an imposing neoclassical façade, the school aimed to further secondary education among white Richmonders as a whole, hence its reputation as "the people's university." By the time Latouche enrolled, the school had so fulfilled such ambitions that its population of more than three thousand students required imposition of two shifts, an overcrowding finally relieved in 1930 with the opening of Thomas Jefferson High School northwest of downtown.[7]

Several former teachers and schoolmates remembered Latouche as an ill-kempt "slum child" who resented his poverty. He also developed a reputation for eccentricity, telling fellow students that he had been born at the stroke of midnight during a thunderstorm on Friday the thirteenth, arriving at a costume ball dressed in a monk's garb and sandals as St. Simeon Stylites, reportedly drinking nearly a gallon of cocoa at a school reception, and coming to class with no shirt under his overcoat. (He would continue to dress unconventionally, with a college profile, for instance, describing his "favorite exercise" as "not putting on a shirt.") One English teacher, Walter Beverly, recalled further that he drew pictures to describe grammatical concepts, while his history teacher Sadie Engleberg remembered how he refused to interrupt his reading Radclyffe Hall's groundbreaking 1928 lesbian novel *The Well of Loneliness* for an exam ("This book is far too important to stop reading for a test," he protested), until she informed him that she too had read the controversial novel, at which point he relented. In early 1931, his peers voted him "most original boy," and when questioned about this honor by his school paper, he responded, "I was greatly surprised as I didn't expect it," before breaking into a British folksong that had the "agonized reporter" scurrying away. As in later years, many felt the force of his unorthodox personality, and by his junior year he had acquired a "coterie." "We regarded him as a genius...," recalled one high school friend in 1939. "He was allergic to discipline, and completely impervious to convention."[8]

At the same time, Latouche became involved in all sorts of high school clubs and activities, joining the Writers' Club, Dramatic Club (also called the Scarlet Maskers), French Society, and Harwood Literary Society (a public-speaking group), and contributing regularly to the school's weekly, the *Monocle*, which began publication during his freshman year, and which, under the formidable supervision of his female English teacher Charles Anthony, quickly won acclaim as one of the best high-school papers in the region. Under the byline Treville La Touche (or alternately, Trevil La Touche), he started a column of his own—initially entitled "The Snoop," but later "Fragments"—that itself received statewide recognition, as did his contributions to the school's literary magazine, the *Record*.

The "Fragments" columns typically included a brief prose poem, some editorial reflections, chatty one-liners about various students and teachers, and a short poem or two. The prose poems suggest some absorption of recent aesthetic currents, as any number of opening lines illustrate: "The sun is a golden bowl that God has hammered out of the laughter of a woman dressed in a silver robe"; "The wan light of these deserted moons, Atrea, throws the whiteness of your hand into a faint memory of rose-petals"; "We will garner roses in newer granaries of dreams: that shall be the accomplishment of newer skies, after noon has gone"; and so on. Latouche's little commentaries, meanwhile, display a certain preoccupation and ambivalence with respect to questions of tradition and modernity; he mocks Victorian prudery and sentimentality (alluding to Joyce Kilmer's "Trees" he writes, "Poems are made by anyone / But only I can make a pun") and rejects the concept of "an All-seeing Providence," but he also parodies dadaist esotericism and at one point writes, "In casting aside old conventions and old fashions, we have cast aside, too, something of the consideration and companionship of the older generation." Such tensions seem to echo the attitudes of some of Richmond's established intelligentsia, including his friends Marie and T. Todd Dabney and his eventual mentor James Branch Cabell, whose influence can be discerned in the young writer's baroque style and arch tone.[9]

These "Fragments" rarely allude to larger world affairs; as an exception, Latouche derides those "boosters" antagonistic to President Herbert Hoover's attempts to provide Europe with some war debt relief. Nor does he discuss specific artists very much, although he has cause to refer to Gershwin's *An American in Paris* as a "blaring, symphonic, tearing, sychophantic, antiphonal cry of Modern Existence," and to share his enthusiasm for the then obscure Emily Dickinson, whose "exquisite" poetry is "full of delicate mysticism and slender beauty that quivers in the reader's mind long after the book has been laid aside" (as an example, reproducing the whole of "I had no time to hate, because"). As for his own verse published here, it tends to be terse and evocative in the style of the Imagists and the early Ezra Pound, as in the tellingly titled "Image" ("This much is known: the wet boughs / Of lilac trees are black in the dawn"); or wittily aphoristic after the fashion of Dorothy Parker or Ogden Nash, as in "Nursery Rhyme" ("No matter what your talents are / If you but own a motor-car / You're certain to be popy-lar"), with one ditty, written in his senior year, even taking note of Nash: "Some people have a pash / For writing like Ogden Guash [*sic*]."[10]

Latouche pursued more serious literary ambitions with his stories and poems for the *Record*, John Marshall's prize-winning monthly literary journal founded in 1909, which during these years operated under the guidance of the English department's Walter Beverly and for which Latouche served as assistant and eventually associate editor. Descended from a literary Virginian family, Beverly (1890–1971), a writer himself, had progressive ideas, as might be inferred from his approving mention of socialist J. B. Priestley in a December 1930 talk bemoaning the state of the union. He and Latouche formed a close bond, and for a December 1931 issue of the *Monocle* that featured faculty contributions, Beverly jumped at the chance to pen a "Fragments" parody in the style of the "petite, inimitable Treville." On his part, Latouche praised Beverly for "fanning the flames of genius in the heads of his staff."[11]

Latouche wrote at least fifteen poems, eleven stories, and two occasional pieces for the *Record*. The earliest of these, an amusing piece about "My First Day at High School" in which the author's anxieties (including hearing his teacher call out his name so as to sound like "Trevilla Touche") overwhelm him, dates from the first semester of his freshman year. However, whereas the "Fragments" columns tend along this line, that is, toward the droll (although not exclusively so: nearing graduation, he writes in his column, "I see that my life is like unto a succession of dark rooms, through which I wander with outstretched arms"), a number of these *Record* publications concern rather unrequited love, youthful disenchantment and alienation, and sadness over the transience and futility of life. Even in the jaunty "Folk Song" for a March 1932 humor issue, the minstrel poet, his heart "sore a-sighing," concludes, "It's devil a bit that I'll be caring."[12]

Some of these poems and stories involve uncanny fantasies of death and time past, with Latouche's peers themselves referring to his work as "Gothic (and rather morbid)." Indeed, with their gloomy shadows and strange music, these writings can be so overwrought as to be faintly ridiculous, perhaps purposefully so. In "Return," a young student tells his high-school girlfriend, "My heart is like brushwood, Jeanne. It is autumn and the great fingers of my soul are beating out the flames of my heart." At the same time, his work exhibits greater restraint over time, as seen in the poem "Two Nocturnes" published at the end of his senior year.

A few tales also reveal an interest in the occult and Eastern spirituality that would survive into Latouche's adult years, as would the racial concerns that surface in several of the stories, including "Black Laughter: A Fragment Torn from the Life of a Negress." This particular story involves a black washerwoman, Cally, who becomes a celebrated dancer, Bama, on Broadway. Her light-skinned boyfriend, Willie, "tired of being called a dinge, a black," resolves to "pass" as a white man, and after taking her money, leaves her. That night, while performing, Cally sees her white audience as wanting to gaze on "a Black making a fool of herself on the stage. A Black contorting herself for the money." The next day, a theatrical notice appears recommending Bama "to all admirers of the bizarre. All through the dance one could see the lightheartedness of her race, the freedom from care. Miss Bama is a striking example of how White Rule is benefiting the Race." Reading this, Cally laughs and shoots herself. Its melodramatic excess notwithstanding, the story reveals an uncommon sensitivity to the destructive effects of racial stereotyping and prejudice.

These *Record* publications further show Latouche steeped in classic literature, from the Bible and the Elizabethans to the Romantic poets and the erstwhile Richmonder, Edgar Allan Poe (whom Latouche apparently admired). William Blake serves as an inspiration for the nature poem "Variations on a Theme by Blake," and Samuel Taylor Coleridge's *Christabel* provides an epigraph for the melancholy story "No Green on the Oak." But Latouche shows some awareness of more contemporary trends as well. In "Return," for instance, the hero, a pianist, plays "a music of banging thuds and shrill staccatos" that the author associates, as the story unfolds, with composers Leo Ornstein and George Antheil, while the story's heroine finds some soothing consolation in the "incoherences" of T. S. Eliot. Plainly, by age sixteen, Latouche had developed some familiarity with some of the day's more advanced artists (although Ornstein's heyday already had passed by some ten years).[13]

The strong autobiographical strain behind these writings—many of the poems use the first person—naturally shed light on the artist as a young man. The three fables that constitute "Three Tales" seem especially revealing in this respect. In the first, "The Sand-boy," a young prince, desirous of both the beauty of a boy and the wealth of a woman, loses both; in the second, "The House," a girl attempts to escape from the grip of her mother and her home; and in the third, "The Cat," the feline protagonist, disgusted with a society tea, resigns herself to a "cat-song of loneliness and despair." These tales can be read in terms of the author's uneasy response to his homosexuality, his family, and his social world, respectively. The objects of thwarted or latent desire in these stories, when specified, tend to be male, and the writing occasionally waxes homoerotic; in one of the "Two Nocturnes," in reference to some boys swimming at night, Latouche writes, "the lake / rushed up to meet their brown bodies with its moist lips"; and in the story "Paul and the Dragon," Latouche says of the protagonist, "His body was a glorious paean of youth! He stretched his young body until the muscles vibrated with tautness." Meanwhile, "Black Laughter," as discussed above, arguably bespoke Latouche's own sense of otherness—a correlation that would help explain his vehement rejection of Southern racism.[14]

Latouche further revealed some social consciousness in correspondence with his schoolmate John Kellogg, who wrote a serial about high-school life, "Dixie Doodle," for the *Record*. At the turn of 1931, Latouche presented Kellogg with a copy of J. C. Grant's 1930 novel depicting the brutal conditions of a British pit village, *The Back-To-Backs*, with a note that read, in part, "Perhaps this will jar you from the saccharine niceties of *Dixie Doodle* and its coterie of brain-offspring. But you are such an illimitable jazz-hound this book will perhaps bore you." Kellogg replied that given the "traditions" of John Marshall High School, a "thoroughly realistic" story would "offend our dear elders, those smug, narrow-minded, intolerant people who refurst [*sic*] to acknowledge that such conditions as I should like to have describe [*sic*] exist in our town, at our own high school." Latouche in turn defended to Kellogg the "outrageous mendacities" that surfaced in his own columns: "My life has consisted of a series of disillusionments calculated to embitter me towards anything existent outside of my own pitiful trauma-existence."[15]

Latouche's success as a writer quickly spread beyond the confines of John Marshall. As early as 1929, he published a poem in the pulp serial *Love Story Magazine* for which he received twenty dollars; and in 1930, *The Black Swan: The Magazine of Virginia*, a short-lived local journal "of literary and human interest," reportedly accepted for publication two poetic snapshots of Richmond street life: "Market Scene," which had appeared in the *Monocle* the previous November, and "Evening Comes to Seventeenth Street." In the end, the magazine published only the latter, a gloomy view of the city's Jewish ghetto.[16]

Latouche made even more of a splash in April 1931 by taking first honors for his story "Strange Dusk" in the First Tournament of Arts and Crafts, sponsored by the newly constituted Richmond Academy of Arts, in the course of which he earned the praise of no less than James Branch Cabell, who served as contest judge and who befriended the young writer. (Latouche subsequently submitted this story, yet another tale of adolescent loneliness, and perhaps his most explicitly homoerotic venture to date, to the little journal *Pagany*, in whose archives the manuscript survives.) That same semester, in addition to winning a Gorgas Medallion from the John Marshall faculty for the best paper on "The Gorgas Program of Personal Health," Latouche received second honorable mention from the Virginia High School Literary and Athletic League for an essay, "Lamp of Beauty," about Lincoln's early love Ann Rutledge. And three of Latouche's early poems appeared in a large published compendium, *Younger Poets: An Anthology of American Secondary School Verse* (1932).[17]

However mannered and overstrung, Latouche's high-school writings evidence a born, even compulsive writer with a sharp mind and a vivid imagination. Moreover, premonitions of his mature work appear throughout. Something of their alternately comical and melancholy tone made their way into a number of later efforts, as did their penchant for lush nature painting, culminating in "Lazy Afternoon" (*The Golden Apple*) and the "Silver Song" (*The Ballad of Baby Doe*). More specifically,

Latouche recycled the images of "wild berries" and a "dragon" for "Windflowers" (*The Golden Apple*), reinvented "pink-fat butterflies" as "fat pink cloud" for "Lazy Afternoon" (*The Golden Apple*), and reformulated the line, "One smile I can't forget," as "I can't forget his smile" for the song "A Rainy Day," while the recitation of nationalities in his portrait of a metropolis, "Traffic Lights," foretold *Ballad for Americans* and other works. Even more explicitly, he reprised his *Monocle* bon mot "Beauty is only skin deep, but Heaven known [*sic*], that's deep enough" in *Ballet Ballads* as "And beauty is only skin deep / For the Elders that was deep enough." In a memorial tribute to Latouche, composer Vernon Duke quoted, as "already indicative" of the lyricist's "manner," the final seven lines of the high school sonnet "Death and the Poet":

> With steady hand and lip I shall depart
> For that dim residence of mossy stone
> Where I might lay aside these vain ideals
> And, rid of this encumbering flesh and bone,
> Be free to lie alone. I shall not feel
> The lack of any love, nor feel again
> Any emotion save lying in the rain.[18]

During his time at John Marshall, Latouche also joined the Dramatic Club and participated in a number of school productions, most under the direction of drama teacher Charlotte Wheeler. He seems to have made his high-school debut in a May 1929 performance of Dan Totheroh's *Pearls*, a turn thought "very humorous" by the school paper. Small in stature, with a handsome profile, a mass of black hair, and sparkling blue eyes, he consolidated his reputation as one of the school's leading comedians in productions of a farce by Adam Appelbud (pseudonym of Carl Pierce), *Oh, Kay!*; a comedy by Zellah Covington and Jules Simonson, *Second Childhood*; and a parody of Simon Gray's melodrama *Little Nell*, in which he played the title role in drag "with charm and grace. When he peered through his maze of golden curls in his wistful little way and bowed with a resounding whack it moved all the audience to tears and hysterics." Particularly active in the French department, he also performed in scenes from Molière's *Le bourgeois gentilhomme* (playing Monsieur Jourdan), the same playwright's *Le malade imaginaire* (playing Monsieur de Bonnefoi), and Jules Moinaux's farce *Les deux sourds* (playing Boniface)—all apparently in the original French. His high-school stage career climaxed with his "somewhat grotesque" performance as the humpbacked dwarf in Stuart Walker's adaptation of Oscar Wilde's *The Birthday of the Infanta*, a production that took top honors in April 1931 at the Tidewater High School Tournament in Williamsburg (see Figure 1). The previous spring, Latouche similarly had been cast as Puck for a production of *A Midsummer Night's Dream*, a seemingly perfect role for this saucy elf, although, probably due to conflicts, another student ultimately took the part. In his senior year, his John Marshall classmates voted him "best actor" as opposed to "most intellectual," "most original," or anything else.[19]

Latouche became involved in community theater as well. Early in his high school career, he even reportedly helped found, with his teacher Charlotte Wheeler and local directors Rose Kaufman (later, Banks) and Arthur Philips, the Children's Theatre, a group that subsequently became a wing of the Richmond Drama Guild. In late 1929, he starred in the ensemble's production of Louise Burleigh Powell's *The Merry Fiddle,* and in early 1930 he appeared in both *Aladdin and His Wonderful Lamp* (performing the title role) as dramatized by Arthur Philips, and *The Pied Piper* as adapted from Browning by Rose Kaufman, who directed both of these later productions. That same spring, he played a Native American boy and wrote the epilogue for a historical pageant, *James,* written by Philips, about the founding of Jamestown; and he also took the role of Dickon the Devil in a Richmond Drama Guild production of Percy MacKaye's popular 1908 play after Hawthorne, *The Scarecrow,* directed by Wheeler.[20]

In addition, in late 1931, a group of John Marshall drama students, under Latouche's leadership and direction, formed the Wigglesworth Players with the intention of performing on radio, making their debut on local WRVA on December 9 in a version of James Branch Cabell's *Simon's Hour.* The Players presented at least four more half-hour shows during that winter season, including Anton Chekhov's farce *The Bear* and Rawlings Percival's *My Last Duchess,* presumably an adaptation of the Browning poem of the same name.[21]

During this same period, in early 1932, the indefatigable Treville joined the cast of a production of Carlo Goldoni's *La locandiera,* sponsored by the Italian Literary Society of Richmond, and presented partly in Italian, partly in English. Much as Latouche's high-school acting career peaked with his rendering of the misshapen dwarf in *The Birthday of the Infanta,* so his community work culminated with his portrayal of yet another dwarf in a Children Theatre's production of *The Golden Dwarf,* adapted from the tale "Rumpelstiltskin." In a preview piece for the latter, local journalist Mary Weston Tucker opined that Latouche "probably does the most artistic work in the city," while in a review of the show, Alice Lichtenstein, also of the *Richmond Times-Dispatch,* praised the young man's "finished characterization" as "sufficiently 'scarey.'"[22]

Meanwhile, Latouche wrote his own plays, including a one-act piece entitled *The Stone Wall* given by the Dramatic Club during his junior year. And on December 23, 1931, his graduating class presented—as entertainment before the afternoon senior dance—another original play, a fantastical piece entitled *Christmas in Ix* (pronounced Icks). Set in the year 2047, the story involves the Emperor of the Moon, who threatens war against King Ixobad of Ix (played by Latouche) unless the children of Ixobad stop "their eternal lamentations and tears." Promised his lady love if he can set things right, the poet Philaster conjures an Old Witch who in turn calls for Santa Claus, who arranges a solution. After the curtain falls, Santa has the curtain open once again so that he can distribute candy to the children and utter the moral, "so long as there is kindness in a human, so long will we be glad." This fable might have been inspired in part by *The Birthday of the Infanta*, which had played so successfully the previous spring, although at the same time, the court names—King Ixobad, Count of Bombixia, Marquis of Saltipratt, and so forth—strongly recall Cabell's fiction, while the play's epilogue suggests even at this early date some connection with the distancing effects of playwrights Luigi Pirandello and Bertolt Brecht.[23]

These extensive and varied theatrical experiences naturally helped hone Latouche's dramatic sensibilities. His involvement with so many stage tellings of fantasies and fairy tales looked ahead in particular to his own many theatrical representations of legends and fables. As Vernon Duke pointed out, playing the Devil in *The Scarecrow* especially set the stage for a lifelong engagement with "the Faust formula and the devil's doing," as evident not only in such shows as *Cabin in the Sky* and *The Happy Dollar*, but his fondness for "sketching little devils on scraps of paper or tablecloths," and for signing some letters, "Beelzebub" (although he seemed far more inclined to draw cherubs and angels).[24]

The production of *The Scarecrow*, meanwhile, brought Latouche into contact with the considerably older Marie Keane Dabney, who played Goody Rickby in the show and who became a good friend. Born to a British father and a French mother, Marie (1866–1953) grew up in Virginia, but was educated abroad. She eventually married T. Todd Dabney, scion of an old Virginian family and inheritor of a coastal plantation as well as property in Richmond. A suffragette and actress, she prided herself as a freethinker, visiting Gertrude Stein in Paris and startling Richmond society with her agnostic views.[25]

In her memoirs, Dabney remembered that she first befriended Latouche—"the only genius I have ever known"—on the set of *The Scarecrow*: "This devil, complete with horns and tail, was a youngster of thirteen [*sic*: Latouche was fifteen at the time] who, as he cavorted devilishly, improvised such apt and clever lines that he stole the show. After shedding horns and tail, he went home with me, and there he stole T. T. [Dabney]'s heart. Even at that early age he was writing poetry, and we encouraged him to come often." In a letter to Marie from the late 1940s, Latouche recalled these visits to the Dabneys' Richmond home, a charming federal style building on North Foushee known as the Little House:

> How well I remember his [T. Todd Dabney's] fine head aureoled in the beams of yellow light in the shining June air as we sat in the garden of the Little House talking about the rights of man and the passing of good manners.
>
> He talked of decency as something that one took for granted, and of that elusive standard—the spirit of humanity—as basically good.
>
> His voice was as remote as silk on an old screen . . . and I, fascinated, was a thin, untidy child with dreams too big for his frail frame, full of questions, and hope, and anger. . . .

> I can recall every word; for he was the first philosophic friend who had entered my life.
>
> You appeared...with your arms full of flowers, and bricks, and play-scripts, filling the place with life in its most fluid and violent form.... The Little House is as unique and lovable as ever.... I dream too much, as ever. Some things do not change. Memory has given them immortality.

The Little House plainly represented for Latouche a haven from his disadvantaged and provincial background, setting a pattern for the sort of refuges he found in later years among other sophisticated and well-to-do friends.[26]

Latouche also enjoyed a lifelong friendship with Marie's daughter Annette Dabney Stone (1890–1960), herself the young man's senior by a good many years. The wife of Walter Maxwell Stone, Annette proved even more daring than her mother, winning some local notoriety by hosting interracial parties and entertaining leftist political ideas; in 1943, she asked the *Richmond Times-Dispatch* to have her name added "to your list of white Virginians who would like to see those laws repealed which discriminate against any race." She also spent a few years in the 1940s on staff at the progressive Black Mountain College, which her son, Frederick, a photographer, attended from 1939 to 1941. After Latouche settled in New York, he retained perhaps closer ties with Marie Dabney and Annette Stone than with any other Richmond friends; indeed, when he joined the military, he named, in the event of death, Annette Stone as his beneficiary after his wife and mother.[27]

During the summer of 1931, between his junior and senior years of high school, Latouche spent a number of weeks in New York, in the words of Rose Kaufman, "scouting about." Two surviving letters that seem to date from this period—one to a close high school friend, the dancer Lillian Loehr, and the other to James Branch Cabell, who had recently come to know and take an interest in the young writer—indicate that he resided part of the time with a friend in Queens, part of the time in a rooming house in Manhattan; and that he happily attended Gilbert and Sullivan's *The Mikado* and *Iolanthe,* probably as presented by the Civic Light Opera; Stravinsky's *Petrushka,* staged by the Dance Centre; and *The Band Wagon,* a new show with music by Arthur Schwartz, lyrics by Howard Dietz, and a book by Dietz and George S. Kaufman that Latouche deemed "one of the cleverest revues I've ever seen."[28]

These two missives remain, along with his few notes to John Kellogg, among Latouche's very few early surviving letters. The one to Loehr, a kind of love letter, recalls the high-flown melodramatics of his high-school poetry:

> My very dear, is the dreamlessness of stars to be attained? Never, never while the hand falters or the foot lingers is the long climb to the silent temple to be gained. The dark night that fills our eyes will some day flee before the dawn, but will the dawn be too late for our too mortal selves? You, in

> whose eyes alone have I yet beheld the eternal flame, have not grasped the thin thread of dream that binds our being together.

At the same time, after going on in this vein for a while, he describes this letter as "one of the most painful concoctions of slop I've yet perpetrated," and finds that he remains "a vain, conceited, depraved, soiled, careless creature whose modicum of talent has been inflated to large dimensions by his sense of showmanship." The more restrained epistle to Cabell essentially requests, in view of his dire financial situation (he interrupts the letter in order to hide under the bed from his landlady), a letter of recommendation to the *American Mercury*, a literary magazine to whom he hopes to sell some of his work; and yet the letter still contains some poetic imagery to which Cabell reasonably might be sympathetic: "now the dusk is creeping into the room, and the long hair of night is blowing over the bosom of the sky." Both letters conclude with Latouche supposing that he is "mad," as indeed seems the case from these frantic reports.

During this visit to New York, Latouche approached a charitable organization, the Joint Application Bureau, located on 22nd Street, alleging that his money had been stolen and that his family could not come to his aid. Whether or not the bureau assisted him financially, they were impressed enough with his "possible genius along literary lines" to introduce him to some contacts at Columbia University with the idea that he might enroll there after graduating from John Marshall. The following summer, after Latouche's return to Richmond for his senior year of high school, the bureau contacted Cabell about finding local Richmond monetary assistance so that the young man could continue his education. Cabell wanted Latouche to attend his alma mater, the College of William and Mary, but financial exigencies seem to have precluded that option. Moreover, Latouche longed to leave Virginia for the big city. In the end, armed with a scholarship and some local support, he departed Richmond after graduation to spend the 1932–33 academic year at Riverdale Country Day School, a preparatory school in New York, apparently with the express purpose of readying himself for college the following year. (About this same time, Edward Cone, later a noted music theorist, similarly attended Riverdale after high school before proceeding to Princeton.)[29]

Located on a sprawling campus in Riverdale, an affluent area of the Bronx, the prestigious Riverdale Country Day School started as a boy's day school in 1907 but opened its doors to boarders in 1920. Latouche naturally partook of the school's good arts program, joining the glee club, once again assuming the lead role in his play *Christmas in Ix* as part of a December holiday program, and appearing as well in a March production of Oliver Goldsmith's *She Stoops to Conquer*. He took classes in English, French, math, and chemistry, learned to play soccer, and continued to write poems and stories—he even had a poem read over WOR Radio on a program devoted to young people's poetry—but none of these early works seems to have survived.[30]

Needing the permission of a relative to leave campus, Latouche claimed as family a Richmond writer who lived in New York, Clifford Dowdey, so that he could gad about Manhattan at will. Dowdey recalled that Latouche—whom he already remembered from Richmond as having "an ebullient personality, an extravagant humor and a fanciful way of expressing himself, and the smooth manners of a born con"—would briefly check in and out with him on these getaways: "On his return from these trips he bore various gifts: I remember a handsome polo coat . . . and an expensive piece of luggage. I never asked and he never volunteered anything." As ever the rapscallion, Latouche nearly found himself expelled from the school "for stealing the school bell and other deviltry."[31]

Latouche occasionally wrote to Cabell while at Riverdale—to boast a bit about his quick study of soccer; to request a photo of the older man to hang on the wall of his dorm room; to tell about a wooden statue he had carved of Horvendile, the demiurge who appears in a number of Cabell's novels—and remained in touch with him after returning to Richmond in the summer of 1933. Latouche's high-school writing already had shown the influence of Cabell, but such personal contact apparently made him all the more appreciative of the older man's books: "The same things that old Hegel squinted over a musty paper to set down, the same thing that Spengler presented to a gaping world, is the thing that *I* (perhaps you did not mean them to be there; perhaps they weren't) have derived my comprehension of what your books were." Cabell continued to tout William and Mary, although even were Latouche to receive a scholarship, he doubted that he would be able to afford to go there because of the lack of possible employment in the Williamsburg area. In any event, he returned to New York in the fall of 1933 in order to attend Columbia University, leaving Virginia behind for good. But he maintained contact with Cabell, and while at Columbia published a thumbnail sketch of his Virginian mentor, whom he fondly recalled sitting "in his comfortable chair, hands folded, talking of death and the stock market and beaten biscuits." After Latouche's death, writer Ruth Yorck told Cabell, "When Latouche talked about his youth and how often by whom he was discovered, he always mentioned you with tender gratitude."[32]

Latouche reportedly received a $1,000 scholarship from Columbia, which would help explain how someone so impecunious managed, in the depths of the Depression, to attend college. According to his college record, he entered Columbia with "superior preparation" in English and French, and "normal preparation" in other subjects, including German. Planning to major in French studies, he took, during his freshman year, French conversation and literature and required courses in early Western civilization and literature, as well as elementary Italian, physical education, and personal hygiene, all three of which he failed.[33]

During his freshman year, Latouche joined Columbia's time-honored literary club, the Philolexian Society, whose members included such new friends as senior John Sturdevant and junior Herman Gund, both of whom he introduced to a Barnard sophomore with literary aspirations, the Russian-born Nora Lourie (later

Gund, then Percival). From a distance of eighty years, Lourie remembered Latouche—still Treville—as not only "very bright and very clever" but warmly sympathetic and demonstrative. After the spring 1934 semester let out, the two of them rented rooms in a home on Brewster Street in Provincetown, the artist's colony on Cape Cod increasingly popular with gays and lesbians, where they met up with Latouche's friends from Richmond, writer Jack Woodford and his daughter, Louella (both of whom apparently had run into Latouche in Provincetown the previous summer). Taking possession of the home's large attic, Latouche further made the space available to such visiting friends as Sturdevant and Gund. "Sturdy [Sturdevant] is very nice," Lourie wrote to Gund during Sturdevant's visit, "and I think him nicer than Treville, who's charming only as long as he's the focus of attention and then becomes a querulous child cutting capers to be noticed."[34]

Lourie also told Gund about the large number of "fags" and "fairies" (terms, she later averred, not used with pejorative intent) at the August 24, 1934, costume ball given by the Provincetown Art Association at Town Hall that she attended with Latouche and Sturdevant, both of whose own homosexuality she had no issue with (indeed, she felt some lesbian attraction herself to Louella Woolfolk). Lourie dressed as a mermaid, Latouche, a Russian nobleman (see Figure 3). "He [Latouche] looked spectacular in a purple bedcover and a black fur collar and a muff on his head," wrote Lourie to Gund, "and he won the men's prize for the most artistic [man's] costume as an Aubrey Beardsley design of a Russian nobleman, and has been strutting ever since."[35]

Returning to New York, Latouche further befriended an incoming Columbia graduate student in English, Florence Wolfson, the precocious and somewhat bohemian daughter of middle-class Jewish immigrants who lived on the Upper East Side. Attending the literary salon that Wolfson hosted in her parents' Madison Avenue apartment, Latouche could have—and presumably did—rub shoulders with a number of outstanding young artists and intellectuals, including poets John Berryman and Delmore Schwartz (along with the latter's future wife, Gertrude Buckman), philosophers William Barrett and Hippocrates Apostle, and the openly gay Gertrude Stein enthusiast Julian Sawyer. These friends, writes Wolfson's biographer, "stayed until early morning, talking philosophy, getting drunk, having little orgies in Florence's bedroom, seeking physical as well as intellectual pleasure." Reflecting on this early stage of her life more than seventy years later, Wolfson herself commented, "The people, the culture, the brains. It's terrible today. Does anybody think and live philosophy?"[36]

As a sophomore, Latouche continued with the Western civilization and literature sequence and enrolled as well in a French literature seminar, an English composition project, a class on the philosophy of art taught by Irwin Edman, and once again elementary Italian and physical education. (In his 1948 Guggenheim fellowship application, he claimed to read, write, and speak French "fluently," and Italian and German "fairly fluently.") However, eager to embark on a professional career, during the spring semester of this sophomore year, he drifted away from his course work altogether—"Treville was writing naughty songs for nightclub singers," recalled Nora Lourie, "and spending less and less time on campus"—and ended the year failing or dropping all his classes.[37]

As in high school, Latouche distinguished himself all the same in extracurricular activities while at Columbia, and became especially active not only with the Philolexian Society and another literary club, the Boar's Head Society, but with the college's little magazine, the *Columbia Review*, serving in his sophomore year as vice president of the Philolexian Society and associate editor of the *Review*. During his freshman year, he also spearheaded the idea of having the Philolexian Society present the American premiere of Jean Cocteau's play *Orphée* (1926), which he was to direct, and for which the group obtained the support of Cocteau as well as Lee Miller, the model and photographer who recently had appeared in the French poet's film *Le Sang d'un poète* ("The Blood of a Poet," 1930), although in the end, the project fizzled for lack of funds.[38]

Concerning the *Review*, Latouche contributed something to all ten issues published during his two years there, including poems, book reviews, a short essay, and some occasional pieces, "Pastiches," whose title alone suggested some continuity with his "Fragments" column for his high-school newspaper. He continued to write under the name Treville Latouche, although by his sophomore year he identified himself on occasion as J. Treville Latouche and John Treville Latouche as well.

Latouche published a total of eight poems in the *Review*, six as a freshman, but only two as a sophomore, already suggesting a waning of interest in producing serious verse. These poems generally address topics that had preoccupied Latouche while in high school—love, time, loss, mortality—in a familiarly disenchanted way; but they are more expansive in form and mature in expression than his earlier work. Published during his freshman year, "Elegy Before Dying" expressly documents this growth, for although it begins almost identically to his high-school poem, "The End of the Song," instead of hearing "a violin playing in the distance / playing a song, a sad song" on encountering "you whom I had never seen before," the poet now writes,

> your head's bright flair
> quiescent, I did not hear your voice.
> I sensed you warily, received your tones
> remotely, as though heard through telephones—

If anything, Latouche's college poems conjure images of doom and destruction all the more, with nature portrayed as pitiless and hostile, and favored imagery including crumbling towers and melting wings.[39]

Relatedly, the poet casts a censorious eye not on Richmond as before, but rather on New York, especially in the two poems published in his sophomore year: "Two

Variations from a Night Club Suite" (1934) and "Legend for a Great City" (1935). Here, along the lines of T. S. Eliot and Hart Crane, he confronts the vapidity and harshness of contemporary life. But he finds as well sustenance in myth: in the legendary cities of ancient times, and in the rising phoenix as opposed to the shrilling peacocks, symbol of modern life, writing in "Legend for a Great City,"

> Be proud, then. Strive to capture while you wake
> the fable deep within you. Let your mind
> erect upon the street a brazen snake,
> or travel through the subway stiles to find
> a crowned swan on the stair, who rest [*sic*] there, weeping
> above the ragged men who lie there, sleeping,
> with tabloids wrapped around them for a cloak.

The general malaise expressed by Latouche in these poems seems reflective of his generation as a whole; perusing an issue of the *Review* from this period, Lionel Trilling, Columbia's most eminent literary critic, noted, "Almost every one of the contributions of fiction or verse deals with the contradictions, the hurts, the confusions of his own (or some self-representing hero's) emotional life."[40]

Latouche's literary collegiate efforts quickly garnered him several impressive awards. In his freshman year alone, he not only shared first place honors for the Columbia Review–Philolexian Prize for the poem "The Gull," published in the *Review* in April 1934, but, for the annual Philolexian Society contest that same spring, he also earned first prize in the poetry division for the poem "Monroe Park," and tied for first place in the prose division for the short story "The Encounter" (two works apparently lost). And the following year, he won first-place honors in a three-way tie for the Boar's Head Society Award for the poem "Legend for a Great City," published in the *Review* in May 1935. Dissension among the judges makes it hard to know how Columbia's premier poet—the much-admired Mark Van Doren, who served on at least some of these juries—felt about Latouche, whom he seems to have had in class as well, although he surely would have rated the young man's work highly. In any case, for an underclassman to snag four major literary prizes against such formidable competition as John Berryman (who won second-place honors for the Boar's Head Award) signaled, at the least, considerable promise.

During these years, with Marxist sentiment gaining ground on the Columbia campus, the Philolexian Society (including Latouche's work) came under some unfriendly scrutiny from some of the more politically engaged leftists on campus, including Mordecai Bauman, later an admired singer among the popular front (and also in time, ironically enough, a champion of Latouche). In response to such concerns, the *Columbia Review* sponsored a symposium, "Art and Propaganda," in the spring of 1934, soliciting essays from Latouche as well as from his colleagues Robert Giroux, later a well-known publisher, and John K. Massey. Whereas Giroux questioned Marxist assumptions, and Massey adopted a Marxist line, Latouche, in a piece entitled "Art and the Artisan," took a somewhat middle ground, viewing the present situation as pitting establishment mavericks like Eliot—whose *The Waste Land* "leaves an artist two solutions: religion or suicide"—against so-called proletarian poets, who display a certain vigor, but in whose work Latouche discerns only "stumbling, inchoate phrases, brutal indictments, verbalized hate." Even among the Russians, he argues, the most vital artists—such as filmmakers Vsevolod Pudovkin and Sergei Eisenstein, and composer Sergei Prokofiev—appear rooted in the past. "Art as an integral force existed long before the rise of either the bourgeois or the proletariat," he concludes. "Whatever the temporary modification, it will continue so long as there are men who wish to see or appreciate what exists beyond the continuing walls of the moment."[41]

Latouche's other critical writings from this period—including reviews of a collection of essays by Pound and volumes of verse by Robinson Jeffers, William Rose Benét, and William Carlos Williams—reveal a similarly high degree of sophistication for a nineteen-year-old, his age at the time of all these pieces but the Pound review, which he wrote at twenty. As was his wont, this criticism also tended to be playful. He opens his Jeffers review by stating, for example, "Perhaps it is my own perversity of mind that enables me to reconcile with perfect ease the misanthropic elements in the poetry of Jeffers with the Marxian position in respect to contemporary politics." Indeed, he sometimes assumes the sort of high-handedness that he decries in Williams and Pound.[42]

Nevertheless, however cool, Latouche displays real appreciation for those older poets under review. Although he professes no "personal admiration" for Jeffers, for instance, he praises the work's rugged beauty. He finds "great charm and grace of line" in Benét's verse, when not merely workaday; and he commends Williams's ability at times "to impress a mood with a paucity of words," even if the poet can be oddly obscure as well. The Pound review similarly shows two minds: the poet's *Cantos* "are fascinating intellectual rubbish-heaps," while his book of essays has "robustness, knowledge, charm, and much nonsense, all pleasant reading."

Meanwhile, Latouche's three "Pastiche" pieces, which he published in his sophomore year, comment on a variety of artists outside of poetry: author Gertrude Stein, composer George Antheil, painter Juan Gris, monologist Ruth Draper, dancer Martha Graham, set designer Frederick Kiesler, comedian Beatrice Lillie, photographer Alfred Stieglitz, and the American Ballet Theatre. These short causeries—one of which Lionel Trilling deemed "good," although he wished "it had more sinew and less Stark Young casualness and ornament"—show the author's impressive cultural breadth even at this tender age. He regards, for instance, Antheil's opera *Helen Retires* (despite its "worthless libretto" by John Erskine) more favorably than the work of Howard Hanson, George Gershwin, and "the Younger Composers" (presumably meaning, at least in part, those contemporaries, including his later collaborator Jerome Moross, then associated with Aaron Copland), and he rates Graham's work higher than both the Denishawn school and Mary Wigman. He similarly draws distinctions between Ruth Draper and Cornelia Otis Skinner; Frederick Kiesler and both Adolphe Appia and Jean Hugo; and Beatrice Lillie and both Charlie Chaplin and the Marx Brothers. These vignettes further suggest, in comparison to his freshman year, when his contributions to the *Review* centered on poetry, a growing preoccupation with the performing arts, with Latouche apparently putting his time away from Columbia to good use.[43]

Akin to this development, Latouche authored the book and lyrics to Columbia's Varsity Show of 1935, *Flair-Flair: The Idol of Paree,* produced by college senior George E. Leonard. An annual event founded in the 1890s as a means of raising funds for school athletics, the Columbia Varsity Show long had established itself as one of the foremost collegiate entertainments in the nation. Indeed, with elegant venues like the Waldorf-Astoria and the Hotel Astor, and near-professional production values, the shows served as important showcases for emerging talent, and over the years a number of prominent artists cut their teeth working on Varsity Shows, including composers Roy Webb and Richard Rodgers, lyricists Oscar Hammerstein II and Lorenz Hart, and novelist Herman Wouk, who worked on the two that preceded Latouche's.

As producer George Leonard recalled in the program book published by Columbia's humor magazine, *Jester,* the play committee, having selected Latouche in the fall of 1934 out of a field of seven candidates to write this show's forty-second edition, gathered in December to hear him read his script. "Before starting, the young author broke down and confessed that he had read the thing that afternoon and didn't think it funny at all, so we all had to make reassuring noises before he went ahead and made us think so, too." Latouche—as J. Treville La Touche—wrote not only the book and lyrics, but the music to two of the songs: "Flair-Flair" and "Ladies of the Evening." Eight other students and alumni contributed music as well, most notably Robert Lawrence, a recent graduate who also orchestrated and conducted the show.[44]

As with previous Varsity Shows, *Flair-Flair* had an all-male cast, with the female roles played by men in drag. This included the much-loved pony ballet, a dance chorus composed of brawny athletic types who, their legs unshaven and their muscles protruding, performed as high-kicking chorus girls, their carefully drilled ensemble work as hilarious as their lapses in synchronicity. The shows similarly featured singing choruses with men dressed as women; John Berryman, not tall enough for the pony ballet, sang in such choruses in both 1934 and 1935. "I don't think it ever occurred to me that there was any homosexual angle to the experience," remembered Berryman's friend E. M. Halliday, who danced in the pony ballet in 1934. Nonetheless, Columbia authorities felt that *Flair-Flair,* which Berryman's parents thought both "very funny" and "very dirty," had gone too far and decided to dispense with female impersonation for the next year's Varsity Show, a break in tradition that, although perhaps a sign of the times, owed a good deal to the bawdiness of Latouche's libretto.[45]

The story, in two acts, each with three scenes, takes place in Paris in 1912 and concerns the romance between George Anderson, a wealthy American tourist, and the eponymous heroine, a Parisian nightclub singer who rises from an obscure Montmartre bistro, the Dead Dog, to stardom at the Folies Bergère. Count Louis de Grandgousier, the villain, attempts to obstruct this romance, but love triumphs at the end, the resolution having to do with the discovery that Flair-Flair, her parentage previously unknown, is the daughter of the Mademoiselle from Armentières—an allusion to the rowdy barracks song popular during the First World War. (This sendup of a classic dramatic contrivance presumably involved the distinguishing liver spot mentioned in coverage of the show by Columbia's newspaper, the *Daily Spectator*.) Other dramatis personae include the Duchess of Tympp-Queeper, the Senora de la Canas y Schmaltz, Prince Boris Btvani, and Francois, Marquis de Foutre. "The play," explained Latouche, writing in the third person, "is a timid satire on the faded morals and ambitions, the bad drama, music and lyrics of 1912 (the last three were alarmingly easy for him to imitate). There is No Real Message in the book." Still, as "a brilliant spoof on the sophisticated world of international entertainment," to quote his friend Nora Lourie Percival, the show represented a marked departure from standard Varsity Show fare, which tended toward Graustarkian fantasy or collegiate satire. "Latouche the unpredictable," observed the *Spectator*, "is the prime mover in this change."[46]

Although neither the script nor the score to *Flair-Flair* appears to have survived, the extant program book includes several of the show's lyrics, excerpts that reveal considerable wit, not to mention the sauciness that won the show its notoriety. In the number "Flair-Flair," for instance, the heroine intimates, among other things, her prowess for both oral and anal sex, with Latouche going Irving Berlin's "She certainly can can-can" from "Heat Wave" one better:

> And even the Croat and the Bulgar
> Gets a lump in the throat when I'm vulgar,
> I haven't as yet met a Mexican man
> Who disliked the way that my can can can-can.

In further identifying herself in this number with Eva Tanguay, the early-twentieth-century actress famous for her unconventional behavior, Flair-Flair can be seen that much more as a prototype for those liberated fin-de-siècle women who populate Latouche's work as a whole, including Helen (*The Golden Apple*), Flora (*The Vamp*), and Baby Doe (*The Ballad of Baby Doe*). Meanwhile, the song's transgressive display of exaggerated femininity, the stuff of drag queens, resonated with Latouche's own skill at female impersonation, from playing Little Nell on the stage in high school to entertaining friends with imitations of such grand dames as Queen Victoria; as late as the 1950s, he enjoyed donning elegant evening gowns, with Kenward Elmslie recalling his penchant for dressing up as Marie Antoinette.[47]

The ribaldry of the song "Flair-Flair" characterizes the score as a whole. In the duet "I'll Remember You," after George sings, "Don't know what to do about this new thrill," Flair-Flair responds, "You will!" "Let's Dance," a parody of the two-step craze of the early 1900s, featured so many double entendres as to make the dance a barely veiled metaphor for sex. Even the ballads had campy overtones: "Gone—the stimulation of love, the intoxication of love— / Now the expiration of love; / Why must there be solitary love?" muses Flair-Flair in "Solitary Love." Latouche clearly set out to mine a large field of risqué humor, as suggested too from the titles of some lyrics not included in the program book, such as "The Sex Life of the Chrysanthemum," this last perhaps a take-off of writer Robert Benchley's popular routine, "The Sex Life of the Polyp."[48]

Martin Manulis, a senior who had played the leading ladies in the 1933 and 1934 editions, in the process making a name for himself as a Mae West impersonator, won the role of Flair-Flair, as expected. Indeed, Latouche wrote the part with Manulis—later a successful Hollywood producer—in mind. John J. Birgel, another senior, played the all-American George, and John E. Lonergan came in to direct. The cast rehearsed for one month, during which time Ethel Merman, Victor Moore, and Vera Dunn, then on Broadway in Cole Porter's *Anything Goes*, attended a rehearsal. "Our author," reported producer Leonard, presumably meaning Latouche, "after being 'baby-faced' and 'angel-childed' around by Vera Dunne [*sic*], scored a two base hit, when he took her home and managed to get a date with her."[49]

After a single runthrough with orchestra that lasted until 4:00 a.m., *Flair-Flair* opened the following day, on March 12, 1935, at the Hotel Astor, "the best first-night in many years," wrote the *Spectator*, "after the worst dress-rehearsal in history." A crowd of about two thousand roared their approval throughout the evening. Wrote Lucius Beebe in the *Herald Tribune*, " 'Flair-Flair' is student musical burlesque in the gay and bawdy old tradition with more than usually happy lyrics and spontaneous raffishness." The *Times*, *Post*, and *World-Telegram* agreed, the last-named writing, "They should have let J. Treville La Touche out in '34, summa cum laude."[50]

In his review, Beebe informed his readers that the show's young author was "reported to be a leading light in the Bohemian circles of Morningside Heights," that is, the Columbia University area. The joking biography of Latouche published in the program—which mentioned his various likes and dislikes, including his rating of E. E. Cummings, George Antheil, and Grant Wood as America's best poet, composer, and painter, respectively—could only have enhanced this reputation. The same might be said of the program's accompanying photograph, which showed Latouche, his hair coiffed, wearing an ascot, holding a cigarette, and generally looking dashingly sophisticated for a college sophomore.[51]

Latouche for some time had been moving away from both his academic studies and serious poetry. But the success of *Flair-Flair*—he even managed to sell some of its songs—no doubt encouraged him all the more to pursue a career in musical theater. Dropping out of Columbia by the end of his sophomore year, the twenty-year-old writer faced the daunting challenge of making his way on Broadway.[52]

3

The Boy Wonder of Broadway

Discussing his reasons for pursuing a career in the theater after dropping out of Columbia in the spring of 1935, Latouche stated in 1949, "When I left college, with a background of poetry and prose awards, I had a choice of concentrating my energies into the 'slim volume,' or of attempting to work in the so-called 'popular' fields. My choice of musical theater was partly due to necessity—I have been self-supporting since I was fourteen—and also due to a real belief that this form is an authentic reflection of American culture." All the same, Latouche continued to write serious poems throughout his life, and in the later 1930s he even aspired to publish a volume of verse, but without success.[1]

Earning a living wage in the theater proved no easy business either, and for a while he barely made ends meet. But he slowly began to find work, thanks largely to the support of various friends, including the Russian-American composer Vernon Duke, who in time became one of his most important collaborators.

Born Vladimir Dukelsky near Pskov, Russia, by the Estonian border, Vernon Duke (1903–1969) came from a prosperous and cosmopolitan family; his heritage was Georgian and Lithuanian on his father's side, Russian, Austrian, and Spanish on his mother's. He attended in his teens the Kiev Conservatory, where under the tutelage of Reinhold Glière he learned to write pieces in the style of Alexander Glazunov, although exposure to Debussy's *Pelléas et Mélisande* and the modal theories of his piano teacher, Boleslav Yavorsky (later an important influence on Shostakovich), suggested more novel ideas. During the civil war that followed the 1917 October Revolution, his family fled their home, first to Odessa, where Dukelsky studied with the Polish composer Witold Maliszewski, and then to Constantinople, where he happily discovered the music of Irving Berlin and George Gershwin. Using pseudonyms, he started writing tunes that "sounded as if they were in the authentic American jazz idiom, but harmonically they weren't."[2]

Arriving with his family in New York in 1921, Dukelsky worked as an arranger, pianist, conductor, and composer in commercial venues even as he pursued loftier ambitions. He found in Gershwin a patron who made it possible for him to go to Paris in 1924, whereupon he also befriended Prokofiev, his other "guardian angel." While in Paris, he further won the backing of the legendary director of the Ballets

Russes, Serge Diaghilev, who in 1925 triumphantly launched Dukelsky's ballet, *Zéphire et Flore*, with choreography by Léonide Massine and sets by Georges Braque. That same year, using the pen name Vernon Duke, which had been suggested to him by Gershwin, he wrote a successful operetta for the London stage, *Yvonne*. His career faltering in Europe, he returned in 1929 to America, where, "back in my element," he attained success both as Vladimir Dukelsky, concert composer, and Vernon Duke, writer of popular songs, including the hits "April in Paris" (1932) and "Autumn in New York" (1934). Eventually adopting the name Vernon Duke for all his work, his music for Broadway and Hollywood, although stylistically distinct from his serious music, showed rare refinement, with experts David Jenness and Don Velsey finding the "harmonic sophistication" of his popular songs "unexcelled."[3]

Duke first encountered Latouche, whom he described as "an astonishing youth," in the summer of 1935 at a Park Avenue party hosted by the young actress Elsa Beamish and her flatmate. Recalled Duke,

> Both girls were under Latouche's spell and invited me over for an exhibition of his talents. Johnny dusted off a few hot epigrams, then sat down at the piano and accompanied himself in a bouquet of night club-type songs—subsequently used by Spivy [LeVoe] and others—containing references to the phenomena of the day. He sang and played atrociously, but the songs themselves, while of the self-consciously "smart" variety, were often amusing and effective.... He [Latouche] was very small, dark and stocky, with the face of a precocious infant. Johnny's mind was ever alert, his wit ever sharp and often merciless; but the boy's essential goodness and kindness shone through his eyes. Extremely erratic by nature, Latouche worked spasmodically and swiftly on his poetry; short periods of work to be followed by long days and nights of blissful laziness and idle gallivanting.

Duke proposed to his friend and collaborator, writer Moss Hart, that the latter hire the young man as a secretary, but in retrospect admitted, "a crazier notion cannot be imagined. Moss, whose amiability, while occasionally strained, is admired by all, gave Latouche an 'interview' and found him very nice, full of talent, but hardly secretary material."[4]

Latouche at least secured some work assisting on the show *Murder in the Old Red Barn*, which opened at the American Music Hall on February 1, 1936. This musical had a roundabout genesis beginning with two Californian producers, who in 1931 mounted a recently unearthed temperance play from the 1840s, *The Drunkard, or The Fallen Saved*; audiences, weary of Prohibition, found *The Drunkard* a hoot—they were encouraged to hiss the villain and cheer the hero—and its success in Carmel encouraged the producers to take this laugh revival to Santa Barbara and Los Angeles, where it opened at a small venue, the Theatre Mart, in the summer of 1933. With some alcohol now legal, *The Drunkard* was presented as a dinner show with beer and other refreshments, and, in the tradition of American minstrelsy, with musical numbers performed between the acts as well as after the play proper. An enormous hit—W. C. Fields, a repeat attendee, featured the production in his 1934 film *The Old Fashioned Way*—the show ran for more than twenty years.

In March 1934, two Broadway producers, John Krimsky and Harry Bannister, launched *The Drunkard* at the American Music Hall, a former church on East 55th Street converted into a dinner theater; they likewise served beer, pretzels, and sandwiches but, with Prohibition now repealed, offered hard liquor in a cellar lounge as well. After the show closed in December, Krimsky and Bannister, in association with journalist Lucius Beebe, found another hoary melodrama to revive, namely, *Maria Marten, or The Murder in the Red Barn*, a nineteenth-century British warhorse attributed to John Latimer.

Maria Marten dramatized one of the most sensational British murder cases of the nineteenth century: in 1827, a young farmer, William Corder, allegedly killed his lover, Maria Marten (and possibly before that, their illegitimate child), and then buried her in a local barn, where she was discovered the following year, her body badly decomposed, after which Corder was found guilty and executed by hanging. The story became the subject of numerous ballads, plays, and films, including a 1928 rewrite by Montagu Slater and a 1935 movie version directed by Milton Rosmer. Having coproduced in 1933 the first Broadway staging of Bertolt Brecht and Kurt Weill's *Die Dreigroschenoper* as *The Threepenny Opera*, Krimsky possibly discerned some kinship between that German masterpiece and this planned travesty of *Maria Marten*.[5]

The resulting satire, *Murder in the Old Red Barn*, proved a hit with critics as well as with audiences, who booed, cheered, stamped, whistled, and shouted through the proceedings. "Hisses and blessings punctuated every declamation and movement of the play," wrote Percy Hammond in the *Herald Tribune*, "all of them proving that the heart of the New York drama lover is, on especial occasions, in the right place." Like *The Drunkard*, the show also presented musical "interludes" between the four acts, here featuring can-can dancers, roller skaters, tumblers, jugglers, and singers, who encouraged the audience to join in on such chestnuts as "Daisy Bell" and "When Irish Eyes Are Smiling." Following the villain's execution at the conclusion of the play proper, the entire cast launched into a rousing rendition of the popular Depression anthem, "Happy Days Are Here Again." Observed Robert Benchley in the *New Yorker*, "It all makes the legitimate theatre seem very drab."[6]

If the score drew largely on popular favorites, the entr'actes in addition contained a few numbers with words and music by Latouche—here appearing as Jean-Treville Latouche—in collaboration with composer-lyricist Richard Lewine (pronounced Le-WEEN, 1910–2005), in later years a noted television producer. In a preview piece about the show, the *Times* reported "that such songs as may flirt with nostalgia are the joint work of La Touche and LeWine, two lyricists imported at insignificant expense from the Tenth Avenue counterpart of the Place Pigalle," or in other words, from shady nightclubs.[7]

Although essentially a joke, this last assertion might have been truer of Latouche than Lewine, a Columbia graduate who at least had two (albeit failed) revues to his credit, *Fools Rush In* (1934) and *Entre-Nous* (1935). But in any case, both Krimsky and Beebe had seen and enjoyed Latouche's college show *Flair-Flair*, and had decided that he and Lewine would make a good team. The program listed two of their songs—"Not on Your Tintype," sung by Marion Butler and Leslie Litomy, and "Don't Throw Me out of the House, Father," sung by the American Music Hallettes—but the title song from *Flair-Flair* turned up in the course of the evening as well.[8]

In his unpublished monograph on Latouche from the 1970s, Andrew Drummond included a few lines from both "Not on Your Tintype" and "Don't Throw Me out of the House, Father," presumably thanks to an interview with Richard Lewine, who in late 1999 recorded these same two jaunty ditties at the piano (along with a third song, "I've Got Designs on the Tattooed Lady") for another Latouche researcher, Erik Haagensen. As sung—apparently slightly misremembered—by Lewine, "Don't Throw Me Out" ended, "Don't turn us out of the house, father / Don't turn us out of the house / You should forgive us for our sins / And thank the Lord that it wasn't twins." Lewine further recalled that for "Don't Throw Me Out," the Hallettes, dressed in Victorian costume, held baby dolls in swaddling clothes that at the conclusion of the number they tossed about from one to the other. Neither "Not on Your Tintype" nor "Don't Throw Me Out" elicited any particular mention in the press, with the exception of the *World-Telegram*'s Robert Garland, who seemed to like them both.[9]

Murder in the Old Red Barn, which charged a cover of $1.65, ran for nearly a year. Krimsky paid Latouche something for his songs—Lewine remembered finding him waiting outside the theater for his tiny royalty, and paying Latouche some small amount from his own pocket—but to what extent the young lyricist might have benefited financially from the show's success is unclear. He remained in dire straits in any case. After *Murder* closed, Krimsky and his brother Jerrold brought another burlesque to the American Music Hall, *Naughty-Naught '00*, which opened in early 1937; for this production, Lewine once again worked on the score, but now in collaboration with the lyricist Ted Fetter, perhaps because by this time Latouche had other obligations, including extensive involvement with Erika Mann's revue *Pepper Mill*.[10]

Starting in the fall of 1936, Latouche also worked briefly for the Ballets Russes de Monte Carlo. His biography in the *Pepper Mill* program gave his position as "research director," and he also identified himself in a newspaper byline as the company's "American historian," but he seems to have been, essentially, an assistant press agent, as he admitted still elsewhere.[11]

Founded in 1931, the Ballets Russes de Monte Carlo, a successor to Serge Diaghilev's famous Ballets Russes, functioned, at least initially, under the leadership of Colonel Wassily de Basil, a man described by Vernon Duke as "devoid of social graces, clumsy in a room, clever in business and with the sketchiest-imaginable knowledge of the arts, especially music. His redeeming features were a strongly developed sense of humor and a certain, rather winning, bonhomie." In the mid-1930s, de Basil and Massine, the ballet master who had choreographed, as mentioned, *Zéphire et Flore*, commissioned Duke to write a new ballet, *Jardin public*, which the company premiered in 1935 and presented in a revised version in the spring of 1936. All this drew Duke into a renewed association with the Ballets Russes; and when the company arrived in New York in October for the start of their fourth American tour, Duke, aware that the impoverished Latouche had had "a series of annoying illnesses" for which he had been hospitalized, "had the bright idea of palming him off on the good colonel as a fifth press agent." De Basil had doubts about employing so young a public relations man, but Duke assured him "that Latouche was a great genius and could make the ballet palatable to cowboys or dockyard workers. This proved the real clincher, and Latouche was hired on the spot, although we had some difficulty in securing a much-needed twenty-dollar advance for him."[12]

Duke further recalled that de Basil and Latouche refused to understand each other, the former speaking French with a strong Russian accent, "whereas Latouche's French had distinctly Southern intonations—not the Midi of France but the Midi of Richmond, Virginia." One evening in Philadelphia, Duke and de Basil witnessed Latouche "discussing the vagaries of the Russian soul" with prima ballerina Irina Baronova, prompting de Basil to say to Duke, "Ach, Dimotchka, Dimotchka, if only your little Babouche would write instead of talking to my ballerinas, we'd get somewhere." An article about Latouche in *Collier's* magazine further reported that on one occasion, the young press agent extravagantly bought drinks for an assemblage and then handed the bill over to de Basil, who subsequently pocketed some amount out of Latouche's paycheck each week with the comment, "Another round for everybody."[13]

Duke remembered that Latouche and de Basil "parted company" two weeks after Philadelphia, which would mean sometime in late November. Perhaps Latouche quit the company specifically in order to be able to work with Erika Mann on *Pepper Mill*, which opened in January. However, Latouche resumed some association with de Basil in the spring, at least to judge from a preview piece he wrote in March for a Richmond paper in anticipation of a Ballets Russes performance there (an article that aimed to demystify ballet by, among other things, presenting premier danseur David Lichine as a former athlete who likes "sudda pops"). Whether Latouche simply had assisted on this particular tour stop because of his ties with Richmond remains unclear. But at any rate, his work on *Pepper Mill* surely took precedent to all else during the late fall and early winter of 1936–37.[14]

Writer and actress Erika Mann (1905–1969) was the oldest child of the German novelist Thomas Mann. In the 1920s, she and her brother Klaus, with whom she often collaborated, settled in Berlin, where Erika became, writes one of her biographers, "a symbol of the daring new woman of the Weimar Republic: the kind of woman who wore short hair, had affairs with men or women, and wrote witty, charming pieces in the popular press." Appalled by the Nazis, she devised and produced an antifascist revue with the assistance of, among others, brother Klaus, who provided some of the material; her lover, actress Therese Giehse, who directed and performed in the show; and composer Magnus Henning, who wrote most of the music and served as music director. Christened *Die Pfeffermühle* ("The Peppermill") by her eminent father, the revue successfully opened in an intimate cabaret in Munich on January 1, 1933. Erika hoped to move the production to a larger theater in Bavaria, but in light of growing Nazi control, she and her troupe repaired to Zurich, where they reopened *Die Pfeffermühle* in the fall of 1933. Loved by some, detested by others, the cabaret subsequently toured Prague, Amsterdam, Brussels, and other cities, eventually giving more than a thousand performances.[15]

In the fall of 1936, Erika, who the previous year had obtained British citizenship through an arranged marriage with the poet W. H. Auden, crossed the Atlantic with Klaus, followed by various company members, in the hopes of bringing *Die Pfeffermühle* to New York and perhaps even touring the country. Under the sponsorship of F. C. Coppicus in association with the Columbia Concerts Corporation, and backed by some local philanthropists, *Pepper Mill*, as it was now called, opened for a limited run on January 5, 1937, at Chanin Auditorium, a 192-seat theater on the fiftieth floor of the Chanin Building located at East 42nd Street and Lexington Avenue. Erika Mann served as master of ceremonies, Therese Giehse directed, and Magnus Henning played piano and apparently at times joined the cast, which otherwise featured four German women, including Mann and Giehse, and three local American men, including Latouche. Although Mann mainly relied on older material, she introduced a few novelties as well, including two numbers sung by Wallace Rooney: the traditional American ballad "Willie the Weeper" (a detail worth noting given Latouche's later dramatization of the song); and "Demagogue," with words by Ernst Toller and W. H. Auden and music by Aaron Copland.

Mann faced two major challenges: securing translations of selected German texts into English, and then familiarizing the German cast members with the English adaptations—all in about two months. For the translations, she turned mostly to Latouche, who adapted a number of songs, mostly by Mann and Henning ("The Yodeler," "Especially for Mr. Winterbottom," "Doctor's Orders," and "The Gangster of the Puppet Show"), but also by Henning and lyricist Klaus Mann ("The Lorelei"), and composer Werner Kruse and lyricist Erich Mühsam ("The Little Revolutionary"). These songs largely deplored and satirized world affairs, especially in Germany. In "The Lorelei," a gloss on the famous Heinrich Heine poem of the same name, the singer finds herself an outcast in her village because she loves a Jew, in one stanza singing,

> My old father threatens a beating,
> Mama says her heart will break,

Because the young man I am meeting
Is old Mr. Levy's son Jake.[16]

How Erika Mann came to entrust all this work to the twenty-two-year-old Latouche remains unknown. By this time, the latter had become friendly with other European émigrés, among them Frederick Kiesler and Goetz von Eyck—Paul Bowles recalled that Latouche "collected German and Central European refugees the way someone else might collect tropical fish; he was always eager to add more to his assortment"—so he and Mann perhaps made contact through the exiled German community. The fact that writer Edwin Denby, a good friend of Latouche, adapted one of the songs suggests another possible connection, as Mann and Denby had been in Berlin and Switzerland about the same time and moved in similar circles; it also seems possible that Copland came to this project by way of Denby, as the two had just collaborated on the opera *The Second Hurricane,* although Latouche just as well could have introduced Denby and Copland to Mann. In any case, Latouche became involved in the revue to the point that he even participated on stage as a singing actor in both solo and ensemble numbers.[17]

Pepper Mill received for the most part terrible reviews. Although the critics seemed appreciative of Mann's charm, most pummeled the show, lambasting the production, the material, and the performers (especially the American cast members) as unprofessional. "A deadlier, more embarrassing evening I have never seen," reported the *Post*; "Plainly, the human race will stand for anything," wrote the *Evening Journal*. With astonishing callousness, the *Billboard* even compared the fate of the refugee cast members to "the fact that they themselves victimize the few American theatergoers who may pay to see their show." Latouche took a double drubbing: he bore the brunt for the assumed notion that the adaptations failed to do the original material justice, and he had his performance singled out by *Variety* as "thoroughly amateur." Perhaps the fact that the critics similarly disparaged the contributions of Auden and Giehse—later to originate the role of Mother Courage—offered the young lyricist some consolation.[18]

At the same time, Arthur Pollock (*Brooklyn Eagle*) rose vigorously to the work's defense: "They [the company] deserve a friendly reception here, for they play in the friendliest spirit, with a kind of warm affection for humanity in general and an unpretentious intelligence. Unfortunately, they have about them nothing that is slick. And New York loves the slick.... It is by far the wisest revue in town." In the face of so many disastrous first-night reviews, Pollock reiterated his support a few days later: "To me it [*Pepper Mill*] seemed, though clumsy in the extreme in the matter of its performance, unostentatiously brave, wise and ingratiating." The entertainment daily *Variety,* the local German weekly *Neue Volkszeitung,* and the new music quarterly *Modern Music* also weighed in with generally good notices. The last two even had kind words for Latouche, with composer Virgil Thomson in *Modern Music* commending the lyricist's "gift for bright words and sharp rhymes." Meanwhile, *Variety* reprimanded the critics for giving "the most completely rude performance of the season. They talked to each other, kidded among themselves and walked out en masse (with a single exception) at the end of the first act. Maybe that had something to do with the fact that the second act was much better and went off much smoother.... On a night-club floor, even as is, it would have a much better chance. With a smart audience, of course."[19]

As Mann remembered, in the course of its first week the revue improved as the German actors became more accustomed to performing in English; but she nonetheless terminated the run following six performances. After the show closed, the New School for Social Research, which had established a University in Exile in 1933 as a haven for refugee academics, invited the troupe to perform at its auditorium on West 12th Street for a few weekends in late January and early February, and Mann extensively overhauled the show for this engagement, which reportedly played well to full houses. But the idea of an American tour now seemed hopeless, and several company members, including Giehse, returned to Europe.[20]

In later years, the company's principal dancer, Lotte Goslar, enumerated four reasons for the revue's lack of success in New York: the constraints imposed by singing in English, the irrelevance of some of the material to local American conditions, the country's isolationist mood, and the lack of familiarity with this type of literary cabaret. However, the show's failure represented only a temporary setback for Mann, Latouche, and others involved in the production, who soon enough found alternate ways to disseminate their antifascist message.[21]

By this time, Latouche also had written, according to Vernon Duke, "a libretto and two ballets," meaning, presumably, ballet scenarios; the young lyricist plausibly went to work for de Basil specifically with the hope of collaborating on a new ballet. His profile in the *Pepper Mill* program further credited him with a forthcoming book of verse. All this material, to the extent that it ever existed, appears to be lost. But some of his cabaret songs from the period survive, thanks to recordings by Spivy LeVoe and Hope Emerson, and corresponding manuscripts found among Andrew Drummond's papers.[22]

The skimpy and inconsistent information about Spivy LeVoe (1906 –1971) alleges that she was born in Brooklyn, the daughter of Russian-Jewish immigrants, although at least one source describes her as "Russian-born." In her youth, as Bertha Levine, she played organ in churches and movie theaters, but in due course established a career as a singer-pianist in speakeasies and nightclubs. As early as 1931, when she appeared on radio, she used the name Spivy LeVoe, but she became better known simply as Spivy, a deep-voiced purveyor of clever chansons of the Noël Coward variety. In 1936, she began a close association with Tony's, a bar-restaurant on West 52nd Street operated by Tony Soma, an Italian immigrant and yoga enthusiast who sometimes entertained customers singing while standing on his head. Soma, who earlier had operated a well-known speakeasy on West 49th Street, long had attracted a smart artistic and literary crowd, including a notable gay clientele, a reputation surely enhanced by having Spivy, a mondaine lesbian with a bracing wit, as his "première diseuse." The designer Frederick Kiesler recalled how he, Latouche, Marc Blitzstein, Jane and Paul Bowles, Virgil Thomson, Aaron Copland, and less often E. E. Cummings would assemble late at night to hear Spivy at Tony's, where in the "exuberant atmosphere," Latouche and Soma sometimes would stand on their heads and sing duets.[23]

Plump and buxom, Spivy performed in Tony's modest back room, usually accompanying herself at the piano. Singing some ten to fifteen selections in a given night, she performed mostly original comedy numbers written especially for her, including many featuring lyrics by Latouche. In a June 1939 *New York Times* review of her act, Theodore Strauss commented, "Spivy's material, witty, acid and tragicomic, is better than most of the essays one hears about town, and her delivery is that of a sophisticated artist on her own grounds. She knows the value of surprise in punching a line, she uses understatement unerringly and her piano accompaniment is superb." Recalled one of her pianists, "She was magic! There was such glee when she sang those saucy lyrics, and her energy was boundless."[24]

In 1940, Spivy opened her own club, a penthouse boîte located on the ninth floor of a building at East 59th Street and Lexington Avenue; she originally planned on calling the place "La Vache sur le Toit" ("The Cow on the Roof"), after Paris's famous Le Boeuf sur le Toit ("The Bull on the Roof"), but the club became known simply as Spivy's Roof. Wearing gowns or dinner jackets glittered with sequins, her hair a lacquered pompadour, Spivy presided over this fashionable East Side club, as writer Irving Drutman recalled, "not unlike some eccentric figure out of Lautrec's Montmartre." In the course of its twelve-year existence, Spivy's Roof presented singers Mabel Mercer and Thelma Carpenter, comedians Sheila Barrett, Martha Raye, and Paul Lynde, and pianist Liberace, among many others, but mostly the proprietor herself. Many of the club's showcased artists were homosexual, and like Tony's, the place became popular with the gay community, although Spivy insisted that her customers comport themselves with discretion. After closing shop in 1951, Spivy spent some years in Paris, Rome, and London before returning to America in the late 1950s, where as Madame Spivy she secured work as a character actress in film and television, including small roles in the movies *The Fugitive Kind* (1960), *Requiem for a Heavyweight* (1962), and *The Manchurian Candidate* (1962), and a star turn in an *Alfred Hitchcock Presents* TV episode, "The Specialty of the House" (1959), which drew on the gay ambience of Spivy's Roof. Her obituary in the *Times* quoted her as saying, "The customer is more usually tight than right."[25]

Spivy seems to have started singing Latouche's lyrics around 1935, sometimes to his tunes or her own or someone else's, and the two quickly became lifelong friends, although their relationship could be tumultuous. In January 1938, for instance, Latouche noted in his journal that Spivy had become his "enemy" (adding, "Poor Spivy—hysterical, glandular, ugly, charming, and so talented"), reporting a few days later that she had "made a semi-settlement of her quarrel with me." And in a letter to Spivy toward the end of the year, Latouche, admitting that he owed her money and lyrics, expressed the hope "that our friendship was a bigger and more sympathetic one than it turned out to be. I'm sorry; you can hardly afford to lose a staunch friend and neither can I. But both of us are always doing things we can't afford." Indeed, although notoriously tight-fisted, Spivy apparently offered Latouche some financial security during these difficult years—she claimed to pay him fifty dollars a week, at least at some point, to write what she called "classical lines tinged with Rabelais"—much as Latouche provided Spivy with the sort of material indispensable for her career.[26]

One of Latouche's earliest songs for Spivy, "I'm Going on a Binge with a Dinge" ("dinge" being rather slighting slang for a black person), for which he wrote both words and music, tells of a biracial woman tired of Park Avenue ("White people / Please don't be offended," the verse begins) and looking to have some fun in Harlem:

I'm goin' on a Binge with a Dinge
Gonna end up in Harlem
With my end up in Harlem
O-O-O....

I'm goin' on a Binge with a Dinge
Mess up my Schiaparelli [Italian fashion designer]
Passing out on my belly.
O-O-O.
Fare thee well!

This particular song, whose lyric survives in typescript along with a fragment of music, proved a favorite with Spivy's audience, and for a period she would conclude each evening with the number.[27]

At about this same time, while on Cape Cod, possibly during the summer of 1935 or 1936, Latouche prepared for Spivy a translation of Paul Verlaine's 1869 poem "Clair de lune" ("Moonlight")—ostensibly so that Spivy could recite or sing the poem, famously set by both Gabriel Fauré and Claude Debussy, to her own piano accompaniment. Surviving in manuscript, Latouche's version has its own characteristic flavor, as seen by way of a comparison of its opening stanza with a recent and somewhat more literal one by Norman R. Shapiro, although both similarly preserve the rhyme and metrical scheme of the original:

Shapiro's version
Your soul is like a landscape fantasy,
Where masks and Bergamasks, in charming wise,
Strum lutes and dance, just a bit sad to be
Hidden beneath their fanciful disguise.

Latouche's version
Your mind is an enchanted country-side
Where masks and bergamasks go charmingly

Playing on lutes, and dancing . . . But inside
Beneath the glitter is melancholy.

This unexpected lyric for Spivy intriguingly points to continuities between New York's club scene of the 1930s and Paris's bohemian cabarets of the preceding century.[28]

By late 1937, Latouche also had started writing songs for Spivy with the German-American composer-pianist Goetz von Eyck (1911–1969). "I wonder," he wrote to Spivy in September 1937 with respect to his many collaborations with Eyck, "that this letter isn't in rhyme. . . . I order my meals in alexandrins, snore in iambic pentameter, and yawn in blank verse." Latouche possibly met Eyck through the latter's lover (and later wife), actress Ruth Ford, the sister of Latouche's friend Charles Henri Ford. In any event, this close working relationship continued into 1938, but subsequently tapered off as Eyck pursued a career on stage and screen, eventually becoming the noted character actor Peter van Eyck.[29]

Of those dozen or so songs released commercially by Spivy, four have lyrics by Latouche: "The Last of the Fleur de Levy" (music by Latouche) and "I Love Town" (music by Eyck), both included on the album *Seven Gay Sophisticated Songs by Spivy* (1939, on the Exclusive Recordings and Commodore Celebrity Series labels); and "Surrealist" (music by Spivy) and "I Didn't Do a Thing Last Night" (music by Spivy), both from the album *An Evening with Spivy* (1947, on the Gala label). Moreover, Spivy cut a demo recording, also in the late 1940s, of a number by Eyck and Latouche, "The Fool in the Moonlight," a vocal score of which survives among Andrew Drummond's papers as well.

"The Last of the Fleur de Levy" tells of a "frowsy" wreck who once had been the Jewish "empress" of a fashionable salon (the title puns Levy, a familiar Jewish surname, with *fleur-de-lis*, the decorative emblem associated with French royalty); "I Love Town" comments facetiously on the attractions of city life; "Surrealist," drawing on the vogue for surrealist art in New York at the time, narrates a love affair, with surrealistic imagery, between a surrealist painter and a bearded lady; "I Didn't Do a Thing Last Night," addressed to a doctor, recounts the singer's varied drunken exploits the previous evening; and "The Fool in the Moonlight" gives vent to feelings of romantic infatuation. For the most part accompanying herself at the piano, Spivy talk-sings her way through these numbers in a parlando manner, although "Fleur de Levy" and "Surrealist" also feature tuneful choruses redolent of barroom ditties, and "The Fool in the Moonlight," both in form and content, more closely resembles a commercial popular song. In short, the literary attractions of these songs, heavy on irony, outweigh their musical interest.

Several of these lyrics show an early fondness on Latouche's part for *abccb* quintains that scan somewhat like limericks, as in this stanza from "Surrealist" about the surrealist painter and bearded lady's courtship:

When they strolled through the park of a Sunday
A rose in her beard she would wear

And he'd look soigné
In a suit made of hay
With a lamb chop in his boutonniere.

"Surrealist" features too a similar rhyme scheme favored by Latouche, one also related to old ballad traditions, namely, *aabccb*, as in this stanza from the number's interlude:

Then he played a gavotte
On an old china pot
And murmured "Now let's go to bed—

For what is more jolly
Than love à la Dali?
Do you mind if I stand on my head?"

As suggested by this sampling, Latouche's songs for Spivy tended to brandish droll and tricky rhymes, other examples including "feel good" and "[John] Gielgud," "snacks smell" and "[Elsa] Maxwell," "arty folks" and "artichokes," "bar one day" and "Dubonnet," and "Thackery" and "daiquiri." Such ingenuity would culminate on a grand scale with Latouche's *The Golden Apple*.[30]

Spivy continued to sing Latouche's cabaret songs for the remainder of her career. On one occasion in 1946 at Spivy's Roof, at which the New York art world gathered to attend the premiere of a puppet show performed by John Bernard Myers to two puppet plays by Charles Henri Ford and Jane Bowles, with music by Paul Bowles and set designs by Kurt Seligmann, Spivy sang a set of Latouche songs including "Surrealist," which, recalled Myers, "brought down the house."[31]

Meanwhile, Latouche involved himself with other cabarets and cabaret artists around town, including a club that opened in late 1937 upstairs from Theodore's, a restaurant on East 56th Street and Fifth Avenue, and that became one of the lyricist's favorite haunts: Le Ruban Bleu ("The Blue Ribbon"). Founded and managed by Herbert Jacoby, a dapper French-Jewish gay refugee affiliated with similar night spots in Paris, Le Ruban Bleu showcased, within its cramped confines, such international talent as Brazil's Elsie Houston, Germany's Lotte Lenya, and Austria's Greta Keller, as well as such African Americans as Jimmie Daniels and Mabel Mercer. (Commenting on a visit to the cabaret in his 1938 diary, Latouche wrote that he "missed Elsie Huston's [*sic*] divine singing and miming—only heard the elegant blackamoor Jimmy Daniels singing suffisticated sawngs. He is grander than an empress, lacking that tremendous simplicity many of his people have.") Naming Cole Porter and Marlene Dietrich among the club's habitués, cabaret historian James Gavin writes, "Jacoby brought together a truly cosmopolitan group of performers and audiences, the likes of which existed no place else in Manhattan."

Jacoby ran Le Ruban Bleu until 1942, when his assistant Julius Monk took over as manager, and the following year opened another nightclub with which Latouche would become associated, the Blue Angel.[32]

Jacoby featured singer Hope Emerson (1897–1960) in Le Ruban Bleu as early as March 1938, when the *Times* reported, "Miss Emerson entertains at the piano with songs and has been mentioned by persons who should know as the fruition of the night clubber's everlasting search for a feminine Dwight Fiske," in reference to a cabaret performer who told humorously lewd stories to his own piano accompaniment. Standing over six feet tall, Emerson already had had something of a stage career, and after the war, would become a familiar presence in film and on television; but she performed as well at various clubs at least into the early 1940s. In May 1939, reviewing the current line-up at Le Ruban Bleu, the *Times* referred to her as "that dynamo among risqué singers, shouting her naughty refrains with inimitable gusto."[33]

In 1940, Emerson, ostensibly accompanying herself at the piano, released on the General label six songs all written—apparently music as well as lyrics—by Latouche: "Oh Sultan!" "Did I Do Wrong?" "What Happened to Me?" "Virtue May Lurk," "Simeon Babbitt," and "Her Name Was Lil." As suited Emerson's personality, these numbers tended to be more antic and bawdy than Latouche's songs for Spivy. In "Oh Sultan!" the singer, on a date with an "oriental gentleman" atop an elephant on 52nd Street, tells her brazen suitor,

> Now you've got a harem
> And you're the head guy with them
> You've made your Bedouins
> Now you go and lie with them.
> Oh sultan, oh sultan, stop your insultin'
> No good will result in you insultin' me.

In "Did I Do Wrong?" the singer tells advice columnist Dorothy Tricks (a parody of the real life Dorothy Dix) about an escapade with a man ("who made me want to sh-riek!") that she met in a bar, coyly punctuating her narrative with the question, "Did I do wrong?" until, in a final stanza that involves some typically ingenious wordplay, she provides her own answer:

> He said his life had been a blank book until we met that night.
> But I gave him such a blank look, dear Miss Tricks, did I do right?
> Then he showed me his bank book, and then I turned out the light.
> Did I do wrong? Well you're god-darn right I did!

In perhaps the most remarkable song in the set, "Simeon Babbitt" (subtitled in Latouche's typescript, "A Fable for Tired People," to which he also added, "from a poem by Robert Lax," a poet whom Latouche probably knew at Columbia, where

Lax wrote for the college humor magazine *Jester*), the eponymous wine clerk, envious of rabbits who frolic in clover, discovers that his dream to become a rabbit has come true—but finds himself with eyes "rather soft for a male" and "a fluffy white tail," that is, "the wrong kind of rabbit!" Finding that he "had changed his position in life," Simeon adopts the name "Simone Simone Lapin" (after the sexy French actress, Simone Simon, and the French word for rabbit, "lapin") and when "every so often he starts feeling funny / Goes off in a corner to toss off a bunny." This "fable for tired people" concludes, "The moral is: People who want to be rabbits / Had first better learn their progenitive habits." Emerson enhances the humor of this thinly veiled tale of transgressive gender and sexual identity by softly reciting the text, composed mostly of couplets, over a tinkling piano accompaniment appropriate to the kind of Peter Cottontail narrative it aims to evoke and subvert. More than any of Latouche's other preserved cabaret songs, "Simeon Babbitt" highlights the homophilic sensibilities of the sophisticated community who gathered to hear Spivy and Emerson at Tony's and Le Ruban Bleu, and who listened to their recordings, which seem to have been intended largely as at-home party entertainment.[34]

About the time Le Ruban Bleu opened in late 1937, Latouche found some much needed additional employment by way of a Federal Theatre Project (FTP) revue, *Sing for Your Supper*. Founded in 1935 as a division of the government's Works Progress Administration, the FTP, under the supervision of Hallie Flanagan, produced—before Congress withdrew funding in the summer of 1939—hundreds of stage works and radio plays, in the process giving modest employment to thousands of theater people, from ushers and janitors to writers and composers, mostly in New York but around the country as well.

In the fall of 1937, Hallie Flanagan and George Kondolf, the director of the FTP in New York, decided to launch a satirical Broadway revue, prompted in part by the success of both *O Say Can You Sing* (1936), a revue Kondolf had launched while heading the FTP in Chicago, and *Pins and Needles* (1937), the runaway hit labor musical on Broadway. However, as the FTP's New York division lacked experience with this type of entertainment, Harold Hecht, the actor appointed to direct the show, found it necessary to recruit writers, lyricists, and composers outside the program. Remembered Ned Lehac, one of the show's composers,

> The first of these [recruits] was a short, dark, young leprechaun who arrived on a very cold night wearing a Navy surplus crew-necked sweater, a pair of beat-up trousers, worn shoes, and the kind of wool cap a sailor dons when he stands watch on the deck of a ship in freezing weather. Hecht had found this brilliant guy down on the Manhattan Bowery in the Mills Hotel, a well-known fifty-cents-a-night flophouse [*sic*: presumably the inexpensive Mills House No. 2 on the Lower East Side]. His name was Johnny LaTouche.[35]

Latouche's involvement with the show can be dated at least as far back as a January 22, 1938, diary entry in which he recounted a meeting with Hecht and his assistant Robert Sour, during which the three discussed not only the planned revue and writings about the Soviet Union by André Gide and Lion Feuchtwanger, but the nature of genius, leading Latouche to reflect, "I hold firmly to my somewhat mystical theory that the creative instinct as born is many sided; environment and inhibitional tendencies thrust it into one—or sometimes two—particular channels." As evidence, he cited Leonardo da Vinci's difficulties in completing projects, thanks to the restrictions of his social milieu, including "the sexual phobias of the petit bourgeois." Such convictions possibly spurred Latouche to pursue, as he did, widely varied projects, and perhaps helped rationalize his own inability to complete many of them. Tellingly, in a radio script written two years later, *No Program Tonight*, Latouche has one character tell another, with respect to the notion that the show must go on, "My dear lady, you're a slave to convention... many lovely things are unfinished, Rodin's statues, Leonardo's paintings, even Schubert's Symphony was never completed."[36]

In a subsequent diary entry from that same month, Latouche further noted that Hecht planned to promote him from "lyric-writer to supervisor" on *Sing for Your Supper*, which did not open, however, until late April 1939. Whatever Latouche's exact responsibilities, aside from a leave of absence in the summer of 1938, he appears to have been on the FTP payroll from late 1937 or early 1938 to the spring of 1939, working an ostensible twenty hours a week for about ninety dollars a month.[37]

Even as Latouche worked on *Sing for Your Supper*, he became involved with the FTP's Variety Unit, working on some of their *Melodies on Parade* shows—ostensibly not the *Melodies on Parade* written by Hans Brune Myer, "a musical review of the Gay Nineties" that played under FTP auspices during the summer of 1937, but rather as scriptwriter for the Federal Theatre's "all-colored" *Melodies on Parade* presented during the summer of 1938, as well as for that show's expansion or adaptation as "a musical drama" set in "the Old West" featuring "songs of the period" that debuted toward the end of 1938.[38]

Like the 1937 edition, the summertime 1938 *Melodies on Parade* appeared under the auspices of the aptly titled Caravan Theatre, a division of the FTP that presented somewhat makeshift productions around New York free of charge. Advertised as a "variety bill," the show opened on August 16, 1938, and gave more than ten performances in different venues, mostly public parks. The *Melodies on Parade* that followed later in the year, whatever its relationship to the earlier show, premiered at the American Legion Hall in the Rosedale section of the borough of Queens on December 10, 1938. This later production featured, in addition to Latouche, the work of director Harry Miller, producer Matt Shelvey, arranger Walter Travers, conductor Ben Roberts, set designer Murette Renwick, and costumer Charles Hawkins.[39]

Latouche's script for presumably this wintertime *Melodies on Parade* survives in the archives of the FTP. A rather slim vehicle on which essentially to hang various songs and dances, this script remains historically interesting as, among other things, the lyricist's first extant musical comedy book. The story, a burlesque of westerns, features a range of comic stereotypes: the city slicker, the country heroine, the wise-cracking aunt, the villainous cattle rustler, the lovelorn maiden, and the charlatan doctor—this last a figure, inspired by W. C. Fields, who runs a traveling medicine show. The characters use such phrases as "sufferin' coyotes" and "jeepers creeps," and the plot, such as it is, concludes with a double wedding. Many of these stock elements, already in wide currency, would surface a few years later in the musical *Oklahoma!* based on Lynn Riggs's 1930 play *Green Grow the Lilacs*, but Latouche handles such elements with more pointed satirical intent.[40]

The script calls for a potpourri of traditional airs like "Red River Valley" and "The Monkey's Wedding," folkish popular music like "Oh! Susanna" and "Home on the Range," and nineteenth-century hit songs like "Fountain in the Park" and "A Hot Time in the Old Town," making the work, according to a student of such shows, an FTP pastiche musical as opposed to one of its revues or book musicals. Whether or not Latouche selected these numbers himself, in the case of the folk-song "Jesse James," he specified the "Lomax version," suggesting some familiarity with the compendium of *American Ballads and Folk Songs* published by John and Alan Lomax in 1934.[41]

In the musical's most politically charged exchange, one of the characters, Unc Jasper, contrasts his town, "a place where people can be free," with the money and power concentrated in the big cities, adding, "But someday the people will change that, too." Another striking moment in the show also occurs in the first act, when Unc Jasper, in a farewell speech to the heroine Clementine, says, "Here we are, part of the people in a state, and that state is a part of a great country, where else in the world would you find as many people, of as many nationalities, religious beliefs, and walks of life, all gathered together happily under one roof, and all being one thing—An American." When Jasper asks the townsfolk where they or their parents come from, and they call out different nations, he suggests that they sing "some of the things our forefathers sang in other lands, songs that we brought over with us, that have become part of the tradition of our country." Several townsfolk duly demonstrate numbers from their varied places of origin, until they all launch into "a real American song," namely, "Turkey in the Straw." Either explicitly or implicitly, the townsfolk show themselves to be of Italian, Irish, German, Chinese, Scottish, Spanish, English, French-Canadian, and Russian background. This portrayal of cultural and ethnic diversity set in the context of an idealized American heartland—oddly inserted in the midst of a spoof—would emerge a central focus of Latouche's 1939 *Ballad for Americans*, while the lyricist would once again cast an ironic eye on the Old West in such vastly more mature works as *The Happy Dollar* and *The Ballad of Baby Doe*.[42]

Latouche's first real break came in late 1938 with the introduction of some of his songs into the musical revue *Pins and Needles*. Playing at the Labor Stage (formerly, the Princess Theatre), a small Broadway house, the show was the brainchild of Louis Schaffer, executive director of Labor Stage, an arm of the education division of the International Ladies' Garment Workers' Union (a mixed-gender union composed mostly of Jewish- and Italian-American women). *Pins and Needles* opened in November 1937 as a weekend entertainment of "social significance" for union members, with garment workers on stage and professional talent behind the scenes. However, the show proved so successful that its schedule expanded to eight performances a week, with the actors given dispensation from their day jobs. The production moved to a bigger theater, the Windsor, in June 1939, and closed a year later after more than one thousand performances on Broadway. Cast members also gave a command performance of excerpts at the White House in March 1938, and traveled the country (although not the segregated South) twice, the second tour ending in May 1941.[43]

Pins and Needles featured mostly the music and lyrics of Harold Rome, who had written some of the material in the mid-1930s while working at Green Mansions, a Jewish resort in upstate New York; but other writers contributed songs and skits as well. Marc Blitzstein, for example, composed a sketch with music that satirized the Federal Theatre, which earlier in 1937 had pulled the plug on his opera *The Cradle Will Rock*. The show further revised, added, and dropped numbers throughout its long run, including producing revamped editions in April 1939 (*Pins and Needles 1939*) and November 1939 (*New Pins and Needles*). This lighthearted revue celebrated union life while poking fun at fascists abroad and reactionaries at home; in response to the 1939 Nazi-Soviet Pact, the show eventually reflected some anti-Stalinist sentiment as well.[44]

In late May 1938, Latouche and composer Berenece (Bernece) Kazounoff temporarily left the Federal Theatre for the Adirondacks in order to write revue material for Green Mansions, where Louis Schaffer heard some of their work and seems to have been particularly impressed with Latouche. Kazounoff, a trained pianist who would later pursue a career as a talent agent and concert manager, previously had composed songs for two Broadway flops, including *A Little Racketeer* (1932), whose score she had written with the composer-lyricist Lee Wainer, one of Latouche's collaborators on the FTP revue in progress, *Sing for Your Supper*. Indeed, Wainer might well have introduced Latouche to Kazounoff, although all three might have known one another simply through theater circles. Little is known about Kazounoff, but one of her later clients, the pianist Seymour Bernstein, described her as "heavyset, eccentrically masculine in manner, and loud-mouthed."[45]

In September, the press announced that *Pins and Needles* would shortly replace Blitzstein's "FTP Plowed Under" with "The Great White Way Turns Pink," a new number by Latouche and Lee Wainer. That song apparently never made it into the show, and seems to have simply disappeared, although the title suggests some satire of Broadway's commodification of the political left. However, toward the end of the year, the revue introduced two other numbers by Latouche, but with Kazounoff:

the sketch and song "Britannia Waives the Rules," and the song "Lorelei on the Rocks." The first of these also involved the collaboration of writer Arnold B. Horwitt (1918–1977), who worked with Latouche on the sketch and the lyrics, although some sources suggest that Horwitt took primary responsibility for the sketch, Latouche for the lyrics.[46]

Both "Britannia Waives the Rules" and "Lorelei on the Rocks" seem lost as well, although fragments and descriptions survive. The former number, inserted into the first act, lampooned Britain's September 1938 appeasement of Nazi Germany over Hitler's claim to the Sudetenland, making the sketch quite topical. The skit featured six men and one woman: British Prime Minister Neville Chamberlain (played by dressmaker Fred Schmidt), three members of his cabinet, a Japanese envoy, a German envoy, and a Miss Beamish (ostensibly named after Latouche's friend Elsa Beamish). The number included, probably in the sketch portion, a clever play on words, with respect to Chamberlain's shuttle diplomacy, that seems classic Latouche—"If at first you don't concede, fly, fly again"—while the lyric similarly contained the very Latouchian rhyme of "potsy" and "Nazi": "We're afraid of going red, / so we spend our time instead, / playing potsy on the Nazi-Roman axis." For its part, "Lorelei on the Rocks" ridiculed Nazi ideology by way of a famous poem, "The Lorelei," by the verboten Heinrich Heine, here parodied not soberly, as in the Klaus Mann lyric that Latouche had adapted for *Pepper Mill*, but farcically; the Lorelei (played in drag by Berni Gould, a cloakmaker), ignoring a storm trooper (once again, Fred Schmidt), sings of the former glories of German art and sighs,

> Since the Nazi Vereine [club]
> Suppressed Heinrich Heine,
> I've fallen on evil ways. . . .
> I long for my merman,
> But I find the new German
> Is too, too Teutonic for me.

One contemporary source described this last song as "a lament over the decline of German culture since the advent of Hitler." As no doubt intended by Louis Schaffer, both numbers helped broaden the presence of international concerns within the context of the revue.[47]

Directed by Robert H. Gordon, both "Britannia" and "Lorelei" went over big. "In the show for about a month," reported the *Brooklyn Eagle*, "they 'wow' the audiences, which used to reserve its main enthusiasm for 'Four Angels of Peace.'" The success of these numbers brought sudden fame to Latouche, more so than to his collaborators. An advertisement for the show from March 1939, for instance, described "Britannia" as "a new hit by the latest 'Pins and Needles' discovery John Latouche (assisted by Arnold Horwitt and Bernece Kazounoff)." Both the *Brooklyn Eagle* and the *New York Post*, impressed with the lyricist's youth and bemused by the idea of so aristocratic-sounding an author as John Patrick Digues Treville LaTouche writing numbers for a union show, presented profiles of the young man. Yet other journals published articles with such headers as " 'Pins' Musical Enriched by La Touche" and "Labor Stage Spots a 'Find' as John Patrick La Touche Comes up with Two Live Ones on 'Pins and Needles' Menu." These features about Latouche, incidentally, mentioned, once again, a forthcoming book of verse that never materialized, as well as his authorship of the English subtitles for Victor Trivas's *Dans les rues*, a 1933 French film that opened as *Song of the Streets* in 1939; this last undertaking pointed not only to Latouche's longstanding interest in film, but his continued engagement with the work of artists, like Trivas, banned by the Nazis.[48]

Pins and Needles removed "Lorelei on the Rocks" from its April 1939 second edition, and then "Britannia Waives the Rules" in September 1939, some months prior to the third edition. The removal of "Britannia" deprived the show of one of its best-loved skits, but Britain's declaration of war against Germany in early September made any parody of earlier appeasement untenable. For Latouche, though, the show already had helped establish his name, setting the stage for greater glory still.

4

The Little Friends

The meager documentation regarding Latouche's personal life during the late 1930s consists of a few weeks of diary entries from early 1938 and some other scattered sources, in particular, the extensive literature surrounding composer-writer Paul Bowles—to the point that "Touche" (as his friends started to call him) seems, at least during this period, more an appendage of the Bowles circle than an agent in his own right. Such a record leaves in the shadows Latouche's developing relationship with, among others, Theodora Griffis, whom he would marry in 1940, but nonetheless rounds out our knowledge of the young man's world.[1]

Born into a cultured middle-class family, his father a dentist, Paul Frederic Bowles (1910–1999) grew up in Queens, New York. Some evidence suggests that his mother's paternal line, the Winnewissers, might have had Jewish roots, a matter to which Latouche jokingly alluded by dubbing him Friedrich von Winewitz. After a few semesters at the University of Virginia, Bowles left school in order to study and write music, touring Europe and North Africa in the early 1930s with his mentor, Aaron Copland. In the ensuing years, he established himself as both a composer and a music critic, including a position at the *Herald Tribune* alongside his close friend Virgil Thomson, who had helped arrange the hire. In the late 1940s, after settling in Tangier, Bowles spent less time on music than on literature, partly for practical reasons. He achieved international acclaim with his 1949 novel, *The Sheltering Sky*, which made him a cult figure among such writers as William Burroughs and Allen Ginsberg; although not sold on his fiction, even Norman Mailer pronounced in 1959, "Paul Bowles opened the world of Hip."[2]

During his freshman year at Columbia, Latouche introduced himself to Bowles following a December 17, 1933, League of Composers concert at which John Kirkpatrick premiered Bowles's Piano Sonatina, and informed the composer that they had a mutual friend in the writer Bruce Morrissette, a graduate of Richmond College whom Bowles had met while attending the University of Virginia, and whom Latouche knew, less well, as a John Marshall High School alumnus who edited Richmond College's literary magazine, the *Messenger*. (Morrissette, a James Branch Cabell enthusiast at the time, later became a noted authority on Rimbaud and Alain Robbe-Grillet.) In his autobiography, Bowles recalled at first thinking

Latouche "a strange little man," but added, "I saw him several times at parties that winter and gradually came to think him brilliant and amusing."[3]

That Bowles and Latouche, with their sharp wit and sophisticated and advanced taste in contemporary literature and music, gravitated to each other hardly surprises. They further liked and attracted many of the same people, forming with Harry Dunham the "founding fathers" of a group dubbed by Thomson the "Little Friends" because of the short height of its core members.[4]

Bowles met Harry Hickenlooper Dunham (1910–1943) in April 1930 on the occasion of a Philadelphia Orchestra concert featuring Martha Graham dancing to Stravinsky's *The Rite of Spring* under the baton of Leopold Stokowski, Dunham's uncle through marriage. The son of a renowned Cincinnati physician, Dunham was then at Princeton, Bowles, at the University of Virginia. The two struck up a friendship, and even before Dunham graduated from Princeton in 1933, they traveled abroad together. After leaving school, Dunham, who had studied architecture at Princeton but become increasingly interested in dance and photography, settled in New York, where he and Bowles saw each other regularly, sometimes even residing together. Bowles presumably introduced Dunham to Latouche, and they too became fast friends; discussing the period around 1936, Bowles wrote, with a slight air of disapproval or jealousy, "Whenever I went to see Harry, I found John Latouche with him."[5]

Virgil Thomson, a friend to all three, remembered Dunham as "surrounded by the white light he seemed always to give off," and further remarked, "Harry was charming, a star presence, and had nothing to do but have a social life." In fact, Dunham pursued an adventurous career in the 1930s as a cameraman and film documentarian in such far-flung places as Samoa, China, and Spain, where he covered the Civil War for Pathé News. (While in Madrid in 1937, he befriended poet Langston Hughes, who stated that the "well-bred" Dunham "had been in the thick of several battles and had taken some daring sequences.") At the behest of no less than Orson Welles and John Houseman, Dunham also created film sequences, with fellow cameraman Paul Dunbar, for an aborted Mercury Theatre production, *Too Much Johnson*. But he indeed had family money and generously aided Bowles during these years, and very likely Latouche as well.[6]

Despite whatever monetary assistance Dunham provided, Latouche and Bowles struggled financially during the 1930s, which helps to explain their frequent moves from one New York address to another. In the summer of 1936, after Alfred Barr, the first director of the Museum of Modern Art, made his East 52nd Street two-bedroom apartment available to Thomson, Latouche, "then impecunious and convalescent," as Thomson recalled, moved in with him for several weeks before departing for Joy Farm, the New Hampshire summer retreat of another distinguished friend, poet E. E. Cummings (where Latouche learned how to drive a car and tell the constellations). During some of 1937 he lived with Bowles in a "wretched little room" on East 53rd Street. When Harold Hecht of the Federal Theatre Project discovered him in late 1937, he apparently was residing at the Mills House No. 2, a low-cost hotel on the

Lower East Side. At some point in the late 1930s, he also shared a room at the Chelsea Hotel with his friend, writer Robert Faulkner. And in the spring of 1939, Latouche further located to a "cheap" and drafty penthouse in Manhattan's Chelsea district previously occupied by the Bowleses. That Paul Bowles, himself an incessant traveler, should describe Latouche's life during these years as "nomadic" says a lot.[7]

The romantic lives of the Bowles-Dunham-Latouche trio proved as complex as their peregrinations. Good-looking young men—Bowles and Dunham were blond, Latouche, dark—all three appeared to have amorous relations with both men and women. Dunham married twice during this period—first to Elizabeth Derby in 1934, then to Marian Chase in 1940—while pursuing affairs with others, including Bowles, Latouche, and impresario Lincoln Kirstein. (Dunham apparently captured Aaron Copland's heart as well: the latter dedicated his 1943 Violin Sonata to his memory.) As for Latouche, after having dinner in early 1938 with the furniture manufacturer and Soviet sympathizer Walter Charak and his wife, Amy, he commented in his diary that he found it "droll" that the Charaks "upbraided" him for his "strict moral code . . . since I have probably had to date more affairs than the two of them combined, and the code worked *beautifully* for that." In contrast, Bowles, who married his and Latouche's mainly lesbian friend Jane Auer in 1938, seemed sexually cautious: "Paul was no good as anybody's lover . . . ," wrote Thomson. "Personally I think he had a low sexual temperament. . . . He made out in his life as if he were queer. But he was completely and consistently disagreeable with all the men in his life and perfectly wonderful with all the women."[8]

These varied attitudes toward love and sex reflected differences in temperament and personality: Dunham, gentlemanly, but recklessly daring; Latouche, impish, impulsive; Bowles, phlegmatic, exacting. Indeed, the spontaneity of Dunham and Latouche disconcerted Bowles. "He [Dunham] is a bit of a wild-man, and has fits of temper which are quite irrational," wrote Bowles to Copland in 1931, "but which he enjoys, quite obviously; so I never interrupt them . . . he is really quite mad at times." As for Latouche, Bowles wrote in his memoirs,

> Touche was nomadic and routineless in his life; he ate whatever he found and slept more or less wherever he was when he got sleepy. I, who lived by immutable self-imposed rules, was voluble in my criticism of his carefree behavior, but he seemed to understand that my disapproval came as much from envy as from anything else. Harry took his irregularities as a matter of course and did not complain if he arrived at four in the morning to announce that he was starved.

After the Bowleses rented a farmhouse in Staten Island in 1939, an extended visit by Latouche wrought such havoc that Paul fled to Manhattan in order to get some work done. And in 1947, when Latouche approached Jane Bowles about staying at her husband's apartment on West 10th Street while the latter was in Tangier, Jane wrote to Paul, "You know his [Latouche's] character and habits of neatness so you cannot blame me for hesitating," adding in a subsequent letter, "I hope Touche doesn't bamboozle us into getting into your place. It will be difficult if he's out on the street but maybe you'd want him there?" For his part, after observing Bowles at a gathering "talking about other subjects but really conveying himself," Latouche wrote in his 1938 diary, "I loved Paul as a friend—we were happy living together in the wretched little room on 53rd St. But he is en route, in that inflexible way that nothing will prevent."[9]

None of this need obscure, however, the genuine affection both men felt for each other; and although they saw one another with increasing rarity after 1940, they remained good friends. After learning of Latouche's death in 1956, Bowles wrote to the composer Peggy Glanville-Hicks, "There is practically no one in New York whom I shall miss more. Whenever we saw each other, I realized that my years of absence had made absolutely no difference; we had not drifted apart at all. And with so many other friends I discover that a time-crack appeared, and I know it will grow wider with each absence." In still later years, Bowles shared with friends fond memories of Latouche's description of cats as "snakes in fur," and the lyricist's impersonation of the imaginary Countess Smegma; Bowles further sang for his biographer Millicent Dillon the line, "Sex has reared its ugly head for everyone but me," from some song Latouche had composed, and went on to say, "He [Latouche] was wonderful. I was very angry with him for dying, for depriving everybody of his person."[10]

Still, the relationship seems to have been somewhat chilly as compared to that between Latouche and Dunham, who wrote to Thomson from Shanghai in early 1937,

> It boils down to hating to be in bed alone. And the least objectionable partner I've ever found is Touche. If you were here we'd have problems, to bed or not to bed. If Paul [Bowles] were here we'd have hungry genius to be fed. . . . If Marian [Chase, Dunham's girlfriend] were here I should be profoundly bored. But if Touche were capering around that bathroom and running naked about the place, I should be pleased as Punch and twice as grouchy. . . . The thought of Marian or Touche positively irritate [*sic*] me to extinction. Touche would be pulling and leaping about for the sun, or worse demanding affection or attention.

For his part, Latouche wrote in his diary a year later, "it is so nice to think there is someone I love as much as I do Harry—nothing psychopathic, nothing lush—but loving both him and what he means almost as thought [*sic*] it were an extension of myself. Sometimes, I wonder if deeply loving someone is not our only immortality—when one is loved back, of course."[11]

Latouche remained extremely attached to Dunham, whose early death—he was killed in action over Borneo in late October 1943 while serving in the army air corps—left him numb with grief. "Harry was one of the people I loved most," he stated in his journal after getting the news in November, "—his is the first death that has cut into my personal world." In a letter to Marian Chase, by this time Dunham's wife, Latouche further wrote, "Certainly I realize that youth has closed its door irrevocably, since Harry was so integrally the symbol of magic and illusion and charm that represented what I loved about being young—you know how otherwise youth was a trying period for me." And yet, he told Chase in another letter, "when it was time to put the masks away, he [Dunham] did so without losing reality: together, you formed a new one, and needing masks no longer, a complete man exited with honor and love."[12]

Latouche, Bowles, and especially Dunham all veered left politically, and became involved in some fashion or other with the American Communist Party (CPUSA). Dunham evidently joined the party around 1935, volunteering as a cameraman for party leader Earl Browder's 1936 presidential campaign, and filming and photographing Chinese provinces under communist control in 1936 and 1937, which resulted in the documentary *China Strikes Back* (1937), produced by Frontier Films. Bowles, who since at least 1937 had been assisting the party by disseminating anti-Trotskyist propaganda, officially joined its ranks around December 1938, as did his wife, Jane. "I thought this the right moment to get into the Communist Party," remembered Bowles, "and told Harry, who was glad I wanted to join. Touche was already in but for some reason would not admit; I discovered the fact later."[13]

This reminiscence, along with an allegation by a "reliable" informant recorded by the navy in 1944, would indicate that Latouche too joined the party, although in voluntary testimony to the FBI in 1954 and 1956 he denied ever being a communist or a member of the Communist Party. He admitted only a general sympathy with some communist ideals and that he attended five to ten Communist Party meetings in order to discuss a Federal Theatre Project play that had been criticized as antisemitic. True, by the 1950s he could hardly deny his many associations with various progressive causes and organizations, but he offered the FBI this among other explanations:

> In the slum neighborhood in Richmond, Virginia, where I lived as a young boy, I observed the rock fights with negroes and the antagonism of Catholics and Jews even in my own family, and all the prejudices and angers which appeared to me to be the product of ignorance and squalor. I tried to absorb the democratic ideals of Jefferson and Thomas Paine and resolved that if I ever were lucky enough to escape from that slum atmosphere, I would always, when possible, align myself on the side of freedom and the dignity of the human being.

Consequently, the "avowed ideology of the Communists, seemingly on behalf of the under-privileged, made a serious impression on me," although he had "serious doubts about collective thinking and collective action as compared with individual thinking and individual action." He further stated that while at Columbia, he refused to join the Young Communist League and publicly had been attacked by schoolmates as a "reactionary aesthete." Asserted Latouche, "Even at that time I had written considerable poetry and had determined to become a professional writer. The subject matter of my writing was, I felt, spiritual."[14]

Such protestations find support in, among other things, Latouche's May 1934 article "Art and the Artisan" for the *Columbia Review*, as discussed earlier. But the overall picture remains murky. Composer Earl Robinson, a party member who collaborated with the lyricist in the late 1930s, stated that Latouche "was neither Communist nor pro-Communist," whereas Gore Vidal recollected Latouche saying that he had been rejected by the Communist Party "as too frivolous and a sexual degenerate." Latouche's partner, Kenward Elmslie, believed that in the event that he joined the party, he would have done so "for about ten minutes." As for the collegiate experiences raised in his FBI testimonials, these seem somewhat moot, considering that after Latouche left Columbia, the political climate changed considerably as the CPUSA embraced the concept of a united popular front under the slogan "Communism is Twentieth Century Americanism," and as friends like Bowles and Dunham became party members. In sum, the evidence points to communist sympathies during this general period, even if remote. At the least, Latouche supported Republican Spain and the communist-affiliated Theatre Arts Committee. And unlike Bowles, who oddly enough decided to sever ties with the party after the German invasion of the Soviet Union in 1941, Latouche remained something of a fellow traveler at least into the late 1940s, although by then, if not earlier, he seems to have become more outspokenly critical of both the Soviet Union and communism.[15]

Meanwhile, three women appeared on the scene in the mid-1930s who would eventually marry Bowles, Dunham, and Latouche, respectively: Jane Auer, Marian Chase, and Theodora Griffis. When Thomson referred to the Little Friends, he largely had these three couples in mind, whereas Frederick Kiesler employed the term to indicate their whole coterie of friends, and Latouche even more broadly seems to have adopted the phrase as a code for homosexuals or homosexual artists.[16]

Born into a well-to-do, non-observant New York Jewish family, Jane Bowles, née Auer (1917–1973), attended private schools in Massachusetts and Switzerland. Latouche seems to have met the aspiring writer, still in her teens, in late 1936, at a club—possibly some gay-friendly establishment, given their shared homosexual predilections. In later years, Jane recognized this initial meeting as a kind of turning point, conferring some special importance to the fact that Latouche wore a necktie instead of a belt to hold up his pants. In any event, the two, both unconventional and waggish, quickly became good friends, often spending their Sunday afternoons that winter at the Greenwich Village apartment of poet E. E. Cummings. Among other things, they shared a deep love of French literature, and enjoyed drinking late into the night, with both of them borderline alcoholics at the least. They also enjoyed playacting and mimicry; their close mutual friend Robert Faulkner remembered in particular a routine in which Latouche played actor Sir Cedric Hardwicke and Jane, his lesbian secretary. "She was rough and gentle and liberating, all at the same time," stated Faulkner. "She would go into people's lives and make some dormant thing inside them come to life." Yet another friend, gallery owner John Bernard Myers, thought her "one of the funniest people I've ever met, but it would be hard to describe her humor or her wit, they are so idiosyncratically her own."[17]

While working on *Pepper Mill* in early 1937, Latouche organized an outing to Harlem with Erika Mann, Jane Auer, and Paul Bowles, on which occasion Latouche and Mann smoked marijuana and talked shop, while Auer and Bowles became acquainted. The latter two subsequently developed a strong attachment, and in February 1938 entered into an open marriage, with Jane pursuing lesbian affairs and Paul's bisexual attachments including a romance with Peggy Glanville-Hicks. "She was far more mysterious to me than Paul was," recalled Copland. "He was reserved, but open with those he knew well. She had a curious childlike quality. She was very sensitive and easily upset, but only at certain things, and you never knew why. You only knew that whatever her response would be, it would be original."[18]

One month prior to the marriage, Latouche wrote in his diary that Jane had talked to him "about her love difficulties with Paul," and added, in a passage suggesting some sense of loss and perhaps jealousy, "I suppose she [Jane] doesn't love me any more. On my way home I saw my reflection in the glass, and wondered how anyone could—I mean desire. But remembered with smug comfort that Hallie Paul [an artist friend] said the night before I looked physically satisfying—in the sense of the artist's eye, of course. So that restored my inflated ego—which is much too easily restored, I am afraid."[19]

A certain caustic edge seemed to mark the relationship between Jane and Latouche. "Here comes Complications Janie," he would say on espying her, while at one gathering, when Latouche, "in his childish voice and with his childish charm," refused to share a bottle of cognac with composer David Diamond, Jane exclaimed, "Touche, you give David a drink! Stop being such a pig." But they maintained a lifelong and important friendship, including staunch support on Latouche's part for Jane's brilliant literary work. At private readings of her novella in progress, *Two Serious Ladies*, for instance, Latouche's appreciative laughter (undaunted by her protestations that he stop) proved encouraging; and in 1941, on completing the manuscript, she wrote to Thomson that Latouche had been "very nice—actually to read the mess I handed to him last year and not to call me on it." (Jane admitted modeling the character of the "stout" Arnold—who has "a pleasant face with wide jowls that protruded on either side but did not hang down as they do on most obese people"—at least physically on Latouche.) Latouche further gave the manuscript of *Two Serious Ladies* to the literary agent who arranged for its eventual publication in 1943; and he traveled to Ann Arbor in the summer of 1953 to attend a tryout performance of Jane's play *In the Summer House*, which he thought "wonderful." Latouche's sudden death proved a grave shock to Jane, perhaps even contributing to her subsequent decline. "Jane and Touche had always had a special feeling for each other," writes one of her biographers, "though they had quarreled often enough. His death was a great blow to her."[20]

The granddaughter of Horace Gair Chase, a prominent Chicago businessman, Marian Putnam Chase graduated the Friends Seminary, a Quaker school in New York, in 1923. Entering the picture around 1936, she seems to have been a favorite of the Little Friends, who admired too her mother Gertrude, a communist. "It will always be one of the wonders of my life," wrote Latouche in his diary, "that Gertrude Chase, one of the most intellectual as well as beautiful women I have know [*sic*], can make such a perfect tomato aspic." Accounts differ as to the nature of Marian's affectional orientation, but she too became infatuated with the dashing Harry Dunham. "As for that Dunham number you seem so attached to," advised Thomson in July 1938, "it might be a very good idea to let Touche have it temporarily and you do one of those fake flights into Lesbia that are fashionable this year." In early 1940, Dunham and Chase married; and after Dunham's death in 1943, Marian became, wrote Thomson, "my closest companion." Marian herself died young of polio on a steamship returning home from Italy in 1951.[21]

Chase very possibly introduced her good friend, Theodora ("Teddy," "Theo") Griffis, to the Little Friends. And if Theodora proved on the whole a somewhat distant presence, she established a special bond with Latouche, whom she married in 1940 and divorced some five years later.[22]

One year younger than Latouche, Theodora Griffis (1915–1956) came from a very distinguished and affluent family. Her mother, Dorothy Nixon, was the daughter of S. Frederick Nixon, a successful businessman who served for a number of years in the New York State Assembly, eventually holding the office of speaker. Her paternal grandfather, William Elliot Griffis, was an eminent minister and prolific author, in particular about Japan, where he taught in the 1870s; her uncle John Elliot Griffis, a composer of modest fame; and her father, Stanton Griffis, a wealthy Wall Street financier who in the 1930s acquired Brentano's (a venerable chain of bookstores) and became chairman of Madison Square Garden and a leading executive at Paramount Pictures. Dorothy and Stanton divorced in 1937, with the latter retaining the large family estate in New Canaan, Connecticut. After contributing to the war effort in various capacities, Stanton served as ambassador to Poland, Egypt, Argentina, and Spain under the Truman administration. Meanwhile, Dorothy died in 1942.[23]

Theodora attended a girl's preparatory school, the Madeira School, from which she graduated in 1934, and then Cornell University, graduating in 1939. How and when she came to know Latouche remains uncertain, but things had so developed that by the time of a February 5, 1938, diary entry, Latouche could speak of going to his "belovèd Theodora's to dinner," where he and her "charming" mother Dorothy "hypnotized each other with talk." That same night, he "kissed Teddy goodnight seriously for the first time." The following day, he further "inducted her [Theodora] to the Marxists" by taking her to a benefit concert for the leftist journal *New Masses*.[24]

Theodora appears to have been, like Latouche, primarily homosexual. Meeting her after her marriage to Latouche at a party given by painter Buffie Johnson in 1942, the young Patricia Highsmith, later the author of *Strangers on a Train, The Price of Salt,* and *The Talented Mr. Ripley,* and also essentially lesbian, thought Theodora particularly masculine in manner, an impression heightened by her wearing cream-colored tights and black boots in the manner of coachman livery. Highsmith at any rate found her more sympathetic than Latouche, whom she thought "horribly, sickeningly flippant," noting that he put his "beefy arms around every woman eventually, with a flip answer for everything," although she welcomed his invitation to visit him and his wife at home, writing in her diary, "Should like to see Teddie and Touche again."[25]

Theodora successively held positions with the financial services firm Morgan Stanley, her father's own investment firm Hemphill Noyes, and Brentano's booksellers, the family business for which her brother, Nixon, also worked. After her divorce from Latouche, she settled in New Canaan, Connecticut, with her lover, Louise Shangle (described by Latouche as "that mildewed millstone... still firmly riveted into her neck"), and died of cancer at New York's Memorial Hospital in early 1956, a half-year before Latouche's own untimely demise. During these later years, she remained distantly friendly with her ex-husband, to whom she left a bequest of ten thousand dollars.[26]

Otherwise, little is known about her. Her brief obituaries reported on her gifts to Mystic Seaport and the New Canaan Library, evidencing her love of both the sea and literature. In a thumbnail portrait, Ruth Yorck warmly recalled the pale, quiet, and beautiful Theodora—dubbed "the nymph" by the Little Friends—as inquisitive, gifted, clever, and secretive. Theodora's nephew remembered also an unconventional streak, including an attraction to Zen Buddhism. In a rare surviving letter, one sent to Latouche's mother, Effie, she apologized for being a "*lousy* letter writer," something that frustrated Latouche, her father, Stanton, and others, and that militates against a fuller picture of one the great loves of Latouche's life. She remains best remembered for Cornell Medical School's Theodora Griffis Faculty Club, established by Stanton Griffis in her memory in 1962, her father choosing to ignore the married name that she herself kept to the end of her life.[27]

The Little Friends formed part of a larger artistic sphere that included composers George Antheil, Marc Blitzstein, Aaron Copland, and David Diamond, but especially Virgil Thomson, whom they called "Papa," and who liked them all, including Latouche. "We all long for Touche," he wrote to Marian Chase from Paris in early 1939, and again, some months later, "*We want Touche.*" Describing the Little Friends in his memoirs as "a quarter mad," Thomson went on to say, "I call these lovely people not quite sane because though not besotted and not corrupted and none of them, God knows, the least bit stupid, all were pursued by fatality, as if the gods would destroy them." Thomson had in mind not only the early deaths of the Dunhams and the Latouches, but Jane Bowles's debilitating stroke at age forty. He attributed this "local curse"—which spared only Paul Bowles—to "Dunham's white-lighted glamour and his unstated but relentless will to die young."[28]

Latouche's relationship with Thomson could be rocky. On one occasion in early 1945, Thomson told Latouche "with great fury and critical acerbity wrapped in the get-it-down sugar of friendship," that the young lyricist had embarked on the "classical Virginia pattern" of love and work frustrations followed by an escape into alcohol (and, he prophesized, drugs), and warned him further that he had developed the reputation for getting "big advances" and then failing to deliver, leading Latouche to reflect, "Such is the feeling that lack of success can engender—Virgil is not a very good friend, altho a brilliant mind. But he becomes more and more papal in his pronouncements—the lightest contradiction drives him into a wattled rage. His resemblance to Queen Victoria is having its inevitable result. But I enjoy seeing him, and his apartment, so like that standard one inhabited by the old maids designed by Mary Roberts Rinehart, is essential Americana." Some months later, after learning that Thomson had told several people that he, Latouche, could not be trusted with producing promised work, the latter again wrote in his journal, "Virgil is attacking everyone recently, and, resorting to a kind of musical blackmail in order to have his mediocre compositions advanced into the public eye (and hair), is causing a resentment of himself to grow like a slow fire among his fellow musicians." And yet, not long after, on repeated listenings to a recording of Thomson's documentary film score *The Plow That Broke the Plains* (1936), he wrote to the composer, "I am filled with present and past love for you."[29]

Latouche gained an appreciation for other composers in this particular circle, many of whom, like Thomson, had studied in Paris with Nadia Boulanger, including Copland, Blitzstein, and Bowles. On hearing Copland's 1937 opera for high school students to a text by Edwin Denby, *The Second Hurricane*, played at a private home in early 1938, he wrote in his diary, "it was excitingly simple—the words, I mean: the music had other beauties"; and after encountering the work again in concert, he found it "still wonderful (with the superb Denby text)." About this same time, attending performances of Blitzstein's *I Got the Tune* and, for a second time, *The Cradle Will Rock*, he described the former as "a very exciting Radio Opera," and the latter, "Still thrilling as ever"; in 1941, now more financially flush, he contributed monetarily to the production of Blitzstein's opera *No for an Answer*. (Blitzstein himself he found "a puzzling person—I feel drawn to him by that violent yet subtle quality of his nature.") He further hoped to arrange for portions of Bowles and Charles Henri Ford's unfinished opera *Denmark Vesey* to be performed on radio, even if he thought these two collaborators "mismated." Regrettably, Latouche himself never had the occasion to provide words for Bowles or any of these other composers, perhaps because they tended to regard him somewhat dismissively as, in Thomson's words, "an author of light verse." Recalled Bowles, "Touche made his living writing song lyrics, although he called himself a poet, and bitterly resented my calling him a lyricist." In truth, Latouche professionally involved himself in a popular milieu at some remove from these composers, although in time, working with Jerome Moross and Douglas Moore, he also proved an outstanding opera librettist.[30]

Latouche actually had approached Bowles, before turning to Earl Robinson, about setting *Ballad for Americans* (1939), but embarrassed by the text's "subject matter" and its "too many concessions to popular taste," Bowles turned down the offer. The latter further recounted that Latouche would later "twit" him by saying, "Wouldn't you like to have written 'A Ballad for Americans'? I came to you and asked you, you son of a bitch, and you wouldn't"—to which Bowles would point out that had he done so, "my music would have made it an entirely different song, which would have had no popular success. This did not please him [Latouche] either, for to him it implied that the music had a preponderant part in the song's creation."[31]

Latouche and Bowles at least worked on some of the same cinematic projects: the silent short *145 W. 21* (1936); the film documentary *Congo* (1945); and the avant-garde films *Dreams That Money Can Buy* (1947) and *8 X 8: A Chess Sonata in 8 Movements* (1957). In the case of the 1936 short, directed by the Swiss-born photographer and filmmaker Rudy Burckhardt, this involved appearing as actors alongside Thomson, Copland, Denby, and actress Paula Miller, the wife of director Lee Strasberg. Shot in three days, the picture took its title from the Manhattan address shared by Burckhardt and Denby, a loft apartment that served as the film's principal mise-en-scène. Created to help raise money for the Henry Street School Settlement production of *The Second Hurricane*, the short was shown, with music (now lost) by Bowles, at a fundraiser, giving everyone, as Copland recalled, "a laugh."[32]

In the film, Denby plays a writer, Miller, his girlfriend or wife, and Copland and Latouche, two handymen (see Figure 6). As Copland and Latouche repair the roof of Denby and Miller's loft apartment, the latter two attend a burlesque show, where Thomson and Bowles also can be seen in the audience. Back at West 21st Street, Latouche, snapping his fingers, suggests to Copland that they burglarize the apartment; ransacking a bureau, Latouche joyously unearths "four smackers." Returning to their ravaged apartment, Denby and Miller find an overlooked twenty-dollar bill. As Copland and Latouche enjoy a steak dinner, Denby and Miller embrace, the final shot showing Burckhardt filming the pair.

Whatever the satiric intentions of this whimsical farce—including the contrast of Miller's reading of a *Modern Romances* magazine with her later attendance at a burlesque show—Latouche's film presence, in the context of this study, naturally holds special interest. Slender, elfin, a good head shorter than Copland, he prances around like a sprite, evoking that "leaping about for the sun" of which Dunham spoke. Burckhardt plainly drew on Latouche's propensity for creating disturbance, especially as the latter tears through a chest of drawers, tossing items every which way, with Copland the hesitant observer. Meanwhile, the final sequence, with Latouche and Copland laughing lustily over beers and a meal, suggests a warm affection between the two.

Latouche's immersion into the world of American contemporary music seems to have helped frame his views on the day's serious musical culture. Discussing the "grrreat Toscannini" (*sic*) in his 1938 diary, he stated, "That he is a great conductor there is no denying, but that he is rather an ass seems just as apparent. The only real thing he ever did was to refuse to conduct in Germany—and of course he had to say he did it for the sake of 'persecuted *musicians*.' Christ, when will people accept the fact that real art has guts, and can face contemporary problems without the 'maestro' flourish." And reflecting on the February 6, 1938, *New Masses* benefit at the 46th Street Theatre, he wrote that everything about the concert "exclaimed, Carnegie Hall is dead! And a good thing, too. Stuffy, arid music playing in a vacuum atmosphere!"[33]

Latouche's composer friends formed only part of a large network of artists and art lovers, including poets Witter Bynner, E. E. Cummings, Robert Hunt, and Muriel Rukeyser (pronounced ROO-ky-ser); writers Jane Bowles, Edwin Denby, Muriel Draper, Robert Faulkner, Charles Henri Ford, Peter Lindamood, and Carl Van Vechten; painters Alexander Brook, Maurice Grosser, Buffie Johnson, Pavel Tchelitchew (pronounced Tchel-EET-chev), and Kristians Tonny; photographers Rudy Burckhardt, Victor Kraft, and Marion Morehouse; designers Frederick Kiesler and Oliver Smith (Paul Bowles's second cousin); producer-director John Houseman; and such cultural arbiters as gallery owner Kirk Askew and his wife, Constance, museum director Arthur ("Chick") Austin, and dance impresario Lincoln Kirstein. By 1939, composer Leonard Bernstein, actress Judith Tuvim (later, Judy Holliday), and such refugee painters as Salvador Dalí and Yves Tanguy (pronounced TAHN-gee) had joined the scene as well (with Latouche purchasing in 1941 Dalí's painting *Anbattet*, as he did some drawings by Joan Miró). Cummings and Morehouse formed a couple, as did the same-sex pairings of Bynner and Hunt, Copland and Kraft, Denby and Burckhardt, Ford and Tchelitchew, and Grosser and Thomson (although both Kraft and Burckhardt eventually led heterosexual lives). Clearly this social world included a considerable number of bisexuals and homosexuals (or what Latouche at the time sometimes referred to as "fairies" or "pansies"); and if Bowles, Dunham, and Latouche all decided to marry, it could hardly be attributed to the absence of alternatives within their set. Indeed, although homosexuality remained a somewhat taboo subject in polite society, the frankness with which some of these artists addressed gay themes—as in the homoerotic drawings of Tchelitchew or the writings of Jane Bowles—clearly paralleled Latouche's own candor in this area.[34]

An open attitude toward homosexuality certainly prevailed among another circle with whom Latouche had some association, one in which the gay architect and designer William ("Bill") Levy Alexander (born Alexander Levy, 1909–1997) assumed a leading role. Latouche became friends with the slightly older Alexander sometime in the 1930s, a decade that witnessed the latter's signature achievement: the so-called Hangover House in South Laguna, California, for his friend, adventurer Richard Halliburton. Although active on the West Coast, Alexander maintained a presence in New York as well, including hosting what one commentator describes as "neo-pagan" rituals on some family property upstate in Coxsackie. There, Latouche joined Alexander and such gay friends of his as writer Paul Mooney and landscape designer Charles Wolfsohn in "nude bathing" and "sleeping under the stars" as well as poetry readings and music listenings. One surviving photograph shows Alexander, Mooney, and Wolfsohn in the nude or semi-nude posing in the woods as the three graces. Photographs from the same period in which Latouche and Theodora, both naked, cavort on the grounds of Stanton Griffis's estate, including one in which the lyricist embraces a nude classical statue, likewise reveal a penchant for nudist display (see Figure 16).[35]

Latouche's few surviving letters and diary entries from these years contain only the passing description of Cummings ("charming"), Ford ("pretty, vacillating, genius-eating"), Hunt ("extremely charming, but *très louche* [French: very shady]"), Lindamood ("red-headed; distrait"), Morehouse ("beautiful"), and Rukeyser ("a fine poetess . . . a black lioness"). Meanwhile, although few of these artist friends left behind written impressions of him, Alexander Brook, Buffie Johnson, and Pavel Tchelitchew painted his portrait, and John Seymour Erwin, Rudy Burckhardt, and Carl Van Vechten photographed him. Brook's somber full-body portrait, *La Touche* (1938), presents its subject—already appearing a good deal heftier than in the 1936 Burckhardt film—in a suit and bowtie, an overcoat casually draped over his shoulders, and a cello and reading material flanking him on either side. Tchelitchew's vibrant head portrait (c. 1940), *John Treville Latouche,* shows the young lyricist, his clothes tattered, his eyes crystalline, his eyebrows bushy, and his head topped by an unruly mass of brown hair, with a small visage emerging from his torso (see Figure 11). In Johnson's 1940–41 painting, *The Poet (John Latouche),* the subject, dressed in black trousers and a sweater of dark plum, lies barefoot and thoughtful on his side in what appears to be a seaside landscape, his hand resting on a book, an overturned sandal by his feet. For all Latouche's reputation as a jester, these three paintings suggest a certain restless melancholy. Meanwhile, in 1937, the Mississippi-born writer-photographer John Seymour Erwin photographed him draped in a luxuriant toga as a regal Tiberius, the picture, like Tchelitchew's portrait, establishing contact with surrealism through its superimposition of what looks like the cut-out of a classical torso (see Figure 7). Van Vechten's marvelous 1944 photo portraits, with Latouche in navy uniform, date from a slightly later period, but some of these too have a somewhat sad quality, whereas others seem more sanguine, even gleeful (see Figure 27). In some contrast, Rudy Burckhardt's 1945 photos of the lyricist, now in his early thirties, capture a sober maturity that seems to signal a new phase in his life.[36]

Of Latouche's relationships with these sundry artists, that between himself and Frederick Kiesler (1890–1965) deserves some special attention on account of its warmth and longevity, not to mention Kiesler's importance in helping to introduce Latouche to that exiled European artistic community with which the latter became so deeply involved. Born into a Ukrainian-Jewish family, Kiesler studied painting and architecture in Vienna and initially became known in avant-garde circles for his "electromechanical" set for a production of Karel Čapek's robot drama *R.U.R.* in Berlin in 1923, and for his Mondrianesque spatial structure, *City in Space,* exhibited in Paris in 1925. Settling in New York in 1926 with his wife, Stefanie ("Steffi"), Kiesler pursued a multifaceted career designing store windows, buildings, and theater and opera sets, his constructivist work evolving in the 1930s, under the influence of the surrealists, to more biomorphic shapes and methods. A larger-than-life personality despite his diminutive size of only about five feet, and a revered figure among adventurous and thoughtful artists across a broad range of disciplines, Kiesler made his mark more as a theorist and visionary than as a designer or architect per se, although his sketches anticipated the work of, among others, architect Frank Gehry, the first recipient (in 1998) of the prestigious Kiesler Prize for Architecture and the Arts. "Being with Kiesler was like touching an electric wire that bore the current of contemporary history," eulogized his friend Virgil Thomson, who added, "Kiesler was the one among us who understood best the work that any of us was doing and who cherished it. Such faith is rare on the part of an artist who knows himself to be advanced." In less adulatory although still respectful reminiscences, John Bernard Myers described him as "Napoleonic in manner," Hans Richter as, "A lovable man, whom it was difficult to love."[37]

Latouche and Kiesler first met after the February 28, 1934, world premiere of George Antheil's opera *Helen Retires,* for which Kiesler had designed the sets. Still only a college freshman, Latouche walked across the empty Juilliard stage and introduced himself to the designer, "releasing a discourse on the modern theater" and the work in particular of André Breton, Jean Cocteau, and Jean Giraudoux. "Stunned" and "delighted" by the young man's "curiosity and knowledge," Kiesler suggested that they meet again, and the two subsequently became dear friends.[38]

During his stint as a cultural reporter for the *Columbia Review,* Latouche left behind an assessment of Kiesler's work that sheds some light on this exceptional relationship. Commenting on the designer's sets for *Helen Retires* and a Juilliard production of *Ariadne auf Naxos,* Latouche, now a college sophomore, wrote, "the wide field Mr. Kiesler has blazoned, with his introduction of the cinema as a component, and his use of the anachronism either as design or as intellectual connotation, is perhaps the most hopeful for the new stage.... I do know that settings as an extension of the idea of the play, and not as a shell in which action takes place, are inevitable, and of these Mr. Kiesler is a sincere creator." On a more personal level, during his service in the navy, Latouche, on hearing from Stefanie about some of her husband's work-related problems, wrote back, "I'm sorry Kiesler must still lock horns with those old crustaceans up at Juilliard.... I wish he were more ruthless about people, but I suppose if he were, some of that profound capacity for love would be dissipated, which would be a pity. I think much of him and of you."[39]

From 1934 to virtually the end of Latouche's life, as documented by Stefanie's diaries, not much time would elapse, generally speaking, without him and Kiesler, both late-night gadabouts, sharing a dinner or cultural excursion of some sort, including outings to see the Eugène Labiche's *Horse Eats Hat* at the Federal Theater (1936), Thomas Dekker's *The Shoemaker's Holiday* at the Mercury Theatre (1938),

Bernard Herrmann's cantata *Moby Dick* at Carnegie Hall (1940), William Saroyan's play *Love's Old Sweet Song* at the Plymouth Theatre (1940), Sergei Eisenstein's film *Alexander Nevsky* at the Fifth Avenue Playhouse (1946), Gottfried von Einem's opera *The Trial* at City Center (1953), and a Frank Lloyd Wright exhibit on the grounds of the Guggenheim Museum's future location (1953). Presumably sometime in the late 1930s, Kiesler designed a storyboard for an avant-garde film, *Aphrodite's Left Turn,* imagined to feature actress Elissa Landi (Aphrodite) along with Edwin Denby (A Young Man), Aaron Copland (A Professor), Theodora Griffis (A Tender Torso), Latouche (Choir-Boy), and Kiesler's cat Sing-Sing; in the early 1940s, he began sketches for a home for Latouche; and during Latouche's final months, the two embarked on a musical theater project, *The First Time.* Kiesler enjoyed just kicking up his heels with Latouche, which he typically did until the wee hours, often without Stefanie. After Latouche died, Kiesler, shocked and devastated by the loss of his "closest young friend," assented at the behest of family and friends to read Carson McCullers's eulogy at the lyricist's memorial service.[40]

As suggested by the forecited letter to Stefanie Kiesler, Latouche—like Jane Bowles, Marian Chase, and the other Little Friends—grew close not only to Kiesler but to "his tranquil wife and comrade," as Hans Richter described her. A remarkable person in her own right, Stefanie Kiesler, née Frischer (1897–1963), assisted refugees from Nazi Germany and war-ravaged Europe during the 1930s and 1940s, many of whom she encountered as head of the French and German collections of the New York Public Library, a position she held for decades. Such kindness extended to her American-born friends as well, with her obituary stating that Latouche "practically lived in her house during his early poor days." One preserved snapshot from around 1940 shows Stefanie smiling at Latouche with utter delight (see Figure 9).[41]

Concerning this circle of artists as a whole, Latouche spent a good deal of time with them in various social settings. Indeed, his 1938 diary intimates an endless succession of such gatherings from noon, about which time he sometimes rose, until as late as four or five in the morning—all busily interspersed with writing lyrics on the fly, meeting with composers and producers, or catching a concert, exhibition, or film, viewing in quick succession, for instance, director Irving Cummings's comedy *Merry-Go-Round of 1938* and Walt Disney's *Snow White and the Seven Dwarfs,* which he deemed "dull, save for the animals and the dwarves. The humans were unworthy of Disney's genius, I thought. Or perhaps I was too tired for fantasy."[42]

Although the Little Friends often congregated in their own apartments, or those belonging to family members, their larger set tended to meet, among other places, at the homes of E. E. Cummings, Muriel Draper, Carl Van Vechten, and especially Kirk and Constance Askew, whose four-story brownstone on East 61st Street became a principal hub for this social network. During the regular season, the Askews entertained throughout the week, but were known especially for their Sunday evening "at homes" at which four or five dozen "notabilities," according to

John Houseman, could be found in the couple's large drawing room and smaller library. Writes Houseman, "Tea was served, also cocktails and whisky, though never in quantities that would interfere with the serious business of the gathering. Shoptalk was permitted up to a point; so were politics, if discussed in a lively and knowledgeable way. Flirtation (homo- and heterosexual) was tolerated but not encouraged." Architect Philip Johnson described the Askew home as "the crossroads of the world for several years," and their salon undoubtedly helped make New York a more cosmopolitan city, especially with regard to trends in fashion and art.[43]

Bowles, who thought that the Askews "ran the only regular salon in New York worthy of the name," might have brought Latouche into this scene; but in any case, Latouche introduced the Askews to Bowles's future wife, Jane Auer, who became a devoted habitué of their parties. In an entry in his 1938 journal, Latouche recounted being "dragged to Constance Askew's salon at midnight"—by whom he does not say—and finding a "very drunk" Jane ("She is lovely, but tonight she looks debauched") and a "very drunk" Kristians Tonny, among other friends and acquaintances. "But where do I reach reality in all this," he asked himself. "I have not the courage now. Tomorrow? Today is always tomorrow—." Returning home drunk that morning after a late-night breakfast with Copland, Thomson, and Tonny and his wife, Marie-Claire Ivanoff, he further reflected, "When I got home, I told myself in the mirror what a fool I was, but narcissistically refused to believe it. Inside I do, and am sad. Goodnight."[44]

During these same years, Latouche concurrently established his inveterate habit of frequenting bars and nightclubs, including some in Harlem, but especially Tony's and Le Ruban Bleu in midtown Manhattan, as discussed earlier. Indeed, the cabaret scene formed a sort of counterpoint to the Askew salon, similarly challenging the accepted mores of the day, and presuming a certain worldliness framed especially by an appreciation of current trends both at home and abroad. At the same time, these two domains made up rather separate spheres. Whereas Broadway celebrities could be found at Tony's and Le Ruban Bleu, the same types were more likely to attend parties hosted by Jules Glaenzer, Elsa Maxwell, and Condé Nast than those of Draper or the Askews, where, as Houseman recalled, "show business was sparsely represented." And whereas the cabarets showcased the irreverent and the bawdy, the atmosphere at the more sophisticated salons, modern art galleries, and new music concerts tended to be more serious and intellectual. Latouche's association with the Little Friends and their extended circle no doubt encouraged a certain boldness of expression and independence of thought, and some of these friends shared his enthusiasm for the nightclub scene, including, as mentioned earlier, Thomson, who even announced his intention, in late 1937, of writing something for Spivy. But cabaret life brought Latouche closer in touch with his real métier, and provided not only a diversion from the sorrow and nostalgia that haunted so many of the Little Friends, but an outlet for his own irrepressible wit and gaiety as well.[45]

5

Ballads for Americans

The appearance of Latouche's work in *Pins and Needles* coincided with his association with the Theatre Arts Committee (TAC). Founded in 1937 by members of the theater community as the Theatre Arts Committee to Aid Spanish Democracy, TAC soon after abbreviated its name as its concerns went beyond support for Republican Spain to advocacy for China and Czechoslovakia as well as progressive causes at home. In May 1938, TAC began staging its own entertainments, Cabaret TAC, under the management of John Proctor, and in July 1938 initiated a monthly organ, *TAC* magazine, under the editorship of Edna Ocko. At its height in 1939, TAC had a membership of more than two thousand, but conflicts between pro- and anti-Stalinists among its broad coalition of leftists precipitated its dissolution in the course of 1940.[1]

In late November 1938, around the same time that *Pins and Needles* adopted "Lorelei on the Rocks," Cabaret TAC featured Norman Lloyd in a presumed version of this same number, "The Last of the Lorelei," described by the *Times* as a "bitterly grotesque lament." And in its January 1939 issue, *TAC* magazine, "glad to introduce John Latouche to our readers," published seven humorous poems by the lyricist with illustrations by William Steig under the header, "New Year's Resolutions." In each of these poems, a certain type in the art world—"Dancer," "Movie Producer," "Movie Queen," "Radio Announcer," "Composer," "Audience Member," and "Critic"—vows to become more committed politically, with the critic, for example, promising not to "damn every drama as hefty / Whose tone is a trifle lefty." In some of these poems, Latouche conflated political with artistic populism; the composer, for instance, whose "Stravinsky was strictly from Minsky," and whose "Bach was worse than my bite," concludes, "So this year to tunes I am swerving / And I'm all for Berlin. (I mean Irving)." (The Stravinsky-Minsky rhyme, already used by Ira Gershwin in *Let 'Em Eat Cake*, would later appear as well in a Lorenz Hart lyric from *Pal Joey*.) Latouche continued to sound a socially conscious note in a book review of Elsa Lanchester's memoirs, *Charles Laughton and I*, published in the following month's issue of *TAC*, in which he noted that the book, although enjoyable, lacked involvement with "the contemporary scene," and failed to recognize "that the creator who withholds himself from participation in active world progress will inevitably become static."[2]

In the earlier January issue, *TAC* magazine mentioned that Latouche, "one of our most promising young political satirists," already had been represented in "various editions of Cabaret TAC," but evidence regarding such participation remains sparse. One edition of the cabaret, presented on the Labor Stage on February 12, 1939, included a song written by Latouche with composer Lee Wainer, "Leaning on a Shovel," destined to appear in the revue *Sing for Your Supper* later in the year. And many TAC events in late 1939 and 1940 featured the lyricist's *Ballad for Americans.* But Latouche likely had other work presented at Cabaret TAC, including perhaps some of those songs he continued to write with Berenece Kazounoff.[3]

Five numbers by Kazounoff and Latouche appeared in any case in one or another edition of *Sunday Night Varieties,* a revue along the lines of Cabaret TAC presented sporadically on several Sunday nights in March and April 1939. Directed and conceived by Nat Lichtman and sponsored by the periodical *New Masses* "for cultural and fund-raising purposes," the show brought together, on a shoestring budget, a young and idealistic company reportedly willing to work for nothing. Several of these journeymen had worked with Lichtman in an area of the Catskill Mountains dotted with Jewish resorts known as the Borscht Belt, including the show's star, an up-and-coming Danny Kaye, who met his future wife, composer-lyricist Sylvia Fine, through this production.[4]

Sunday Night Varieties contained mostly the music of Kazounoff, collaborating alternately with Latouche and David Greggory, but also included several songs by Sylvia Fine and some sketches by writer Sam Locke. The Kazounoff-Latouche songs, mostly lost, included "Blasé," a lampoon of cafe society; "Physical Culture," a satire of Bernarr Macfadden's fitness regimen; "Home Is Where You Hang Your Heart," a celebration of love; and two other songs, "Tattooed Lady" and "Times Have Changed." A surviving copy of "Home Is Where You Hang Your Heart," its title a play on the phrase, "home is where you hang your hat," preserves a rare example of Kazounoff's music, in this instance, tuneful and bluesy, but not particularly memorable. The song engages a favored topic of the period, with the lyric at one point stating, "You may be poor and insecure / But if your love is there / You're like a millionaire at home." Harold Rome had written a similar number, "Sunday in the Park," for *Pins and Needles,* and Latouche and Kazounoff well might have hoped that that revue would pick up "Home Is Where" or one or another of these other songs; indeed, a February 1939 advertisement for *Pins and Needles* announced that Latouche was at work on some new sketches for the show. At the same time, "Home Is Where" reveals a certain wit—"You may have to climb to the roof for a view / Maybe there's a note that the rent's overdue"—that distinguishes the song from more sentimental numbers in this vein.[5]

Sunday Night Varieties—alternately called *Left of Broadway*—opened on March 5, 1939, in a loft nightclub, dubbed the Keynote Theatre, on West 52nd Street. The premiere largely went unnoticed in the press, although a critic for the *Daily Worker* found it to contain "more intelligence, humor, pulchritude, and entertainment" than "any show I've seen this season on or off Broadway." After a few performances at the Keynote—the police shut down the last scheduled performance because the *New Masses* lacked the requisite license—the revue moved to a small stage in the Barbizon-Plaza Hotel on Central Park South for a single performance on April 9. Reviewing this latter opening, *Variety* imagined that the "staid, conservative, and plush-lined" Barbizon-Plaza "must have had a case of capitalistic jitters... when the proletarian 'Sunday Night Varieties' got through with the so-called upper strata," but nonetheless recommended the show, with its cheap admission price of one dollar, as "a sock addition to the meager Sunday night offerings." Unable to secure the Barbizon-Plaza for Sunday nights, Lichtman attempted to find a Broadway house, but financial backing proved an obstacle, and that seems to have been the end of it.[6]

In late 1939, a similarly young cast, the Promenaders, included three of the songs from *Sunday Night Varieties*—"Blasé," "Physical Culture," and "Home Is Where You Hang Your Heart"—along with another Kazounoff-Latouche number, "Slap On the Grease Paint," and a song for which the lyricist himself apparently wrote the music, "Blues," in an intimate revue entitled *Two for Tonight*. Presented at the Cherry Lane Theatre in Greenwich Village, the show opened on December 28 to largely tepid reviews, although the critics singled out for praise both "Home Is Where" and "Blues," which targeted "hot songs and people and things in the public eye," including anti-union journalist Westbrook Pegler. Around this same time, Latouche contributed some "specialty numbers" as well to the third annual "Stars for Spain" benefit for Republican Spain, held at New York's Mecca Temple on December 10, 1939.[7]

On June 20, 1939, a troupe of Austrian refugees, calling themselves the Refugee Artists Group, premiered an evening of sketches and songs, *From Vienna,* at the elegant Music Box Theatre on West 45th Street. Herbert Berghof directed the cast of fourteen, accompanied, as in *Pins and Needles,* by an orchestra of two pianos, with pianist-composers André Singer (using his pseudonym Otto Andreas) and Hans Herberth in the pit. The show contained new material in English as well as older items translated from German, including a play, consuming most of the first act, by Jura Soyfer, *Der Lechner-Edi schaut ins Paradies,* adapted by Latouche as *Journey to Paradise,* the lyricist's only credited contribution to the production.

Many members of the Refugee Artists Group were Jewish, leftist, or both, and had been associated with Vienna's provocative Kleinkunstbühne ("Cabaret Theater"), a company, established in 1933 under the guidance of architect Victor Gruenbaum, that specialized in humorous songs and satirical sketches. After some initial success on the legitimate stage, the Kleinkunst was barred by Austria's increasingly authoritarian government from playing in larger theaters; and so for several years, they divided into smaller groups and performed in cellars and coffee shops until, totally doomed by Nazi control of Austria, they disbanded just prior to the Anschluss of

March 1938. Gruenbaum subsequently emigrated to the United States and helped Kleinkunst members and other actors regroup in New York, where they found employment as best they could as waiters, clerks, cooks, handymen, and so forth.[8]

In December 1938, the troupe performed some of their material for an impressed Beatrice Kaufman, who rallied to their cause a group of sponsors that included her husband, playwright George S. Kaufman, along with such other Broadway luminaries as Irving Berlin, Edna Ferber, Sam Harris, Lorenz Hart, Moss Hart, and Richard Rodgers. These supporters, many Jewish themselves, raised enough money for the troupe to start rehearsing a new revue, and in April, after a successful audition at the St. James Theatre, Irving Berlin and Sam Harris offered them the use of their Music Box Theatre free of charge. Director Charles Friedman, set designer Donald Oenslager, costume designer Irene Sharaff, and lighting director Hassard Short—all outstanding figures—similarly agreed to work on the production on a nonprofit basis. The Artists Group hoped not only to make ends meet, but to raise funds for colleagues trapped abroad.

For this revue, originally called *It Happened In Vienna*, the Artists Group decided to duplicate the Kleinkunst practice of interpolating a somewhat serious musical play—the *Mittelstück* ("Centerpiece")—into the proceedings, and selected for this purpose Jura Soyfer's popular *Der Lechner-Edi*, first performed in 1936. A journalist, poet, and playwright, Soyfer (1912–1939) came from a Russian-Jewish family who found their way to Vienna following the October Revolution. A strongly committed Marxist, he became one of the most celebrated satirists of his time, supplying the Kleinkunst with much-prized *Mittelstücke*. While attempting to flee to Switzerland after the Anschluss, he was arrested and sent to concentration camps, first Dachau and then Buchenwald, where he died of typhus on February 16 at age twenty-six.[9]

Soyfer's work with the Kleinkunst brought him into a collaborative relationship with the forementioned André Singer (1907–1996), a Hungarian-Jewish pianist-composer who used the pen name Otto Andreas for his cabaret activities. After some time in Paris and London, Singer moved to the States in August 1938, and apparently collaborated with Latouche on the latter's adaptation of *Der Lechner-Edi*. During the war, Singer served in the army, and in 1946, joined the faculty of Sarah Lawrence College, where he taught music theory, composition, and piano.

Latouche likely came to be entrusted with adapting the Soyfer play on the basis of the work he had done on Erika Mann's revue *Pepper Mill*. In any event, he submitted a rather finished draft of *Journey to Paradise*, minus song lyrics, for copyright in late December 1938. The Artists Group had hoped to present the play in January, largely in order to help raise money for Soyfer's release from Buchenwald; but such plans came to naught, and the adaptation appeared only after Soyfer's death as the centerpiece of *From Vienna*.[10]

A kind of science-fiction fable, *Der Lechner-Edi* concerns the unemployed Edi Lechner, who having lost his job at a shoe factory, blames his machine at work for displacing him. The machine, called Pepi, appears and, himself antiquated, takes Edi and his girlfriend Fritzi progressively back in time in an attempt to stem the scientific and cultural advances that have led to this current crisis. Persuading Luigi Galvani, Galileo, Columbus, Gutenberg, and Orpheus to renounce his invention or art, the three finally arrive at the Garden of Eden. There, after Edi urges that man not be created, and Fritzi argues otherwise, the Gatekeeper brings the story to an end by announcing that the choice between good and evil will remain in the hands of mankind. Also including two songs, "Wanderlied der Zeit" ("Time Traveler's Song") and "Moritat im Paradies" ("Gruesome Ballad of Paradise"), the play inhabits a Viennese comic tradition derived from Johann Nestroy, among others, but shows the influence of Brecht as well.[11]

Calling the main couple Eddie and Betty (later renamed Tony and Annie), and the machine Joe Gadget, Latouche freely adapted the Soyfer text, drawing on native vaudeville traditions for some of the humor, and sporting an occasional rhetorical flourish somewhat akin to Clifford Odets. Unencumbered by the sort of Austrofascist censorship that confronted Soyfer, Latouche also proved more pointed in his satire. In the Soyfer text, for instance, Edi dissuades Galvani from inventing electricity by subjecting him to a montage of contemporary radio programs, whereas in Latouche's version, Eddie, after a joke about his month's electric bill, reveals to Galvani the horrifying use of electric wire during the First World War. (In a subsequent version, Latouche substituted the more familiar Benjamin Franklin and his kite for Galvani and his frog legs.) Similarly, Latouche managed to incorporate cracks about fascist Italy and Spain; and for the "Moritat" lyric that he eventually supplied, he wrote two additional stanzas, one excoriating dictators, the other lamenting the fate of the refugees. His script ended more optimistically as well, Eddie stating not just "it's all up to us," as in the original, but rather "it will be ours." Horst Jarka, who in later years translated the play himself, opined that Latouche's adaptation inescapably lost something of the work's original flavor, in particular the "comic linguistic contrast between Edi the 'little guy' and the famous eggheads," but thought that the new stanzas for the "Moritat" gave the song added "immediacy," and that an original lyric composed by Latouche for the work's finale remained true to Soyfer's "spirit."[12]

From Vienna opened to excellent reviews, including a near rave by Brooks Atkinson in the *Times*. Observed *Life* magazine, "a first-night audience which had been prepared to feel merely sympathetic toward a mediocre show found itself instead delighted by first-rate entertainment." The critics particularly marveled that a group of political exiles should present a revue neither bitter nor gloomy, but rather gentle and captivating. Concluded Atkinson, "It is a shock to realize that people like these can be refugees from any part of the civilized world. For they are the grace and delight of civilized living. But they are among friends now. All of us were deeply moved last evening by this quiet incident in the code of human relations." Indeed, the opening-night audience erupted at the show's conclusion with warmhearted cheers and shouts of "Bravo!" All this throws into question, to say the least, historian Cecil Smith's 1950 description of the show as "a pathetically ineffectual collation."[13]

The striking difference between the reception of *From Vienna* and that of Erika Mann's *Pepper Mill* can be explained in part by their materials, one full of Viennese charm, the other, Weimar bite. Tellingly, the *Brooklyn Eagle*'s Arthur Pollock, one of the few critics who admired *Pepper Mill,* weighed in with one of the more critical reviews of *From Vienna,* finding it "timid" and lacking in "edge." But *From Vienna* had other advantages over *Pepper Mill,* including more polished production values. In addition, the performers as a whole had greater familiarity with English thanks both to their longer residency and to the expert coaching of Arthur Lessac, who had helped mainstream the New York accents of the *Pins and Needles* cast. By the time the Artists Group appeared at the Music Box, only mere traces of their Austrian accents could be discerned.

The critics generally agreed that *Journey to Paradise* formed the weakest segment of the show, although they liked the performances of leading man Paul Lindenberg, who was thought to resemble a livelier Charles Boyer, and leading lady Illa Roden, who was compared to Janet Gaynor. They especially found its length, an obvious oddity for a Broadway revue, the major sticking point, making this something of a cultural problem; whereas Viennese audiences, according to Horst Jarka, "had enjoyed the jump from the light numbers to the serious *Mittelstück*," here the play proved, as Atkinson noted, "too long for our impatient taste." Even so, the *World-Telegram* thought the play contained some of the "cleverest" material in the show, and *Variety*, "an imaginative morality piece," while the *Nation* commented as to the entire revue, "There is not a dull or tasteless moment, and scenes which may seem strange to an American audience add freshness to the experience."[14]

From Vienna closed in the red on August 26, 1939, after seventy-nine performances. An hour's worth of televised excerpts appeared on NBC's fledgling W2XBS station on September 26, and a retooled version of the show, without *Journey to Paradise* or any other *Mittelstück*, was presented at the 92nd Street YMHA on December 9. Having learned something about American sensibilities, when the troupe, now called the American Viennese Group, staged a follow-up revue, *Reunion in New York*, in February 1940, they prepared numbers that Atkinson found suitably "brief and pithy." The Soyfer play apparently made nonetheless a lasting mark on Latouche, who seems to have adopted something of its picaresque, allegorical approach, especially in *The Golden Apple*.[15]

Meanwhile, *Sing for Your Supper*, the Federal Theatre Project musical revue that Latouche had been associated with virtually from its inception in late 1937, finally opened in April 1939. A number of factors had caused various delays. For one thing, the FTP undertook to recruit and train an interracial cast of well over one hundred performers, not helped in this regard by what seems to have been some ineptness on the part of the revue's director, Harold Hecht. Moreover, as the show endlessly rehearsed all over town, discontented company members, including composer Harold Rome and actor Dan Dailey Jr., quit the production, often necessitating script and casting changes. Further complicating matters, the FTP's New York director, George Kondolf, having promised Broadway producers that he would stage only one large show at a time, seemed hesitant about replacing the FTP's big moneymaker at the Adelphi Theatre, Arthur Arent's *One-Third of a Nation,* with an untried musical revue.[16]

In late October 1938, *Sing for Your Supper* finally moved into the Adelphi with the expectations of a December premiere, but a slashed FTP budget resulted in various dismissals and the need once again to postpone an opening in order to recast and re-rehearse the show. In the midst of this chaos, Charles Friedman, the successful director of *Pins and Needles,* arrived to help stage at least the larger production numbers, including the two finales, "Papa's Got a Job" and "Ballade of Uncle Sam."[17]

(One incidental confusion involved the late November 1938 opening of Rodgers and Hart's *The Boys from Syracuse,* which contained a hit number also entitled "Sing for Your Supper." Rodgers and Hart averred that they had taken their title not from the FTP revue, which they claimed to have known nothing about, but rather, like the FTP itself, from the nursery rhyme, "Little Tommy Tucker." The FTP considered lodging a complaint, but ultimately decided that the popularity of the Rodgers and Hart song could only help advertise their own show.)[18]

Unfortunately, every production setback for *Sing for Your Supper* meant a potential sacrifice of topicality, leading in a vicious circle to writers often having to update material, thereby causing further delays. Two early surviving scripts indeed contain many sketches that never made it to Broadway—enough songs and skits to provide at least another full show. Latouche might well have written several of these unattributed sketches, some of which seem characteristic of his work, although the show's principal writer, Robert Sour, had a similar wit and craft. In any case, the revue early on adopted the idea of having Uncle Sam, America personified, arrive backstage to learn about the theater, and then return throughout the show (although in the final version he appeared only in the opening and closing scenes). In conjunction with this conceit, the writers penned a number of parodies of familiar plays, including three spoofs that never made the final cut—"One-Third of a Mitten" (*One-Third of a Nation*), "Our Borrowed Substance" (*Our Town*), and "You Can't Take the Pulitzer Prize with You" (*You Can't Take It with You*)—as well as two, both by Latouche, that did: "Legitimate" (*Pins and Needles*) and "Perspiration" (*The Cradle Will Rock*). Along these same lines, the show also lampooned, with a number entitled "At Long Last," its own protracted rehearsal period. Otherwise, the revue engaged in more general social and political satire, with the tone more irreverent than sectarian, and largely without the sort of agenda that characterized *Pins and Needles,* let alone *The Cradle Will Rock.* Tellingly, one of the more daring numbers, "It All Adds up to One," an argument for racial harmony that would have had the white and black ensembles dance at first combatively and finally in unison, ultimately gave way to such less provocative sketches as “Opening Night,” an homage to the black musical *Clorindy*, and “The Last Waltz,” an Anna Sokolow dance, with music by Alex North, depicting the sinister rise of fascism in central Europe.[19]

Latouche had four numbers in the show as it opened at the Adelphi, all in the second act: “Legitimate, “Perspiration,” and “Leaning on a Shovel” (all three with music by Lee Wainer), and “Ballade of Uncle Sam” (music by Earl Robinson). Although the texts to these four numbers survive, often in multiple versions, the music for the three Wainer numbers appears to be lost, with the exception of two pages from the verse to “Legitimate.” In that particular song, at one point intended for Peggy Coudray (who created the role of Mrs. Mister in *The Cradle Will Rock*) but sung at the Adelphi by another of the show's stars, Virginia Bolen, the singer, in a sendup of *Pins and Needles*, finds success on the stage only after going to work in a garment factory:

> At last I'm on top place in wonderful dramas
> And all I can say is
> The actress's way is not agents
> But knitting pajamas.

The surviving bit of music—perhaps the only extant example of Wainer's work with Latouche—indicates a composer of some charm.[20]

The more elaborate “Perspiration,” for which Latouche wrote the mini-libretto, satirized not only Marc Blitzstein's *The Cradle Will Rock* and its stripped-down staging by Orson Welles, but the work's suppression by the Federal Theatre, with an announcer introducing the piece, an opera by one Marmaduke Schnook originally entitled “Sweat,” by saying, “There is no censorship on the WPA. The new title is, ‘Perspiration.’ ” The opera takes place in Struggle Town (after Blitzstein's Steeltown) and the story involves button and buttonhole workers, their boss (Mr. Bankbook), and a union organizer (Mr. Zipper), with composer Schnook—at one point slated to be played by Wainer himself—narrating the action and describing the scenery à la Blitzstein (“The sky is grey, with probably thundershowers later”). Picketers appear throughout the sketch with such signs as “Act Two Is Unfair to Act One” and “This Opera Is Unfair to Verdi.” At the end, declaiming “Mr. Schnook is unfair!” the stagehands protest the absence of scenery; the idle musicians, the unoccupied pit; and the actors, the lack of costumes and makeup. For this “Perspiration” sketch, which reportedly imitated Blitzstein's music as well, Latouche wrote a “mutter mutter mutter” chorus of the type that would turn up in *Ballet Ballads, The Golden Apple*, and *The Ballad of Baby Doe*, as well as an Ogden Nash–like rhyme that he also would recycle in various ways:

> When you're near I'm feeling physical.
> The touch of your hand is aphrodisical.

I also like you in ways that are mental—
But that is purely incidental—[21]

Like the revue generally, "Perspiration" and "Legitimate" both employed Yiddish phrases and syntax for comedic purposes, a reminder of the strong presence of Jewish creators and audiences with regard to the period's left-leaning satirical theater especially. In "Legitimate," the singer, now known as "la divine Schmaltz," recalls her days in the garment factory, where "Mr. Shapiro my hero, / Was an expert on Arthur Pinero." And in "Perspiration," worker Tessie, in a parody of Blitzstein's "Moll's Lament," sings, "I work ten hours I repeat.... And by me hurts the feet," while she and fellow worker Bessie, using the Yiddish words for "bastard" and "thief," sing of their boss, "He's worse than Czar Romanoff— / He's a momser—he's a gonof." Latouche's Jewish background plainly came in handy in this context.

The work's penultimate number, "Leaning on a Shovel," mocked Republican censure of the allegedly profligate Works Progress Administration by having a quartet of "WPA boys," holding toy shovels, facetiously claim to have built the Boulder Dam and other public works "by leaning on a shovel!" (see Figure 12). The lyric further satirized accusations by the House Un-American Activities Committee (HUAC), chaired by Martin Dies, of communist subversion within the WPA:

We didn't lift a finger
To build the parks
That you see in every city.
At home we always linger
And read Karl Marx
If you don't believe us—ask the Dies Committee.

Boldly mocking for a government-funded revue, this song helped set the stage for the patriotic uplift of the finale, "Ballade of Uncle Sam," the show's only number to feature the music of Earl Robinson.

A Seattle native, Earl Robinson (1910–1991) studied composition with George F. McKay at the University of Washington, where he learned to appreciate both Wagner and Duke Ellington. A cross-country trip in 1934 awakened him to the depth of the Depression's awful toll, and on arriving in New York, he became a lifelong socialist, including more than twenty years of membership in the Communist Party. Writing incidental music for left-wing theater and political songs for communist camps, he also studied on scholarship with Aaron Copland at the Downtown Music School during the 1935–36 academic year. Some association with the New York Composers' Collective furthered his receptivity to mass song as represented by the German composer Hanns Eisler, and then, with the establishment of the popular front, native folk music as exemplified by the African-American singer-guitarist Huddie ("Leadbelly") Ledbetter. Speaking of this era in later years,

Robinson said, "If we found no fault with the Soviet Union, we had at the same time a tremendously open and positive approach to America, its revolutionary past and its ongoing history. There would be a socialist America one day, coming about through struggle, possibly revolution." In the summer of 1936, he composed two songs, "Joe Hill" (about the slain labor leader) and "Old Abe Lincoln," both with lyrics by Alfred Hayes, that became favored anthems in leftist circles; and in 1937, he married a Jewish New Yorker also active in the Communist Party, and founded the American People's Chorus. During these same years, he earned his living primarily as a copyist and composer for the Federal Theatre.[22]

Robinson recalled that after meeting Latouche in early 1938 through the Federal Theatre, the two decided to write a work for *Sing for Your Supper* that would take American history as its subject. Remarked the composer, "In a real sense Latouche and I had been looking for each other. . . . John had already been thinking of writing a history of this land." Latouche himself asserted that the piece, "Ballade of Uncle Sam," often referred to as a cantata, bore some relation to his 1935 poem, "Legend for a Great City," although he admitted that the connection was remote. Indeed, the work would remain somewhat unique in the context of Latouche's career, indicating that he angled his text to Robinson's particular gifts and interests, to the point of closely reworking the couplet "This republic never will be free / till the black man's out of slavery" from "Old Abe Lincoln" as "Man in white skin can never be free, / While his black brother is in slavery."[23]

Latouche and Robinson wrote the work rather quickly during the first half of 1938, Latouche taking some two weeks for the text, Robinson, about a month for the music. The two never became particularly close socially, yet they worked together well, and after the great success of "Ballade of Uncle Sam" as *Ballad for Americans*, they produced two more choral works, namely, *Battle Hymn* and *Forward, America* (both 1942), but not the folk opera occasionally alluded to in the press.

For the "Ballade," Latouche decided to feature the show's unifying figure of Uncle Sam, and devised a text that had two soloists—Uncle Sam and another figure variously identified in different drafts—alongside a choral ensemble that included a few solos as well. Throughout the several versions, the work's structure remained largely intact, opening with the two principal soloists, sometimes assisted by the chorus, who commemorate the struggle for democracy in the context of four phases of American history: the Revolutionary War (represented by a quote from the Declaration of Independence and by sundry political figures, although eventually omitting the names John Adams, Tadeusz Kościuszko, and Israel Putnam); westward expansion (represented by various frontiersmen); emancipation (represented by Abraham Lincoln, with a quote from the Gettysburg Address, and a musical quote of the phrase "Let my people go" from the spiritual "Go Down Moses"); and the "machine age," meaning industrial capitalism. Following this, in response to questions from the chorus, Uncle Sam identifies his many occupations, ethnicities, and religions, and the previously skeptical chorus, inspired by America's national heritage, respond with renewed confidence:

Out of the cheating,
Out of the shouting,
Out of the murders and lynching,
Out of the windbags
The patriotic spouting
Out of uncertainty and doubting,
Out of the carpet bag and the brass spittoon
It will come again
Our marching song will come again.

At the conclusion, the chorus reveals itself as "America!"[24]

Regarding the work's form, Latouche explained, in his preface to the published libretto, that he alternated the "familiar loose quatrain" characteristic of the "folk ballad" with a "counter theme" that expands on "the interruptions and interjections which always arise from the audience of a ballad," all "culminating in a mass participation that completes the structure, reflecting at the same time the unity of thought implicit in the text." The "loose" quatrains—or more commonly, quintains—typically contain perfect, often single rhymes, whereas the "interruptions" tend toward spoken dialogue, and the finale contains, appropriate to its function as a "culminating" synthesis, a variety of techniques.[25]

The three surviving drafts of "Ballade of Uncle Sam" differ most in their beginnings. In the earlier versions, Latouche prefaced his history lesson with a dejected chorus who proclaim, "There's bad things happening in this land," although by the third draft, he and Robinson chose to omit this introduction and launch directly into the narrative. But Latouche also made smaller changes in the libretto over time, including sometimes moderating the text in deference to director Harold Hecht, who had final say in such matters. For instance, he changed the line "Some [frontiersmen] were honest and some were sons of bitches" to "Some liked to loaf while others dug ditches"; and the phrase "Out of imperialist monopolies" to "Out of uncertainty and doubting." He also reined in a more expanded critique of the machine age, including some play with the phrases "rugged individualism" and "ragged individualism." Added at the suggestion of Robinson, the catalog of Uncle Sam's religions, including "atheist," came at a relatively late stage as well. (In at least one of Robinson's manuscript scores, the phrase "Orthodox Jewish," published as such, appears "Orthodox, Jewish," indicating, as probably intended by Latouche, two separate religions rather than one denomination.)[26]

According to contemporary sources, Latouche "was moved to write his words after watching the inroads of the Silver Shirts in Virginia," a reference to William Dudley Pelley's fascist and antisemitic Silver Legion based in Asheville, North Carolina. In the preface to the published 1940 text, Latouche further explained that the cantata "was written during a time of nebulous doubts and cloudy issues, when people were divided by the fear that the democratic system of government would not survive. The intention of the 'Ballad' is an affirmation against negativist thinking, pointing to the historical progress of democratic thought as the integrating force in the future development of that history."[27]

Robinson reflected the text's fundamental dialectic by contrasting a largely major-mode refrain reminiscent of American folk music (and less obviously Beethoven's "Ode to Joy") for the historical narrative, with a marchlike chant in a modal minor more redolent of Hanns Eisler for the resolve of the "nobodies" to "keep the faith." About ten minutes in length, the work largely stays in its primary key of E major, but occasionally ventures into other tonalities for some of these marchlike chants as well as for some of the individual historical vignettes. Aside from the machine-age section, with its use of modernist dissonance for programmatic purposes, the music largely employs familiar chords, including many triads, although handled freely. The chorus tends to sing in unison, with textural variety provided by, among other means, the use of spoken lines, speech-song, humming, and whistling. The marchlike coda arguably constitutes the most effective portion of the work, including some exciting harmonic shifts before a return to the E-major tonality for the final exchange, "Who are you?" "America!"

Sing for Your Supper premiered at the Adelphi Theatre on April 24, 1939. Abe Feder provided lighting; Herbert Andrews, the sets; and Mary Merrill, the costumes. Fred Hoff led the Federal Theatre Orchestra, and Walter Paul arranged and orchestrated the music, including "Ballade of Uncle Sam." In addition to Coudray and Bolen, the cast featured Paula Laurence, who played Tessie in "Perspiration," and Gordon Clarke, the Uncle Sam in the "Ballade."

Notwithstanding a few good reviews, and some appreciative words in particular for "Papa's Got a Job," "Legitimate," and "Perspiration," the critics largely thought the show "dull," "clumsy," and "raucous," Brooks Atkinson writing in the *Times*, "Much of the material is third-rate stuff with songs that are frequently lost in the tumult of a noisy orchestra and to lyrics that can hardly be heard." However, because the show, which already ran long, started nearly a half-hour late, most of the reviewers left before the "Ballade," and thereby missed what the *Catholic World* and *Theatre Arts*, whose notices did not appear until June, thought a "stirring" ending. This not only deprived the "Ballade" of some public recognition, but meant short-changing the revue as a whole, although Arthur Pollock (*Brooklyn Eagle*), who stayed for the "Ballade," found the piece merely "a pretty projection of the idea that Uncle Sam is the product of all the races on the globe and not just a tall, gaunt, goateed gentlemen [*sic*] who got here first."[28]

Even without consideration of the "Ballade," Robert Coleman (*Mirror*), who disliked the show, admitted that the audience "laughed heartily and often. And their applause was frequent and robust." But the "Ballade" proved especially effective with the public, who reportedly greeted each performance with a cheering standing ovation. So strong a finale undoubtedly helped make the show a popular success, as did the ticket prices, which dipped as low as twenty-five cents for a balcony seat, and prospects for a long run looked good.[29]

Unfortunately, the poor reviews—several of which suggested some bias against the Federal Theatre—played into the hands of congressmen who for some time had been waging a crusade against the FTP, including HUAC, which thought the Federal Theatre riddled with communists, and the House Committee on Appropriations, who faulted the unit for waste and inefficiency. With its extended rehearsal period and its considerable cost (estimated at between $250,000 and $500,000)—not to mention reports of interracial dancing and lewd dialogue—*Sing for Your Supper* became a favorite whipping boy for politicians eager to shut down the program. Holding up the script of the show during one hearing, Congressman Clifton Woodrum famously pronounced, "If there is a line or a passage in it that contributes to the cultural or educational benefit or uplift of America, I will eat the whole manuscript, and I am not particular fond of that kind of diet." In order to preserve funding for other WPA programs, in June 1939 the Senate struck a deal with the House and reluctantly agreed to withhold support for the FTP, which terminated all productions by month's end. On July 30, *Sing for Your Supper* accordingly gave its sixtieth and last performance. "The cast never sang 'Ballade' with more fighting spirit than they did that night," recalled press agent Anthony ("Tony") Buttitta, who thought that the revue could have run another year or two. Discussing the decision by Congress to close the FTP, composer Ned Lehac similarly remarked, "If this had not happened, I firmly believe that *Sing for Your Supper* might well have been a landmark in theatrical history, and a brilliant example of what a subsidized musical theatre could create in our country, as it had been doing for decades in Europe."[30]

The "Ballade" might well have slipped into obscurity but for a happy turn of fate. Having led performances of the piece with his American People's Chorus, Robinson realized that the work could stand on its own as a concert work, and approached the noted radio commentator Norman Corwin about getting it on the air. Corwin thought the piece right for *The Pursuit of Happiness*, his new 1939 radio show on the Columbia Broadcasting System, and had Robinson successfully audition the "Ballade" for some CBS executives, who agreed that the work would make a perfect vehicle for the outstanding African-American bass Paul Robeson, the singing actor who had thrilled audiences in productions of *The Emperor Jones* and *Show Boat*, and who recently had returned to America after several years abroad. Robeson liked the piece, which accorded with his own taste and convictions, and after a week's rehearsal with the composer, performed the work on the third episode of *The Pursuit of Happiness* on Sunday, November 5, 1939, following a broadcast by the New York Philharmonic (see Figure 14). Ralph Wilkinson rearranged the score, Lyn Murray prepared the interracial chorus, Mark Warnow conducted, and Corwin penned an introduction, read by the show's host, Burgess Meredith, which included the lines, "Democracy is a good thing. It works. It may creak a bit, but it works."[31]

The piece as broadcast differed in a number of ways from the latest of the surviving drafts of "Ballade of Uncle Sam," although some of these changes might have been made even before *Sing for Your Supper* opened. Robinson, presumably in consultation with Latouche, conflated the two principal solos into one large solo, no longer identified as Uncle Sam, making the piece, retitled *Ballad for Americans* at Corwin's suggestion, more of an abstract vehicle for baritone and chorus as befitted its new context. Further, at the end, the soloist, not the chorus, is identified as representing "America!" in a revelation echoed by the chorus. And finally, at Robeson's insistence, the composer transposed the music downward, although he eventually published the cantata in the original key of E major.

The radio premiere—which aired some two months after the outbreak of hostilities in Europe—elicited an extraordinary response. The studio audience stood up and cheered for a few minutes on the air, and then kept applauding for another fifteen minutes or so. Enthusiastic listeners jammed the CBS switchboards in New York and Hollywood, and over the ensuing days, hundreds of letters and wires poured into the network's "amazed" offices. Some of this sensational response presumably involved not only Robeson's performance per se, but the spectacle of a great African-American voice representing the entire nation and its history. At the same time, the work soon enough would prove hugely popular with white soloists as well.[32]

The piece's wildly successful radio premiere promptly led to a contract with Robbins Music, which the following year published the work both as a vocal score, arranged by Domenico Savino and subtitled "A Modern Cantata," and as a poem, subtitled "A Modern Narrative." These publications marked the beginnings of an important relationship between Latouche and Robbins Music, which with its affiliates Leo Feist and Miller Music formed a conglomerate (the Big Three Music Corporation), by this point controlled by the Metro-Goldwyn-Mayer company. In contrast to some rivals such as Max Dreyfus, whose Chappell-Harms company published the work of leading Broadway composers, Jack Robbins (1894–1959), the head of Robbins Music, shrewdly cultivated close ties especially with dance bands, the school trade, and the film industry, leading to MGM's acquisition of the Robbins catalog in the mid-1930s. Described by Vernon Duke as "that erratic, unpredictable, almost too colorful, but withal lovable leprechaun of popular music," Robbins closely evaluated and critiqued the words and music of the scores he published, the kind of supervision, as in the case of Max Dreyfus and other major publishers of the period, that for all its importance remains largely undocumented. Headquartered at 799 Seventh Avenue, he worked closely with his chief editor, Domenico Savino, an Italian-American composer-conductor described by Duke as "a skilled musician with a 'classical' background and a flair for Italianate, extravagantly colored 'lush' orchestration." Having left Dreyfus for Robbins in 1939, Duke himself served the latter as composer and editor, and took credit for selling *Ballad for Americans* to the firm, although Robbins himself surely recognized the work's potential for school and radio use.[33]

Following the cantata's legendary radio premiere, Cabaret TAC presented the *Ballad*, with Michael Loring the soloist, at the 92nd Street YMHA and at the Manhattan Center in late 1939; and CBS accommodated the many requests for an encore by broadcasting the piece on Corwin's show on New Year's Eve, with Robeson once again featured. Many other performances followed, especially in the early 1940s. The work remained especially associated with Robeson, who continued to sing the solo part on the air, including a performance on an August 26, 1940, pilot radio program for CBS, *All God's Children*, in which the music appeared at the end of a comic sketch in which Robeson, representing pre-Columbian America, confronts black minstrel comedian Eddie Green, playing a burlesqued Columbus. "The coming of the white man will bring much sorrow to this country," Robeson tells Green, "but even so we welcome you, because in time to come the people who will follow into this new land will bring forth a shining hope for the whole world."

Robeson also sang the work in concert to hugely enthusiastic crowds around the country, including the South, numerous times, both in recital and with orchestras. Perhaps most notably, he performed the piece with the New York Philharmonic at Lewisohn Stadium before many thousands every summer from 1940 through 1943. At the first such account, on June 25, 1940, with the combined choral forces of Hugh Ross's Schola Cantorum and the black Wen Talbot Choir under the baton of Mark Warnow, Howard Taubman of the *Times* spoke of the work as having "coursed through the country like a powerful west wind." Just the opening introductory bars of the piece played by Robeson's accompanist at a sold-out 1940 recital at Carnegie Hall elicited "wild" ovations from the crowd (which included a small black contingent), while the work itself, according to the *Times*, brought "no end to the applause." Reviewing another high-profile event, Robeson's performance of the cantata at the Hollywood Bowl with the Hall Johnson Choir before a jam-packed crowd of about twenty-three thousand, Isabel Morse Jones of the *Los Angeles Times* spoke of its "commanding and powerful message," while actor Clarence Muse, writing in the African-American *Chicago Defender*, stated, "It was an inspiration and a sincere gesture to awake sleeping Americans and assure them that Mr. and Mrs. nobody, the etcetera and even the anybodies are important in our social fabric.... I wish every Negro in the world could have been there."[34]

Other soloists performed the piece as well, including on radio such prominent singers as the black baritone Jules Bledsoe, the white tenor James Melton, and the white baritones Lawrence Tibbett and Robert Merrill. The work became especially popular with high school choruses and college glee clubs, community groups, and church and professional choirs, with the composer preparing an unaccompanied version for the famed Westminster Choir in 1940. As perhaps a sign of its wide dissemination, in 1941, the director of music for New York's public schools, George H. Gartlan, took the unusual step of barring performances of the piece in the schools, partly because of its use of such street jargon as "and that ain't all," partly for fear that the work might undermine authority; but Robinson and Latouche worked together to help overturn this ban. The writer and well-known Texan entrepreneur H. Stanley Marcus had no such reservations, dispensing seventy-five copies of Robeson's recording of the work to the Dallas school system.[35]

Politically, the *Ballad* proved remarkably multipurpose. The Republican Party featured the piece, with Ray Middleton as soloist, at their national convention in Philadelphia in June 1940, while a few weeks earlier, the same work reportedly had appeared at the national convention of the Communist Party in New York. Not to be left out, Democrats, including First Lady Eleanor Roosevelt, extolled the piece as well. Plainly tickled by the Republican Party's adoption of the *Ballad*, the *New Yorker* ran a "Talk of the Town" item, "Ballad for Republicans," in which they quoted Latouche as saying, "We wrote the song for everybody, not for Republicans alone," Robinson adding, "Especially not for Republicans alone." (In a letter to Jerome and Hazel Moross, Latouche confessed, in a somewhat ironic way, that the work's adoption by the Republican Party had left him "completely shattered.")[36]

As a supporter of the Nazi-Soviet pact, Robinson also proved less than sanguine about the work's inclusion at an early 1941 benefit to aid war-torn Britain, writing to Abraham Olman, the general manager of Robbins Music,

> I wrote the Ballad for Americans (I am speaking for myself entirely and not Latouche) because I truly believe America is and can be a great and truly democratic country. And I wrote it because it is a peaceful country. To have the Ballade [*sic*] used to whoop up war spirit and to involve us in the imperialist conflict on either side seems to me entirely and [*sic*] wrong and contrary to my deepest convictions and principles.... I think we and the Ballad should be a force for keeping us out of the war instead of helping get us into it.

On the other hand, the composer surely had no qualms about the work's use by the U.S. Army Negro Chorus for two concerts at the Royal Albert Hall in late September 1943 specifically intended to defuse racial tensions both within the American military and between American forces and the local British population. Corporal Marc Blitzstein coached the chorus, Sergeant Hugo Weisgall conducted the London Symphony, and Private Kenneth Cantril, the recital's only white singer, performed the solo part. The concert also featured a new orchestral piece by Blitzstein, *Freedom Morning*, and a selection of spirituals, among other works, but *Ballad for Americans* captured the lion's share of attention by the critics, who praised it lavishly, as did subsequent notices of performances of the work by the Negro Chorus in Manchester, Glasgow, and Edinburgh.[37]

Indeed, British wartime response constituted a high-water mark in the history of the work's critical reception. Whereas Americans often regarded the cantata's novel interplay of song and speech as simply characteristic of radio drama, the British found the form, as the *London Times* reported, "noteworthy, since nothing quite like it in form or substance has appeared in European music.... this narration to orchestral accompaniment swung easily and naturally from speech to song, told a political and historical story of struggle for freedom, incorporated interjections, questions, and even an ironical whistle, all of it bubbling with American vitality and bluntness of speech," the *Evening Standard* adding, "There are great hopes for a nation which applauds and upholds its heretics as its heroes." Blitzstein arguably absorbed something of the work's form and style in his own *Airborne Symphony* (completed 1946), as Copland had done in *Lincoln Portrait* (1942), although the latter composer thought the work's refrain, "And you know who I am," according to Robinson, "too schmaltzy-commercial."[38]

The *Ballad* early on made its way onto disc, with both Paul Robeson and Bing Crosby recording the work in 1940, the former with the American People's Chorus under Nathaniel Shilkret for RCA Victor, the latter with the Ken Darby Singers and the Victor Young Concert Orchestra for Decca. And in 1944, John Gaius Baumgartner and the Westminster Choir, under the choir's founder John Finley Williamson, recorded the work's unaccompanied version for Columbia Records. Reviewing the Robeson release, journalist William Gottlieb thought it to constitute not only the "most stirring contribution to records" since Billie Holiday's recent recording of "Strange Fruit" of the previous year, but "one of the finer products of the new 'national consciousness' inspired by the European war." Poet Archibald MacLeish, hoping to enlist Latouche for a radio project at the Library of Congress, wrote the lyricist in July 1940, "I have been playing your ballad over and over to myself with increasing admiration. And I started out with very great admiration indeed." Several decades later, jazz critic Nat Hentoff also spoke "affectionately" of this "exhilarating" recording: "It was all there, both the salty exposure of multiform domestic injustices and the heady assurance that if we all pulled together...we'd beat the bosses and the racists and all those other malignant forces that were soon, though we didn't know it, going to gang up on Paul Robeson himself. It was such a buoyant piece of music that the kids in my neighborhood memorized it, then improvised on it, all of us wishing we could sing like Robeson." Meanwhile, the imprisoned Ethel Rosenberg wrote to her husband, Julius, on July 6, 1951, that hearing the Crosby recording of "this immortal masterpiece," along with the Frank Sinatra recording of Robinson's "The House I Live In," on an Independence Day broadcast helped give her "courage, confidence and perspective."[39]

Like the Robbins sheet music, the Robeson and Crosby recordings sold tens of thousands of copies—a financial bonanza for all concerned. In addition, in early 1940, MGM, the parent company to Robbins Music, acquired the rights to the work for $4,000, an amount split evenly between Robbins, Robinson, and Latouche, who for a while went about "startling his friends by casually pulling out of his pants pocket a $1,000 bill." MGM initially announced plans to feature the work in one of their Mickey Rooney–Judy Garland musicals, prompting Latouche to write to his mother, "It will probably be horrible because they [Rooney and Garland] are not my idea of [John] Barrymore and [Eleonora] Duse"; but MGM used the *Ballad* rather as the centerpiece for a film along those general lines, *Born to Sing*, starring Ray McDonald and Virginia Weidler and directed by Edward Ludwig. Released in 1942, this far-fetched musical concerned a group of youngsters who, abetted by gangsters, stage a musical revue in an abandoned social hall of the German American Bund in order to vindicate the revue's swindled composer, an ex-convict on parole for an accidental death. (In its review of the film, the *Baltimore Sun* felt obliged to assure its readers that unlike the film's fictitious composer, neither Robinson nor Latouche had ever served time or killed anyone.) Much like *Sing for Your Supper*, the film concluded climactically with the *Ballad*, with white baritone Douglas McPhail the soloist, the whole rather faithfully rendered save, most notably, for the glamorized coda. Reflecting the *Ballad*'s emphasis on social diversity, choreographer Busby Berkeley, who directed this segment, uncharacteristically emphasized the individuality of the chorus members—at least until the very end, when his trademark synchronicity suggested the achievement of some national unity. *Variety* deemed the finale "absurdly over-produced" and Earl Robinson likewise described this sequence as "outlandishly choreographed," although the *Christian Science Monitor* claimed, conversely, that the number had been "produced simply," and that its "effects" had been "obtained mostly by the use of steadily changing camera angles."[40]

Latouche himself gave an impromptu performance of the *Ballad* at the piano at the Ruban Bleu nightclub in 1944, and recorded the poem without music on July 2, 1946, for the Library of Congress—a recording that happily preserves his lilting Virginian speech, with the opening phrase, "In seventy-six the sky was red," sounding something like, "In sevendy-six the sky was rehd." For this latter reading, Latouche delivered the poem simply, with the final "America!" almost anticlimactic in its quiet understatement—a far cry from its full-throated musical setting. Still, although others likewise "chanted" the work without music, Latouche modestly claimed that "the words require Mr. Robinson's magnificent score to give them a living quality."[41]

After the war, interest in the work waned, a development hardly helped by the blacklisting of Robinson, Latouche, and Robeson in the 1950s. Performances continued nonetheless, including recordings, variously orchestrated, that featured Odetta (1960), the New Christy Minstrels (1968), and Brock Peters (1976). Composer Earl Robinson often sang the solo part himself, as in a performance dedicated to Latouche's memory in May 1960 and a 1986 recording that revealed some textual changes, among them appending Native American tribes and notables to the section about the western frontier, replacing "housewife" with "househusband" in the list of occupations, and adding a few ethnicities in the catalog of nationalities. For a fiftieth anniversary performance in 1989, the composer additionally mentioned, among his description of Americans, "people of all sexual persuasions, gay, straight, and lots more!" The New York City Labor Chorus, a group composed mostly of city employees who recorded the work both in 1993 and 2000, further tweaked the text, including adding "Moslem" to its list of religions, and addressing ecological concerns. Reviewing the Labor Chorus's 2000 release, along with the 1940 Robeson recording (which had been inducted into the Grammy Hall of Fame in the "traditional pop" category in 1980), Faith Petric commended the *Ballad* as "especially valuable for teachers; children are bound to remember the lessons taught by this powerful and beautiful song, especially if given a chance to learn it!"[42]

Despite its marked decline in popularity, *Ballad for Americans* over the years retained the attention of critics and historians, although few seemed to have studied the music or text all that closely. Rather, the piece became largely a cultural symbol, including, for some commentators, an example of the vulgarity and sentimentality of midcentury American "middlebrow" culture. As early as 1944, James Agee—who wondered about "the judgment of a man [Paul Robeson] who, over and over and over, to worse and worse and worse people, has sung the inconceivably snobbish, esthetically execrable *Ballad for Americans*"—saw the work as typifying a corrupt strain in American culture that he labeled "pseudo-folk." And in a 1947 article, Robert Warshow, emerging from a similar *Partisan Review* milieu, more sweepingly considered the work emblematic of the entire communist-infected culture of the 1930s. In later years, Kevin Jack Hagopian similarly opined that the work, for all its good intentions, embodied the sort of "fatal flaw" endemic to popular front art, while Annegret Fauser critiqued the piece as "a propagandistic celebration of American exceptionalism."[43]

Other commentators, including in recent times Michael Denning, Robert Cantwell, Lisa Barg, and Michelle Stephens, proved more sympathetic to the work. Such observers typically pointed to the work's delineation—right from the start, with its inclusion of the Jewish financier Haym Solomon, the African-American slave Crispus Attucks, and the French military officer Lafayette among the founding fathers—of America's occupational, ethnic, and religious diversity; its implication of the darker sides of American history, including racial and economic oppression; and its depiction of the American dream as, in Langston Hughes's famous phrase "a dream deferred," but one that "will come again." Denning concluded that the *Ballad* "should be understand [*sic*] not as an emblem of middlebrow patriotism, but as a synecdoche for the extraordinary flowering of the historical imagination in Popular Front fiction, film, music, and art," as exemplified by works by John Dos Passos, Orson Welles, Paul Strand, Duke Ellington, John Steinbeck, and others that "mediate on the absence of the people: on the martyrs, the losses, the betrayals, the disinherited." Tellingly, Agee and other detractors grouped the *Ballad* with the work of many of these same artists, revealing that the critical rift over the *Ballad* signaled a more profound fissure with respect to, in Warshow's words, "the legacy of the '30s."[44]

Meanwhile, many topics concerning the *Ballad* remained largely unexplored, including matters of style and technique, with Barg proving unusual in noting felicitous details in Robinson's score. Otherwise, hardly any attention was paid, for instance, to the work's tonal or poetic structure, or to its innovative fusion of speech and song; or to how its popular modernism reflected the influence of such artists as Gertrude Stein, Hanns Eisler, Aaron Copland, and Marc Blitzstein (although poet H. R. Hays noted a remote resemblance to Brecht, "carried out on the Hollywood, radio, Tinpan [*sic*] Alley, commercialized folksy level"). Nor has much consideration been given to the work's original theatrical context, of how on a certain level the piece arose as part of a didactic dialogue between the government and the theatrical community. By having the piece staged in *Born to Sing* by poor, talented urban youths, MGM seemed more responsive to this aspect of the work than did many professional critics.[45]

The work's social meanings also could be clarified by more nuanced readings of the text. The phrase "out of the murders and lynching," for instance, must have registered, for listeners of the time, not only racial and antisemitic violence—with lynching a pressing concern as Congress repeatedly refused to enact anti-lynching legislation—but the slaying of labor leaders and striking workers. Similarly, within its small confines, the frontier section presented a far more complex picture of western expansion than, as sometimes suggested, an endorsement of manifest destiny. Moreover, critics often seemed oblivious to the work's defiance—"But who cares what they say, / When I am on my way"—and almost wholly insensible to its irony, partly communicated musically, but also in the text, as in the chorus's "Paul Revere had a horse race" or the soloist's "Czech and double Czech." Indeed, in his memoirs, painter Jimmy Ernst recalled architect Frederick Kiesler telling him, apropos Latouche's "problem" with the work's reception, "He [Latouche] hates the idea of it being treated as a patriotic hymn. He can't convince people that it was meant to be a satire on Americanism. He's had trouble of that kind with a lot of his work. It always seems just to miss. I always thought he should have chosen Paul Bowles to write the music for 'Ballad.'"[46]

Whatever its enduring value, *Ballad for Americans* remains a compelling phenomenon of its time. As an extended composition—if only ten minutes in length—of some seriousness, the work, with tens of thousands of listeners at home and abroad cheering its presentation on stage and screen and over the air, perhaps can be compared in the history of twentieth-century American concert music only to such works as Gershwin's *Rhapsody in Blue* and Copland's *Lincoln Portrait,* even if the cantata's popularity, which basically coincided with the war years, proved largely ephemeral. At a particularly critical time in world history, the *Ballad* affirmed, with humor and grace, some of the humanistic ideals at stake, and helped to unite in common purpose citizens of various stripes and antagonisms.

6

New Friends

His financial situation considerably improved thanks to *Ballad for Americans*, Latouche during the winter of 1939–40 moved to a five-room apartment at 12 Minetta Street, a quaintly curved block linking Minetta Lane and Bleecker Street in Manhattan's bohemian Greenwich Village. He also hired a secretary and a cook, according to an October 1940 feature about him in *Collier's* magazine, which contained a photo of the lyricist at home seated in front of a large portrait of Jane Bowles by Maurice Grosser, Virgil Thomson's companion. Noting his short height and stocky build, *Collier's* further reported that his resemblance to "a milk-fed edition of John Garfield of the movies" occasioned his frequently signing Garfield's name "in anybody's autograph book," to which he "always adds, generously, 'Be sure to visit me for a day or two when you're out in Hollywood.'" As for his erratic lifestyle, *Collier's* quoted him as saying, "I never plan anything. Things just happen to me. Wheee!"[1]

Latouche took in as a roommate his good friend Robert ("Bu," or to Latouche, "Bubu") Faulkner, a writer-editor with whom he previously had lived at the Chelsea Hotel. "He [Faulkner] is very charming," wrote the lyricist to his mother in February 1940, "and I am sure you will like him when you meet him." In a letter to his parents, Paul Bowles described Faulkner as "an alcoholic who at any moment goes off the track," while Ned Rorem, in his memoirs, remembered him as "hysterically funny" and "a court jester, like John Latouche without the talent." Not much is known about Faulkner, who also enjoyed a particularly close relationship with Jane Bowles. A reference to him by painter Jimmy Ernst as Latouche's "companion and roommate" suggests that their friendship involved some romantic intimacy.[2]

At the same time, Latouche maintained an amorous relationship with Theodora Griffis, whom he married on October 30, 1940, and to whom, according to one source, he had been "secretly engaged for two years." Latouche's newfound success presumably made it more feasible for him to marry into the Griffis family, although what reasons he and Theodora had for marrying in the first place remain uncertain given their basic homosexuality. Perhaps the marriages of a number of close friends, including the similar pairings of Paul and Jane Bowles and Harry and Marian Dunham, had some sway in this regard. Moreover, as suggested by Ruth Yorck in her biographical portrait of Latouche, the lyricist apparently found it amusing to marry into so prestigious and moneyed a family, much as the rebellious Theodora welcomed the notion of wedding an unconventional artist. But the union seems to have been no mere marriage of convenience, but rather to have had its deeply emotional and even ardent side, as in the "serious" kiss mentioned earlier that Latouche gave Theodora while dating. In any event, Theodora's tycoon father Stanton apparently brooked no objection; on the contrary, he seems to have been fond of Latouche, who ironically would address him as "Massa," and with whom he played cards.[3]

John and Theodora's small chapel wedding took place at the Fifth Avenue Presbyterian Church (five days after the successful opening of Latouche's musical *Cabin in the Sky* on Broadway) in a ceremony officiated by the Reverend Ralph Nesbitt. Paul Bowles served as best man, and Virgil Thomson composed special music for the event. The next day, the newlyweds left for a honeymoon in Mexico, where they spent several weeks in Taxco, the temporary home of Paul and Jane Bowles; there, they met up with Robert Faulkner, and met Natalie Scott, the grande dame of Taxco's expatriate community, who wrote the Latouches letters of introduction to anthropologist Frances Toor in Mexico City, and preservationist Martha Robinson in New Orleans. "Touchey [*sic*] has a grand sense of humor, very witty; but also very intelligent, widely read and sensitive . . . ," wrote Scott to Toor. "You'll like them [the Latouches], so I don't feel apologetic as I sometimes do when I give people letters,—which isn't often." In a postcard to Thomson from Taxco, Latouche wrote, "Trip lovely. Mexico City like Gary, Indiana wrapped in a serape. Taxco wonderful. Mariposas. Burros calling at night. Jane [Bowles] and Bob [Faulkner] blooming. Sunshine. Music. Spanish. Sex. Moons."[4]

On the married couple's return to New York, after they settled into what Latouche called "our cote on Minetta Street," Stanton Griffis held a black tie reception for the newlyweds at his apartment on East 57th Street near Sutton Place. Then, in the fall of 1941, the couple moved to a house at 217 East 49th Street, where Latouche held, according to one gossip columnist, a three-night housewarming "to accommodate the overflow," and where he lived until joining the navy in 1943, although he and Theodora regularly retreated to Stanton's estate in New Canaan, Connecticut, as well. In a letter to her mother-in-law, Theodora described her and John's new seven-room quarters—"a wonderfull [*sic*] house now up in a civilized part of town"—as a happy improvement over the Greenwich Village apartment, with "*lots* of light" and a kitchen "three times the size of the one downtown." This missive—one of Theodora's few surviving letters—also informed Effie that John had been working "like one demented" and that she had not seen "much of him" over the last few weeks, referring to herself as "bearing up under my widowhood," a phrase that, although whimsical in context, points to some real dissatisfaction that presumably played no small part in the collapse of their marriage.[5]

With his new wealth, celebrity, and social connections, Latouche suddenly found himself, at a still tender age, a patron of the arts and a frequent invitee to high-toned affairs. But his intimate set stayed essentially filled with struggling young artists and European émigrés. The group associated with the Little Friends remained a core contingent of this social world, although their center seemed to shift from the Askew salon, more than ever dominated by French surrealist painters, to one of the various places occupied by either Latouche or Jane Bowles, who often resided apart from her less social husband.

A number of still younger artists attached themselves to this group, including not only Leonard Bernstein and Judy Holliday, as already mentioned, but the painter Jimmy Ernst (1920–1984), which left Latouche and Jane Bowles bewailing the fact that they were no longer the babies of their crowd. A refugee from Germany who had arrived in New York in 1938, Ernst, his parents divorced, lost his Jewish mother in the Holocaust, but managed to help rescue from France his gentile father, the celebrated painter Max Ernst. Trying to establish himself as a painter while working as a clerk at the Museum of Modern Art, Jimmy—who in time emerged as an eminent artist in his own right—found the Latouche-Bowles circle, which he came to know in the course of 1940, extremely congenial, describing their synergy as follows: "These friends, not all of them young, but all involved in some aspect of the performing or creative arts, were finding each other, like spokes of a wheel radiating from a center. The center was a shelter from the aesthetic and moral dicta of a society deaf or blind to innovation and afraid of deviations from imagined norms. It was also an energizer, a core of reassurance that no one need to be alone in dissent or diversity."[6]

The young Ernst received one of his first commissions when, at the suggestion of Vernon Duke, Latouche asked him to paint a mural in his Minetta Street apartment's large bathroom, which Latouche thought, as Ernst recalled, "just too damned depressing." Forming a "Jimmy Beautification Society," Latouche solicited funds from such friends as Jane and Paul Bowles, Aaron Copland, Frederick Kiesler, Virgil Thomson, and gallery owner Julien Levy to help pay for Ernst's painting supplies. Aside from Friday nights, when Latouche could be counted on to attend the Askew salon, Ernst often found a steady parade of persons—from poet E. E. Cummings to striptease artist Gypsy Rose Lee—streaming into the bathroom as he worked, although he never could be quite sure whether to observe his progress or to use the facilities. "My dear, you'll have to leave me alone for a minute," actress Stella Adler told him on one occasion. "This lady has to pee!" After the completion of the mural, which represented a breakthrough for Ernst, bringing him closer to his father's work, the painting provided the background for a photo shoot of Latouche at work by setting up the bathroom as a study, including having a desk block the toilet on which the lyricist sat (see Figure 15).[7]

With the 1941 move of Paul and Jane Bowles and Oliver Smith to 7 Middagh Street in Brooklyn Heights, near the Brooklyn Bridge, the Little Friends found another base of operations, if short-lived: the February House, so called because of the February birthdays of a number of its occupants. Since mid-1940, the four-story brownstone had served as a residence for an extraordinary assemblage of young artists: mostly writers, including Carson McCullers, George Davis, Gypsy Rose Lee (at work on a mystery), Thomas Mann's son Golo, and W. H. Auden and his American lover, Chester Kallman, but also two musical British expatriates, composer Benjamin Britten and his companion, tenor Peter Pears. When McCullers and Lee vacated the house, at least temporarily, the Bowleses took their spots until leaving for Mexico that summer.[8]

One chronicler of the February House refers to Latouche as a "continued presence" there, which easily can be believed, although if the Britishers thought the Bowleses a disruptive force, they surely would have found Latouche that much more unsettling. Auden in any case maintained a seemingly disdainful attitude toward *Ballad for Americans*, reportedly telling Oliver Smith, apropos the suggestion that he and Britten provide a more "upbeat, patriotic ending" to their operetta in progress, *Paul Bunyan*, "I don't want to sound like John Latouche," although some observers have suggested that the *Ballad* might well have "left its mark" on the work after all. In turn, Latouche's greater familiarity with Auden arguably made him more susceptible to the latter's influence.[9]

Whatever his relationship with the Britishers, Latouche developed a particularly warm rapport with the Georgia-born Carson McCullers (1917–1967), understandable enough given, among other things, their shared status as iconoclastic and strongly antiracist Southerners. Three years younger than Latouche, McCullers published her first novel, *The Heart Is a Lonely Hunter*, during this period, in early June 1940, a sensational debut that quickly established her as one of the country's foremost writers. The novel, moreover, had some intriguing parallels with Latouche's contemporaneous work, even hinting at some mutual influence. The story's rebellious Jake Blount, for instance, echoed *Ballad for Americans* when he states, "And I'm Dutch and Turkish and Japanese and American," and when he says of the founding fathers, "They fought so that this could be a country where every man would be free and equal." Conversely, the book's portrayals of African Americans looked ahead to *Cabin in the Sky*, with the novel's Portia in particular resembling the musical's Petunia; tellingly, Ethel Waters, the star of both the stage and screen versions of *Cabin in the Sky*, also appeared in the stage and screen adaptations of McCullers's *The Member of the Wedding*. McCullers spoke with deep admiration of both Latouche and his work in a moving eulogy composed on the occasion of his death, while Latouche reciprocated such high regard, to judge from the fact that he sent Virgil Thomson a copy of McCullers's *The Ballad of the Sad Café* with a note that read in part, "see if it contains any channel for your music."[10]

In the early 1940s, Latouche established another close friendship with painter Brion Gysin (1916–1986). Described by Ned Rorem as "tall and Anglo-Saxon, suave and open and educated," Gysin grew up in Canada and Britain before moving to Paris, where he exhibited with other surrealist artists and became acquainted with Jane and Paul Bowles. After arriving in New York in June 1940, he met

Latouche, "a marvelously funny, generous friend with whom I was very intimate indeed." Although engaged to be married, Latouche "was all for" their becoming lovers, but Gysin declined, "stupidly perhaps." Latouche became a mentor to the slightly younger man, finding him work as a costume assistant for Irene Sharaff on the show *Banjo Eyes,* aiding him financially, and more generally supporting and guiding his career, including helping to promote his literary aspirations and hone his skills as a writer. On seeing some of Gysin's illustrations in 1947, Latouche's sardonic pronouncement, "the impotence of being [Max] Ernst" (a pun on Oscar Wilde's *The Importance of Being Earnest*), helped resolve Gysin's determination to pursue a literary rather than an art career, including writing a book and lyrics for an unrealized Broadway musical based on *Uncle Tom's Cabin.*[11]

Around the time that Latouche befriended Gysin, he also met the writer William S. Burroughs (1914–1997), with whom Gysin later would have an important friendship and working partnership. At this point, however, Gysin knew about Burroughs only from Latouche, who presumably met the writer through his assistant, Burroughs's first wife, a divorced German-Jewish refugee named Ilse Herzfeld Klapper, whom Burroughs married in 1937 so that she could escape to New York. After coming to America, but before employment by Latouche, Ilse served as a secretary for the German writer Ernst Toller and then, after his death, for the Austrian actor-producer Kurt Kasznar. Latouche accordingly could have met her through either Toller or Kasznar, both of whom he knew; but in any case, she came to work for him in the early 1940s, perhaps after Kasznar left for military service in 1941. Gysin recalled one instance when, after Ilse answered the telephone at Latouche's apartment, the lyricist told her, "If that is your husband William Burroughs, don't let him up here because he's got a gun!" and explained to Gysin, "She's married to this dangerous lunatic." Indeed, Latouche, "famous for his skits," reportedly would do one about Burroughs, saying, "I'm Bill Burroughs and I've got a gun. Don't come near me." (This jesting proved tragically prescient, as Burroughs would fatally shoot his second wife in what appears to have been a drunken mishap.) In later years, Burroughs adapted some of his literary techniques, as in his best-known work *Naked Lunch* (1959), from Gysin, whom he regarded as "the only man I have ever respected.... the only person of either sex. He was completely enigmatic because he was completely himself.... They [people] saw in him a threat, a deadly threat. Rightly so, I think." If Latouche helped guide Gysin's artistic development, as appears the case, he can with reason be regarded as at least an indirect influence on Burroughs as well.[12]

Long after he had settled in Tangier in 1950, Gysin recalled the roisterous times that he and Latouche had had in the 1940s, when they would "clown around for seventy-two hours on end. Being young and tough in those days we went on all kinds of binges.... We really toured, man. We toured downtown, uptown, we were on the Eastside, Westside, Harlem, Brooklyn, every place like that." Gysin specifically remembered how singer Billie Holiday obliged their search for some marijuana by giving them the key to her apartment and telling them where they could find two joints. After the war, Gysin and Latouche continued their "binges" out in the Hamptons, that cluster of villages in eastern Long Island becoming increasingly popular as an art colony.[13]

Among other things, Latouche and Gysin shared an interest in otherworldly phenomena. "Touche was the only person with whom I ever took an oath that I or he would attempt to make contact from beyond the grave," asserted Gysin, who also reported that they shared a good friend in the Irish medium Eileen Garrett (1893–1970), as suggested by Latouche's journals as well. Having grown up hearing voices and seeing visions, Garrett developed her presumed psychic abilities under the guidance of the socialist poet and gay activist Edward Carpenter and the parapsychologist and psychic researcher James Hewat McKenzie. After the disastrous crash of the British dirigible *R101* in 1930, she conducted a series of closely observed séances in which she reportedly channeled information from some of the deceased crew members, helping to make her one of the most famed mediums of her time, although she herself retained a good deal of skepticism regarding the notion of a spirit world. In 1940, she landed in New York, where she established the Creative Age Press and *Tomorrow* magazine, both dedicated to paranormal phenomena, and eventually the Parapsychology Foundation as well.[14]

Gysin related some colorful stories, not necessarily reliable in all their details, concerning Garrett and Latouche. On one occasion, while on furlough from the Canadian Army, probably in late 1944, he stayed with Latouche at the latter's new quarters at 29 Washington Square West—where Eleanor Roosevelt maintained a Manhattan residence as well—and attended a party there at which the guests included not only Garrett, but painter Bessie Lasky, palmist Margaret Mamlok, actor Yul Brynner, and an unnamed astrologer, among others. (Latouche also invited to this gathering Bob Gregory—a British wrestler and the former husband of Princess Baba of Sarawak—because, as Latouche explained to Gysin, "he's doing hypnoanalysis for the American Air Force," but Gregory phoned to cancel.) "I'm gonna have *all* the weird ladies who're into the fourth dimension," Latouche allegedly told Gysin about the party, expressing the hope that "Eleanor [Roosevelt] will come too." Gysin recounted another incident, probably dating from 1945, at which Garrett invited him and Latouche to her apartment to witness the surrealist writer Maurice Sandoz produce the stigmata, leading Latouche to touch the red marks that appeared on Sandoz's hands "like Doubting Thomas."[15]

Gysin further recalled how skillfully Latouche, whom he thought "one of the most extraordinary mimics I've ever known," imitated Garrett's "affected way of speaking," to the point that Gysin once rudely addressed Garrett on the phone thinking it was Latouche impersonating her. "Touche used to call her 'the Fiddler Crab,'" he continued, "because she always came dancing and darting in at you sidewise with all her psychic antennae snapping at you as she gave you the insidious old elbow, cradling her huge tits in her arms as she advanced. In Killarney green satin she was a sight." Garrett herself recalled bringing together the Irish writer and raconteur Oliver St. John Gogarty, the Irish author of ghost stories James Reynolds, and Latouche, taking mischievous pleasure in observing Gogarty and Latouche "reduce to ashes Jimmy [Reynolds]'s pretensions about his great and noble birth." Apparently taking to heart Latouche's dubious claims about his Irish ancestry, Garrett thought that with these three writers "the Irish past became alive again."[16]

Another friend of Latouche involved in occult practices included the forementioned hand analyst Margaret Mamlok, whom Latouche possibly met through Bessie Lasky, the wife of the noted film producer Jesse L. Lasky. Mamlok (1878–1953), after studying palmistry in Berlin, emigrated to New York in 1937, a refugee from the Nazis, with her husband, the prominent dentist Hans Mamlok. In her memoirs, Lasky remembered Mamlok as "a mature, brilliant, German cultured woman" who was "warm, gracious, and had a keen awareness toward life and people." Latouche spoke fondly of her as well, and reported further, in a June 20, 1944, journal entry, about a hand reading with her: "Mrs. Mamlok . . . informs me that I have the hand of a genius. But says also that I have never been in love: that my palm shows no personal influence. God knows—I *don't* know."[17]

As for the unnamed astrologer at the Latouche party mentioned above, that might well have been Natacha Rambova (1897–1966), another friend during these years. Born Winifred Shaughnessy in Utah, Rambova, who married four times, remains widely remembered as the second wife of matinee idol Rudolph Valentino, but she had her own remarkable career as a dancer, art director, costume designer, and authority on dreams, mythology, astrology, and world religions, amassing an important collection of Egyptian artifacts in the process. In 1944, during a period in which Latouche saw her with some regularity, she co-wrote a book, *Technique for Living*, whose breathing and physical exercises, related to yoga and aimed at fostering serenity and mental clarity, gives an idea as to the kind of regimen Latouche attempted under her supervision. He also consulted with her about his astrological chart, as he did for several years with another leading astrologer, Charles Jayne (1911–1985), who recalled in particular discussing the lyricist's creative problems in connection with those of poets Keats and Shelley and the composer César Franck. However seriously he took astrology, Latouche seems all the same to have kept a sense of humor about such things: "A heavy block seems to lie between me and my work," he wrote in his diary on August 16, 1943. "Natacha [Rambova] calls it the influence of the planet Saturn. I call it just plain lead-in-the-ass."[18]

Even as he maintained his association with the Little Friends, Latouche cultivated another, somewhat overlapping set of friends that contained a pronounced number of émigrés; and much as the history of the former group remains in large part documented by the literature surrounding Paul and Jane Bowles, so that of this contiguous circle comes in good measure through the diaries and correspondence of Leo Lerman.

Born into a poor, Jewish immigrant family, Lerman (1914–1994) worked as an actor and stage manager before establishing himself as a writer in the early 1940s, in due course becoming editor at such fashionable magazines as *Mademoiselle* and *Vogue*. An autodidact of enormous culture, Lerman wrote widely on the arts, but became especially well known for his Sunday-night parties at his Lexington Avenue apartment on the Upper East Side, which brought together, as noted by the editor of his diaries, "different sets of people on a spectrum that included art, music, theater, literature, film, society, and demisociety, as well as the shopkeeper down the street." At Lerman's memorial service in 1994, producer-director Harold ("Hal") Prince stated, "The quality of those evenings was remarkable because, though it was rare, it wasn't as rare in New York life as now, alas." Indeed, these gatherings resembled those hosted by Latouche in the 1940s and 1950s.[19]

Lerman's occasional references to Latouche in his published journals indicate a warm but not particularly intimate relationship. When their paths crossed in June 1941 at a performance of Jean Cocteau's *La voix humaine*, featuring their mutual friend Eleonora Mendelssohn in an English version that Latouche had prepared for the German actress, Latouche reminded Lerman that they had met some six years earlier, suggesting that prior to this diary entry they had not had much contact. However, by 1944, Latouche could describe the "nervous and marvellous" Lerman as one of the "people strong in me," and Lerman write in his own diary, "Today I lunched with Touche, whom I love very much for his gentle little-boy qualities, and we talked of our hauntings and of panic, each of us having such enormous panic." At the same time, the friendship seems to have had a somewhat strained quality. In 1956, Latouche's closest friends nixed the idea of having Lerman read McCullers's eulogy at the lyricist's memorial service in favor of Frederick Kiesler, who wrote in his journal, "We liked to forget that he [Lerman] had been critical the past few years of John's life and work." Indeed, in the immediate wake of Latouche's death, Lerman delivered the sad news to his ex-lover Richard Hunter (whom Latouche also liked) with a comic sideswipe: "So Touche is dead—passionately dead, I am sure—and rebelliously—and as ever unable to resist an invitation—and mostly not too sure of keeping it on that date and at that moment." In the end, Ruth Yorck and Eleonora Mendelssohn, two of their most beloved friends, seem to have bonded Latouche and Lerman as much as anything.[20]

The niece of the prominent German publisher Samuel Fischer, Ruth ("Rut") Yorck, née Levy (1904–1966), came from a Jewish family from the Berlin area and adopted her mother's maiden name, Landshoff, while in her teens (she still remains better known in Germany as Ruth Landshoff or Ruth Landshoff-Yorck). With various degrees of success, Yorck took up writing, painting, modeling, and acting, appearing on both stage and screen, including a small part in F. W. Murnau's classic horror film *Nosferatu* (1922), but she won special notoriety as the epitome of the so-called new woman of Weimar Germany, or as her biographer Thomas Blubacher describes her, the "glitter girl, style icon, and poet's muse" of 1920s Berlin. A short-haired, cross-dressing bisexual, she befriended a large number of celebrities, from entertainer Josephine Baker, film star Charlie Chaplin, actress Marlene Dietrich, and playwrights Bertolt Brecht, Gerhart Hauptmann, and Ernst Toller to scientist Albert Einstein, writer Thomas Mann, film director Josef von Sternberg, artist Oskar Kokoschka (who drew her portrait), and photographer Otto Umbehr (who photographed her). For many years the lover of the writer Karl Vollmoeller, whose many credits included the screenplay of *The Blue Angel* (1930), she helped the relatively unknown Dietrich land the film's lead female role, thereby playing a pivotal part in the latter's career.[21]

By the time of her 1930 marriage to Count David Yorck von Wartenburg, Yorck had become focused on a serious career as novelist, playwright, and poet, producing work that explored "radical ideas of gender and sexuality." After 1933, she began the process of emigration, eventually arriving in New York in 1937, about the time of her divorce from Yorck. Residing in Manhattan, she attracted a coterie of bohemian friends appreciative of her writing as well as for "her general moral support of all things experimental." During her last years, this group of friends extended to artist Andy Warhol and such pioneers of off-off Broadway as Joseph ("Joe") Cino, who ran Caffe Cino, and Ellen Stewart, the African-American founder of the La MaMa Experimental Theater Club. Yorck died at the Martin Beck Theater in Stewart's company while awaiting the curtain to a performance of Peter Weiss's play *Marat/Sade*.[22]

Much as Yorck transformed her modest surroundings into "make-believe splendor" by using fruit crates for furniture and aluminum foil for wallcover, so, argued Lerman, she turned "prosaic prose into strong, moving, unhackneyed writing—at least for the moment she prodded you into writing, really writing. If you had a spark, the merest glimmer, she bellowed it into a roaring fire. She did not suffer mediocrities: She endured geniuses. She had the power of making you greater than yourself." Lerman also admired Yorck's "wonderful, very Jewish laughter," and the way she generously offered advice to those artists who "came to her as if she were a trysting place.... She came to be the living, gallant, courageous expression of pre-Hitler vanguard Europe to the generations of post-Hitler-war American boys and girls. And the miracle of it was that she never dated: She was always younger than the youngest rebel, speaking their language because she had already invented it years ago for them." Yorck herself would say, "I am rediscovered every year, but, like Persephone, I always return underground."[23]

Beginning in 1940, Yorck apparently began to work for Latouche, as suggested by the forementioned *Collier's* piece, which alludes to his having a "countess" as a secretary. "The countess," reported *Collier's*, "can't of course, take shorthand, and her grammar is purely intuitive, but she plays a stunning game of backgammon. 'My secretary,' John says proudly when confronted by a garbled word, 'spells entirely by ear.' " Moreover, a surviving check register of Latouche's from March to April 1941 reveals regular payments to Yorck in the amount of fifty dollars per month. Whether Yorck's position consisted more of a sinecure than actual employment remains unknown; she at least helped Latouche improve his German, a language he never mastered, although he enjoyed writing to German friends in his own fanciful version of Suetterlin script. In any case, Latouche continued to support Yorck in one way or another for the rest of his life, including housing her for a period in 1953 as she recovered from a bout of cancer. Indeed, in 1957, Lerman wrote Richard Hunter that Latouche's death boded poorly for Yorck: "No matter how they fought, he inevitably helped her."[24]

Yorck's importance to Latouche can be gauged somewhat by the frequency with which she appears in his diaries, as in an August 1943 entry in which he mentions their reading T. S. Eliot at home together. In February 1944, while serving in the navy, he even took the unusual step of pasting a photograph of her in his journal (see Figure 17), with some accompanying thoughts that included these: "sweet and startling Ruth, full of despair and wonder, so ready for tomorrow—so unprepared for today. Yet her faith in me when I had none in myself will have me always in her debt.... Ruth is genius without discipline, Love with its bandage removed, but too far-sighted to perceive the nearest kisser." Respectful of Yorck's abilities, on the occasion of the 1945 release of her book *Lili Marlene: An Intimate Diary*, Latouche wrote to her publisher, "This penetrating portrait of the complex and ill German mentality illuminates much of contemporary history that has puzzled American minds like my own. I congratulate you on publishing such a courageous and fascinating document, and I hope it will find a wide audience in the postwar period, where enlightenment of the citizens of all countries is so urgently required for the problems confronting them."[25]

Yorck, for her part, deeply loved and respected Latouche, even attempting to publish a commemorative omnibus following his death. In an unpublished appreciation of the lyricist, "The Sinister Doodles of John Latouche" (the title a reference to his ubiquitous drawings of devils and other fantastic creatures, as in Figure 40), Yorck wrote, "Latouche has a pretty sizable talent for the arts, besides his main talent, which can be described best by stating, that he is capable of filling a shallow dish with deep waters. That way he makes poetry available to all and sundry.... Latouche is not alone in believing and proclaiming that in our time poetry belongs in a musical. And that is where he hides it, or presents it. After the doodles of the manuscripts have been eliminated." And in an intimate although factually somewhat inaccurate portrait of Latouche in a book of "biographical impressions" published in German in 1963, Yorck further stated, "He was my best American friend, but one really cannot say that, because he was also European, as otherwise only Thornton Wilder is"—and this although Latouche, as she noted, never traveled to Europe. Yorck attributed such cosmopolitanism to Latouche's extensive knowledge of world literature (she emphasized his indebtedness to Brecht), but also to his immigrant friends, who helped equip him with a European education. She admitted that the lyricist could be vain and difficult, but extolled his energy, intelligence, charm, generosity, and "sparkling" ("sprühend") conversation: "He was a joy!" This warm friendship between Yorck and Latouche surely played its part in the transplantation of progressive European styles and ideas to America.[26]

A friend of Yorck's from the old country, Eleonora von Mendelssohn ("Ellie" to Latouche, "Ela" to Lerman, 1900–1951) was born into a particularly wealthy and distinguished German family, the daughter of a partly Jewish banker descended from the philosopher Moses Mendelssohn (with composer Felix Mendelssohn an uncle many generations removed) and a gentile Italian pianist, herself the daughter of an accomplished painter. Eleonora's godmother, the Italian actress Duse after whom she was named, inspired her to pursue an acting career, and she made a name for herself performing in both classic and modern drama in Germany and Austria, all the while cultivating friendships with the likes of Rainer Maria Rilke, Hugo von Hofmannsthal, and especially Max Reinhardt, with whom she had an affair. (According to Lerman, the morphine administered to her after she aborted a child conceived with Reinhardt left her addicted to the drug, although Reinhardt's son Gottfried claimed rather that she turned to morphine out of unrequited love for his father.) With her father deceased and her mother in Florence, Eleonora and her homosexual brother, Francesco, a cellist who for a while was engaged to Ruth Yorck, made their ritzy villa in Grunewald available to Berlin's artistic elite and maverick demimonde, including many gay friends. "Beauty, intelligence, money and the background of Italian, German and French culture could have given Francesco and Eleonora a leading role in Berlin society," wrote their friend, actress-writer Salka Viertel, "—but they preferred the friendship of actors and bohemians." Recognizing the precariousness of their position in Nazi Germany, the Mendelssohn siblings (the subject of yet another book by Thomas Blubacher) made their way in 1935 to New York, where Eleonora, although finding some work in the theater, felt obliged to sell some of the family's extraordinary art collection, including works by Van Gogh, Pissarro, Sisley, and Manet, not only in order to maintain a fairly lavish lifestyle, but to help needy refugees and to care for the troubled and often institutionalized Francesco.[27]

Having already wed three times—to the Swiss pianist Edwin Fischer, the Hungarian military officer Emmerich von Jeszenszky, and the Austrian actor Rudolf Forster—Mendelssohn married in 1947 a fellow German émigré, the homosexual Martin Kosleck, a character actor whose Hollywood career had the couple shuttling back and forth between Los Angeles and New York during these years. At the same time, she maintained a romantic relationship with conductor Arturo Toscanini. In 1951, she died in what appears to have been either a suicide or a drug overdose.

In an affectionate portrait of Mendelssohn, Gottfried Reinhardt remembered his father's lover as "defenseless against the basic currents swirling around her, valiant to the point of self-destruction, sustained only by her own enthusiasm and by continuously being in love, always with the best, the best people and the best ideas—and broken on them." Lerman similarly wrote, "Eleonora somehow became for us . . . a symbol of European culture and civilization then fast being trampled. She assumed heroic stature, for we knew she could, in her frail, star-driven person, endanger herself out of loyalty. . . . Duke or dustman's daughters, none of that much mattered to Eleonora. What mattered to her was genius. She was a pushover for genius and, of course, for charm." Her good friend, the famed actress Elisabeth Bergner, described her further as "the most beautiful, classy, accomplished, beloved, unhappy person I ever met."[28]

The close friendship of Latouche and Mendelssohn dated at least back to 1941, when the lyricist adapted for her Cocteau's monodrama *La voix humaine* as *The Human Voice*, which Mendelssohn performed at the 92nd Street YMHA on June 11, 1941, on a triple bill that also included works by Gerard Willem van Loon and Gustav Wied. They might have met originally through Ruth Yorck. Surviving evidence suggests, in any case, a particularly intimate relationship. In a letter sent to Mendelssohn during his 1942–43 trip to the Congo, Latouche wrote of missing her "acutely," and in a 1945 letter composed on his way to Los Angeles, he wondered if he had kissed her "warmly enough" at the station "to protect your cheek from harsher lips until my return," a homecoming of which he spoke eagerly: "In the evenings we will read [Joachim] Ringelnatz, and I shall knit you a hallway snare to catch maestri in" (an apparent reference to Toscanini). A 1946 article about Mendelssohn cited her appreciation for Latouche as someone "who helped her find her way in a new world," while a 1949 feature on Latouche spoke of the Biedermeier furniture in his West 12th Street apartment on loan from Mendelssohn. Latouche also became friendly with her brother Francesco, attending the latter's wild parties at his place on East 83rd Street, ten blocks north of Eleonora's apartment on East 73rd Street. Acknowledging Latouche's close friendship with Eleonora, Leo Lerman asked him to read an elegy by Rilke at her funeral.[29]

Like Frederick Kiesler and Ruth Yorck, Mendelssohn surely introduced Latouche to some of her celebrated friends, including the Austrian-Jewish film and theater director Max Reinhardt (born Maximilian Goldmann, 1873–1943), a frequent guest artist in Hollywood and New York before settling in the United States after the Nazi occupation of Austria. One extant photograph, apparently from the early 1940s, shows Reinhardt, Mendelssohn, and Latouche together, with the lyricist's gaze fixed intently on the Austrian director. Reinhardt's death in October 1943, learned about while in the service, left Latouche "extremely depressed," as he wrote Stefanie Kiesler: "I admired him enormously as a person, and he was about to return to his earlier period of the small intimate dramas, which I think would have given him a new impetus toward living. He seemed tired when I last saw him, quiet and tired. Certainly, he was not an old man, and his death is a loss to the post-war theater, which he would have adjusted to more easily than the rigors of between-war Broadway."[30]

A few other émigré friends might be mentioned in connection with this social circle: actor Yul Brynner, singer Marlene Dietrich, writer Anaïs Nin, and physician Max Jacobson. Born in far eastern Russia, Brynner (1920–1985), who achieved great fame on stage and screen in the 1950s as the star of Rodgers and Hammerstein's *The King and I*, spent his teenage years in Paris, where he accompanied himself on the guitar singing Russian and Gypsy songs in cabarets. Arriving in the United States in 1940, he found similar work in New York, including at the Blue Angel, where Latouche might well have made his acquaintance, although he could have met him through Mendelssohn and her friend, actress Ilse Bois, as well. In any case, in Latouche's diaries from the 1940s, he often mentions spending time with "Youl Bryner," as the actor then spelled his name, intimating a particularly warm relationship. Indeed, in 1985, Lerman, who claimed that Brynner had affairs with both men and women—including another member of this group, the German-born Marlene Dietrich (1901–1992)—recalled finding Brynner "Narcissus naked" in Latouche's bed in the latter's Washington Square apartment, suggesting even a sexual side to this friendship. Meanwhile, Latouche seemed to entertain the notion of a liaison with Dietrich himself, to judge from this June 1944 journal entry: "For the past week have been enchanted by the ambience of Marlene Dietrich, whose natural charm and deep sweetness are at complete variance with the sequin elegance of her public personality. She seems to like me very much, but I am helpless when I think of the difficulties involved in making a direct move into a relationship." After Brynner's marriage to actress Virginia Gilmore in 1944, Latouche grew close to the latter as well, writing in his diary, "I always respond to her indefinable personal magic, which is made up of blondeness, of retreating personality, and of a shifting quality that I cannot name—I suppose it is just that old-fashioned thing 'glamor.' "[31]

Although a more distant acquaintance, Latouche also became friends during these years with the refugee writer and diarist Anaïs Nin (1903–1977). Born in Paris to Spanish-Cuban parents, she grew up in a musical family, with her father, Joaquín Nin, a notable composer-pianist; her mother, Rosa Culmell, an accomplished mezzo-soprano; and her younger brother Joaquín Nin-Culmell, a rising composer in his own right. Following an adolescence spent in Paris, Barcelona, and New York, she made Paris her home until the outbreak of war prompted a return to America. By this time, she had released her debut book, the symbolist prose-poem *House of Incest* (1936), and had begun her lifelong series of diaries whose publication in the 1960s and 1970s helped make her a feminist icon.[32]

Latouche and Nin apparently became friends soon after the latter's arrival in New York from Europe in December 1939, for in an April 1940 journal entry, she reports how her "young friends"—Latouche along with the poet Hugh Chisholm and his wife, Bridget (later, the painter Bridget Tichenor)—took her to a party to meet the Greek surrealist poet Nikolaos Kalamares, writing, "John Latouche is delightful, full of playfulness and fantasy. He made up a language which sounds like French but is a gibberish equivalent. He talks to me in this at length, and I answer in fake Japanese. We deliver fervent speeches, outdoing Joyce with our double talk." Nin seemed to move only tangentially among Latouche's friends, but the particularly close relationship she established with Gore Vidal in the postwar period must have kept her and Latouche in touch during these later years as well.[33]

If the Little Friends had their fair share of heavy drinkers—including Jane Bowles, Robert Faulkner, Carson McCullers, and Latouche himself—Latouche's refugee friends showed a distinct proclivity rather toward psychoactive drugs. Passing mention has been made of Mendelssohn's addiction to morphine; but along with Yorck, Brynner, Dietrich, and Nin—that is, virtually all the exiles discussed above—she also took stimulants, as did Latouche, under the medical supervision of the controversial Dr. Max Jacobson.

Another German-Jewish refugee, Jacobson (1900–1979) received his medical training in Berlin, where he practiced medicine before making his way to New York in 1936. Setting up shop in Manhattan, "Miracle Max" specialized in energy-boosting serums that combined vitamins, hormones, steroids, enzymes, amphetamines, and other ingredients, and that he administered to his patients (as well as to himself) by way of hypodermic needles, although many learned to inject his potions on their own, with the doctor's office providing needles and vials. One of his clients, writer Truman Capote, described these elixirs as inducing "instant euphoria. You feel like Superman.... Ideas come at the speed of light.... You don't need sleep, you don't need nourishment. If it's sex you're after, you go all night. Then you crash—it's like falling down a well." To his evident satisfaction, Jacobson counted as his patients many prominent figures in various walks of life, including Marilyn Monroe, Mickey Mantle, lyricist Alan Jay Lerner, and both John and Jacqueline Kennedy. According to a 1970 statement that he himself apparently prepared, Jacobson claimed to be "particularly interested" in using "methods to counteract the severe physical and emotional stresses of those who live and work in environments of continual high pressure."[34]

In 1972, a front-page *New York Times* article helped bring Jacobson's practice under public scrutiny, part of an ongoing reassessment with respect to the growing dissemination of amphetamines especially. Jacobson claimed that he used only small and harmless amounts of amphetamines in his concoctions (a position since challenged in the medical literature), and several past and present clients came to his defense, citing the doctor's kindness and the therapeutic effects of his regimen. Tennessee Williams, a former patient mentioned in the *Times* exposé, wrote to the paper's editor, "I am inclined to believe that he [Jacobson] was a brilliant experimenter but that in certain cases, including mine, the experiments—perhaps like all medical experiments—happened to involve a good deal of hazard. I think his motives are humanitarian." (Some years later Williams claimed that he found Jacobson's shots "marvelously stimulating to me as a writer.") Others spoke more critically of both the physician and his practice, mentioning in particular psychotic episodes induced by amphetamine withdrawal. Wrote Alan Jay Lerner's assistant,

"Max [Jacobson] was not a simple charlatan. He was a far more complicated one, brilliant, mysterious in his power to manipulate and orchestrate all the body systems and the mental ones as well. . . . But he was corrupt to the core." After extensive review, in 1975, the New York State Board of Regents revoked Jacobson's license, citing a host of infractions, including endangering the health of his patients and misrepresenting his practice to drug suppliers.[35]

A patient of Jacobson's as early as 1942, Latouche likely learned about Jacobson through friends like Yorck and Nin, who had been treated by the doctor back in Europe. In any case, a number of entries in Latouche's journals indicate that he continued to see Jacobson throughout his life, and that he helped him edit his medical writings. They even collaborated on a planned book, for which transcripts of two discussions recorded a week apart in the spring of 1949 survive among Latouche's papers.[36]

These two transcripts—both supplemented with a very few remarks by, in the first instance, Jacobson's wife, Nina, and in the second, Ruth Yorck—remain remarkable in several ways, not least in preserving Jacobson and Latouche in conversation, both men erudite and witty, the former, however, considerably more imperious. Latouche steers the sometimes rambling conversation to some consideration of the health effects of overcrowding, central heating, air conditioning, automated work, sedentary living, poor eating habits, alcohol abuse, and other features of contemporary American life, presumably the focus of their proposed book. In his responses, Jacobson emphasizes psychological and environmental conditions, rather than hereditary factors, in causing illness, attributing, for example, the genetic susceptibility among Ashkenazi Jews to Buerger's disease to the stress of ghettoization and the effects of poor diets. Aside from a partiality to vitamin supplements, he further expresses deep skepticism toward a range of medical treatments, including prescription drugs, psychoanalysis, and physical therapy, advocating rather good nutrition, sexual activity, and, in general, harmony with nature as the road to good health—a far cry from the notorious "Doctor Feelgood" depicted in later exposés. Jacobson's holistic principles, incidentally, appear not unrelated to Latouche's dedication to the idea of an integrated lyric theater, and when the lyricist tells Jacobson, "They have lost their view of the whole," he could be speaking not only of medical specialists, but artistic ones as well.[37]

Meanwhile, the use of Jacobson's elixirs—Kenward Elmslie recalled Latouche regularly giving himself shots—could explain some of Latouche's behavior, his animated and talkative presence, for instance, or his propensity for staying up all night, although he seemed capable of acquiring stimulants on his own; in a diary entry of February 1944, while in the navy, he mentions feeling "spry as a fox" after taking some Benzedrine, an amphetamine often used by military personnel. Similarly, the notion that the use of Jacobson's potions might have played some part in Latouche's demise—and Leo Lerman considered Jacobson somewhat responsible for the deaths of both Latouche and Yorck—must be weighed against Latouche's other habits, including excessive use of alcohol and cigarettes, indulgences Jacobson strongly warned against. All the same, Latouche might have resorted more than otherwise to alcohol and cigarettes in order to help counteract the anxiety and tension induced by amphetamines. Latouche and many of his friends in any event seemed to use psychoactive drugs as a matter of course, without much regard for their risks one way or the other.[38]

7

Radio and Patriotic Work, 1940–1945

The tremendous success of *Ballad for Americans* over the air helped Latouche gain employment as a radio writer, a vocation that occupied him especially in the months leading up to the October 1940 premiere of his musical comedy *Cabin in the Sky*.

One early reference to such radio work appears in connection with an April 21, 1940, show, *The American Family Discusses War*, aired over the NBC Blue network station WJZ (currently WABC) on behalf of the Children's Crusade for Children (CCFC), a drive by American youth that helped raise money for refugee children; for this broadcast, which starred Howard Lindsay and Dorothy Stickney, Latouche adapted a short dramatic piece by Dorothy Canfield Fisher, the national chairman of the CCFC. More generally, he secured in the course of 1940 a staff appointment with NBC Radio, one source reporting a weekly salary of $500; this position included supervision, along with writers Ranald R. MacDougall and Albert N. Williams, of a new NBC series, *The Listener's Playhouse*, which ran from June 1940 to January 1942, although Latouche's participation in the show seems to have ended long before then.[1]

The Listener's Playhouse used radio's familiar term "playhouse" but represented a novel attempt on the part of NBC to develop, along the lines of CBS's *Columbia Workshop*, a somewhat elite audience for radio drama by broadcasting every week a new half-hour play by Latouche, MacDougall, or Williams. Dispensing with any advertising sponsors, which only added to its elevated stature, the program aired Saturday nights at 8:30 on—at least initially—NBC's Red network station WEAF and its many affiliates.[2]

Latouche wrote four shows for *The Listener's Playhouse*, all of which premiered in 1940: "No Program Tonight, or The Director's Dilemma"; "Benedict Arnold: Portrait of a Traitor" (also known as "The Traitor"); "Men with Wings, or Flight into Darkness"; and "The First Dance." For all these shows save "Benedict Arnold," which had a score by George Maynard, NBC's staff arranger Tom Bennett provided the music—a crucial ingredient in radio drama. Recordings of these four programs survive, as do, among Latouche's papers, the scripts for "Benedict Arnold" and "Men with Wings."[3]

In "No Program Tonight" (aired July 13, 1940), a Pirandellian lark, an actor in a radio soap opera, overwhelmed by the pointlessness of such "drivel," stops in the middle of a performance and, while still on the air, engages the other cast members in a discussion about their personal lives—to the outrage of the show's director (played by Norman Lloyd), whose asides provide much of the show's humor ("Oh, Stanislavsky, you should be living at this hour"). After several of the station's crew members weigh in, some local citizenry appear and argue for the importance of radio to the public. This program in particular offered what audiences might have expected from the author of *Ballad for Americans*.

In "Benedict Arnold" (aired August 17, 1940), perhaps Latouche's strongest radio drama, the exiled American turncoat (played by Santos Ortega) recalls various episodes in his life, conjuring a vivid psychological portrait of a disillusioned soul. This sort of flashback structure, although especially congenial to radio, remains perhaps most familiar today through such works as Clifford Odets's stage play *Waiting for Lefty* (1935), Marc Blitzstein's opera *The Cradle Will Rock* (1937), and Orson Welles's film *Citizen Kane* (1941)—works that suggest the permeating influence of radio during this period, and in the case of the final scene of Latouche's *The Ballad of Baby Doe* (1956), its lingering impact as well. As the *Brooklyn Eagle* reported, "Benedict Arnold" further employed "blank verse, rhythmic prose and a Greek chorus to establish its tragic mood," with the narrator stating at the start of the show, for instance,

> These are days of shadowy understanding
> When the air holds currents of unexpectedness
> And words fall like bullets on the civilian ear:
> Warnings hold us frozen:
> Men with blue eyes, beware of men with grey.[4]

Latouche's next program, "Men with Wings" (aired September 7, 1940), an allegorical adaptation of the Icarus story, similarly featured a heightened, somewhat portentous poetic style, here recalling the author's 1934 poem "The Gull." In this dramatization, Icarus foresees the future destruction caused by air warfare, and, before his fall, climbs toward the sun in order to blot out such fearful visions; states the Greek chorus, "A legend must not look at reality / Or it is destroyed." Latouche dedicated this episode to writer-pilot Antoine de Saint-Exupéry (at the time, mistakenly thought shot down in the war) and "to the many / For whom you spoke, the pilots / And aviators of free countries, / And to their dead companions." (While serving in the navy, Latouche actually would lunch with Saint-Exupéry and his wife in San Francisco.)[5]

For his final *Listener's Playhouse* show, Latouche penned a more lighthearted playlet, "The First Dance" (aired October 5, 1940), about a sixteen-year-old girl, Angelika. On the way to her first dance at the local country club with her nagging mother and babbling aunt (played by Hope Emerson), Angelika, upset with her boyfriend, compensates by dreaming about becoming a great actress, then a nurse during wartime, and finally a tough gangster, "Angie the brain." One additional episode, providing a central social context, concerns not a fantasy but the girl's distraught recollection of some hoodlums attacking a Jewish peddler (the man's ethnicity only implied) and the inaction of the police. However, the story ends happily as Angelika reconciles with her boyfriend. If some of Latouche's other radio plays evoke his early poetry, this one recalls his high school tales of adolescent alienation.

Even as he provided scripts for *The Listener's Playhouse*, Latouche undertook other radio projects. He wrote, for instance, an *Ode to Radio*, with music by Tom Bennett, to kick off a "gigantic tribute to radio broadcasting" that aired on August 3, 1940, on the occasion of the annual convention of the National Association of Broadcasters (NAB). This commission subsequently caused some discomfiture when the NAB realized that Latouche belonged to the organization's perennial adversary, ASCAP, at least according to the lyricist, who recalled writing a letter to the president of the NAB that read, "Dear Sir: I made application for membership to ASCAP long before I wrote the Ode. I'm sorry it embarrassed you and would like to return the money you paid me. Enclosed please find my personal check for ten dollars. The nine hundred and ninety seems to have slipped away."[6]

And on October 12, 1940, about a week after "The First Dance" aired, NBC Radio also presented Latouche's *New Walls of China*, a radio piece on behalf of the relief agency China Aid Council. The published version of the play by Trans-Pacific News confusingly attributed the work to no fewer than six authors—the three *Listener's Playhouse* writers (Latouche, MacDougall, and Williams), along with Norman Corwin, Arch Oboler, and William Saroyan—but then, on another page, solely to Latouche. Perhaps Latouche took primary responsibility for the piece and various colleagues assisted in some capacity or other. In any case, the drama embodied a complex form in nine parts that used an array of Chinese and American voices and characters, and that alternated poetic chanting with short dramatic vignettes. Aiming to dispel quaint stereotypes, the piece rather presented the Chinese as heroic, resourceful, and unified in their successful attempt to stem Japanese occupation, Latouche quoting Sun Yat-sen as he had Thomas Jefferson and Abraham Lincoln in *Ballad for Americans*. In one of his earliest forays into explicit wartime propaganda, Latouche subsequently published a related but more straightforwardly journalistic piece about Chinese resistance, slightly retitled "New Walls for China," two years later in *Harper's Bazaar*, further evidencing his primary authorship of the original radio work. States this article near its conclusion, "Now China is building a new wall, not a wall to isolate themselves, but a wall of education and faith and force that makes them part of the wall against tyranny being built all over the world."[7]

With the successful launching of *Cabin in the Sky* on October 25, 1940, Latouche's work in radio seemed to slow; but he intermittently continued to have some involvement with radio as late as 1949. He wrote and read some commentary celebrating America's ethnic diversity, for instance, as part of an elaborate tribute, *One Nation Indivisible*, complete with broadcast messages from Eve Curie, Maurice Maeterlinck,

Thomas Mann, Lin Yutang, and others, which aired on NBC on January 20, 1941, on the occasion of Franklin Roosevelt's inauguration to a third presidential term. He penned some text for a program, *China on the March*, broadcast on March 20, 1941, by CBS in support of United China Relief. And on March 30, 1941, *The Silver Theater*, a CBS program sponsored by the International Silver Company, broadcast an episode, "One Step Ahead," based on an original story by Latouche adapted by staff writer True Boardman; a noirish tale about an unhappily married couple told from the perspective of the husband (played by Orson Welles), the drama concludes with the wife, always "one step ahead" of her husband, dying of heart failure before he has the chance to murder her. Highly uncharacteristic of his work, this last effort plausibly projected some tensions plaguing his recent marriage to Theodora Griffis.[8]

In March 1941, Latouche moreover published an intriguing article, "The Muse and the Mike," in *Vogue* magazine that argued for radio's potential for poets in particular. Indeed, radio needs the poet "since he has an innate understanding of the natural laws controlling the theatrics of the ear. In the new art-forms of radio . . . the poet will again find his place." For Latouche, the radio work of W. H. Auden, Norman Corwin, Archibald MacLeish, Albert Williams, and Arch Oboler, "the most spectacular [radio] dramatist to date," not only reflected the technical advances of an industrial society, but promised to fulfill poetry's age-old function as a wide disseminator, like the folk ballad, of knowledge and wisdom: "To stir people's deepest understanding, the poetic medium must be invoked." Citing such things as the use of the commentating chorus in radio dramas, he further noted similarities with earlier forms of poetic theater, including the ancient Greek and Elizabethan stage: "At last, through radio, poets can speak again in many ways. The surface is scratched; there are only the spaces, waiting to be filled in."[9]

After American entry into the war, Latouche's sporadic radio work focused that much more on the Allied cause. This included serving as a staff writer for the *Treasury Star Parade* (1942–44), a widely aired fifteen-minute show that employed some of the country's best actors and writers, typically working pro bono, in sketches aimed at promoting the purchase of U.S. treasury bonds and stamps. Radio historians, whatever their thoughts regarding the use of the airwaves for such government propaganda, consider these *Treasury Star Parade* programs to constitute an "impressive" achievement, "because in the space of a fifteen-minute time slot," as one commentator observes, "they couple the art of the drama with audio technology to produce highly charged infusions of national pride, support for the war, a determination to combat fascism, and a motivation for buying War Bonds."[10]

The *Treasury Star Parade* entrusted Latouche to write its premiere show, "The Statue of Liberty," which aired around the country in February 1942 and re-aired later in the fall, an unusual distinction. This minidrama took the shape of an extended conversation between the Statue of Liberty (portrayed by the Australian Judith Anderson) and a recent French immigrant, Jean (played by another distinguished actor, the British Maurice Evans). Liberty reminds Jean of freedom's ongoing challenges at home and abroad, and, quoting Whitman's *Leaves of Grass,* sends out a message to the world's peoples, including both Jews, "scattered over the earth, your children starved, your property stolen," and Germans, "your poets in prisons, fighters underground and exiled."

Anderson included "The Statue of Liberty" and a "song-poem" by Latouche, "Fog," on a 1944 RCA Victor release, *Judith Anderson in Dramatic Sketches,* which also contained a dramatization of Lincoln's letter to a war widow, and passages from the Sermon on the Mount. Latouche originally wrote "Fog" as a melodrama for speaker and musical accompaniment in collaboration with composer Vernon Duke and choreographer George Balanchine as a vehicle for the latter's wife, Vera Zorina, who danced to the piece at a sold-out benefit concert, Carnival for Britain, at Radio City Music Hall presented after midnight on February 22, 1941, in order to raise funds for British War Relief. The poem gives voice to the famed London fog, now helping to shield the capital from German bombers: "How many times have I come with my grey embrace / To the city that I love." That April, actress Gertrude Lawrence recited this song-poem on the radio program *Friendship Bridge to England,* accompanied by Duke at the piano; and the following year, Judith Anderson presented the work on the *Treasury Star Parade,* with Duke's effectively atmospheric music, at times reminiscent of Debussy, played by the Al Goodman Orchestra. In contrast, the RCA Victor release of Anderson's renditions of "The Statue of Liberty" (with a supporting cast including Gene Leonard) and "Fog" dispensed with any orchestral underscoring, but more simply framed these accounts with choral snatches of American and British patriotic airs, respectively—a real impoverishment with regard to "Fog" especially. This RCA album, incidentally, received unenthusiastic notices in the press, the *Times* commending the "sentiments" of "The Statue of Liberty" and "Fog," but finding neither to possess "the ring of sincerity that made Mr. Latouche's *Ballad for Americans* an exciting piece."[11]

In the course of 1942, Latouche wrote at least two more programs for the *Treasury Star Parade*: the short story "Mrs. Murgatroyd's Dime" and the play "Two-Way Passage." In addition, toward the end of the year, the *Treasury Star Parade* presented an adaptation by Malcolm Meecham of a "dramatic poem" by Latouche, "From America to Archangel." All three programs featured incidental music by David Broekman, with whom Latouche would later collaborate on some songs.

"Mrs. Murgatroyd's Dime," read by actor Robert Montgomery, then serving as a lieutenant in the U.S. Naval Reserve, tells its tale not from the perspective of the Statue of Liberty or the London fog, but from a dime as it changes various hands; in due course a cleaning woman, Mrs. Murgatroyd, buys a war stamp with the money, helping the government to purchase a torpedo that sinks an enemy destroyer. "Two-Way Passage," adapted from a 1941 novel of the same name by the Slovenian-American writer Louis Adamic (1898–1951), concerns a German immigrant to the Midwest, John Schmidt (played by Paul Henreid), who attempts to maintain some distance from his native homeland but, in the face of threats from local Nazi partisans, chooses to return to the old country in the hopes of teaching Europeans the American ideals of "life, liberty, the pursuit of happiness, equality, tolerance, decency, faith: all of the things that make life beautiful, that we have learned and made work here"; in a recent discussion, historian Lorraine Lees described this show as communicating the idea "that *Americanized* immigrants could make a unique contribution in the fight" against fascism. "From America to Archangel," recited by Vincent Price with the assistance of some actors and a chanting chorus, advocated support for the Soviet Union, with the story's twist involving the arrival into an American port of a Russian merchant marine manned by a crew of women (with writer Malcolm Meecham probably providing the dramatic vignettes interspersed in the course of the prose-poem proper).[12]

Both "The Statue of Liberty" and "Mrs. Murgatroyd's Dime" also made their way into print as part of a collection of *Treasury Star Parade* scripts that featured pieces as well by Thomas Mann and Thomas Wolfe, among others, and a grateful introduction by Henry Morgenthau Jr., secretary of the Treasury. In his preface to "Mrs. Murgatroyd's Dime," William Bacher, the *Treasury Star Parade* producer who edited this anthology, described Latouche as "a short, swarthy, amiable chap—a little lazy, I think. Why is it that all the likable people are the lazy ones? Anyway, if John had never written anything else, I would have liked him immensely for this little piece that follows."[13]

Latouche further adapted some of "The Statue of Liberty" for his cantata for speakers and chorus, *The Marseillaise*, composed in 1942 for a Bastille Day celebration in support of the Free French community in New York. Composed in free verse (versions of the script—not all complete—exist in both English and, as *La Marseillaise*, in French), this concerted work followed along the lines of *Ballad for Americans*, with the nation's voice personified not by Uncle Sam but by the Marseillaise, who succinctly chronicles France's republican ideals, defeats, and triumphs from 1792 to 1942. In this instance, however, Latouche imagined more of a multimedia presentation, with film clips and slide projections, including a portrait of Walt Whitman in conjunction with a recitation of that poet's "O Star of France." Although Latouche composed the English original, he seems to have received help from his friend Ruth Yorck on the French version, which assigned the reading of the Whitman poem to the refugee poet Yvan Goll, who conceivably might have helped on the French translation as well. The details of the cantata's performance remain unknown but for Yorck's recollection that she staged this "épopée" (French: epic poem), which she considered one of Latouche's most beautiful works; and that the piece, which also involved the participation of another friend, Eleonora Mendelssohn, brought the audience to tears. The work possibly appeared as part of the final "tableau" at a rally of an estimated five thousand supporters of Free France at the Manhattan Center on July 14, 1942, honoring not only Bastille Day, but the 150th anniversary of "La Marseillaise."[14]

In the course of 1942, Latouche penned another two works in the tradition of *Ballad for Americans*, both with that earlier work's composer Earl Robinson: *Battle Hymn* and *Forward, America*.

Battle Hymn took its inspiration from President Roosevelt's first wartime State of the Union Address on January 6, 1942. With Latouche for the moment unavailable, Robinson initially drafted the libretto himself, but later turned to the lyricist to help him "fix the words," with the result that they both received credit for the text. The libretto, in fact, did not so much quote Roosevelt's speech as dramatize its major themes, including a summary of fascist aggression and aims, a confirmation of Allied unity, a reiteration of the principles at stake, and an inventory of the materiel needed to defeat the enemy. Stylistically, the work, like *Ballad for Americans,* formed a kind of melodrama, with sung lines alternating with spoken ejaculations.[15]

On April 30, 1942, the Almanac Singers presented a preliminary tryout of the piece, here entitled *A Report of the State of the Union,* at Detroit's Institute of Arts, with Robinson at the piano. The following evening, on May 1, the Treasury Department, as part of its war bond drive, broadcast an apparently more elaborate version of the work, advertised as *The Roosevelt Cantata: A Report of the State of the Union,* with the participation of baritone William Hargrave, actors William Adams and Henry Hull, a chorus prepared by Ray Bloch, and the Treasury Orchestra under Al Goodman. And on May 10, 1942, baritone John Wright DeMerchant and the Ray Bloch chorus, accompanied by pianist Robinson and led by Simon Rady, performed the piece, now called *Battle Hymn,* at the Alvin Theatre on Broadway as part of a concert, "Music at Work," for Russian War Relief.[16]

Organized by composer Marc Blitzstein, "Music at Work" featured a rich sampling of music, dance, drama, and film, with *Battle Hymn*—which the *Daily News* thought "very badly presented"—offered as an example of radio music. Discerning reminiscences of *Ballad for Americans* and Carl Sandburg's 1936 collection of poems, *The People, Yes,* respectively, Louis Biancolli (*World-Telegram*) and Olin Downes (*Times*) thought *Battle Hymn,* if not as "strong" as these predecessors, similarly "rousing," whereas Virgil Thomson (*Herald Tribune*), although deeming Robinson's musical prosody "quite often apt," found the piece "a shade stuffy." "I think rhyme would have given it wings, perhaps," he added. "'In any case, I kept remembering all the time a satirical song of Latouche's that is equally patriotic but somehow more fun, a marching ditty about the ladies' auxiliary corps, called, 'Nelly, pull your belly in; it's for the U.S.A.'" (Thomson seems to have confused the song, "Nelly, Pull Your Belly In," by Charlotte Kent and Louis Alter with a Latouche parody for Spivy, "One-Hundred Percent American Girls," which included the lines, "Annie, pull your fanny in, it's for the U.S.A.")[17]

A week later, on May 17, 1942, Paul Robeson sang the solo part in a radio performance of *Battle Hymn,* eliciting congratulatory letters to Earl Robinson from Robeson's wife, Essie, as well as from Eleanor Roosevelt, who wrote the composer that she and the president both thought the whole program "magnificent." So encouraged, Robinson attempted to enlist Eleanor Roosevelt's help in getting the work published. Apparently, Latouche's publisher Jack Robbins refused to allow Robinson's publisher Max Dreyfus, the head of Chappell Music, to issue the score, prompting Robinson to ask the First Lady, in the interest of the piece's patriotic value, to write Robbins and "bring a little pressure to bear on him to lift this legal stranglehold." Robinson further explained to Roosevelt that Robbins had been "very hysterical about the whole thing," and had refused to discuss the situation with either him, Latouche, or Dreyfus. However, such proposed intervention became unnecessary as Robbins finally agreed to allow Chappell to publish *Battle Hymn* in exchange for the rights to another 1942 choral work by Robinson and Latouche, *Forward, America* (which went unpublished and appears lost). Reviewing the score to *Battle Hymn* in the April 1943 issue of *Music Educators Journal,* Marion Knoblauch thought the work "one which, in addition to being timely, carries an important message that must be understood by all who want to deserve the winning of this war and take a place in the world reconstruction to follow."[18]

Subsequent performances of *Battle Hymn* included one with Robinson conducting baritone Mordecai Bauman, the Schola Cantorum, and the New York Philharmonic at Madison Square Garden on June 10, 1943. This latter concert, free to the public and part of a drive to recruit civilian defense volunteers, featured an extravagant simulation of an air attack on New York staged by Norman Bel Geddes and Max Reinhardt, with the Robinson chorus serving as a grand finale, complete with service men marching down the stage steps waving the flags of the united nations at the work's end. But as a piece of topical propaganda—down to the number of airplanes and tanks needed to conduct the war—*Battle Hymn* quickly lost relevance. Robinson himself struck a defensive note about the work, telling Eleanor Roosevelt as early as November 1942 that as "a political tract" that attempted to "give all the answers," the piece "tried a little too hard."[19]

Just a month or so after the radio and concert debuts of *Battle Hymn,* Robinson and Latouche unveiled yet another patriotic choral work, the previously mentioned *Forward, America.* The piece premiered over WJZ Radio on June 16, 1942, directly following *Soldiers of God,* an army tribute to chaplains in the service narrated by Vincent Price, and starring actors William Holden and Jeffrey Lynn, at the time both serving in the army. This debut of *Forward, America* featured the versatile baritone Conrad Thibault and the celebrated all-black 372nd Infantry Choir under the direction of Lieutenant David Bray. A press photo showing Latouche attending a "script conference" for *Soldiers of God* suggests that he likely contributed to the spoken portion of the show as well as the concluding number (see Figure 25). Neither the broadcast nor the choral work is known to have survived.[20]

In an article published in the September 1942 issue of *Mademoiselle* magazine, Latouche sounded less sanguine about radio than he had some seventeen months earlier in *Vogue,* admitting that he had been disappointed with most of the programs aired over the previous summer. Still, he had praise especially for Arch Oboler's dramatic series *This Precious Freedom,* as well as for Stephen Vincent Benét's *They Burned the Books* and such programs as *We the People*: "Exactly why one is interested in Miss Sympharosa Snell, who has devoted her life to making a replica of the Taj

Mahal out of human teeth, is a debatable question: the fact remains one is." Objecting to radio's use of "play-technique," Latouche advised rather a "direct line from the speaker into the mind of the air audience," lauding comedian Henry Morgan's fifteen-minute show, *Here's Morgan*, as embodying "the real essence of radio's evanescent art."[21]

Before leaving to serve in the navy in the fall of 1943, Latouche wrote a few other patriotic works that might be mentioned here. In 1941, for instance, he rewrote the text to the 1775 anthem "Bunker Hill" (music attributed to Andrew Law, words taken from Nathaniel Niles's sapphic ode, "The American Hero"), a song he deemed "applicable to our present war for survival against the Axis powers as it was to the courageous fight of our Founding Fathers," although here rewritten to address, among other things, the concerns of American youth: "Out of the ruins a fairer world is rising / We will achieve it." The Rutgers Glee Club premiered the number at a November 11, 1941, rally of American Youth for Freedom in the grand ballroom of New York's Hotel Waldorf-Astoria.[22]

In addition, Latouche collaborated with Domenico Savino in 1942 on a patriotic work for chorus and band, *Marching Along: A Fantasy*, published in 1943. For this piece, Savino arranged a medley of familiar military tunes—"Marching Along Together," "Anchors Aweigh," "Marines' Hymn," and "Over There"—interspersed with connecting material for which Latouche provided sung and spoken interjections, including some noble sentiments reminiscent of *Ballad for Americans*: "A race of many races, / A people of many peoples / A nation of many nations living in unity and freedom." Reviewing the published score for *Music Educators Journal*, Ruth Jenkin wrote, "Would make an exciting ending for a concert to sell bonds. Not much work, but fine effect. Use a large chorus. The pianists will have fun, too." In 1943, Latouche also provided the lyrics for a song for the Navy Air Corps, "Anchors in the Sky," with music by Peter De Rose; a journal entry of September 16, 1943, suggests that, typically enough, he wrote the words to this stolid march in the vein of "Anchors Aweigh" in a single sitting.[23]

After his release from the Seabees in 1944, Latouche continued to do some radio work for the Treasury, including writing the show "To the People of America," aired by the program *Treasury Salute*, as part of the government's Seventh War Loan Drive, which followed the defeat of Germany in the spring of 1945; based on a story by Allen J. de Castro, this episode celebrated both America's diversity and its pervasive "instinct for liberty" as expressed in the nation's baseball games, church meetings, political rallies, and circus sideshows, as well as in the recent flag raising at Iwo Jima. Also in 1945, Latouche appeared as a guest on a program sponsored by another bond-drive show, *Music for Millions*, on which baritone Robert Merrill and a men's chorus, accompanied by Mark Warnow's Orchestra, performed both an abridged version of *Ballad for Americans* and Latouche's adaptation of "Bunker Hill." By the time of this 1945 broadcast, the country was well on its way toward the astonishing wartime achievement of selling about $185 billion worth of securities—an achievement that helped to both finance the war and stem inflation, and that owed a significant debt to radio writers like Latouche.

How Latouche's intensive if relatively brief involvement with radio influenced his work in theater and film remains more a matter of speculation, but something of the styles and techniques characteristic of the medium seem to have left their mark on his output generally, including his first Broadway book musical, *Cabin in the Sky*.

8

Cabin in the Sky

In 1940, following *Ballad for Americans*, John Latouche wrote the lyrics for *Cabin in the Sky*, a work that, if only a modest commercial success, represented another triumph—its distinguished composer, Vernon Duke, deemed it "the all-time high in my Broadway career"—and that gave further proof of the young lyricist's impressive talent.[1]

The show's originator and bookwriter, Lynn Root (1905–1997), grew up in a small Minnesota town, and had had some success on Broadway both as an actor and as a playwright, especially with his 1934 comedy *The Milky Way*, before settling in the late 1930s in Los Angeles, where he worked as a screenwriter, mostly for Twentieth Century-Fox and RKO Radio. Root based his *Cabin* script on an original story, "Little Joe," the show's working title until about a month before its October 25, 1940, opening, when—partly to distinguish the work from Rodgers and Hart's forthcoming *Pal Joey*—the name was changed to *Cabin in the Sky* after one of the show's songs. How Root came to write a musical comedy book, in an African-American folk idiom no less, remains unknown, although his son recalled his fine ear for dialects and his special regard for the expressivity of black speech. In any event, he prepared, as Vernon Duke recalled, that rarity of the period, "a workable book complete with song cues."[2]

This script made its way to Duke circuitously. The author's wife, Helen, apparently asked her friend Dorothy Hart, the wife of actor Theodore ("Teddy") Hart, to get the book to the latter's brother, lyricist Lorenz Hart, who gave it to his friend and advisor Milton Bender, who passed it on to the eminent choreographer George Balanchine, who in turn showed it to Duke, thinking that the two of them—two cosmopolitan Russian-Americans who had worked together before—could collaborate on this property.

"On reading the script," recalled Duke, "my first impulse was to turn it down because much as I admired the Negro race and its musical gifts, I didn't think myself sufficiently attuned to Negro folklore. Yet, I loved Lynn Root's book and couldn't tear myself away from it." Encouraged by both the enthusiasm of his octoroon maid and, more defiantly, the admonitions of his publisher Jack Robbins, who protested that he already had a Duke in his stable—Duke Ellington—to write "colored shows," Vernon Duke decided to take on the project.[3]

Duke and Balanchine found a willing producer, and eventually codirector as well, in the Polish-born Albert ("Al") Lewis (1884–1978). They also hoped to enlist as lyricist Ira Gershwin, with whom they had collaborated both in Hollywood and on Broadway, and whose work on *Porgy and Bess* made him a natural candidate for this vehicle. But Gershwin, already committed to working with Kurt Weill on *Lady in the Dark*, suggested rather his good friend E. Y. Harburg or the Georgia-born Johnny Mercer. According to Duke, Harburg "turned down" the book "for [its] lack of significance, social or otherwise," although Harburg claimed that he simply thought Duke the wrong composer for the material—hence, his willingness to collaborate with Harold Arlen on the work's later movie adaptation. Duke approached Mercer as well, to judge from the fact that in November 1939 news surfaced that the two would compose the show's score; but for whatever reason, Mercer declined as well. Duke reasoned that perhaps another Southerner, his young friend John Latouche, "might be the man for *Cabin*. I tried the notion on Larry [Hart], Doc [Bender] and Balanchine, my co-conspirators in the venture, and they all thought it a good gamble; Johnny himself was willing, nay, enthusiastic." Producer Lewis must have agreed as well, and in June, Root, Duke, and Latouche duly signed a contract that provided each a $250 advance against royalties, earmarked as 3½ percent, 1½ percent, and 1 percent of box-office receipts, respectively.[4]

Around this same time, George Abbott (1887–1995), who had written, directed, and produced Rodgers and Hart's *The Boys from Syracuse* (1938), based on Shakespeare's *The Comedy of Errors*, commissioned Duke and both Latouche and lyricist Theodore ("Ted") Fetter (c. 1907–1996) to provide the score for an adaptation of another of the Bard's plays, *Much Ado About Nothing*. The idea of teaming up Latouche and Fetter presumably originated with Duke, who had collaborated successfully with the latter on the 1936 revue *The Show Is On*, and who clearly liked the actor-lyricist, whom he described as "a baby-faced, ever-cheerful young man (he was in the *Garrick Gaieties* cast in 1930), Cole Porter's cousin and the son of a Princeton professor." Duke, Latouche, and Fetter presumably completed something of a draft for this Shakespeare musical in the course of the year, for a December 1940 article referred to the score as "long completed," although by this time Abbott, preoccupied with launching *Pal Joey*, seems to have lost interest in the show. Only fragments of the book and a handful of song lyrics, all co-written by Fetter and Latouche, seem to survive in any case.[5]

As for *Cabin in the Sky*, producer Albert Lewis, in need of capital, secured the assistance of, in Duke's words, "the affluent and well-liked Vinton Freedley," who had produced a number of George Gershwin and Cole Porter musicals, and who invested $5,000 in this new show. Lewis and Freedley lined up some other notable backers, including fellow producers Martin Beck, Sam H. Harris, Gilbert Miller, and W. Horace Schmidlapp, although the production opened on a tight budget, with estimates ranging from $30,000 to $70,000.[6]

Early on, Lewis engaged the Ukrainian-born Boris Aronson (1898–1980) as set and costume designer, and over the summer, arranged—in a move perhaps inspired by George Gershwin's pilgrimage to the Georgia Sea Islands for *Porgy and Bess*—for Aronson, Duke, Latouche, and Balanchine to travel South in order to experience, as one article reported, "the groove of Negro life and folklore." Guided by Latouche—the group's one Southerner, not to mention its only native-born American, although he shared with the other three some Slavic heritage—the four spent some time in the lyricist's home town of Richmond, Virginia, before Latouche and Duke retreated to Virginia Beach in order to work on the show. "Latouche was as erratic as ever," recalled Duke; "would work hard one day and loaf even harder the next—but we returned to New York full of fried chicken, Smithfield ham and with a rough draft of the score." After arriving home, Duke and Latouche more or less completed the piece by early fall, working part of the time in Westport, Connecticut, in a house rented by the composer.[7]

Duke took a blasé attitude with respect to his and Latouche's venture South, saying, "there wasn't much to imbibe in Virginia Beach except highballs." He claimed to have learned more—as the score itself would suggest—from attending jam sessions in "jive joints" in Harlem and Chicago, although one contemporary source mentions that while in Virginia, "he listened to typical Negro music as played in funny little cafes and even in so-called 'dives,' before he was ready to compose the 'Cabin in the Sky' numbers." Still, in the end, Duke and Latouche largely went their own way: "Thoroughly saturated with southern talk and Negro spirituals," stated Duke, "we decided to stay away from pedantic authenticity and write our own kind of 'colored' songs."[8]

Perhaps having more need to do so, Aronson seems to have taken the trip South more seriously, visiting and photographing the homes of poor blacks in Richmond. "Without being conscious of it," observed Aronson, "they were artists, because they had free taste and courage. It was this flavor of poverty mixed with sun, misery, and imagination that I sought to capture [in *Cabin in the Sky*]." As for Balanchine, he became, reported one impressed journalist, "somewhat of an authority on Negro dialects and inflections." All the same, the creative team, including author Lynn Root, tended to rely on Latouche for details of authenticity.[9]

Cabin in the Sky marked the start of an important professional relationship between Duke and Latouche, who would collaborate on two more shows as well as on several smaller items, although after 1941, their paths largely diverged. Their friendship could be tempestuous, thanks to the considerable temperament of both men (in later years, Latouche, drafting a list of composers for an imagined project, wrote alongside Duke's name, "Oy!"); but the two remained throughout their lives on congenial social terms and deeply respectful of each other's talent.[10]

They made nonetheless an unusual pair, and their contrast in comportment alone—Duke, tall, thin, polished, outfitted in tailored clothes, monocle, and walking stick, looking, as one *Cabin* cast member stated, "like a Russian nobleman"; Latouche, short, stout, boisterous, with tousled hair and rumpled clothes, "having," commented Duke, "the appearance of an unmade bed"—amused not only observers, but the artists themselves. Duke recalled one episode in particular in which Latouche turned up at a "bediamonded and beminked" backer's audition for *Cabin* at Lorenz Hart's home in some typically "outlandish" outfit—Duke cited "dirt-stained blue jeans and sneakers," although a contemporaneous piece mentioned rather "a rayon play suit in a bright shade of green"—prompting the composer to ask, "Good heavens, John, aren't you overdoing it a bit?" to which Latouche replied, "Not at all... at least I look alive. I don't know how you always achieve that freshly embalmed effect."[11]

The press seemed to enjoy reporting on so "incongruous" a pair. One report mentioned that their publisher, Jack Robbins, greeted them by saying, "Hello Overdressed and Underdressed." Others relayed ribbing of the sort quoted above, with Earl Wilson of the *New York Post* observing the two in "some row" over a composition while at work in their studio at the Robbins Music headquarters, Duke yelling, "My heart! My heart! You'll force me to go to Mexico City again for the altitude!" Duke himself recounted a similar incident, although one in which Latouche did the shrieking. Acknowledging their differences, the *Milwaukee Journal* described them nevertheless as "two parts of a whole falling perfectly into place," adding that they enjoyed cooking together, the paper providing readers with recipes to a favored Russian meal of stuffed eggplant and cooked apples, and an accompanying photograph showing them at work in the kitchen, Latouche's shirt widely open at the collar, his sleeves rolled up, Duke in an apron and tie.[12]

Their working habits correspondingly at odds, Duke seemed less than happy about having as a collaborator "a none-too-willing worker" who "wrote in spurts" and "was exceedingly unreliable," frustrations also felt by many of Latouche's collaborators, and reminiscent as well of other notable songwriting teams, such as Rodgers and Hart. At the same time, they worked effectively side-by-side, one journalist of the period describing their compositional method as follows: "Duke plays 'mood music' fitting the sort of thing they have to write and La Touche dreams up phrases to fit the notes and the idea." The two further shared a rare sensitivity to matters of dramatic integrity and finesse; soon after *Cabin* opened, Duke stated,

> One does not write a great play for a performer. One should write the play as a play. One should write the music as music, and both should fit together, the music helping to further the plot and the plot giving the proper setting for the songs. That is why for years I have been searching for a chance to do a musical play with characters and with a story and with a worth of its own not dependent on the players.

Cabin in the Sky provided Duke and Latouche with just such an opportunity.[13]

Cabin takes place in the "present," that is, around 1940, although only a few references so situate the play, underscoring the show's fablelike character. Similarly, both the script and the program book vaguely identify the setting as "somewhere in the South," although producer Lewis imagined the action taking place in "a back alley in Memphis or Atlanta." The entire dramatis personae would seem African-American, as suggested explicitly by the script's occasional racial references, and more implicitly by its extensive adaptation of black Southern dialect.[14]

Act I, scene one. Exterior of the Jacksons' home, somewhere in the South. Night. As friends pray for "Little Joe" Jackson, mortally wounded by Domino Johnson after being caught cheating in a game of craps, Georgia Brown—Joe's mistress (and an entertainer at a local saloon, John Henry's Cafe)—approaches the house, but the attending physician, Dr. Jones, shoos her away ("God's A-Gwineter Trouble De Water," traditional spiritual, for chorus).

Scene two. Little Joe's Bedroom. As Joe dies, Lucifer Jr. (also called the Head Man) and his Imps come to claim the shiftless, gambling, womanizing Joe, but his wife, Petunia's, ardent prayers prompt the intervention of The Lawd's General and his band of angels ("The General's Song," for The General and Saints). As Lucifer Jr. and The General both claim Joe, whose spirit nervously awaits its fate, Fleetfoot, one of the angels, arrives with God's verdict: Joe will be granted a six-month reprieve to redeem himself, but will have no recollection of this bargain; rather, his conscience will be tested as Lucifer Jr. and The General wrangle for his soul ("Pay Heed," for The General and Saints). Petunia exults in Little Joe's recovery ("Taking a Chance on Love," for Petunia).

Scene three. The Jacksons' Backyard. One month later. Two of Little Joe's cronies—Dude and the saloon owner John Henry—attempt to collect some gambling debts, but Petunia, taking advantage of their greed and mendacity, outwits them in a game of dice. Little Joe resolves to get a job and relieve Petunia of having to take in washing, and she and Joe reflect on heavenly and earthly delights, respectively ("Cabin in the Sky," for Petunia and Little Joe). Brother Green, a parson, arrives with his flock, and Little Joe repents, to the satisfaction of The General and the displeasure of Lucifer Jr. ("Holy Unto the Lord," traditional gospel hymn, and "Dem Bones," spiritual by James Weldon Johnson, both for the ensemble).

Scene four. The Head Man's Office in Hades. Three months later. With only two months left, Lucifer Jr. and his three "idea" men plot to corrupt Little Joe by having him win the Irish sweepstakes. Jubilant, Lucifer Jr. delivers a rousing broadcast to mankind ("Do What You Wanna Do," for Lucifer Jr. and Imps).

Scene five. The Jacksons' Front Porch. Urged on by Lucifer Jr., Little Joe purchases a sweepstakes ticket from Dude. Petunia permits this indulgence and the two leave for a church meeting, Lucifer Jr. laughing softly (reprise of "Taking a Chance on Love," for Petunia).

Act II, scene one. The Jacksons' Backyard. One month later. The Lawd's General and his angelic soldiers reflect on man's fall as they battle with Lucifer Jr. and his henchmen ("Fugue," for The General and Saints). Returning home from his job slinging sugar sacks, employment that has enabled Petunia to quit her laundry service,

Joe imagines the home he hopes to procure for the two of them ("My Old Virginia Home on the Nile," for Little Joe and Petunia). As Petunia leaves to do some shopping, a napping Joe dreams about Georgia Brown ("[Vision] Egyptian Ballet," for Georgia Brown and dancers). The Devil's Messenger arrives with a winning sweepstakes ticket, but Little Joe, unable to read the ticket and under the sway of The General's counsel, throws the paper away, to the chagrin of Lucifer Jr. ("It's Not So Bad to Be Good," for The General). Georgia Brown enters, but Little Joe spurns her advances ("Love Me Tomorrow [But Leave Me Alone Today]," for Little Joe and Georgia Brown). Before departing, Georgia finds the discarded lottery ticket, and Joe takes his good fortune as heavenly reward for his marital fidelity; but as he and Georgia innocently embrace, Petunia enters, and misunderstanding the situation, orders them both to leave ("Love Turned the Light Out," for Petunia).

Scene two. Exterior of John Henry's Cafe. One month later. Staged in front of a curtain, people gather to the strains of a jazz pianist.

Scene three. John Henry's Cafe. Couples dance ("Lazy Steps" and "Boogy Woogy," for dancers). Little Joe, flush with his lottery winnings, enters with a flashily dressed Georgia Brown ("Honey in the Honeycomb," for Georgia Brown and dancers). Petunia, elegantly attired, appears, claiming half of Joe's money and ridiculing Georgia Brown ("Savannah," for Petunia). Domino Johnson and Little Joe fight over Petunia, whose prayers give rise to a destructive storm. During the ensuing mayhem, Domino Johnson shoots Petunia inadvertently and then Little Joe.

Scene four. At the Pearly Gates. Petunia regretfully realizes that she had misjudged Little Joe. At first denying Little Joe entrance into heaven because of the manner in which he spent money throughout his life, The General reverses his decision after Fleetfoot appears with word that Georgia Brown has repented and donated Joe's lottery winnings to a church. As Joe drops a pair of dice on the floor, he receives a final celestial slap before The General and Petunia ascend the heavenly stairs followed by Little Joe and others ("Finale," including a reprise of "Cabin in the Sky," for the ensemble).

A parable placed in the somewhat clichéd context of the sacred and profane within African-American society, *Cabin in the Sky* recalled after a fashion *Porgy and Bess*, but even more so white writer Marc Connolly's Pulitzer Prize–winning dramatization of biblical stories, *The Green Pastures*, which opened on Broadway in 1930, with an acclaimed film version released in 1936. Nearly every review of *Cabin in the Sky* at the time of its premiere compared the musical to *The Green Pastures*, a work Lynn Root surely had in mind while writing *Cabin*; it could hardly be coincidence that *The Green Pastures* and *Cabin in the Sky* had angelic characters named Flatfoot and Fleetfoot, respectively. The banter between The General and Fleetfoot in *Cabin* particularly resembled that between De Lawd and Gabriel in the Connolly play, much as the destruction of the cafe by heavenly forces evoked similarly apocalyptic cleansings in *The Green Pastures*. Root's whimsical and imaginative use of stage black dialect further recalled Connolly's play, although *Cabin* tended at times more in the direction of popular burlesque.[15]

Gallery 1 (captions are on pages ix–xii)

Figure 1

Figure 2

Figure 3

Figure 4

Figure 5

Figure 6

Figure 7

Figure 8

Figure 9

Figure 10

Figure 11

Figure 12

Figure 13

Figure 14

Figure 15

Figure 16

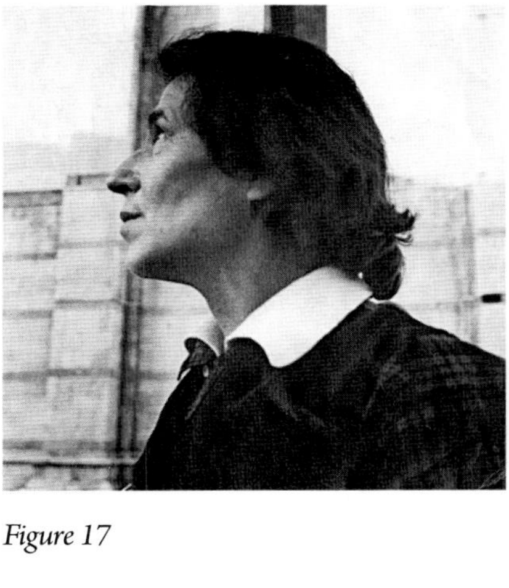

Figure 17

Figure 18

Figure 19

Figure 20

Figure 21

Figure 22

Figure 23

Figure 24

Figure 25

Figure 26

Figure 27

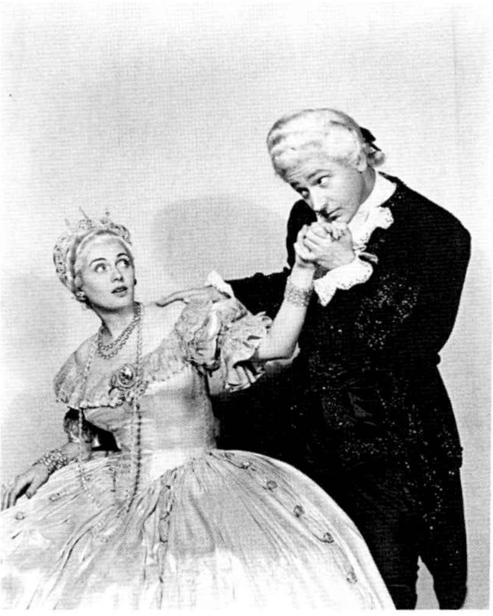

Figure 28

Cabin also often reminded critics of *Everyman, Faust,* and Ferenc Molnár's *Liliom* (later, the source for Rodgers and Hammerstein's *Carousel*) sooner than *Porgy and Bess,* although even from the show's first scene—with Georgia Brown's entrance echoing Bess's appearance at Robbins's funeral—many comparisons with the Gershwin opera could be drawn. The musical also made contact with a whole range of more popular entertainments, including such cartoons as the Merrie Melodies short *Sunday Go to Meetin' Time,* produced by Warner Brothers in 1936, and Walt Disney's *Donald's Better Self,* released by RKO in 1938 during Lynn Root's association with the studio. But the work seemed, perhaps most decidedly, an American retelling of the ancient Greek tale of Orpheus and Eurydice, only with the genders reversed: an entreating woman wins back her husband from the dead, only to lose him again through a lack of trust, with a happy ending wrought, as in Monteverdi's operatic version, through the contrivance of a *deus ex machina.* (In 1948, Balanchine, perhaps not coincidentally, created an *Orpheus* ballet with Stravinsky, who attended a performance of *Cabin in the Sky,* and who might have related, as might have Balanchine and Duke, to the show's semblance to Russian folk tales.)[16]

In line with its mythic qualities, the piece avoided, as mentioned, contemporary references, thereby obscuring any topical significance. But the opposition of, on the one hand, Lucifer Jr. and his henchman, and on the other, The General and his soldiers, resonated nevertheless with the current world war, in some instances, directly so. For instance, in the scene in Hades—which also could be read as a satire of Hollywood (indeed, in his original script, Lynn Root described the set for this scene as resembling "a movie producer's office")—Lucifer Jr. complains that he is "stuck wid a bunch of 'B' idea men. All da 'A' boys am over in Europe." And near the play's end, the Devil's Messenger similarly reports to Lucifer Jr. that, as punishment for losing Little Joe, "He [Satan] gonna send you to Europe. He say dere's a couple o' human bein's over dere dat kin furder yo' edication." Moreover, the final tableau, with Petunia and Little Joe surviving amid the rubble of a ruined cafe, strongly evoked wartime devastation, with the couple's ascent to a "cabin in the sky" representing an escape from the surrounding turmoil.

As with so many morality tales, *Cabin*'s principal characters—Petunia, Little Joe, and Georgia Brown—do not embody good or evil in any absolute way, but rather mirror tensions between virtue and sin, the latter variously represented by sloth, greed, lust, and anger. At the same time, all three protagonists ultimately find redemption, Petunia and Little Joe through their love and devotion, Georgia Brown, through repentance. As several scholarly critiques of the show's film adaptation have observed, such moral ambiguity provided a certain complexity to the show's appropriation of African-American stock figures—a complexity more manifest in the show than in the film, thanks in large part to the Duke and Latouche score largely gutted by Hollywood.[17]

Indeed, Duke and Latouche shaded the drama with considerable nuance, helping to set mood, limn character, and further the action—all making the show a notable, if underappreciated, exemplar of the so-called integrated musical comedy.

"For once," notes Ethan Mordden in his survey of the Broadway musical, "a musical isn't a novelty act... but a deeply felt story unfolded in a special atmosphere that of itself inspires unique songs, dances, and jokes." At the same time, although the intermittent use of traditional black music enhanced the folklike atmosphere, the score proper generally underplayed the book's more rustic flavor in favor of something more urban and worldly, with Duke evoking city blues and jazz (music suggestive to some first-night critics of the stylish all-black Broadway revues associated with Lew Leslie) rather than spirituals and folksongs, and Latouche skirting about Root's black dialect in favor of an ethnically attuned but more hip, less quaint verbiage: "If romance is so nice / You can keep it on ice," Little Joe tells Georgia Brown, who later counters, "Better grab what you got / While the iron is hot" ("Love Me Tomorrow").[18]

The score further foregrounded the play's basic moral argument. The General makes his case in "Pay Heed" and "It's Not So Bad to Be Good," and Lucifer Jr., more winningly perhaps, as is often the way with devils, in the infectious "Do What You Wanna Do," which reads like Latouche's credo, including the line, "Go on and live / Like a crazy elf / Put your inhibitions upon the shelf." (In a contemporary profile of the lyricist, one journalist wrote, "He [Latouche] seeks just one thing—to do what he likes, when he likes and without interference.") Latouche further explored this basic dichotomy in the duets "Cabin in the Sky" and "Love Me Tomorrow" as different characters express opposing viewpoints.[19]

"My Old Virginia Home" and "Savannah" encompass a different sort of dialectic, with each juxtaposing stereotypical imagery in ways that ultimately affirm African-American culture. "My Old Virginia Home," published as "In My Old Virginia Home on the River Nile," warrants special attention in this respect, in that some later productions, like the 1964 revival at the Greenwich Mews, excised the song as racially objectionable, although the number—one of the most delightful in the entire score, and one that entered the repertory of black cabaret singer Bobby Short—seems crucial in establishing Little Joe's affection for his wife. Moreover, this duet—whose verse begins, "My people ain't no ordinary people / I'll have you understand / My people are extraordinary people / From Egypt land"—in fact subverts the traditional plantation song by replacing familiar African-American tropes with a string of fanciful Egyptian images: " 'Stead of mammies, we'll hear mummies softly hum." "Savannah" accomplishes something similar with respect to black pride, although conversely, by having Petunia tout the appeal of Southern black over Cuban customs: "When those banjos are softly strumming / They beat those humming guitars."[20]

Although faithful to the simplicity of the story, with Duke and Latouche restraining the kind of chic often found in their work, the score additionally featured a sophistication unusual for such light entertainment, with Latouche, for his part, showing skill at developing a single overarching idea through metaphor and allegory. Consider, for instance, the gambling allusions in "Taking a Chance on Love"; the contrasting dark and light imagery in "Love Turned the Light Out"; the long list of foods with sexual overtones in "Honey in the Honeycomb" (for which Duke claimed to have written the first chorus); and the compilation of the negative consequences of sin in "It's Not So Bad to Be Good" (a number possibly modeled after "It Ain't Necessarily So" from *Porgy and Bess,* and apparently added only after the show opened).[21]

Some of the score never made it to Broadway. Duke originally fashioned, apparently at Balanchine's suggestion, a dirgelike vocalise for the opening chant, but ultimately retained only a fragment of this music as a complement to the spiritual "God's A-Gwineter Trouble De Water." (What involvement Duke had, incidentally, with the traditional African-American music presented in the first act and the "Lazy Steps/Boogy Woogy" episode in the second act remains uncertain; given that *Time* magazine reported some "true, improvised boogie-woogie" performed by the pianist in the pit orchestra, and that the dancing for the "Lazy Steps/Boogy Woogy" sequence derived from the concert repertoire of co-choreographer Katherine Dunham, at least this particular segment apparently featured some improvised jazz or some music associated with the Dunham company or both.) Duke and Latouche also cut two songs slated for Little Joe's deathbed scene: the whimsically devilish "Little Poppa Satan," intended for Lucifer Jr.; and the sweetly gentle "We'll Live All Over Again," a lullaby intended for Petunia to sing to Little Joe, and replaced at the eleventh hour with the more upbeat "Taking a Chance on Love."[22]

In making some of these and other changes, Duke and Latouche, as well as Root, often deferred to the wishes of the show's headstrong star Ethel Waters (1896–1977). Even before signing on, Waters, an outstanding singing actress who recently had wowed Broadway audiences in Dorothy and DuBose Heyward's *Mamba's Daughters,* insisted that the musical cast Little Joe in a less unsavory light, as she could not imagine Petunia praying for such a rascal. "After some of the changes I demanded had been made I accepted the role," she recalled in her autobiography, "largely because the music was so pretty. But right through the rehearsals and even after the play had opened, I kept adding my own lines and little bits of business to build up the character of Petunia." Waters also vetoed the notion of casting Eddie ("Rochester") Anderson as Little Joe, and similarly requested some of the cuts mentioned above, including replacing Duke's dirge with a traditional spiritual, and "We'll Live All Over Again" with some other number, which led to the last-minute creation of "Taking a Chance on Love."[23]

"Taking a Chance on Love" proved not only one of the great showstoppers in Broadway history, but a huge hit independent of the show, indeed, the most popular song that John Latouche ever wrote, and one of Duke's most famous as well. Discussions of this storied interpolation typically mention Waters's dissatisfaction with her opening number, but neglect to note that, according to producer Lewis, a need also arose for a number at stage front at the end of the scene in order to accommodate a set change, a function "Taking a Chance on Love" could serve more easily than "We'll Live All Over Again," meant to be sung to Little Joe at his bedside.

At any event, in Duke's seminal telling, he salvaged from his trunk a number called "Fooling Around With Love" that he had written with Theodore Fetter for the aborted *Much Ado* musical, and played it for Latouche, who "fell for the tune" and relyricized the song, retitled "Taking a Chance on Love," with "some assist" from Fetter (although this leaves unexplained how Latouche, as co-lyricist on *Much Ado*, would not already have had some familiarity with the number). After hearing the rewritten song, Waters and Vinton Freedley voiced their approval and Latouche composed four more choruses, so the lyric essentially can be said to represent his own work, although Fetter in due course received credit as coauthor. The song proved, in any case, dramatically apropos, expressing Petunia's joy in Little Joe's miraculous resurrection in imagery concordant with the gambling theme found throughout the show as a whole.[24]

"Taking a Chance on Love" proved an instant success, the first-night audience insisting on encore after encore, with Waters singing the last of its five choruses, to the best of Duke's recollection, at least three times. Each *A* section of the song's *AABA* choruses features triple rhymes that help evoke the thrill of rejuvenated love, all to a melody that falls stepwise from the fifth note of the scale until, at the word "Taking [a chance on love]," it arrives at the tonic pitch—an example of German music theorist Heinrich Schenker's famed *Urlinie,* here wedded to a deliriously giddy lyric:

Here I go again
I hear those trumpets blow again
All aglow again
Taking a chance on love.

In some contrast, the *B* sections typically express, in smart response to the music's harmonic structure, past sadness giving way to present happiness, as in this neatly symmetrical bridge from the second chorus (note "dreamed" and "dream," and "bets" and "playing the numbers"):

I never dreamed in my slumbers
And bets were taboo
But now I'm playing the numbers
On a little dream for two.[25]

The book for *Cabin in the Sky* in the end differed considerably from Root's original three-act *Little Joe,* at least in its details if not in its basic plot and dialogue. For a start, Duke and Latouche, working with Root, had to find and contextualize song spots, for Root's cues consisted mostly of references to traditional African-American spirituals at the end of scenes (more proof, if any needed, that he modeled his piece after *The Green Pastures*), although Root's titles for a "torch song" for Petunia ("Love

Has Broken My Heart") and a "swing song" for Georgia Brown ("I Gotta Taste for Sweet Things") not only prefigured the placement of "Love Turned the Light Out" and "Honey in the Honeycomb" in the show, but their animating poetic ideas. Root's revised book also placed greater emphasis on the human as opposed to the supernatural characters, with certain changes, including the deletion of any references to domestic violence, suggesting some sensitivity to Waters and her concerns in particular. Root relatedly toned down the script's more cartoonish qualities, omitting, too, such offending phrases as "darkies" and "nigger rich."

Lewis, Freedley, and Balanchine provided Waters with a fine supporting cast, although plans to have Cab Calloway play Lucifer Jr. in what would have been his Broadway debut fell through, apparently because of a lack of funds; that part went rather to Rex Ingram, who had played, ironically enough, De Lawd in the film version of *The Green Pastures*. Arthur ("Dooley") Wilson took the role of Little Joe, a breakthrough opportunity that helped initiate a notable film career, including a featured turn as the nightclub entertainer Sam in *Casablanca* (1942). Todd Duncan, an accomplished operatic singer who had created the role of Porgy in Gershwin's *Porgy and Bess*, was cast as The Lawd's General. And J. Rosamond Johnson, another alumnus from *Porgy and Bess*, appeared as Brother Green, while his choir, the J. Rosamond Johnson Singers, several of whom also assumed minor roles, formed the show's chorus.[26]

Perhaps the most noteworthy casting involved the hiring of Katherine Dunham and her dancers. Born in Chicago, Dunham (1909–2006) studied both classical and modern dance; but encouraged by such teachers as Ruth Page, and inspired by her graduate studies in anthropology at the University of Chicago, including field work in the Caribbean, she developed a unique choreographic style that conjoined aspects of African, African-American, Afro-Caribbean, and Latin-American dance, music, and folklore. Having seen the Dunham company perform in New York in March 1940, Balanchine viewed them again in Chicago that summer, and made the unexpected decision to recruit the whole troupe for *Cabin*, including Dunham as Georgia Brown—even though she had relatively little experience as a singer—and the rest of the company as dancers and for smaller roles. Featured in the "Egyptian Ballet"—with Dunham dressed as Nefertiti (see Figure 21)—as well as in "Lazy Steps" and "Boogy Woogy," the Dunham dancers also performed in other numbers, including "Dem Bones," "Do What You Wanna Do," and "Fugue," with one of Dunham's lead male dancers—the lithe and charismatic Archie Savage—partnering Ethel Waters in "Savannah."[27]

Although Balanchine oversaw the entire production, he and Dunham extensively collaborated on the choreography, to the point that the show essentially interpolated some of Dunham's concert repertory, including the "Lazy Steps/Boogy Woogy" sequence, as noted. At times, tensions between the two choreographers arose. Dunham nixed, for instance, Balanchine's idea of dressing her as a mummy in the "Egyptian Ballet" and unwinding her on stage; she also took offense at the casting of some light-skinned blacks for the cafe scene in order to offset her own darkly complexioned company. But by most accounts, the two worked together amicably (as opposed to Dunham's difficulties with Ethel Waters), and succeeded in creating highly novel and effective stage movement strikingly distinct from the kinds of tap-dancing and hoofing associated especially with all-black shows.[28]

As also mentioned, Boris Aronson, one of the period's most brilliant stage designers, supervised the sets and costumes, assisted in the latter task by the celebrated costumer Barbara Karinska as well as by Dunham's soon-to-be husband, John Pratt, who created the costumes for Dunham and her dancers. Hugh Martin—the future co-composer of the movie musical *Meet Me in St. Louis*—served as vocal coach and arranger, including creating a countermelody for Ethel Waters to sing in a repeat chorus of "Cabin in the Sky" that met with Duke's approval and that can be heard in Waters's 1940 recording of the song. Latouche, meanwhile, helped coach Dunham on her songs, the start of a close friendship between the two. (Latouche might well have introduced Dunham to his doctor Max Jacobson, whom the dancer credited with having "saved my life over and over again during my many years of stressful travels.") Under Duke's watch, a notable team of musicians—Domenico Savino, Charles Cooke, Joseph ("Fud") Livingston, and Nathan Van Cleve—provided the orchestrations, supplemented at times by Dunham's Cuban and Haitian drummers on stage. Max Meth conducted the orchestra.[29]

Lacking the resources for out-of-town tryouts, *Cabin in the Sky*—advertised in some instances as a "musical fantasy" or a "Negro fantasy"—opened after a few preview performances at the Martin Beck Theatre on October 25, 1940, with ticket prices ranging from $1.10 to $3.30 for evening performances, somewhat less for matinees. The critical reception proved mixed but generally positive, with one of the best reviews luckily coming from the influential drama critic for the *New York Times*, Brooks Atkinson, who stated, "Perhaps 'Cabin in the Sky' could be better than it is but this correspondent cannot imagine how. For this musical fantasy... is original and joyous in an imaginative vein that suits the theatre's special genius. Lynn Root began it by writing an extraordinary fresh book about heaven, hell, and the common earth where black people work out their destiny. By great good fortune everyone associated with him has met him on equal terms." In a follow-up piece, Atkinson, mindful of less enthusiastic notices, admitted that the piece failed to break Broadway's "Negro formula" to the extent that *The Green Pastures* and *Porgy and Bess* had; but he averred that African Americans had "a special genius for this kind of theatre skylarking," and that the show remained, in his estimation, "the best Negro musical this column can recall and the peer of any musical in recent years." In a July 1941 retrospective, George Jean Nathan, the magisterial critic of the *American Mercury*, indeed deemed *Cabin in the Sky* the "best musical show" of the preceding season, one that included such formidable rivals as *Pal Joey* and *Lady in the Dark*.[30]

As a whole, the critics, even those with reservations, commended various aspects of the production. Writing for *Newsweek*, for instance, John O'Hara, author of the forthcoming *Pal Joey*, observed "a great deal of exciting dancing" and some "pretty funny" lines, although he did not particularly like any of the principals except Katherine Dunham—a decidedly minority opinion given all the bouquets flung at Ethel Waters. In the weeks following opening night, columns by experts appeared detailing the excellence of the dancing (John Martin in the *Times*), the score (Robert Lawrence in the *Herald Tribune*), and the sets and costumes (Lillian Johnson in the *Baltimore Afro-American*).[31]

Such approbation extended to Latouche, the reviews deeming his lyrics "crisp and jaunty," "excellent," "gracious," "of real distinction," "smart," and "clever"—plainly an auspicious debut for the lyricist's first Broadway musical. Having orchestrated and conducted Latouche's 1935 Columbia Varsity Show, music critic Robert Lawrence could place this achievement in perspective better than others: "He [Latouche] has gone far since then [1935], and his latest work reveals a sureness of touch and a feeling for musical cadence that is most gratifying." Lawrence further admired how well Duke and Latouche fitted the songs "into the flow of the plot," with the exception of "Savannah," which he thought superfluous. Virtually every critic praised in particular "Taking a Chance on Love," which Nathan declared the season's "best musical show tune," but many also commended "Cabin in the Sky," "My Old Virginia Home," and "Honey in the Honeycomb." Meanwhile, *Time* magazine proved rare in actually quoting some of Latouche's lyrics, namely, the laugh line, "There'll be doin's in those ruins when we come," from "My Own Virginia Home" (a line very possibly adapted by Cole Porter in *Kiss Me, Kate* as, "What scandalous doin's in the ruins of Pompeii!").[32]

On the more negative side, a number of reviews complained of dull and contrived patches in the second act, particularly the denouement. But the most contentious aspect of the show involved its folk and racial dimension, including charges of stereotypical depictions of African Americans. A related disagreement revolved around whether the production's "brassy sophistication," to cite Wolcott Gibbs's review for the *New Yorker*, operated "against the spirit of Lynn Root's simple fable." Some, in this context, spoke of the musical as debasing the dignity of *The Green Pastures*, and even Atkinson, who did not subscribe at all to this notion, claimed that the show failed to capture the "universal loveliness" of the Connolly play.[33]

The harshest such reviews came from white critics writing for progressive publications, such as Louis Kronenberger (*PM*), Joseph Wood Krutch (*Nation*), Alvah Bessie (*New Masses*), and especially Ralph Warner (*Daily Worker*), who stated, regarding the first-night audience, "Truly the slave holders love to watch their own conception of the Negro come to life on the stage." (Warner, no doubt aware of Latouche's standing among the left, perhaps showed some bias in exempting the lyricist from this general indictment while at the same time implicating the anti-communist Duke: "I want to make clear that John LaTouche's lyrics do not suffer from this fault [apparently meaning racial stereotyping]. He has written several excellent sets of words to the less than exciting music of Vernon Duke, whose other name is Vladimir Dukensky [*sic*], one-time Russian exile, now an American citizen.") Notwithstanding his admiration for the quality of the performances, Alvah Bessie similarly advised his readers to "skip" the show, explaining, "this is the usual Broadway chauvinism and restates the usual assumption that Negroes are charming clowns whose main interests in life are sex, religion, gambling, and personal ostentation in clothes." By contrast, the black press—as represented by the *New York Amsterdam News*, *Chicago Defender*, *Atlanta Daily World*, and *Baltimore Afro-American*—seemed generally pleased with the work. Dan Burley (*Amsterdam News*) posted a particularly enthusiastic notice, describing the musical as "the answer to a show-goer's prayer, and a sudden and marvelous antidote for the blues which afflict so many of us, [in] these dark, uncertain days," and stating again at year's end, "There's something about 'Cabin in the Sky' that brings you back again and again."[34]

Miller Music, an affiliate of Robbins Music, published no fewer than ten songs from the show, that is, all the solo songs aside from those for The Lawd's General. And Ethel Waters recorded four of these songs with Max Meth and the Martin Beck Theatre Orchestra. But for all the excellent reviews and the popularity of some of its individual numbers, *Cabin in the Sky* closed on March 8, 1941, after only 156 performances. That the contemporaneous radio ban of ASCAP composers by the broadcast industry played some part in shortening the work's run seems likely, although *Panama Hattie*, *Pal Joey*, *Lady in the Dark*, and other similarly affected shows commanded considerably longer runs. In any case, *Cabin* at least had a triumphant and profitable 1941 tour of Boston, Toronto, the Midwest, and the West Coast, with held-over engagements in several cities.

The touring show even garnered more consistently excellent notices than in New York; Cecil Smith (*Chicago Tribune*), for example, grouped the work with only two others he had reported on over the previous three years that "fully exploited the best possibilities of the musical stage in their beauty and imagination, their pointedness and wit, their richness of conception and excellence of execution," an assessment that prefigured his discussion of the show in his milestone 1950 text *Musical Comedy in America*. The black press once again seemed especially fond of the work—the *Chicago Defender* in particular followed the tour assiduously—although *PM* magazine approvingly quoted a local Los Angeles African-American weekly, the *Inter-Church Tribune*, which accused the show of "pandering to the white man's liking for Negro caricature, to his affection for a disenfranchised personality called Uncle Tom." Meanwhile, Bostonians debated the propriety of the dancing, with local censors insisting that Katherine Dunham cover her exposed midriff in the "Egyptian Ballet."[35]

Latouche accompanied the tour during at least part of its successful summer 1941 run in Los Angeles, cryptically describing California as "an extraordinary and possessed country" to the poet and art collector Edward James. Probably about this time, the lyricist—or so it would appear—drafted a story outline for an unrealized dance drama with songs for Katherine Dunham and her company, called *Lilith, or*

The Deadliest Sin, copies of which survive among both his and Dunham's papers (the typescript of which includes only Dunham's name, although the content strongly points to Latouche's authorship). This scenario follows three archetypes—Adam, Eve, and Lilith—down through the ages, with the Adam figure, for instance, appearing as King Solomon, Napoleon, and a modern henpecked husband, and the Lilith figure correspondingly the Queen of Sheba, Josephine, and a nightclub entertainer. Latouche imagined Dunham as Lilith, but white actors as Adam and Eve (either Robert Benchley, Frank Fay, or Roland Young as Adam, and possibly June Walker as Eve), with Dunham Company members joining the white dancer Paul Draper in an Italian Renaissance scene, and someone to play the black emancipator Harriet Tubman. The boldly interracial dimension of this entire concept looked ahead to Latouche's *Beggar's Holiday*, while the interest in Adam, Eve, and Lilith as archetypes—already explored after a fashion in *Cabin in the Sky*—anticipated Latouche's very final musical, the unfinished *The First Time*.[36]

In the spring of 1943, MGM released a film version of *Cabin in the Sky* produced by Arthur Freed, then at the beginning of his career as the preeminent midcentury producer of movie musicals. The picture seemed, at least in part, a response to urgings from the Office of War Information that the Hollywood studios increase and elevate the roles for African Americans in their films. Purchasing the movie rights for $40,000, MGM began production near summer's end in 1942 and completed the film that autumn for about $650,000, a modest amount for a Freed musical, but a sizable budget for an all-black film.

Ethel Waters and Rex Ingram, from the original Broadway cast, appeared in the movie, as did some of Dunham's dancers (although not Dunham herself), and Albert Lewis served as associate director. But by and large, the film involved a notably different pool of talent: Joseph Schrank, who had written sketches for *Pins and Needles*, revised the script, assisted by an uncredited Marc Connelly; Cedric Gibbons and Leonid Vasian served as art directors; Irene Lentz designed the costumes; Vincente Minnelli, making his feature film debut, directed, assisted by an uncredited Busby Berkeley; and in addition to Waters and Ingram, the all-star cast included Eddie ("Rochester") Anderson (Little Joe), Lena Horne (Georgia Brown), Louis Armstrong (one of Lucifer Jr.'s henchmen), John W. ("Bubbles") Sublett (Domino Johnson), and Butterfly McQueen (Petunia's friend Lily), along with the Hall Johnson Choir and the Duke Ellington Orchestra.

Freed further hired the team of composer Harold Arlen and lyricist E. Y. Harburg, with whom he had worked on *The Wizard of Oz* and *Babes in Arms* (both 1939), to revamp the score. In his autobiography, Minnelli explained, with reference to the film's mid-1942 production schedule, "The original composers weren't available. Vernon Duke was in the service, and John Latouche was working on another show." What show that might have been remains a mystery, as Latouche produced no musical between *The Lady Comes Across*, which opened in January 1942, and his departure for the Congo on behalf of the Belgian government in October of that same year. However, in late May 1942, the *Times* reported on a Broadway adaptation in progress of a 1933 German operetta by the Austrian-born Ralph Benatzky (1884–1957), *Bezauberndes Fräulein,* to be presented by Philip Adler, Alfred Bloomington, and Peggy Fears as *The Enchanting Lady,* with Rowland Leigh mentioned as lyricist, Latouche, as bookwriter. So possibly this was the show—an aborted undertaking with which Latouche's friend Dawn Powell also became involved—that allegedly prevented the lyricist from journeying to Hollywood to work on the Minnelli film (assuming that MGM would have wanted Latouche independent of Vernon Duke, who was then stationed in the Coast Guard in New York).[37]

But even had Duke and Latouche been available, Freed might have opted to have Arlen and Harburg revise the score anyway, so as to compensate—in light of Arlen's close association with black singers especially—for what the producer perceived as the musical's lack of "Southern songs." Minnelli had his own dissatisfactions with the original score, citing "several production numbers put in for showy effect, but having nothing to do with the simple story." In the end, the film retained only four numbers from the stage show—"Taking a Chance on Love," "Cabin in the Sky," "Honey in the Honeycomb," and "Love Me Tomorrow" (the last used only as background music in the cafe scene)—and added three songs by Arlen and Harburg—"Li'l Black Sheep," "Happiness Is a Thing Called Joe," and "Life's Full o' Consequence"—along with the popular 1910 chestnut "Shine," and some music by Duke Ellington, including the instrumental "Goin' Up."[38]

The movie further reframed most of the action as a dream of Little Joe, with people from his waking life appearing as Lucifer Jr. and The Lawd's General, a device that strongly recalled *The Wizard of Oz,* whose stock footage of a tornado reappeared at the film's climax. Again echoing *The Wizard of Oz,* the picture concluded with a happy reunion between Petunia and a reawakened Little Joe rather than with, as on Broadway, the couple's ascent to heaven. All the same, the movie adopted the show's basic structure and even much of its dialogue, although the filmmakers juggled the song spots, so that, for instance, Petunia's "Happiness Is a Thing Called Joe" took the place of "Taking a Chance on Love," and her reprise of "Honey in the Honeycomb" substituted for "Savannah." The only markedly gratuitous interpolation involved "Shine," clearly added as a vehicle for John Sublett so as to feature—like Bill Bailey's dancing in "Taking a Chance on Love"—just that sort of hoofing eschewed in the stage version.[39]

All this left the film without any songs for either The Lawd's General or Lucifer Jr., thereby eliminating the central binary provided by "Do What You Wanna Do" and "It's Not So Bad to Be Good." Nor did the revised score allow as much music for Little Joe, whose love for Petunia went musically unexpressed. Such changes significantly altered the tone of the musical, as the cut songs were precisely those numbers—including also "In My Old Virginia Home" and "Love Me Tomorrow"—that had provided the Broadway show with much of its wit and style. And regarding even those retained songs, the film arguably changed some lyrics to their disadvantage.

Such deletions and alterations hardly could be compensated fully by the sentiment of "Happiness Is a Thing Called Joe," the drollery of "Life's Full o' Consequence," and the exuberance of "Shine."

Cabin in the Sky premiered in Dallas on March 11, 1943, and then enjoyed wide distribution throughout the country in April and May. The film's critical reception resembled that for the stage show, with many admiring reviews and a few damning ones, including Barry Ulanov's in *Metronome* and Ramona Lewis's in the *Amsterdam News*. Differing opinions could be found among black audience members as well, according to the *Atlanta Daily World*, who cited a Tuskegee graduate praising the picture for capturing "real folklore," and a local reporter who criticized the film as perpetuating negative stereotypes. The few comparisons between the stage original and the movie adaptation proved similarly divergent; the *Times* thought the film "as sparkling and completely satisfying as was the original stage production," whereas the *Wall Street Journal* felt that the picture "somehow fails to fully capture either the inspired sincerity or the broad and spontaneous humor of its stage predecessor." But however adept and imaginative Minnelli's direction, and however endearing the performances, including Louis Armstrong's marvelous cameo, without the Balanchine and Dunham choreography, the Aronson sets and costumes, and the full Duke and Latouche score, the film clearly represented a less sophisticated and daring enterprise than its stage predecessor, making the extensive and often penetrating scholarly criticism about the film relevant to the stage musical only up to a point.[40]

Although the film version—which Duke called "trite"—eclipsed the popularity of the stage show, the latter held the boards by way of periodic revivals. In August 1953, for instance, the Sea Cliff Summer Theatre—a small venue on Long Island that burned down in late 1956—presented a weeklong run, under the direction of Latouche's friend Herbert Machiz, of what the *Amsterdam News* called "one of the great pieces of Negro Americana." Produced by two novices, Louis Macmillan and Thomas Ratcliffe, the cast featured Juanita Hall, who had originated the role of Bloody Mary in *South Pacific*, as Petunia; nightclub entertainer Julius ("Nipsey") Russell as Little Joe; and Dunham disciple Josephine Premice as Georgia Brown, with members of the Dunham Company also in tow. Billy Strayhorn and Luther Henderson, who both had helped arrange Latouche and Duke Ellington's 1946 musical *Beggar's Holiday*, provided the two-piano accompaniment, assisted by Dean Sheldon on drum kit and bongos.[41]

Latouche apparently helped guide this summer-stock production, which presented the dialogue in standard English as opposed to stylized dialect. Moreover, the show not only reordered the musical numbers, but restored some of the music cut from the original score and recycled as well "Not a Care in the World" from Latouche and Vernon Duke's 1941 musical *Banjo Eyes*, an insertion that became rather standard (and whose urbanity raised a slightly false note in context).[42]

This 1953 revival opened to excellent reviews and played to packed houses, leading producers Macmillan and Ratcliffe, whom Duke thought "two very nice and literate Harvard alumni," to initiate what became an exceedingly fractious attempt to return the show to Broadway. For whereas Duke and Root supported this initiative, Latouche strongly resisted the idea because of certain differences with the two producers, and welcomed, rather, his old friend Oliver Smith's offer to produce the show instead. In the fall of 1953, all parties agreed to have Smith coproduce the work with Macmillan and Ratcliffe, but when Smith withdrew from the show in early 1954, Latouche backed out as well. After numerous phone calls and letters involving agents and lawyers, in the fall of 1954 Duke and Root initiated arbitration proceedings against Latouche with the Dramatists Guild, prior to which the attorney for the petitioners, L. Arnold Weissberger, reported to Duke a telephone conversation in which he had told Latouche to stop "acting like an obstinate damn fool. He [Latouche] said that the idea of an arbitration fascinated him, and I told him to continue to write fascinating lyrics and stop trying to be fascinating in an arbitration."[43]

After the guild's arbiters—playwrights Marc Connolly, Philip Dunning, and Samuel Spewack—ruled in favor of the petitioners, Latouche still demurred, concerned that the proposed contract bound him to the majority decisions of Duke and Root. Wishing Duke and Root, "a very Happy, Latoucheless New Year," on December 30, Weissberger reported that Latouche's disregard of the arbitration outcome had "blasted" his reputation, adding, "it will be a long time before anybody is going to want to enter into any kind of contract with him." Only under threat of contempt of court did Latouche finally sign a contract in early 1955.[44]

Then, in March 1955, came a remarkable volte-face, as coproducer Macmillan told Duke not only that he had he come to terms with Latouche—"I find him," wrote Macmillan, "the kind of guy who returns sincerity with sincerity and who once admits his error will come over and be completely cooperative"—but that he wanted Latouche to direct the show as well, and further outlined some major revisions that already suggested the lyricist's guiding hand. Duke, outraged, fired back:

> I am perfectly willing to believe that he [Latouche] may have great talent in that department [directing]; but don't forget that the man's obstructing tactics were due entirely to his colossal ego and to his burning desire to be the headman at all costs. All you have to do is put him in the position of this tremendous responsibility—as the play's director, as he will grab the opportunity to make mincemeat of Lynn and myself, not to mention you and your partner.

Deferring to Duke, Macmillan proposed other directors—including at one point, Jerome Robbins, also deemed unacceptable to the composer—before the entire project fizzled out in late 1955, by which time Duke, Root, and Latouche seemed pleasantly reconciled, as if this prolonged battle, which in the end came to naught, had been a mere passing storm.[45]

In the late 1950s, after Latouche's death, Root prepared a new version of the book "indicative of the times," purging the script of its broad African-American dialect in favor of more standard English, without totally sacrificing the ethnic flavor of the original. Conscious of the hackneyed association of blacks with razors and dice, Root relatedly eliminated Petunia's game of dice with Dude and John Henry, and created a back story in which Domino Johnson shoots Little Joe over Georgia Brown rather than slashing him over a crooked game of craps. As for the topical jokes, Root adjusted them to fit the context of the Cold War as opposed to World War II.[46]

Presumably in consultation with Duke, Root also tweaked the score, reinstituting "We'll Live All Over Again" and "Little Poppa Satan" in the deathbed scene, and including an instrumental reprise of "Love Me Tomorrow" for the episode formerly occupied by "Lazy Steps" and "Boogy Woogy." In addition, the revised show featured a new song, "Living It Up," with both words and music by Vernon Duke, for Little Joe to sing in the cafe scene—an idea perhaps suggested by the interpolation of "Shine" at a similar spot in the film adaptation. The number, which Duke described as the solo for Little Joe that Latouche "always meant to write, but, somehow, didn't," suited the general tenor of the show, although its allusion to Princess Grace dated the song in a way Latouche had avoided in his own lyrics.[47]

Producers St. John Terrell and T. Edward Hambleton independently expressed interest in the revised show, but nothing materialized until 1964, when the Greenwich Mews Theater, an interracial company based in Greenwich Village, launched a production starring Rosetta LeNoire (Petunia), Tony Middleton (Little Joe), and Ketty Lester (Georgia Brown). Directed by Brian Shaw with musical arrangements by Eric W. Knight, the production doctored the show some more, dropping "Little Poppa Satan" and "My Old Virginia Home," for instance, but, as at Sea Cliff, adding "Not a Care in the World." The production also adapted "Living It Up" as a duet for Little Joe and Georgia Brown, and, in response to new sensitivities regarding the word "pickaninny," replaced Latouche's image of Cupid as "a sinful pickaninny" in "Love Me Tomorrow" with the more correct but less jingly "artful little demon." At some point, the producers, Arthur Whitelaw and Leo Friedman, considered incorporating some of the songs by Arlen and Harburg from the film version as well, an idea surely dismissed not only by Duke, who thought Arlen's songs unbefitting dramatically, but by the lyricist's mother, Effie, who expected new productions, in keeping with her son's contract with Duke, to avoid "any musical or lyrical deviations" from the original score.[48]

The Greenwich Mews revival opened on January 21, 1964, and closed on March 1 after forty-seven performances. The critics, including Candace Womble of the *Amsterdam News,* largely found the show enjoyable, with the *Journal-American* deeming the work "a small classic in our time," although the *Times* and the *Herald Tribune* both thought the sound level deafening, and the *World-Telegram* similarly found the musical's "quiet dignity and integrity" compromised by "vaudeville humor and outright caricature." Despite the show's short run, Capitol Records released a cast album under the direction of the jazz bandleader and arranger Melvin

("Sy") Oliver, who reorchestrated the piece for a big band larger than the pit ensemble used at the Greenwich Mews. Not particularly adept vocally, and a good distance from the original Broadway sound orchestrally, the recording nonetheless had its high points, such as Tony Middleton's robust performance as Little Joe, including a delightful rendition of "Love Me Tomorrow" with Ketty Lester.[49]

Several of the show's songs retained some presence among both vocalists and instrumentalists independent of any production. Jazz trombonist Curtis Fuller even released a long-playing record, *Cabin in the Sky* (1962), of selections from the score arranged and conducted by Manny Albam, part of a vogue for jazz albums built around Broadway shows. "Taking a Chance on Love" assumed special prominence in this respect, climbing to the top of the charts as performed by Helen Forrest and the Benny Goodman Orchestra in 1943, the same year that another Vincente Minnelli MGM musical, *I Dood It*, used the song as a featured spot for the African-American pianist Hazel Scott. Countless other jazz and popular artists covered the song, most of whom, like Lester Young, Frank Sinatra, Ella Fitzgerald, Dizzy Gillespie, Bud Powell, Tony Bennett, Rosemary Clooney, Rod Stewart, and Michael Feinstein, performed the music, as had Waters herself, in a lightly swinging vein, although some, like Sonny Stitt or Chet Baker with Gerry Mulligan, pushed the tempo faster, whereas others, like Stéphane Grappelli, Clark Terry, Johnny Mathis, and Barbra Streisand, conversely treated the song as a slow ballad. The show's title song also established itself as a standard, although more as an instrumental than a vocal number, while still other numbers from the show occasionally surfaced in clubs and cabarets as well.

Meanwhile, various companies continued to mount the show, such as Tidewater Dinner Theatre in Norfolk (1979); Theatre Under the Stars (TUTS) in Houston (1985); Musicals Tonight! in New York (2003); Lyric Stage in Irving, Texas (2006); and Encores! at New York City Center (2016). In all these productions, the line-up of musical numbers varied considerably, with Encores! including "Little Poppa Satan," "Fugue," and Arlen and Harburg's "Happiness Is a Thing Called Joe," but neither "Not a Care in the World" nor "Living It Up." Thanks to support from the Joseph S. and Diane H. Steinberg Broadway Musical Restoration Fund, this last production occasioned a particularly ambitious restoration, with music director Rob Berman and (for the spirituals) vocal arranger Linda Twine rounding out the incomplete surviving score; orchestrator Jonathan Tunick replacing the lost orchestrations with those of his own, although with an eye to Ethel Waters's recordings with the Martin Beck Theatre Orchestra; choreographer Camille A. Brown designing historically informed dances; and stage director Ruben Santiago-Hudson and the artistic director of Encores! Jack Viertel, aside from rendering the original script into standard English, only slightly altering the book in light of contemporary sensibilities.

Reviews of these later productions by and large found the piece well worth reviving, with Latouche's lyrics often commended as "witty" and "brilliant," even if the continued bowdlerization of his work took a bit of a toll. More negative response to the show generally focused on white appropriation of black folkways, although without much cognizance of the roles Ethel Waters, Katherine Dunham, J. Rosamond Johnson, and other African Americans had played in the work's creation. Reviewing the Encores! production, Judd Hollander (*Epoch Times*) proved unusual in unearthing a "deeper message" to the musical, namely, "that even the most devout person can forsake righteous ways, while even the most confirmed sinner can choose to be reborn."[50]

9

Banjo Eyes

During the summer of 1940, while at work on *Cabin in the Sky* and various radio projects, Latouche managed some involvement with a revue, *Crazy with the Heat*, produced by the Viennese émigré actor Kurt Kasznar (born Servischer, 1913–1979). Kasznar had worked with Max Reinhardt in Europe, and after appearing in the latter's production of *The Eternal Road* (1937) on Broadway settled in New York, where he met and married Cornelia Woolley, the daughter of a prominent philanthropist—an alliance that presumably helped enable the twenty-seven-year-old actor to launch his own show.

Kasznar initially presented *Crazy with the Heat* at small summer venues, opening on July 29, 1940, at the Red Barn Theatre in Locust Valley, Long Island, where the show played for two weeks before moving to the Theatre-By-the-Sea in Matunuck, Rhode Island, and the Cedarhurst Playhouse in Cedarhurst, Long Island. Advertised as an "intimate revue," the production featured a cast of seventeen headed by mimic Sheila Barrett and accompanied by two pianos, with Kasznar as director and Eugene Loring as choreographer.

In this early guise, the show included four numbers by Latouche, all with music by the revue's primary composer, the French expatriate Rudi Revil, and all introduced by relative unknowns: "One Hour for Lunch" (the lyrics co-written with John Cleveland and Luther Davis); "Day Before Yesterday"; "Old Ghosts for Ancient Castles, Extended, Ltd." (adapted from the chanson "Le fantôme du manoir," lyrics by Charlys); and "Walking with Miss Darkness" (the lyrics co-written with Kasznar). In addition, the revue contained a sketch by Latouche entitled "Air Conditioning." Lead sheets for the sprightly "One Hour for Lunch" and the somber "Day Before Yesterday" survive, as do two other Latouche songs very possibly intended for this revue: the Brazilian-flavored "At a Masquerade in Rio," also with music by Revil, and the romantic "The Other Side of the Moon," with music by Gershwin's female protégée Dana Suesse (pronounced Dayna Sweess).

Born Rudolf Heinrich Weil in Strasbourg to German-Jewish parents, Rudi Revil (1916–1983), Latouche's principal partner in this venture, had studied music with Nadia Boulanger and, although still only in his early twenties, had enjoyed notable success as a popular songwriter in his native France before emigrating to the United States in 1939. Like so many of Latouche's collaborators, he traversed the worlds of popular and serious music, including composing a ballet, *Zodiac* (1947), for Lincoln Kirstein's Ballet Society. Described by one commentator as "suave, witty, and elegantly mannered," the handsome young composer also became known as a connoisseur of fine art and antiques. How Kasznar, Revil, and Latouche discovered one another remains unknown—at the time of the revue, Revil apparently was staying at the home of Latouche's friend Francesco Mendelssohn—but at any rate, Latouche once again found himself working with urbane émigrés.[1]

The team of Revil and Latouche attracted positive notice, with a feature article in the *Post* finding their songs to contain tunes "of the kind that stick in the mind," and a review of the Kasznar show in *Variety* singling out some of their numbers in a mostly otherwise unenthused review. However, by the time Kasznar brought the show to Broadway, after further tryouts in New Haven and Boston, he had cut—along with much else—all the Latouche material. Far from the modest revue with "sophisticated pretentions" mounted over the summer, this newly conceived show—which opened at the Forty-Fourth Street Theatre on January 14, 1941, to dismal reviews, and gave seven performances before closing on January 18—cost over $100,000 and boasted a cast of about eighty headlined by the old-time comic Willie Howard. Sinking another $20,000 or so into the production, journalist Ed Sullivan presided over yet another rewrite, including a spot for comedian Victor Borge making his Broadway debut, and the show reopened on January 30, but the critics remained unimpressed: "A souffle, once fallen, seldom rises again," commented John Anderson (*Journal-American*). Although the revamped production eked out a total of ninety-two performances, and continued to play the vaudeville circuit after closing on April 19, it ultimately lost tens of thousands of dollars. Kasznar and Revil subsequently put this flop behind them, the former becoming a well-known and highly regarded character actor both on Broadway and in Hollywood, the latter eventually repatriating to France, where he produced such song hits as "Le petit cordonnier" ("The Little Shoemaker") and "Marjolaine."[2]

During this same period, Latouche worked on another revue, the *Ice-Capades of 1941*, the first of what would become a popular series of ice shows known simply as the Ice Capades. Thanks in large part to the technical wizardry and show-biz savvy of the superstar Norwegian figure skater Sonja Henie, ice shows had become increasingly popular in America in the 1930s not merely as exhibition displays, but as bona fide theatrical events, with all the trappings of the traditional Broadway revue, including elaborate sets, comedy routines, and orchestrated musical scores. The day's leading drama and dance desks not only regularly covered such entertainments, but often did so with rare enthusiasm. Reviewing a 1939 Sonja Henie show at Madison Square Garden, the *Times* dance critic John Martin wrote, for example, "There is definitely something of great interest to be developed in the realm of the ice ballet, and amazingly enough here is one experimental art where there is a large and wildly enthusiastic audience to watch the experiment and fight for the privilege of paying the bill."[3]

In 1940, as this vogue approached its zenith, New York's recently completed Rockefeller Center redesigned its thirty-five-hundred-seat Center Theatre specifically to present ice shows on a proscenium stage as opposed to an arena, the traditional venue for such spectacles. For the refitted Center's inaugural *It Happens on Ice*, which premiered in October 1940, the show's producers, Sonja Henie and Arthur Wirtz, consulted with music publisher Jack Robbins, who in turn commissioned Vernon Duke and others in his atelier—although not Latouche—to provide material for this revue. Meanwhile, earlier that same year, the Arena Managers' Association decided to launch their own touring ice show independent of Henie, the *Ice-Capades of 1941*, and they, too, approached Robbins, who seems to have cornered the market with respect to such events, and who commissioned in this instance a score from composer Peter De Rose and lyricists Mitchell Parish and Latouche.

By this time, Peter De Rose (1900–1953), a now largely forgotten American singer, pianist, and composer of popular music, had scored his greatest hit, the 1934 piano solo *Deep Purple*, lyricized by Mitchell Parish in 1939. Although De Rose had little background in theater per se, Robbins presumably recognized in "Deep Purple," whose rights he held, the sort of music apropos an ice show; indeed, some of De Rose's work appeared in *It Happens on Ice* as well.

The *Ice-Capades* company and crew, including the songwriters, gathered in Atlantic City in early July 1940 in preparation for the show's premiere at the local Convention Hall on July 19. According to the souvenir program, De Rose and Latouche attended rehearsals "and then locked themselves in a room with a piano to write the special lyrics and tunes for the show." The revue, which contained solos, pair skating, comedy skits, and big production numbers, some with exotic and lavish settings, starred Henie's principal rival, the British figure skater and dancer Belita Jepson-Turner, as well as some other noted skating talent, including the comedy team of Larry Jackson and Bernie Lynam. Radio City's Russell Markert, who had founded the Rockettes, directed the cast of about seventy-five, creating yet another ensemble of precision dancers, the Ice-Rockettes. Earl Moss and Jerry Mayhall prepared the musical arrangements, with the latter conducting the apparently amplified orchestra and vocal soloists.[4]

Five numbers with lyrics by Latouche written for or otherwise associated with this show survive: four with music by De Rose ("Somewhere," "Yippi-I-Ay!" "Oriental Moon-Rise," and "Swing Me a Lullaby") along with one, "Yankee Doodle Polka," composed with Vernon Duke. Another song by De Rose and Latouche from this same time period, "Mis Amigos," might have been written for this production as well. The program book listed only two song titles—"Somewhere," sung by George Byron during the first-act ensemble number ("The Garden of Roses"), and "I Hear America Singing," a song by De Rose and Parish performed in the finale—but the show doubtless featured other numbers by Latouche as well. "Oriental Moon-Rise," also performed by Byron, might well have surfaced in the opening "Arabian Nights" segment, described as "a fantasy of love and jealousy in the harem of the Sultan";

"Yankee Doodle Polka," possibly during "Yankee Rhythm," one of Jackson and Lyman's routines; and "Yippi-I-Ay!" perhaps during the finale in which the entire cast appeared, according to the *Billboard*, "in the most garish cowboy and cowgirl costumes conceivable." And if indeed used, "Mis Amigos" might have accompanied the solo entitled, "The Tango."[5]

This colorful score seemed aptly pitched to the novel requirement of writing songs for skating dancers and clowns, and as the *Ice-Capades* traveled to more than twenty cities during the 1940–41 season, the critics praised the music along with most everything else about what the *Boston Globe* called a "nimble, imaginative, and above all gracefully beautiful . . . extravaganza." Financial motivation aside, for Latouche work on an ice show presumably represented not only another opportunity—as in his radio dramas—to explore the poetic possibilities of a newly popular artistic medium, but a means specifically to experiment with novel combinations of word, music, movement, and spectacle, the sort of preoccupation that would culminate in his late theatrical work.[6]

Robbins Music published "Somewhere," "Yippi-I-Ay!" and "Yankee Doodle Polka," as well as De Rose and Parish's "I Hear America Singing," whereas "Oriental Moon-Rise," "Swing Me a Lullaby," and "Mis Amigos" went unpublished and apparently survive only as lead sheets. Ray Eberle and the Glenn Miller Orchestra recorded "Somewhere," as did Dinah Shore, among others, while two dance bands, Gray Gordon and his Tic-Toc Rhythm, and Lou Holden and his Disciples of Rhythm, both recorded "Yankee Doodle Polka." After the revue completed its tour in May 1941 in Los Angeles, Republic Pictures featured the company in a film also entitled *Ice-Capades of 1941*, but that movie, released over the summer, contained a different musical score.

Although Latouche spent most of 1941 working with Vernon Duke on two new shows, *Banjo Eyes* and *The Lady Comes Across*, they collaborated as well on several smaller efforts in addition to "Yankee Doodle Polka." One such, "The ASCAP Song," presumably composed at the request of the performance-rights organization to which both belonged, the American Society of Composers, Authors and Publishers, happily asserted that songwriters, thanks to ASCAP, no longer needed to die a pauper's death as had Stephen Foster; Duke and Latouche probably wrote the number as some sort of a morale booster, given ASCAP's current travails with both the broadcasting industry and the federal government. Other surviving Duke and Latouche songs include "Tonight at Sundown" (1941), possibly written for the *Ice-Capades of 1941*, and "Two Sparkling Eyes" (1942), one of their final collaborations. The two also prepared a few items for the Allied cause, including some adaptations of traditional Chinese songs for a benefit for United China Relief and, as discussed earlier, "Fog" for British War Relief.[7]

Duke and Latouche furthermore collaborated on a risqué routine for the British entertainer John Buckmaster presented in the spring of 1941 at Felix Ferry's Manhattan nitery, the Monte Carlo, in which Buckmaster impersonated varied speakers, assisted by strippers, delivering lectures about three birds identified as the Ritzicum Floosibus, or Yellow-crested Cinch; the First Basisbus Easiorum, or Southern Clinger; and the Tomatokins Lushivus, or Night Flyer. As Duke recalled, "the three ladybirds," accompanied by bandleader Ted Straeter, "stripped down to essentials, while chanting our lascivious roundelay, 'Sisters Under the Skin' " (a number apparently lost). Having burlesque queens appear at so tony a club as the Monte Carlo struck observers as, in the words of one correspondent, "about the wackiest thing yet," but the act—presented at 12:30 a.m. as the first of Buckmaster's two shows—proved a hit with audiences and critics alike.[8]

Banjo Eyes, Latouche's second show with Vernon Duke, was the brainchild of the singing comedian Eddie Cantor. Born Israel Iskowitz in New York, the son of Russian-Jewish immigrants, Cantor (1892–1964) emerged from humble beginnings to become one of the most celebrated stars of his time. Rolling his eyes, shaking his head, clapping his hands, singing humorous and sometimes sexually suggestive songs, and prancing and swishing about the stage with enormous gusto, often in blackface, he typically played the impish fool, as in the Broadway hit *Whoopee* (1928) produced by Florenz Ziegfeld, and the Hollywood film *The Kid from Spain* (1932) produced by Samuel Goldwyn.

In 1940, Cantor sought to return to Broadway after an absence of more than ten years, and pondered various projects, including a musical dramatization of his career to be called, after his trademark peepers, *Banjo Eyes*; but he ultimately decided to feature himself rather in a musical adaptation—also under the title, *Banjo Eyes*—of John Cecil Holm and George Abbott's popular 1935 farce *Three Men on a Horse,* thereby fulfilling an ambition of some standing, as he had hoped to star in Warner Brothers' 1936 film version of the play. He no doubt felt that the role of Erwin Trowbridge, the comedy's bullied and vamped hero, nicely could accommodate his stage persona. In 1941, he persuaded Jack Warner, on behalf of Warner Brothers, who owned the rights to the play, to co-finance the musical with him fifty-fifty, and to have Albert Lewis—who had presented *The Nervous Wreck* (the source for *Whoopee*), *The Jazz Singer,* and *Cabin in the Sky* on Broadway—produce the show. Warner and Cantor further agreed that the latter would star in any Warner Brothers film version of the musical.[9]

Over the summer, Cantor and producer Lewis engaged Joseph Quillan and Irving ("Izzy") Elinson, staff writers for Cantor's popular radio show *Time to Smile,* to adapt the Holm and Abbott comedy. As they intended no mere musical farce, but rather a Ziegfeldian extravaganza in the tradition of the *Follies* and *Whoopee,* with variety acts, beautiful chorines, and elaborate set designs, Cantor and Lewis also recruited a large cast along with the three-person team who earlier that same year had created the stunning dream sequences in Kurt Weill's *Lady in the Dark,* namely, set designer Harry Horner, lighting designer Hassard (Hazzard)

Short, and costume designer Irene Sharaff. In the end, Cantor and Warner Brothers spent a hefty amount on the production, estimates ranging as high as $160,000.[10]

Cantor originally had wanted Rodgers and Hart to write the score, but after they declined, management hired, as the press announced in August, Duke and Latouche, likely on the recommendation of Lewis, who had worked with the two on *Cabin in the Sky*. With rehearsals scheduled to begin in early October in order to meet an expected Broadway opening by Thanksgiving, this left Duke and Latouche only two months or so to prepare the score, and to do so, moreover, while preoccupied with another show, *The Lady Comes Across*. Meanwhile, bookwriters Quillan and Elinson, conferring with the songwriters at Cantor's suite in the Essex House, completed a draft of the book in mid-September.

In his memoirs, Duke provided a droll and revealing anecdote with respect to Latouche's failure to turn up at some of these conferences:

> Doc Bender [Lorenz Hart's friend, Milton Bender] and I were worried about Latouche's chronic nonattendance of the Essex House powwows; rumors of his life of rural splendor were all over town and the producers began shaking their heads portentously. We borrowed Larry Hart's car and chauffeur and motored to [the Stanton Griffis estate in] New Canaan to track down the recalcitrant lyricist. . . . After questioning the major-domo, the butler and several fleet-footed footmen, we were escorted to an attractive formal garden. A group of earnest-looking German and Viennese refugees in summer garb were reclining on the grass listening with rapt attention to Latouche, their host, striking in baby-blue jeans, a white bandanna tied around his head, reading poems obviously not meant for either *Banjo Eyes* or *Lady Comes Across*. There was prolonged applause after the offering and the German accented voice of a countess [presumably Ruth Yorck] was heard to exclaim: "Zere iss only one Tchann Cocteau in France, only one Tchonnee Latouche in America!". . . The seance over, Latouche greeted us effusively and volunteered the information that grouse and Romanee-Conti would be featured at dinner, [and] also requested that one of the footmen show us to our rooms. The rooms were splendid, the dinner even better, but our every effort to divulge the reason for our mission to the host fell on a deaf ear. . . . After breakfast the next morning, Doc went in search of Latouche, found him, pushed him next to the piano, where I was sitting, a prop smile on my lips, and said resoundingly: "There—now get to work, you two, or there'll be nothing but trouble." Johnny, pouting disagreeably, produced a pad and a pencil and we began wrestling with a rhumba Cantor intended to sing to one of the race horses in the play. I played a chorus; Johnny made a face. I tried another; he shook his head disdainfully. "All right, listen to this—it's the best of the lot," I said, ductile to a degree, and played yet a third rhumba. "Good heavens, Vernon!"

> Johnny shrieked in disgust, "If you only had a little less agility, and a little more ability!" A frightful fracas ensued, Bender and the butler participating energetically. Somehow, peace was restored and we all went back to New York with a fourth and final rhumba for Eddie Cantor's horse.[11]

Having such sophisticates as Duke and Latouche write a star vehicle for a clown who had made his career singing the likes of "If You Knew Susie" and "Ida (Sweet as Apple Cider)" had its incongruities, not to say risks, but the two songwriters assumed, at least publicly, a lofty view of the matter. Latouche stated in late September, for instance, "Fundamentally, I consider myself a poet. I think poetry should be heard over the radio and in musical comedies; it shouldn't be limited to the slender volumes which never reach anybody.... Why, Shakespeare wrote lyrics. Now naturally I'm no Shakespeare, but I'm trying to put some poetry in the music Duke and I are writing for... Eddie Cantor's new musical, 'Banjo Eyes.'" Duke similarly proclaimed—as he had with respect to *Cabin in the Sky*—the seriousness of his aims:

> That is why it is so wonderful to work with Mr. Cantor. We [he and Latouche] wrote two songs for him that are as different as black and white and he found them extremely acceptable. He has a wide range and a great ability for adapting himself.
>
> Songs should not be dragged in by the hair. They should further and accentuate—punctuate in other words—the story and stress the stage dynamics rather than hinder them. Mr. Cantor has wonderful ideas and appreciates all these things.

All the same, in January 1942 Latouche told Charlotte Dieterle, the wife of film director William Dieterle, that he "hated doing" the show, and that he had not attended a performance since the New York premiere back in November.[12]

Duke and Latouche at least had some amusing material to work with. The meek and upright Erwin Trowbridge, the protagonist of *Three Men on a Horse*, lives with his wife, Audrey, in suburban Ozone Heights, New Jersey, and commutes to New York, where he makes a modest living creating doggerel for a greeting-card company. Upset with both Audrey's spendthrift ways and her obnoxious brother Clarence, Erwin plays hooky, gets drunk, and winds up at a bar in a New York hotel, where three gamblers—Charlie, Frankie, and Patsy—learn that he has made a hobby of accurately predicting the outcome of horse races. The gamblers talk him into a partnership, helped in this endeavor by Patsy's girlfriend Mabel, a former showgirl. At the play's climax, Patsy forces Erwin to bet all his earnings in a race, which—now that he has "doped" a horse for money rather than for fun—causes him to lose his powers of divination. In the end, Erwin asserts himself, standing up to Clarence, Patsy, and even his tyrannical boss, Mr. Carver, who offers him a new office and a big raise.[13]

Whereas the movie version remained faithful to the play, the musical adaptation prepared for Cantor retained only the basic shell of the stage original. Sidetracked by the need to feature Cantor in a medley of his famous hits near the end of the show, Quillan and Elinson seemed to lop off or at least drastically abridge the play's denouement in which Erwin loses his ability to pick horses, confronts the gamblers and his boss, and earns a promotion at work; they introduced rather a new focus, that of an impending baby for Erwin and Sally. The musical further deleted the character of Erwin's brother-in-law, the chief catalyst for the play's action, but rather had his boss Mr. Carver fulfill some of those functions. The three gamblers stay central to the action, as does Patsy's girlfriend Mabel, but Charlie's now on furlough from the army and has a girlfriend of his own, Ginger, who wants him to give up gambling. Finally, the bookwriters provided the potential for spectacle by making space for a lavish display at Mr. Carver's greeting-card company, various entertainments at the midtown hotel (where Mabel and Ginger perform as showgirls), dream episodes in which a horse called Banjo Eyes provides Erwin with the names of winning horses, an interpolated scene at an army base, and a grand finale at the races at Belmont Park.

Cantor seems to have supervised the casting himself, assigning to his mistress Jacqueline Susann, who years later would author the bestselling book *Valley of the Dolls*, a small speaking role: Miss Clark, the mistress—fittingly enough—of her boss, Mr. Carver. Other cast members included June Clyde (Sally Trowbridge), Bill Johnson (Charlie), Romo Vincent (Frankie, replaced before New York by Ray Mayer), Lionel Stander (Patsy), Audrey Christie (Mabel, replaced during the New York run by Collette Lyons), Sara Ann McCabe (Ginger, replaced before New York by Virginia Mayo), the horse pantomimists Nonnie Morton and Andy Mayo (Banjo Eyes), and Virginia Mayo (Banjo Eyes' trainer). (The sister-in-law of Andy Mayo and later a Hollywood star, Virginia Mayo had been hired as part of Morton and Mayo's horse act.) The production also featured African-American hoofer Bill Bailey and the dance team of Sally and Tony De Marco, as well as, by the time of its arrival on Broadway, specialty dancers Gloria Gilbert, Tommy Wonder (who left the show during the New York run), and the Canadian trio Lynn, Royce, and Vanya. Albert Lewis directed the book, and Hassard Short, the musical numbers. Domenico Savino supervised the orchestrations and Ray Sinatra (a cousin of Frank Sinatra) conducted the orchestra.[14]

The show had its world premiere on November 7, 1941, at the Shubert Theatre in New Haven, where it played for two days. The work at this point featured ten songs by Duke and Latouche: "Greeting Cards," for various soloists; "I'll Take the City," for Erwin and chorus; "Don't Let It Happen Again," for Mabel, Frankie, and chorus; "A Nickel to My Name," for Charlie and soloists; "Hushabye Land," for Frankie; "Who Started the Rhumba?" for Erwin, Banjo Eyes, and the ensemble; "I Always Think of Sally," for Erwin; "Song Without Words," for Ginger and soloists; "Banjo Eyes," for Erwin, Bill Bailey, Banjo Eyes, and the ensemble; and "Not a Care in the World," for Frankie (later, Charlie) and the ensemble. Another song, "What

Every Young Man Should Know," apparently intended for Erwin, failed to make it even this far, but would find its way into Duke and Latouche's next show, *The Lady Comes Across*.

"A Nickel to My Name," "Not a Care in the World," and "I'll Take the City" show Duke and Latouche in particularly fine form. In the lightly romantic "A Nickel to My Name," presumably inspired by the telephone booth that functions as an important prop in the play, Charlie regards the nickel that allows him to speak to his girlfriend Ginger on the phone worth more than all of Rockefeller's millions: "Life is really swell," states the verse just prior to the chorus, "and love can weave a spell / Thanks to Alexander Graham Bell." In the chorus's bridge section, Latouche deftly complements the music's growing harmonic tension, with the climactic word "up" arriving alongside an aptly dissonant chord before the apologetic "I'm sorry" and the music's return to more familiar harmonic terrain:

> I'm as happy as a pup
> As you tell me foolish things
> Till the operator rings—
> "Your time is up . . . I'm sorry."

(As with other songs from the show, the lyric for this number as found in the script differs from that in the printed sheet music, with, for instance, soldier Charlie's "You can't be a Rockefeller / When you're wearing the khaki, fella" appearing in the sheet music more generically as, "I am not a Rockefeller / With a million bucks in my cellar.") The breezy "Not a Care in the World," at one point intended for Frankie but later sung by Charlie, unfolds an unusual rhyme scheme, with the emphasis on internal as opposed to external rhymes, as in this phrase from the bridge section: "As Kate the Great used to state long ago, 'Nichevo!' " (a laugh line that obviously assumed knowledge of the common Russian expression for "Don't worry!"). "I'll Take the City," sung by an exasperated Erwin to his boss and wife as he expresses his intention to go on a spree, features a similar wit, while neatly fitting Cantor's manic stage presence: "I'll drink in Oscar Levant's room / I'll put a juke box in Grant's Tomb / And I'll go truckin' on down."

Some of the songs featured a horse motive in order to provide some thematic unity: "Hushabye Land," sung in New Haven by Frankie probably to lull Erwin to sleep, pictures a land of equine contentedness; "Who Started the Rhumba?" attributes that popular Latin-American dance to the movement of horses; and "Banjo Eyes" conflates praise for the eponymous horse with that for both Erwin and the famed entertainer playing him. As for the show's other numbers, "Greeting Cards," the one song whose music does not seem to have survived, satirizes both greeting-card platitudes and Ziegfeldian extravagance in its representation of various holiday greetings. "Don't Let It Happen Again," for the sparring Mabel and Frankie, contains a Gershwinesque verve, whereas "Song Without Words," a ballad in which a melody's need for a lyric becomes a metaphor for romantic coupling, has a sort of Rodgers and Hart sweetness, recalling in particular "With a Song in My Heart," although the conceit itself also resembles Vernon Duke's song with Ira Gershwin, "Words Without Music." And both "I Think of Sally" and "What Every Young Man Should Know" seem cognizant of such Cantor hits as "Margie" and "Makin' Whoopee!" with, however, the respective sentiment and bawdiness of these chestnuts taken to a higher level of wit. During the musical's creation, Latouche especially acknowledged the influence of Ira Gershwin on his work, stating, "Ira is the person who taught me the most about lyrics."[15]

Duke recalled that the New Haven premiere lasted until close to 1:00 a.m., "with practically no one except the chorus girls' mothers, the backers and their families remaining in their seats for the finale." The show actually received rather good notices, with the *Hartford Courant* deeming the lyrics "deft in the fantastic fashion of string incongruities which seems to be the law in the word-world right now," although *Variety* warned that future success would depend on a funnier script and a better score. After moving to Boston's Colonial Theatre, where *Banjo Eyes* opened on November 11, the production again received generally positive reviews, although mixed with respect to the score; the *Boston Post* thought the show to contain songs the "poor public" could not "hum as they leave the theatre," whereas the *Evening American* admired "La Touche's witty, literate, sometimes entrancing lyrics and Vernon Duke's enchanting music."[16]

Cantor arranged for producer Max Gordon and writers Moss Hart and George S. Kaufman, as well as John Cecil Holm, the co-author of *Three Men on a Horse*, to attend the Boston opening, and consulted with them about the show afterward. Holm remained on hand to help doctor the book, and Duke and Latouche set about revising the score, which Moss Hart found lacking. "Latouche was now the archvillain," remembered Duke; "he and Hazzard Short, our director, didn't see eye to eye, Short dismissing every new lyric with a deprecating, 'If it's by Latouche it can't be good.'" After a few days of attempting to write another "If You Knew Susie," Latouche, as Duke recalled, "was ousted and replaced by Harold Adamson, a quiet and philosophical chap with many 'commercial' achievements behind him." Indeed, Adamson (1906–1980), much more of a Hollywood than a Broadway lyricist, already had received two of the five Academy Award nominations he ultimately would earn in the best original song category. Latouche presented the situation somewhat differently, telling choreographer Ruth Page in late December that he "walked out of it [*Banjo Eyes*], because they wanted such vulgar and old-fashioned words that I rebelled. That was fireworks and lawyers and agents whirling about." In any case, as Duke and Adamson prepared a few new songs, *Banjo Eyes* remained an extra week in Boston for a total of three weeks; and canceling a scheduled Washington engagement, the show traveled rather to Philadelphia, where it opened on December 2 for another two weeks, extended to three by popular demand.[17]

As in New Haven and Boston, the Philadelphia critics generally welcomed the show but not necessarily the score, which, despite the insertion of a few new Duke and Adamson numbers calculated to appeal to a mass audience, the local *Daily News* savaged in a notice headed, "Comedy in Search of Music." On the other hand, the *Inquirer*, in its rave review, spotted a few possible song hits and further described the show's lyrics as "pretty—well—pungent."[18]

By the time the show finally arrived in New York, four Duke and Latouche songs ("Don't Let It Happen Again," "Hushabye Land," "I Always Think of Sally," and "Song Without Words") had been dropped, and three Duke and Adamson songs ("It Could Only Happen in the Movies," for Erwin and Mabel; "Make with the Feet" for, eventually, Mabel, Tommy Wonder, and the De Marcos; and "We're Having a Baby," for Erwin and Sally) had been added, although not the Duke and Adamson song "Taxi" for Frankie, a hit in Philadelphia, but presumably cut in conjunction with Romo Vincent's replacement by Ray Mayer. One seemingly new dance number in the Broadway production, "I've Got to Hand It to You," perhaps represented a version of the cut "Don't Let It Happen Again," a conjecture supported not only by their similar placement in the show, but by their titles, which scan alike.

During the Philadelphia run, the musical also added a patriotic number to the Camp Dixon scene. Quillan and Elinson, perhaps at Cantor's suggestion, originally had included this scene, which featured some slapstick humor, as an apparent nod to the increasing number of young men drafted under the Selective Service Act of 1940, the impetus as well, no doubt, for making Charlie a soldier. Indeed, the musical from the start had incorporated some topical political sentiment, including some barbs hurled at Nazis and communists alike; the New Haven premiere even had concluded with the national anthem. But in the wake of America's declaration of war against the Axis in the second week of December, the show further incorporated into the Camp Dixon scene a marchlike victory song for The Captain and his troops, "We Did It Before and We Can Do It Again," a newly composed number with music by Cliff Friend and lyrics by Charles Tobias, Cantor's cousin through marriage.

Banjo Eyes opened on Broadway on Christmas day at the ornate Hollywood Theatre, a former movie palace owned by Warner Brothers (later, the Mark Hellinger Theatre, and currently, the Times Square Church). Latouche appropriately received primary billing as the show's lyricist, with Adamson credited with "additional lyrics." A surviving script helps document the work's scenario as it seems to have appeared at its New York premiere, as follows, with music by Duke and lyrics by Latouche unless otherwise indicated.

Act I, scene one. The Display Salon of the Carver Greeting Card Co. The company hosts an elaborate display of greeting-card verses for representatives from exclusive department stores ("The Greeting Cards," for various soloists). Mr. Carver refuses to give his principal verse writer, Erwin Trowbridge, a raise, and Erwin's wife, Sally, thinking that the names of race horses in her husband's little black book refer to girlfriends, unjustly accuses him of infidelity. Incensed, the mild-mannered Erwin decides to go on a tear ("I'll Take the City," for Erwin, Boys, and Girls).

Scene two. The Bar in a Midtown Hotel ("I've Got to Hand It to You," for Tommy Wonder, Leona Olsen, and other dancers). Charlie, a soldier in the army, reunites with his girlfriend Ginger, a showgirl at the hotel, where he also finds his old gambling buddies Frankie and Patsy. Erwin enters drunk, and Frankie and Patsy discover that he has an uncanny ability to pick winning race horses, although Erwin himself never gambles. Charlie calls Ginger on the phone ("A Nickel to My Name," for Charlie and soloists). Wanting to keep Erwin as a tipster, Frankie and Patsy carry him away after he passes out.

Scene three. Mabel's Room, in the same hotel. Frankie and Patsy install Erwin in the hotel room of Patsy's girlfriend Mabel, another showgirl, who lulls Erwin to sleep.

Scene four. The Dream Pastures. Erwin dreams of the race horse Banjo Eyes, who gives him some hot tips ("Who Started the Rhumba?" for Erwin, Banjo Eyes, and the ensemble).

Scene five. Mabel's Room. Erwin attempts to make his escape as Mabel tries to get the inside dope from him ("It Could Only Happen in the Movies," for Erwin and Mabel, lyrics by Harold Adamson). As Sally and Patsy enter, they find Mabel and Erwin in a compromising position.

Act II, scene one. The Bar. Mabel and others dance ("Make with the Feet," for Mabel, Tommy Wonder, and the De Marcos, lyrics by Adamson). The gamblers leave in search of a missing Erwin.

Scene two. Erwin's Home, Jackson Heights. Erwin returns home to Sally and happily learns that his wife is pregnant ("We're Having a Baby," for Erwin and Sally, lyrics by Adamson).

Scene three. The Dream Pastures. In another dream, Erwin hears from Banjo Eyes that the latter will win the forthcoming Gold Cup Race ("Banjo Eyes," for the ensemble).

Scene four. Erwin's Home. The gamblers descend on Erwin and through a series of contrivances Erwin, stripped of his clothes, borrows Charlie's uniform in order to meet his wife.

Scene five. Camp Dixon. Picked up by the military police, Erwin finds himself at an army camp and attempts to fall in line during drill ("We Did It Before and We Can Do It Again," for The Captain and Boys, music by Cliff Friend, lyrics by Charles Tobias).

Scene six. The Clubhouse, Belmont Park. In deference to Ginger, Charlie refrains from placing any bets ("Not a Care in the World," for Charlie and the ensemble). Rescued from the army by Patsy and Frankie, Erwin inadvertently gives them the name of the winning horse.

Scene seven. The Grandstand, Belmont Park. After Banjo Eyes wins the race, Erwin entertains the crowd with his Eddie Cantor impersonation, singing some of the star's best-known hits in blackface (medley, including "Margie," "Ida," and "If You Knew Susie," for Erwin, with "Makin' Whoopee!" an encore, music and lyrics by various artists). All celebrate (reprise of "We're Having a Baby" and "Banjo Eyes," for the ensemble).

The New York critics widely greeted *Banjo Eyes* as a deluxe, boisterous, often hilarious entertainment, and a personal triumph for Cantor; in its evaluation of the reviews posted by New York's nine biggest dailies, the *Billboard* reported that all recommended the show. The *Billboard* itself considered *Banjo Eyes* one of the best musicals of what seems to have been a humdrum season. At the same time, no one made any great claims for the work; "It's no great shakes," stated the *Billboard*, while Wolcott Gibbs wrote in the *New Yorker*, "'Banjo Eyes' has practically every characteristic of a superior musical comedy except the subtle qualities of wit, taste, and imagination which distinguish the best of them." The press, incidentally, took Cantor's use of blackface in stride, without any comment even by the noted African-American critic Dan Burley in a piece about the musical for the *Amsterdam News*; on the contrary, Burley described Cantor as a "a man who has a deep aversion to color lines and all other lines having to do with a person's race, place of birth, color or prestige."[19]

With respect to the score, Brooks Atkinson (*Times*) reported, in his particularly favorable review, "Vernon Duke has written a vibrant score of metallic music and John Latouche has done some witty handsprings for the lyrics." But like a number of the out-of-town critics, most of the New York critics (who understandably seem to have been unaware as to who wrote which lyrics) thought the score, if at times "pleasant" and "tuneful," largely "undistinguished" and "commonplace." Louis Kronenberger even concluded his notice in *PM* with a slam at Latouche's lyrics, which seemed to him "as disappointing as Mr. Duke's music; they not only lack sparkle, they even indulge in some appalling false rhymes" (although Kronenberger easily could have confused Latouche's work with that of the show's other lyricists). Of all the numbers, only Duke and Adamson's "We're Having a Baby" made much of an impression, even becoming something of a showstopper. A year later, Duke's publisher Jack Robbins, who brought out no fewer than nine songs from the show, including some that never made it to Broadway, wrote to the composer, "Cantor probably would have closed the show if he did not have that 'Baby' song. He had nothing else to hold on to. The song also saves your neck."[20]

Because Cantor's *Time to Smile* radio show aired on Wednesdays, *Banjo Eyes* stayed closed that day of the week, but instead offered performances on Thursday (later changed to Sunday) afternoons and Sunday evenings. Aside from opening night, with its top price of $7.70, the most expensive ticket cost $4.40. In the course of the show's Broadway run, Cantor and company continued to tinker with the score, including adding the George Sumner song "The Toast of the Boys at the Post" for Mabel and soloists to sing in the first act, substituting Peter De Rose and Harold Adamson's "The Yanks Are on the March" for "We Did It Before" in the second act, and interpolating a new

Duke and Adamson number, "Leave My Women Alone," into the comedian's blackface medley. Cantor improvised in other ways, as evidenced by an incident recalled by composer Stephen Sondheim: "He [Cantor] was an acquaintance of my family, and when my father took me at the age of eleven to see the show [*Banjo Eyes*], Cantor surprised both of us by urging his stage wife, June Clyde, to get dressed quickly because 'We're going to the Sondheims' for dinner.' It remains one of the most thrilling moments in my theater-going experience." Moreover, since most other Broadway shows closed on Sunday nights, theater celebrities sometimes showed up at a performance of *Banjo Eyes* to take a bow or sing a song, including Gertrude Lawrence and Sophie Tucker, currently in *Lady in the Dark* and *High Kickers*, respectively. One Sunday night, Danny Kaye, who had left the cast of *Lady in the Dark* for a star turn in Cole Porter's *Let's Face It!*, made an unexpected appearance as a recruit in the Camp Dixon scene, to the surprise of Cantor and the delight of the audience.[21]

The show seemed headed to run at least through the summer, but closed prematurely on Sunday, April 12, after 126 performances, due to Cantor developing some undisclosed malady—reportedly a bad case of hemorrhoids—that required medical attention and several weeks' rest. However, many doubted that this alone accounted for his resignation, especially given the allegedly minor nature of his ailment. Some pointed to such other factors as his dissatisfaction with management and boredom with the show. In any event, some two hundred actors, dancers, musicians, and crew members found themselves, to their general displeasure, suddenly out of work, although at least for Virginia Mayo, tired of the show herself, the end of the run came as "a relief."[22]

Meanwhile, about $50,000 in advance sales had to be refunded, and in the end the show lost, by one estimate, $100,000. Management hoped eventually to reopen the show with either Cantor or perhaps comedian Jack Haley, but such intentions came to nothing; indeed, the notion of Haley or anyone else assuming so personalized a star vehicle seems hard to imagine. Nor did Warner Brothers ever produce a film version of the show, as originally planned.[23]

In one of the few recent assessments of this show, Cantor biographer Herbert Goldman writes, "*Guys and Dolls* [1950] would be the show that *Banjo Eyes* might well, and should, have been. Cantor likewise would have fared much better had his songs been tailored to the character of Trowbridge; what he got were mediocre Eddie Cantor numbers." At the same time, the emphasis on spectacle, not to mention the interpolation of old Cantor favorites, left little room for songs that might limn character or advance the story, with most of the major characters—including Patsy, Frankie, Ginger, and, but for a brief moment, Sally—given nothing to sing whatsoever. For all this, recent commentators like Goldman and Ethan Mordden have painted a bleaker account of the show's history than warranted. In 1961, producer Lewis even wrote a letter to *Variety*, bristling that the current reviews of *Let It Ride!*, another musicalization of *Three Men on a Horse*, should refer to *Banjo Eyes* as a failure, writing that, but for Cantor's departure, the production "was most certain to continue its successful run indefinitely."[24]

Eddie Cantor recorded "We're Having a Baby" with June Clyde in 1942 during the run of the show, and performed it again with Nora Martin in the 1944 film *Hollywood Canteen*; and Desi Arnaz sang that same number on a popular 1952 episode of the *I Love Lucy* television series, "Lucy Is Enceinte" ("enceinte," the French word for "pregnant," adopted in response to puritanical television codes), in which Lucy announces her pregnancy to Desi. But the protests of Jack Robbins notwithstanding, some of the songs by Duke and Latouche proved in the end more enduring, especially "A Nickel to My Name" and "Not a Care in the World." In 1941, Jan Savitt recorded both numbers with his Top Hatters, as did bandleader Bob Chester, with Bill Darnell on "A Nickel to My Name" and Betty Bradley on "Not a Care in the World," the latter song also recorded by Peggy Lee with the Benny Goodman Orchestra. In later years, stylish singers continued to perform both songs, with Bobby Short, Richard Rodney Bennett, Dawn Upshaw, and Klea Blackhurst all recording "Not a Care in the World," and Bennett in addition recording "A Nickel to My Name." (Those later performers who sang the verse to "Not a Care in the World" tended to rewrite the offending line, "My future is dark as Harlem by night.") A few other Duke and Latouche numbers from the show continued to appear as well. "I'll Take the City," performed by Arthur Siegel, turned up, for instance, on the second volume of *Ben Bagley's Vernon Duke Revisited*, and "Song Without Words," sung by Kaye Ballard, on the third volume of that same series. "I'll Take the City" also resurfaced in the revue *Taking a Chance on Love*, where Jerry Dixon performed the song in the biographical context of the young Latouche—an artist determined to make New York his own, not unlike the beleaguered suburban hero of *Banjo Eyes*.

10

The Lady Comes Across

In early 1941, quickly following the success of *Cabin in the Sky*, Latouche and Duke started work on another musical comedy, eventually called *The Lady Comes Across*, with the press reporting in March a planned opening in late June; but due to various delays, the show would not have its New York debut until January 9, 1942, about two weeks after *Banjo Eyes* premiered on Broadway. Latouche and Duke consequently found themselves working on both musicals at once, "a perilous procedure," conceded the composer in his memoirs, "and we should have known better; but the producers of the two shows were so persuasive that it became difficult not to give in." It would seem more accurate to say, given that Latouche and Duke had agreed to work on *The Lady Comes Across* long before *Banjo Eyes*, Albert Lewis, the producer of the latter show, needed to do most of the persuading. But the songwriters felt an indebtedness to Lewis for producing *Cabin in the Sky*, and Latouche particularly tended, in any event, to spread himself thin.[1]

The Lady Comes Across had an unusual genesis. On December 30, 1940, a show called *She Had to Say Yes* (which apparently had nothing to do with the 1933 Loretta Young film of the same name) opened on the road in Philadelphia to poor reviews and expired some two weeks later at a whopping loss estimated at about $120,000. The show's producer and lead, the British operetta singer Dennis King, sold the expensive Stewart Chaney sets and costumes to George Hale, a prominent dance director recently turned producer, with the idea that King and Hale would create an entirely new musical around the designs of the old show, "a rather novel notion," as Duke observed. Dumping the old score by composer Sammy Fain and lyricist Al Dubin as well as the book by Bob Henley and Richard Pinkham, Hale by late February had recruited for this purpose not only Duke and Latouche, but choreographer George Balanchine and bookwriter Fred Thompson, a British-born playwright who had written successful musicals for Broadway in the 1920s and the West End in the 1930s. As the year progressed, and as Dennis King withdrew from the venture, the press further announced one co-writer after another: first Guy Bolton, Thompson's partner of long standing, followed by Arthur Sheekman, George Marion Jr., and finally by June the brilliant satirist Dawn Powell, who remained with the show—variously called "Dreams Come True," "Listen, Lady!" "Nice Dreaming," and finally "The Lady Comes Across"—virtually to its ill-fated end, and who became a close friend of Latouche in the process.[2]

Born in Mount Gilead, Ohio, Dawn Powell (1896–1965) graduated from Lake Erie College and in 1918 made her way to New York, where she pursued a writing career and married a poet and critic with whom she had a disabled son eventually needing institutional care. A prolific author more critically than financially successful, Powell produced over time essays, short stories, plays, and especially novels, taking her native Ohio and her adopted New York as her principal milieux. Her sharp and mordant wit led some to regard her as the Dorothy Parker of Greenwich Village, with Powell holding forth at the Hotel Lafayette as Parker did at the Algonquin Hotel. But her good friend, critic Edmund Wilson, discerned a more telling resemblance to the "high social comedy" of such British novelists as Anthony Powell, Evelyn Waugh, and Muriel Spark, writing, "Miss Powell's books are more than merely funny; they are full of psychological insights that are at once sympathetic and cynical, and they have episodes that are rather macabre, which seem to hint at something close to embitterment." For his part, Gore Vidal—who met her through Latouche—thought her comparable to such outstanding American contemporaries as John Dos Passos, F. Scott Fitzgerald, and Ernest Hemingway as well as to the French master Honoré de Balzac.[3]

Given that Powell never had worked on a musical comedy before, her appointment as co-author seems somewhat surprising; but she had written satirical sketches for the ribald nightclub entertainer Dwight Fiske, as producer Hale presumably knew, and her dialogue in general crackled with the kind of sassy, irreverent wit one could imagine brightening a musical comedy. From her perspective, with her limited income and the expense of caring for her son, Powell certainly could use the money—a windfall, should the show prove a success. And she would be joining a distinguished creative team.

Meanwhile, casting proved especially uncertain, with a string of actors mentioned as potential leads, including for a while Dennis King himself. But by August, Hale had arranged for the celebrated British singer-dancer Jessie Matthews to star in the show, assisted in this matter by film producer Charles R. Rogers, who hoped to showcase her subsequently in Hollywood movies. Sometimes thought of as a British Marilyn Miller or Ginger Rogers, although arguably more like Eleanor Powell, Matthews had achieved stardom on the transatlantic stage in the 1920s and then in British cinema in the 1930s. By this point, however, she had not appeared in a stage musical for some ten years, so that *The Lady Comes Across* represented an undertaking somewhat parallel to *Banjo Eyes*, which marked a similar although ultimately far more successful comeback for Eddie Cantor.

When Matthews arrived in America in early September, the show still lacked a lead comedian, although the press mentioned, among others, Bobby Clark and Jack Haley as possible candidates. In early October, Hale finally secured the services of Ray Bolger, the gangling song-and-dance man who had played The Scarecrow in the

1939 film *The Wizard of Oz*; but dissatisfied with the script, Bolger resigned by the end of the month, shortly after rehearsals had begun. Alluding to such casting vagaries in a sardonic postmortem of the show, "The Birth of Comedy," published in the *Times* the day after *The Lady Comes Across* closed, Dawn Powell recalled, "Wires hum with big name possibilities.... Producer instructs writers to do new version to fit each hum of the wires. Composer and lyricist rush changes to fit changing line-up.... Except for Miss Matthews, no name ever mentioned before appears at rehearsal." In the end, the musical featured, along with Matthews (replaced before the Broadway opening by Evelyn Wyckoff), comics Joe E. Lewis and Mischa Auer; the nightclub dance team of Gower Champion—at the start of his memorable stage career—and Jeanne Tyler; the Martins (a vocal quartet consisting of songwriters Hugh Martin and Ralph Blane, along with sisters Phyllis and Jo Jean Rogers); singer Wynn Murray, described by Duke as "siren-voiced, callipygous"; actors Stiano Braggiotti and Ruth Weston; and ballet dancers Eugenia Delarova, Marc Platt, and Lubov Rostova. Hale further hired actor-director Romney Brent as stage director, and Morrie Ryskind—who had co-authored with George S. Kaufman the books to Gershwin's three so-called political operettas, and had provided scripts as well for the Marx Brothers—as general production supervisor (which involved working on the book with Thompson and Powell). Domenico Savino supervised the orchestrations and arrangements, Jacques Rabiroff served as musical director, and the Stewart Chaney sets and costumes made their return appearance.[4]

As early as September, Powell expressed some repugnance with what she called the "incredible cheapness of [the] musical comedy field," writing in her diary, "Cruel exploitation of egos. All men engaged in it mercilessly make use of their advantage, call in girls for auditions—or boys, if that's their taste." However, all this provided at least grist for Powell's sharply satirical pen. After the show's New Haven world premiere, but shortly before it opened in Boston, she published a humorous article, for instance, delineating two ways in which writing a novel differed from writing a musical comedy book. First, whereas a novelist produces something on paper, a bookwriter writes out loud, marching and pacing. "Morrie Ryskind, for instance," she explained, "who is supervising the production of 'The Lady Comes Across' is pacing Fred Thompson and me. By the time we've marched out nine or ten acts, all of us going off in different directions and coming together in the middle, the act looks like a Boy Scout flag drill." She granted that up to a certain point, one could in fact set down material, but only until the rehearsal period:

> Fred Thompson wrote the original idea a few hundred times by himself first, then I joined in and we wrote it a few more dozen times, and all this was quite all right, even encouraged, as it kept us from making the wrong sort of social contacts (a mutual hobby). But once the cast was assembled we were on the march. We could whisper lines, shout lines, signal them, tap them out in Morse, but never must we offend with great packs of written matter.

The other difference, she averred, lay in the fact that the novelist had to shoulder either praise or censure on his or her own, whereas the musical comedy bookwriter could dispense blame in the event of a flop or take full credit should the show succeed:

> Already I see my collaborator, Fred Thompson, fading into the distance and as I look back on it I did everything myself, even to sharpening his pencils. The work of Morrie Ryskind, who tramped over the book barefoot, fades away too, and as I look on it in the big way, it seems to me I hummed those melodies of Vernon Duke all myself and I spelled out those lyrics to Johnny La Touche one summer afternoon as I dandled him on my arthritic knee. That is, I did all this if the show goes over.[5]

Within weeks of the show's closing in January 1942, Powell similarly parodied her experience working on the musical by way of a short story, "Audition," about two bookwriters who, holed up in a hotel suite, await the producer of some Broadway musical. Near the tale's conclusion, as they interview a rather pathetic young actress, one of the writers tells her about the role in question:

> Your biggest comedy scene is laid in a lighthouse. You're stranded there with a Mae West character, a Bert Lahr character, a Betty Hutton, and say, a straight man, Tony Martin type. They start some crossfire, you give it right back, it's a howl; the West character gives you a sock line, voom and out. Lahr has a typical Lahr line, voom and out. Then three fast cracks, one right after the other, from Hutton, voom and out. Your juvenile looks at you—audience still howling, see—he gives you one terrific line, voom, and blackout. What do you say?

To which the actress, Miss Mink, replies, "It sounds cute all right. Would I have to wear tights?" (The mocking mention of the lighthouse setting and, earlier in the story, a "lighthouse scene," no doubt drew on Powell's having to write a script around built sets.) In a 2001 interview about the musical, Zachary Solov, one of the production's young ballet dancers cast by Balanchine, expressed comparable disdain: "At that time, because I was so artistic (ha, ha, ha), I thought those sketch writers were just the most vulgar, horrible guys in the whole world. One time in New Haven, I happened to be in a room that was on the same floor as them. They would come flying out of their rooms stark naked and fly into the other guy's room and scream the new joke that came to them and fly back all naked."[6]

Perhaps because of extensive revisions undertaken under Ryskind's supervision, and Hale's decision, after the Boston opening, to have director Edgar MacGregor and choreographer Charles Walters help restage the show, more than the usual confusion reigned throughout the tryout period. In her memoirs, Jessie Matthews recalled,

> Most musicals have to be beaten into shape. *The Lady Comes Across* was very nearly battered to death. The script had to be changed and they'd left it a little late.... In the original script I was cast as an English girl who gets mixed up in a spy ring. Each morning new pages of dialogue were handed to the cast, and we looked to see who was left in and who'd been cut out.... I was still a spy-catcher, I still had to master the odd sentence in French, German and Swedish, but I hadn't a clue whom I was supposed to catch.
>
> Organization was non-existent. The book of the play was hacked to pieces and none of the joins met... it was unbelievable chaos. New dialogue and new lyrics for the songs arrived monotonously every morning. I used to pin the lyrics on my muff, my handbag, anywhere for quick study, for there was no time to learn them.[7]

The Lady Comes Across debuted at the Shubert Theatre in New Haven on December 11, 1941, the day America declared war on Germany and Italy, and then played Boston's Shubert Theatre for ten days beginning December 17 before moving to New York. Although the script seems to have disappeared, the broad outline of the story can be gleaned from newspaper reviews, a situation, however, complicated by the fact that the critics themselves hardly understood the action. Jill Charters (Jessie Matthews), a British actress looking for work in the States, applies for a position with the FBI, mistaking the acronym for a radio station, and the bureau hires her to infiltrate a ring of fifth columnists who operate out of an exclusive dress shop under the sway of the villainous Alberto Borel/Zorel (Stiano Braggiotti). Because of her clairvoyant abilities, Jill proves a crackerjack spy, with her allies in counterespionage including her love object, federal agent Tony Patterson (Ronald Graham), along with Otis Kibber (Joe E. Lewis) and perfume salesman Ernie Bustard (Mischa Auer). The story romantically paired not only Jill and Tony, but Otis and the wealthy dowager Mrs. Riverdale (Ruth Weston), and Ernie and the brassy Babs Appleway (Wynn Murray). At the conclusion, evidence incriminating the fifth columnists turns up in Mrs. Riverdale's girdle. One review thought the play a "satire on the F.B.I.," and although this description proved singular, the show seems to have been largely mocking in tone, with Balanchine's ballets apparently veering toward the farcical and dreamlike. Jessie Matthews recognized in particular some resemblance to *Lady in the Dark*, and it seems likely that, given the titles and stars of both shows, the creators of *The Lady Comes Across* to some extent had in mind, perhaps parodistically, the Kurt Weill musical, which had opened in January 1941.[8]

Several Boston critics thought the show's premise had potential, but nearly all agreed that the story turned painfully dull as the musical progressed, and that in the end the plot merely served as scaffolding for some dances and songs. Wilella Waldorf

(*New York Post*) even described the piece, upon its Broadway debut, as "actually more revue than musical comedy, if you care to go in for fine distinctions.... It is very loosely flung together in breathless style, giving the impression at times that it might be operating on the principle that the first people to reach the stage got first crack at the songs and dances." One of the show's leading dancers, Marc Platt, relatedly recognized in the work an approach that he believed had seen its day:

> Georgie Hale was from the old school, twenty-five, thirty years before, when you'd get a lot of beautiful showgirls and some acrobats and some magicians and they'd slap together a few little scenes and somebody would write the songs, and the whole show was put on and concocted in a way that nothing really very much led into anything else, supposedly organized by the seams in the songs. It was a very loosely put-together show. That's the way Georgie Hale worked.... This was at the end of that period, and they [viewers] were looking for changes.[9]

Whatever the script's limitations, Duke and Latouche supplied an ample and quite attractive score, fleshed out further by some material by the team of Danny Shapiro, Jerry Seelen, and Lester Lee (or just Shapiro and Lee) that Joe E. Lewis had brought with him. The line-up of musical numbers as presented on Broadway (all by Duke and Latouche unless otherwise indicated) follows: "Three Rousing Cheers" (for Souvenir Hunters, Autograph Seekers, Reporters, and others); "Feeling Lucky Today" (for Jill and Otis); "Modes in Manhattan" (for Models and Photographers); "You Took Me by Surprise" (for Jill, Tony, and the Martins); "Hit the Ramp" (for Babs, Ernie, and the ensemble); "February" (for Otis, music and lyrics by Danny Shapiro, Jerry Seelen, and Lester Lee); "Eenie Meenie Minee Mo" (for Ernie, Babs, Otis, and Mrs. Riverdale); "Tango" (for Ernie, Ballerina Comique, and the ensemble); "Lady" (for Tony, Models, Campbell and Kay [Gower Champion and Jeanne Tyler], and the ensemble); "The Queen of the Opera" (for Mrs. Riverdale); "Coney Island Ballet" (for Ballerinas, Premiere Danseur, and the ensemble); "This Is Where I Came In" (for Babs, and Campbell and Kay): "You Can't Get the Merchandise" (for Otis, music and lyrics by Shapiro and Lee); "Summer Is a Comin' In" (for the Martins and the ensemble); and "Daybreak" (for Jill and The Phantom Lover).

Miller Music published four of these songs—"You Took Me by Surprise," "Lady," "This Is Where I Came In," and "Summer Is a Comin' In" (as "Summer Is A-Comin' In")—as well as one number cut on the road, "I'd Like to Talk about the Weather" (for Jill, Tony, and Boys). Another excised song, "What Every Young Man Should Know" (for Otis, and apparently composed originally for *Banjo Eyes*), survives in manuscript, as do lead sheets for "Feeling Lucky Today" and "Modes in Manhattan," and the lyric for yet another cut song, "Upsala" (for Otis, Jill, Ernie, and the ensemble, its music reportedly "in the manner of a Tyrolean landler"). Otherwise, the score, like the script, seems lost, although "The Queen of the Opera" (for Mrs.

Riverdale) might well have been a rehearsal for Latouche's hilarious "A Nail in the Horseshoe" composed some ten years later with John Strauss.[10]

Aside from the breezy duet "Feeling Lucky Today," the sendup of models "Modes of Manhattan," and the ersatz Swedish college anthem "Upsala," the surviving numbers concern romantic love in one way or another—usually seen as problematic or irresistible or both. In "You Took Me by Surprise," the lovers, once "confident" and "wise," find themselves "out on a limb"; in "Summer Is A-Comin' In," a parody of the medieval round "Sumer is icumin in," all nature yields to love when summer arrives; in "This Is Where I Came In," Bab finds that her cavorting has made "a dog a' me / I'm going back to monogamy"; and in "What Every Young Man Should Know," Otis advises steering clear of sex altogether:

> When you are on the town with pretty sweeties,
> If you are wise, be deaf to their entreaties
> Go home by ten, and eat a bowl of Wheaties
> That's what ev'ry young man should know.

How these songs fit the larger narrative remains unclear, but the theme of sexual temptation and resistance that largely unites them apparently served a story, as suggested by reviews, in which the women needed to win over reluctant men.

For all its romantic preoccupations, the world war hangs, albeit lightly, over the score as it does the plot. In the best-known number from the show, "You Took Me by Surprise," the entire lyric ingeniously uses military imagery to depict love's onslaught, with a verse that begins, unusually enough for a love song,

> Looking at hist'ry since wars began
> One lesson we all have learned
> Countries fell ev'rywhere
> When they neglected to prepare.

And in "I'd Like to Talk about the Weather," the singer, unable to think of anything but his beloved, states, in reference to the prominent union leader John L. Lewis (not to be confused with the show's co-star, Joe E. Lewis), "I should discourse on John L. Lewis / Or praise the U. S. of A."

If lacking the charm of *Cabin in the Sky* or the liveliness of *Banjo Eyes*, the score nonetheless has an elegance and flair of its own, so much so that even though the show proved a dismal flop, some of the songs continued to be heard in clubs and on recordings. Duke, who credited the song "Lady" with having "a fine lyric," thought at least three of the numbers ("You Took Me by Surprise," "Summer Is A-Comin' In," and "This Is Where I Came In") "equal to anything in *Cabin*." Subtleties abound, not only in the many striking lyrics, but in those pungent melodies that led a number of critics to complain about the score's lack of hummability. "This Is Where

I Came In"—with its suave syncopated, chromatic melody matched to an opening stanza that reads, "I'm doing the town up brown like before / I find it such a bore / This is where I came in / Ho-hum"—epitomizes the score's swank sophistication.

For its part, "Summer Is A-Comin' In," which in 1955 Duke still considered "probably Latouche's top achievement to date," featured archaic English modernized to comic effect, a contrivance also exploited by Ira Gershwin, Lorenz Hart, and Cole Porter, although Latouche went his distinctive way with a series of wacky and bawdy couplets that closely match the meter of the original Middle English text: "Balmy breezes smell like gin, / Why the heck don't you give in," "Each Libido goeth pop! Margret [*sic*] Sanger [the birth control activist] closeth shop," "Lovebirds snuggleth cosily, / Strippeth Gypsy Rosie Lee," and so on. Duke heightened the spoof by quoting the British folk tune "Country Gardens" at the reference to clubwomen planting forsythia and hydrangea, much as he had quoted "Yankee Doodle" in "Yankee Doodle Polka," and Mendelssohn's Wedding March in "Don't Let It Happen Again" (*Banjo Eyes*). Years later, Latouche apparently wrote some additional text for Charlotte Rae's adoption of the number in the mid-1950s, including the lines, "In every dark and stagnant pool / the primitive amoeba, / Divides and says 'Ich liebe.' "[11]

The Lady Comes Across had an overlong New Haven premiere plagued with glitches that lasted until 1:30 a.m. or so, but then a smoother Boston opening. Given all the havoc behind the scenes, these tryout debuts received surprisingly good reviews, with the critics especially praising Joe E. Lewis, but also admiring much else, including Latouche's "satirical" lyrics. In perhaps the best review the show would receive anywhere, the *Boston Globe* described the entertainment as "joyous and irresponsible, gilt-edged and sophisticated." But most found the book haphazard and the score in need of better voices. Nor did Matthews make much of an impression beyond the fact that she seemed nervous, an obvious handicap for a star vehicle.

Indeed, Matthews, who had a history of nervous breakdowns, was struggling to maintain her mental equilibrium. The pressure of returning to the stage after so long an absence and of carrying a show in such constant turmoil, not to mention the trauma she had suffered as the result of German bombing raids back home and the anxiety of being separated from her family, took its toll. Complicating matters, the show's plot apparently stoked her predisposition toward hallucinatory paranoia and she began to imagine herself pursued by pro-German spies. A nervous wreck by the time the run ended in Boston, she collapsed and entered Columbia-Presbyterian Medical Center, thus dashing any hopes of a rejuvenated American career.[12]

Management postponed a planned December 30 Broadway debut and hastily cast as Matthews's replacement Evelyn Wyckoff, a young unknown then appearing in a minor role in Weill's *Lady in the Dark*. Granted permission to leave the Weill show, Wyckoff had but a week to prepare the part. The creative team now had to make further changes, including making the heroine American rather than British. The show also eliminated one of her numbers, "I'd Like to Talk about the Weather," and in general curtailed those dance routines created specifically for Matthews.

Meanwhile, Joe E. Lewis substituted a topical wartime number by Shapiro and Lee, "You Can't Get the Merchandise," for the Duke and Latouche song, "What Every Young Man Should Know."

The show opened at the Forty-Fourth Street Theatre on January 9. In attendance for the premiere, Cole Porter went backstage after the performance to congratulate Duke and Latouche on their score. But although the critics once again lauded Joe E. Lewis, and agreed that Wyckoff performed commendably under the circumstances, they generally found the show mediocre at best. Whereas *Banjo Eyes* had received, according to the *Billboard*'s reading of the major dailies, a positive endorsement of 100 percent, *The Lady Comes Across* managed an approval rating of only 11 percent.[13]

Neither the music nor the lyrics seemed to make an impression one way or the other—as in Boston, the Shapiro, Seelen, and Lee number "(Poor Little) February," sung by Lewis, proved by far the hit song of the evening—although Wolcott Gibbs, in his review for the *New Yorker*, concluded his review with a swipe at Latouche's reference to Ernest Dowson's famed poem "Non Sum Qualis Eram Bonae Sub Regno Cynarae" (1891), in the verse to "This Is Where I Came In," writing, "There was nobody in the cast called Cynara. It was just one of those literary allusions." The lyric in question, misquoted by Gibbs, actually reads,

> I once was prone to carousin'
> Till I fell for you, pal
> Now the gutter has got me again,
> But just like old Ernest Dowson
> And his Cynara [pronounced SIN-a-ra] gal
> In my funny fashion I've been faithful.

By conjuring Dowson's celebrated poem inspired by Horace, and its refrain, "I have been faithful to thee, Cynara! in my fashion," Latouche intended no mere show of erudition, but rather, in a song about the conflict between lust and fidelity, aimed to establish humorous contact with a literary tradition that dated back, as mentioned, to Horace. "We should not be frightened by literate pieces," Latouche wrote Duke after the show folded, "purely because of Mr. Woolcott [*sic*] Gibbs' crack about literacy—I suppose you know he wrote me a three-page apology for his review, blaming the mistake he made on his broken arm. I was extremely amused."[14]

On January 10, after the show's third performance, Hale informed the cast that the show would close immediately. The players "wanted to play ball," Hale told the *Times*, but he told them that, given the poor reviews, "there was no sense in going on." That left a cast and crew of about 125 unemployed, and a financial loss estimated by Hale at about $80,000. "You'd think that, after all his perseverance, Mr. Hale would have persevered just a little longer in an effort to beat the notices," wondered the *Billboard*, "particularly since the cast reportedly offered to co-operate in keeping the show going. By that time, tho, maybe the scenery was getting on his nerves." Years later, Gower Champion's dance partner in the production, Jeanne Tyler, claimed that *The Lady Comes Across* would have been a hit had Matthews stayed with the show.[15]

Duke and Balanchine drowned their sorrows at a Russian nightclub with "a bevy of dancing beauties" and then escaped to Florida. Remaining in New York, Latouche wrote to his friend Charlotte Dieterle that despite the show's failure—which he attributed "chiefly to an inept and old-fashioned book by that Aristophanes of your glittering city of Hollywood, Mr. Morris Ryskin [*sic*]"—he enjoyed doing the show. And in a letter to Duke, he also looked ahead to future projects with the composer, but cautioned, "We certainly must be very careful about the level of shows we do from now on.... But don't be afraid of giving them too much distinction, if we reverse our technique and provide over-simple scores to good books, we will run into the same difficulties. However, I think it is impossible for either one of us to be corny, without trying awfully hard."[16]

Meanwhile, Latouche and Dawn Powell continued to see each other with some regularity, as evidenced primarily by the latter's diaries. On January 22, 1942, for instance, Latouche took Powell and director Robert Lewis to the 1-2-3 Club, a fashionable new restaurant-lounge at 123 East 54th Street, where the lyricist "table-hopped, chatting with everyone," leaving Powell "shocked at the rather naïve opportunism of this very charming boy." And in April 1945, Powell wrote Edmund Wilson that she visited Latouche at home, where she found him "sick in bed with strep" reading Wilhelm Reich's recently published *The Function of the Orgasm* (a book that would help spur the sexual liberation movement in postwar America). She further kept tabs on Latouche's work, finding *Ballet Ballads*, as performed in the lyricist's apartment in 1946, "very stunning," and *The Golden Apple*, after a similar playthrough at his home in 1953, "a very thrilling experience." Attending the premiere of *The Golden Apple* at the Phoenix Theatre in 1954, she again commended the piece as "thoroughly fresh and delightful."[17]

Powell grew quite admiring of this "extraordinary young man" himself. On returning home from a visit to Ohio in late 1942, she reflected, "Away in [the] provinces, I missed Latouche, since he impersonates New York itself—alive, eager for every phase of the city, foreign to, but eagerly interested in, the provinces. This is what often makes love—the absent one is missed not for what he or she is but the life they represent." At the same time, she cast a sharp eye on his eccentricities and foibles, as she typically did with those she most loved. "Deporting himself like a celebrity," she wrote in 1953, "and actually being treated as one—not really his fault he has so little time to write, everyone surrounds him, strangers sit at his table." Not unlike Paul Bowles, she also found that he simply drained her, impeding her own work. In a diary entry from September 1942, she wrote,

> Latouche came out Saturday and Sunday and left me exhausted. He is so multi-gifted that he seems to leave people as worn as if they'd been to a

> circus, and while he shoots sparks in all directions, in the end it is the others who are depleted and he is renourished.... It is unconsciously deliberate on his part. He wants people not-to-do, just as he doesn't-do. He likes their doing well—no envy there—but it is the actual *doing* he minds.

Even a letter from "the naughty fellow" read later in the year left her unable to do any work. "Fond as I am of him," she wrote in 1944, "he drags the last drop of blood out of you."[18]

On his side, Latouche seemed to take unmitigated pleasure in the relationship. While stationed in California in 1944, he received one letter from Powell "so brilliant that I cultivated a reputation for insanity by rolling with laughter on my bunk, at sporadic intervals." He plainly strove to amuse her in turn, perhaps more so than with any other friend; for although he often indulged in inspired nonsense in his correspondence with, among others, Virgil Thomson, Eleonora Mendelssohn, and Ruth Yorck, none of his relatively few extant letters seem as manic and fanciful as those to Powell, addressed variously as "Porkchop," "Crush," and so on. A letter from the Belgian Congo dated December 23, 1942, and addressed, "Dere Santa," opens, for example,

> i fink I will dwop oo a line to tell oo what I dam well better det in my stokin dis Kwismas, or oo will dit my ickle copper-plated toe up oo wed flannel behind. One I want a sled wif Ickle Snort on it in dold leaf, and two a demountable girl just like the one dat mawwied dere old Dad and fwee dont twack up my nice clean floor wid oo's fuckin reindeers!
>
> Sweet cuz, it is sad to be spending Xmas in the tropics: the only streak of lavender-and-old-Woollcott that I have left is the small-town reverence for holidays...I salute on July 4th, pray on Easter, discover Brooklyn on Columbus day, dance marxist dances around the maypole on May first, get pregnant on Mother's Day, lay wreaths on Memorial day, lay wraiths on Halloween, get laid on St. Fallopian's Day; even Maundy Thursday finds me fumbling through my GREATcoat for a groat to give the fellows. So imagine being trapped in hibiscus and white sunshine, when all I want is to see a spavined old Santa up to his withers in dirty snow tinkling for pennys.

The letter continues, densely typed, with barely an indentation, in this vein for pages (little wonder Powell found herself worn out by such displays). In a lengthy postscript dated January 12, Latouche further included two off-color limericks composed by Powell's friend, writer Emily Hahn, that illustrate his delight in playing the "naughty boy" to Powell's "Mums," with one of the ditties as follows:

> I'm sorry, Mrs. Nettleby-Gore!
> I just can't go ON anymore!

I'm covered with sweat
And you haven't come *yet*
And the clock says it's quarter past four!

Powell's papers relatedly preserve a dadaistic three-page poem-story by Latouche, "Major Minor: An Incident and a Novel," in thirteen minuscule parts; reads one segment, "No nein na ne nada sorry so sorry indeed." Latouche plainly could share with Powell a certain side of his creative personality as with few others.[19]

After Latouche died, Powell, in addition to ruminating on his life and work privately, wrote to a friend a letter that also touched on *The Lady Comes Across* in a way that brought the story of their relationship full circle:

> Latouche's death was a shock and seemed a cruel incredible trick to keep mediocrity safe for mortality. He will make a tough, indestructible little ghost, though. How time softens minds! For instance for years none of us (he or I or anyone connected) ever mentioned our embarrassing connection with that monster musical *Lady Comes Across*. Certainly never Latouche, me, Gower Champion, Vernon Duke, Mischa Auer, Joe E. Lewis, et cetera. Then in Touche's obit the credit crept in. And today the terrible little producer of it, Georgie Hale, died, and after tyrannizing over all of us, only got ¼ obituary space that Latouche did, but mentioning *Lady Comes Across* as part of his triumphs. Then I have been called to Theatre Guild TV department lately to discuss adapting short stories from *Sunday, Monday and Always* for the Steel Hour, and the director says, "Our lawyer is most insistent that we get you for this as he says you and Latouche did such wonderful work on some musical!" The lawyer was also Georgie Hale's at the time and never protected us from the mess or insults at the time.... The gist of this is that your successes are forgotten but your failures become successes, so why worry?[20]

After a whirlwind of activity—preparing no fewer than three shows with Vernon Duke in little over a year—Latouche's career in the theater slowed as he helped research a film documentary in the Congo and then served in the military. Not until *Rhapsody* opened in the fall of 1944 would he have another musical to his credit.

Meanwhile, he involved himself with several projects, few of which came to fruition. In August 1941, the *Times* reported, for instance, that he had signed with RKO Radio to write a "sequence" in "'chant' form" for director William Dieterle's forthcoming *Syncopation* (1942), a feature film exploring the development of jazz through the lives of jazz musicians. Latouche apparently had become friendly with Dieterle and his actress-writer wife, Charlotte, in the course of 1941, very possibly through Eleonora Mendelssohn. An illustrious filmmaker admired by Brecht, Dieterle (1893–1972) had left his native Germany in 1930 for Hollywood, where he and Charlotte (1896–1968) established themselves as leading progressive intellectuals in the community. "May I say again how thankful I am that there is someone like you in Hollywood," Latouche wrote Dieterle in late 1941. At about this same time, Latouche published a highly laudatory review of Dieterle's 1941 film *All That Money Can Buy* (later retitled *The Devil and Daniel Webster*) in *Modern Music*, although he apologized for the notice in a letter to Charlotte: "It [the review] is badly written for which I am sorry, because I had to do it in fifteen minutes before catching a train to Boston, but the spirit is there. As a matter of fact, I got into a quarrel with the magazine, because I said that Bernard Herrmann's score was magnificent. The lady-editor [Minna Lederman] said, 'In an intellectual magazine nothing is *magnificent*, neither Bach, Beethoven, nor God.'" But although Latouche wrote something entitled "American Poem" (apparently lost) for Dieterle, that effort never made its way into *Syncopation*.[21]

Some Bertolt Brecht–related projects date from these years as well. Indeed, the Dieterles—along with, presumably, another of Latouche's German friends, writer Ruth Yorck—seem to have played some part in bringing Latouche and Brecht together after the latter's arrival in America in 1941, although one source reports that Latouche had met Brecht during the playwright's previous trip to New York in 1935. In any case, Latouche appreciatively wrote William Dieterle in the fall of 1941, "Meeting Brecht was a great experience for me, after admiring him so much for years." About this same time, Latouche translated and published two poems by Brecht (actually parts two and three of the poet's "To Posterity") in collaboration with Yorck (who used her more familiar German name, Ruth Landshoff) in the October 1941 issue of *Decision* magazine, a short-lived journal based in New York and edited by Klaus Mann. The esteemed director Erwin Piscator further proposed to Brecht that Latouche, who hoped to translate other poems and plays by the German writer, adapt *The Good Person of Szechwan* for the New York stage, a suggestion, however, that came to naught. Latouche in particular dreamed of translating *The Threepenny Opera*, and during this period often would try out his versions of some of the play's songs for friends, as painter Jimmy Ernst reminisced:

> Some of these floating social evenings seemed to have as their tradition John LaTouche's endless quest to come up with adequate translations of Bertolt Brecht's German lyrics for Kurt Weill's *Threepenny Opera*. Sometimes ignored, but never for long, Touche, impish in size and face, would plunk himself down at the piano and play Weill's music, trying to find fitting counterparts to Brecht's sardonic German original. All of this was delivered in a falsetto frog-voice that certainly caught the sarcastic flavor of the songs but hardly ever came close to the bite of the words. At the end of his experimentation he invariably sat back, compressing his lips into a thin-lined smile that reached from ear to ear, and waited for applause and approbation. Instead he'd become the object of critical, good-natured banter.

Years later, Kenward Elmslie remembered that Brecht, as not only a brilliant poet who wrote for the musical theater, but an outstanding embodiment of Weimar culture, greatly attracted Latouche, who reportedly offered some counsel to Marc Blitzstein on the latter's landmark translation of *The Threepenny Opera.*[22]

In the course of 1941, Latouche also explored the possibility of working with choreographer Ruth Page on a ballet. During these years, an interest in combining serious dance with the spoken or sung word took wing, a trend for which the work of Stravinsky, including *The Soldier's Tale* (1918) and *The Wedding* (1923), remained a benchmark, but one that also informed such varied works as Marc Blitzstein's *Cain* (1930, and a piece that Latouche thought sounded "exciting" after hearing about it from the composer in 1938), Weill's *The Seven Deadly Sins* (1933), David Diamond's *Tom* (1936), Jerome Moross's *Frankie and Johnny* (1938), and Hunter Johnson's *Letter to the World* (1940). Latouche already had participated in this development himself by way of another work by Moross, *Susanna and the Elders* (1940), a piece, yet to be discussed, that would form the cornerstone of one of the most notable exemplars of this entire movement, Moross and Latouche's *Ballet Ballads* (1948). Such fusions of ballet or modern dance with speech or song had precedents and parallels not only in much non-Western theater, as often noted, but in Broadway musicals as well. Indeed, in *The Lady Comes Across,* Gower Champion elicited critical attention for the integration of movement and speech in his dance routines, although in the case of ballet and modern dance, the physical demands made of the dancers typically precluded them from speaking or singing themselves.

Based in Chicago and supported by Thomas Fisher, her well-heeled attorney husband, Ruth Page (1899–1991), one of the era's most prominent choreographers, had pioneered just such fusions of movement and song, as in the forementioned *Frankie and Johnny* with Jerome Moross. At the recommendation of Virgil Thomson, she approached Latouche in early 1941 about lyricizing six jazzed-up arrangements of Chopin for a ballet she already had created, *Chopin in Our Time,* the words meant to be more spoken than sung. In late March, Page premiered such a ballet, but with one John McGee reciting his own lyrics against jazzy renditions of Chopin played at the piano by Owen Haynes. Latouche's lyricizations of Chopin would have to wait for the 1945 operetta *Polonaise,* although Page's program note for *Chopin in Our Time* seems worth noting in the context of that somewhat later work as well: "Only the hope of romance is left; only the dreams of a once normal world; Chopin in our time."[23]

By May, Page had come up with another suggestion: a ballet on biblical stories as told by the famed early-twentieth-century evangelist Billy Sunday, with music by her friend Weill and words by Latouche. Weill confided to Page a preference for working rather with writer Paul Green, with whom he had collaborated on the musical *Johnny Johnson* (1936); but with Green unavailable, the composer met with Latouche and reported favorably to Page, "He seems to be a nice guy, very busy with twenty different projects, but apparently quite versatile." Latouche, for his part, thought Weill "extremely charming and intelligent," and imagined that they would work "extremely well" together, further telling Page, "I am using a new (I hope) development of the ballet-opera technique and God help us all if it does not come off right."[24]

Weill soon enough developed doubts about Latouche. "Every time I meet him he has a terrible hangover," he wrote Page in late June, "but he says that is purely accidental. Of course, he hasn't written a line yet, but his ideas, although rather vague, sound very nice and I think if we ever get him to write it, he'd probably do a good job." By mid-August, Weill simply concluded that he "couldn't work with anybody so dishonest and unreliable as a worker and as a person," explaining to Page that he had discovered, through some undisclosed source, that contrary to Latouche's assertions, the lyricist had some sort of exclusive arrangement with Vernon Duke, "who probably thinks I'm trying to snatch his precious little lyric-writer. So let's forget about that little louse."

Page and Latouche nonetheless continued to correspond about the ballet, which the lyricist described as "a semi-longish, rather important work, I think, at least I hope," although in December, Latouche heard from Weill that neither he nor Page had any interest in working with him. "I was rather startled at his [Weill's] brusque tone…," he wrote Page. "Since I had no exact contract with you, only a great desire to do something as exciting as this; and also to work with you and with Weill, whom I think the best contemporary composer—I was rather set back at being made to appear guilty just because I had badly planned my working life."[25]

In fact, Page had not shut the door on a possible collaboration with Latouche, and over the summer of 1944, with some encouragement from Thomas Fisher, Latouche approached Jerome Moross about possibly writing a triple bill for the choreographer, with one act devoted to the Billy Sunday idea, a proposal that quickly inspired, from Moross, the notion of a Red Riding Hood ballet, thus setting into motion a concept that would evolve into Moross and Latouche's *Ballet Ballads* (which ultimately involved other choreographers). Meanwhile, Page held out some hopes for a Billy Sunday ballet with Weill and Latouche as late as 1946; but with the two of them preoccupied with Broadway shows, she created *Billy Sunday* the following year with composer Remi Gassmann instead.[26]

Another apparently unrealized Latouche project from this period, *Nutcracker Jive*, recalled Page's Chopin ballet in its basic premise of jazzing the music of a classical composer, although here Tchaikovsky rather than Chopin. According to press items in the fall of 1943, this planned Broadway Christmastime extravaganza, the presumed brainchild of the marionette master Frank Paris (the creator of the Howdy Doody puppet), was to feature 145 puppets each standing about two feet high, with dialogue co-written by Paris and Fred Keating, Tchaikovsky's music arranged by Herbert Kingsley, and lyrics by Latouche. Intended for adults, the show was to include a marionette striptease to the "Dance of the Sugar Plum Fairy," which presumably would have resembled Paris's filmed puppet fan dance to Debussy's "Clair de lune." Whether Latouche contributed anything to the *Nutcracker Jive* submitted for copyright by Paris in April 1944 seems unlikely, given his military service in the fall of 1943 and winter of 1944.[27]

During this same period, Latouche also entertained, according to press reports, continued collaborations with Vernon Duke, including musical adaptations of Aristophanes' *The Clouds* (with sets by Salvador Dalí), S. N. Behrman's *Serena Blandish,* Edwin Justus Mayer's *The Firebrand,* Ferenc Molnár's *The Good Fairy,* and Michael Sadleir's *Fanny by Gaslight,* not to mention a Barnum & Bailey circus show with dances by Balanchine; but none of these projects saw the light of day either. Sometime in 1944, Latouche proposed to producers Paul Feigay and Oliver Smith that he collaborate on *The Firebrand* not with Duke but rather with Leonard Bernstein, at least according to Dawn Powell, who wryly reported the producers' reaction as follows: "They liked Lenny; Lenny had talent; but he had no name. This was big stuff, see—no amateurs. Latouche protested—Lenny would be all right; why not go over to Lenny's place and listen to some songs he had written—really good. Well, sure, they'd let Lenny have a try but they had too big a production in mind for little Lenny." As it happened, Feigay and Smith launched Bernstein's musical *On the Town* with lyricists Betty Comden and Adolph Green later in the year, and Max Gordon, a *Firebrand* musical—*The Firebrand of Florence*—with music by Kurt Weill and lyrics by Ira Gershwin the year after that.[28]

The closest Latouche came to working again with Vernon Duke on another musical occurred in the 1950s as the composer, along with the playwriting team of Jerome Lawrence and Robert E. Lee, sought to adapt Theodore Pratt's 1945 satirical novel about Hollywood, *Miss Dilly Says No,* for the musical stage as *Dilly*. Duke planned to write the lyrics in collaboration with Lawrence and Lee, but he wanted to use two of his trunk songs, one with a lyric by Latouche ("Time Passes By"), the other with a lyric co-written by Latouche and Theodore Fetter ("I'm About to Become a Lover"), and in discussing the matter with Latouche in the fall of 1953, persuaded him to join the team. However, after signing a contract in early November, Latouche walked away from the show, explaining to Duke, "I have the greatest fondness for you, and would like the show to be a success, which it can be. Lawrence and Lee are very clever (and also very nice people, which is a rare accompanyment [*sic*] to talent) and the lyrics of theirs I've heard are witty and beautifully constructed. Added to your own baroque tendencies lyrically, I think you have a combination that outweighs my own misty creative efforts.... Let's do a show from scratch soon!" Doubtful about Lawrence and Lee as lyricists, Duke pleaded with Latouche, "Johnny, we love you and we need you; need I say more?" But although Latouche came to an agreement with Duke with regard to the two trunk songs in question, and stayed a friendly consultant on the show, he maintained his ground, Duke's producer Gala Ebin explaining to the composer, "John actually was very sweet and apologetic about it all, and retains the friendliest feelings and good wishes for all of us and the project,—but the Muse has left him as far as *Dilly* is concerned, and that's that." The fact that the show (which never materialized) seemed destined to involve the work of so many lyricists, including Fetter, Duke, Lawrence, and Lee, seems to have been a major deterrent.[29]

Latouche's decision to forsake *Dilly*—as with his wrangling over the aborted Broadway revival of *Cabin in the Sky*—irked Duke, whose regal manner Latouche continued to mock by referring to him as the Duchess of Dishwater; but none of this seemed to affect Duke's essential fondness and admiration for his erstwhile collaborator, with whom he shared the stage for a final time in 1956 with *The Littlest Revue*, and for whom, in the wake of the lyricist's death, he penned two deeply appreciative memorial tributes.[30]

11

To the Congo and into the Navy

"New York is very exciting in war time," Latouche wrote Charlotte Dieterle in early 1942. "The people are finally gay again and the theatre particularly has taken a new lease on life, this late in the season.... New York has become a young and irridescent [*sic*] metropolis with an elderly substrata of last-minute farewells." Receiving a military classification of 1A, he himself faced the prospect of armed service; but thanks to the intervention of Franklin and Eleanor Roosevelt, both admirers of his work, he received a year's deferment so that he could travel to Africa in order to help prepare a documentary about the Congo sponsored by the Belgian government.[1]

Home to about twelve million blacks and thirty thousand whites, the Belgian Congo (now, two nations: the Democratic Republic of the Congo, and the Republic of the Congo) had been a private colony of King Leopold II of Belgium for almost a quarter century (1884–1908) before international outcry over administrative mismanagement and cruelty led to a takeover by the Belgian government, which subsequently ran the colony for over another five decades (1908–1960). After Nazi Germany occupied Belgium in May 1940, the Congo not only remained loyal to Belgium's government-in-exile, ensconced in London, but actively supported the Allied cause, sending their segregated military, the *Force Publique,* to fight in various campaigns, and supplying Great Britain and the United States with such valuable raw materials as rubber, tin, copper, and uranium, deposits of which helped the United States create the atomic bomb. Accordingly, Britain, the United States, and the exiled Belgian government all had compelling reasons for maintaining good relations with the Congo, including promoting a positive image of the country's colonial administration, whose reputation had been tarnished by a long history of violent repression, especially under Leopold's rule. In this context, Belgium's Minister of Colonies Albert De Vleeschauwer and Foreign Minister Paul-Henri Spaak, further concerned about the effect American world hegemony might have on their control of the Congo after the war, commissioned the Belgian filmmaker André Cauvin to create a documentary about the Congo in particular for American distribution.[2]

Cauvin (1907–2004) already had established himself as not only one of Belgium's leading documentarians, but one especially familiar with the Congo, having created two short films about the country in 1939: *Nos soldats d'Afrique* and *Congo, terre d'eaux vives*. He arrived in New York in July 1942 to find and assemble a crew, including an American to write the film script. Cauvin reportedly heard good things about the twenty-seven-year-old Latouche through friends in the émigré community, and deemed him suitable for the job at hand, his fluency in French, the Congo's official language, no doubt a strong point in his favor. Latouche's reputation among liberals and leftists offered the additional advantage of helping to counteract the perception that this undertaking represented an exercise in imperialist propaganda, as suggested by the fact that from the start the mission aimed to disclose, according to the *Richmond Times-Dispatch*, "that all the stories told about the behavior of the Belgians in the Congo are not true, show how far civilization has been brought in that land and how greatly the Congo can help the United Nations by producing war materials."[3]

Offered a salary of $500 per month plus expenses, Latouche joined a team that also included the British cameraman Arthur Fisher, assistant Peter (Pierre) Navaux ("a young Greek and Latin scholar from London," noted Latouche), and secretary Lucienne Harvey Meurisse, a close friend of Cauvin's (and described by Latouche as a "sweet curly blonde"). The group aimed not only to prepare a documentary, but broadcast radio shows from Leopoldville (now, Kinshasa), and gather material for possibly two books: a volume of captioned still photographs and a study of Congolese folklore. In the end, the venture resulted in a short film documentary, *Congo*, and a single travel book, also called *Congo*, with a text by Latouche and photographs by Cauvin (both released 1945, with a French edition of the book appearing in 1949).[4]

Departing by boat at different times, the team rendezvoused in Leopoldville in late October 1942. On his arrival, Fisher became ill with bladder cancer, and was flown to England, where he died shortly after; unable to find a replacement, Cauvin took responsibility for the camera work himself. Assisted by some seven native helpers, the remaining foursome traveled—by plane, automobile, river-boat, and other vehicles—the enormous length and width of the colony, nearly one-third the size of the contiguous United States. They visited villages and cities, schools, medical clinics, mining towns, an army base, a silkworm farm, an elephant training camp, and a leper colony, all the while observing and recording native songs, stories, and dances. Aside from the tragic loss of Fisher, the mission proceeded relatively smoothly, notwithstanding a car accident, some theft of property, and other mishaps. Cauvin had imagined the trip lasting two or three months, but the crew wound up spending about seven months on location.[5]

Latouche gained some elementary knowledge of two Bantu languages—Bangala and Swahili—and assumed the role of amateur journalist and anthropologist, interviewing colonialists and natives alike, and in some instances transcribing native songs and stories. He read history books and travel memoirs, and kept a diary of his own, now lost, although remnants survive in his *Congo* book. And characteristically, he enjoyed simply immersing himself in the country's life and landscape. His few surviving letters from the Congo complement his more formal published account of his experiences there. "Africa a pippin . . . ," he wrote Virgil Thomson, for instance, "Nice food, gay people, bright cities, indigenous natives very much so." After visiting an elephant training camp, he told his friend Eleonora Mendelssohn about how the latter would "immediately weep" on seeing the "little jumbos" violently separated from their mothers, and about a Yiddish folksong he had learned from a Polish refugee pianist living in the area. He wrote especially uninhibitedly to Dawn Powell, alluding to drinking parties and "prowls in the bush," and stating, with respect to his health, "I've been trekking around the native quarter, and I've probably got beri-beri, tse-tse, or one of those double diseases. Maybe it's somebody I ate." He further informed her, "Cauvin has been filming, with a zest that makes me feel languid, all the phenomena that glitter here under the black sun."[6]

On January 3, 1943, in the midst of this African sojourn, various newspapers, including the *Atlanta Constitution*, the *Baltimore Sun*, and the *Los Angeles Times*, published a short story by Latouche, "This One Weakness," akin to the author's radio playlets, illustrating the reciprocity among his work in different mediums. The story tells of a German soldier, trained from childhood to be a fighting machine, on a mission to destroy a dam in enemy territory; encountering an old woman and a young couple, the soldier raises his pistol with the intent to shoot, but an allergic reaction to ragweed allows the three civilians to apprehend him—the moral involving the futility of attempting to create "a human devoid of almost every instinct except the combative one." Having this story published around the nation in the midst of war, with himself many thousands of miles away, seems just another of the lyricist's improbable feats.[7]

While in Africa, Latouche also wrote some poems, two of which later appeared in the 1943–44 issue of *Hemispheres*, a quarterly of French and American poetry edited by Yvan Goll. A distinguished writer and poet of Alsatian-Jewish heritage, the exiled Goll (born Isaac Lang, 1891–1950) ostensibly had befriended Latouche even before the latter left for Africa, given not only his involvement in Latouche's *The Marseillaise*, as mentioned earlier, but the fact that he also published his own French translation of a poem by Latouche, "Ce temps n'est pas pour nous" ("This Is Not Our Time"), in the November 3, 1942, issue of *La Voix de France* ("The Voice of France"), a French resistance paper published in New York during the war. The original English version lost, this earlier poem would seem to reflect on Latouche's deteriorating relations with his wife in the context of wartime destruction abroad, although the poem ends optimistically with the thought, "Le temps viendra pour nous" ("The time will come for us").[8]

On his return to New York, Latouche apparently showed several of his recent poems to Goll, who published a pair of them as *Two Poems from Congo*. Latouche wrote the first, "Yangamgit," in February 1943; the second, "Pelican Song," the month before. The meanings of these two deeply felt poems, both rich in jungle imagery, remain elusive, especially the abstruse "Pelican Song," which reminds literary historian David Perkins of the early Robert Lowell. The more accessible "Yangamgit" reads in part,

> Come, Come proud love
> Through the plantations of night gathering stars
> Come in disguise of unchanging season and clement wind
> To justify the avid avatars
> That for gay union our two selves designed

The publication of these poems, released during his time in the navy, came as a surprise to Latouche, who regretted that they bore no dedication to Cauvin as intended. Indeed, as evident from his correspondence with the Belgian filmmaker, Latouche held Cauvin in tender regard.[9]

For his part, Cauvin, who thought of Latouche as "an American Rimbaud," came to greatly admire the lyricist, not only his wit—he especially relished his impersonation of Queen Victoria in the lavatory, with the pulling of the chain a high point—but his amazing memory, shrewd insight, and profound originality. "It was an extraordinary mind," he later recalled. "Through John Latouche one can get into the psychology and spirit of a man who is outstandingly gifted. Very few people can comprehend and appreciate Latouche's gifts. While we were together I went into his heart, and became, I believe, his substitute father." At the same time, Cauvin found Latouche childlike and exasperating, writing in his diary in March 1943,

> John is a spoiled child. Particularly in the morning. He presents himself at breakfast like a boxer who has lost his last match... he has a very sure instinct to ask for the food that is precisely impossible to obtain—and that gives him a case for argument. He nearly never raises his voice but turns his head from left to right while his blue eyes follow the strange curve of his feelings. I have the impression of finding anew yesterday's comedian who tries to become the dramatic actor.[10]

After Latouche returned home in July, such gossip columnists as Leonard Lyons and Earl Wilson occasionally commented flippantly on the mission. Two anecdotes in particular made the rounds. In one, the papers quoted Latouche as saying that he expected to find "savages" and "cocoanuts" in the Congo, but found instead Pittsburgh. Another story—which possibly originated at a dinner party hosted by Sara and Gerald Murphy, with Dorothy Parker and Dawn Powell in attendance—concerned Parker, who quipped, in reference to the popular series of Broadway shows *New Faces*, that Latouche had traveled to the Congo to prepare an all-leper review called *No Faces*.[11]

In late August 1943, Cauvin presented a rough cut of some 40,000 feet of silent film for an invited audience that included Belgian officials. The *Times* announced that the completed picture, with a narration by Latouche, would be ready for distribution in another two months, but the documentary would not be released officially until February 1945. Part of the delay concerned Latouche's dawdling, which although characteristic enough perhaps indicated some ambivalence about the whole project. In February 1944, while stationed in California, he finally completed a draft of the scenario, but about this same time, Cauvin, impeded by Latouche's absence, hired dialogue director Frank Beckwith to help co-write the script, with both Latouche and Beckwith receiving credit for the film's narration.[12]

Meanwhile, Latouche persuaded Paul Bowles to write the film score; and although the latter wondered "whether it was logical, or even ethical, for me to associate myself with a vehicle of colonialist propaganda," he took some comfort in knowing that Paul Robeson was to read the commentary, even if that task ultimately went to the radio actor Truman Bradley. Cauvin assisted Bowles by providing him with recordings of Congolese music, which found their way into a soundtrack that showed at times the influence of Copland. Bowles allegedly subverted the film's intentions by transforming the Belgian national anthem into "a strident conqueror's march," but the score, at least as heard in a cut version released by Warner Brothers that might have bowdlerized the original music, seems to oblige the film's rhetoric, with a stirring rendition of the said anthem at the film's end.[13]

The picture, to its credit, implied some integrationist sentiment, as in the phrase "black hands working with white hands," and conceded, moreover, the enduring value of some aspects of traditional Congolese culture, such as "the principle of equal distribution"; but the narration essentially put forth a standard colonialist discourse by presenting, in stark duality, tribal Africa as primitive and quaint and the industrialized Congo as enlightened and progressive. Nor did the picture—at least in the version released by Warner—address the issue of foreign occupation and governance, let alone exploitation. However, given the script's coauthorship and editorial oversight, Latouche's precise involvement concerning all this remains difficult to gauge.

Latouche's *Congo* monograph, described by the author in 1949 as a "too-hastily written view of an important variation on the colonial theme," proved more nuanced and personal than the documentary in a variety of ways. For one thing, with its translations of native songs and lyrics, it revealed a more profound engagement with the traditional culture of the indigenous Congolese, notwithstanding some unconcealed expressions of otherness. (Of one tribal festival, for instance, he wrote, "I longed to leave the correct island of civilization on which I sat so firmly in their midst; I wished to leave my companions, and merge myself into the dark, anonymous body of many heads, arms and legs that shivered and shook with a terrifying unity before me. But it was too late, centuries too late.") Moreover, disclaiming any "affection for imperialism," Latouche undertook some critique of colonial rule, observing that the country's progress "would be quicker still if the profits not already substantially diminished by governmental taxes were turned back into Congolese improvements, rather than flowing into the oubliettes of abstract absentee fortunes."[14]

At the same time, Latouche noted, under the Belgian "experiment," advances in public health, education, and welfare as well as in the protection of the land itself, applauding the formation of Albert (now, Virunga) National Park, the continent's first wildlife sanctuary. More controversially, the book presented admiring portraits of Leopold II and Henry Morton Stanley—the author pointed, rather, an accusing figure at the Arab slave trade, which Leopold, in fact, dismantled—and while not "in any sense" condoning former "brutalities," castigated critics of the Congo Free State for using the colony as a "whipping boy" and for cultivating a "holier-than-thou" attitude (mentioning, in this context, America's shameful treatment of its own native population). Nor did Latouche detail more recent abuses, going only so far as to say, "Quite often I saw things that irritated or puzzled me, but these things were so unimportant in comparison with the impressive scale of the human effort evident everywhere, that my desire grew to give a positive interpretation of the Congo picture." All in all, the book embodied tensions not only between noble ideals and wartime exigencies, but also between tradition and modernity. "As we evolve," remarked Latouche, musing on Congolese customs, "we must take forward with us the good that has been into the next phase of evolution. Or else we move into a darkness with no compass at all to guide us."[15]

Although his close friend Ruth Yorck thought the travelogue, released in July 1945, a disappointment, especially as compared to the author's personal accounts of his travels, *Congo*—published by Willow, White and Company, and distributed by Duell, Sloan and Pearce—received generally good reviews, including approving notices in the *New York Times* by both the South African writer Stuart Cloete and the distinguished African-American author W. E. B. Du Bois, who wrote, "While one may question the optimism in some of the conclusions, and the estimates of such men as Stanley and Léopold II, there is no denying the value of the book—if only as an eye-opener to the resources of a still-dark continent." As suggested from the latter review as well as by those published by the *Amsterdam News* and the *Chicago Defender*, African-American readers seemed inclined to share Latouche's admiration for the colony, although the *Defender* noted that the author's "African idyll contradicts more authoritative reports, which must be believed until La Touche and the Belgian government can show more conclusive evidence that they have changed their ways." As for Latouche's skill as a travel writer, the *Herald Tribune* discovered "phrases worthy of Poe... and descriptions of Africa in the raw that outmatch [H.] Rider Haggard," whereas the *Saturday Review* thought Latouche's "letterpress" not quite at the level of the "wonderful" photographs, which showed the men and women of the Congo as "unmistakable and diverse human personalities."[16]

Stating a preference for Latouche's travelogue over anthropologist (and Paul Robeson's wife) Eslanda ("Essie") Goode Robeson's *African Journey* (also published in 1945), Paul Engle, writing for the *Chicago Tribune*, thought that the author's "exact reporting" drove him "into the amusing position of having to say good things for imperialism" after "he had satirized it in earlier writings." But perhaps the most evocative review came from the *Madison Quarterly*'s Sue Quinn, who saw the book as an example of the author's ability, as in *Ballad for Americans*, to translate "the reality of ugliness, evil, and defection into the ideal of beauty, goodness, and perfection," an accomplishment in part drawn from a repugnance with American racism that dated back to the author's early years growing up in the South. Quinn elaborated on this perceived connection between *Congo* and the *Ballad* by writing, "He [Latouche] sings, in fact, the ballad of beauty for a land he learned to love," and by comparing his art, in this context, to the visionary idealism of such varied figures as Martha Graham, Eugene O'Neill, Arnold Schoenberg, Thomas Wolfe, and Grant Wood.[17]

Correspondences similarly could be drawn between the *Congo* and Latouche's subsequent work. The integration of song, dance, and fable discovered in Congolese ritual found an echo in *Ballet Ballads,* although even before his African sojourn, Latouche had experimented with such amalgams in the earliest of the ballads, *Susanna and the Elders*. (Indeed, on the occasion of the premiere of *Ballet Ballads* in 1948, he remembered his "surprise" during a Batwa ceremonial dance that the natives had been using what he considered such "new" forms "since the dawn of their culture.") Moreover, a major theme of the *Congo* book—the impact of the metropole and modernity on traditional ways of life—formed a principal concern of *The Golden Apple* and, to an extent, such other works as *The Vamp* and *The Ballad of Baby Doe*.[18]

Awarded a knighthood ("Chevalier de l'ordre de la couronne") for services to the Belgian government, Latouche remained involved with Africa after his return from the Congo, including publishing reviews of two books on African topics for *Saturday Review*: a February 1945 review of Hassoldt Davis's account of his experiences with the Fighting French in Africa, *Half Past When: An American with the Fighting French* (1944); and his own August 1945 review of Eslanda Robeson's *African Journey* (1945). Latouche plainly liked both books, *Half Past When* for its "candor," *African Journey* for its "charm," both for their "humanity and passion," to quote the review of the Davis volume. But with the war over by the time of the Robeson review, Latouche seemed freer to strike an anticolonialist note, writing, for instance, "the Negro's status in Africa—socially, industrially, and economically—is insecure and unfair even in the most hopeful locales."[19]

Latouche's appointment to the Council on African Affairs (CAA) allowed him to address such concerns in the political arena. Founded in 1941 by the black activist Max Yergan as an outgrowth of the International Committee on African Affairs, the CAA aimed to improve the social welfare and political freedom of Africans through various activities, including staging rallies and benefits, organizing conferences, airing radio programs, and publishing pamphlets and a monthly journal, *New Africa*. Led by such outstanding black figures as Yergan, Du Bois, Paul Robeson, and W. Alphaeus Hunton, the council also included a small, mostly Jewish white minority, including by the mid-1940s not only Latouche but his friends Leonard

Bernstein and John H. Hammond, a jazz record producer, civil rights activist, and heir to the Vanderbilt fortune.[20]

On April 25, 1947, Latouche joined thousands of others in a mass meeting organized by the council, then at the height of its influence, that both celebrated the recent birthday of an increasingly vilified Paul Robeson and advocated "Freedom of the African Colonial Peoples—Through a Strong United Nations." Held at the Seventy-first Regiment Armory, the event featured a pageant by Latouche that depicted the "world-wide struggle against imperialism," according to contemporary sources, who also quoted the author as saying, with respect to his recent African mission, "As I met them [the African people] and later on, as I read the dismal figures on education, medical care, economic development, etc, one statement rang out: they will no longer submit to the domination of Great Britain or Belgium or any other power for imperialist purpose.... There is no escaping the fact that this is 'One World' and colonial freedom is a 'must' for world peace. And that involves us." Some friends, he acknowledged, had warned him against speaking out on such issues for the sake of his career, but he maintained that silence entailed the bigger risk. "Since the rally at which he [Robeson] will speak, incidentally marks his birthday," he added, "I want to present the play [the Armory pageant] to him as my birthday gift."[21]

Latouche subsequently became entangled in an internal rift that tore through the council as the Cold War escalated in the course of 1948. During that year, Max Yergan attempted to suppress council critiques of anti-Soviet and anticommunist policies in an attempt to maintain popular support, while others, including Robeson, in turn accused Yergan of red-baiting. On May 15, in the midst of this struggle, Latouche submitted a detailed four-page letter to Robeson and the council's executive committee that he had co-written with two elder African-American statesmen and fellow council members, Mary Church Terrell and Henry Arthur Callis, and that charged Yergan with a long list of grievances, including alleged misrepresentation of the group's aims and questionable handling of the organization's finances. Although the letter generally avoided the matter's larger political context, a reference to those council members "who insist upon the defense of the African peoples against the intensified exploitation and oppression entailed for them under the so-called European Recovery Program ('Marshall Plan')" indicated precisely the pro-Soviet bias that Yergan had attempted to quash. Some of the letter's language suggests Latouche as perhaps its lead writer, as does the fact that his name heads the list of signatories. In any case, this document played some part in the council's decision to suspend Yergan's membership later in May and then to expel him in September. By this point, the council, in response to an increasingly hostile political climate, had begun to maintain a low profile, leaving behind no record of Latouche's later participation, if any, with the organization.[22]

A rather different picture of Latouche's involvement with the council, however, emerges in two sworn affidavits that he gave to the FBI in 1956. For a start, he claimed that his dramatic piece for the 1947 Armory rally—which he referred to by the title *Science versus the Jungle*—had no political intent other than to illustrate "the principle that science and education would alleviate conditions in Africa by helping the natives help themselves," and he denied the remarks attributed to him on that occasion, including the assertion that he meant the piece as a birthday gift to Robeson. Moreover, he claimed that Robeson and V. J. Jerome, the Communist Party's cultural commissar, had come to him with "trumped up" charges against Yergan and that he subsequently resigned from the council because Robeson "was trying to use the Council as a sounding board on domestic issues which was contrary to the purposes for which the Council was set up"—the sort of argument that Yergan himself leveled against Robeson. But the evidence suggests that Latouche either misremembered or more likely misstated his role with the council in his sworn testimony. Indeed, if he commonly stretched the truth as a matter of course, how much more likely would he have been to prevaricate to the FBI, especially in light of the political tribulations he endured in the intervening years.[23]

"Touche got back from Africa having zigzagged in a boat for six weeks so no one knew what had happened to him," Dawn Powell wrote to a friend on July 11, 1943. "He was welcomed by his draft board, income-tax collectors, process servers, editors who had not received the promised material, and long-faced representatives of his bank. This has left him somewhat crushed, but he exubers up if out of his orbit."[24]

Powell further reported, "Touche said his wife looked so beautiful when he got back that he almost had a go at her himself," with the lyricist's extant diaries—which resume in August 1943 after a five-year gap—indeed suggesting some continuation of conjugal relations, at least to judge from such entries as that from August 17, in which he wrote, "I romped with Theo at bed-time, and scared her by making werewolf faces." The two at least enjoyed reading aloud Philip Wylie's best-selling *Generation of Vipers* with designer Frederick Kiesler and his wife, Stefanie, and socializing with Theodora's brother, Nixon, and his fiancée and soon-to-be wife, sculptor Martha ("Toni") Hughes. But in truth the marriage had begun to unravel. "We lay in the light, and I tried to reach her," Latouche wrote in his September journal, "but I was too deeply still in the setting of my own fear—my sense of inadequacy swept off balance, and hampered comfort"; and again in October, "Theo was remote and odd: I tried to reach her without success; a wall wavered between us." By this time, they had thought to divorce, although Latouche, about to leave for military service, harbored the hope that the marriage still could be salvaged.[25]

Latouche assumed much of the blame for the collapse of his marriage, with his unpredictably manic behavior surely taking its toll. On one occasion, as reported in his diary, he startled Theodora by running about the apartment "naked and joyful" shouting "Joy! Joy! Let us be free!" (an episode capped by reading Lao-Tzu's *Tao Te*

Ching in the bathroom). And at dinner one night, he surprised his wife, along with Nixon and Martha, by announcing, "I think I've outgrown you all." In general, although he hoped to complete a number of projects, including a treatment of the Hiawatha story for Walt Disney, he often found himself creatively blocked, which left him dejected and moody, as did the war itself, which caused him in one instance to "tumble off the wagon." He might well have vented some of these frustrations when he met in August for coffee with fellow lyricist Lorenz Hart, whom he found "nervous and so sad." Alike in many ways, the two lyricists presumably discussed, among other things, the blockbuster success of *Oklahoma!* which Hart's former partner, Richard Rodgers, had written with Oscar Hammerstein, and a performance of which Latouche attended with painter Buffie Johnson shortly before leaving for service.[26]

His reprieve at an end, Latouche over the summer underwent a military physical examination—which put his height at about 5 feet 3 inches and his weight at 154 pounds, and noted as physical defects myopic astigmatism of the left eye (20/100), two missing back teeth, and an operated hernia—and was found fit for duty. On October 2, 1943, he was inducted as an apprentice seaman into the U.S. Navy Construction Battalion, the "Seabees," a division of the armed forces responsible for such duties as storing and transporting materiel, and building bases, hospitals, roadways, and airstrips, including repairing damaged and destroyed equipment in the Pacific theater. (This division acquired its nickname "Seabees" by way of a pun on the initials for Construction Battalion, C. B., with "sea" alluding to their status as sailors, and "bee," their reputation as "busy bees," their logo showing a bee holding a drill, a hammer, and a wrench; in training camp, Latouche noted that the "bewildered, awkward men" themselves privately defined C.B. as "Confused Bastards," adding, "we live up to it.") With his background in radio propaganda, it would seem that Latouche would have made an especially good candidate for intelligence work, but he joined the navy, he asserted, specifically because the army would have given him a desk job. "I wrote plenty of words before the war," he stated in July 1944, "and I expect to fill tons of paper after, but when the German fortified his ideas with tanks, I can't fight back with a pen."[27]

In the second week of October 1943, Latouche left for Camp Peary, outside of Williamsburg, Virginia, for some grueling basic training, about which he nonetheless wrote enthusiastically to his mother, whom he continued to assist financially, and to such friends as Frederick Kiesler, with whom, in a rare letter documenting their relationship, he indulged in some black irony: "I have also learned how to eviscerate a Jap with a machete; how to cut a Nazi throat with a hand bayonet, wiping off the blood onto the uniform; how to slice up with a trench knife, and side-step the guts as they fall out; how to burn bush and shoot down the enemy as they run out; how to kick the testicles in hand-to-hand fighting; and other bits of useful knowledge." He especially exulted in his popularity among his mates, who called him

"Butch," and who helped him learn how to properly make a bed and to roll and fold clothes. "I never realized how useless I was before," he told Kiesler.[28]

However, in November he received some distressing news that dampened his spirits. First, with respect to a planned visit to New York, he heard from Theodora that she did not want to see him, "a brutal slap in the face" for which he turned to the writings of Emerson for consolation; and then, once arriving in the city, where he stayed at the Algonquin Hotel, he learned about Harry Dunham's death in the Pacific—a double blow that left him deeply depressed.[29]

Assigned to the 131st Naval Construction Battalion, Latouche arrived at the Camp Parks naval base in Shoemaker, California, in early December after "a grisly trip across the continent in a dusty train." At Camp Parks, located about thirty miles southeast of Oakland, Latouche spent much of his time in drill—on one ten-mile hike, he occupied himself by imagining paintings by Camille Corot, André Segonzac, and Salvador Dalí, and music by Mozart, Johann Strauss, and Igor Stravinsky—when not performing such menial tasks as moving supplies, digging ditches, and cleaning latrines. Much of this work he found tiring and tiresome; hearing a truck driver sing "Oh, What a Beautiful Mornin" (*Oklahoma!*) while transporting lumber one miserably cold December day left him "close to homicide." In mid-December, he came down with catarrhal fever and spent about a week in sick bay. "It's amazing to traverse Africa without illness," he wrote to André Cauvin, "and then fold up in healthy California." In January, he contacted the Office of Strategic Services, the government's intelligence agency, about a possible transfer.[30]

His situation improved in early 1944 as he began to write for the battalion newspaper, the *Skipper*, and received a promotion from seaman second class to storekeeper third class, whose rank he likened to that of an army sergeant; and when offered a desk job with the local public relations staff in February, he decided to stay with his unit, partly out of esteem for his commanding officer, Edward Dunham, and partly because he hoped to find "the actual pulse of the war" once his battalion shipped out to the Pacific. "I am very anxious to get into action," he explained to Cauvin. However, in late March, a week after arriving at the Seabees base at Mauna Loa Ridge on the Hawaiian island of Oahu, Latouche learned from Cauvin that the Belgian embassy, in conjunction with the military, had arranged for his release so that he could complete work on the Congo documentary. "I have applied for three months leave, in lieu of a discharge: I have no desire to leave the service until the war is over," he wrote in his journal. "However, I will be delighted to finish the film, and have the opportunity to write a few articles and to swell my low finances. And to see New York again." After some delays, Latouche returned in mid-April to California, where he received an honorable discharge "by reason of his own convenience."[31]

While with the Seabees, Latouche made some friends with whom he could play cards and horse around. "This contact with ordinary people has done me a great deal of good," he wrote to his friend Marian Dunham, although in his diary, alongside sympathetic character studies of his fellow troops, he occasionally expressed exasperation with their backwardness and bigotry. On one occasion, teased about his name in chow hall at lunchtime, he threw a fork at one of his mates, an action that left him "deeply ashamed of myself." He also decried the level of navy culture, describing the hit song "Pistol Packin' Mama," for instance, as "a repellent example of the moronic ditty that occasionally is celebrated as a public mass to mediocrity," and *Superman* and other comics as "another example of our degradation of ancient instincts." Yearning for "civilized talk," he eagerly looked forward to letters from home; he especially thought about Theodora, whose correspondence he found "charming and extremely moving, in a terse way." "I long to be with her, to sustain her, to have her comfort me, to grow together with her, to feel the seed flowering into majesty," he wrote in his diary in March, although he also told Marian Dunham at about this same time, "I love her deeply. But I must say it's all quite a bore. If we separate or divorce, I haven't any intention of being friendly or getting together later on...that's a noelcowardish idea, and really indicates that Theo wants to have her cake and sleep on the side it's buttered on, too. We will all have serious work to do after the war, and there isn't any time to run around barefoot in each other's egos as it was pleasant to do when we were younger."[32]

In his spare time, Latouche wrote poems, studied mapmaking, and learned chess; left-handed, he also practiced writing with his right hand. As always, he read voraciously, noting in his journal lists of authors read, including Saint Augustine, Max Beerbohm, S. N. Behrman, Helena Blavatsky, Thomas Carlyle, Alexis Carrel, G. K. Chesterton, John Collier, Confucius, Emerson, Kathryn Forbes, Robert Graves, Muriel Bruce Hasbrouck, Gerald Heard, Aldous Huxley, Thomas Jefferson, Thomas Mann, Somerset Maugham, Clifford Odets, I. A. Richards, Booker T. Washington, Eudora Welty, and Edith Wharton, as well as mysteries by Rex Stout and many others. His interest in several of these publications, not to mention the *Bhagavad Gita* and the Bible, evidenced his keen and diverse spiritual preoccupations; in a rating of one compilation of books, only Augustine's *Confessions* (although read only in part) received four stars. Latouche even became active in the Christian Men's Service League at Camp Parks, explaining in a letter to Dunham,

> I dropped in to the meetings (you know my fondness for hymns—particularly sung in our own peculiar manner, and the zeal with which I joined in the singing must have impressed my mates that I had more piety than I seemed to have, because several meetings later I was voted in as battalion vice-president—which means delivering short bible-readings, etc.). I have leapt into the part with amusement, and the rather bewildered chaplain finds the bible texts leading inevitably at every meeting to the social issues of the day. However, being a left-wing Methodist, he is not displeased.[33]

About this same time, reflecting in his journal on Schopenhauer's maxim "The greatest of follies is to sacrifice health for any other kind of happiness," Latouche referred to himself, at least by implication, as a "spiritual traveller," writing,

> Running across this [maxim] in crusty old fogy Schopenhauer reminds me of the paradox that we must seek truth not only among those who have observed it, but among those who violate it. So many philosophies are denigrated because the promulgators did not practice what they preached (Rousseau, Nietzsche). But these men knew more than any others what hells resulted from the flaunting of natural laws: out of their flaming pits, they shouted warnings to the spiritual traveller—*because* of their derelictions rather than *in spite of* they should be listened to with care and awareness.

In another diary entry, Latouche similarly wrote of Hitler and Nazi collaborators Pierre Laval and Vidkun Quisling, "We should hold a measure of bitter gratitude for these men: without them we might have gone on our whole lives vegetating, accepting the wrongs and shortcomings of our selves and the dubious society we have created out of these selves.... Their evil has forced us to the extreme of creating an at least temporary good." Latouche would develop this line of thinking in the opera *The Golden Apple*, as encapsulated by Mother Hare's "Without evil, how can the good ever change? Without change how can any man ever grow?"[34]

During his time at Camp Parks, Latouche also regularly visited San Francisco, where he spent time with Seabee sidekicks and "alcoherent amours," went to the movies (including a double feature of two horror films, *Son of Dracula* and *The Mad Ghoul*), and attended operas and concerts, although he regretfully missed a Milhaud premiere with the San Francisco Symphony, explaining to Virgil Thomson, "I adore Milhaud's music." "At first it [San Francisco] seemed dreadful," he further informed Thomson, "because it's overcrowded with service men—and I confined my sightseeing to those centers catering to them. Now I've struck out and found all sorts of giddy endroits that have flavor and mystery." While stationed on Oahu, he similarly made excursions into Honolulu, where he enjoyed the company of the "vain, affable, and extremely charming" British actor Maurice Evans, then serving in the army's entertainment section. During his brief time on the island, he characteristically investigated native Hawaiian legends as well.[35]

In his war journal, Latouche often expressed the hope that his time in the military might help him better structure his life. On New Year's Day 1944, he resolved "to learn orderliness" and "to achieve concentration," adding,

> These two lacks in my mental equipment will have to be acquired against a potent natural indolence, and an affection for the irons-in-the-fire mode of life. Also, cultivation of moderation and order will be a hard pull for one as prone to extremist thinking as I am. But perhaps the difficulty of achieving

> these aims will compensate for their humdrum character. I shall borrow from Benjamin Franklin the habit of a daily check-up, in order to be able to estimate my progress.

Some two weeks later, he further wrote that his service in the Seabees "had not been futile up to now: it has given me a framework upon which to base a badly needed organization of my scattered resources." Among other things, he aimed to moderate his extreme moodiness, very possibly the result of some kind of bipolar disorder.[36]

Latouche often placed such attempts at self-improvement in the context of his artistic aspirations, which never seemed far from his mind. At one point, he spoke of "the service I hope I shall render in the post-war world," stating elsewhere, "I pray fervently for the end of the war, so that I may resume those responsibilities I so lazily avoided during the past two years." He frequently sketched ideas in his journals for stories and theater pieces, and imagined possible collaborations with Alfred Hitchcock and Bing Crosby, among others. He stayed particularly close throughout this period with composer Jerome Moross, with whom he planned an opera based on Ben Jonson's *Volpone*.[37]

After returning to New York in May for an assumed three-month leave from the navy, Latouche largely neglected his diary, making it more difficult to chronicle his life for the remainder of the year. He worked on his *Congo* book, for which he received the sizable sum of $4,000 paid out in various installments, and spoke eagerly about returning to military service, but the navy never recalled him. He seems not to have gone back to his 49th Street apartment either, to judge from a June 20, 1944, journal entry in which he mentioned occasionally meeting with Theodora for lunches and dinners, although the statement, "our talk is passionless so far," implied perhaps continued hopes for the marriage.[38]

In this same June 1944 journal entry, Latouche also referred to sporadic sessions with the pioneering behavior therapist Andrew Salter (1914–1996), at thirty years old about six months Latouche's senior. With no more than a bachelor's degree, Salter already had published his first book, *What Is Hypnosis: Studies in Auto and Hetero Conditioning* (1944), a Pavlovian treatise that proposed conditioning neurotic behavior through hypnosis. (The novelist Richard Condon drew on Salter's work for his 1959 political thriller, *The Manchurian Candidate*.) "Those of us who knew Salter personally," wrote Gerald Davison on the occasion of the psychologist's death, "appreciated his sheer brilliance, his wit, his warmth, decency and consideration for others, his supportiveness, his keen intuitive grasp of human nature, his infectious zest for life, his love of art and literature, and his devotion to family and friends." That Latouche's consultations with Salter formed part of a larger effort toward self-improvement on his part finds ample evidence in a compilation of personal "liabilities" and "assets" listed near the end of his 1944 diary, with his "problem" identified as the need to "conquer self, or be destroyed by it," and the "solution" necessitating "self-discipline" and "self-control"—reflections supplemented with quotes from Muriel Hasbrouck's *Tarot and Astrology: The Pursuit of Destiny*.[39]

In one June diary entry, Latouche admitted that Salter, with whom he presumably practiced hypnotic and relaxation techniques, had "done little for me so far," but he apparently remained at least lifelong friends with the psychologist, who inscribed a copy of his 1955 revised version of *What Is Hypnosis* "to John Latouche, a past master himself, with the best wishes of Andrew Salter." The two men also collaborated in early 1945 on a two-act play, *The Wax Flower*, a nearly complete typescript of which survives, and a project apparently resuscitated as late as 1954 with the additional input of Latouche's partner, Kenward Elmslie.[40]

Latouche and Salter based their play on George du Maurier's 1894 novel *Trilby*, about the eponymous young woman's rise to operatic fame under the mesmerizing influence of the Jewish hypnotist Svengali—a story that also helped inspire Gaston Leroux's 1910 novel *The Phantom of the Opera*, famously adapted in 1925 as a film starring Lon Chaney. *The Wax Flower* concerns Jim Poynton, a psychologist interested in hypnosis, and his fiancée, Sylvia, who under the spell of a crackpot hypnotist, Rengo, becomes a zombified cabaret celebrity, Stella, the "wax flower" of the title—her change of name symbolic of her transition from her natural state to artificial stardom. Assisted by his friend Chuck, a veteran and a painter, Jim rescues Sylvia from Rengo, who dies, although in what appears to be the play's final scene his ghost ominously returns.

The Wax Flower seems to have provided its coauthors an opportunity to explore, if not exorcise, personal conflicts. In Salter's case, this involved the uses and abuses of psychoanalysis and hypnotism, including mishandling of his signature contribution to the profession, assertiveness training—a concern epitomized in Jim's observation, "Science is a two-edged sword: In the hands of irresponsible persons it destroys as well as creates. Airplanes can bring a world closer, or bomb its cities into oblivion overnight." For Latouche, the play seemingly offered a means with which to vent his feelings about Theodora, including demonizing her own therapist. "I do not love Jim," Sylvia/Stella says in a trance induced by Rengo. "Men are bad. I must think only of you, Rengo." That Salter and Latouche meant to project themselves as dual heroes seems further suggested by the fact that the play's two male protagonists consist of a psychologist and an artist.

Although more biographical implications easily could be teased out of this script, the authors intended the play as no mere psychological exercise, but rather a work of art in its own right. Not only did they copyright the play; they seemed to have secured a tryout performance in the summer of 1946 with the Montowese Playhouse in Branford, Connecticut, which on July 30 of that year premiered as part of their regular season *Figaro*, a Pierre Beaumarchais adaptation by Latouche that he reportedly hoped to bring to Broadway—one of the lyricist's sundry works that seems to survive in name only. Reviewing this particular production, which starred Gino Caimi as Figaro, the *New York Post* reported that the material, further adapted by director

William Whiting and presented in the style of the commedia dell'arte, showed "potential charm."[41]

By this time, Latouche had long moved on with respect to his marriage. Over the summer of 1944, he even appeared on the radio show *Blind Date*, a program produced by Tom Wallace and hosted by Arlene Francis, in which, on a divided stage, three women—typically actresses or models—would converse each by telephone with two servicemen on leave, and then select the one she preferred; the three losing men received consolation prizes, the winning couples, a chaperoned night out on the town at the Stork Club. No details about Latouche's appearance have surfaced, but according to producer Wallace, he became the first Seabee to go on the show.[42]

Near the end of this same summer, Latouche found himself in a joyous new relationship, writing in his journal on August 24, "A wild, unexpected love has come—a love which makes me sure, instead of happy, which lifts me up, instead of chute-the-chuting. A strange love from the sweeping winds of the world." And in September, he moved into an apartment of his own at 29 Washington Square West, a multistory complex facing Washington Square Park. A new period in his life had begun.[43]

12

Rhapsody

In the early 1940s, Latouche's career as a popular song lyricist took a somewhat different tack from his previous work in cabaret, thanks largely to his newly established association with music publisher Jack Robbins. Many of his popular songs from these years involved providing Robbins, sometimes in apparent response to the radio industry's 1941 boycott of ASCAP composers, with lyrics for previously written music, including "Zombie: Cancíon Bolero" (1941), music by the Cuban bandleader Xavier Cugat, with an original Spanish text by Pedro Berríos; "Cae Cae" (pronounced Ky-Ky, 1941), music and Portuguese lyrics—as sung by Carmen Miranda in the film *That Night in Rio*—by the Brazilian composer Roberto Martins; "Day Dream" (1941), after a 1939 instrumental by Billy Strayhorn, with Duke Ellington receiving credit for the music as well; "Twilight Rhapsody" (1941), music by the Italian songwriter Giovanni D'Anzi; "No Greater Love" (1941), music adapted by Robbins Music's staff arranger Domenico Savino after Tchaikovsky's First Piano Concerto; "Forever and a Day" (1943), adapted with lyricist Robert Musel (and "with the choleric assistant collaboration" of Jack Robbins, according to Latouche) from the 1915 hit song, "Ich muss wieder einmal in Grinzing sein," by Ralph Benatzky, an Austrian operetta composer recently emigrated to America; and "The Beauty Hula" (1944), a popular 1935 hula instrumental by prominent Hawaiian musicians John Kameaaloha Almeida and Johnny Noble.[1]

Latouche probably undertook these largely workaday projects as a favor to Robbins and to make some money. That he felt some compunction about such activity might be inferred from his occasional use of the *nom de plume* John Digges (a pseudonym that derived from his alleged full name, John Patrick Diggs Treville Latouche), as in, for example, "No Greater Love," which featured one of his most banal lyrics ("No greater love can I feel / than I am feeling for you / All other loves are unreal / Your love alone is always true," and so forth). Robbins presumably hoped that this particular song, whose melody had become especially familiar through its use as the signature music to Orson Welles's *Mercury Theatre on the Air*, might rival "Tonight We Love," an adaptation of the same Tchaikovsky melody by Ray Austin and Freddy Martin, with words by Bobby Worth, which rose to the top of the charts in the fall of 1941. But whereas Austin and Martin molded the melody to fit a duple meter, Savino retained the triple meter of the original, making it less useful for dance purposes.

Latouche's sporadic penchant for anonymity might help explain the anomaly of another number, "Racing with the Moon," a huge hit for the crooning bandleader Vaughn Monroe. According to the manuscript of the song's chorus deposited for copyright in early 1941, Monroe, Latouche, and Johnny Watson collaborated on the number, a slightly altered version of which appeared in print later in the year with the music credited to Watson and the words to Monroe and one Pauline Pope, perhaps a pseudonym for Latouche. In any event, the lyric, with its changing landscape serving as a metaphor for lost love, recalled Latouche in his more purplish vein, as found, for example, in "Love Turned the Light Out" from *Cabin in the Sky*.

Latouche's best popular song from this period, "Day Dream," marked the beginnings of an important relationship with Duke Ellington (1899–1974) and William ("Billy") Strayhorn (1915–1967), one that in time would yield a full-length musical, *Beggar's Holiday* (1946). A native of Washington, D.C., Ellington by this time had achieved international recognition as the time's foremost jazz band composer, arranger, and conductor; Strayhorn, who grew up in the Pittsburgh area and had a more formal musical education than Ellington, early on fashioned himself as a crossover artist in the mold of his idol, George Gershwin, and only recently had become a staff composer and arranger for the Ellington band, a position he held almost uninterruptedly from 1939 to his death.

Ellington and Strayhorn worked together very closely, almost telepathically, on many projects. "Billy Strayhorn was my right arm, my left arm, all the eyes in the back of my head, my brainwaves in his head, and his in mine," wrote Ellington in a tribute to the man he described as "the biggest human being who ever lived, a man with the greatest courage, the most majestic artistic stature, a highly skilled musician whose impeccable taste commanded the respect of all musicians and the admiration of all listeners." Working with Ellington and Strayhorn in the recording studio, producer Irving Townsend observed, "Little of what either writes is left unchanged by the other." This partnership flourished in large part due to Strayhorn's command of what he called the "Ellington effect" and his uncanny ability to intuit the older man's intentions. What unique qualities Strayhorn brought to their working relationship remains less studied, although as a man of broad culture whose enthusiasms included Stravinsky, he helped Ellington achieve, according to some observers, an elevated refinement and sophistication; Ellington biographer James Lincoln Collier even argued, in a discussion that, in light of Strayhorn's homosexuality, seemed to register some homophobic overtones, that Strayhorn in this sense had a deleterious influence on Ellington by encouraging the latter's "tendency—weakness if you will—toward lushness, prettiness, at the expense of the masculine leanness and strength of his best work." In any case, the modest and easy-going Strayhorn functioned largely in Ellington's shadow, appreciative of the fact that

Ellington treated him so equitably, although the lack of artistic autonomy sometimes rankled, leading to occasional tensions and rifts.[2]

Originally composed as an instrumental by Strayhorn in 1939, "Day Dream" had been recorded as such by alto saxophonist Johnny Hodges and His Orchestra, a small unit of Duke Ellington's band, in late 1940, with Ellington at the piano, and released the following year. Lyricizing the number in mid-1941, Latouche likely collaborated in person with either Strayhorn or Ellington or both, in part because the song, at least to judge from the Hodges recording, still needed an introductory verse. At any rate, the lyricist developed a warm friendship with both Ellington and Strayhorn; rumor even had it that Latouche and Strayhorn, both young gay men who enjoyed speaking French and bar-hopping, became romantically involved.[3]

Knowing that at least the music for the chorus of "Day Dream" preceded the words—a compositional method common to many popular lyricists, but not necessarily Latouche, who often wrote his lyrics either prior to or in tandem with the music—allows an appreciation of his agility in tailoring his verse to a given melody. For the leaping octave that begins each *A* section of the song's *AABA* chorus—a gesture that resembles the opening of Harold Arlen and Yip Harburg's "Over the Rainbow" (1939), although Strayhorn's music more decidedly recalls Claude Debussy's famous piano piece *Rêverie* (itself converted into a 1938 popular song, "My Reverie")—the phrase "Day dream" seems to have been a given; but for each of these *A* sections, Latouche shows his distinctive hand by matching the melody's threefold phrase structure with triple rhymes, one of which also involves an internal rhyme ("rosy glow"):

Day Dream
Why do you haunt me so
Deep in a rosy glow
The face of my love you show.

Latouche displays similar skill and sensitivity by locating an evocative dissonance (a sharpened fifth degree) as the site for the word "haunt," and by devising for the bridge section, whose chromatic wanderings, as Walter van de Leur observes, look back to Chopin and Gershwin, appropriately disoriented imagery:

Don't know the time
Lordy, I'm in a daze
Sun in the sky,
While I moon around feeling hazy.

More generally, the languid lyric, which anticipates especially "Lazy Afternoon" (*The Golden Apple*), nicely reflects the music's wistful mood, with the phrase "don't break my reverie" underlining, consciously or not, the song's connection to the forementioned Debussy piece.[4]

Although slower to establish itself as a vocal than as an instrumental number, "Day Dream" became one of Latouche's most enduring songs, with recordings by such outstanding vocalists as Tony Bennett, Betty Carter, Ella Fitzgerald, Johnny Mathis, Helen Merrill, Linda Ronstadt, Audrey Silver, Jo Stafford, Sarah Vaughan, and Nancy Wilson. (Several singers, apparently insensible to the subtle charm of the text's sun-moon dichotomy, replaced the phrase "moon around" with such prosaic phrases as "go around," "roam around," and "sit around.") Van de Leur had special praise for Strayhorn's "breathtaking" 1957 arrangement of the number for Ella Fitzgerald and the Duke Ellington Orchestra: "As if to mirror the experience of dreaming while being awake with a similar duality in music, the arrangement of *Day Dream* parallels the airy and sensual atmosphere of John LaTouche's lyrics with the use of so-called polychords." At times, as in the case of Betty Carter's 1994 release, the song even became a means to explore altered mental states at least somewhat congruent with a certain side of Latouche's own psyche.[5]

During this period, Latouche collaborated on other popular songs as well, including three surviving unpublished numbers with composer Walter Donaldson: the waltz "I Met You in a Dream," the ballad "Forgive Me Again," and the fox-trot "Baby, That's for Me." Born in Brooklyn, Donaldson (1893–1947) rose through the ranks of Tin Pan Alley to become, often in league with lyricist Gus Kahn, one of the most prolific and successful songwriters of his time, his many hits including "Carolina in the Morning" (1922), "Yes Sir, That's My Baby" (1925), and "Makin' Whoopee!" and "Love Me or Leave Me" from the Broadway show *Whoopee* (1928). In the 1930s, he moved to Los Angeles, where he wrote mostly for the movies and enjoyed continued good fortune. However, after his death, his name—if not his music—became largely forgotten, leading such connoisseurs of the popular song as Alec Wilder and Allen Forte to regard him as a neglected master.[6]

Donaldson, who often traveled to New York during his later years, probably met Latouche through Jack Robbins; the manuscripts of the three songs that he and Latouche wrote together all bear a Robbins Music copyright of 1942. Robbins himself might have suggested the collaboration, knowing especially Donaldson's interest in working with rising lyricists. At any rate, these Donaldson and Latouche songs simply gathered dust until unearthed in the early twenty-first century by the composer's daughter Ellen Donaldson, who had them transcribed and recorded. The poignant "Forgive Me Again," whose melody, like that of "Day Dream," features a haunting diminished sixth interval, and whose lyric appears to resonate with Latouche's marital difficulties, seems the best of these three numbers.[7]

As a favor to his friend Marianne Oswald (born Sarah Alice Bloch, 1901–1985), the Franco-German-Jewish chanteuse exiled in New York, Latouche also translated, shortly before leaving for service in the fall of 1943, the cabaret singer's signature piece "Anna la bonne," a 1934 *chanson parlée* (French: spoken ballad) written for her by Jean Cocteau. "She has all the shivers of ecstasy that she can summon about it...," wrote Latouche to Frederick Kiesler about Osborne's reaction to this presumably lost adaptation. "I wont be surprised if she suddenly turns up disguised as an Admiral to get another poem out of me. She's capable of it. I'm horrified she'll find out that I did it in a half-hour, before my last dinner at home." After the war, Latouche, incidentally, wrote a warmly appreciative review of Oswald's memoirs, *One Small Voice* (1945), for the leftwing journal *Free World*, in which he discerned in the "outmoded puritanism and bigotry" Oswald encountered growing up in a small French-German border town parallels to his own childhood in Richmond.[8]

One more number from this period, Leonard Bernstein's "It's Gotta Be Bad to Be Good," might be mentioned here because of past questions of authorship that also permit some consideration of Latouche's early relationship with the composer. Considered at one point for use in Bernstein's 1944 musical *On the Town* (and eventually replaced by the more farcical torch song "I'm Blue"), "It's Gotta Be Bad," originally composed in 1942, came to public notice by way of a 1975 off-Broadway revue, *By Bernstein*, and a 1981 recording, *Ben Bagley's Leonard Bernstein Revisited*, with Bernstein credited for both the words and the music, as in the case of the 2010 published score. However, according to Bagley, Betty Comden (with whom Bernstein collaborated on the musicals *On the Town* and *Wonderful Town*) surmised that Latouche "might have worked on" the number with Bernstein, who had settled in New York after graduating Harvard in 1939 and the Curtis Institute in 1941.[9]

This supposition seems plausible, at least hypothetically. Latouche and the slightly younger and primarily homosexual Bernstein had become chummy during these years, very likely through Paul Bowles and Aaron Copland. In July 1943, for example, Bernstein wrote to Copland about "a long cocktail party" that he attended with Latouche, Bowles, and several others: "Occasion: triumphant return [from Africa] to these parts of one LaTouche. Great to-do. It went on all night, mostly me and Touche and Paul, and wound up at Peter Monro Jacks' [read: Jack's] (horrid) and we finally left Touche there in his four o'clock cups. He's a terror if there ever was one. I sort of like him in a weird way, especially when he's sentimental in that mountebank manner. It's a wonderful aggressiveness."

Not long after, in response to a proposal that he write the lyrics for a musical adaptation of the play *The Firebrand*, Latouche suggested, as mentioned earlier, that he collaborate with Bernstein, touting some of the composer's songs to the skeptical producers, Paul Feigay and Oliver Smith. Nothing came of that, but after Feigay and Smith decided to adapt Bernstein's ballet with Jerome Robbins, *Fancy Free*, which premiered in April 1944, as the musical *On the Town*, the press periodically announced that Latouche would write that show's lyrics, with Betty Comden, Adolph Green, and sometimes Robbins named as bookwriters. (During this same period, Latouche heard Bernstein conduct his *Jeremiah Symphony* at Lewisohn Stadium, describing the work in his journal as "a rich and powerful piece, derivative in the early sections, but evolving into a harsh originality at the end.") However, Comden and Green in the end took responsibility for both the show's book and lyrics. According to Bernstein biographer Humphrey Burton, Jerome Robbins actually wanted Arthur Laurents to author the book, and Latouche, the lyrics, but he deferred to Bernstein's insistence that Comden and Green write both. On the other hand, Vernon Duke claimed Latouche himself "turned down the job... fearing that the management would want him to write conventional lyrics, not poetry," another unverifiable claim.[10]

Whatever the case, Comden probably had something of this background in mind in suggesting that Latouche might have had a hand in "It's Gotta Be Bad to Be Good." Moreover, the lyric contains some phrases redolent of Latouche, starting with the title, which closely recalls the similarly paradoxical "It's Not So Bad to Be Good" from *Cabin in the Sky*. However, an extant manuscript score credits the words to Hughie Prince, a lyricist of the period best remembered for "Boogie Woogie Bugle Boy" (1941), which would seem to settle the matter, although Bernstein ostensibly revised both the words and music subsequently. A collaboration between Bernstein and Latouche—at least a known one—would have to wait another ten years.[11]

Not working on *On the Town* at least freed Latouche to write the lyrics for *Rhapsody*, an operetta adapted from the work of Fritz Kreisler that opened on Broadway on November 22, 1944, about a month prior to the Bernstein musical. The decision by the show's journeyman producer, Blevins Davis, and its principal backer, Lorraine Manville Dresselhuys, to present a work by Kreisler formed part of a renewed interest in European operetta—and its American off-shoots—in New York in the early 1940s. During these years, even as the genre waned in Hollywood, operettas by Jacques Offenbach, Johann Strauss, Oscar Straus, and Franz Lehár—as well as Americans Victor Herbert, Reginald De Koven, Rudolf Friml, and Sigmund Romberg—enjoyed more or less successful revivals in New York. In the opinion of critic Cecil Smith, this renaissance of light opera bespoke the need for wartime escapism, although it seems to have been related as well to the influx of European refugees to America and especially New York, for these exiles included, in addition to a welcoming audience, such operetta luminaries as composers Ralph Benatzky, Fritz Kreisler, Robert Stolz, Oscar Straus, and Emmerich Kálmán, who produced one of his last operettas, *Marinka* (1945), for the Broadway stage.[12]

The time's hospitable response to operetta further could be placed in the context of the success of Rodgers and Hammerstein's *Oklahoma!* (1943) and *Carousel* (1945) and the triumphant return to Broadway in 1942 of Gershwin's *Porgy and Bess* (with much of its sung recitative now spoken), not to mention several new shows based on nineteenth-century classical music, including *Carmen Jones* (after Bizet, 1943) and *Song of Norway* (after Grieg, 1944). According to one source, *Song of Norway* in particular inspired Blevins Davis to produce *Rhapsody*.[13]

The celebrated Austrian violinist Friedrich ("Fritz") Kreisler (1875–1962) differed somewhat from many of the cited émigrés in that he and his American wife had had a close association with New York that dated back to the early years of the twentieth century. Born into an at least partly Jewish family, but raised Catholic, Kreisler studied both in his native Vienna and in Paris, and quickly achieved great fame for his superbly lyrical violin playing as well as for his delightful encore pieces and eighteenth-century hoaxes. Edward Elgar dedicated his Violin Concerto to Kreisler, who premiered the piece in 1910. But Kreisler had success as a theater composer as well, writing two well-received operettas: *Apple Blossoms* (1919), with composer Victor Jacobi and librettist William Le Baron, for Broadway; and *Sissy* (1932), with librettists Ernst and Hubert Marischka, for Vienna. *Apple Blossoms,* set in New York, accommodated local taste by absorbing something from Victor Herbert, whereas the utterly Viennese *Sissy,* set in nineteenth-century Bavaria, fell more squarely in the tradition of Strauss and Lehár.[14]

In May 1944, Blevins Davis (1903–1971) reached an agreement with Kreisler's general manager, Charles Foley, that allowed him the use of the composer's music for a new show, with Kreisler essentially retaining the rights to the material. Armed with lavish support from Lorraine Dresselhuys—an asbestos heiress and former actress then married to her third husband, a Dutch banker—Davis commissioned Broadway's foremost orchestrator and arranger, Robert Russell Bennett (1894–1981), to adapt Kreisler's music, in particular the score to *Sissy,* whose orchestrations Bennett had prepared at the time of its Viennese premiere, and which itself had recycled some music from *Apple Blossoms* and several of the composer's most famous violin pieces. As with *Carmen Jones,* whose musical score he also had prepared, Bennett stayed close to his original source material, in contrast to the more freewheeling adaptations undertaken by Robert Wright and George Forrest for *Song of Norway* and later *Kismet* (after Borodin, 1953) and *Anya* (after Rachmaninoff, 1965).[15]

Davis further hired the exiled Austrian drama critic Alois M. Nagler (1907–1993) to create a scenario for the show. Since arriving in the United States, Nagler, a leading authority on Viennese theater, had carved a niche for himself as a teacher and researcher for several American colleges, notably Yale University, whose faculty he eventually joined. Indeed, Davis possibly met Nagler through shared Yale contacts. In any case, he wrote Nagler that the latter "might as well save a great deal of time" and model his scenario after *Sissy,* although he advised further that the story be brought "up to date in tempo and situation."[16]

Based on the 1931 play *Sissys Brautfahrt* ("Sissy's Bridal Journey"), Kreisler's *Sissy*—like its 1936 Hollywood adaptation, *The King Steps Out,* a vehicle for Grace Moore directed by Josef von Sternberg—takes as its subject the 1854 marriage of the young Elizabeth von Wittelsbach (the "Sissy" of the title) to Emperor Franz Joseph I. Nagler retained the idea of a romantic comedy set against the background of the Hapsburg court, but placed the action back some one hundred years, with the historical personages including Emperor Francis I, Maria Theresa, and the adventurer Giacomo Casanova; and reconfigured the heroine as a commoner in love with a rebellious actor. Nagler's convoluted story and its many variants, alternately called

Rhapsody and *May Wine*, suggest the influence of *Der Rosenkavalier* and other works by the Viennese poet and librettist Hugo von Hofmannsthal, about whom Nagler often lectured.[17]

Davis entrusted the actual dialogue to Arnold Sundgaard (1909–2006), a playwright then best known for a controversial Living Newspaper drama about syphilis, but later to make his mark primarily as a librettist for Kurt Weill, Douglas Moore, and others. The show's director, Henry Wagstaff Gribble (1896–1981), worked on the script as well. Davis, who started to write the lyrics himself in collaboration with Bennett before entrusting them to Latouche, also engaged David Lichine as choreographer, Oliver Smith as set designer, Frank Bevan as costume designer, Stanley McCandless as lighting designer, and Fritz Mahler as musical director.

Latouche apparently joined the show rather late in the game, perhaps even after the operetta went into rehearsal in late September, for the earliest references to him as such seem to date from October. Davis ostensibly came to realize the advantages of having a professional lyricist on board, especially someone of Latouche's particular abilities. For his part, Latouche presumably signed on at least partly for financial reasons, but his closeness to the émigré community and his fondness for operetta surely factored in as well. "I like sentiment, but my own kind, not the kind I'm told I should have . . . ," he wrote in his journal the previous year. "I want to be free to like [Engelbert] Humperdinck and Victor Herbert and [A. A.] Milne."[18]

Originally scheduled to debut, without any out-of-town tryouts, on October 30 at the recently refurbished and newly named New Century Theatre, the premiere was postponed, reportedly because of book trouble, first to November 6; then, after the departure of Gribble and the assumption of the stage direction by Lichine, to November 11; and finally to November 22. Already an expensive production—what with its elaborate sets and costumes, large cast, orchestra of some forty players, and numerous stagehands, not to mention the high rent at the capacious New Century Theatre—these delays, including the need to settle with Gribble, meant ever-increasing outlays of cash, with some sources reporting the show's cost as high as $300,000 and even $400,000, more than twice the original budget of $150,000.[19]

During the extended rehearsal period, radio writer Leonard L. Levinson (1904–1974), in collaboration with Sundgaard and Latouche, revamped the book, although to what extent remains difficult to say. In later years, in a note to fellow producer George Freedley that accompanied this revised script, producer Davis disdainfully commented, "As you know I never approved this tripe. Am delighted to send it to you as an example of Leonard Levinson's writing. He, like *Lichine*, is good in his field as a gag man—the latter the dance—but in a musical with *great music* he was out of place." Levinson at least seems to have helped simplify the book, which remained rather convoluted nevertheless.[20]

Rhapsody takes place during the reign of Maria Theresa in Vienna, from noon to midnight on the shared birthday of Emperor Francis I and the young Lili Hugenhaugen.

Act I, scene one. Music Room of the Hugenhaugen Home. The daughter of Vienna's court master of ceremonies Lotzi Hugenhaugen and court ballet mistress Tina Hugenhaugen, Lili Hugenhaugen furtively embraces her lover, Charles Eckert, who presides over the entertainment at a suburban tavern, the Maywine Pavilion. Tina informs Lotzi that in honor of the Emperor's birthday, the diva Madame Boticini has arrived courtesy of France, and a ballet troupe, courtesy of Russia. Casanova, an aging libertine enamored with Lili, pays a call ("They're All the Same," for Casanova, Ilse, and women soloists). Charles invites Lili to celebrate her birthday at the Maywine Pavilion ("My Rhapsody," for Lili and Charles). Boticini and Casanova, spies and agitators in the service of Madame Pompadour, hope to incite a royal scandal ("Scherzo," for Boticini).

Scene two. Gardens at Schoenbrunn Palace. Emperor Francis reflects on his happy married life ("Heaven Bless Our Home," for Francis). Boticini attempts to seduce the Emperor, her efforts foiled by the arrival of Maria Theresa ("The World Is Young Again," for Maria Theresa and Ladies of the Court). A ballet in honor of the Emperor follows ("Presentation," for Maria Theresa, Francis, Boticini, Captain of the Guard, and the ensemble; and "Chinese Porcelain Ballet," for Ilse, Ivan, Rickshaw Man, and women of the corps de ballet). Boticini and Casanova arrange things so that during the royal treasure hunt the Emperor will find himself alone with Boticini ("To Horse," for Boticini, Casanova, Lotzi, and Tina).

Scene three. Maywine Pavilion Outside Vienna. Merrymakers sing and dance ("The Dandy's Polka," for The Dandy; and "May Wine Polka," for the corps de ballet and the ensemble). Charles and Lili express their love ("Take Love," for Lili, Charles, and the ensemble). A danced enactment of the royal treasure hunt follows ("The Hunt," for Ilse, the corps de ballet, and the ensemble). Boticini's young black servant, Demi-Tasse, seeks his freedom. A satirical dance proceeds in defiance of an official decree that Charles desist from any theatrical presentations ("The Roulette Game," for Sonya, assisted by featured dancer Nicholas Beriozoff, the corps de ballet, and the ensemble). Imperial guards arrest Charles against the protests of his friends ("Song of Defiance," for Charles and the ensemble).

Act II, scene one. The Jail. Lili and her friends help Charles escape from jail ("Because You're Mine," for Charles; and "When Men Are Free," for Charles and the ensemble).

Scene two. Apartment of Casanova in the Palace. Maria Theresa suspects her husband of infidelity ("Happy Ending," for Maria Theresa). Boticini once again tries to seduce the Emperor ("Rosemarin," for Boticini). Lili and Charles expose Boticini and Casanova to the Empress, who banishes the schemers from Austria.

Scene three. The Ballroom of Schoenbrunn Palace. Maria Theresa and Francis share a tender moment ("Caprice Viennois," for Maria Theresa and Francis). All ends happily ("Midnight Ballet," for Ilse, Ivan, Sonya, and the corps de ballet; and "Finale," including a reprise of "Happy Ending," the lyric modified, for the entire company).[21]

Such an Austrian lovefest on Broadway as *Rhapsody* might seem odd in light of America's contemporary struggle against a greater Germany, but the script significantly alludes to the threat of Prussian armed intervention, and the show as a whole—as with the rekindled interest in Viennese operetta more generally—can be seen in the framework of a growing perception of Austria as the first nation to fall victim to Nazi aggression, as expressed in late 1943 by official Allied rejection of the German annexation of the country as null and void and by inclusion of Austria in the "overrun countries" series of commemorative stamps released by the U.S. Post Office. Nagler took pains to censor character names that he thought sounded too Prussian, and the bookwriters duly responded to such concerns by changing, for instance, the hero Charles Wagner to Charles Eckert, and the maid Gretchen to Greta. Moreover, the theme of subversive theater suppressed by official mandate resonated with actual developments in Austria—as Latouche well knew from his ties with the Refugee Artists Group—and implied support for Austrian resistance, even giving the operetta a strong political overtone. That Demi-Tasse—although descended from Mohammed, the Marschallin's servant in *Der Rosenkavalier*, and still a figure of some hackneyed racial humor—should collaborate with the rebels to attain his freedom reflected some related progressive social trends as well.[22]

Latouche provided the lyrics to nearly all the songs, including "They're All the Same," "Scherzo," "Heaven Bless Our Home," "The World Is Young Again," "To Horse," "Take Love," "Song of Defiance," "Happy Ending," "Rosemarin," "Caprice Viennois," and perhaps others, as well as at least one song not used in the production, "The Way They Do It in Paris." Although attuned to old-fashioned sentiment, these lyrics exhibited an uncommon sophistication, especially for an operetta text. A comparison, for example, between Latouche's lyrics for two Kreisler violin pieces—*Liebesleid* ("Love's Sorrow") as "The World Is Young Again," and *Caprice viennois* as "Caprice Viennois"—and the lyricizations of these same melodies by the Marischka brothers in *Sissy*, or Dorothy Fields in *The King Steps Out*, or Tommie Connor in a later, more faithful English adaptation of *Sissy* entitled *Lisa*, reveals Latouche's distinction both poetically and dramatically. In "The World Is Young Again," for instance, rather than write a conventional love lyric, Latouche evoked the seasonal return of summer as an apt metaphor for Maria Theresa's renewed feelings of love:

The season of my heart has begun
Summer brings her gifts one by one
Joyful is the shimmering sun
All the world is young again.

In "Caprice Viennois," a duet originally intended for the Emperor and his seductress, but later given to Francis and Maria Theresa, Latouche created a compelling narrative about adulterous love—"I fell in love, and my love was complete / I thought the magic was through / Then you appear, so enchantingly sweet / Singing a song that is new"—a lyric that well suited the sensuous whimsy of the music, and that contained, moreover, a line that a few years later would form the title of a Latouche song written with composer Rudolph Goehr: "All of a sudden it's you."[23]

The show afforded some outlet for Latouche's wit as well. One number, "They're All the Same," a catalog song that lists some of Casanova's conquests, anticipated Cole Porter's similarly saucy "Where Is the Life That Late I Led?" (*Kiss Me, Kate*), in particular, the lines, "There's darling Lisa back in Pisa / We were in the leaning tow'r the night she fell." And in "Rosemarin," a lyricization of Kreisler's violin piece *Schön Rosmarin,* the refrains of "la's" not only accommodated the piece's violin figuration, but added some slyness to this winsome ballad about the pursued village maiden Rosemarin:

She got the carriage trade
As well as marriage trade
And none could ever guess
The key to her success
To men embracing her
Or madly chasing her
Or else unlacing her
She['d] smile and say,
La la la la la, etc.

The November 22, 1944, premiere at the New Century starred Annamary Dickey (Maria Theresa), George Young (Emperor Francis I), Gloria Story (Lili), John Hamill (Charles), Rosemarie Brancato (Boticini), Eddie Mayehoff (Casanova), and others, including featured dancers Patricia Bowman (Ilse), Alexandra Denisova (Sonya), and Jerry Ross (The Dandy)—a diverse group drawn from opera, ballet, musical comedy, and in the case of Mayehoff, radio comedy. Aside from opening night, for which a premium ticket cost as much as $12.00, admission ranged from $1.20 to $6.00, depending on the day and so on. The program named Sundgaard and Levinson as the show's bookwriters, and Latouche as lyricist, with unspecified "additional lyrics" by Davis and Bennett.

The critics liked the music but not the script, which Wilella Waldorf (*Post*) thought "laboriously smutty and monumentally dull," and Ward Morehouse (*Sun*), "the dreariest book within memory." Waldorf and Morehouse loathed the show in general, the former calling it, "a ponderous, pretentious, preposterous mess," and the latter, "a theatrical calamity of major proportions," whereas several other critics looked more kindly on at least certain aspects of the production. But aside from *Cue* magazine, which unaccountably handed this "charming operetta" a rave, virtually all the notices thought the show a colossal waste of talent and expense: "As an example of what money can't do, it's a masterpiece," stated Robert Garland in the *Journal-American*.[24]

The scant critical attention paid the lyrics tended to be dismissive—John Chapman (*Daily News*), for instance, called them "quaintly awful," and Wilella Waldorf similarly thought them to possess the "faintly nauseous, coyly leering quality of the book"—but the sporadic praise of certain numbers, including "Take Love," suggested tacit approval of at least some of Latouche's work. Moreover, the generally harsh assessment of the lyrics seems mitigated by the fact that the production's weak voices and poor acoustics made it often difficult to understand the words.

Kreisler attended opening night, "beaming good-will at every one upon the stage," according to the *Daily News,* although he allegedly thought the whole enterprise dubious, claiming that Lorraine Dresselhuys "made the mistake of wanting to manage everything." "*Rhapsody* was never approved by Fritz," recalled Kreisler's manager, Charles Foley. "I refused to attend rehearsals after I had had one look at the affair. Fritz also had nothing to do with it except that, as a courtesy, he attended the opening night."[25]

Rhapsody closed deep in the red on December 2, 1944, after only fourteen performances. Dresselhuys donated the show's sets and costumes to New York City Center, and Davis and Sundgaard undertook yet more revisions on the script in the hopes of a performance there in the spring. But the show remained unresurrected and quickly drifted into oblivion.[26]

Although several reviews intimated the commercial possibilities of a few numbers, the fact that Foley sold the music rights to publisher Max Dreyfus but Latouche remained under contract to Jack Robbins, who, reported *Variety,* "made an issue of the matter," seems to have impeded the publication of any of the songs from the show. In any event, nothing from the score circulated after the operetta closed, although the combination of Kreisler and Latouche, so full of charm and good humor, might yet find its way to listeners "free to like Humperdinck and Victor Herbert and Milne."[27]

13

Polonaise

As the war came to its end, Latouche viewed the world with alarm. The repudiation of Henry Wallace by the U.S. Senate and the death of President Roosevelt depressed him, as did the "appalling complacency and ignorance" of American youth (for all their "physical beauty") and the similarly "complacent jingoism and rotarian zeal for the Big News Thrill" as represented by such publications as *Life* and *Time* magazines and the Hearst newspapers. "The atomic bomb is a fitting achievement for an epoch which has already produced fascism, political tortures, segregation and sexual anarchy," he wrote on August 7, the day after Hiroshima. Out of such bitterness came "You Live a Little Longer That Way," one of several songs written with composer David Broekman in early 1945, not to mention *Willie the Weeper* and *Beggar's Holiday*. At the same time, he managed to dispel such gloom with an optimistic anthem, "Wait for Tomorrow," from his 1945 operetta *Polonaise,* a song vaguely comparable to "You'll Never Walk Alone" from *Carousel,* which had opened earlier that year.[1]

Latouche certainly showed no complacency about his own life. On the contrary, he frequently chastised himself for his impulsiveness and indolence (he concluded, at least, that he worked best in the early morning and late at night) and expressed dissatisfaction with what he had accomplished thus far, readying himself rather for the "big work" that lay ahead. This involved delving still deeper into spiritual and psychological matters; he read books and pamphlets on yoga and psychic phenomena, spent time with the likes of medium Eileen Garrett and hypnotist Andrew Salter, and kept a record of his dreams. In January, he offered this summation of his philosophical outlook, one that revealed his affinity to Epicureanism and Eastern mysticism:

> I know... that there is no fixed state: that Lucretius and the Eastern theorists were closer to truth than our fine stodgy Steam-Boiler Socrates's and Machine-Made Marx's. Yet it is not a circle of repetition, but a swooping and descending spiral, that moves through dark and light impassively, discarding the wornout civilizations, dreaming out the old conceptions, reweaving grass and earth into a new combination of meadow; reshaping bodies and impulses into new shades of involution and evolution.

Latouche also drew inspiration from an eighteenth-century French writer, the Marquis de Vauvenargues, some of whose aphorisms he copied out in his journal, including the maxim, "The falsest of all philosophies is that which, under pretext of freeing mankind from the toils of passion, councils [*sic*] indifference, resignation, and self-forgetfulness."[2]

Relatedly, Latouche welcomed—after military service and the dissolution of his marriage—the prospect of some time alone, but he seemed to find himself surrounded, as ever, by scores of people, including apparently several male lovers. Some new acquaintances signaled shifts in the cultural terrain. In January 1945, at a cocktail party hosted by his friend Ruth Yorck, for instance, he met the French writer and philosopher Jean-Paul Sartre, observing in his journal, "A tiny, sedate gargoyle with a sick, brilliant mind: I liked him." Still, he found his interest at the reception focused rather on another guest, the composer-writer Maurice Sandoz, who told the lyricist that he could produce the stigmata in a matter of minutes.[3]

Latouche became particularly intrigued with composer John Cage, who since moving to New York in 1942 with his wife, Xenia Kashevaroff, had cultivated a social circle that overlapped with his own, including mutual friends Virgil Thomson, Peter Lindamood, Marian Dunham, and Paul and Jane Bowles. Latouche had met Cage before entering the military, "but it was about work," as he wrote Dunham while in the service, "and he was quite subdued. I found him very nice altho he seemed a Chawlie Fawd [probably a reference to their Mississippian friend, poet Charles Henri Ford] stepped up with a hormone of two: tales of his wit and charm reach me by several channels. At any rate, I'm glad SOME of the new youngs are gay [meaning presumably spirited and not necessarily homosexual]." Latouche's allusion to "work" perhaps involved his success, during the summer of 1943, in persuading Herbert Jacoby to offer to showcase Cage at the cabaret the Blue Angel, an invitation Cage ultimately declined: "I am so completely on fringe of acceptability," the composer explained to his lover, choreographer Merce Cunningham, "that such an action would remove what of doubt remains in bourgeois heads."[4]

Back in New York after his military discharge, Latouche, along with his friend, designer Oliver Smith, subsidized a prepared-piano recital of Cage's music performed alternately by the composer and duo-pianists Arthur Gold and Robert Fizdale at the New School for Social Research on the afternoon of January 21, 1945; at a post-concert party at Virgil Thomson's, Latouche presented Cage, "as a token for the excitement of his work," a watch that Paul Bowles had given to him. Three days afterward, Cage visited Latouche, who, feeling that "concert halls are dead forms," suggested that the composer stage an event at a boxing ring or a basketball court, so that the audience, sitting in bleachers, would be able to look down and observe the prepared piano. The following day, at the forementioned gathering for Sartre, Latouche found both Cage and Jane Bowles "stand-offish and terse," but he remained friendly with Cage and his wife, who invited Latouche to a party at their place toward the end of the year.[5]

As for new collaborators, in early 1945 Latouche worked with composer David Broekman on a series of songs, seven of which survive in manuscript among the papers of Latouche's agent, Lucy Kroll. Born in Leiden, the Netherlands, Broekman (1899–1958) studied at the Royal Conservatory of The Hague and conducted regional orchestras before arriving in New York in 1924. In the late 1920s and early 1930s, he worked in Hollywood directing the music for numerous films, but in the late 1930s he returned to New York, where he pursued a career as conductor and composer for radio, television, and the concert hall. Reviewing the premiere of his one-act "folk opera" *Barbara Allen* (1953), to a libretto by Edward Eager, *Times* critic Harold Schonberg deemed the work comparable to Kurt Weill's *Down in the Valley*, although superior "in matters of prosody and dramatic force."[6]

Latouche and Broekman could have met through any number of contacts, but probably knew each other best through their shared radio work, including those Latouche *Treasury Star Parade* shows for which Broekman had written the music. In any case, the surviving seven songs they wrote together—with Latouche, in at least one instance, knocking out a lyric in a single session—tend decidedly toward American and in particular African-American folklore, with "Grey Goose" adapting a folksong popularized by Huddie Ledbetter in the 1930s, and "The Lord and Me" resembling a spiritual; "I'm Walking Beside You," a gospel hymn; "Till My Man Comes Home to Me," the blues; and "My Home Behind the Sun," a bluesy lullaby. The humorous "Sunday Go to Meetin' Time" and caustic "You Live a Little Longer That Way" brandish a certain downhome quality as well. At the same time, these numbers fall more in the category of the folkloric concert song than either more rustic or commercial genres.

During these same years, Latouche grew particularly close to a young gay composer named Donald Fuller (1919–1975), although their only extant collaborations seem to date from a later period. Born in Washington, D.C., to a wealthy family, Fuller studied music at Yale with Richard Donovan and David Stanley Smith, but quit school before completing his degree. He subsequently studied composition with Bernard Wagenaar at Juilliard, Aaron Copland at Tanglewood, and Darius Milhaud at Mills College.[7]

In the early 1940s, Fuller joined the staff of *Modern Music*, the venerable quarterly devoted to contemporary music founded by the League of Composers in 1924 and published under the supervision of Minna Lederman. Remaining with *Modern Music* until it folded in 1946, Fuller assumed the "arduous task," in Lederman's words, of reporting on new music in New York, which meant reviewing every season dozens of concerts, including many important world and American premieres. He in due course became associate editor of the magazine as well.[8]

Fuller's reviews for *Modern Music* bespeak a high regard not only for his teachers Donovan, Wagenaar, Copland, and Milhaud, but for Bartók, Stravinsky, Prokofiev, Poulenc, and at least certain pieces by Schoenberg, Ives, Martinů, Hindemith, Sessions, Revueltas, Blitzstein, Shostakovich, Cage, and many others. These articles might not boast the profundity or wit of some of the magazine's best writers, like Blitzstein or Virgil Thomson, but they reveal nonetheless a maturity and sophistication remarkable for someone in his midtwenties; Minna Lederman would not have entrusted him with so crucial a job without the approval of such a friend and advisor as Aaron Copland. No doubt Latouche's friendship with Fuller helped ensure the lyricist's continued familiarity with a wide diversity of serious new music.

Following the collapse of *Modern Music*, Fuller continued to earn his livelihood primarily as an editor, although he pursued, at least for a while, a compositional career as well, including writing songs with Latouche. Unfortunately, for all his gifts, his alcoholism—Ned Rorem recalled that Latouche would refer to Fuller as "his drunk composer"—seems to have helped sabotage his ambitions. In any case, the last years of his relatively short life remain shrouded in obscurity.[9]

How Fuller and Latouche met remains unknown, but the relationship apparently became romantic for a while. Discussing with Andrew Drummond the time—probably just after the war—when he and Latouche lived together, Fuller recalled an exhausting round of moves and social events as well as tantrums and spats, including one instance when the two "grappled on the kitchen floor at the height of a party for over one-hundred people." He further recollected his being moved to tears by Latouche's renditions of folksongs at the piano, and their shared love for reading aloud horror comic books. After they parted, Fuller maintained a warm friendship with Latouche, whom he thought, for all his large social circle, an essentially lonely person who had trouble relating well to others.[10]

In early 1945, the novice producer W. Horace Schmidlapp announced a new show for the fall, *Polonaise*, about the Polish military hero Tadeusz Kościuszko, with a book by Gottfried Reinhardt and Anthony Veiller and a score adapted from Chopin by Bronislaw ("Bronek") Kaper, a project that eventually involved Latouche as well. Born in Berlin, Reinhardt (1913–1994), the son of the famed director Max Reinhardt, and like his father a good friend of Eleonora Mendelssohn, had coauthored scripts for Broadway adaptations of Strauss's *Die Fledermaus* (*Rosalinda*, 1942) and Offenbach's *La belle Hélène* (*Helen Goes to Troy*, 1944), although he worked mostly as a writer and producer in Hollywood. His co-writer, Veiller (1903–1965), a New York native, similarly had established himself in Hollywood, primarily as a screenwriter. Like Reinhardt and Veiller, the Polish-born composer Kaper (1902–1983), a graduate of the Warsaw Conservatory, also worked mainly in film, first in Berlin and Paris, but by the mid-1930s, in Hollywood, where he embarked on a long and distinguished career, his many notable film scores including *Lili* (1953), which earned him an Oscar. For a while, the veteran producer Vinton Freedley joined forces as well, but in late May, citing the expense of a show slated to cost somewhere between $150,000 and $200,000, he bowed out, his position as co-producer assumed by Harry Bloomfield.[11]

The adaptation of especially nineteenth-century musical classics for use in popular song and musical theater had by this point a long history. The work of Frédéric Chopin (1810–1849) already had yielded the hit song "I'm Always Chasing Rainbows" (1918) as well as a musicalized depiction of the composer's life, *White Lilacs* (1928), itself a response to an operetta about Schubert, *Blossom Time* (1921), a work so popular as to enjoy periodic Broadway revivals, including one in 1943. As mentioned in the context of Latouche's *Rhapsody,* based on the music of Fritz Kreisler, the early 1940s witnessed an upsurge of such practices on Broadway, especially in the wake of *Carmen Jones* (1943), after Bizet's *Carmen,* and *Song of Norway* (1944), about Edvard Grieg's life and work; indeed, in July 1945, the *Times* cited a conspicuous number of current and planned Broadway musicals based on classical music, including not only *Song of Norway* and *Polonaise,* but adaptations of Mendelssohn, Tchaikovsky, and Dvořák.[12]

Chopin seems to have been particularly in the air. In early 1945, about the time Schmidlapp announced plans to launch *Polonaise,* Columbia Pictures released *A Song to Remember,* an acclaimed motion picture about Chopin that according to a contemporary observer prompted "phenomenal" and "unprecedented" interest in the Polish composer. "Chopin provided for American viewers of the 1940s," writes Ivan Raykoff in a recent study of the film, "an allegorical figure of resistance to Nazi aggression in the overrun nations of Europe, and a model of selfless sacrifice in the cause of freedom." The composer's A-flat major Polonaise, which served a symbolic function in the movie similar to that of the Grieg Piano Concerto in *Song of Norway,* became especially popular, not only as recorded by José Iturbi and other concert pianists, but as arranged for piano and dance band by Carmen Cavallaro—a predecessor to the even-better-known Liberace—as *Chopin's Polonaise* (1945), and as arranged and lyricized by Buddy Kaye and Ted Mossman as "Till the End of Time" (also 1945), a big hit for crooner Perry Como and others. "Making pop music out of the polonaise cleverly tapped into the reservoir of politicized connotation and wartime nostalgia that was generated by the piece," comments Raykoff.[13]

Tadeusz Kościuszko (1746–1817)—one of the world's most honored Poles, and one whose name during the Second World War marked a squadron of the British Royal Air Force manned by Polish flyers—cut another emblematic figure. Born in the Polish-Lithuanian Commonwealth, Kościuszko fought as a commanding officer under George Washington in the American Revolutionary War and then for Polish independence in the Polish-Russian War of 1792 and the Kościuszko Uprising of 1794. A student of art and architecture, a champion of the rights of minorities and the dispossessed, an enlightened freethinker who enjoyed a close friendship with Thomas Jefferson, Kościuszko came to represent over the years, writes historian Halina Filipowicz, "a man positively overflowing with stock Polish attributes: love of freedom, courage in adversity, passionate, selfless generosity, and especially 'that most engaging quality of his nation, what we may term the Polish sweetness,' " this last phrase taken from a 1920 biography by Monica M. Gardner that for decades served as a chief source in English about the Polish hero. That the creators of *Polonaise* would think of conflating Kościuszko and Chopin—the two most potent symbols of Polish nationalism—seems understandable enough, notwithstanding their many differences, including the fact that they belonged to different generations. The polonaise—a stately Polish dance that by the late eighteenth century had acquired strong political resonance—itself united them, Kościuszko in having polonaises attributed to and named after him; Chopin, in writing a splendid series of polonaises for the piano.[14]

From the start, Schmidlapp seems to have had in mind for the role of Thaddeus Kosciusko (as the operetta spelled his name), the Polish tenor Jan Kiepura (1902–1966), not coincidentally a good friend of Bronislaw Kaper, who also had co-written one of Kiepura's first big hits, "Ninon." Then at the height of his fame, the dashing Kiepura had appeared in opera houses around the world but had achieved success in film and light opera as well, sometimes partnering with his wife, the beautiful Hungarian film and operetta star Marta Eggerth (1912–2013). Married in 1936, Kiepura and Eggerth, both Jewish on their maternal sides, found refuge in 1938 in the United States, where for several years they worked apart, Kiepura singing leading lyric tenor roles at the Metropolitan Opera, Eggerth working for MGM as a featured artist in two Judy Garland musicals. But in 1943, they reunited for an acclaimed Broadway revival of *The Merry Widow*, with choreography by George Balanchine, which set the course for their future. Ultimately performing *The Merry Widow* hundreds of times, Kiepura found the Lehár operetta closer to his "real temperament" than opera, stating, "I do not like to kill, and opera is full of killings. Always killing Carmen, bah. I do not like to kill women, I like to kiss them." After signing Kiepura, Schmidlapp considered Risë Stevens and Theodora Lynch as potential co-stars for some future film adaptation of the show, but by the summer, he naturally enough had contracted Eggerth to play against her husband on stage.[15]

Although he only recently had weathered the dismal fate of the all-too-similar *Rhapsody*—another costume drama based on classic European melodies—Latouche agreed in early April to write the lyrics. "I finally gave up and signed a contract to do *Polonaise*, a musical produced by Vinton Freedley," he wrote in his journal on April 3. "It is not yet the time for my release into my big work—the foundation stones must be laid more solidly." (This entry suggests a closer connection to Freedley, who had co-produced *Cabin in the Sky*, than with Schmidlapp, who also had been involved with that earlier show as an investor.) In late April, Latouche rented a house in Los Angeles from screenwriter Jesse Lasky Jr., the son of his friends Jesse and Bessie Lasky, and spent much of May and June working on the operetta in Los Angeles. On May 25, he wrote in his diary, only sporadically maintained at this point, about "a horrifying evening" at Chasen's, a popular restaurant near Beverly Hills, with Schmidlapp and his soon-to-be wife, actress Carole Landis; Gottfried Reinhardt and his wife, Silvia; Curt Bois, the German-Jewish refugee actor scheduled to play the operetta's main comic character; and Bronislaw Kaper. "They all behaved like lunatics," wrote Latouche in his journal, "—and I did not feel like a lunatic—a dangerous point of view, because earlier I *did*. . . . Oh hell, when will all this miasma that haunts our time be clarified."[16]

Leaving Los Angeles, Latouche spent most of July in rural Pennsylvania with composer Jerome Moross and his wife, Hazel, and their young daughter, Susanna. As he worked with Moross on *Willie the Weeper* (from *Ballet Ballads*), he avoided alcohol, resumed his yoga exercises, took inventory of his anxieties, including his "mild persecution complex," and enjoyed Hazel's cooking and Moross's Mozart at the piano, played "with conviction and excitement." "Haunting, penetrating, the persistent elegance of his [Mozart's] music," reflected Latouche; "through the decaying worlds it travelled, and travels yet, signing its poignant name over and over on each new evening." Moross appeared distraught himself, contending one evening that Jews would lose their civil rights in the United States, as they had over the centuries in Europe, and as Japanese-Americans had during the current world war.[17]

At the end of the month, Latouche returned to New York to prepare for the Broadway opening of *Polonaise*. In addition to Kiepura (Kosciusko), Eggerth (Marisha), and Curt Bois (Sergeant Wacek Zapolski), the show starred, at least during tryouts, operatic soprano Rose Inghram (Countess Ludwika Zaleski); actor Ferdi Hoffman (General Boris Volkoff); the dancer and former collegiate fullback Rem[ington] Olmsted (Wladek); and ballerina Tania Riabouchinska (Tecla), the wife of the show's choreographer, David Lichine. The production also featured stage direction by Edward Duryea Dowling, sets by Howard Bay, costumes by Mary Grant, orchestrations by Don Walker, choral arrangements by Irving Landau, and musical direction by Max Goberman, although, as with the cast, some of this personnel changed on the road.

Latouche arrived in Hartford, Connecticut, in early September with the company in anticipation of the world premiere at Bushnell Auditorium on September 13. After a rocky opening, marred by, among other mishaps, a delayed curtain and an ailing Kiepura, the show gave three performances in Hartford before moving on to Ford's Theatre in Baltimore on September 17 and the National Theatre in Washington on September 24. Helped by Kiepura and Eggerth's recent triumph in *The Merry Widow*, business at the box office proved brisk, although aside from a strong endorsement from the *Billboard*, the notices tended to be negative. Above all, the reviews, even while praising the production, which cost about $180,000, as attractive and colorful, criticized the book as plodding and humorless, and the score—except for the "Heroic" Polonaise, which patrons hummed and whistled on their way out of the theater—as tuneless and unmemorable. The *Hartford Courant* mentioned in this context the challenge of adapting classical piano music for the lyric theater: "It doesn't suit the highbrows or purists and it does not get over to the average theater goer." Moreover, as the *Courant* discovered during an informal poll taken during intermission, many in the audience, probably thinking of *Song of Norway* or *A Song to Remember*, expected a show about Chopin's life as opposed to a somewhat obscure Polish military hero.[18]

Before the musical opened on Broadway, management instituted a number of changes, replacing Edward Dowling with Stella Adler as director, Max Goberman with Ignace Strasfogel as musical director, and Ferdi Hoffman with Harry Bannister as Volkoff, among other cast alterations. In addition, the book was shortened, and some numbers were cut.

A tentative synopsis of the show as it more or less arrived at the Alvin Theatre on Broadway, based on an early script and other materials, follows below, with the parenthetical attributions to Chopin's work determined from various playbills as well as from the score, most of which survives, with one lost number, "Hay, Hay, Hay," apparently derived from a Polish folksong. (As in *A Song to Remember*, the Chopin used drew largely on some of the composer's most familiar music.)

Act I, scene one. The Ramparts—West Point, 1783. General George Washington informs the Polish soldier Thaddeus Kosciusko that he has been promoted to the rank of general for his service during the American Revolution. Kosciusko and his sidekick, Sergeant Wacek Zapolski, resolve to return to Europe to fight for Polish independence.

Scene two. The Waterfront—New York. The philandering Zapolski says his farewells to his various amours.

Scene three. A Hayfield near Cracow, Poland. Some time later. Kosciusko and Zapolski, disguised as Romanian silk merchants, make their way to the estate of Count Casimir Zaleski near Cracow. As peasants pitch hay, Marisha, "a comely peasant girl with a great and infectious gaiety"; her brother Wladek; and others join in song ("Autumn Songs," for Marisha, Wladek, and Peasants, from Chopin's "Życzenie"). Tecla, "the village belle, a flirtatious wench with a roving eye," dallies with Zapolski ("Laughing Bells," for Tecla and Zapolski, music by Kaper). Kosciusko sings of his homeland ("O Heart of My Country," for Kosciusko, from Chopin's Nocturne in E-flat major, op. 9, no. 2). Marisha finds herself attracted to Kosciusko ("Stranger," for Marisha, music by Kaper). The Russian officer, General Boris Volkoff, attempts to molest Marisha, but Kosciusko comes to her defense. Kosciusko reunites with Count Zaleski, who invites him back to his manor house where other anti-Russian insurgents have gathered.

Scene four. The Road to the Manor House. Tecla and Zapolski plan a rendezvous for that night.

Scene five. The Manor House. That evening, Zaleski's wife, the "vivacious and beautiful, if shallow" Countess Ludwika Zaleski, recalls her youthful infatuation with Kosciusko ("Au Revoir, Soldier" for Ludwika, music by Kaper). The Count and Countess host a peasant harvest festival ("Meadow-lark," for Kosciusko and Peasants, from Chopin's Mazurka in B-flat major, op. 7, no. 1; "Mazurka," for Tecla, Wladek, and Peasants, from various themes of Chopin; and "Hay, Hay, Hay," for Zapolski).

Scene six. The Road to the Hayfield. The festivities continue.

Scene seven. The Hayfield—that night. Kosciusko and Marisha express their love ("Just for Tonight," for Kosciusko and Marisha, from Chopin's Etude in E major).

Tecla succumbs to the romantic atmosphere ("Moonlight Soliloquy," for Tecla, from Chopin's Nocturne in F-sharp major, op. 15, no. 2). Kosciusko and other revolutionary leaders assemble a people's republican army ("Finale," for the ensemble, from Chopin's "Heroic" Polonaise in A-flat major and "Revolutionary" Etude in C minor).

Act II, scene one. The Royal Palace, Warsaw. A few weeks later. As Kosciusko and his followers prepare to lay siege to Warsaw, the members of the imperial court hold a dance ("Gavotte," for Courtiers, from Chopin's *Variations on a French Air* [*sic*]; and "Exchange of Lovers," for the corps de ballet, from various themes of Chopin). Having previously spurned the revolutionaries, Ludwika now abets the rebels, who storm the royal palace ("Polonaise," ballet pantomime, with pianist Zadel Skolovsky featured in Chopin's "Heroic" Polonaise in A-flat major). Kosciusko and Marisha share a romantic moment ("Now I Know Your Face by Heart," for Kosciusko and Marisha, from Chopin's "Minute" Waltz in D-flat major). Ludwika looks forward to a better future ("The Next Time I Care [I'll be Careful]," for Ludwika, music by Kaper). Other numbers follow ("Tecla's Mood" for Tecla and Girls, from various themes of Chopin, including the Scherzo in B-flat minor; "Motherhood" for Zapolski and the Four Princesses, music by Kaper [cut during the run]; and "Wait for Tomorrow," for Kosciusko, from Chopin's Ballade in A-flat major and Piano Sonata in B minor).[19]

Scene two. A Street in Warsaw. Marisha reflects on her love for Kosciusko ("I Wonder as I Wander," for Marisha, from Chopin's Ballade in G minor and *Fantasy-Impromptu*).

Scene three. The Battle of Macijowice (*sic*). A battle unfolds ("Battle Ballet," for the corps de ballet, from four Chopin etudes).[20]

Scene four. Volkoff's Headquarters. After the Battle. Kosciusko surrenders to Volkoff, but admits only temporary defeat (reprises of "Just for Tonight," for Kosciusko and Marisha, and "Wait for Tomorrow," for Kosciusko).

Scene five. The Waterfront—Philadelphia. Some time later. Having been granted his freedom by the Russians, Kosciusko returns to Philadelphia with Marisha ("Finale," for the ensemble).

In devising their script, Reinhardt and Veiller used a central episode in Kościuszko's career, the Kościuszko Uprising, as their primary focus, framed by the Pole's departure from America in 1784 and his return there in 1797. Kościuszko indeed organized a people's army in Cracow in early 1794 and led a rebellion against the Polish state in an attempt to establish a republic, although the operetta incorporated into this episode the hero's earlier 1791 role in helping to form a constitutional monarchy. As also depicted in the show, Kościuszko in fact suffered a crushing defeat at the Battle of Maciejowice near the conclusion of the uprising, one whose end led to the dismemberment of the country. Otherwise, much of the story seems to have been largely imagined, even while drawing on historical personages, with the character of Ludwika, for instance, ostensibly modeled on an early love of Kościuszko, Ludwika Sosnowski, whose real-life husband, Prince Joseph Lubomirski, fought, like Count Zaleski, on the side of the rebels.

As with *Rhapsody, Polonaise* had as a principal subtext the struggle for liberation in Nazi-occupied Europe (although by the time the show opened, the war already had ended). The script tellingly took a few swipes at both Prussia and antisemitism. It also glorified Kościuszko's democratic ideals, including his willingness to identify with both peasants and Jews. "All of us . . . alike," the hero states, at least in an early draft, "Poles, Lithuanians, Ukranians [*sic*], Jews . . . there is no difference now. Prince or peasant, we have embraced one goal . . . freedom."[21]

Although not as literal as the work Robert Russell Bennett had performed for *Carmen Jones* and *Rhapsody*, Kaper hewed closer to the selected Chopin melodies than did many popular adaptations of the classics, resulting in a lyricism that at times brought the score in range of Italian composer Giacomo Orefice's 1901 opera based on Chopin's life and work, *Chopin*. This presented Latouche with the task of writing text that not only would suit the tone of the music and its dramatic context, but also would fit the phraseology of rather complex melodies, many pianistically as opposed to vocally conceived—a challenge deftly handled. In "O Heart of My Country," based on Chopin's most famous nocturne, and here used to express Kosciusko's love for Poland, Latouche, for instance, placed the word "hope" at the phrase's highpoint, and created the tag "that fills the winterland with spring" for the cadential flourish that follows:

O heart of my country
More dear to me than lover
In you I discover
Sweet hope that fills the winterland with spring.

He demonstrated similar dexterity in the first-act finale, to take another example, by accommodating the pianistic bravura of the "Heroic" Polonaise with patter that rolls off the tongue: "Victory! / There is victory in view! / We were living in the shadow but the dawn is breaking through!" Such lyricization of Chopin's melodies plainly called for irregular meters and rhyme schemes, as seen further in the climactic stanza from the operetta's big romantic duet for Kosciusko and Marisha, "Just for Tonight," derived from the Etude in E major:

How can we deny this tender
Moment of complete surrender,
When the night in all its splendor calls,
And will not wait,
Whispers it is late.
One that I adore
Forever more!

The handful of original songs afforded Kaper and Latouche the opportunity to express themselves more freely, with particularly happy results with "The Next

Time I Care," in which Ludwika's cynicism cannot conceal, as intimated in the final couplet, the hurt of a hopeless romantic:

VERSE
The April of my love was fair and gay
Then April wept and danced away,
Now I have strong defenses
My youthful hopes have fled.
I find the game of love is quite an art
I'll play the fool but I'll be smart,
Though I may lose my senses,
I'll never lose my head.
CHORUS
The next time I care I'll be careful,
The next time I fall I'll be wise.
My lips will be warm but my heart will be cold
For someone who's easy to have and to hold.
The next time I care I'll be wary,
I won't keep my head in the skies.
Yet all of the time I'm completely aware,
That this is the last time I'll care.

In light of the recent collapse of Latouche's marriage, and the fact that he often played the fool himself, this lyric can be seen as particularly personal, although its undercurrent of wit helps offset its pathos.

Polonaise opened at the elegant Alvin Theatre on October 6, 1945. The critics, who reported that Rose Inghram stopped the show with "The Next Time I Care," by and large found a thing or two to praise about the production—Arthur Pollock (*Brooklyn Eagle*) seemed particularly impressed with its "big and lusty moments"—but generally outdid one another in clobbering an entertainment widely perceived as "embarrassingly ludicrous," "acutely tiresome," "pompously dull," and "solemn, stodgy, and disjointed." "The best I can say for the thing as a whole," wrote Louis Kronenberger (*PM*), "is that it appalled me enough at times to keep me from being bored. The show has simply spared no expense to gum itself up in every possible way." And Wolcott Gibbs (*New Yorker*) wryly remarked, "In the end, the lovers are reunited happily, though in Philadelphia, and the audience is given its freedom."[22]

Jan Kiepura's wooden acting and stagey grandstanding came in for special ribbing. "His favorite spot is in the middle of the stage at the edge of the apron," wrote John Chapman (*Daily News*), "and there must be some kind of mark there for him so he won't fall off." George Jean Nathan (*Theatre Book*) even referred to Kiepura as "notorious for what is known in the acting profession as temperament," and asserted that the tenor "drove the present management [Schmidlapp and Bloomfield] and the original director, Edward Duryea Dowling, out of their heads by insisting upon hogging attention for himself," thus intimating one reason for Dowling's withdrawal from the show.

The other cast members, especially Eggerth, fared better, as did the score, with only a rare critic like Kronenberger so punctilious as to find the music, as he had with *Rhapsody*, troublingly anachronistic for its subject matter. Bob Francis of the *Billboard*, for instance, deemed Kaper's arrangements of Chopin "canny" and Latouche's lyrics "excellent," while John Chapman similarly regarded the music and "some of the lyrics" as among the show's few assets. In contrast, *Time* magazine thought the Chopin melodies, although the best thing about the show, "vulgarized into schmalzy [*sic*] songs," and Lewis Nichols (*Times*) dismissed the lyrics as "undistinguished." However, as in the case of *Rhapsody*, difficulties in understanding the cast—here clearly due to, in the words of Wilella Waldorf (*Post*), the "formidable accents" of some of the stars—obviously made such evaluations provisional. Howard Barnes (*Herald Tribune*) even found it hard to discern the language in which Kiepura and Eggerth sang, leading him to conclude that it might have behooved the producers to have presented the piece as an opera in Polish. Indeed, Wolcott Gibbs's expressed disappointment with Latouche's lyrics seemed undercut by his admission that "O Heart of My Country" sounded to him like "The Hot of My Corn Tree" (a witticism that must have amused Latouche, who took to calling the song that himself).[23]

With notices even worse than those for *Rhapsody*, *Polonaise* might have been expected to close with comparable alacrity; Robert Garland (*Journal-American*) noted in his review that by the time the show reprised "Just for Tonight," the number "sounded ominously like the piece's theme song." But thanks in part to strong advance sales, the operetta, with ticket prices ranging from $1.20 to $6.00, survived for three months.

Soon after the show opened, Bloomfield acquired Schmidlapp's interest in the property and continued to oversee various changes in the production, including reordering and changing numbers, and replacing Curt Bois with Rex Weber until a series of grievances brought before the Dramatists Guild by the show's composer and two bookwriters led to Bois's reinstatement. Moving to the less glamorous Adelphi Theatre on December 3, the show closed there on January 12 after 113 performances.[24]

In spite of financial problems, Bloomfield, aided by a loan from producer J. J. Levinson, launched a road tour starting in Philadelphia and Boston in January. The reduced company still starred Kiepura, Eggerth, and other members of the original cast, but among other changes, Betty Kean replaced Tania Riabouchinska; Ann Dennis, Rose Inghram; and eventually T. C. Jones, Curt Bois, who quit the show in Chicago. The box office receipts in Philadelphia and Boston proved better than expected, with the show even getting a rave from the *Christian Science Monitor*. Bloomfield attributed the operetta's newfound success to its revised script—comic writer Charles Sherman had a hand in the rewrite—as well as to an increased interest in Chopin, with the producer even establishing a tie-in with RCA Victor to have albums of Chopin's music released in conjunction with the tour.[25]

But as the production moved on to Buffalo, Detroit, Chicago (from where Claudia "Acidy" Cassidy, who despised the show, wrote in the *Tribune*, "This thick but far from succulent slice of Polish ham is equally uncharitable to history, music, and stage, and the audience"), St. Paul, Minneapolis, and Milwaukee, producer Bloomfield—who had planned a six-month tour, followed by a reappearance in New York—experienced continued difficulty making payroll, and the show folded in St. Louis in May.[26]

In 1945, RCA Victor released an album of several selections from the score slickly arranged, featuring Al Goodman and His Orchestra and the Guild Choristers, with Rose Inghram singing, as on stage, "The Next Time I Care," but with Earl Wrightson and Mary Martha Briney standing in for Kiepura and Eggerth. Various numbers also appeared over time on recorded compilations: the duet "Just for Tonight," performed by Nelson Eddy and Ann Jamison; "The Next Time I Care," recorded by both Betty Bennett and Richard Rodney Bennett; and "Wait for Tomorrow," performed by Scott Ailing. Meanwhile, when in 1954 RCA Camden reissued the 1945 album on a long-playing record paired with selections from Victor Herbert's *Eileen* (with Al Goodman billed as Harold Coates), the recording company advertised the work—surprisingly enough, considering that Latouche's name hardly had appeared in any of the reviews for the original show—as "John Latouche's *Polonaise*," a fair indication of how much his name had come to mean in the intervening decade.

14

Beggar's Holiday

In late 1946, a new musical, *Beggar's Holiday*, opened on Broadway, featuring, for the first time, a full-length book as well as lyrics by John Latouche, with music by Duke Ellington. Like *Banjo Eyes* and *Polonaise*, the show managed only a modest run of a little over three months, but proved a far more significant event in the annals of American musical theater.[1]

The idea for *Beggar's Holiday* originated with Perry Watkins (1907–1974), an African-American painter turned technical director and scenic designer who had worked extensively in New York for both the Federal Theatre Project and commercial Broadway productions, becoming in 1939 the first black member of the United Scenic Artists. In the course of 1945, Watkins and co-producer Dale Wasserman (1914–2008), the manager of the Katherine Dunham Dance Company, decided to produce a show of their own, namely, an adaptation of John Gay's classic eighteenth-century musical comedy *The Beggar's Opera*, with an interracial cast and crew (a January 22, 1946, press release mentioning Malaysian, Chinese, and Japanese in addition to black and white participants). Watkins and Wasserman probably knew one another through, among other connections, the ill-fated all-black revue *Blue Holiday* (1945), which featured Katherine Dunham's troupe; and it was likely through Dunham that Wasserman had some acquaintance with Latouche as well.[2]

Watkins and Wasserman seem to have had Latouche in mind for the show early on, at least to judge from Watkins's recollection that when he approached Ellington about the idea, he mentioned Latouche's name. As further recounted by Watkins, Ellington readily accepted the proposal, although he pleaded ignorance with respect to both *The Beggar's Opera* and Latouche, leading Watkins to comment, apparently thinking in particular of his unfamiliarity with Latouche, "And I realized all of a sudden that Duke never went to the theatre very much, but he was probably pulling my leg, too."[3]

Indeed, Ellington's supposed unfamiliarity with Latouche seems implausible given not only the popularity of *Ballad for Americans* and *Cabin in the Sky*, in whose 1943 film version Ellington had appeared, but the fact that Latouche so successfully had lyricized the Billy Strayhorn–Duke Ellington number "Day Dream" in 1941. In any event, looking back on *Beggar's Holiday* in 1967, Ellington referred to Latouche as "one of the great writers of all time" and as someone who wrote the show's "broken" and "wonderful" lyrics; and in 1973, he further stated, "It was a great experience writing with a man like him [Latouche], a man who is so imitated today by other people writing shows. He was truly a great American genius, and he was recognized as such, but he was not an aggressive man and took it all in his stride like a true artist." For his part, Latouche no doubt welcomed the opportunity to collaborate with Ellington, a musical master in his prime and one eminently suited for the project at hand.[4]

Luther Henderson, a black graduate of Juilliard who helped Billy Strayhorn orchestrate and arrange *Beggar's Holiday,* once remarked that Ellington "wanted the recognition of writing a Broadway show more than he wanted to write a Broadway show." Such statements as these have led some commentators to presume a certain lack of interest in the lyric stage on Ellington's part, although the bandleader had participated in theatrical productions for virtually his entire professional life. True, many of these activities simply involved the introduction of a few numbers in some uptown or downtown show, but he had launched his own successful full-scale revue, *Jump for Joy,* on the West Coast in 1941, and for some years had occupied himself with various story musicals, most recently, *H.M.S. Times Square* (1943–45), an unfinished adaptation of Gilbert and Sullivan's *H.M.S. Pinafore.* All the same, Ellington never had had a book musical produced, much as Latouche never had written a musical comedy script for the Broadway stage, so the producers displayed a certain boldness on both counts.[5]

In September 1945, the *Times* announced that Ellington and Latouche—both of whom received a $2,500 advance against royalties and a promised 4 percent of box-office receipts—had begun the process of "converting John Gay's classic into the modern idiom," with a planned February premiere and a production budget of $150,000. Coincidentally, about the same time, another interracial songwriting team—Kurt Weill and Langston Hughes—embarked on a new show, *Street Scene,* that would arrive on Broadway in early January 1947, some two weeks after the Broadway debut of *Beggar's Holiday.* Over the summer of 1946, Latouche and Ellington themselves had considered calling the show "Street Music," and only later rechristened the work *Beggar's Holiday* during rehearsals in the fall (a title that echoed not only the forementioned *Blue Holiday* revue, but two earlier shows from the late 1930s, namely, *The Shoemaker's Holiday* and *Knickerbocker Holiday*), then *Twilight Alley* for its out-of-town tryouts later in the fall, and finally *Beggar's Holiday* for its Broadway premiere at the end of the year. Ironically, but hardly unexpectedly, *Beggar's Holiday* came closer than *Street Scene* to Weill's own Weimar-era adaptation of *The Beggar's Opera,* namely, *The Threepenny Opera,* written in collaboration with Bertolt Brecht.[6]

Beggar's Holiday also could be placed in the context of the vogue for jazzy updates of British classics with African-American casts, including several rival productions of *The Mikado* in the late 1930s, two swing versions of *The H.M.S. Pinafore* in the early 1940s (including Ellington's own aborted *H.M.S. Times Square*), and a 1939 jive adaptation of *A Midsummer Night's Dream* called *Swingin' the Dream*, which featured Louis Armstrong as Bottom. But the legacy of *The Threepenny Opera* towered more decisively, even though the work had flopped in English translation on Broadway in 1933 and would remain more fabled than familiar in the English-speaking world until Marc Blitzstein's adaptation appeared in 1954. As mentioned earlier, Latouche himself for some years had been essaying for friends his own translations of songs from *The Threepenny Opera*. Moreover, Watkins presumably knew something about Clarence Muse's failed attempts during the war to launch an all-black production of the German work in English; Muse's ambitions possibly even helped point Watkins in the direction of *The Beggar's Opera* in the first place.[7]

A friend of Jonathan Swift and Alexander Pope, playwright-poet John Gay (1685–1732) wrote *The Beggar's Opera* (1728), a so-called ballad opera that established practically overnight the prototype for the modern Anglophone musical comedy. Like many operas of that period, the work opened with a prologue, though one presenting not lofty allegorical figures but rather a Beggar, the opera's presumed author, who discusses his work with a Player. As the action proper begins, Peachum, a fence and extortionist, and his wife, Mrs. Peachum, learn from Filch, a young man in Peachum's employ, that their daughter, Polly, has married Captain Macheath, the leader of a gang of thieves and an irrepressible lady's man. Concerned that Macheath might rob him, Peachum arranges, with the assistance of Jenny Diver and several other of Macheath's prostitute girlfriends, for the highwayman's arrest. Incarcerated in Newgate Prison, Macheath makes his escape thanks to another of his lovers, Lucy, the daughter of the corrupt jailor Lockit, a crony of Peachum's. Lucy, pregnant with Macheath's child, unsuccessfully attempts to poison Polly. Betrayed by one of his gang and recaptured, Macheath faces execution, but in response to the Player's objection to so tragic an ending, the Beggar provides a reprieve for Macheath, who reunites with his wife, Polly. In the course of the play's three acts, Gay interpolated no fewer than sixty-nine songs, putting new lyrics to borrowed melodies from a broad repertoire that included folksongs, theater songs, and operatic airs—numbers subsequently arranged and orchestrated by Johann Christoph Pepusch for theatrical presentation.

A work of scathing satire as well as, at times, mock pathos, *The Beggar's Opera* functions allegorically on a number of levels: as a burlesque of both Italian opera and English sentimental romantic comedy, as a withering sendup of British fashion and society, and as a cynical indictment of a topsy-turvy world in which greed and lust undergird presumptions of moral superiority. As part of his research into the work, Latouche scrutinized William Eben Schultz's 1923 study of the opera, jotting in the margins of the book, "my error!" after reading Schultz's observation, "The play is never bookish."[8]

Influential on such nineteenth-century writers as W. S. Gilbert and Oscar Wilde, *The Beggar's Opera* maintained its drawing power with twentieth-century audiences, especially, it would seem, during those disillusioned periods that followed both the First World War, as most famously evidenced by *The Threepenny Opera*, and the Second World War, as witnessed by Benjamin Britten's arrangement of the original score (1948), Peter Brook's film adaptation of the work starring Laurence Olivier (1953), and Marc Blitzstein's long-running English version of *The Threepenny Opera* (1954), not to mention Stravinsky's *The Rake's Progress* (1951), an opera inspired by Gay's contemporary William Hogarth, whose paintings and engravings themselves owed a great debt to *The Beggar's Opera*. "Gay continues to supply a relevant structural and thematic model for understanding the institutional world and social and individualized sensibility that have come into being since the Enlightenment," states Dianne Dugaw in her recent study of *John Gay and the Invention of Modernity*.[9]

Among sundry unpublished notes that Latouche prepared during the musical's genesis, he ventured his own reasons for the work's appeal, including its function as a "social cathartic," and the fact that "it invites an exciting range and variety" for designers, performers, and others. He also commented, with regard to his proposed show, "Properly done, 'The Beggar's Opera' can do for that sterile, sad, retrogressive form of theatre known as musical comedy what it did for the grand opera of 1720. It can, by demonstration of the virtue of proper marriage (of libretto and music), make an honest woman of the whore." All the same, he distinguished his aims from those of Brecht and Weill:

> My intention is to make a contemporary version based on these two Eighteenth Century works [Gay's *The Beggar's Opera* and its suppressed sequel, *Polly*], which will, I hope, retain the pungent, cynical humor of the original, but which will at the same time emphasize its timeless satire.... The bitterness can be overdone. The version by Brecht and Weill, which captured so admirably the desperate cynicism of German audiences after the last World War, reflects how far this interpretation can be carried—but the present American mood demands a different interpretation. It should partake rather of that anxiety, that mixture of dread and hope, which is the keynote of this transitional period.[10]

As to his collaboration with Ellington, Latouche further noted that although both *The Beggar's Opera* and *The Threepenny Opera* "made musical history," there "still remains the wide-open golden opportunity for a native American composer to create both a score and a new musical idiom. It has enormous range—patter songs, satiric musical commentary, blues, chants, love songs, and pure orchestral creation for production, dance, and mood. The possibility for style, rich, free, versatile. It should be a rebuke to existing musical comedy; it should date it." On another occasion, he wrote, "Musically, it [*Beggar's Holiday*] will be a 'jazz' opera, rather than a folk work, although certain folk elements will be retained, depending on the need of the characters." No doubt thinking of the Ellington band, but perhaps, too, of Weill's lean orchestration for *The Threepenny* Opera, he further proposed skillful use of smaller groups of instruments "rather than mass sound to impress," and in addition hoped to narrow the distance between stage and pit by having individual characters play certain instruments, in early drafts specifying the use of piano, guitar, hurdy-gurdy, and harp on stage.

Latouche's unpublished notes outlined many other ideas and concerns. He imagined, for instance, a set evocative of a cluttered waterfront that could revolve, thereby suggesting other settings. In contrast, the "more elaborate costumes," he wrote, "should provide the glitter of the production, through the use of extravagant color and extreme design." Furthermore, he envisioned highly choreographic stage movement throughout, without dance numbers inserted arbitrarily: "The net result of physical production scheme should be a vindication of the fluid, shifting, imaginatively lighted stage as contrasted with the grossly mechanical, ponderous style of physical setting." Tellingly, Latouche, who ultimately anchored the show in the context of Hollywood film noir, underlined a passage in the William Schultz study that compared the "numerous scenes" and "brisk, staccato sort of movement" of Gay's work to motion pictures.[11]

Regarding the notion of an interracial as opposed to an all-black cast, Latouche commented, "The 'Opera' is characteristic of no race more than any other. It's [*sic*] vices are man's. But an all Negro production, for instance, might invite an undesirable association in the minds of the already prejudiced. The solution is this: the cast shall be mixed, and if justification is needed let it exist in the use of a locale where races are naturally heterogeneous"—a reasoning that at one point led Latouche to consider setting the work in old Louisiana. As for his principal characters, he described Macheath as "not overburdened with intelligence, but makes up for it in audacity"; Polly as "petite and lovely, but not very bright"; Lucy as "tall and gorgeous, with depth and an intelligence put to depraved uses"; and Jenny as "wild[,] barbarously attractive in an arrantly sexual way." In short, with respect to virtually all aspects of the production, Latouche assumed a guiding hand.[12]

In February 1947, some six weeks after *Beggar's Holiday* opened on Broadway, Latouche once again, though publicly this time in a *New York Times* article entitled "Letter to John Gay," reflected on the show's relation to *The Beggar's Opera.* He drew a parallel between Gay's satire of Italian opera as a means of lampooning Britain's upper classes with his own appropriation of gangster films and "so-called comic magazines that would startle the Marquis de Sade" to critique "a contemporary type, the huckster of power," whose "antics and contradictions cannot disguise his emotional deep-freeze, his moral bankruptcy" (although Latouche found to his surprise that some of his "most obvious travesties on the zipper-lip school of writing were taken literally—possibly because it is difficult to burlesque a style which has already become a parody on itself"). He concluded, "my fundamental aim was to write an entertainment in terms of the world we live in, rather than the gaudy Ruritania once held essential as a locale for musical happenings."[13]

In late 1945, Watkins and Wasserman approached John Houseman (1902–1988) about directing the show, then still in progress. The British-American producer-director, born Jacques Haussmann in Bucharest, had had no experience directing musical comedy as opposed to opera and straight drama, but he had worked extensively with black artists, including directing the all-black premiere cast of Virgil Thomson's *Four Saints in Three Acts,* heading the Negro Unit of the Federal Theatre Project, and producing such integrated shows as Richard Wright and Paul Green's *Native Son.* Ellington and Latouche auditioned some of the score for Houseman, who thought the bandleader "one of the world's great spellbinders," and who tentatively signed on before leaving for film commitments on the West Coast.[14]

Press releases in January 1946 announced that Ellington and Latouche had entered the final writing of their "jazz opera"—now budgeted at $200,000—and that Latouche would join Ellington on tour in February in order to complete the work. How much time the two actually spent on the road together remains unclear, although Latouche reportedly planned to stay with the band until he and Ellington finished the score. Nor does much information survive concerning their working method; according to one source, the words came first, as certainly seems the case in at least a few instances, although to judge from the reminiscences of Perry Watkins, composer and lyricist worked side-by-side as well. At any rate, Watkins assured Houseman in the course of the spring and summer that the two writers were "cooking with gas." In the interim, Latouche's involvement with outstanding jazz musicians took something of a detour with the creation of a "lyrical accompaniment for a drum concerto" for Gene Krupa (1909–1973), scheduled for a May 16, 1946, premiere at New York's Aquarium cocktail lounge, the details of which remain unknown.[15]

In September, Houseman arrived in New York with his assistant Nicholas Ray—later the acclaimed director of *Rebel Without a Cause* (1955), among other films—to assess the musical's progress in anticipation of a planned opening later in the year. In his memoirs—initially in *Front and Center* (1979) and then slightly revised in *Unfinished Business* (1989)—Houseman recalled that after meeting with the producers,

> Nick [Ray] and I . . . were made aware of several things—none of them good. Latouche was not only lazy but he was drinking and he had been working on several other projects during the summer. He had written a number of lyrics but only the roughest draft of our first act and almost nothing of the second. Ellington, teeming with tunes and mood pieces, still had not faced the necessity of composing a musical score. Added to these unpleasant discoveries were others of which I soon became aware: our producers were not only inexperienced and inefficient—they were desperately short of money. Finally, owing to the Duke's enormous list of future commitments, we had no leeway at all but must start rehearsals within four weeks or not at all.

Nevertheless, Houseman and Ray decided to undertake the show, and the two swung into high gear in preparation for rehearsals, which began on October 21:

> We spent our days casting and planning the production, our nights in a desolate penthouse I had rented on the roof of the Chelsea Hotel, slaving away at the script, trying to give it some semblance of shape and motion. Latouche was of little help to us. He argued and whined in defense of his non-existent script. Then he vanished for ten days. When he reappeared he quibbled with us over what we'd done in his absence. A week before rehearsal we had the semblance of a first act: it remained fairly close to Gay's original text, ending with MacHeath's [*sic*] betrayal by Jenny Diver. The second act was chaotic: it remained so during rehearsals and throughout our New Haven, Hartford, Boston and New York engagements....
>
> Rehearsals began deceptively well. The quality and color of Ellington's music and the energy of our mixed cast almost made us forget the inadequacies of our book and the absence of a structured score. When we needed additional music Ellington's arranger Billy Strayhorn ... would run up to the Duke's apartment and fish out of a drawer, crammed with unperformed music, whatever tune seemed to fit the scene. Some were wonderful and, with Latouche's lyrics, remained for years in the repertory of Lena Horne and other well-known singers. But this did not make up for the absence of the score we so sorely needed.

Although Latouche often vexed collaborators by disappearing on the job, a letter from him to a friend dated September 17, 1946, in which he described himself as "slaving away at the script of the *Beggar's Opera*" would seem to question the accuracy of some of these recollections. But whatever its veracity, Houseman's account—echoed in both Bernard Eisenschitz's biography of Nicholas Ray and David Hajdu's biography of Billy Strayhorn, which concluded that all the songs were "composed either by Ellington in collaboration with Strayhorn or solely by Strayhorn"—seems more than misleading, especially as concerns the authorship of the musical's book and music.[16]

To start with, the contributions of Houseman and Ray formed only part of an extended creative process lasting many months. Latouche left behind, in addition to various sketches and literally dozens of song lyrics, two nearly complete scripts and a finished one that can be said to represent his own work however edited. The earliest of these scripts, which Latouche labeled a "first draft," possibly dates from the summer of 1946, at the time when he considered calling the piece "Street Music," for the typescript's cover page has that title scribbled over the words "The Beggar's Opera." An interim script, the one that Houseman and Ray apparently helped edit in the early autumn, presumably squares more or less with the show as presented in rehearsal and tryout. A completed late script, ostensibly written after director George

Abbott replaced Houseman during the show's Boston run, more closely conforms to the version subsequently seen on Broadway and even more so to that mounted for the show's short post-Broadway Chicago run. Concludes Daniel Caine in his study of the show, "Internal evidence—the handwritten ms [manuscript] which accompanies the various typescripts of *Beggar's Holiday*—leads to the conclusion that Latouche was the major, if not sole, author."[17]

All this material further calls into question the description of Latouche as "lazy," although the lyricist, by his own admission, often struggled with periods of indolence. Recalling that Latouche "wrote and wrote," Ellington took umbrage when, at a staff meeting after a matinee performance in Boston in which the orchestra drowned out the singers, the composer was asked for a new song, responding, "Well, listen now, I love to write music. Let's put ten new songs in the show. I'll sit here and write 'em tonight. But here is a man (Latouche) who has written the lyrics for over fifty songs. I just saw the matinee, and I couldn't hear the words." Added Ellington, "I got into a big thing about it, and they let that go by."[18]

As to the music, Ellington, who spent his life tirelessly touring with his band, clearly had Billy Strayhorn serve in New York as his deputy for long stretches, including for much of the rehearsal and tryout period. Moreover, when asked if Ellington gave the show his full attention, Luther Henderson replied, "No. No indeed. By no means. No way. He just didn't, you know." All the same, Ellington and Latouche had been working on the score since the fall of 1945 and had completed a large number of songs before the show went into rehearsal. Moreover, Ellington accepted a four-week engagement at the Aquarium in October so that he could be near at hand during casting and the early rehearsal period. In addition, Watkins recalled that during the tryout period, he arranged for Ellington, then on tour, to fly in so that he could write a needed song, an extravagance and inconvenience that would have been unnecessary had Strayhorn been expected to assume all such responsibilities.[19]

Even while away, Ellington stayed in close touch with Strayhorn, who consulted with the bandleader over the phone, so that, among other things, Strayhorn's occasionally riffling through Ellington's trunk seems to have been at the latter's instruction. Rooming with Strayhorn during tryouts, Henderson himself remembered the time in New Haven that Strayhorn phoned Ellington concerning a needed dance sequence for the show: "They must have talked and hummed and so forth for an hour or more, you know. And Stray[horn] [said], 'All right, o.k., oh great,' and got himself a little beer and some coffee and wrote it that night.... It was about a five minute ballet but he did it over the phone." Henderson concluded that although Strayhorn "did a great deal of the exposition" (apparently meaning arranging and developing material), Ellington wrote "all the tunes." Copyright registrations and attributions accompanying published music and recordings, not to mention sketches and manuscripts, would seem to confirm Ellington's essential authorship of the music.[20]

This does not answer all questions of provenance, many of which at this late date might well be nearly impossible to answer. Nor does it deny the possibility that

Strayhorn composed or co-composed some of the songs, especially as the show approached its premiere in New Haven in late November 1945. At the least, Strayhorn apparently resented not receiving more credit for his work on the musical, which, as Walter van de Leur suggests, possibly played some part in his distancing himself at least temporarily from Ellington after the show opened. However, whatever assistance they received, Ellington and Latouche can be said with assurance to be the authors of *Beggar's Holiday*.[21]

Latouche's three surviving books—a "first draft," an interim script, and a late script apparently created sometime between the Broadway premiere and the post-Broadway Chicago run—possess, for all their myriad differences, more or less the same structure, one so closely derived from *The Beggar's Opera* that in a few instances the author modeled some dialogue and song texts after the Gay original. At the same time, Latouche retooled the material in various ways, setting the story in modern times and, according to one précis, "anyplace in the United States where the political corruption is taken for granted even by honest citizens." Macheath became a gangster; Peachum, a ward heeler; and Polly, a debutante. (Latouche's first draft supposed Peachum a former pimp; Mrs. Peachum, a retired whorehouse madam; and Polly, a graduate of reform school, her crimes having included shoplifting and smoking marijuana.) The characters most altered included Lockit, still Peachum's pal, but now a police chief (a revision perhaps suggested by Tiger Brown in the Brecht version); Lucy, still Lockit's daughter, but early on Sweet Lucy, a prostitute, and ultimately, a stenographer; and Filch, still in Peachum's employ, but now an aspiring gang member renamed Sneaky Pete and eventually Careless Love, who spies on Peachum on behalf of Macheath. Latouche also created a new character, a prostitute named The Cocoa Girl, who gained greater presence over time as a vis-à-vis to Careless Love.[22]

The character of the Beggar went through some particularly notable transformations. Latouche initially imagined this figure—called, along the lines of Brecht's Street Singer, the "Ballad Singer"—as someone who "looks, acts and sings like Leadbelly [Huddie Ledbetter]. In fact, he should be Leadbelly." He further conceived the character as "a cryptic figure, playing somewhat the same role as the Solo in *Ballad for Americans*—asking questions of which he already knows the answers; commenting with wisdom and tolerance on the hectic saga which is actually being dreamed up in his mind." This conception accorded with the first draft, in which the Beggar appears throughout the action, guitar in hand, singing folklike quatrains that respond to the action, and telling Macheath at the play's climax:

> You see how it is, Mac. Look at the lathered pack of mankind, hysterical, jittery, anxious—jumping this way and that, snapping and biting at whatever passes before their furious jaws... looking for a blame in this man's color, a scapegoat in that man's race, running frantically before the shadow of their illogical fear—trapped in the arid gulleys of their hatred... and

> always refusing to track it down to where it hides—in the secret shadows of his own heart. The deed has been done by all of us—the hates hated by all of us—the bombs released, the triggers pulled, the mines laid, the victims destroyed—by all of us. The one thing we equally share in this inequal world is guilt.

Earlier in this same script, Macheath does a little philosophizing of his own: "Each man preys upon his neighbor, and yet we herd together in overcrowded, uncomfortable cities, anxious, nervous, waiting for the moment when we too will fall under the tooth and claw."[23]

However, by the time of the interim script, Latouche had settled rather on the idea of having the same actor play both the Beggar and Macheath, underscoring the notion established early on that the drama constitutes not the Beggar's play, as in the Gay original, but rather his dream—a dream, moreover, related not so much to opera as to film noir, with Macheath the Beggar's alter ego. As early as the first draft, Latouche had conceived the idea of placing the condemned Macheath, near the play's end, in an electric chair on a raised dais, and then, following a brief blackout, showing him seated in a "gaudy juke-box chair," a humorous take on *deus ex machina* stagecraft; but in the subsequent scripts, when the lights go up, the Beggar appears in Macheath's stead and explains (in the late script) that he "can't go bumping off that hero—not in a musical comedy!" Then, after righting things, he removes his hat and cloak to reveal his identity as Macheath, Peachum giving the audience advance warning: "Get this—this is the novel twist!" This dramatic conceit had precedent in Latouche's *Willie the Weeper* (1945), in which the eponymous chimney sweeper espies his *doppelgänger* in various glamorous roles; that Latouche eventually adapted the lyric "I've Got Me" from *Willie the Weeper* for *Beggar's Holiday* only underlined such connections. In conjunction with this reconception of the Beggar's role, Latouche turned his attention more to psychological concerns, especially in the interim script, which featured some surreal interludes in which the Beggar and Macheath converse with each other, with the latter pleading at one point, "Let me come back to myself!" to which the Beggar answers, "Not until you've worked it all out inside yourself."[24]

Notwithstanding its overarching parody of film noir, the script in all its phases eschewed explicit social satire or allegory, a point of distinction from *Of Thee I Sing*, *The Cradle Will Rock*, *West Side Story*, and other musicals to which the work over the years has been compared. Taking his cue more directly from *The Beggar's Opera*, Latouche focused more generally on the corruption and hypocrisy of a debased society, making his points through facetious dialogue and preposterous situations. At the same time, the musical occasionally derided some national foible or institution for a laugh. For instance, at Lockit's suggestion to Peachum that they frame the criminal "Gutsy Tortoni," the latter replies, "No foreigners this year—even crime has to be truly American." And arriving at the gang's hangout, one of the prostitutes,

Baby Mildred, remarks, "I haven't been on an outing in ever so long—the last one was a picnic sponsored by the Elks." The American news media came in for some ribbing as well. But all this seemed somewhat incidental to Latouche's main project.

Assuming that Latouche and Ellington worked more or less in tandem, by the time of the first draft they had completed around thirty numbers, about half of which would make it to Broadway, albeit not necessarily as performed by the same character. The texts of a few of these numbers—including "Rooster Man" and "Ore from a Gold Mine" as well as others eventually cut—derived from *The Beggar's Opera* (in "Rooster Man," Gay's "how do you do," for example, becoming "how do you do daddy"), but Latouche moved away from such literal reworkings over time. Perhaps thinking of Brecht's borrowings for *The Threepenny Opera,* he also adapted, virtually verbatim, W. B. Yeats's lyric "Brown Penny" for the bittersweet ballad so titled, Latouche tweaking the text only so as to fit a female rather than a male speaker. The lyricist himself penned an unusually poetic number, "Inbetween," to open the show, its verse reading,

> Between the twilight and nightfall
> There's a time that's outside of time
> When you feel yourself standing nowhere at all
> And you watch the shadows lazily climb
> Where there was once the sun,
> And now there is none.

Such elegiac poignance formed a nice complement to Yeats's "Brown Penny," which in the context of the show practically could be taken for a Latouche lyric. At the same time, "Inbetween" conveyed a distinctively somber note—"with nostalgic seriousness," wrote Latouche on one early draft of the lyric—thereby offsetting the raucous comedy that follows in such a way as to make the work very much a postwar enterprise.

The musical's other lyrics at this preliminary stage ranged from the playfulness of "TNT," the ironic sentimentality of "When I Walk with You," and the sassiness of "The Wrong Side of the Railroad Tracks" to the sarcasm of "Lullaby for Junior" and the cynicism of "The Scrimmage of Life," "Tooth and Claw," and "Women, Women, Women." Some brief quotes hint at the sort of sharp wit characteristic of these songs: "It's a sweet house that we sing about / Where the plumbing never plumbs, and the children shout / And the food's so bad that the rats eat out / We wonder what the other side is like?" ("The Wrong Side of the Railroad Tracks"); "What a nice fate for Junior / To be cradled in a cribhouse crib / Conceived in sin / And weaned on gin / And educated ad lib" ("Lullaby for Junior"); "When you climb on a back, / how much taller you are! / Stand on somebody's forehead / and reach for a star!" ("The Scrimmage of Life"); and "The foolish, the pious / Insist it ain't so / But suckers supply us / With plenty of dough / The phonus balonus is always a draw /

So here's a toast to tooth and claw!" ("Tooth and Claw"). Even while absorbing black popular traditions, Latouche made no effort, as he had in *Cabin in the Sky*, to evoke African-American dialect or culture per se, but rather accommodated his lyrics to the interracial intentions of the show as a whole.

Over the years, the musical gained a reputation for containing a number of jazz patters and recitatives, and several numbers indeed involved such an approach, sometimes in ways that recalled Broadway operetta practices as found in, say, Gershwin's *Of Thee I Sing* or Weill's *Lady in the Dark*. But the great majority of titles, even at this early stage, consisted of full-fledged songs with verses and choruses. Moreover, these numbers drew on a variety of genres, including folksongs, hymns, blues, and show tunes, with the music for the gang and the prostitutes, as opposed to the Peachums and the Lockits, tending more consistently toward jazzy idioms. Some of these numbers, like the Gay Nineties–styled waltz "Tooth and Claw," sounded less like Ellington than Latouche, suggesting that the bandleader might have taken some cues from his lyricist with regard to the music. At any rate, the songwriters mined a good deal of humor through stylistic incongruity, as in creating a college fight song parody for the caustic "The Scrimmage of Life" or a sentimental waltz for the acerbic "Lullaby for Junior." Likewise, the lovely romantic ballad "When I Walk With You," with its theme "And for me there is no one but you!" held just enough exaggerated sentiment so as to enhance the absurdity of having the womanizing Macheath sing such a number to Polly, let alone of having him reprise the song to Polly, Lucy, and Jenny en masse, with separate stanzas addressed to each of his three lady loves.[25]

From the start, the show's songs deviated from standard musical comedy practice not only in their tone, but in their harmonic and formal structure. For example, in "Inbetween," a song that bears some musical resemblance to the "Come Sunday" music from Ellington's *Black, Brown and Beige*, the verse concludes with a firm cadence, whereas the chorus ends with an open-ended harmony, the very opposite of typical Broadway procedure, as musicologist James O'Leary has observed. However, by the time of the work's New York premiere, Ellington and Latouche had written several new songs that not only gave certain principals, especially Macheath and Jenny, more to sing, but that in part also seemed aimed at supplying the score with more potential song hits. Tellingly, of the eleven songs published by Chappell from literally dozens of numbers composed for the show—"Girls Want a Hero" (published as "Where Is My Hero?"), "He Makes Me Believe" (published as "He Makes Me Believe He Is Mine"), "I've Got Me," "I Wanna Be Bad" (published as "Wanna Be Bad"), "Maybe I Should Change My Ways," "Take Love Easy," "Tomorrow Mountain," "Brown Penny," "Tooth and Claw," "When I Walk with You," and "The Wrong Side of the Railroad Tracks"—all but the last four seemed to date from a later stage in the work's history.[26]

These newer songs also tended to bring the show closer to romantic comedy, although in different ways, from the wry commentary of "Girls Want a Hero" (for Lucy, cut on the road, but reinstated in Chicago), and the knowing self-delusion of

"He Makes Me Believe" (for Jenny, added in Boston and cut in New York), to the ironic narcissism of "I've Got Me" (for Macheath, added in New York), the world weariness of "Maybe I Should Change My Ways" (for Macheath), and the hardboiled advice of "Take Love Easy" (for Macheath in tryout, for Jenny in New York). As for "I Wanna Be Bad," that song provided a comic turn for Careless Love, "Tomorrow Mountain," a lively finale for the ensemble.

However, even in these more conventional numbers, Ellington and Latouche maintained the sort of exuberant irony characteristic of the score as whole. "Girls Want a Hero" and "I Wanna Be Bad," for instance, both open with prim verses that humorously serve to foil the transgressive fantasies expressed in their respective choruses. Similarly, the songwriters provided a sardonic undercurrent to the affecting "Maybe I Should Change My Ways" by answering Macheath's doubts ("If I anchored down my heart / Would the magic start?"), sensitively depicted with chromatic chords, with a final shrug of a resignation ("But something deep inside me says / that love undying is a sham / I guess I'll stay the way I am!") expressed by a pat cadence.

As the finale to both of the show's two acts, "Tomorrow Mountain" deserves special note. Developed from an earlier finale, "Utopiaville," itself indebted to the folksong "Big Rock Candy Mountain," this number presents a despondent verse adapted from the chorus to "Inbetween" (with the line "We are trapped in Twilight Alley / There is no place we can run" supplying the show's title for a while) and an optimistic chorus derived, conversely, from the verse to "Inbetween," a neat way to frame the entire musical. The lyric taps, in a singular way, a longstanding trope of comic utopias by envisaging a crooked world with "a Scotch-and-Soda fountain" where "you will be a lucky sinner / with no conscience for your guide." Ellington did his part by, for example, moving to a surprisingly bright tonality for the chorus, thereby heightening the lyric's droll sarcasm. In the spirit of both Gay's play and *The Threepenny Opera,* the number provides a festive ending even while satirizing the theatrical convention it inhabits, namely, the uplifting final chorus—an impulse slightly anticipated in *Cabin in the Sky*, but turned much more provocative here.[27]

Perry Watkins and Dale Wasserman made good on their promise to assemble an interracial cast. As early as December 1945, the press often mentioned Lena Horne as the leading lady, and Latouche and Ellington possibly wrote the character of Sweet Lucy with her in mind; the producers also thought to recruit the British actor Michael Redgrave, presumably for the role of Macheath. Although neither hope materialized, the nonetheless stellar cast featured white performers Alfred Drake (Macheath), Libby Holman (Jenny), Zero Mostel (Mr. Peachum), Dorothy Johnson (Mrs. Peachum), and Jet MacDonald (Polly Peachum); and black performers Avon Long (Careless Love), Rollin Smith (Chief Lockit), Mildred Smith (Lucy Lockit), and Marie Bryant (The Cocoa Girl). Subsidiary players proved similarly diverse, with such white performers as Marjorie Belle (later, Marge Champion), Paul Godkin, and Herbert Ross sharing the stage with such performers of color as Tommy Gomez, Archie Savage, and Royce Wallace.[28]

Latouche became particularly good friends with Libby Holman, the production's Jenny. Holman (born Elizabeth Holzman, 1904–1971) had achieved fame as an unconventional torch singer on Broadway—she helped popularize the strapless dress—before in 1931 marrying Zachary Reynolds, heir to the Reynolds tobacco fortune; after Reynolds's mysterious death the following year, she found herself indicted for murder, although charges eventually were dropped. Holman subsequently married actor Ralph Holmes in 1939, from whom she separated in 1945, and then artist Louis Schanker in 1960. Although she appeared infrequently on stage after her marriage to Reynolds, among other undertakings in the early 1940s she collaborated with the black singer-guitarist Josh White in concerts and recordings of traditional African-American blues and spirituals, a background that presumably helped win her the role of Jenny in *Beggar's Holiday*.[29]

During the show's tryout in Hartford, Latouche introduced Holman to Paul and Jane Bowles, and they all joined a circle of friends, including also Tallulah Bankhead, Truman Capote, Tennessee Williams, and Holman's lover Montgomery Clift, who regularly gathered at Holman's Connecticut estate, Treetops, with its three-storied, neo-Georgian manor house on a large wooded parcel of land, now part of Mianus River State Park. "She was great fun to be with and had a private glamor all her own. And life in her house was wonderful," recalled Paul Bowles, to whom the bisexual Holman proposed marriage in 1948, with the idea that the two of them and Jane could all live together.[30]

As for the production of *Beggar's Holiday*, Oliver Smith assumed responsibility for the settings; Walter Florell, the costumes; Peggy Clark, the lighting; Valerie Bettis, the choreography; Max Meth, musical direction; and Billy Strayhorn, the orchestrations. Producer Watkins had done some designs for the show himself, but once the musical went into rehearsal, Houseman insisted that those be "turned over to Oliver Smith, who, in less than a week, delivered designs of such imaginative beauty that he repeated most of them years later (fire escapes and all) in *West Side Story*. Costumes were created by a wild male *modiste* with gold-lacquered hair named Walter Florell. They were extravagant and scandalous and exactly right" (see Figures 31–33). Smith's stark sets and Florell's flamboyant costumes, as well as Bettis's use of what dance critic John Martin called "incidental movement," suggest that the production staff responded in various ways to Latouche's early concept of the work as outlined above.[31]

According to Houseman, the show faced other problems besides the ones specified earlier concerning the script and the score: "Alfred Drake was charming but never quite tough enough; Libby [Holman] was nervous and less sultry than I remembered her; our ingenue [Jet MacDonald] was pretty but pale, overshadowed by a young dancer who later became known as Marge Champion. Nick [Ray] and I seriously considered switching them after the first week, but by then Alfred [Drake] was enamored of the ingenue and it couldn't be done." Meanwhile, Watkins, who expressed no small disappointment that he in particular failed to interest any African-American investors in the show, had trouble meeting an ever-growing budget that eventually grew to about $325,000. However, in October, he managed to attract a backer described by Houseman as "a small, ill-favored, timid alcoholic," John R. Sheppard Jr., a dental-supply heir who helped keep the production afloat, and who subsequently purchased producer Dale Wasserman's interest in the property once the latter, describing himself as "psychologically tired," bowed out in mid-November.[32]

Financial woes prevented a timely delivery of the sets in New Haven in advance of the world premiere of *Twilight Alley* (subtitled "A Parallel in Tempo to John Gay's 'The Beggar's Opera'"), so that the cast and crew had only one incomplete dress rehearsal before opening at the Shubert Theatre on November 21. "Even in a town that was used to impromptu openings ours was unusually calamitous," wrote Houseman, who recalled that Drake and the cast essentially improvised the final twenty minutes of the show. Afterward, the creative team held an all-night conference at a suite in the Taft Hotel. "Everything was discussed and argued about over whiskey and sandwiches except the obvious fact that we had no book and no score," stated Houseman, plainly exaggerating the situation considering that the show listed no fewer than thirty-nine numbers in the program. "Ellington sat smiling until his wife took him to bed. Touche passed out. Nick [Ray] and Valerie [Bettis] decided to elope and made reservations for a flight to Cuba but were intercepted."[33]

Management originally had thought to take the show next to Newark and Philadelphia, but after four sold-out performances in New Haven, *Twilight Alley* moved instead to Hartford, Connecticut, where it opened on November 27. The musical's early notices proved none too auspicious. *Variety*, covering the New Haven world premiere, thought that the production had some excellent assets, including a "tuneful score" and "a moderately interesting book and some nice lyrics," but found that the whole had yet to gel into "solid entertainment." In a review of the Hartford opening, the local *Courant* even more severely faulted this "sleepy show" with "a dull book badly wanting for humor, and a score which never really gets off the ground."[34]

By the time *Twilight Alley* arrived in Boston on December 3 for a three-week engagement at the Opera House, several numbers had been reordered, some cut, and still others at least temporarily added, including two urbane songs for Jenny, "He Makes Me Believe" and "My Reward," and a number for Macheath adapted from a 1935 song for which Strayhorn had composed both lyrics and words, "Let Nature Take Its Course," an interpolation no doubt undertaken in extremis. The show seemed to Houseman in better shape, but the reviews remained tepid nonetheless. The Boston drama desks, who actually admired many aspects of the production, including the music and the lyrics (to the extent that they could be heard), leveled the brunt of their criticism at the book, which they found tedious and incoherent, without the satirical thrust of the Gay original. Most reviews appeared further perplexed and bothered—as did, reportedly, the audience—by the play's tone and intent. "There seems to be some confusion as to whether the plot is to be taken a mite seriously," reported Cyrus Durgin (*Boston Globe*). "The style shifts so often that it is difficult to know what total effect is intended," agreed L. A. Sloper (*Christian Science Monitor*), continuing, "If satire, it misses. If bawdy entertainment, it may attract a public when it has been smoothed out and stepped up." Elliot Norton (*Boston Post*) echoed these concerns, writing, "John La Touche seems to be jeering only at his own story," and wondering, "is this burlesque instead of mere satire?" The *Billboard* too had trouble classifying the work: "It's a confusion of styles, being something of an opera, ballet, operetta, musicomedy, and play with music."[35]

Soon after the Boston opening, management arranged for Houseman to hand over the reins of the show to writer-director George Abbott. Houseman could not remember whether he had quit or been fired, but his departure seems to have been civil, with his assistant Nicholas Ray staying on to help with the transition; indeed, notwithstanding Abbott's eleventh-hour redesign of the show, Ray received sole credit as director once the musical arrived in New York.[36]

Abbott oversaw the reordering and removal of many numbers, including the three forementioned songs added in tryout, although the show, now once again called *Beggar's Holiday*, still arrived in New York with an impressive thirty-one numbers (including reprises) listed in the program. This revised line-up featured one new song, "I've Got Me," a humorous opening number for Macheath, the lyric, probably under the pressure of the moment, adapted from Latouche's *Willie the Weeper* composed the previous year, affording the opportunity to compare Ellington's setting of the words with that of Jerome Moross.

Abbott further replaced Libby Holman, the only cast member who consistently had received poor notices, with Bernice Parks, and helped tailor the script more in conformity with musical comedy practices. The revised production also seemed to make more of Bill Dillard, the black singer-trumpeter who played one of Macheath's gang, his character's name now changed from Deep Ellum to The Horn. A synopsis of this revamped *Beggar's Holiday* as it more or less appeared on Broadway follows.

Act I, scene one. Exterior of Miss Jenny's. Twilight descends on a shadowy area of the city ("Inbetween," for Lucy; and "The Chase," a dance for The Pursued and Policemen). As the Beggar invites the audience to enter his movie-inspired fantasy, people gather in front of Miss Jenny's, a bordello ("When You Go Down by Miss Jenny's," for Citizens and Girls). Giving a girlfriend the brush-off, Macheath, the leader of a gang of thieves, revels in his independence ("I've Got Me," for Macheath).

Scene two. Interior of Miss Jenny's. One of the bordello's prostitutes, The Cocoa Girl, sings a racy ditty ("TNT," for The Cocoa Girl). Jenny, the brothel's madam, counsels Macheath's gang about love ("Take Love Easy," for Jenny); she herself jealously suspects that Macheath's "insurance" regarding his control of the corrupt political boss Hamilton Peachum involves a girl. Macheath's men make Careless Love, a young fellow placed in Peachum's employ by Macheath as a spy, a member of their gang ("I Wanna Be Bad," for Careless Love). Careless Love tells Macheath that Hamilton Peachum's daughter, Polly, awaits him outside, confirming Jenny's suspicions ("Rooster Man," for Jenny).

Scene three. Exterior of Miss Jenny's. Macheath and Polly agree to marry ("When I Walk with You," for Polly and Macheath; "Wedding Ballet," for dancers; and reprise of "I've Got Me," for the First Girl).

Scene four. At Hamilton Peachum's. Needing to find a criminal in order to distract the district attorney from their own illicit dealings, Chief of Police Lockit and Hamilton Peachum decide to arrange for Macheath's arrest ("The Scrimmage of Life," for Mrs. Peachum, Peachum, and Lockit). Mrs. Peachum frets that Polly might be in love with Macheath ("Ore from a Gold Mine," for Mrs. Peachum). After discovering that Polly has married Macheath, the Peachums urge her to inform on him for the reward money, but she refuses to do so ("Finaletto," for Polly, Mrs. Peachum, and Peachum). Polly warns Macheath of impending danger (reprise of "When I Walk with You," for Macheath and Polly).

Scene five. A Street. In an extended pantomime, Lockit, Peachum, and the cops search for Macheath, who eludes capture.

Scene six. A Hobo Jungle. Two days later. In their deserted hide-out, the gang express their philosophy of life ("Tooth and Claw," for Mac's Gang). Careless Love tells Macheath about his contentedness with The Cocoa Girl, prompting the gang leader to reflect on his own romantic life ("Maybe I Should Change My Ways," for Macheath). As the prostitutes arrive, The Cocoa Girl and Careless Love describe their slum home ("The Wrong Side of the Railroad Tracks," for The Cocoa Girl, Careless Love, and The Horn). Macheath promises all a criminal's paradise ("Tomorrow Mountain," for Macheath and the ensemble). Tipped off by Jenny, who disarms Macheath with the assist of The Cocoa Girl, Lockit and his men arrest the gang leader and take him away. Jenny initially throws aside the reward money given to her by Lockit; but reconsidering, she picks up the cash and, putting it in her stocking, exits (reprise of "Tomorrow Mountain," for the ensemble offstage).

Act II, scene one. The Street. Chief Lockit's daughter, Lucy, reflects on love ("Brown Penny," for Lucy). The town anticipates Macheath's appearance in court ("Chorus of Citizens," for the ensemble). (In the surviving late script, as in the post-Broadway Chicago run, this scene opened with a "Chorus of Citizens," followed by "Girls Want a Hero," for Lucy, with "Brown Penny," also for Lucy, sung later in the act after Macheath's "Fol-de-rol-rol.")

Scene two. Chief Lockit's Office. Peachum expounds on the vagaries of the law (reprise of "Tooth and Claw," for Peachum and Reporters).

Scene three. The Jail. On a visit to Macheath in jail, Jenny scorns his romantic overtures ("Lullaby for Junior," for Jenny). Lucy falls for Macheath, but finds a rival in Polly ("Quarrel for Three," for Polly, Lucy, and Macheath; and "Fol-de-rol-rol," for Macheath). Macheath escapes from jail with Lucy's help, and Peachum and Lockit blame each other for his breakout. The prisoners denounce women as untrustworthy ("Women, Women, Women," for Prisoners).

Scene four. The Street. The betrayal of Macheath leaves Careless Love embittered (reprise of "Women, Women, Women," for The Cocoa Girl and Careless Love).

Scene five. Jenny's Bedroom. Polly, Lucy, and Jenny compare notes concerning Macheath, who suddenly appears and makes love to all three (reprise of "When I Walk with You," for Macheath).

Scene six. Under the Bridge. The police, with the forced assist of Careless Love, capture Macheath ("Ballet," for dancers; and "The Hunted," for Macheath).

Scene seven. Finale. As the police strap Macheath to an electric chair, the stage darkens and then lightens again to reveal the Beggar sitting in his place, the electric chair gaily lit and decorated. After the Beggar discloses himself as Macheath, he happily gives himself to Polly, Lucy, and Jenny ("Finale," including a reprise of "Tomorrow Mountain," for Macheath, Jenny, Polly, Lucy, and the ensemble).

After final benefit previews on December 24 and 25 for, respectively, Sydenham Hospital, a health care facility in Harlem serving the African-American community, and the Council on African Affairs, with which Latouche, as discussed earlier, had some affiliation, *Beggar's Holiday* opened in New York at the Broadway Theatre on December 26, 1946. Many notices still thought the musical only so-so, with kind words for Oliver Smith's sets, Bettis's choreography, Latouche's "intelligent" and "clever" lyrics, and cast members Avon Long and Marie Bryant, but objections to what many regarded as the show's muddled plot, slow pace, vulgar humor, inept score, and miscast performers, especially Zero Mostel, whose zany antics proved controversial. George Jean Nathan summed up this majority opinion with his description of *Beggar's Holiday* as "only intermittently amusing."[37]

However, the show also garnered several highly enthusiastic notices, suggesting that the extra three weeks under Abbott's guidance made a considerable difference, or that the material found a more responsive audience among at least some of Broadway's critics, or both. A good third of the reviews could be described as at least highly favorable, to the point that by the time the show closed three months later, critics like Douglas Watt (*Daily News*) could speak of the work as a "succès d'estime" (a verdict with which Ellington agreed, except that he elaborated, calling the musical, "a tremendous *succès d'estime*"). Perhaps significantly, one of the most laudatory reviews came not from any of the drama desks but from a music critic, Robert Bagar (*World-Telegram*), who singled out Ellington and Latouche as the show's "two especially brilliant stars," writing, "Together, the music and text combine in as felicitous a wedding as the Broadway stage has offered in months." Brooks Atkinson (*Times*) similarly began his review with the salvo, "Let appropriate salutes be fired in honor of Duke Ellington and John Latouche," and concluded it by stating, "Mr. Ellington and Mr. Latouche have given Broadway a score and lyrics we can be proud of."[38]

Such proponents of the work, whatever their reservations, tended to emphasize the work's novelty and originality. Discussing this "important" score, for instance, John Chapman (*Daily News*) described Latouche's lyrics as "admirable in refusing to follow the Tin Pan Alley formula." In an article published in late January, in which he restated his esteem for Latouche's "brilliant lyrics," which featured "the sharpness and wit of the best modern rhyming," and Ellington's "wry, dissonant, contemptuous and biting score," Brooks Atkinson lauded the show, along with Burton Lane's *Finian's Rainbow* and, in passing, Kurt Weill's *Street Scene*, both of which had opened two weeks after *Beggar's Holiday*, for breaking with formulaic musical comedy. Rosamond Gilder pressed similar claims for all three shows in *Theatre Arts* magazine. And in a retrospective about the state of ballet on Broadway, *Times* dance critic John Martin relatedly opined that Bettis's choreography "matched the rhythmic originality of John Latouche's lyrics and Duke Ellington's music with equal originality of her own." Even critics not particularly enamored of *Beggar's Holiday* acknowledged that "nothing quite like it has been seen around here before" (Arthur Pollock in the *Brooklyn Eagle*) and that it "travels its own road" (Louis Kronenberger in *PM*).[39]

In his review for the *New Yorker*, Wolcott Gibbs, who himself did not like the show, recognized that such diverse reaction to *Beggar's Holiday* came down to personal taste, and cited some qualifications required for an appreciation of the work, among them, a capacity to enjoy "a kind of music that is apt to be described as interesting rather than as melodious" and a book "that frequently discards intelligibility altogether in favor either of a kind of disjoined symbolism or else of a modernized version of the old movie-chase technique, stimulating but essentially maniacal"; a broad-mindedness "to the point where one of the most explicitly and genuinely depraved sporting-house scenes ever staged will cause him no moral uneasiness"; and a fondness for "the frantic, strangulated comedy of Zero Mostel." As could be inferred by Gibbs's review, a major fault line in the work's reception touched on an amenability toward modernity, including sexual candor, with Louis Kronenberger, for instance, opining that Latouche "showed too much taste for sex, and very little taste beyond that," and Richard Dier in the *Baltimore Afro-American* touting, among the show's other virtues, "plenty of sex." Tellingly, Euphemia van Rensselaer, in the *Catholic World*, disapprovingly found "the general atmosphere of *Beggar's Holiday* about on a par with *No Exit*," the 1944 Jean-Paul Sartre play that had opened on Broadway in late November 1946. However compromised his original vision—a matter alluded to by Eric Bentley in a March 1947 article entitled "Broadway and Its Intelligentsia"—Latouche, in collaboration with fellow adventurers, at least had succeeded in challenging the Broadway establishment.[40]

One of the most expensive shows on Broadway—comparable to Irving Berlin's far more ingratiating *Annie Get Your Gun*, which had opened the previous May—*Beggar's Holiday*, long beset by financial problems, closed, after a last-ditch recourse to Sunday matinees, on March 29, 1947, after 111 performances. In later years, reflecting on this modest showing, Houseman took personal responsibility for "what should have been a triumphal theatrical novelty" by saying that he agreed "to go into rehearsal with a show that was nowhere near ready," and that neither he nor Ray had the needed experience with musical comedy to set things right. In his own memoirs, Abbott stated, "I think I could have made a hit show out of *A Beggar's Holiday* [*sic*] had I been able to have the proper changes of cast. But having extravagantly squandered hundreds of thousands of dollars, the management now suddenly became penurious and was unwilling to squander a little more to salvage what they had already wasted. As a result, they lost it all." Luther Henderson, who remembered *Beggar's Holiday* as a "fantastic" and "beautiful" play, apportioned blame to both producer Watkins, who "just had stars in his eyes," and director Houseman, who "did the best he could but it just wasn't his milieu." And Ellington, who also thought the show "a gorgeous play," suggested that its unprecedented interracial casting, including having a black man play a police chief, struck audiences as "silly." Mildred Smith similarly attributed the musical's lack of success to the fact that its racial dimension broke new ground, saying, "any time you do this kind of thing, you have some kind of conflict."[41]

These statements regarding how racial attitudes might have affected the show's reception remain difficult to verify. According to Kenward Elmslie, an eyewitness to the Boston tryout, the interracial romance between Macheath and Lucy led some patrons to leave the theater. On the other hand, the press seemed widely appreciative of the work's casting, with *Variety* specifically commending the show for not stereotyping blacks: "It is laudable that a police chief, for instance, is a Negro; a Negro girl loves a white man with all the dignity of a white woman." But such casting likely heightened those disquieting features of the work that often seemed to confound or antagonize viewers.[42]

After closing on Broadway, *Beggar's Holiday,* its content reflecting some modifications undertaken during the New York run and its personnel slightly altered, opened in April for a scheduled twenty-week engagement at Chicago's Shubert Theatre. But the show met with mediocre notices and closed after a disappointing two weeks, dashing the company's hopes for a tour of other American cities and possibly even London.[43]

Plans for a 1947 cast album with Musicraft also came to naught, as did those for a 1964 Columbia recording that would have reunited Alfred Drake, Zero Mostel, and Libby Holman. Fortunately, however, two sets of demo recordings survive. The first, made relatively early in the show's history, employed such noncast members as Ellington singer Marion Cox, with Latouche apparently introducing some of the numbers and singing "Tooth and Claw" himself. By contrast, the second demo, eventually released commercially in 1989 by Blue Pear Records, featured virtually all the principals of the Broadway cast except for Zero Mostel. Beyond their obvious historical value, these recordings remain satisfying in their own right, preserving delightful performances by Drake, Avon Long, Bernice Parks, and others. Meanwhile, sometime in her sixties, Libby Holman recorded, in her whisky contralto, "Inbetween" as part of a compilation of bluesy songs released in 1974 by Monmouth Evergreen and later reissued on the Blue Pear album.[44]

In the course of 1947, the Ellington band also recorded five songs from the show with featured vocalists: "Women, Women, Women" with Ray Nance (as "Women [They'll Get You]"); "Brown Penny" with Kay Davis; "He Makes Me Believe" and "Take Love Easy" with Dolores Parker; and "Maybe I Should Change My Ways" with Chester Crumpler (as "Change My Ways"). Of these numbers, only "Take

Love Easy" became something of a standard, with recordings by such singers as Ella Fitzgerald, Shirley Horn, Lena Horne, Bobby Short, and Nancy Wilson, although other songs from the show enjoyed the occasional airing as well, including "Tomorrow Mountain," which proved a congenial vehicle for Horne, Frankie Laine, and Jo Stafford. Instrumentalists also performed music from the show, including alto saxophonist Johnny Hodges, who in 1959 recorded "Brown Penny" with Ellington and his Award Winners, as found on the reissues of the albums *Blues in Orbit* (2004) and *Back to Back* (2010), and the acclaimed French pianist Jean-Yves Thibaudet, who devised a *Beggar's Holiday Suite* consisting of "Inbetween," "Brown Penny," and "Take Love Easy" for a release entitled *Reflections on Duke* (1999).[45]

Meanwhile, the Karamu House, an historic interracial theater company based in Cleveland, periodically considered staging the show in the early 1950s, and Perry Watkins, who retained a great fondness for the work's "brilliant" score, similarly attempted to launch a revival, possibly starring Shirley Bassey and Tom Jones, in the early 1970s; but the musical, after closing in Chicago in 1947, did not receive another hearing until 1992, when the Smithsonian Institution's National Museum of American History mounted a concert version of the work. For this venture, spurred by the institution's 1987 acquisition of the Ellington papers, the museum's director of programs Dwight Bowers oversaw a painstaking reconstruction of the score from archival and other sources; he further devised the concert to simulate an early rehearsal for the 1946 production, with a small cast presenting twenty-one numbers from the show, and a fictional stage manager serving as narrator. Initially given at the museum's intimate Carmichael Auditorium on the first two days of February 1992, the production, directed by Ron O'Leary, with Thomas Henry McKenzie as Macheath, received a strongly positive review from *Washington Post* critic Richard Harrington, who lauded the composer more than the lyricist, stating, "Latouche is clever in his writing, but Ellington is masterly." A few more performances of this concert version followed in 1992 and 1993.[46]

About this same time, Dale Wasserman, the producer who had pulled out of the show in 1946, and who since had adapted for the stage Ken Kesey's novel *One Flew Over the Cuckoo's Nest* (1963) and penned the book to the musical *Man of La Mancha* (1965), planned his own revival of *Beggar's Holiday*, revamping the work with reported permission of the Ellington and Latouche estates. As part of his redaction, Wasserman, who attended one of the Smithsonian's 1993 concert renditions, resurrected songs that long had been discarded, shifted and redistributed numbers as a whole, and tweaked many lyrics. In addition, he rewrote the book, although he used Latouche's script as a template, and furthermore adapted much of the original dialogue, belying his claim to be the show's sole author.[47]

The Pegasus Players, under the direction of Dennis Courtney, debuted Wasserman's edition in Chicago on October 12, 1994, with Kevin McIlvaine as Macheath. Although critical of this "third-rate production," the *Chicago Tribune*, like the *Washington Post* a few years earlier, had nothing but kudos for the score.[48]

Later stagings of the Wasserman version included those by the York Theatre off Broadway (1999); the Marin Theatre Company in Mill Valley, California (2004); and the Opera Theater of Pittsburgh (2009), as well as a French production in English, *Beggar's Holiday, ou Le rêve d'un mendiant*, presented at Paris's art complex, Espace Pierre Cardin (2012). This French production, further adapted by the show's Macheath, David Serero, occasioned the musical's first commercial cast album, an apparent vanity project that had little to recommend it. The publicity attendant to these revivals, drawing on information provided by Wasserman, helped disseminate, incidentally, some false or unsubstantiated claims, including the notion that protesters picketed the original production because of its interracial cast.

The dearth of performances and recordings naturally hindered critical attention and commentary. Of the many books devoted to Ellington, some hardly took notice of the work, and those that did, such as studies by James Lincoln Collier (1987), Harvey Cohen (2010), and Terry Teachout (2013), proposed that the bandleader's "pedestrian" and "undistinguished" score showed the marks of an unschooled musical dramatist, one who, according to Teachout, "knew nothing about how to write an *Oklahoma!*-style 'book show' whose songs drive the action." Latouche, his lyrics deemed "awful" by Collier and "riddled with clichés" by Cohen, came in for special censure, with Teachout describing the lyricist as "a poisoned chalice, a gay-alcoholic with a hard-earned reputation for unreliability." However, the ostensible lack of deep familiarity with the musical and its history made this critical tradition tenuous.[49]

Music theater historians, although generally more respectful, also tended to give the work only brief consideration. Cecil Smith, who had attended a performance in Chicago, remembered *Beggar's Holiday* as successful "in a measure," but handicapped by Latouche's "love of verbiage," which "got the better of him in his lyrics," and Ellington's music, which "revealed an almost complete inability to relate his compositions to dramatic situations." Lehman Engel, who likely saw the show as well, claimed that the "failure" of *Beggar's Holiday* demonstrated the limitations of jazz as a "firm exclusive basis of a theater-music score." More sympathetically, Ethan Mordden credited Latouche with "as so often trying to habilitate Broadway to the boldest art before Broadway was quite ready," and Ellington with some noteworthy songs, but concluded nonetheless that "the dead score killed it [the show]." And Gerald Bordman suggested that "much of Latouche's sting and Ellington's intimacy was lost in the cavernous auditorium of the large, inconvenient Broadway Theatre," an observation that raised the question of whether this lavish musical might have met with a kinder fate had it been more modestly produced along the lines of, say, Blitzstein's adaptation of *The Threepenny Opera*.[50]

In the context of its general neglect, the work's few specialized studies proved particularly valuable. In an article published in 1987, the first serious investigation of the musical, Daniel Caine proposed that "despite some serious flaws," Latouche's "lyrics and libretto provided a witty and effective commentary on the modern city Big Time, particularly when wedded to music by that most quintessentially urban of modern composers, Duke Ellington," although the author noted a disconnect between Latouche's original vision and commercial realities: "The problem facing Latouche, then, was that he was an original playwright with a serious, 'revolutionary' message: that crime is the very foundation of capitalization; while at the same time, the economic forces meant that a Broadway success must generally adhere to an accepted formula: say nothing that could possibly offend anyone." Nevertheless, concluded Caine, *Beggar's Holiday* stood out as "radical" in the context of rival Broadway musicals and "truly ahead of its time."[51]

In another important study, part of a monograph devoted to *Duke Ellington's Music for the Theatre* (2001), John Franceschina offered a corrective to longstanding allegations concerning Ellington's incompetence as a musical dramatist, in part by spotlighting several cogent details in the score. Franceschina found further confirmation of Ellington's stage savviness in some of his jottings made during the show's tryout: "Ellington's notes have more than curiosity value as they demonstrate his interest in, and understanding of, dramatic rhythm and in the ability of music to complement, and control, that rhythm.... He was no dilettante, not simply a songwriter hoping to impersonate a theatre composer. He knew how to tell a story through the use of music."

More recently, James O'Leary, in his 2012 dissertation on "Discourse and Politics of the American Musical, 1943–1946," explored conflicts in the musical deemed "highbrow" and "lowbrow," including satire versus burlesque and classical versus jazz performance styles, and concluded that the show "blurred" such "boundaries" in an attempt to forge "a new kind of political expression in the theater that would be appropriate in a post–World War II aesthetic climate," although like Daniel Caine, he found such aspirations undercut by the restrictions of the Broadway stage.[52]

Despite these helpful discussions, *Beggar's Holiday* remained not only underappreciated but highly misunderstood with respect to its authorship, content, and reception. Part of this involved a certain amount of misinformation surrounding the work and its history, but perhaps more to the point, personal preference and expectation. Critics and scholars looking for song hits of the kind found in the popular 1981 Ellington revue *Sophisticated Ladies,* which had no use for any of the numbers from *Beggar's Holiday,* no doubt would be as disappointed in the show as those looking for a musical akin to Rodgers and Hammerstein. Rather, the work needed to be faced on its own terms. Whatever the show's flaws or compromises, Ellington and Latouche produced one of the most courageous works in the history of the Broadway musical, a giddy romp that provocatively and wittily explored, both in music and word, the venality and vapidity of contemporary society and the mystery and complexity of the human heart.

15

Film Work

In his later years, Latouche collaborated with the German-American director Hans Richter on two landmarks of avant-garde cinema: *Dreams That Money Can Buy*, first viewed in 1947, but not released until 1948; and *8 x 8: A Chess Sonata in 8 Movements*, released in 1957, one year after the lyricist's death. Moreover, Latouche worked with the Swiss-American director Herbert Matter on a short documentary (1949–50) about the sculptor Alexander Calder, and in the 1950s started his own film unit, which produced a few shorts, including a cartoon adaptation of his children's poem "The Peppermint Tree" (1955) and a work by the experimental filmmaker Maya Deren, *The Very Eye of Night* (1956).

Latouche long had shown an interest in vanguard cinema, writing, for example, in a 1941 review of William Dieterle's film *All That Money Can Buy* (adapted from Stephen Vincent Benét's story "The Devil and Daniel Webster"), "For many years now, experimental films have been demonstrating how closely the medium is related to fantasy. But Hollywood, with its own fixed ideas of what the public wants, has released production after production relentlessly molded to box-office categories." Accordingly, in the Dieterle film, and in a contemporaneous release, *Here Comes Mr. Jordan*, he found some welcome movement away from the industry's "run-of-the-mill," even if he thought the success of the latter film depended more on "its antic dialogue and Robert Montgomery's magnificent performance" than on "its fantastic subject." Latouche as a matter of course would have welcomed the opportunity to work with the outstanding film experimenter Hans Richter, whom he might have come to know through, among others, their close mutual friend Frederick Kiesler.[1]

Born into a German-Jewish family, Hans Richter (1888–1976) studied art in his native Berlin as well as in Weimar and Paris. In the course of the 1910s and 1920s, as a painter, sculptor, and eventually filmmaker, he immersed himself in all the latest artistic trends, although he found the study of Bach under the guidance of Ferruccio Busoni "really the basis of my future development." He spent the years 1931–1933 in the Soviet Union working on the never-completed anti-Nazi film *Metall*, and then lived in the Netherlands, France, and Switzerland before emigrating to the United States in 1941. Settling in New York, he joined the faculty of City College's newly established Institute of Film Techniques, where he taught experimental and documentary filmmaking until his retirement in 1956, after which he divided his time between studios in Connecticut and Switzerland.[2]

Richter began his film career in the 1920s with the creation of abstract shorts, but in the course of the decade he increasingly employed figurative imagery, sometimes in collaboration with such composers as Darius Milhaud and Paul Hindemith. The filmmaker viewed these Weimar-era shorts, which pioneered such techniques as multiple exposure, stop motion, and rapid intercutting, as an outgrowth of his art work:

> The spirit in which I made these films, the motives which inspired me, and the methods by which I made them were not, properly speaking, part of the art of film-making; the spirit, the motives, the method arose less from literature than from painting.
>
> That's it: I am a painter, and I will remain a painter who makes films, just as did my friends [Fernand] Léger, Man Ray, [Marcel] Duchamp, [Francis] Picabia, [Viking] Eggeling and the others.... I came to film... against my will, impelled to celluloid, away from the canvas, by the logic of the esthetic development of modern painting.

None of this betokened an indifference toward social content; on the contrary, Richter, who viewed the documentaries of Sergei Eisenstein and Roberto Rossellini as complementary to his own work, proved highly engaged in matters of civil concern.[3]

Soon after Richter's arrival in New York, a local movie theater expressed interest in showing several of his shorts on the condition that he create a unifying story that would tie the various films together; and to this end, the director raised funds from the wealthy American gallery owner and art collector Peggy Guggenheim as well as from the innovative Scottish filmmaker Kenneth Macpherson. However, the French painter Fernand Léger proposed that he and Richter use the money instead to create an entirely new film, *Folklore à l'americaine*, which would include a love story between storefront mannequins. Inspired by this suggestion, Richter decided to produce a whole new series of short films not only with Léger but with other surrealist artists currently in New York: the Americans Man Ray and Alexander Calder, the Frenchman Marcel Duchamp, and the German Max Ernst, then married to Peggy Guggenheim. In the end, he created six episodes "based on drawings, objects and suggestions" by these artist friends along with an original sequence of his own, working too with various musicians as follows: "Desire," after Ernst (music by Paul Bowles); "The Girl with the Prefabricated Heart," after Léger (music and lyrics by Latouche); "Ruth, Roses and Revolvers," after Ray (music by Darius Milhaud); "Discs and Nudes Descending the Staircase," after Duchamp (music by John Cage); "Ballet," after Calder (music by Bowles); "Circus," also after Calder (music by David Diamond); and "Narcissus," after an idea of his own (music by Louis Applebaum). The project, which proved a stellar showcase for surrealist art, occupied Richter for some four years, from 1944 to 1947.[4]

Three of the shorts presented actors in some sort of narrative, generally with monologues and dialogues rendered as voiceovers: "Desire," written by Ernst and derived from his collage-novel compiled from Victorian engravings, *Une semaine de bonté* (published in 1934), concerns sexual yearning (with Ernst himself appearing in the film along with gallery owner Julien Levy); "Ruth, Roses and Revolvers," after a story by Man Ray, parodies audience identification with film heroes by having movie patrons mimic the gestures of an on-screen figure; and "Narcissus," with dialogue by Richter and Richard Huelsenbeck (using the name Charles Hulbeck), reimagines the Greek myth of Narcissus by having the protagonist, who turns blue in the course of the episode, look "not only *at* his own image but *into* it and into the world which is mirrored in him." (Relating the autobiographical overtones of this last sequence to Richter's concealed Jewish background, and observing further the suppressed Jewish identities of Man Ray [Emmanuel Radnitzky] and Tristan Tzara [Shmuel Rosenstock] and the gentile Duchamp's inclination to adopt, conversely, a Jewish name, commentator Milly Heyd regards such masquerading as central to the very essence of the surrealist movement; given Latouche's hidden Jewish background, this argument would seem relevant to his own involvement with surrealism.) Three other episodes—"Discs and Nudes Descending the Staircase," "Ballet," and "Circus"—deal more in abstraction, without any verbal commentary, although "Discs" uses a model to simulate, through superimposition, Duchamp's famed *Nude Descending a Staircase*, no. 2 (1912); and "Circus" features, through stop action, Calder's miniature circus, *Cirque Calder* (1926–31), in motion.[5]

Standing somewhat apart, "The Girl with the Prefabricated Heart" unfolds a clearly shaped tale as narrated by the accompanying sung ballad written by Latouche, and illustrated on screen by mannequins in stop action interspersed with shots of Léger's painting *Julie, la belle cycliste* (1945). This episode plainly drew on a mythic tradition involving animated statues, dolls, marionettes, and automatons, with the story especially recalling E. T. A. Hoffmann's tale "The Sandman," later adapted by Delibes as *Coppélia* and Offenbach in *The Tales of Hoffmann*; but the sequence further exemplified the particular fascination that mannequins held for the surrealists, as manifest in the work of Giorgio de Chirico, not to mention the twenty decorated mannequins installed at the Paris International Exposition of Surrealism in 1938. "The mannequin seems to have been intended especially for our industrialized, dehumanized age, whose strengths and weaknesses it symbolizes so well . . . ," notes Willard Bohn concerning this phenomenon. "It appears to be the absence of compassion, more than anything else, that makes this character so threatening to the modern sensibility—itself partly shaped by the numerous cold-blooded social and political crimes of our century."[6]

Latouche's tale about the mannequin Julie in "The Girl with the Prefabricated Heart" can be more accurately described as a ballad than a song per se, not only because its long narrative clocks in at about eight minutes, but because its meter and form, including its choral refrain, evoke balladry, as in this opening stanza:

Oh Venus was born out of sea-foam
Oh Venus was born out of brine
But a goddess today
If she is Grade A
Is assembled upon the assembly line.
CHORUS
How divine. Rise and shine.
Upon the assembly line.

For variety, some of the stanzas feature couplets, as in this description of Julie, still nude and bald:

Her chromium nerves and her platinum brain
Were chastely encased in cellophane
And to top off this daughter of science and art
She was equipped with a prefabricated heart.

Donning a wedding gown, Julie marries a male mannequin dressed in a tuxedo, after which the music briefly stops as she and her husband converse (although still in verse); but his lovemaking so exasperates her that she cries out, "Oh, this is ridiculous! Sisters, come to my aid!" at which point two other female mannequins appear and the ballad resumes, "Her Amazon sisters were passing that way / They rushed to her aid and saved the day." Julie leaves her mate "bereft and wifeless / And he fell to the ground quite lifeless," as she bicycles away, the lyric ending,

And so she rides on through the evening
As pure as she was at the start
For there's no man alive
Who could ever survive
A girl with a prefabricated heart
A love-proof unbreakable heart.

This ballad—and by extension, this entire film sequence—appears an ironic dramatization of Latouche's failed marriage, at least from his perspective. For he no doubt thought of himself as the impetuous husband left "bereft and wifeless," and Theodora/Julie as the heartless wife, even alluding to his wife's lesbianism by way of her "Amazon sisters" who "rushed to her aid and saved the day." As mentioned earlier, Latouche similarly seems to have projected Theodora as the possessed Stella in *The Wax Flower*, the play he wrote with his psychiatrist Andrew Salter about this same time.

That Latouche also composed the music for this sequence has gone unnoticed, an understandable oversight considering that neither the opening titles nor the end credits made any such attribution. Rather, the film identified him simply as the author of the episode's lyrics, with Libby Holman and Josh White mentioned as the ballad's two soloists, and Norma Cazanjian and Doris Okerson as the two back-up singers. However, as Louis Applebaum, the film's Canadian musical director, indicated in the picture's souvenir program book, and as confirmed by a surviving manuscript vocal score, Latouche wrote not only the ballad's lyrics but its music, a rollicking ditty reminiscent of some of his cabaret songs. Applebaum remembered that he initially heard this "flamboyant music" in Holman's apartment: "From the first, when it was boisterously sung by John Latouche to his own piano accompaniment, through its decoration and development by Luther Henderson and this writer, the song seemed unable to disengage itself from the pleasant environment that nurtured it. It finally had to leave for more mundane surroundings when it was recorded by Miss Holman and Josh White, and two capable sopranos [Cazanjian and Okerson] from Juilliard supplying the Salvation Army–Valkyrie commentary to the song's preachment." Whatever refinements of melody and harmony subsequently imposed, the original manuscript, in Latouche's hand, shows the lyricist a capable tunesmith of a folklike bent, with the alternation of major and minor modes providing a certain bittersweet resonance.[7]

Latouche's participation in the film extended further—although similarly unacknowledged—to the frame story eventually devised by Richter in collaboration with David Vern, Hans Rehfisch, and Joseph Freeman, in which the separate episodes came to constitute the dreams of mostly neurotic people. Drawing on the detective fiction of Raymond Chandler and Dashiell Hammett, whose work Richter apparently liked, the film's prologue, which satirizes not only film noir and hardboiled mysteries but psychiatry, consumerism, and modern art, introduces a war veteran named Joe (Jack Bittner), who, discovering that he has the ability to unearth dreams by looking into people's eyes, turns his apartment into a dream dispensary. A series of clients arrive: a timid bank clerk ("Desire"), a prim young woman ("The Girl with the Prefabricated Heart"), the bank clerk's discontented wife ("Ruth, Roses and Revolvers"), a gangster ("Discs and Nudes Descending the Staircase"), a young girl ("Ballet"), and the girl's blind grandfather ("Circus"). The story concludes with Joe's own dream ("Narcissus") and his realization, "There is so much ahead of me... so much, so much I have to find out." The clients sometimes pay for their dreams—hence, the film's title, *Dreams That Money Can Buy*—but other times not. In the case of the gangster, played by Latouche, the client, hoping for some horse racing tips (shades of *Banjo Eyes*), demands his dream at gunpoint, at the conclusion of which he pistol-whips Joe and steals his money; in the case of the blind grandfather, the client simply offers to share his dream with Joe.

Virtually all the monologues and dialogues that accompany, unsynchronized, these interstitial episodes seem to have been written by Latouche. Once again, the film's titles obscured this contribution by crediting Richter with having "written and designed" the picture, making exceptions only for Man Ray, who supplied the "story" for "Ruth, Roses and Revolvers," and Richard Huelsenbeck, who co-wrote the "dialogue" with Richter for the "Narcissus" episode; only in the end credits does the vague acknowledgment, "Dialogue by John Latouche," appear. However, even without knowing that a 1948 *New York Times* article named Latouche as author of the film's narration and dialogue, the rhymed screenplay itself would suggest as much, as its style and wit show his fingerprints: "It's terrific," Joe tells himself after seeing a vision in his own eyes. "Here's something on which you can really pride yourself. You've discovered that you can look inside yourself. You're no longer a bum. You're an artist." Or consider Joe's poetic counsel to the bank clerk: "Let memory of mortgages, loans and property sales, dissolve into the cries of nightingales." If Latouche, as seems probable, took Theodora as his model for writing the dialogue for the prim woman (with the actress who played her on the screen, Valerie Tite, even looking somewhat like Theodora), he surely had himself in mind for the gangster role that he played in the "Discs and Nudes" sequence, the narration stating prior to the gangster's dream, "Here's the problem: He [the gangster] has no conscience, he has no subconscience. That's why he wants to have a dream.... He wants what he wants when he wants it"; and afterward, with even greater irony, "Imagine an active type like that having such a delicate dream. If he wasn't so much of an extrovert he might have been a poet."[8]

The episode with the prim woman accordingly sheds light on Latouche's political sensibilities during this period. In what appears to be a parody of political activism, the young woman asks Joe to "sign up," offering him such choices as "Pamphlet to Perpetuate Citizens in Public Life," "League to Discourage Citizens in Public Life," and "Action Committee for the Abolition of Abolition." At Joe's reluctance, she muses, "He doesn't understand. He has to belong to something. Otherwise, how will he ever know who he is?" Consistent with the film's emphasis on self-analysis, this satire accords with a growing interest, on Latouche's part as well as many others on the political left, in addressing societal concerns more through psychic well-being than political action, a merging of Marxist and Freudian ideas sometimes called Freudo-Marxism. That the film as a whole views the separate dream episodes not merely in the context of individual neuroses but as part of larger communal issues finds evidence not only in the antifascist subtexts found in some of the episodes, but in the mocking portrayal in "Desire" of the bank clerk's bourgeois wife and the fleeting images of social chaos and violence seen outside Joe's office door at that episode's conclusion.

Although a seeming oddity in the context of Latouche's career up to this point, *Dreams That Money Can Buy* in fact made extensive contact with his life and work, including his longstanding contact with surrealism, and his preoccupation with dreams both in his journals and in his work from his earliest stories to most recently *Willie the Weeper* and *Beggar's Holiday*—a cut song from which, "He Makes Me Believe," even contains the line, "The dreams that he sells me are second hand." Knowing more about the film's history—including how and when Latouche became involved with the picture, although this presumably happened before Léger's return to Europe in 1945—accordingly could help illuminate how works like *Beggar's Holiday* might have been shaped by the lyricist's association with progressive trends in art and cinema; or conversely, how Latouche might have influenced Richter's film over and above those factors already cited. At the least, he brought Paul Bowles on board, as he likely did Libby Holman and Luther Henderson, two of his *Beggar's Holiday* associates. Whether or not he contributed to the picture in still other ways, between writing lyrics, music, and dialogue, lining up talent, and acting in the film, he well deserved his description in the film's souvenir program book as "one of the main collaborators of *Dreams That Money Can Buy*," an achievement unrecognized in the extensive literature about the work.[9]

Presiding over Art of This Century Films, a small production company established just for this enterprise, Richter directed most of the picture with borrowed cameras and with the assistance of Miriam Raeburn and Arnold Eagle, among others, in and around a loft at 34 East 21st Street in New York's Flatiron district. Shot in 16 mm, the film cost in the end about $25,000, a remarkably low budget for a full-feature color movie over an hour in length, thanks to a cast and crew who, the *Times* reasonably supposed, would have cost Hollywood millions of dollars, but who for the most part worked on this project gratis (with both Richter and Applebaum covering some expenses out of their own pockets).[10]

Richter sought widespread distribution for the film, arguing that the work could be seen as comparable, after a fashion, to Walt Disney's *Fantasia* (1940), although he set his sights on a potential audience of a few million as opposed to many millions. Richter, whose hopes might have been bolstered by the fact that Alfred Hitchcock had recently collaborated with Salvador Dalí on *Spellbound* (1945), perhaps adapted the film's title from another Hollywood production, *All That Money Can Buy*, a picture that, as mentioned, Latouche admired. At any rate, the film's co-opting of Hollywood, even if ironic, proved a sticking point with a critic like Parker Tyler, who in 1949 described the work as "a glaring commercial effort to popularize esoteric art" and "a vitiated product of experimentalism."[11]

Given an award for "best original contribution to the progress of cinematography" at the Eighth Venice International Film Festival in 1947, *Dreams That Money Can Buy* previewed at the small Fifth Avenue Playhouse in Greenwich Village on April 22, 1948, as the initial presentation of the newly formed Cinema 16 Film Society, and then officially opened at the same theater on the following day, although under less-than-ideal circumstances; the film, as *Variety* reported, occasionally wandered off the screen onto the ceiling to "whistling and clapping," with further disturbance caused by people coming and going. Then, too, the high admission price of eighty-five cents, with the program book costing an additional twenty-five cents, seemed to *Variety* "likely to arouse resentment."[12]

Although somewhat sympathetic to Richter's ambitions, the New York reviews generally found the film "monotonous," "unintelligible," and, so far as concerned the leftist *Worker*, short on "mature substance" and "social understanding." At the same time, the critics enjoyed the "amusing" Léger sequence with its "new John LaTouche song," described as "dandy" and "catchy." Significantly, one of the picture's best reviews came from a music critic, Harold Schonberg, who naturally paid special attention to the score; declaring the film "fascinating" and "a synthesis of the arts that is also good entertainment," he described Latouche's music and lyrics for "The Girl with the Prefabricated Heart" as "in the best Kurt Weill tradition... alert, somewhat formalized but not too held down."[13]

After about three months at the Playhouse, the film moved further uptown to another art house, the Fifty-fifth Street Playhouse off Seventh Avenue. Distributed by Films International of America, the picture also had short runs throughout the year in such cities as Los Angeles, San Francisco, Boston, and Washington, all the while receiving mixed reviews as in New York. Whereas the *Washington Post* lampooned the picture by posting a surreal notice that concluded, "Crazy not am I dream just," and the *Boston Globe* observed attendants "sleeping peacefully" during this "bizarre" and "pretentious" movie, the *Christian Science Monitor* and *Los Angeles Times* largely praised the film, with the latter declaring the Léger episode "as delightful as a scene from 'Alice in Wonderland.'" By September, the film had recouped about 75 percent of its investment, but the picture ultimately failed to make a profit.[14]

In time, *Dreams That Money Can Buy* established itself nonetheless as a classic of its type, with showings appearing over the years in theaters and museums worldwide. The film proved influential as well, not only on such local filmmakers as Jonas Mekas, but possibly also on Federico Fellini. If anything, the film's reputation grew as the work came to appear, as film historian A. L. Rees argued in 1999, "uncannily prescient of a contemporary post-modernist sensibility." Indeed, director David Lynch cited the picture as a particular favorite of his, commenting with regard to the Léger episode, "The film [sequence] feels like a modern day music video. And I'm sure that the music was done before the film. And the feeling is to me very absurdly humorous and also frightening.... I guess anything that looks human but isn't is frightening."[15]

In April 2005, on a commission from the National Film Institute (later, the British Film Institute), and at the suggestion of Marek Pytel, a specialist in combining film with live performance, the Real Tuesday Weld, a British band founded by lead singer Stephen Coates, rescored the film. First presented at London's National Film Theatre in April 2005, this revamped version contained the original text as narrated and sung in person by Clive Piper and Cibelle Cavalli, but featured new live music, mostly composed by Coates, that "interacted" with the original score. Jettisoning so diverse and distinguished a soundtrack naturally impoverished the film, but the jazzy new music at least helped foreground some of the picture's more whimsical qualities. The Real Tuesday Weld subsequently performed this revised version at the Tate Modern's Turbine Hall and at film festivals in Belfast, Bath, and Moscow, where the picture included Russian subtitles in Cyrillic. Concurrently, the British Film Institute released both the Real Tuesday Weld as well as the original version on DVD, further providing Latouche's work with rare international exposure.[16]

Latouche had much less to do with Richter's next major picture, *8 x 8: A Chess Sonata in 8 Movements* (1957). The filmmaker undertook this project at the suggestion of Marcel Duchamp, a chess enthusiast, after *The Minotaur*, a planned sequel to the "Narcissus" episode of *Dreams That Money Can Buy*, failed to secure funding, although *8 x 8* engaged similar concerns in its attention to the "unforeseen obstacles you had to overcome," as Richter said of *The Minotaur*. "Chess is so universal," wrote Richter to Jean Cocteau about this new project, "that practically every human situation has its corresponding move among the countless possibilities of chess. This is really what fascinated me about the theme, and that is why I got involved in it in the first place." The filmmaker further recognized a kinship between the work, which took its title from the layout of a chessboard, and Lewis Carroll's *Through the Looking-Glass*, even beginning the movie with a title that read in part, "This film deals with the world of fantasy. It is a fairy tale for grown-ups. It explores the realm behind the magic mirror which served Lewis Carroll 100 years ago to stimulate our imagination."[17]

8 x 8 initially took shape as a short film shot on the grounds of Richter's Southbury, Connecticut, home in the spring of 1952, a short that would become the second sequence, "Black Schemes," of the completed eight-part color picture. Taking this short with him to Europe, the filmmaker found such friends as artist-poet Jean Arp, patron Peggy Guggenheim, and graphic designer Willem Sandberg eager to help with other episodes, with Jean Cocteau contributing one sequence, "The Queening of the Pawn," in which the chess maneuver of a queened pawn becomes a metaphor for gender variance. Filmed once again with cameraman Arnold Eagle, and in such far-flung places as Paris and Venice, as well as on the grounds of Libby Holman's estate, the picture premiered in 1957.[18]

"Black Schemes," the only sequence with which Latouche seems to have been involved, concerns the failed entrapment of the white queen (Jacqueline Matisse, the artist Matisse's granddaughter), who, as the white king (Marcel Duchamp) sleeps, triumphs over a bishop (the French painter Yves Tanguy), a rook (the German poet Richard Huelsenbeck), a knight (the American art dealer Julien Levy), and, finally, the black king (the Greek poet Nicolas Calas). Dressed in costumes suggestive of medieval dress, the characters enact their struggles in the woods, with the prop of an eight-ball providing yet more use of the color black and the number eight.

Richter, who oversaw and sometimes designed the soundtrack himself, clearly wanted this particular episode to evoke medieval times and Latouche accordingly provided him with a number, "Mock Madrigal," more or less appropriate to this end in both tone and word. As a song about the power of Venus, this madrigal seems comparable, for all their differences, to "The Girl with the Prefabricated Heart," which conflates the goddess of love with a store mannequin as opposed to a chess piece. In this instance, the number appears during the episode only sporadically, mostly at those moments in which the amorous knight attempts to seduce the queen; but the song, which brings the episode to a close, helps structure the entire sequence.

At least in the version of the film currently circulating, "Black Schemes" uses only six of the eight stanzas found in the song's published version, among other discrepancies. In a jaunty trimeter, each six-line stanza unfolds a lilting *aabccb* rhyme scheme, as in the last two stanzas heard in the film:

So lackaday my coney
Stay at the ceremony
Sing out with faltering breath.
O blest eternal daughter.
Though you're the lamb she'll slaughter
'Twill be a lively death!

And so she's still evading
In endless masquerading
Through every shifting scene.
We're lost within the mazes
Of all her lunar phases:
The harlot, dame, and queen.

The reference to "mazes" in this last stanza implies some connection between Richter's intentions in this film and those of the abandoned *Minotaur*. Meanwhile, "harlot, dame, and queen" displays a familiar Latouchian turn of phrase, as seen also in "traitor, spy, fifth columnist" from the radio play "Benedict Arnold," and "husband, father, child" from the "Farewell Song" (*The Ballad of Baby Doe*).

For this "Mock Madrigal," Latouche wrote a charming melody in duple meter, somewhat in the style of an English madrigal, with a neoclassical accompaniment of some sophistication, rounded off by extended "roulades," as Latouche terms them, more fully extended in the published song than in the film. Marked "pompously," the printed version contains two footnotes to performers, advising, first, that the singer emphasize the "flat dipthong [*sic*] sounds" of the melismas "for comic effect," and, second, that the "inflated pomposity" of the song be "less [Henry] Purcell and more Moody-Sankey," in reference to American hymnodists Dwight Lyman Moody and Ira David Sankey—both footnotes in the spirit of the film's irreverent playfulness. Composer Robert Abramson, an expert in the Dalcroze method, reharmonized and scored the song for harpsichord and recorder, and folksinger Oscar Brand recorded the vocal part. Abramson further developed Latouche's melody in some of the soundtrack's purely instrumental sections as well.

Originally scheduled to open at the Fifth Avenue Playhouse on March 4, 1957, the film encountered a delay when Richter came to loggerheads with the state censorship board, who wanted some brief female nudity edited out, prompting a defense of the film in the *Times* by film critic Bosley Crowther. Ultimately, Richter and the board compromised by agreeing to present the offending imagery in soft focus, and the film premiered as such on March 15. In several ways more adventurous than *Dreams That Money Can Buy*, with subtle transitions linking the episodes rather than a frame story, the film received a few good reviews from some of the New York dailies, with the *Post* finding the music of the Latouche episode "hauntingly effective," but the work never gained much of a toehold even among aficionados of avant-garde cinema. Latouche's delightful "Mock Madrigal" accordingly remained obscure as well, although in 1956 the piece appeared, along with songs by Ben Weber and Ned Rorem, in the final issue of Daisy Aldan's little magazine, *Folder*.[19]

Meanwhile, Latouche also wrote a brief narration for *Works of Calder*, a twenty-minute film about Alexander ("Sandy") Calder (1898–1976) released in 1950 and directed by the sculptor's good friend Herbert Matter (1907–1984), a Swiss-American photographer who had arrived in the United States in 1936 and who would begin a long tenure as professor of photography at Yale in 1952. Commissioned by the Museum of Modern Art and produced by Burgess Meredith, who read the narration, the documentary also featured a score by John Cage for prepared piano, percussion, and tape. As with *The Last Joan*, discussed forthwith, Meredith likely invited the lyricist to work on the film, much as Latouche in turn might have recommended Cage for the music.

The picture attempts a fresh look at Calder's work by viewing it through the eyes of a young lad (played by Herbert Matter's son, Alex), who, after exploring the beach on a windy day, wanders into the artist's studio. States the narration in part,

> He [Calder] worked hard as though in a factory, but the things came out different. And sometimes they [his mobiles] moved all around him and he enjoyed that; it was like having his own private sky. The boy watched them so long he got rather dreamy, and the things he saw in the house and the things he had seen outside got mixed up together in his head. The man said, that was what they were supposed to do.

By juxtaposing shots of the natural world with those of Calder's sculptures, the film underscored the relation of the artist's work to the shapes and rhythms of nature.

As a 16 mm color noncommercial film intended for educational purposes, *Works of Calder* received little attention and to this day remains obscure, although the award-winning Cage score has enjoyed performances and recordings as a work in its own right.[20]

In 1951, Latouche started his own small film unit, A&M Productions (later, Aries Productions), largely underwritten by such friends as Alice Bouverie and Libby Holman. As reported in early 1952, this outfit included, besides Latouche, composer

Donald Fuller, actress Carol Channing, animator Willis Pyle, writer and cartoon voice John Ployardt (the pseudonym of John Fraser McLeish), and designer Nicholas Gibson (with Latouche's friend Harry Martin apparently serving in an administrative capacity). The press further cited a number of color shorts in production or at least planned, including *The Peppermint Tree*, an animated film based on a poem by Latouche; a stop-action picture, *Harlequinade*, with direction by McLeish, "commedia dell'arte dolls" designed by Reginald Massie, and music possibly by Stravinsky; *The Blues*, with singer Holman under the direction of photographer Gjon Mili; a film about the sculptures of Elie Nadelman, narrated and directed by Lincoln Kirstein; two separate pictures featuring the work of *New Yorker* cartoonists Charles Addams and Saul Steinberg; a film based on two brief Gertrude Stein plays, *Ladies' Voices* and *What Happened*; and a Maya Deren short choreographed by Anthony Tudor. Although only *The Peppermint Tree* and the Maya Deren film (*The Very Eye of Night*)—along with portions of an unfinished short, *Presenting Jane*, also produced under the auspices of Aries Productions—ever saw the light of day, this proposed lineup nonetheless reveals a good deal about Latouche's interests and ambitions.[21]

Latouche's acquaintance with Maya Deren (born Eleanora Derenkowskaia, 1917–1961) dated back to 1941, when the latter worked as a personal assistant to choreographer Katherine Dunham, then on tour with *Cabin in the Sky*. Named, like Latouche's friend Eleonora Mendelssohn, after the great actress Eleonora Duse, Deren and her Ukrainian-Jewish family emigrated in 1922 to the United States, where they settled in Syracuse, New York; the family surname shortened to Deren, Eleanora further changed her first name to Maya in her early twenties. After some study in Geneva during adolescence, Deren immersed herself in radical politics while attending sundry schools, including Smith College, from which she received a master's degree in literature. On leaving Dunham's employ and marrying her second husband, film director Alexander Hammid, a recent Czech exile, she began in 1943 to make films herself, creating in the course of her brief life a small corpus of work regarded as a cornerstone in the history of experimental filmmaking.[22]

Latouche might have kept abreast of Deren's filmmaking activities through their mutual friend Leo Lerman, who sometimes appeared in her films, including *At Land* (1944), which Lerman thought "effective" although somewhat pointless. In any event, Latouche featured a screening of Deren's film short *Ensemble for Somnambulists* at a Halloween party at his apartment in 1951, with Lerman observing some bizarre costumes among the guests, including the host "in a sort of space suit."[23]

Latouche presumably admired *Ensemble for Somnambulists*, whose incorporation of dance and film paralleled his own synthesis of dance and theater, for Aries Productions subsequently commissioned Deren to create a work along similar lines, *The Very Eye of Night*, in which spectral dancers—here ballet students choreographed by Anthony Tudor—appear to float among the stars. Deren began work on the project in 1952, agreeing to split the profits forty-sixty with Aries; but between a slow start and unexpected expenses and delays, including complications concerning the musical score by her third husband, Teiji Ito, she did not finish the film until 1956, although she unveiled a near-final edit in Haiti in 1955. By this time, she had long since gone through her advance of a few thousand dollars and had been funding the project at her own expense amid strained financial conditions. Prior to distribution, Deren hoped to renegotiate the original terms of her contract so as to grant herself a larger share of the profits, but Latouche died before any such agreement could be formalized, leaving her to work out the details with his estate. Released in early 1959, the fifteen-minute short, Deren's last completed film, earned the praise of *Times* critic Howard Thompson, who deemed it "an original and haunting fusion of choreography and movie making."[24]

Some fanciful lore contends that because of certain conflicts arising over the unwillingness or inability of Aries Productions to meet Deren's request for further funding, the filmmaker, a student of Haitian culture, put a voudou curse on Latouche, resulting in his death; and that after Latouche's demise, his friends in turn placed a fatal curse on Deren, who similarly died tragically young. But as Deren wrote to the lyricist in September 1953, she understood that in view of his own precarious finances, Latouche could do only so much to help her, and further believed that her own poor judgment had given him reason to feel "pained and outraged" by what appeared "to be a betrayal," leaving her "overwhelmed by a sense of guilt of traumatic proportions." Moreover, in June 1956, shortly before Latouche's death, she assured him that the film's titles would carry his name "beautifully lettered," writing,

> In spite of the tension and somewhat disturbed atmosphere between us, from time to time, I have never forgotten that it was your initiative and initial support and confidence that got this film under way, and I know that, with just a little more luck in your affairs in this past period, you would have seen it through to the end, and I'm glad that I was able, finally to turn out the film that you had had such confidence in.[25]

Indeed, a letter from Deren to Leo Lerman written soon after Latouche's death, and with that event presumably in mind, suggested a close identification with Latouche right to the end: "You [Lerman] should do a book on 'Our bunch'—this pressured bunch that is dying off so early because upon them lay the burden of bridging over from the exhilarations and spectacular rebelliousness of the 'Lost Generation'—to the ones who are coming after us now—the first Cosmopolitans in the best sense of the word.... We are the *atomized generation*." In this context, film scholar Sarah Keller's discernment of some essential commonality between *The Very Eye of Night*, which "fixates on humankind in relation to heaven," and Latouche's *The Golden Apple*, which "takes up mythological themes in a present-day vernacular," seems all the more telling.[26]

Meant to be read aloud to children, Latouche's poem "The Peppermint Tree," ostensibly written in 1949, initially appeared in the March 1950 issue of his friend Eileen Garrett's magazine *Tomorrow*, and later was reprinted in a somewhat shortened version in the 1954 Christmas issue of *Good Housekeeping*. The story follows. In "a town called Onceuponatime, / Where Dreaming was a serious crime," the citizens "Were certain-sure they knew it all." Only one man "could not have been dumber. / This social outcast who wasnt brainy / Was Doctor Addlepayte O'Zany." A famous astronomer who knows the names of the planets, stars, and clouds, O'Zany "was fine up there in the universe / But once down to earth, he couldnt be worse." Among his wife's complaints, "He carefully places his clothes in bed / And hangs *himself* in the closet instead." One early spring, determined to have a garden, O'Zany purchases pumpkin seeds and peppermint drops at the general store, but to the amusement of his neighbors, he plants the drops and eats the seeds. That night, as he sits alone and feels ashamed of himself, an encouraging star appears, singing a song that begins, "Follow your particular star / And you'll rise and shine where the others are," and ends, "Be true to your star your whole life through / And your star will be true to you." The next morning, discovering a "marvelous beautiful Peppermint Tree" that "had grown in his garden overnight," the town cheers Doctor O'Zany, whereupon

> Doctor O'Zany smiled, "Dear me
> It's just as simple as A.B.C.
> You can do it too, whoever you are...
> Just believe in your particular star."[27]

Whatever associations this fable might have held for readers at the time, including astrological overtones that would have made *Tomorrow* magazine an appropriate venue for its debut publication, or echoes of the song "When You Wish upon a Star" from Walt Disney's popular feature film *Pinocchio* (1940), Latouche recognized some relation to Dante, inscribing a copy of the poem to a friend with the question, "is this your idea of a juke-box Dante at work?" Presumably Latouche had in mind the advice Dante receives in the *Inferno* from his former mentor, Brunetto Latini, "Follow your star and you, will certainly / come to a glorious harbor"; whether he also saw some special significance in Latini's counsel coming from someone consigned as a "sodomite" to the seventh circle of Hell, "The Peppermint Tree" carried strong autobiographical resonance, not only in terms of the portrayal of Doctor O'Zany as an eccentric dreamer, but in such details as his "blue eyes" and his disgruntled wife, who "packed her bags and left him flat" after his fiasco in the garden.[28]

Perhaps inspired by *Gerald McBoing-Boing* (1950), a celebrated United Productions of American (UPA) cartoon based on a similar story by Dr. Seuss about a misfit who achieves glory, Latouche decided to adapt "The Peppermint Tree" as an animated short with Aries Productions, and to this end, he commissioned Donald Fuller, his erstwhile collaborator, to write the music; actress Carol Channing to narrate the poem; and experienced animators John McLeish, Nicholas Gibson, and Willis Pyle to design and illustrate the cartoon.

In the fall of 1951, Channing made a masterful demo recording of the work, reciting the text with an impressively wide range of voices to depict the utterances of Doctor O'Zany, his wife, the star, and various citizens (with some overdubbing to simulate a crowd); and singing—reportedly with Jerome Moross at the piano—Fuller's setting of "The Star Song," the film's one musical number. This five-minute demo recording, which happily survives, varies slightly from the original published version, including an additional couplet that might have been suggested by *Gerald McBoing-Boing*: "And all the folks who used to laugh / Now ask him for his autograph."[29]

Using Channing's recording as a template, John McLeish created the storyboard, Nicholas Gibson, the backgrounds, and Willis Pyle, with the help of a few assistants, the animation. The artists set up a makeshift studio in Latouche's East 67th Street apartment—to Pyle's dismay, for he often would arrive early in the morning to find the place littered with debris from the previous night's party, his drawings scattered about and stained with the residue of cocktail glasses. Pyle further recalled how Latouche, appearing at around eleven o'clock in a white silk robe, would comment on the cartoonist's regular early morning work schedule by saying, "Your life must be terribly dull." Although the twelve-minute film appears, at least for the moment, lost, Pyle remembered the animation, which occupied him for about eight months, more in the style of his work for UPA than for Disney.[30]

After some delay in getting the cartoon scored by local musicians, Latouche placed the short with the noted agent Charles Feldman, who in 1953 attempted to sell it to producer Jack Warner, but to no avail. The film finally opened in 1955, playing at various venues, including the Sutton Theater, an art house on Manhattan's East Side, where it settled into a long run as a curtain raiser to the critically acclaimed picture *Marty* (1955). Paid a regular salary while working on the short, Pyle tried to collect some promised additional money once the film opened, but, rebuffed by Latouche (who, he recalled, had "a terrible temper"), he instituted legal proceedings against the lyricist, a suit eventually dropped.[31]

In contrast to the film, the poem, a delightful example of Latouche's art at its most childlike, remained in circulation. A group of high school students in Westfield, New Jersey, for instance, gave dramatized performances of the poem to young children in hospitals, elementary schools, and other venues in 1986. Eminently deserving a reprint, perhaps as an illustrated children's book, a critically aware edition would want to take stock of the slight differences as found not only in the *Tomorrow* and *Good Housekeeping* printings but in Carol Channing's demo recording as well.[32]

In the summer of 1952, with funding from Aries Productions and the assistance of Harrison Starr (b. 1929), a cameraman (and future movie producer) whom he met through Maya Deren, Latouche himself began directing a film short, *Presenting Jane*, for which he also devised the scenario. The project originated by way of a short play so titled by poet James Schuyler (pronounced SKY-ler) that consisted of poetic and nonsensical exchanges by three characters named after Schuyler's friends, painter

Jane Freilicher (the "Jane" of the title) and poets John Ashbery and Frank O'Hara—a social circle with whom Latouche had grown friendly during these years. After a reading of the script by these associates at his apartment, Latouche excitedly resolved to use the poet's dadaist playlet as the basis of a short film.[33]

Latouche cast Freilicher, Ashbery, and O'Hara as themselves, but created a part as well for Schuyler as a kind of watchful spy. Filming began in July 1952 at the home of artist Matsumi ("Mike") Kanemitsu and model Lenore Pettit (a friend of Latouche's) in East Hampton on Georgica Pond, where Latouche, cameraman Starr, the four-person cast, and friends Kenward Elmslie, Harry Martin, and John Bernard Myers all converged, and on whose grounds painter Larry Rivers also had a studio; Elmslie would later recall his surprise at finding Ashbery, Freilicher, and O'Hara in bed one morning, and Freilicher and Rivers in the same bed the next.[34]

Only several days of filming ever seem to have taken place, with some participants on location simply for a weekend or two. "The whole thing," recalled Schuyler, "was a total disaster.... Everyone quarreled with everyone else, no one cooperated, Touche was in a rage, always bawling everybody out." Starr found himself particularly at odds with his "flamboyant" director: "To put it bluntly, I was a pretty fractious guy, and I didn't like Latouche, and I didn't think he knew, to put it even more bluntly, shit from shinola." Although the film was never completed, clips from the work accompanied a reading of Schuyler's script at the February 25, 1953, inauguration of the Artists' Theatre, an off-Broadway enterprise founded by John Bernard Myers and his companion, director Herbert Machiz, at the Theatre de Lys in Greenwich Village, with the program crediting both Latouche and Starr for the film.[35]

Long thought lost, rushes of the film surfaced among Harrison Starr's effects in 2013, with a restored print subsequently prepared by the Harvard Film Archive in cooperation with the Woodberry Poetry Room. The extant film includes footage of Ashbery, Freilicher, O'Hara, and Schuyler driving up to a country house in a Buick Roadmaster convertible—possibly the one Latouche purchased from Tennessee Williams—with Schuyler sitting alone in the back seat like a ghostly presence, comically carrying out all the luggage on their arrival. (Latouche can be seen hovering in the background of one outtake from this scene.) Ironic depictions of the artists—O'Hara typing, Freilicher drawing, Ashbery reading—follow. At one point, Freilicher ambles on a barely submerged dock so that she seems like Venus rising from the sea, an allusion that would have been all the more telling had some reverse motion footage originally employed in this scene survived. The Poetry Project presented these cinematic remnants, with Latouche and Starr named as co-directors, as part of a 2014 posthumous ninetieth birthday celebration for Freilicher at St. Mark's Church in the East Village; in a review of the event for the *Times*, Holland Cotter wrote that the image of Freilicher appearing to walk on water against a sunset "lingered in the mind."[36]

16

Ballet Ballads

Latouche early on found a particularly like-minded collaborator in Jerome Moross, with whom he wrote two of his most significant works: *Ballet Ballads* (1948) and *The Golden Apple* (1954).

Of Russian-Jewish heritage, Moross (1913–1983) grew up in Manhattan and Brooklyn, and started playing piano and composing at a young age. While at DeWitt Clinton High School, he became good friends with a slightly older student, Bernard Herrmann, later a famous film composer for Orson Welles and Alfred Hitchcock. Moross continued his education, like Herrmann, at New York University, where he studied with Philip James and Vincent Jones (and graduated at age eighteen in the spring of 1932), and at Juilliard, where he worked with Bernard Wagenaar, Albert Stoessel, and George Volkel. During these same years, Moross and Herrmann immersed themselves in the new music scene, joining Copland's Young Composers' Group, and becoming especially devoted to the still rather obscure Charles Ives, whose music they enthusiastically played and championed. They also befriended composer Henry Cowell, whom Moross thought "a good, honest, fabulous man."[1]

Within these circles, "Benny-and-Jerry" became notorious for their brusque dismissals of other composers, with Moross himself stating in later years, "Benny [Herrmann] could probably be the rudest man that ever lived and he could also be the most charming man that ever lived." Moross remained rather disdainful toward much contemporary music throughout his life, deeming twelve-tone music, for instance, a sort of "idiocy," and the only-somewhat-preferable minimalism, "a kind of a madness." He even found over time his admiration for Ives slightly "diminished." But he stayed steadfastly loyal to Copland. Recalling a soirée in Los Angeles in the late 1930s, Oscar Levant wrote, "One of my most pleasant recollections of the occasion was the zealous and undeviating loyalty of Moross to Copland. This was emphasized by his unfailing habit of remarking, with a wide and pleased grin, about any new work that was played: 'That's a baad [*sic*] piece.' This applied to anything from Debussy to Schoenberg, always, of course, excluding Copland." "You can't help being cordial with Aaron [Copland]," explained Moross late in life; "he's a *great* man, a man of warmth and dignity who had a genuine interest in seeing American music grow."[2]

Moross initially made his name with adventurous works like *Paeans* for chamber orchestra, a short piece published in 1933 by Cowell, who called its young composer "a vigorous experimenter . . . not afraid to go as far as his imagination can carry him in exploring new orchestral sounds, slides, and rhythms." But by 1934, as his leftist ideals helped point him in the direction of the larger public, his music acquired a new accessibility, as evidenced not only by his arrangement of Louis Moreau Gottschalk's *The Banjo* for two pianos (1934), but by such original pieces as *Biguine* for orchestra (also 1934), a work that suggested the influence of the Mexican composer Silvestre Revueltas. Moross relatedly busied himself in the theater, including composing music for the satirical revue *Parade* and Bertolt Brecht's play *Mother* (both 1935), as well as providing dance scores for the Doris Humphrey–Charles Weidman Company and the Chicagoan choreographer Ruth Page. Recalling the many "exciting operas and shows" he had seen while in Berlin and Vienna in 1932, he envisioned a comparable revitalization of musical theater at home, calling for "the combined talents of every force available in the theatre," lyrics worthy of W. S. Gilbert and Brecht, and "skeletal" settings, all rooted in "our own indigenous minstrel and vaudeville shows"—an agenda strikingly similar to Latouche's own, and one thought to offer a bulwark against fascism.[3]

The jazzy ballet score *Frankie and Johnny* (1937–38), written for Ruth Page under the auspices of the Federal Theatre Project, proved a watershed; "in the midst of writing it . . . ," stated the composer, "I suddenly realized that I was really being myself. I was being like nobody else I knew." Indeed, in its folkloric elements, broad humor, variation form, and blend of ballet and song, the work proved highly characteristic, as did, too, its "sheer physicalness," a trait of the composer's, singled out by Copland, that naturally attracted dancers. Inspired by his travels cross-country, Moross at the same time began to cultivate a certain rustic sound evocative of the American West, first given dedicated expression in *A Tall Story* for orchestra (1938), but most famously realized years later in his Oscar-nominated film score to *The Big Country* (1958). "The composer must reflect his landscape," he said near the end of his life, "and mine is the landscape of America."[4]

In 1939, about the time Moross began to collaborate with Latouche, he married Hazel Abrams (1905–1983), with whom he had one child, Susanna (b. 1940); and in order to make ends meet, in the early 1940s, he took employment in Hollywood, first as an orchestrator, then as a composer. But unlike Herrmann, who energetically pursued a movie career, Moross did just enough film work to be able to return regularly to New York and pursue his great love, the lyric and concert stage. After 1969, he gave up Hollywood altogether and spent his final years residing in New York and Miami, where both he and his wife died in 1983. Although his two operas with Latouche rate among his most ambitious and important achievements, he remains best remembered for his film scores, which garnered the praise of connoisseurs like Christopher Palmer: "This [Moross's] freshness of melodic invention—together with the bouncy, sexy rhythms derived from dance, i.e. from body-language—make for a virile music which irresistibly celebrates life, the sheer joy of being alive."[5]

Latouche and Moross began their association with the dance-cantata *Susanna and the Elders*, which they wrote rather quickly in late 1939 and early 1940, and which eventually became the first of the *Ballet Ballads*, a four-act work completed in early 1947. According to one source, the two men met at a party and decided to collaborate after realizing that "they shared a common desire to write a new form of musical which would utilize all the facilities of song, dance, lyrics and music to tell a story," but the actual circumstances regarding the creation of *Susanna* remain essentially unknown. A 1941 newspaper article reports that they wrote the piece for the Schola Cantorum, a choral ensemble based in New York and directed by the British-American Hugh Ross, who eventually would conduct the first performances of both *Ballet Ballads* and *The Golden Apple*. At the same time, a *New York Times* item of November 1939 announced that choreographers Felicia Sorel and Helen Tamiris planned "a novel type of dance revue" for the Labor Stage that would involve a number of varied artists, including Moross and Latouche, a project that never came to fruition, but that might have helped spur the creation of *Susanna* as well. In any case, Moross later related,

> From the first, John Latouche and I knew exactly what the other was striving for because we had been experimenting separately along the same lines.... We both felt that the limitations the popular stage imposed on its writers and composers and the hothouse atmosphere in which so much modern opera was being produced were equally restrictive. Our particular approach to the lyrical theatre was to use the best in musical comedy, opera and ballet forms with gay abandon, and we were both convinced that the resulting mixture would allow us both to entertain and say what we had to say.[6]

In his preface to the published libretto to *The Golden Apple*, Latouche provided, moreover, a rare account of their working method:

> When I was writing the lyrical texts for *Ballet Ballads* and *The Golden Apple* I would carefully map out the action with Jerome Moross.... I then would write the scenes to interior melodies of my own devising, so that the words would be singable rather than speakable....
>
> The melodies I invented to give the individual lyrics a unified dramatic flow have been heard only by the unhappy few nearest and dearest to me, who assure me they are among the worst they have ever heard. Jerome Moross finally forbade me to give tongue to them in his hearing, with an ominous gleam in his eye that had lethal reflections. But these personal tunes are useful if not pretty, because they preserve the lyric line of the collaboration without permitting the script to invade the usurping domain of poetry.

Latouche further expressed his "surprise" and "delight" with Moross's settings of his words: "Very often phrases which seemed commonplace are lifted into the unusual by a sudden turn of melody. Even more often, the music brings a wild humor of its own when the laughter is fading in the script." Moross returned the compliment in his own introduction to the *Golden Apple* libretto, praising the text as "a wonder of wit and invention," and adding, "His [Latouche's] lines are always written so that they may be set with the greatest clarity, and his scenes are conceived so that they may be easily molded into formal structures."[7]

The particular notion of placing the biblical story of Susanna in the rural American Midwest possibly originated with Latouche, who in discussing the work's genesis, wrote, "I remembered having heard a remarkably vivacious sermon about the wicked elders one hot Sunday afternoon in a Holy Roller revival tent." The idea also might have received some impetus from a 1938 painting by Thomas Hart Benton, *Susanna and the Elders,* which featured two older men (one modeled after Benton himself) spying on a naked young woman, and which caused such a stir as to prompt a February 1939 *Life* magazine spread on the artist's nudes (although back in 1934, the twenty-year-old Latouche had judged Benton a "mediocre artist"). The Susanna story seems generally to have been in the air; a satire of early American utopian communities by Lawrence Langner and Armina Marshall, similarly entitled *Suzanna and the Elders,* premiered on Broadway in October 1940.[8]

A portion from the Book of Daniel generally considered noncanonic by Jewish and Protestant tradition, the Susanna text probably dates from the first or second century BC and has two main variants (with Latouche apparently consulting the English version of one of these as found in the King James Bible). Set against the background of the Babylonian exile, the tale concerns Susanna, the lovely and virtuous wife of Joachim, a wealthy and respected member of the diasporic community. As Susanna prepares to bathe in the privacy of her garden, two lustful elders approach her with the ultimatum that unless she yield to their desires, they will accuse her of adultery with a young man. As she cries out, the elders publicly denounce her. Brought before a community tribunal, Susanna receives a sentence of death, the penalty for such infidelity, whereupon the young Daniel appears and questions the two elders, asking each privately under which tree Susanna committed adultery. When each names a different tree, Daniel reveals them as perjurers and condemns them to the same punishment that they willed for Susanna: death.

Moross and Latouche reconceived the tale as a sermon told by a preacher, The Parson, at a backwoods American tent revival meeting, with soprano and baritone solos and mixed chorus performing diverse dramatic functions: the baritone assumes the roles of the preacher, the two elders (here named Moe and Joe), and The Angel (as the opera conceives Daniel); the soprano, who emerges from the chorus, plays the part of Susanna; and the chorus, as the congregation, helps The Parson narrate events, but at other times represents the ancient diasporic community, with the tenors and basses sometimes enacting the words of the two elders as well. The score also calls for eight solo dancers: four to portray Susanna, Moe, Joe, and The Angel, respectively, but in addition two dancers holding a cloth to symbolize the wall in Susanna's garden, and two others with green boughs to depict the incriminating trees in her garden (here designated as The Cedar from Lebanon and The Little Juniper Tree).

Some of these distancing effects, as in the case of Aaron Copland and Edwin Denby's *The Second Hurricane* (1937), reflected modern theatrical trends, with its amalgam of ballet and opera in particular recalling landmark works of Stravinsky and Weill, not to mention Moross's own *Frankie and Johnny*. Moross himself asserted that he and Latouche had in mind a "choral ballet" like Rimsky-Korsakov's 1909 *The Golden Cockerel*—presumably as staged by Michel Fokine in 1914—although the degree of interaction between dance and song here proved exceptional, especially as *Ballet Ballads* evolved as a whole.[9]

At the same time, as with their modernist predecessors, Latouche and Moross found common ground in folk traditions, the text adopting, for instance, something of the meter and language of Isaac Watts and other hymnodists, as in the opening of Susanna's public defense:

> High above in His cloudy tent
> The Lord of Hosts can see
> These men on my destruction bent
> With lies have troubled me.

"It was important not to imply any mockery of primitive faith on our part," wrote Latouche in 1948. "Accordingly I shaped my lines after the earthy psalmodies I had absorbed during a Virginia childhood." As for the plot, Latouche hewed closely to the biblical telling; and although he omitted, among other details, the damning implication that the elders had a past record of such misdeeds, he implied a criticism of entrenched corruption in other ways, as in the final chorus in which the congregation observes how the "proud" towers of Babylon have turned to "dust" and "rust"—an allegorical critique of the modern metropolis that recalled some of Latouche's early poems.

Moross set the libretto in an analogously folksy manner, with echoes of traditional American folksong, barbershop music, and hymnody, as well as touches of vaudeville, especially for the elders, and Jewish chant, especially for Susanna and the diasporic community, so that the work can be said to epitomize the composer's Jewish-American background. Divided into eight discrete sections, the separate movements tend to feature strophic songs with choral refrains, which enhances the work's folklike ambience, and the whole concludes with a sort of small-town Handelian chorus, perhaps as a nod to Handel's own *Susanna* oratorio. Simple and direct to the point of plainness, Moross creates some dramatic and poetic resonance, as generally in his mature style, through muted dissonance in the accompaniment (derived especially from unstable treatment of the third and seventh degrees of diatonic scales) and swift and unprepared changes of key.

Susanna and the Elders received a performance, presumably with piano accompaniment, by an African-American ensemble that included the Juanita Hall Choir and dancer Clarence Yates, on May 8, 1940, at a benefit concert for the Spanish Children's Relief Fund at New York's Mecca Temple, with Howard Taubman describing this "modern oratorio" in his *Times* review as "a broad, modern take-off on the biblical tale." Moross, however, regarded a subsequent May 9, 1941, account in Los Angeles conducted by film composer Alfred Newman, with soprano Eloise Rawitzer, baritone Robert Brink, and chamber orchestra, but apparently without dancers, as the work's official world premiere. Produced under the auspices of the Music Council of the Hollywood Theatre Alliance, this Los Angeles rendering "elicited loud bravos and applause from the audience," according to the *Los Angeles Times*, with Moross himself publicly commending Newman's "excellent performance."[10]

Following *Susanna and the Elders*, Moross hoped to compose a piece with Latouche based on Ben Jonson's 1606 satire of greed and corruption, *Volpone*. To this end, in late 1943, the composer sent Latouche, then in the navy, an elaborate nine-page scenario for a three-act opera, tentatively entitled *Mr. Fox and Mr. Fly*, that took Jules Romains and Stefan Zweig's popular 1928 adaptation of the Elizabethan play into account, and that called for a small cast and a modest orchestra suitable for either Broadway or "an orthodox opera-house at some later date when it [the work] is a museum piece." Moross followed up in early 1944 with an encouraging letter to Latouche, saying, "I still think you are wonderful and the best probable opera poet in America," to which the lyricist responded, "I adore you, and think you are a charmer with the psyche of a porcupine"; but although "pleased you think I'm the best 'opera poet'—since I have written no opera libretti up to now—and its [*sic*] lovely to have clairvoyant appreciation," he explained that he would need more in the way of a cash advance to undertake so ambitious a project.[11]

However, Moross persisted and Latouche finally gave way, signing a contract, dated February 14, 1944, to write a "grand opera libretto" based on Moross's *Volpone* scenario; and on his return in April from service in Hawaii, he traveled to Los Angeles to work with the composer on the piece. But progress proved torturous: "Jerry and I quarrel in the same violent way we always did," the librettist wrote in his journal. "It disturbs me—particularly the violence of his temper, which shakes me in much the way that mine must have shaken Theo[dora Latouche], who certainly was more insecure at that time than I am now." Discussing their explosive relationship, Moross told Latouche, "I don't think you've ever loved anyone," to which the latter reflected in his diary, "Perhaps that is true. Certainly, least of all myself." Ultimately, the two abandoned the venture, although they sporadically returned to the notion of some sort of *Volpone* opera as late as 1947.[12]

A very few sketches for this *Volpone* adaptation, imagined to take place in Louisiana in 1848, with Bovino (apparently, the renamed Bonario), a "wounded and angry veteran" of the Mexican War, survive among Latouche's papers, including a lyric about money for the greedy Volpone and his servant Mosca, and an exchange between Volpone and the more idealistic Bovino, in which Volpone sings,

> As long as a guy
> Likes a wife *and* a *mis*tress
> Wants the slice *and* the pie
> There's gonna be distress
> A five-buck cravat
> To wear in his collar
> Will always mean that
> Somebody will holler—
> Oh the root of all evil
> Is the fruit of the devil
> Our eternal friend—the dollar... [emphasis in original]

The hardboiled cynicism of this material, not to mention the presence of an angry veteran, and the idea, jotted among these sketches, of having singer Libby Holman possibly play "the whoremistress" of the storied New Orleans brothel Rising Sun, would seem to date this material to about the time of *Beggar's Holiday* (1946).[13]

Moross and Latouche also co-wrote the scenario to another unrealized musical work, *Great Lucifer,* which likewise dates, it would appear, from the immediate post-war period. The tale partakes of a long storytelling tradition that places a heavenly or demonic figure among humankind. In this case, the protagonist, Beelzebub, one of Lucifer's minions, volunteers to inhabit the body of a murdered man while demons attempt to retrieve the man's missing soul. Beelzebub tries corrupting the man's fiancée, but winds up falling in love with her, and as punishment is sentenced to life on earth as a human. One scene in particular—Beelzebub's moral education regarding the seven deadly sins as found in contemporary New York through a series of episodes—looked ahead to the Big Spree sequence from *The Golden Apple,* while the general theme of redemption through love proved for Latouche a lifelong preoccupation.[14]

Meanwhile, Moross and Latouche decided to expand on *Susanna and the Elders* by collaborating on some additional one-act "dance-operas" on traditional American themes, Latouche stating in 1948, "Our intention was to blend several elements of the American theatrical, dance and musical heritage into a pattern adapted to the contemporary stage." With regard to friends who viewed their planned subjects "as suspiciously resembling 'Americana,' Latouche commented, "This self-conscious term puzzled me. No other national group I know of has isolated its historical or cultural past into such a neat and discouraging category. However, instead of being discouraged, we [he and Moross] decided to avoid as much as possible the quaint and cute overtones in such a label and to aim for the direct statement."[15]

Over the summer of 1944, Moross proposed to Latouche as one idea that they adapt the fairy tale *Little Red Riding Hood*, writing, "The whole atmosphere must be a combunation [*sic*] of the Disney Silly Symphony and a slightly lascivious version of an American children's classic." (Launched by Walt Disney in 1929, the Silly Symphonies were animated shorts with risible orchestral scores that drew ironically on classical music, with a 1934 Silly Symphony already featuring "a slightly lascivious version" of Red Riding Hood, *The Big Bad Wolf*.) Soon after making this suggestion, Moross started in on an instrumental piece, *Variations on a Waltz*, that ultimately formed part of the Red Riding Hood dance-opera completed with Latouche in early 1947, *Riding Hood Revisited: A Silly Symphony in E-flat Major*, but that the composer also eventually brought forth as a separate concert work in 1966, making the histories of these two pieces inextricably intertwined.[16]

Even before finishing *Riding Hood Revisited*, Moross and Latouche composed two other one-act dance-operas: *Willie the Weeper*, after an urban black folksong, completed in 1945; and *The Eccentricities of Davy Crockett*, based on the legendary frontiersman, completed in 1946. Grouping their four one-acters so that together they contained something of the dynamics of a traditional symphony—first movement (*Susanna and the Elders*), slow movement (*Willie the Weeper*), scherzo (*Riding Hood Revisited*), and finale (*The Eccentricities of Davy Crockett*)—Moross and Latouche titled the whole *Four in Hand: An Evening of Ballet Ballads*, although when the work (sans *Riding Hood*) appeared off Broadway and then on Broadway in 1948, they simply called the piece *Ballet Ballads*, a title that continued to be used for any combination of these dance-operas, with single performances of any one of them identified rather by their individual name.[17]

When Moross and Latouche spoke about *Ballet Ballads* (sometimes in the context of the 1948 premiere, and therefore without *Riding Hood Revisited* necessarily in mind), they underlined their intention to reinvigorate musical theater through the synthesis of music, text, and dance "into a new dramatic unity," although Latouche realized that not only Batwa tribal dance but Hindu and Dionysian ceremonial rites "had also beaten us to the punch by some few centuries. It still seemed like a good idea, however." Moross and Latouche further emphasized how over the course of the work's four acts, the vocal and dance elements become ever more integrated, apparently thinking not only of how the chorus members increasingly function as dancers, but how finally, in *Davy Crockett*, the principals both dance and sing. But whatever the relation of dance, music, and text among the pieces, each unfolds an essentially uninterrupted musical form, with even those vocal solos that veer most toward freestanding song—"I've Got Me" from *Willie*, "Come Be with Me" from *Riding Hood*, and "My Yellow Flower" and "Ridin' on the Breeze" from *Davy Crockett*—embedded into the musical texture, without enough finality to prompt applause.[18]

In the words of Latouche, *Willie the Weeper*, in contrast to *Susanna and the Elders*, "concerns itself with the desires and fears of the present day, rather than a nostalgic past," with the action taking place in Willie's "untidy mind." Opening with a prologue that introduces the eponymous hero, a poor chimney sweeper who would "liefer smoke a reefer" and who goes "down to the teahouse one Saturday night" to smoke his "magical weed," the seven episodes that follow ("Rich Willie," "Lonely Willie," "Famous Willie," "Baffled Willie," "Big Willie," "Contented Willie," and "Sexy Willie") depict Willie's fantasies of wealth, fame, power, and sex when high on marijuana—the "keynote of the piece," as Latouche wrote in his script—and his anxious feelings of loneliness and confusion otherwise. The piece ends quietly, with Willie described as a man who "dreamed himself silly" and whom "no one ever knew."[19]

Latouche and Moross wrote the work for tenor and mixed chorus, with the soloist functioning both as narrator and as Willie, and the chorus, both as patrons of the teahouse and as commentators. In addition, they devised a Dancing Willie to serve as the chimney sweeper's imagined self, a figure who incarnates Singing Willie's desires and fears, and with whom he often interacts; in the song "I've Got Me" from "Contented Willie" (the same lyric used by Duke Ellington in *Beggar's Holiday*), for example, the two Willies dance side by side, whereas at the very end, they slowly approach each other—"So undecided / Always divided"—and stand face to face as the lights fade and the curtain falls. At the work's marvelous climax, "Sexy Willie," another dance soloist takes the part of the beguiling Cocaine Lil—"Here's your ideal dame / Your innamorata / Your alter-ego / Your this-a and that-a," sing the tenors and basses—with the altos giving voice to Lil's seductive allure: "I'm just a jelly-jelly fish a-swimmin' in the brook / And to catch me, Daddy, you'll have to bait your hook."

Latouche based *Willie*'s libretto to some small extent—most notably in the prologue and the "Rich Willie" sequence—on the traditional song "Willie the Weeper" as published in Carl Sandburg's *The American Songbag*, a popular anthology that likewise had provided the text to Moross's *Frankie and Johnny*. Latouche changed Willie from an opium to a marijuana smoker, and furthermore incorporated a variant folk lyric to the same tune as also found in the Sandburg collection, "Cocaine Lil," for the "Sexy Willie" episode, in particular, making use of the stanza about "a cocaine dog and a cocaine cat," the image of "snakes and elephants silver and gray," and, more or less, the names of Lil's druggy friends. (When director Ernst Aufricht proposed once again making Willie an opium smoker for the work's 1954 German premiere, arguing that "German audiences wouldn't understand the reefer sequence," Latouche told him, "You can't. The after-effects are opposite.") But Latouche composed most of the text himself, a searingly ironic study of modern life, as in the depiction of Rich Willie's rise to fortune, in which he made his way "By hook or crook / But mostly crook" and "took bus'ness from the gutter / And raised it to the curb," or as in this more extended excerpt from the prologue:

> But how he [Willie] loved the wonderful weed—
> A puff is enough and your mind is freed
> From the steel and the stone, the nickel telephone,
> The chippies and the sharpies and the two-bit harpies,

The chiselers and the chasms and the store bought spasms
When the jim jams, the flim flams
The old razzle dazzle has worn you to a frazzle
The forgetful weed
Will get for everyone the kinda fun
They need.[20]

Moross designed around this text a driving set of variations on a boogie-woogie theme that eventually explodes into an unexpected key, triple fortissimo, for Cocaine Lil's dramatic entrance. The bluesy music deftly complements Latouche's snazzy lyrics, as in this refrain from "Sexy Willie," which, using simple interjections, slyly encapsulates a casual sexual encounter:

'Cause it's oh, Baby
And gee, Baby
And mmm, Baby, and ah—
And it's well, well, Baby
And swell, Baby
Then goodbye, Baby
Goodbye—ta-ta.

In "Famous Willie," in which Willie fancies himself a famous saxophone player, Moross also winks at the growing vogue for twelve-tone melody, apparently in response to Latouche's reference to "twelve-tone Willie."[21]

The most humorous and in several ways most unusual of these dance-operas, *Riding Hood Revisited,* features three principal singers in the roles of Mrs. Nature (contralto), The Good Humor Man (tenor), and Granny (soprano); three principal dancers who play Red Riding Hood, The Wolf, and Cupid; and a choral-dance ensemble who portray the trees, flowers, and animals of the forest. Latouche and Moross intended their version as a comically fractured version of the popular folk tale as variously related by Charles Perrault and the Brothers Grimm, in which a young village girl, on her way to her grandmother's house, pays the price for divulging too much information and for straying from the straight and narrow.

The work opens with an instrumental "Overture" in which the flora and fauna of the forest "execute a raucous spring dance." In "Rhumba," the next of its five sections, Mrs. Nature and the chorus observe the arrival of spring with apprehension, with Latouche sporting the kind of larkish humor he had employed in "Summer Is A-Comin' In" ("The guppy-fish look soulful / They want another bowlful / They're there to do their worst / Till June the twenty-first"). In "Pastorale," Mrs. Nature espies Riding Hood, "a modern teen-ager with a bored manner," and, waving her wand, causes The Good Humor Man to appear; smitten with Riding Hood, he serenades her, in a travesty of Christopher Marlowe's much-parodied "The Passionate Shepherd to His Love," with the prospect of domestic bliss:

Come live with me and be my love.
We'll join the younger married set,
With dining-nook and kitchenette,
We'll tête-a-tête from morn to night.

After the two ride off together in his cart, a long instrumental section punctuated with song (as in Disney's Silly Symphonies) ensues, "Waltz and Variations" (more or less equivalent to the orchestral piece *Variations on a Waltz*) in which Riding Hood leaves The Good Humor Man for The Wolf, an elderly Viennese roué with whom she enjoys the pleasures of the city—represented by a sextet of dancing skyscrapers *en pointe*—until The Wolf, exhausted by Riding Hood's sexual demands, seeks to escape to Granny's house, Mrs. Nature observing,

When you've had your fun
They [the young] have just begun—
It's a most unequal drama.
It's unwise to cling to a sweet young thing,
You'll be safer with her grammaw.

Getting to Granny's house first, Riding Hood shoves Granny into the closet and continues to pursue The Wolf when he finally arrives, until The Good Humor Man and Cupid appear and set things right; all ends happily as the two couples—Riding Hood and The Good Humor Man, Granny and The Wolf—reunite. In a coda, Mrs. Nature counsels the birds and the bees, "Don't let this confuse you all / Carry on as usual."

Moross set this delightfully loopy text in his most exuberant and gamesome manner, with farcical cartoonlike treatment of a host of familiar musical tropes, including a parody of Beethoven for Granny at home. The piece overall looks ahead to such fairy-tale parodies as Mary Rodgers's *Once upon a Mattress* (1959) and Stephen Sondheim's *Into the Woods* (1986), but seems even more so a rehearsal for Moross and Latouche's opera *The Golden Apple* (1954), as in sundry ways do all the *Ballet Ballads*, including the novelty of a through-composed rhymed libretto.

Unlike the other *Ballet Ballads*, Moross and Latouche based *The Eccentricities of Davy Crockett* on a historical personage, although so mythologized as to make him a fitting companion to Susanna, Willie the Weeper, and Little Red Riding Hood after all. (Before settling on Crockett, Moross and Latouche considered for this particular dance-opera another famed American figure, namely, John Brown; whether either knew, incidentally, that in 1938 composer Kurt Weill had begun, but never completed, a musical treatment of H. R. Hays's 1936 play for the Federal Theatre, *The*

Ballad of Davy Crockett, remains unknown.) Born in Tennessee, David Crockett (1786–1836) became a successful hunter and backwoodsman as well as a member of the Tennessee militia, which he joined in 1813 under the command of Andrew Jackson, and in which he eventually rose to the rank of colonel. After a few years in the Tennessee state assembly, he was elected in 1827 to the U.S. House of Representatives as a Jacksonian Democrat and served three nearly consecutive terms, following which he faced defeat first in 1831 and again in 1835. Soon after the Texas Revolution broke out in late 1835, Crockett made his way to San Antonio, where he died at the Alamo in early 1836.[22]

Even during his lifetime, Crockett, a colorful personality, became the subject of fanciful yarns, as found in, for example, the book *Sketches and Eccentricities of Colonel David Crockett of West Tennessee* (1833), which portrayed the frontiersman as capable of superhuman feats (and whose title Moross and Latouche adapted for their own dance-opera). Far-fetched stories about Crockett and his wife, Sally Ann Thunder Ann Whirlwind (in actuality, Crockett married Mary Finley, and after her demise, Elizabeth Patton), circulated widely after his death, and over time he took his place with Johnny Appleseed, Daniel Boone, and such fictitious characters as Paul Bunyan (the subject of a lost Moross ballet from 1934) as one of the fabled heroes associated with America's westward expansion. Although several of these tall tales contained crudely racist humor, Crockett's real life defense of squatters' rights and his opposition to the Indian removal bill indicated a man sympathetic to the poor and disenfranchised, and he "came to symbolize," as one historian writes, "a rough egalitarianism, a wild freedom of opportunity, and a solid reaffirmation of the cherished principles of the Declaration of Independence," a perspective enshrined in midtwentieth-century biographies by Constance Rourke (1934), Irving Shapiro (1944), and Meridel Le Sueur (1951).[23]

Combining fact and fiction, Latouche's text for *The Eccentricities of Davy Crockett* recounts the life of Davy Crockett in a manner similar to that used in *Susanna and the Elders*, although the chorus participates more thoroughly in the action, with the principal roles of Crockett (baritone) and his wife, Sally Ann (mezzo-soprano), supplemented by a number of smaller roles, including The Mermaid (contralto) and the Ghost Bear (bass), and with dancing and singing that much more integrated. Highly episodic, the piece follows Crockett from his infancy in eastern Tennessee to his death at the Alamo, with separate sections devoted to his courtship and marriage of Sally Ann; settling the frontier; participation in the Creek War; married life ("My Yellow Flower," for Sally Ann, with some whistling for Crockett); encounter with a sexy mermaid from Memphis (this derived from fables surrounding Crockett's storied sidekick, sailor Ben Hardin); skirmishes with Halley's Comet, a brown bear, and a ghost bear; service in Congress; and departure for Texas ("Ridin' on the Breeze," for Crockett).

From its very opening—"Oh the western star is riding low"—the libretto displays familiar ease with frontier lingo, with such phrases as "rassels with bears," "a-flashin' and a-splashin'," and "pizen rattler" providing the piece with tang and authenticity. Latouche's Virginian background presumably stood him in good stead in this regard, although he plainly absorbed the Crockett literature as well, as in his adaptation of the frontiersman's boast, "Ain't I the yaller flower of the forest? And I am all brimstone but the head and ears, and that's aqua-fortis" (from *Sketches and Eccentricities*), for Sally Ann's love song:

> You're my yaller flower of the forest
> Bloomin' in the steamy, dreamy mud—
> You're made of brimstone except for your head and ears,
> And those are made of vinegar and blood.

At the same time, Latouche's use of such folklore proved distinctively poetic, as seen in the above lyric, or in Crockett's touching farewell to Sally Ann:

> So saddle up the breeze—steady—steady—
> And dry your eyes, my lady gay
> The wind that bears me far away
> Will blow me back some day
> For to claim you...
> But now it's ridin' high
> And I must say goodbye
> Goodbye![24]

In the tradition of tall tales, *Davy Crockett* also sports some bawdy humor, such as Crockett's "I'll go bang some bushes / With my rifle-iddle-i-oh" and The Mermaid's "I'm something in a river bed," but the work has its more serious side as well, one that treats the story of Crockett as symbolic of American history and values (with the episode about Halley's Comet likely reflecting contemporary fears of nuclear annihilation). The piece early sounds a somber note during the consecration of Crockett's frontier home, as the chorus sings, very much in the spirit of *Ballad for Americans*, "Yet they [Crockett and Sally Ann] foreshadow in the lonely places / The coming of their children, free, unfettered— / A nation of nations and a race of races." Catching the contradictions of Crockett's career, Latouche portrays a man who laughs his way into battle, but then, chastened by his encounter with the ghostly victims of religious and racial intolerance, enters politics with high ideals; disgusted with Washington, he finally leaves for Texas, Sally Ann remarking, "For a dream called him onward." The chorus echoes this invocation of the American dream by stating, apropos Crockett's death, "But the people will tell you that he never really died. / When a dream calls them onward, he is riding by their side." In an inspired final stroke that came to Latouche late in the creative process, he ended the work with a recollection of the line, "Colonel Davy Crockett was his name," heard in the opening chorus, but changed to "Colonel Davy Crockett *is* his name" (emphasis added), so as to suggest his enduring legacy, further enriching this original and socially engaged take on a familiar Western trope.[25]

Markedly different from Kurt Weill's 1938 music for his unfinished musical about Davy Crockett, Moross's score features that brash frontier ambience the composer already had evoked in *A Tall Story* for orchestra, but with some of the sharper edges smoothed over. All the same, the score achieves some harmonic interest and contrast both through the employment of the octatonic scale in the instrumental passages, and more generally, through modal and chromatic uses of simple triads, techniques that point to the influence of Stravinsky, although filtered through Copland, whose occasional imprint can be felt throughout the score. Otherwise, Moross shows himself rather impervious to both modernist and commercial currents, a highly individual stance that suggests the lingering influence of Charles Ives.[26]

In total, the *Ballet Ballads* purposefully draws on assorted regional American traditions (comparable in this sense to Samuel Barber's four-movement *Excursions* for piano) that might be summarized as hymnody and the rural Midwest; the blues and city life; cartoon music and Hollywood; and cowboy song and the frontier. At the same time, the work as a whole achieves unity not only through shared stylistic and technical features, but through a common concern with the perils posed by the metropole: all four dance-operas similarly view the city as a site of injustice, decadence, sin, and corruption, while presenting too an idealized pastoral as variously represented by Susanna in her garden, Willie in a state of contentment, The Good Humor Man in his cart, and Davy Crockett and Sally Ann at home. This dialectic of town and country, evil and good, clearly held considerable interest to both composer and librettist, forming a central theme of their next project, *The Golden Apple*, and surfacing in works that they wrote independently of each other as well.

Meanwhile, three of the dance-operas—*Willie the Weeper, Riding Hood Revisited,* and *The Eccentricities of Davy Crockett*—embodied another sort of unity in that their principal musical ideas in large part derived from the same abandoned work, namely, *A Cow in a Trailer*, a 1939 musical theater piece with a libretto by playwright Lynn Riggs and his lover and protégé, the Mexican painter-playwright Ramon Naya (born Enrique Gasque-Molina), for which Moross completed about half the music, some of which premiered on the CBS Radio show *The Pursuit of Happiness* in late 1939. Indeed, Moross and Latouche seem to have created their three companion pieces to *Susanna and the Elders* specifically with an eye toward repurposing the music from *A Cow in a Trailer*, with still other sections of the unfinished score finding their way into Moross's Symphony (1940–42). In any event, *Ballet Ballads* as a whole accordingly can be dated, at least as concerns much of its main musical material, back to 1939, with the Riggs and Naya text supplying some context for the three later dance-operas, not to mention the symphony.

In the mold of John Steinbeck's novel *The Grapes of Wrath* (1939), *A Cow in a Trailer* follows an impoverished family cross-county from Connecticut to California, but here joined by a cow, Bessie (played by a woman wearing a tiara with small horns), who along the way encounters another cow, the insouciant Miss Spot, blithely on her way to the Chicago stockyards, and a romantic interest, the bull Blacky. At the end, the family arrives in Hollywood, where Bessie becomes a star, rechristened Mooella Glee. Throughout the play, four Time Belt Boys, representing the country's four time zones, frame the story, underlining the allegorical nature of the piece, including the metaphor of the American populace as so much cattle. Whereas Riggs outfitted the text with the sort of folkloric humor displayed in his 1931 play *Green Grow the Lilacs*, which would serve as the basis for Rodgers and Hammerstein's 1943 musical *Oklahoma!*, Naya seems to have contributed something of its pointed political edge.[27]

Moross and Latouche adapted, with respect to *Willie*, Bessie's "The Slaughter House Blues" (which specifies at one point "self-consciously negroid") as the work's principal theme, and the cow's farewell to Blacky as "I've Got Me"; with respect to *Riding Hood*, Bessie's pastoral rhapsody, "A Cow in Clover," as the overture, Bessie and Blacky's "Rhumba" as Mrs. Nature's "Rhumba," and Bessie's meeting with the ghost of Miss Spot in the stockyards as the waltz pantomime; and with respect to *Davy Crockett*, the very start of *A Cow in a Trailer* (in which Riggs and Naya called for music that "blares out briefly, harsh, sardonic, but gay, as if announcing an acrid but exciting voyage of discovery") for the opening music and the mermaid episode, and a love duet between two young people, Gracie and Joe, as "Ridin' on the Breeze." Latouche went his own way with regard to the words ("Down in Massachusetts lived a man" became, for instance, "Oh the western star is riding low"), but assuming he knew the work, as seems likely, he possibly borrowed something of its tone and whimsy for *Ballet Ballads*, including Crockett's encounter with ghosts. As the co-author with Gore Vidal in later years of the unrealized film scenario *A Horse Named Gladys*, Latouche presumably would have found so offbeat a satire at least congenial.[28]

Latouche and Moross happily discovered in Lucy Kroll (1909–1997) a dedicated talent agent ready to promote their novel collection of dance-operas. Born Lucy Rosengardt in Brooklyn, Kroll had trained as a ballet dancer and worked for Warner Brothers in Hollywood before returning in 1945 to New York, where she established herself as a talent agent, her clients over the years including Martha Graham, James Earl Jones, and Carl Sandburg. Kroll would continue to represent Latouche, one of her first clients, for the remainder of his life, with her vast repository of papers at the Library of Congress duly containing a wealth of material concerning the lyricist's career. Speaking about Kroll in 1955, Latouche wrote to a collaborator, "She does not undertake anything unless she has a great enthusiasm for it, and once she begins she continues with a perseverance and sense of integrity that are indeed rare."[29]

Finding a producer for what Kroll called Moross and Latouche's "Americana Musical" proved difficult, however. Early on, producer Mike Todd (born Avrom Goldbogen, 1909–1958), encouraged by his assistant Harriet Kaplan, took an option on the show, and in the course of 1945 and early 1946 the press occasionally reported on some such forthcoming Todd production, with Helen Tamiris mentioned as a possible choreographer. But in late May 1946, Latouche and Moross, who found their experience with Todd "harrowing," declined to extend his option for another year.[30]

In the spring of 1946, as Kroll engaged the services of director Mary Hunter, she attempted to sell the show to other producers, including George Abbott, Horton Foote, Sol Hurok, Billy Rose, and Oscar Serlin, with Moross and Latouche giving "endless auditions" of the piece. "Mr. Moross's over-eager piano and my barbaric yawp might have discouraged the less perceptive," recalled Latouche, "but even those persons interested had doubts about the reaction of the public." Playwright Horton Foote, who helped manage productions at the King-Smith School in Washington, D.C., during these years, seemed particularly regretful about turning the work down, but mentioned in addition to certain prohibitive expenses the difficulty in lining up good ballet dancers.[31]

Finally, in the fall of 1947, thanks in large measure to Cheryl Crawford, the American National Theatre and Academy (ANTA) agreed to launch the piece. A nonprofit organization chartered by Congress in 1935 in order to promote superior theater around the country and support drama education in the schools, ANTA had floundered in a rather hostile environment for a number of years, but after the war regrouped and, among other activities, began underwriting alternative theater under its Experimental Theatre wing, an initiative that helped lay the groundwork for a vital off-Broadway scene in New York. Finding Moross and Latouche's dance-operas "delightful," Crawford, an esteemed producer whose recent credits included *One Touch of Venus* and *Brigadoon*, and one of ANTA's guiding lights, persuaded a somewhat chary ANTA board to fund a week's run of the show under the auspices of their Experimental Theatre, although the production went forward without *Riding Hood*, and with the title *Four in Hand* accordingly changed to *Ballet Plays* and ultimately *Ballet Ballads*.[32]

When Mary Hunter and Horton Foote initially suggested dropping *Riding Hood* back in 1946, Moross argued that if any act be cut, it should be *Susanna*, which he deemed the "least interesting of the four from a musical viewpoint," and "the least integrated of the four" as well. But financial considerations no doubt dictated otherwise; even shorn of the relatively elaborate *Riding Hood*, the production, with its cast of sixty singers and dancers, cost some $20,000, almost double the $11,000 allocated by ANTA, and this notwithstanding costumes purchased off the rack; sparse sets consisting of a cyclorama and mobile bleachers; use of two pianos rather than a pit orchestra; and assorted allowances made by the unions, including low salaries. (Dancer Sharry Traver, who had a few small solos, and who later as Sharry Underwood published a key article about this production, recalled that she earned nothing for six weeks of rehearsal and then eight dollars for each of the show's seven performances at the Maxine Elliott's Theatre.) Finding its budget "excessive," Vinton Freedley, the president of ANTA, insisted on outside funding to cover the difference, leading to some scrambling for money at the last minute.[33]

Surely Moross and Latouche had hoped for less spartan conditions for so generously conceived a work, although ANTA productions had been known to make their way to Broadway, as would happen in this instance as well. In any case, in a seminal piece about *Ballet Ballads* published soon after its premiere, Latouche wrote that he and Moross thought themselves "extremely lucky to find a resourceful producer, three gifted choregraphers [*sic*], and a talented and patient cast who sweated through six weeks of hectic rehearsals with uncommon energy and sacrifice." By "producer," Latouche presumably meant Nat Karson, the show's Swiss-born scenic and lighting designer placed in charge of the production; but although he neglected to mention the show's director, Mary Hunter, her involvement seems to have been fortuitous as well, at least according to Sharry Underwood, who thought her the sort of "exceptional director, knowledgeable in music and dance as well as in theatre," required by so complex an undertaking.[34]

Long understood that the production would spotlight different choreographers, in the months leading up to rehearsals the press reported various such possibilities, in one instance naming Felicia Sorel for *Susanna*, Anna Sokolow for *Willie*, and Michael Kidd for *Davy Crockett*, and in another Jerome Robbins for both *Susanna* and *Willie*, and Eugene Loring for *Davy Crockett*. In the end, ANTA enlisted Katherine Litz for *Susanna*, Paul Godkin for *Willie*, and Hanya Holm for *Davy Crockett*.

Katherine Litz (1912–1978) had been a soloist with the Humphrey-Weidman Company and had danced in *Oklahoma!* and *Carousel* as well. Assuming the role of Dancing Susanna, she "took a cue from Charles Weidman's kinetic mime," according to Underwood, and treated this particular dance-opera like a game of charades.[35]

Paul Godkin (1914–1985), who similarly cast himself as Dancing Willie, had more of a ballet background than Litz, but he also had danced in shows, including *Beggar's Holiday* and *High Button Shoes*. Godkin came recommended by Jerome Robbins, who helped advise this fledgling choreographer, although "the final choreography was Paul's," according to Underwood, who further stated, "As Paul's characters were depressed and self-absorbed, he used a kind of jazz movement sympathetic to the blues, sensuous and sinuous isolations with off-beat rhythms. He exaggerated the 'stoned' character of his night citizens and in their manic scenes went as far as parody."[36]

The more established and esteemed Hanya Holm (1893–1992) would play a particularly important role in Latouche's career, as she also later staged *The Golden Apple* and *The Ballad of Baby Doe*, the lyricist's two most ambitious efforts. Born Johanna Eckert, Holm had trained in her native Germany with the influential modern dancer Mary Wigman and had arrived in New York in 1931 in order to establish a branch of the Wigman school. Her monumental dance *Trend* (1937), to music by Wallingford Riegger and Edgard Varèse, catapulted her to the front ranks of America's choreographers. Stimulated by the incorporation of native traditions in the work of such colleagues as Martha Graham, Doris Humphrey, and Helen Tamiris, Holm similarly began to explore the heritage of her adopted country, a development reinforced by her establishment in 1941 of a summer festival in Colorado Springs at Colorado College, where she collaborated with her composer colleague Roy Harris on the folkloric *Suite of Four Dances* (1943) and choreographed a dance to the music of Elie Siegmeister that helped establish her reputation in this area, *Ozark Suite* (1947), a work that might have helped secure her the *Ballet Ballads* commission. At any rate, *Ballet Ballads* opened the door to a successful career in popular musical theater, Holm's later credits including *Kiss Me, Kate*; *My Fair Lady*; and *Camelot*.[37]

Holm agreed to choreograph *Davy Crockett* in late April, a mere two weeks or so before opening night, after conferring with Moross and Latouche (who on their first meeting in his West 12th Street walkup greeted her while standing on his head in a yoga posture). Recalled Holm,

> I looked through the script and could accept libretto and music but not the stage direction, which were done from a purely literary point of view. I had to have something more three-dimensional. John Latouche had a different stage conception from what I thought Davey [*sic*] Crockett should look like, but he was very quickly convinced that the way I wanted to do it was the better way of doing it. I encountered no difficulties; on the contrary, I received the best cooperation imaginable from everyone concerned.

In her detailed description of the choreographer's working method, Underwood, who danced the part of Ann (*sic*) Hutchinson in *Davy Crockett*, extolled Holm's meticulous attention to space, her exhilarating sense of motion, and her penchant for improvisatory methods.[38]

In addition to Katherine Litz (Dancing Susanna) and Paul Godkin (Dancing Willie), the principal cast of *Ballet Ballads* included Richard Harvey (The Parson), Sheila Vogelle (Singing Susanna), Robert Lenn (Singing Willie), Ted Lawrie (Davy Crockett), Barbara Ashley (Sally Ann), Betty Abbott (The Mermaid), and the show's one semistar, the Japanese-American dancer Sono Osato (Cocaine Lil and The Comet), recently seen on Broadway in *One Touch of Venus* and *On the Town*. Given the more integrated nature of *Davy Crockett*, singer Ted Lawrie, wrote Underwood, "was also called on to dance well enough to keep up with the trained dancers," adding, "Somewhat to the chagrin of the male dancers, he did." Hugh Ross served as choral and musical director, and John Mesko and Mordecai Sheinkman provided the two-piano accompaniment. "One of the delights of the original Ballads was that everyone was new," wrote Moross to Lucy Kroll in 1958. "It was a first theatrical experience for almost everyone involved and it gave the whole thing an air of freshness. Not that they were novices. But for Hanya [Holm] and Paul [Godkin] and most of the kids doing the big parts it was the first big chance."[39]

Underwood, in turn, spoke of the respect with which the cast held librettist and composer, "Latouche for his warmth, vigor, and wit; Moross for his fresh diatonic invention, lyricism, and easily assimilated rhythm." Speaking of the "good-humored braggadocio" of *Davy Crockett,* Underwood further noted, "Corny, yes, but never camp, for this was not ridicule. As in all of the ballet ballads, Latouche's lyrics describe the characters and their actions with the mix of amusement and affection of a humanist." She also appreciatively recalled the "frequent presence" of Moross and Latouche at rehearsals, which "kept interpretations lively and fresh." Hanya Holm likewise remembered the lyricist fondly as cultivated, clever, trustful, and sensitive. "In fact he was almost too sensitive," she stated in 1973. "This Watergate thing [scandal] would have destroyed him."[40]

Ballet Ballads opened at the Maxine Elliott's Theatre, situated on 39th Street slightly south of the theater district, on May 9, 1948, for a scheduled six performances, extended to seven by popular demand. Although the show was reviewed in the main by drama critics, the city's two foremost papers, the *Times and the Herald Tribune,* sent their dance critics, John Martin and Walter Terry, to cover the event—at least at first, for by the end of this initial run the *Times* also posted a notice by theater critic Brooks Atkinson, and the *Tribune,* by music critic Virgil Thomson. Having the work so reviewed by the town's drama, dance, and music desks itself spoke to the show's uniqueness.

Ballet Ballads received extremely good notices, with kudos showered on Moross and Latouche for a score thought to rival if not surpass anything on Broadway. Attention naturally focused on the work's innovative fusion of music, drama, and dance, and although several felt that the piece could use greater polish and cohesion—Cheryl Crawford herself remembered the show as "altogether charming and original, if not quite perfect"—and not a few thought *Davy Crockett* generally superior to *Susanna* and *Willie,* the critics deemed the whole a great success, an adventurous experiment that also managed to be good fun ("A happier time was seldom had," enthused Gilbert Gabriel in *Theatre Arts*). "The result," reported Richard Watts Jr. (*Post*), "is a winning amalgamation of three arts of the theatre into a finely integrated whole." Walter Terry accorded Latouche special commendation in this regard, observing the way his lyrics in *Davy Crockett* "lend themselves to melody and to the potential imageries of dance."[41]

The only major dissenting voice came from the *Times*'s John Martin, who thought the material essentially "unchoreographic"—"the ears are kept so occupied with listening for Mr. Latouche's often clever lyrics," he said of *Susanna,* "that the eyes have little time to watch the slender movement theme"—and suggested rather a concert version "without any stage action." In something of a rebuttal, Walter Terry, in a follow-up piece to his *Herald Tribune* review, maintained that the work represented "the first, or at least the most successful, experiment in fusing not two but three theatrical arts," with lyrics "well suited to the kind of choreography desirable for such a production." Brooks Atkinson entered the conversation by confessing that he had been "thoroughly delighted by these singing and spinning whimsies which are original in theme as well as in form"; and Virgil Thomson, although reluctant to comment on the dance, praised the libretto for "verbiage" thought "comical in the familiar Latouche manner and often ingenious" as well as the music: "The sustaining of musical interest in so limited a style over so extended a time places Jerome Moross... as a master workman. In 'Davy Crockett,' the sweetness of his melodic expression and the delicate fancy of his accompaniments make him clearly a composer of more than ordinary charm, too." John Martin remained unconvinced, however, writing to agent Lucy Kroll's husband that he believed that Rodgers and Hammerstein's *Allegro* (1947), "a fairly vulgar Broadway production with no 'experimental' connotations, accomplished far more in the direction of a genuine synthetic theatre form, in spite of its many weaknesses and downright crudities."[42]

The overwhelmingly positive response to *Ballet Ballads* encouraged ANTA to transfer the work to Broadway, and after once again gaining some concessions from the unions, and finding two backers, T. Edward Hambleton and Alfred Stern, willing to invest about $35,000 into an enhanced production, the show reopened at the Music Box Theatre on May 18, only a few days after closing at the Maxine Elliott's. This reopening, the tickets priced from $1.80 to $4.80, prompted an even more rapturous round of reviews, the work's charm and intelligence apparently shining that much brighter amid the "flashy showmanship" of Broadway. "In its progressiveness and invention," stated Rosalyn Krokover in the *Musical Courier*, "it stands in its field far above anything that has appeared on Broadway in recent years." The words "fresh" and "freshness," already common enough among the first set of reviews, appeared virtually everywhere, Harold Clurman, for instance, claiming in the *New Republic* that the work exhibited "a freshness of appeal that no criticism of the separate parts can diminish. Despite the malice and sophistication of the best of Latouche's lyrics, the show as a whole is almost dewily naïve." Critics showed specific appreciation for the show's remarkable form, Miles Kastendieck of the *Journal-American* finding its "fusion... a crystallization of something in the making for almost a quarter of a century—a new art form American in creation."[43]

Latouche's work received particular approbation, both immediately and in the months ahead. William Breyer (*School and Society*), who deemed the show "the artistic high spot of the year," lauded the librettist for having "splendid originality, resourcefulness, dramatic instinct, and a buoyant, invigorating penchant for comedy," and George Jean Nathan (*Theatre Book*) similarly thought the text to have "humor, wit, delicacy and, when called for, dramatic force." Reporting in late May the results of their annual poll of New York drama critics, *Variety* named Latouche both best lyricist and best librettist of the 1947–48 season, and Moross, best composer. Such recognition included a personal letter to Moross from composer Randall Thompson, who extended his compliments not only to the former but to Latouche: "I think we can look to him for more and more fine works."[44]

For all the critical acclaim, *Ballet Ballads* faced an uphill battle on Broadway. First, most of the major dailies chose not to cover a work that had been widely reviewed a week or so earlier. Moreover, the show arrived late in the season, and further could claim neither a marquee name nor anything much even resembling a hit song. Nor did the notion of a mixed bill of dance-operas have much mass appeal. Indeed, although deeming the work "artistically . . . one of the finest on Broadway this or any other season," *Variety* suspected that the production "may be a little caviarish for the run-of-mine Rialto theatergoer."[45]

After the show's weak start at the box office, theater mavens began to wonder if the "longhair" title itself posed a liability—"a hard name to sell," averred the *Herald Tribune,* that "didn't even reflect the quality of this song and dance piece." In his defense, Latouche claimed that *Ballet Ballads* had been intended only as a working title, and that he would have preferred to call the show *Triple-Decker* or *Promenade,* while Nat Karson, evoking popular Broadway revues of years past, suggested renaming the work *Ballet Ballads of 1948*. Producers Hambleton and Stern even invited the public to write to them care of the Music Box Theatre with suggestions for a new title. But the name held.[46]

A concerted effort was made in any case to keep the production afloat. Cast members took to restaurants, hotels, and the streets distributing handbills and hanging posters; Moross and Latouche consented to a reduction in their royalties; the choreographers, director, and ANTA waived their percentage of box office receipts; and Irving Berlin, part owner of the Music Box, arranged for a discounted theater rental. A four-page photo spread about the production in the June 7 issue of *Life* magazine gave the show a much needed boost, and by mid-June, the show seemed headed toward some financial equilibrium. But as the hot summer season set in, traffic at the box office slowed once more, not helped by the show's one headliner, Sono Osato, leaving the cast and being replaced by the lesser known Olga Lunick, who as Cocaine Lil seemed, thought Sharry Underwood, "a long drink of water next to Sono's belly-deep sensuality." In early July, with Hambleton and Stern having expended their investment, Latouche raised just enough money to keep the show going for another week; but the production finally expired on July 10 after a total of sixty-nine performances, including the seven at the Maxine Elliott's. Underwood recalled that following the final performance, Latouche "held a smashing closing-night party" at his Greenwich Village apartment.[47]

Producers Hambleton and Stern hoped to take *Ballet Ballads* on the road and possibly to bring the show back to Broadway as well, this time with the addition of *Riding Hood Revisited* and under the original title, *Four in Hand,* but such plans came to nothing. Meanwhile, the influential music editor Albert Sirmay, who had found *Ballet Ballads,* as he telegrammed Moross, a "wonderful new and original work," helped arrange for Chappell Music to publish the vocal score as a "gesture of encouragement" to a quality off-Broadway musical. Chappell also released three songs from the show, "I've Got Me," "My Yellow Flower," and "Ridin' on the Breeze," and in time published the vocal score of *Riding Hood Revisited* as well, although none of this music sold very well. In addition, after *Ballet Ballads* moved to the Music Box, assistant stage manager Richard Grayson prepared a production script, now housed at the New York Public Library, that remains an invaluable resource with regard to the study and possible recreation of the show as initially presented.[48]

The success of *Ballet Ballads,* even if more critical than popular, presumably helped encourage Moross and Latouche to undertake another project together despite the tensions that plagued their collaboration. Indeed, back in October 1946, on one of his intermittent returns to Hollywood, Moross had written Lucy Kroll that he planned to meet with Christopher Isherwood as part of an effort to find another writer and thereby free himself of Latouche. "If I don't find anybody to work with I will try Touche again," he wrote, "But the last time was so difficult!" However, in the aftermath of *Ballet Ballads,* Moross seemed prepared to work once more with Latouche, as evidenced by further correspondence with Kroll, who wrote to the composer in late June 1948,

> The news of Touche coming around is, of course, only due to the great contribution you have made as his collaborator in bringing him up to the very best of his talent. He is in a better frame of mind, has more money to pay his bills with and has been sugar and honey for the past ten days. He is bringing his mother on to manage the affairs, cook his meals and pay the bills. This sits right with me and if he gets out of hand, I'll talk to her.

Responded Moross, "I am very happy that Touche is going to work with me. I know all his faults and I remember all the agonies. But he can do what I want, and I suppose I have to do it the hard way. It won't be easy, but I think it will be good."[49]

In 1950, while working on this subsequent work with Latouche, *The Golden Apple,* Moross co-produced with Bruce Savan a revival of *Ballet Ballads* at the Century Theatre in Los Angeles. Robert Trout and Frank Seabolt, who had played Joe and Moe in New York, adapted Katherine Litz's staging for *Susanna;* Esther Junger rechoreographed *Willie;* and Olga Lunick, cast as Dancing Susanna as well as Cocaine Lil and The Comet, restaged Holm's choreography for *Davy Crockett.* Some other veterans from the New York production also participated, including Betty Abbott, but the cast otherwise featured mostly newcomers, including Marni Nixon (Singing Susanna), Jerry Duane (Singing Willie), Bert May (Dancing Willie), Theodor Uppman (Davy Crockett), and Joan Spafford (Sally Ann). A new production team prepared the music, settings, costumes, and lighting, and Eugene Feher and Gershon Kingsley provided the two-piano accompaniment.

Produced for under $20,000, the show opened on October 10, 1950, to excellent reviews, and closed after an extended engagement on November 25. In the course of the run, the media espied such movie celebrities as Tony Curtis, Janet Leigh, Donald O'Connor, and Shelley Winters in attendance, with the last-named reported as saying, with respect to her seeing the show three times, "I guess I just like to see people on their toes." (Walt Disney apparently became aware of the work as well, because during the planning stages of his hit television miniseries *Davy Crockett,* which premiered in late 1954, he offered Moross and Latouche $7,500 for their own *Davy Crockett,* a proposition that the composer and librettist indignantly turned down, saying that they would not "sell it to him for that.") Moross hoped for a tour of this Los Angeles production, including perhaps a return Broadway engagement, but to no avail. Fortunately, an audio tape of this production survives, revealing stirring performances by the soloists, and a high level of music making generally.[50]

Some later revivals surfaced without necessarily involving all three dance-operas seen in New York and Los Angeles. In 1950, for instance, Mordecai Bauman directed two of the pieces, *Susanna* and *Davy Crockett,* with the Peninsula Players in rural Ohio; in 1951, the Karamu House in Cleveland presented *Susanna* and *Willie* along with a new work by composer J. Harold Brown and librettist Kenward Elmslie; and in 1964, Karamu once again revived *Susanna* and *Willie,* only this time with *Davy Crockett.* Meanwhile, in 1950, the Choreographers' Workshop attempted to premiere *Riding Hood Revisited* at Hunter College, but during the dress rehearsal, a piece of scenery fell on the heads of lead dancers Dody Goodman and Tommy Rall, leaving them, reported the *Times,* "sufficiently hors de combat to force canceling the performance."[51]

In the early 1950s, Ernst Josef Aufricht, the German-Jewish émigré who had produced the original *Threepenny Opera* in 1928, decided to mark his return to German theatrical life with a production of *Ballet Ballads* as part of the 1954 Berlin Festival. Aufricht initially thought to launch all four dance-operas, but ultimately dropped *Davy Crockett,* presuming that German audiences would miss the point of the work. Finding Ruth Yorck's translation of these pieces, undertaken at Latouche's behest, largely unstageworthy, Aufricht hired Egon Monk, who had served the Berliner Ensemble as Brecht's assistant, to either adapt Yorck's text, as with *Susanna und die Alten* ("Susanna and the Elders"), or create his own, as with *Der greinende Willie* ("Willie the Whiner") and *Rotkäppchen 54* ("Little Red Riding Hood [19]54"). Aufricht also arranged for the esteemed artist George Grosz, a German-American exile like himself, to design the costumes. Writes Andrew DeShong in his study of Grosz's theatrical designs, "The return of two of the Weimar Republic's culture heroes [Aufricht and Grosz] could only excite the press," even if in the end the production's "pretty and gay" costumes (the characters Moe and Joe wore blue and orange spirit gum beards) disappointed those viewers expecting something closer to Grosz's acerbic work of the 1920s.[52]

Presented as *Bilderbogen aus Amerika* ("Illustrated Broadsides from America"), and subtitled "Drei Ballett-Balladen von John Latouche," the production opened at the Komödie am Kurfürstendamm on September 22, 1954, for a two-week run, with *Riding Hood Revisited* finally receiving its world premiere as translated into German. The part-Javanese Dutch dancer Wiet Palar performed the roles of Susanna, Cocaine Lil, and Riding Hood, with the program crediting only the choreographers for *Susanna* (Jens Keith) and *Willie* (Gert Reinholm). Ekkehard Grübler designed the sets, and Mordecai Sheinkman came from the States to join Horst Göbel at the two pianos. The Berlin critics generally admired both the production and the work, which they widely compared to their own epic theater and cabaret of the Weimar years, with one critic likening Latouche to the librettist's German contemporary, songwriter and satirist Klaus-Günter Neumann. However, in contrast to the American reviews, which largely found *Susanna* the weakest of the set, some German critics stated a preference for that particular piece, "because it seems to us," explained the *Berlin Telegraf*, "the most American."[53]

In 1961, tyro producer Ethel Madsen Watt, a singer who before her marriage to theater critic Douglas Watt had performed in the original production of *Ballet Ballads*, launched the last high-profile staging of the work to date, an off-Broadway revival that presented *Riding Hood*, *Willie*, and *Davy Crockett* in that order. Costing about $25,000, the production debuted at the East 74th Street Theatre on January 3, with choreography by Mavis Ray, a last-minute substitute for Todd Bolender (*Riding Hood*); John Butler, a versatile choreographer who had trained with Martha Graham (*Willie*); and Glen Tetley, a star ballet dancer who had assisted Hanya Holm on the work back in 1948 (*Davy Crockett*). Concerning this revival, Watt and Tetley seemed as motivated by memories of the recently deceased Latouche as anything else, stating, "There was something unforgettable about Mr. Latouche.... He was loved for his outstanding talent and enthusiasm."[54]

The show received highly mixed reviews, in the sense that the critics panned *Riding Hood*, or at least its choreography, but seemed generally admiring of *Willie* and *Davy Crockett*, and particularly enthusiastic about the African-American dancer Carmen de Lavallade's performance as Cocaine Lil and The Comet. The most sustained critique came from the *Herald Tribune*'s drama critic Walter Kerr, who argued, like John Martin some thirteen years earlier, that the words and the dancing interfered with each other, making the work something of a "taffy-pull." Ironically, Kerr's dance colleague on the *Tribune*, Walter Terry, who in 1948 had countered this argument by declaring the work, as remarked, "the first, or at least the most successful, experiment in fusing not two but three theatrical arts," now came to Kerr's defense, writing, "The late Mr. Latouche's lyrics are witty, intricate and in many passages, evoke such strong images on their own that heightened dance action seems to intrude." Terry's volte-face seemed related in part to the intervening arrival on Broadway of *West Side Story*, which, the dance critic suggested, might have been anticipated by *Ballet Ballads*, but which represented a synthesis enacted "through extension rather than through intrusion."[55]

Talent agent Lucy Kroll privately opined that this production simply failed to do the work justice, as she wrote to producer Dorothy Olim: "I thought 'Red Riding Hood' was miserably done, and terribly miscast as well as misinterpreted.... I shudder to think of what poor Johnny [Latouche] would have felt if he had seen it. As to 'Willie the Weeper' and 'Davie [*sic*] Crockett,' they fared better, but I thought they were all over-produced, over-choreographed, though there was some brilliant dancing and some good voices." Moross himself found the production to contradict "the entire aesthetic of the work," and refused permission to allow the show to travel after it closed on February 5.[56]

In 1966, Moross, who had orchestrated *Susanna* early in the work's history, orchestrated all the *Ballets Ballads* in anticipation of a planned CBS Television production of the work that never transpired. He nevertheless took advantage of the occasion to rework the "Waltz and Variations" section of *Riding Hood Revisited* as *Variations on a Waltz* for orchestra, recorded as such by JoAnn Falletta and the London Symphony Orchestra in 1993. A 2000 performance of the orchestrated *Willie the Weeper* by tenor John David De Haan and the Hot Springs Music Festival Chorus and Orchestra under the direction of Richard Rosenberg also found its way onto compact disc, a rendition unfortunately not as adroit and compelling as the 1950 account preserved on tape.

By 1970, Moross imagined that *Ballet Ballads* had become "too expensive to mount" as a stage work, and hoped for at least concert performances of the piece, arguing that, with their self-contained forms, they had no need of "the choreographic element." But aside from the rare concert rendering of especially *Willie the Weeper,* such as the one mentioned above, the work largely went unperformed, notwithstanding the sampling of individual songs included in the revue *Taking a Chance on Love* (2000) and the album *Windflowers* (2001).[57]

Chroniclers of dance, opera, and musical theater generally neglected the work as well, for the understandable reason, perhaps, that the piece did not clearly fit any of these categories. At the same time, the work's resistance to any sort of easy classification itself stimulated some critical commentary over the years as it had from the very start. In an early appreciation of the work, for instance, Winifred Kahn (1950) considered the "lyric theatre" of *Ballet Ballads* a welcome alternative to "opera, musical comedy, the straight play." In later years, Ethan Mordden (1999) cited *Ballet Ballads,* along with *Allegro* (1947) and *Love Life* (1948), as one of three works that anticipated the so-called concept musical, a subgenre indebted to the theater of Bertolt Brecht, and popularized by Stephen Sondheim's *Company* (1970), that favored the allegorical over the narrative, the stylized over the realistic, and the episodic over the linear. Mark Grant (2004) and Pamyla Alayne Stiehl (2008) similarly noted how *Ballet Ballads* looked ahead to the "dansicals" of Bob Fosse, Susan Stroman, and others, with Grant mentioning too the "megamusicals" of Andrew Lloyd Webber, although he drew an "all-important difference" with regard to both dansicals and megamusicals in that "Latouche and Moross, both highly educated, cultivated sensibilities, created and controlled the concepts. They—not the director, the choreographer, or the producer—were the authors of their shows.... Their innovation of through-sung, through-danced musicals has been vulgarized and miscarried by post-1980 Broadway." And in a particularly probing study, James Rogers (2010) underscored the singular importance of *Ballet Ballads* by arguing that the work represented a truer milestone than either *Show Boat* or *Oklahoma!* in terms of the development of an integrated musical theater: "Eliminating the ruptures between speech and song, *Ballet Ballads* opened up the possibility of expanding musical theatre into a through-composed—and through-choreographed—vernacular operatic form. By uniting the arts of pantomime, song, and dance in the bodies of the performers . . . the show insisted on the integrated nature of the arts by thematizing their integration within the performers themselves."[58]

For all these intriguing observations, the legacy of this "obscure little work that almost nobody saw and absolutely nobody ever mentions," as Ethan Mordden put it, remains hard to gauge. In 1970, Moross claimed that the work had been "very influential" among the city's intellectuals, observing further, "every time I go to a show now I see something which developed out of *Ballet Ballads*," although he added, "Actually, in technique and style they are still way ahead of the time." Commentators widely agreed in any case that *Ballet Ballads* anticipated nothing so much as *The Golden Apple*, Moross and Latouche's next and final effort together.[59]

17

More Fables

For a few years after the war, Latouche moved about from place to place. In 1946 and 1947, he stayed at the Chelsea Hotel; in 1948, he took up residence at a brownstone at 120 West 12th Street; in 1949, he repaired to an apartment at 49 Park Avenue, not far from Grand Central Station; and in 1950, he relocated to 11 East 77th Street, all the while spending extended periods at the country homes of various friends, eventually including Alice Bouverie, who made her rooms at New York's Gladstone Hotel available to him as well. Finally, in 1951, he settled into a sixth-floor penthouse apartment, with three bedrooms, a large living room, a glassed-in dining room, and an outdoor terrace, at 136 East 67th Street in the Lenox Hill section of Manhattan, which would serve as his home for the remainder of his short life.

Although he apparently continued to see Donald Fuller, Latouche also became romantically involved with an attractive Italian-American veteran, Frank Merlo (1922–1963), whom he reportedly met at the Everard Baths, a gay bathhouse, in 1946 or thereabouts. A workman at the time, but also an aspiring writer, Merlo moved in for a while with Latouche, a living situation allegedly not entirely to the younger man's liking. Introduced to Tennessee Williams by Latouche in 1947, Merlo soon after became that playwright's domestic partner.[1]

Latouche also seems to have cohabitated in the late 1940s with Walter Stane, a young dancer who appeared in various Broadway productions during this time, including *Ballet Ballads*. Latouche at first thought Stane, as he wrote in his journal in September 1948, "eminently agreeable" and "enchanting—or rather, always sunny and charming," adding, "W.[alter] is anything I have ever wanted, from the point of view of *desirability*: aside from a few irritants which are ordinarily unimportant," although even at this point he found himself "withdrawing, stalemating, looking for excuses to interrupt the normally warm flow I feel" and wondering if he himself was "basically hostile, as a personality." By December 1949, he found it "impossible to have a good time with him [Stane]. Too much sense of guilt, too much *social* embarassment [*sic*], not enough meeting-ground—but certainly something is terribly wrong." He and Stane bickered over such things as to what food to keep in the icebox and which motion pictures to attend (on one occasion, given Stane's preference for foreign films, and Latouche's for "old comedies," they compromised by seeing *Sorrowful Jones* with Bob Hope). Latouche's exasperation with Stane seemed part of an overall displeasure with his friends during this stage in his life: "My withdrawal from people, like Charity, begins at home," he noted in June 1949.[2]

Indeed, although Latouche once admitted turning to his diary "only in moments of stress, and then only fleetingly" in an attempt to "deflect my creative instincts onto myself, to make up for the lacks that have distorted my inner purpose since childhood," his sporadic journal entries from these years indicate particularly keen feelings of malaise and anxiety. Among other things, he suffered from dire financial distress as he scrambled to secure loans from friends or advances from associates in a vicious cycle of assuming new debts to pay for old ones. His bank account frequently overdrawn, he sometimes found himself with nothing but spare change in his pockets, although he somehow managed the services of a personal secretary, Elsie Anderson, and other help, and always seemed ready to assist those in need. All the while, he berated himself for his sloth, unreliability, anger, and other perceived failings, writing on June 9, 1949, for instance, "One fact I might as well face brutally and fearlessly—if the two emotions can be combined: I am *not* an artist in the finest sense of the word, and my critical side will not be content with my talents as they are. Greed—(arising from, perhaps, insecurity)—for some sort of importance through my work seems to be more what I work for than the work itself." And on February 14, 1950, he wrote to Gore Vidal, a new and cherished friend, "Four straight years of disaster, with a few prestige plums along the way, have so rattled me I cant even get my hack-work out on time." Receiving a Guggenheim fellowship in April 1949 merely provided a transitory "cheerful note."[3]

As usual, he sought some relief through sexual trysts, binge eating, and excessive use of drugs and alcohol. On June 15, 1949, at the end of a particularly "terrible day," he confessed, "I repeated an old pattern: the movies, the slump, the prowling, the wallowing in old impulses, the divided drama, the cloaca thrill—ah God, how many years now this wheel of exaltation and abasement, and in me no ability to stop either the process or the shame." Plagued as well by some health problems, including colitis, he undertook time and again healthy diet and exercise regimes, including the practice of yoga with Blanche De Vries, in an effort to bring some order and calm to his life. In addition, he continued to receive medical care from Dr. Max Jacobson as well as "treatments in suggestion" from the psychiatrist and neurologist Edward Spencer Cowles.[4]

Although preoccupied with personal problems, Latouche's spotty journal entries from these years offer a glimpse into some of his more worldly activities and concerns. He thought the choice of Thomas Dewey as Republican presidential nominee, for instance, "the final triumph of mediocrity," recoiled with "sick horror at the mental state of New York" after witnessing an attack on the city streets, and responded apprehensively to the imminent signing of the Atlantic Pact establishing NATO in April 1949 with just a single word: "Holà!! [French: Whoa there!]" He further alluded in a mostly desultory manner to books read (Fredric Wertham's *The Show of Violence*, James Hanley's *Boy*, Sax Rohmer's *The Insidious Dr. Fu-Manchu*, P. D. Ouspensky's *In Search of the Miraculous*) and shows attended (Arthur Miller's play *Death of a Salesman*, Irving Berlin's musical *Miss Liberty*, Jay Gorney's revue *Touch and Go*, and a Somerset Maugham adaptation, *Rain*, starring stripper Margie Hart, which he saw in Hoboken, New Jersey). Whereas the "rave reviews" for *Ballet Ballads* left him feeling "listless," the "hideous reviews" for *Miss Liberty* offered, in contrast, some real satisfaction: "nothing ever pleased me more than seeing the smug hierarchy of [Irving] Berlin, [Robert E.] Sherwood, and [Moss] Hart bite the difficult dust. The *new* spirit must be allowed to enter." All in all, this seems to have been a low period in his life.[5]

At the same time, Latouche's frequent self-chastisement over his laziness seems at least somewhat belied by the work he actually accomplished. For during these years, he not only wrote two operas, *Ballet Ballads* and *The Golden Apple*, and busied himself with Hans Richter's film *Dreams That Money Can Buy*, but composed popular song lyrics, adapted plays, and worked on several new musicals, including *Mooncalf* (later, *Golden Ladder*) and *The Happy Dollar*.

He also remained somewhat active, at least through 1948, in social causes, as evidenced by not only his participation on the Council on African Affairs, as discussed earlier, but his joining in early 1947 a delegation of artists in protest against congressional easing of wartime rent controls; his hosting, according to columnist Walter Winchell, a "hush-hush" fundraiser for the Hollywood Ten, presumably in 1948; and his signing on to Henry Wallace's 1948 presidential campaign, including writing material for the cabaret *Show-Time for Wallace*. Two other works from this period further underscore his continued association with the progressive left, in particular, the movement for nuclear disarmament and world government: *Unhappy Birthday* and *The Last Joan*.[6]

The half-hour radio program *Unhappy Birthday*, sponsored by ABC Radio in cooperation with Americans United for World Government (AUWG), debuted on August 6, 1946, in commemoration of the first anniversary of the bombing of Hiroshima. Founded in 1944 as Americans United for World Organization, the AUWG urged the establishment of a world government beyond the limited purview of the United Nations in order to neutralize the threat of nuclear war. Produced and directed by Martin Andrews, and written by Larry Menkin, *Unhappy Birthday* took the form of a sort of docudrama in which a narrator (Clifton Fadiman) tries to persuade an unsure veteran (John Beal), through the exhortations of such guests as novelist Fannie Hurst and radiation biologist Howard Curtis, about the need for global disarmament.[7]

For this broadcast, Latouche wrote a ballad called "Unhappy Birthday"—a contrafactum of Henry Work's classic 1876 song, "Grandfather's Clock," about a clock that "stopped short, never to go again" at the death of the singer's ninety-year-old grandfather. Latouche presumably decided to adapt this song, at least in part, because of the show's use of an alarm clock as a symbol of impending doom. In any case, he wrote several verses, interspersed throughout the program and sung and played by Josh White, with the final verse and chorus as follows:

FINAL VERSE
Now if you're like the rest
And you live in a place
That you'll hope will continue the same
There's a great many questions
It's time you should face
Or they'll write the answer for you in flame.
There's a world bright and new
Our destruction in view
It's a united world if you are wise
For it stops—short—never to start again—
When the bombs fall from the sky.
CHORUS
Oh, the bomb keeps a-murmuring
(Tick, tock, tick, tock)
They're telling the citizens
(Tick, tock, tick, tock)
When we all—stop—never to start again—
When the old dream dies.

Variety extended its praise for this "important" program to the Latouche ballad, which they thought "gave the show the fillip that brought it right down to earth."[8]

The idea for *The Last Joan* originated with either actor Burgess Meredith (1907–1997) or author John Steinbeck (1902–1968), who at least agreed to write a play as a vehicle for Meredith and his wife, actress Paulette Goddard, to be performed at Dublin's Abbey Theatre, about a modern day Joan of Arc who advocates for nuclear disarmament. In early 1947, Steinbeck prepared a ninety-two-page three-act scenario, replete with dialogue, which survives among Latouche's papers, and whose story follows. Inspired by a navy veteran (presumably the role for Meredith) who dies of radiation poisoning from an atomic test blast, the sixteen-year-old Joan Archer (admittedly, a tender age for Goddard, approaching forty) takes her crusade for the demilitarization of nation states through the creation of a world government all the way to the U.S. president's office; but subjected to a psychiatric exam during a Senate committee hearing on subversive activity, she subsequently is institutionalized and, on attempting to escape, murdered by lethal injection.[9]

After Steinbeck destroyed a draft of his play as "no good"—"John [Steinbeck] never really saw what the play was about," Meredith would later comment—Meredith turned the scenario over to Latouche. In July 1948, the *Times* reported that Latouche planned to treat the material "in 'realistic terms' with a background of 'chanting and singing,'" along the lines of *Ballet Ballads*. Meredith hoped to film the Latouche script the following year, but his impending 1949 divorce from Goddard, not to mention the heightening of Cold War tensions, made any such notion rather quixotic. Nothing Latouche may have written for this aborted enterprise seems to survive in any case.[10]

Meanwhile, Latouche's popular songs from this period included two numbers published in 1947 by Chappell ("All of a Sudden It's You," with music by Rudolph Goehr, and "Angel," with music by Joe Glover) and three published in 1948 by Robbins ("Sirocco," with music by Louis Varona and Domenico Savino; "Love Is Love [In Any Language]," co-written with Jack Meskill, with French lyrics by Cécile Chabot, and music by Leo Edwards; and "He Makes Me Believe He's Mine," actually composed some years earlier with Duke Ellington for *Beggar's Holiday*, as mentioned above).

Latouche's collaborators on these songs characteristically formed a diverse group. The Italian-born Domenico Savino (1882–1973) had studied piano and composition at the Naples Conservatory before emigrating to the United States, where he served Robbins Music not only as their chief editor and arranger, but as a composer as well, in this instance partnering with the Cuban jazz musician Louis (Luis) Varona. Leo Edwards (born Leo Simon in Poland, 1886–1978) already had passed his heyday as a popular tunesmith, but as recently as 1939 had enjoyed a modest success (in some sort of a collaboration with both bandleader Paul Whiteman and Jack Meskill, Latouche's co-lyricist on this song) with his Borodin adaptation "My Fantasy." (For this new Edwards song, "Love Is Love," Robbins apparently included French lyrics by the Quebec writer Chabot because, as advertised on the sheet music, the French chanteuse Lucienne Boyer, for whom the song might have been intended, "introduced" the number; perhaps all involved hoped for another "Parlez-moi d'amour," Boyer's big hit from 1930.) Duke Ellington (1899–1974) was a towering jazz pianist, composer, and bandleader. Joe Glover (1903–1969), a student of Ernst Toch and Joseph Schillinger, mostly worked as an orchestral and band arranger. And Rudolph Goehr (1906–1969), part of a distinguished German-Jewish family (which eventually included his nephew, composer Alexander Goehr, and his great-niece, philosopher Lydia Goehr), after narrowly escaping the Nazis with the assistance of his former teacher Arnold Schoenberg, reestablished himself in America as a pianist and composer in a variety of ways.[11]

Latouche doubtless thought of at least several of these songs as some of the hackwork alluded to above, but a distinction could be drawn between, on the one hand, the rather vapid "Love Is Love" and "Sirocco," and on the other, the more personal and stylish "All of a Sudden It's You" and "Angel," the last two tellingly published by Chappell as opposed to the generally more pedestrian Robbins, notwithstanding the excellence of the Ellington song. The two Chappell numbers furthermore employed a conceit dear to Latouche, that of the sleeping heart unexpectedly awakened by love, found as well in such earlier songs as "Caprice Viennois" (which actually contained the line "All of a sudden it's you"). At the same time, in light of Goehr's émigré status, the use of the phrase "old world" in "All of a Sudden It's You" seemed to hold some special meaning:

And so,
To this old world that I know
You bring a different glow
Ev'rything's breathlessly new
All of a sudden with you.

Following his Beaumarchais adaptation, *Figaro* (1946), for the Montowese Playhouse, Latouche also continued to rework scripts, producing, most notably, a version of the Swedish writer August Strindberg's 1888 one-act masterpiece *Miss Julie: A Naturalistic Tragedy* for a touring 1947 double bill produced by Paul Czinner and staged by the brilliant Russian-American director Theodore Komisarjevsky, which also included Anton Chekhov's comedy *The Proposal*. Both plays starred Czinner's wife, Elisabeth Bergner, with *Miss Julie* featuring her in the title role, supported by Raymond Burr (later, a well-known television star) as Jean, and Joan Field as Christine.

A German-Jewish actress sometimes compared to Greta Garbo, Elisabeth Bergner (born Elisabeth Ettel in Ukraine, 1897–1986) had had a thriving career in Germany before the rise of the Nazis forced her and Czinner to seek their fortunes in London, New York, and Hollywood. In these later years, she starred in the 1935 British film *Escape Me Never*, for which she received an Academy Award nomination, and the 1943 Broadway production of *The Two Mrs. Carrolls* (during which time she developed a relationship with a young actress that later inspired Mary Orr's 1946 short story "The Wisdom of Eve" and the 1950 film *All About Eve*). But back in Europe, she had won special acclaim for her work in classic theater, including performances of *Miss Julie* in Berlin in 1923 and Vienna in 1924; and Czinner presumably devised the 1947 double bill in order to showcase this side of her talent.[12]

Prior to this production, Strindberg's *Miss Julie*, a remarkably forward-looking study of social and sexual pathology as embodied in the love-hate relationship between Julie, the daughter of a count, and her father's valet, Jean, had received very few professional showings in America, including hardly any presence on Broadway, which remains the case to this day. (The *New York Times* greeted the work's 1913 Broadway premiere with a review headed, "A Revolting Play.") Doubtless aware of the difficulties posed by the piece, and likely finding the available English translations too old-fashioned for contemporary American taste, Czinner had Latouche—whom he and Bergner would have known through their mutual friends Frederick Kiesler and Eleonora Mendelssohn—prepare an "American acting version" of the play, the kind of service Latouche long had extended to European émigrés. Meanwhile, Czinner left the adaptation of the Chekhov farce to director Komisarjevsky.[13]

Although bearing neither a date nor an author, the heavily marked-up typescript of *Miss Julie* preserved among Komisarjevsky's papers at Harvard University surely constitutes Latouche's version, as evidenced not only by the mention of Raymond Burr's name in the margins, but by a line from the script—"When the upper classes bend, they bend pretty low"—quoted in a review of the 1947 production. From the play's start, with the use of the phrase "real crazy" in Jean's opening line, "She's acting crazy tonight—real crazy," Latouche struck a distinctively modern American note, subsequently reinforced by the use of such slang as "egg him on," "monkey suit," "green around the gills," and "bats in your belfry." He took other, sometimes far-reaching liberties with the text, including interpolating his own material; to take a rather extreme example, compare the beginning of one of Julie's speeches as rendered in a rather literal 1970 translation by Walter Johnson, and then as elaborated by Latouche:

JOHNSON'S VERSION

JEAN: You know you are strange!

JULIE: Perhaps. But so are you!—Besides, everything is strange! Life, people, everything, is dirt that's driven, driven on, on the water until it sinks, sinks! I have a dream that keeps coming back again and again, and I recall it now. I'm sitting on a pillar....

LATOUCHE'S VERSION

JEAN: You are a strange person, Miss Julie.

JULIE: Perhaps I am. But so are you, so is everything—strange and cold and frightening—I feel as if I were drifting on a ship without a rudder—before me tomorrow rises up out of the mist like an iceberg moving through the lonely waters with only a third of it showing above the surface—and most of it hidden below the icy waves—very dangerous—a white floating death is tomorrow.

JEAN: (Who doesn't follow her) Don't think that way. Have some beer.

JULIE. Did you ever hear of anybody dreaming the same dream over and over? I have such a persistent devil of a dream. I seem to be sitting on top of a column that rises hundreds of feet up in the air....

At the same time, like other early translators, Latouche excised some of the play's boldest strokes, such as its allusions to menstruation and bestiality, and in the end, limited by the lack of an authoritative text even in Swedish, and likely sensitive to censorship concerns as well, Latouche soft-pedaled some of Strindberg's daring, somewhat vitiating the play's full force and stature.[14]

Miss Julie premiered at the Forrest Theatre in Philadelphia on January 21, 1947, and after a brief run there, opened in Boston's Plymouth Theatre on February 3 and New Haven's Shubert Theatre on February 13. The critics widely praised Bergner's performance, but responded more cautiously to the play itself, with several reviews regarding the work, for all its poetry, as too much the dated melodrama for Broadway presentation, *Variety* pointblank stating that the work "cannot be classed, by any stretch of the imagination, as boxoffice." Latouche's adaptation similarly elicited mixed reaction, with on the one hand, the *Billboard* and the *Boston Globe* describing the play as "cleverly adapted" and "cleverly modernized," and on the other, the *Christian Science Monitor* finding the introduction of "American slang in an attempt to make the play more accessible" as "not too successful." In any event, ticket sales proved sluggish, and although Czinner hoped to continue to tour and eventually bring the production to Broadway with some revisions and recasting, including Donald Cook as Jean and Lynn Kendall as Christine, the production folded for good in New Haven.[15]

Around this same time, as vaguely suggested by a diary entry from November 1948, Latouche also possibly considered adapting Luigi Pirandello's *Trovarsi* ("To Find Oneself"), a 1932 play whose unpublished Jane Hinton translation he seems to have acquired courtesy of the Pirandello estate's American agent, the Romanian-born playwright Saul Colin, who had planned to launch Hinton's version back in 1939; perhaps Colin hoped that Latouche might further revise the piece, whose story concerns a great actress's struggle to find her true self apart from the characters she plays on the stage. A successful adaptation might have brought some well-deserved attention to this neglected play, but nothing materialized.[16]

Finally, in early 1949, Latouche authored radio treatments of two plays, Ring Lardner and George S. Kaufman's *June Moon*, and Sidney Howard's *Alien Corn*, for the *Theatre Guild on the Air* (1945–53), a prestige hourlong radio program that presented condensed versions of outstanding plays performed by leading stage and screen actors, and that was sponsored, like its television successor, the *United States Steel Hour* (1953–63), by the United States Steel Corporation.

Latouche perhaps thought of these adaptations as more hackwork, at least to some extent, although he presumably felt some affinity to these particular plays. Indeed, his early enthusiasm for *The Band Wagon* (1931), not to mention his own style of humor, would more than suggest a fondness for Kaufman's work. *June Moon* offered the additional attraction of not only skewering the popular music business, but also pitting old-fashioned mores against cosmopolitan fashion, a principal theme of Latouche's major coeval undertaking, *The Golden Apple*.[17]

June Moon concerns Fred Stevens, an aspiring lyricist, who en route to Manhattan to begin a working partnership with composer Paul Sears meets his soul mate, an equally sweet and naïve rube from upstate New York, Edna Baker. Paul, on the payroll of Mr. Hart's music publishing firm, has composed only one hit song, "Paprika," and hopes that Fred might help reinvigorate his listless career. In the course of the action, as Paul and Fred in fact produce a hit song, "June Moon," Paul's disgruntled wife, Lucille, begins an extramarital affair, while Lucille's manipulative sister, Eileen (having been jilted by Mr. Hart), almost succeeds in getting Fred to the altar. In the end, the treachery of Lucille and Eileen are exposed, and Fred and Edna reunite, helped in this matter by the shrewd Maxie Schwartz, a song plugger and arranger for the Hart publishing firm.

Premiering in 1929, *June Moon* featured the novelty of several song parodies, with music and lyrics both by Ring Lardner: "Montana Moon," a song by Paul and his earlier lyricist, Fagan; "Life Is a Game," a cheerful lyric by Fred to Maxie's improvisation; "June Moon," Paul and Fred's hit song; and two hilariously outrageous songs by the pesky young songwriter Benny Fox, "Hello, Tokio!" and "Give a Child a Name."

Accommodating this three-act play to a one-hour radio spot, Latouche abridged the script accordingly, including eliminating the delightfully annoying Benny Fox and dispensing with the subplot involving Lucille's adultery. He accommodated the radio format in other ways, for example, interpolating a sequence of nightclub scenes for Fred and Eileen on the town. And faced with finding an aural equivalent for the wonderfully mimed conclusion of the second act, with Maxie washing a window as the Window Cleaner picks at notes at the piano, he settled on Maxie saying, "I'm in the wrong business. Wonder if it's too late to take up taxidermy!" In addition to numerous other changes, Latouche also updated many of the popular culture references, so that, for instance, when the clueless Fred tries to remember who sang "Swanee River" in *Show Boat,* rather than respond, "You're thinking of Sophie Tucker in 'Strange Interlude,'" Maxie says, "You're thinking of Gypsy Rose Lee in 'Streetcar Named Desire'" (a crack that also proved one of the script's inside jokes, as stripper Gypsy Rose Lee was the sister of June Havoc, who played Eileen in this radio adaptation).[18]

Latouche went further than this, rewriting dialogue and devising his own one-liners, including creating such imagined song titles as "Take That Ice-Pick out of Your Ear, Brother Dear—You're Too Old for the Draft." In collaboration with radio composer Harold Levey (1894–1967), who had worked on Broadway in the 1920s, he also rewrote all the Lardner songs, reconceiving "Montana Moon" as "Montana," and "Life Is a Game" as "Boy, What a World," and making "June Moon" more of a travesty:

> When I thrill to your caress
> I'm just a tongue-tied loon
> Because I can't express
> The magic things you're doin'. . .

And whereas Lardner included only a line from "Paprika"—"Paprika, Paprika, the spice of my life"—Latouche provided the number with this ending:

> My dreams were a hopeless goulash
> Until your kisses added a new dash
> Oh, Paprika, Paprika—
> I'm in a stew—
> I wish I were in it with you.

For the interpolated nightclub scene, Latouche moreover recycled the title song—for which he had written both the words and music—from *Flair-Flair*, his 1935 Columbia Varsity Show.

June Moon aired on Sunday evening, March 27, 1949, with a star-studded cast that besides June Havoc (Eileen) included Eddie Albert (Fred), Kenny Delmar (Hart), Sam Levine (Maxie), Rosemary Rice (Edna), Karl Malden (Paul), and Mary Wickes (Lucille). In addition, Paula Laurence, whom Latouche would have known from his days at the Federal Theatre, assumed some bit parts and sang "Flair-Flair." The broadcast apparently attracted little notice and remains, like the *Alien Corn* adaptation, unavailable, if not lost.

Written by Sidney Howard (1891–1939), a Pulitzer Prize–winning playwright best remembered, perhaps, for posthumously winning an Academy Award for the screenplay to *Gone with the Wind*, the modestly successful *Alien Corn* opened on Broadway in 1933 as a vehicle for the celebrated actress Katharine Cornell. The play's young protagonist, Elsa Brandt—an accomplished pianist recently appointed music instructor at a women's college in the Midwest—came to America from her native Vienna as a child with her mother, a noted operatic soprano, and her father, a distinguished violinist. During the First World War, she and her parents were interned in a camp for aliens, where her mother died of influenza, and her father, Ottokar, for whom she now cares, crippled himself trying to commit suicide. Elsa and her father dream of returning to Vienna, where she might continue her music studies and launch a career as a concert pianist. Supported by a small group of friends, including two men enamored with her—the single Julian Entwhistle, a neurotic and frustrated colleague in the English department, and the married Harry Conway, the well-to-do son of the college's founder—she agrees, as a way of raising money for study abroad, to give recitals in collaboration with Harry's wife, Muriel, an amateur singer who, out of jealousy, ultimately sabotages Elsa's plans. Both Julian and Harry offer to marry and support Elsa, but after a spurned Julian kills himself, she rejects Harry as well, and resolves to leave the college and return to Vienna with her father. Howard derived the title of his play, as did Somerset Maugham for a 1931 story called "The Alien Corn," from Keats's response to the nightingale's song in "Ode to a Nightingale": "Perhaps the self-same song that found a path / Through the sad heart of Ruth, when, sick for home, / She stood in tears amid the alien corn."[19]

In view of his close association with German and Austrian emigrants, Latouche presumably could relate to the play's uninhibited affection and nostalgia for German *Kultur*. Moreover, he might well have harbored some sympathy for its overwrought melodrama, with its many characters in a nearly constant state of turmoil. Indeed, the story's love triangle between Elsa, Harry, and Muriel anticipated *The Ballad of Baby Doe*, with some of Latouche's adaptation sounding like a rehearsal for that work; compare for instance, Muriel's "If you don't steer clear of her, I'll raise a squawk this town will never forget," with Augusta's threats of causing "a scandal"; or Harry's

"I assure you nothing has happened for us to be ashamed of," with Baby Doe's "We have done nothing / We should be ashamed of."[20]

Although assisted by a précis provided by Irving Forbes and editorial oversight by S. Mark Smith, Latouche had his work cut out for him adapting *Alien Corn* for radio; the Howard play featured, on stage for long periods, a number of minor characters, mostly male faculty members, who would be very hard to distinguish over the air. Latouche duly adapted the work as essentially a five-character play for Elsa, Brandt, Harry, Muriel, and Julian, with many lines of dialogue reassigned to one of these major characters, and much else simply invented. He also moderated the work's Germanophilia, with, for example, Elsa pursuing her studies in Rome (as opposed to Vienna), and no ranting from Brandt about his daughter's decision to program the Belgian-French César Franck on her debut recital. Moreover, Elsa's mother perishes not in an American internment camp, but rather a German concentration camp, a change that also made the play more current, even as it complicated the story's chronology.

Starring Bette Davis (Elsa) and Kirk Douglas (Harry), *Alien Corn* aired on April 24, 1949. Although as with *June Moon* little commented on, the broadcast nonetheless occasioned a satirical piece by syndicated columnist John Crosby, who viewed the play as indicative of a literary trend, exemplified also by Fay Kanin's comedy *Goodbye, My Fancy*, and John Horne Burns's novel *Lucifer with a Book*, that implausibly portrayed American schools as cauldrons of intrigue and high emotion. ("The only visible drama at my school was the time my chemistry teacher had two Manhattans at a faculty party, fell into the bathtub and broke his ankle.") Recalling the original 1933 stage play as "a lot of malarkey" to begin with, Crosby found that the radio adaptation "only emphasized the malarkey, and in the place of Miss [Katharine] Cornell, it contained Bette Davis, of the movies, whose Viennese accent in moments of passion moved abruptly into New England."[21]

Meanwhile, Latouche juggled or at least contemplated various musical theater projects in the late 1940s, including a few ideas reported in the press that seemed to go nowhere: a "Negro version" of Brandon Thomas's classic 1892 farce *Charley's Aunt,* to star Lena Horne and Eddie ("Rochester") Anderson (this in 1947, in advance of Frank Loesser's *Where's Charley?*); a musicalization of André Picard's 1918 French comedy *Kiki* (adapted in 1921 for Broadway by David Belasco), with the Russian-born French composer Michel Emer (born Rosenstein, 1906–1984), best known for his songs for Edith Piaf; and a revue planned by Walter ("Wally") Wanger and Gene Doctor entitled *Crosstown.* What Latouche might have prepared for any of these proposals remains unknown.[22]

In the fall of 1947, news similarly surfaced that Latouche had agreed to create a "revised story outline" for Seymour Zweibel's planned but unrealized Broadway adaptation of *Kaiserin Josephine* ("Empress Josephine"), the 1936 Viennese operetta about Napoleon and Josephine by the Hungarian-Jewish composer Emmerich

Kálmán (1882–1953). Hoping to launch the work as a vehicle for the Czech-American operatic soprano Maria Jeritza, Zweibel engaged Edward Eager—later Jerome Moross's collaborator on *Gentlemen, Be Seated!*—to write the book and lyrics, with the press anticipating rehearsals to begin in mid-November and a budget over $200,000. Things developed so far as the completion of a rather finished draft, *Poor Josephine!* by Eager "from a scenario by John Latouche," a draft, however, that stayed so close to the original Paul Knepler and Géza Herczeg libretto as to obscure the extent and nature of Latouche's contribution, although Josephine appeared more the devoted wife in this newer guise. This adaptation, in any case, never got off the ground.[23]

A script likewise survives for another aborted show from the late 1940s associated with Latouche, *Tamborito*. The work seems to have originated with Oscar Hammerstein II's younger brother, Reginald ("Reggie") Hammerstein (1896–1958), a stage director and manager who in late 1947 brought together the rather unlikely combination of composer Ernesto Lecuona (1896–1963), bookwriter Milton Herbert Gropper (1896–1955), and Latouche in an attempt to produce a musical of his own. By this time, Lecuona, who had studied music in his native Cuba with the pianist-composer Joaquín Nin (the father of Latouche's friend, writer Anaïs Nin), had achieved international stardom as a pianist, band and orchestra leader, and prolific composer of songs, theater and film scores, and light concert works, including the enormously popular *Malagueña* from his *Andalucía* suite for piano (completed 1927)—an output that variously showed the influence of Spanish popular and concert music and Viennese operetta, along with some pioneering absorption of Afro-Cuban styles. Far less known, playwright Milton Gropper had had several Broadway hits and misses, including two 1924 flops co-written with Oscar Hammerstein II, followed more successfully that same year by his single-authored *Ladies of the Evening*, a romantic drama whose 1930 film adaptation as *Ladies of Leisure*, directed by Frank Capra, helped jump-start the career of actress Barbara Stanwyck.[24]

Literally meaning "little drum," *Tamborito*, the anticipated Lecuona musical announced in the *Times* and elsewhere (erroneously as *Tamborita*) in September 1947 took its name from a traditional Panamanian genre of folk music and dance especially associated with carnival. The peripatetic Lecuona arrived in New York in December to work on the show with Latouche and Gropper; but how much the creative team actually accomplished before forsaking the piece, aside from the preserved script, which includes song titles but no lyrics, and possibly the song "Tamborito" that survives among the composer's papers in Cuba, remains unknown. When asked in 1949 why he dropped the musical, Hammerstein simply said that he had "a good score and first act, but no second act."[25]

The two-act extant script, preserved among Latouche's effects, constitutes something of a conundrum; not only does the book, although presumably written by Gropper, bear no attribution, but its second act appears to belong to an earlier draft than the surviving first act. The two acts combine, nonetheless, to form a relatively cohesive narrative.

The action takes place in Panama during carnival. The cynical and hedonistic Miguel Velasquez, an American-educated young man who recently has inherited his great-uncle's Panamanian fortune, heeds the advice of his deceased uncle's worldly-wise mistress (named Rosita Garcia-Vidal in act one, Mercedes in act two) and decides to give some structure and purpose to his life by attempting to aid those in need, including helping a desperately poor dancer, Natalia, avoid becoming a prostitute. Appalled by the seeming arrogance and ingratitude of those he endeavors to assist, Miguel concludes that the poor should be kept in their place; but in the end, his idealism reaffirmed, he proposes marriage to Natalia.

Although the basic idea of a young patrician rescuing a woman in distress accords with a favored Milton Gropper topic, the book's campy zaniness suggests at least some input on Latouche's part. Gore Vidal, surely the inspiration for the name if not the person of the saucy Rosita Garcia-Vidal, might have had a hand in this musical burlesque as well, considering that during these years he and Latouche collaborated on several projects, including an unidentified musical comedy; moreover, as a frequent traveler to Guatemala, he specifically hoped to write something with a Central American setting.[26]

In any case, the action and tone of the script resembles far more closely the screwball comedies and satirical revues of the 1930s than the popular musical plays of the postwar period. The lower-class characters, for instance, spout a comically exaggerated pidgin language (as in Natalia's lament, "And disgrace that it is to me, this Velasquez save me from the dance failure that I would succeed to make") that seems a parody of popular stage and screen portrayals of Latin Americans, including Hollywood's *Carnival in Costa Rica* (1947), a film that featured the Lecuona Cuban Boys and that possibly provided a starting point for this travesty. In total contrast, the upper-class Panamanians speak a stylishly arch English, with, for instance, Rosita telling Miguel, "The only disadvantage of being a mistress is that you can not bear children without making your lover uncomfortable." Such clashes of language underline, for all the folderol, the play's serious theme of class conflict and exploitation. The second act becomes at times particularly farcical, with a group of prostitutes protesting the closure of local brothels with signs such as "We Offer the Efficiency That Comes Only from Experience," and "We Are *Not* Communists! We Believe in the Freedom of Every Body to Express Itself!" Little wonder management might have wanted a different second act.

By contrast, two other musicals involving Latouche from this time—*Mooncalf* and *The Happy Dollar*—succeeded in making it to the boards, if not to a Broadway stage as hoped.

Actually, Latouche had only a fitful association with *Mooncalf*, and little to do with the musical as it finally debuted in 1951, after a tortuous history, as *Golden Ladder*. As the work's composer, Lehman Engel, recalled, two young producers, Thomas Hammond and Jeff Bailey, and the director Mary Hunter approached him in the summer of 1948 about writing the music for a new show based on a script by

Alexander King (born Koenig, 1899–1965), a writer and illustrator (and in due course, a popular television personality) who had emigrated in his teens from Vienna to New York. Intrigued by the material—a retelling of the biblical Joseph story set among black sharecroppers in the Deep South, its title, *Mooncalf*, derived from its portrayal of Joseph as a "mooncalf," that is, an absentminded dreamer—and tempted by a $2,000 advance, Engel quickly composed the score over the summer with King, who wrote the lyrics.[27]

Born into a Jewish family in Jackson, Mississippi, Lehman Engel (1910–1982) studied in the early 1930s at Juilliard with Rubin Goldmark and privately with Roger Sessions. He further joined, like Jerome Moross, the Young Composers' Group formed by Copland, who recognized that the "extremely prolific and facile" Engel might not be " 'hopelessly' a composer"—a prescient observation, for although Engel continued to write especially choral and incidental music, he increasingly devoted his time to conducting, becoming one of the time's foremost conductors of musicals in particular. He relatedly emerged a leading theorist of the Broadway musical by way of a series of publications that championed the mechanics of a canonic literature largely focused on the works of Rodgers and Hammerstein and other midcentury hits. Such activities also gave rise to his establishment in 1961 of the BMI Lehman Engel Musical Theatre Workshop as a training ground for young artists working in musical theater.[28]

In early September 1948, the *Times* announced a fall mounting of the all-black *Mooncalf*, with music by Engel, book and lyrics by King, sets by Boris Aronson, and direction by Mary Hunter. But no such staging appeared. By the start of the new year, the producers must have felt the need to doctor the show, for in February 1949 they enlisted Latouche to write some new lyrics; but he apparently revised some old ones as well—what his agent, Lucy Kroll, referred to as his "cleaning up the lyrics for *Mooncalf*"—and when not long afterward, on March 25, Cooper Union presented excerpts of the musical at a symposium entitled, "An Evening on the Theater," Latouche, also on hand as narrator, received sole recognition for the lyrics, with King credited only for the book.[29]

The musical subsequently disappeared from view, but in the spring of 1951, after a gap of two years, the press once again announced a forthcoming Thomas Hammond production of the work, with the lyrics still by Latouche, but with King's script now adapted by actress-playwright Joanna Roos (1901–1989). However, still unable to raise enough funds for a Broadway mounting, Hammond arranged to have the work tried out at Cleveland's Karamu House, where the musical premiered on May 28, 1953, as *Golden Ladder* (after another working title, *Brother Joe*, had been rejected as too suggestive of Joseph Stalin). This final version credited the book to Roos "after an original play" by King, and the lyrics to King and Abel Meeropol (using his pseudonym, Lewis Allan, 1903–1986), the composer of the anti-lynching song "Strange Fruit," and the adoptive father of the orphaned sons of Julius and Ethel Rosenberg. That Latouche's unexplained disassociation from the musical represented a fairly recent development seems suggested by an April 4, 1953, letter from Engel to the director of the Karamu House, Rowena Jelliffe, in which he wrote, "New lyrics also will replace the few which you have read by John LaTouche."[30]

Benno Frank directed the Karamu production, which featured a sizable, presumably all-black cast accompanied by two pianos. The show received some excellent reviews—the *Cleveland Plain Dealer* thought the "captivating" show, with its echoes of *Green Pastures*, more of "an authentic Negro folk opera" than *Carmen Jones*—and played for five weeks as scheduled, closing on July 2. Engel and others hoped for a Broadway or off-Broadway production, but none occurred, and the show drifted into obscurity. Rereading the script in 1980, Roos wrote to Engel, "Perhaps this isn't the time to present blacks as sharecroppers in the early part of this century, but I can't help thinking that one of these days it might have the same impact, in its way, as 'Fiddler on the Roof,' " to which Engel responded, after his own "nostalgic" review of the text, "I think that the whole thing is good but dated.... I think that *Mooncalf* is best left for the libraries."[31]

Along with some of the music from the score, which exhibits a folkloric quality somewhat comparable to Kurt Weill's *Down in the Valley*, three undated scripts to the show survive among Engel's papers: one with book and lyrics by Martin Kieran, presumably a pseudonym for Alexander King; another with book by Roos and lyrics by Latouche; and a third with book by King and Roos, and lyrics by King and Allan (that is, Meeropol). The first of these probably represents an early version from around 1948, the second an interim script as it took shape in the years around 1950, and the third the version ostensibly used by Karamu in 1953.[32]

Throughout these various drafts, *Mooncalf/Golden Ladder* retained more or less the same story and even some lyrics, making the show fundamentally the work of King, although the later two scripts—which provide the basis for the following summary—reduced the number of Joseph's brothers and instituted some other changes as well. Set in the Mississippi delta in the early years of the twentieth century, the pious Jacob oversees a country tabernacle on the grounds of his farm, worked by his sons. However, his favorite son, Joseph, prefers dreaming and singing to farm work, to the resentment of Joseph's brothers and their wives. As a medicine show run by Pettypurr and in need of a singer comes through town, Joseph's brothers, offered $100 by Pettypurr's wife, Valerie, allow the troupe to abduct Joseph, who subsequently falls in love with Miriam, a member of the company. After Joseph spurns Valerie's sexual advances, she accuses him of rape and tells a stunned Joseph about his brothers' betrayal of him.

In the second act, an incarcerated Joseph accurately predicts the release of his cellmate Milo, who works for Faro, the owner of a nightclub, the Egyptian Garden. At Milo's behest, Faro arranges for the release of Joseph, who becomes the nightclub's manager and who marries Miriam, with whom he has a son. With his newfound wealth, Joseph purchases his father's farm with the intent of punishing his brothers, but in the end, he forgives them.

A postwar study in optimism and forgiveness, the musical closely follows the trajectory of the biblical Joseph story, with Pettypurr substituting for the Egyptian captain, Potiphar; Valerie, Potiphar's wife; Milo, the Pharaoh's butler; and Faro, Pharaoh. Over time, the show moved closer to conventional musical comedy, but remained basically a somber melodrama with touches of minstrelsy.

A comparison of the three extant scripts suggests that while Latouche revised many of the original words, several lyrics, all found only in the interim script, appear entirely his own, including "The Promised Land," for Miriam; "Let's Play the Fool," for Valerie; "Store-bought Suit," for Joseph and Jacob; and "We Got a Star," for Joseph and Miriam. Their authorship would seem confirmed by certain telltale rhymes and images, including Miriam's "feather in the air" from "The Promised Land" (see "Inbetween" from *Beggar's Holiday*), while with respect to "Store-bought Suit," the entire lyric reappeared, albeit revised, in *The Golden Apple*, Joseph's "I've got a store-bought suit / With a rainbow plaid" becoming Ulysses' "I've got a store-bought suit / With a fancy plaid." Adapting an idea from King's script, Latouche also seems to have written the strikingly spectral second-act melodrama for Jacob's daughters-in-law.

These original contributions stood out in the context of the show not only in terms of style, but in their ability to limn character and thus enrich the drama. Miriam's act-one solo, "The Promised Land," for example, quickly thrusts her from the shadows to center stage as she tells Joseph of her dreams and aspirations:

> Did you ever see a brown leaf driftin'
> On a gentle autumn breeze
> Or a line of wild geese liftin'
> High up over the trees.
> If you ever saw a blue star burnin'
> And wished you could journey there
> You'll know how my mind keeps turning
> Like a feather in the air.

Although *Golden Ladder* essentially dispensed with Latouche's lyrics, the show retained the daughters-in-law melodrama that he seems to have penned, while the overhauled words to "Store-bought Suit" and "We Got a Star"—now, "Bran' New Look" and "I See a Star"—plainly showed traces of his work as well.

The similarly extended saga of *The Happy Dollar* proved more straightforward, at least in terms of authorship. The show seems to have originated with its bookwriter, Lee Falk (born Leon Gross, 1911–1999), best known as the creator and author of the successful newspaper comic strips *Mandrake the Magician* and *The Phantom*, but also active in the theater as author, producer, and director. In 1947, Falk wrote a musical comedy script, *Hero Hill*, which would become the basis of *The Happy Dollar*, and which piqued the interest of fledgling producer James Dunn (1901–1967), an accomplished actor who considered starring in the show himself.

For this reimagining of the Faust story as a western, Dunn hoped to reunite the team of composer Harold Arlen and lyricist E. Y. Harburg, sensing some connection between Falk's play and Arlen and Harburg's *Bloomer Girl* (1944)—and perhaps, too, with *Finian's Rainbow* (1947), a recent hit by Harburg and Burton Lane. However, with Harburg unavailable, Dunn recruited by the end of 1947 an enthusiastic Latouche, whose *Cabin in the Sky* with Vernon Duke resembled this new vehicle even more closely. Indeed, when Latouche proposed to Duke that they collaborate on this show, the latter, although he liked Falk's book, turned down the offer by explaining that they had "already concocted a colored 'Cabin in the Sky' . . . Why bother with a white one?" In the end, as Duke further recalled, Latouche "handed the book" to William Friml, "who wrote a charming score to a great set of lyrics."[33]

Still only in his twenties, pianist, arranger, and composer William Friml (1921–1973)—the "gifted son," as Duke wrote, of operetta composer Rudolf Friml and his third wife, actress Elsie Lawson—had studied music from an early age, giving piano recitals while still a boy. After some time at the University of Southern California, service in the army, and marriage to actress Shelby Payne, Friml established himself largely in Los Angeles as an arranger for a number of popular singers, although he maintained some involvement with the theater as well, including helping composer Burton Lane revamp the Broadway musical *Flahooley* as *Jollyanna* in 1952. According to his son, also named William, financial worries and chronic pain drove him to take his life at age fifty-one.[34]

Latouche and Friml collaborated on the score during the first half of 1948, and according to one source, completed the work—retitled *The Happy Dollar*—in June, with a production by Dunn in association with Don Medford, later a noted television director, and James Colligan, a theater manager, announced for the fall; but postponement followed postponement. In November, the press mentioned a possible leading role for operetta baritone Earl Wrightson; in December, a planned West Coast tryout with film stars Eddie Bracken and Vivian Blaine (the latter soon to create the role of Adelaide in *Guys and Dolls*); and in January, a production under the direction of Charles Friedman. But nothing along these lines panned out, and in the fall of 1949, after months of struggling to raise enough money, James Dunn forfeited his option on the show, which had to wait another five years before a production materialized.[35]

The synopsis that follows collates especially two early scripts as opposed to a third and somewhat abbreviated version adapted by Richard ("Dick") Ott that dates from later in the work's history.[36]

Act I, scene one. The Happy Dollar Saloon, a frontier bar and casino in Northern California. Turn of the century. Miners, lumberjacks, and cowhands carouse with saloon owner Sal Bean and the saloon girls ("Happy Dollar," for Sal and the ensemble). Sal's old paramour, the rough-and-tumble Boddy Lane, returns after a year's absence, and shares his thoughts about women as so much "surplus baggage" ("I Don't Need No Wimmin'," for Boddy). An elegantly dressed stranger, Scratch, enters looking for the saloon's meek young waiter, Stacky Lee. As the action freezes, Scratch—the devil himself—explains that Stacky's shiftless father Ike, at the moment of his death, had cursed his baby son to hell; and so Scratch reasons that he has a good chance to claim Stacky's soul, notwithstanding the godly influence of the boy's deceased mother, Maggie, a virtuous and hardworking woman who would sing to Stacky and his childhood sweetheart, Susie Tannehill, ballads about legendary American heroes on mythic Hero Hill ("Way Away up Yonder," for Maggie, Stacky, and Susie).

Scene two. The Happy Dollar Saloon. Despite promises made to the "lovely, sweet and spunky" Susie to give up gambling, Stacky loses at roulette and finds himself only deeper in debt. Sal tells Boddy about her ideal mate ("Maybe You're My Man," for Sal). Boddy and Stacky, antagonists since childhood, scuffle over Susie, with Stacky taking a beating (reprise of "Happy Dollar," for the ensemble).

Scene three. Before curtain. Stacky and Susie comfort each other ("No One but You," for Stacky). Remembering his mother's impoverished life, Stacky determines to become rich before he marries Susie. Scratch offers Stacky a white cowboy hat that will provide him with worldly delights in return for his soul ("Scratch's Bargain," for Scratch). Stacky agrees.

Scene four. The Crabapple Tree. Susie, wary of Scratch, quarrels with Stacky and, alone, dreams of future happiness ("The Crabapple Tree," for Susie).

Scene five. The Happy Dollar Saloon. Boddy mocks the locals for their superstitions ("Lucky Lovin' You," for Boddy, Sal, and the ensemble). Stacky arrives newly empowered in his white hat (reprise of "I Don't Need [No Nothin']," for Stacky) and wins the Happy Dollar Saloon in a bet with Sal; but in the midst of his triumph, he takes off a boot and all discover to their horror that his foot has become a hoof ("Stacky Lee," for Stacky and the ensemble).

Act II, scene one. The Happy Dollar Saloon. One month later. Although customers have stopped coming to the saloon, Sal and the saloon girls rehearse a number ("Howdy Stranger," for Sal and the women). Tipped off by Scratch, Sal schemes to wrest the saloon back from Stacky with the help of Boddy, who has decided to become a proper husband ("Family Man," for Boddy). Scratch rehearses Stacky in a song of seduction ("Live for the Moment," for Stacky).

Scene two. Before curtain. A bewitched Susie reveals her erotic side (reprise of "Maybe [I'm That Girl]," for Susie). Stacky regrets his bargain with Scratch ("Whatever Happened," for Stacky and Susie). Sal and Boddy enlist Susie to their cause.

Scene three. In Front of Little White Church. The town gathers for Sunday church service ("Sunday Go to Meetin' Time," for Scratch and the ensemble). Unable to enter the church, Stacky flings aside his hat, which Boddy grabs, upon which Stacky shoots Boddy, wounding him, and then flees. Sal realizes that Scratch intended this outcome from the start.

Scene four. Nearby Woods. As a posse searches for Stacky, Scratch, assisted by the imp Bub and other minions, plans to claim Stacky's soul at midnight ("[Ya Gotta] Give the Devil His Due," for Scratch and Bub).

Scene five. At Crabapple Tree. An exhausted Stacky lies asleep at the base of the crabapple tree, dreaming (reprise of "Way Away up Yonder," for Maggie). Awakening, he finds Susie, who has retrieved the enchanted hat (reprise of "No One but You," for Susie). Prompted by Susie, Stacky dons the hat and wishes to go to Hero Hill (strains of "Way Away up Yonder" segueing into the "Hero Hill" chorus).

Scene six. Hero Hill. Dawn. In a saloon on mythical Hero Hill, such fabled Americans as Johnny Appleseed, Pecos Bill, Daniel Boone, Paul Bunyan, Kit Carson, Davy Crockett, Mike Fink, Hiawatha, and Wild Bill Hickok cavort ("Hero Hill," for The Heroes). Several of the heroes relate their storied deeds ("Tall Tales," for Paul Bunyan, Bill Hickok, Hiawatha, Pecos Bill, Johnny Appleseed, and Mike Fink). Stacky reunites with his repentant father Ike, who works serving drinks to The Heroes. Taking advantage of a clause in his contract that allows him to engage Scratch in personal combat in order to save his soul, Stacky, with his father's help, triumphs over Scratch and redeems himself.

Scene seven. Front of Happy Dollar Saloon. His hoof now gone, Stacky reunites with Susie and reconciles with Sal and Boddy ("Finale," reprise of "Way Away up Yonder" and "The Happy Dollar," for the ensemble).

Over and above the age-old American use of the name "Scratch" for the devil, Falk's adaptation of the Faust legend seemed particularly indebted to Stephen Vincent Benét's 1936 short story "The Devil and Daniel Webster" and its 1941 film adaptation, which so impressed Latouche. Similar to Benét's hero, Jabez Stone, Stacky Lee makes his pact with the devil largely in order to prevent his beloved from suffering the sort of poverty endured by his mother. A sort of holy fool, Stacky remains even more virtuous than Jabez, resisting temptation at nearly every turn and shooting at Boddy, as he eventually explains, only to prevent the latter from falling under the hat's demoniac power. Moreover, Falk, like Benét, placed his morality tale in the context of American history, although whereas Benét's story culminates in a display of notorious national villains, Falk's concludes with a pantheon of national heroes—a conceit that naturally would appeal to the author of *Ballad for Americans* and *The Eccentricities of Davy Crockett*.

At the same time, elements of the script—not only the deal with a devil called Scratch, but the magical cowboy hat, the hero's superhuman breath, and even the names Stacky Lee and Boddy Lane—tapped a body of songs and tales associated with the legendary African-American badman Stackalee (also called Stagger Lee, Stack O'Lee, and so forth). Initially disseminated in the early years of the twentieth century, this lore—popularized by such varied songsters as Mississippi John Hurt, Woody Guthrie, and in later years Bob Dylan—derived from an 1895 incident in St. Louis in which Lee Shelton, a black pimp known as Stack or Stag Lee, shot and killed William ("Billy") Lyons after an altercation in a saloon in which Lyons grabbed Shelton's cowboy hat. In the story's many tellings, Shelton/Stackalee becomes an avatar of bravado and defiance; his Stetson a symbol of male virility. As a native of St. Louis especially, Lee Falk well might have been familiar with this popular legend from an early age, but his adaptation of the tale points in particular to B. A. Botkin's 1944 compendium *A Treasury of American Folklore*, the likely source, too, for some of the musical's portrayals of the celebrated figures on Hero Hill (although not Hiawatha, who does not appear in the Botkin book).[37]

Falk's script relatedly accommodated a tradition even closer to home, namely, the cartoon superhero. As a weakling transformed into a powerful agent with superhuman abilities, Stacky recalled Joe Simon's Captain America, Jerry Siegel and Joe Shuster's Superman, and, given his magical hat, Falk's own Mandrake. That these and other popular superheroes of the time largely represented the work of Jewish-American artists, partly in response to antisemitism, partly in response to national hopes, provides further context for a musical that conflates the story of Faust with Anglo-American and African-American folklore and comic-strip fantasy.[38]

Although none of Friml's music seems extant in notated format, a demo tape of the score for solo piano and, even more remarkably, a makeshift film of the show in rehearsal, both recently discovered by Richard Ott's daughter Anne Melville, survive, preserving the music to most of the numbers. Several of the tunes seem informed by American folk music and the blues as filtered by a kind of elegance reminiscent of the theater work of Vincent Youmans and Arthur Schwartz, along with some of the operetta tradition that Friml seems to have inherited from his father.[39]

In tandem with Friml, Latouche cultivated two contrasting idioms so as to highlight the show's fundamental conflict between good and evil: a romantic one for Maggie, Stacky, and Susie, and a more ironic one for Scratch, Sal, and Boddy. Scratch especially supplies much of the show's humor, including his lyric "Ya Gotta Give the Devil His Due," in which he reminds the audience of his various qualities:

When you kiss a maid who's young and cute—
I'm the breach of promise suit
When you eat so much it is a sin
I'm that extra double chin
When you race your buggy down the line
I'm the cop behind the sign
When you're in a jam and tell a lie
I louse up yer alibi.

Sal, a Mae West type, also provides some sassy comedy, as in "Maybe You're My Man":

The kind of a guy I could follow
Will be a lovin' Apollo
He'll be as tough as a tanker
And rich as a banker
But leaner and lanker.

His chest will be double-barreled
And he'll be neatly appareled
And he'll be simple but arty
A dope, but a smarty
The life of the party.

Meanwhile, the extended Hero Hill tableau displayed an earthier, folksier humor, with Paul Bunyan, to take an example, boasting in his narrative,

Gals go for me, I
Mow 'em down like timber
I'm mighty limber
When it comes to fun.
Once on a spree I
Over-celebrated
And populated
Half of Oregon!

This heroic panorama found room, too, for the gentleness of Johnny Appleseed:

Folks tended my trees in the way that I taught 'em
Till there were apples your hunger to feed
Now when you wander through orchards in autumn
Those are the gardens of John Appleseed.

Some of the show's lyrics seemed a bit reworked—with "Maybe You're My Man" reminiscent of "Girls Want a Hero" (*Beggar's Holiday*); "No One but You," a straight-faced echo of "When I Walk with You" (also *Beggar's Holiday*); and "Sunday Go to Meetin' Time," largely taken from a 1945 song written with David Broekman (with Friml adapting the music as well), although with an added sardonic chorus for Scratch ("Six days you mess up / One you 'fess up / Sunday you're pure as snow again")—but nevertheless exhibited considerable flair and wit.

On April 24, 1954, Theatre Incorporated, an ambitious new theater company in Houston, presented the world premiere of *The Happy Dollar*, thanks to the initiative of baritone Richard Ott, a native Texan who in earlier years had sung with big bands, including the Jimmy Dorsey Orchestra. While living in New York in the 1940s, Ott became involved with trying to raise money for *The Happy Dollar*; and after settling in Houston in the mid-1950s, he persuaded Johnny George, the dynamic female director of Theatre, Inc., to launch the piece. Ott further presided over a revision of both the script and the score, including interpolating a number presumably written by Friml and Latouche, "Cleavin'," while cutting several other songs.[40]

Directed by Johnny George, with sets by Earl Ehret, costumes by Cecilia West, choreography by Vivien Altfeld, and a small combo led by Bill Knight, the production, which seemed to have added Calamity Jane and Annie Oakley to the assembly of legends in the Hero Hill scene, starred local performers Bobby Larr (Stacky Lee), Nancy Phillips (Susie Tannehill), Jay Froman (Scratch), Caroline Richter (Sal Bean), and Richard Ott, using his stage name Dick Culver (Boddy Lane). Presented at Theatre, Inc., the show garnered glowing reviews in both *Variety* and the local papers, with the *Houston Chronicle* lauding Falk's book as combining "extremely witty lines, humorous situations, tenderness, the underlying horror of the 'hell-bound' and the fantasy of folk legend in a way that approaches sheer genius." A popular success as well, the show ran in Houston for a little less than five weeks.[41]

The following year, Ott took the musical for an additional tryout at Dallas's Courtyard Theater in a revamped production directed by himself and starring newcomer Ted Stanford as Stacky Lee along with several members from the original Houston cast. Opening to a rather withering review in the *Dallas Morning News*, the show nevertheless did well at the box office, and extended its planned ten-day run by an additional week. About this same time, Latouche persuaded Falk and Friml to allow his agent, Lucy Kroll, to represent them, writing, "For a work like *The Happy Dollar*, which has a wider appeal [than *Ballet Ballads* and *The Golden Apple*], as well as a high calibre, I think she could work wonders very quickly."[42]

After ironing out some issues with Kroll, the freewheeling Richard Ott next presented *The Happy Dollar* in Los Angeles, where the show debuted on July 9, 1956, at the Los Palmas Theatre with future western film star Ben Cooper as Stacky Lee, and closed at a loss of about $25,000 several weeks later, just days before Latouche's death. Recalled Vernon Duke some months afterward,

> The show opened with no advance reputation, no word-of-mouth appraisal, good or bad. The Hollywood first-nighters, rather to their surprise, saw an integrated musical play of high professional quality, with arresting dialogue and an engaging score. The cast of zealous young Texans and Californians gave it all they had—and they had plenty—but the star of the evening was John Latouche. His lyrics were never more imaginative, never more in key with the story. One single scene—the one called "Hero Hill"—had three show-stoppers in it, flowing on each other's heels. Next day's notices read as though the critics, caught unaware and liking the show in spite of themselves, compromised by admitting that it wasn't bad. The modest musical went deeper and deeper in the red each week and finally folded; so dismal were the show's finances that the theatre was forced to close its doors and went up for sale.[43]

The production indeed received generally favorable reviews by the local press, the *Mirror-News*, for instance, finding the musical "stocked with talent, some good tunes by William Friml, smart, fresh lyrics by John Latouche and an amusing if slightly overworked book by Lee Falk." All the same, critical opinion widely sensed that the musical had little chance of making it to Broadway, partly because of perceived deficiencies with the material, but also because public interest in Faustian tales had surfeited with such recent shows as the musical *Damn Yankees* and the comedy *Will Success Spoil Rock Hunter?* (both 1955). Relatedly, although not stated per se, the work's folklorism must have shown its age; the new Fausts aspired to become celebrity athletes or corporate leaders, not saloon owners. Moreover, as producer T. Edward Hambleton wrote to Vernon Duke, without Latouche around to help guide the musical, the work had that much less of a chance of success. Richard Ott, who went on to found and direct the Houston Music Theatre (now, the Arena Theatre), and who remained very fond of *The Happy Dollar,* thought to revive the show in the 1970s, but never did.[44]

Latouche's varied enterprises from the late 1940s disclosed his continued but intensified involvement with world myth and native folklore, although hardly limited to that. Such aims and impulses soon enough reached a culmination of sorts with his and Jerome Moross's musical adaptation of the Homeric epics, *The Golden Apple,* which happily enjoyed a greater success than any of these other efforts.

18

The Golden Apple

In 1949, following the successful launching of *Ballet Ballads,* Latouche and Jerome Moross, each armed with a $3,000 grant from the Guggenheim Foundation, started in on a new work. Moross's Guggenheim fellowship represented the extension of a grant he had obtained from the foundation in the spring of 1947 for various projects, but his 1948 renewal request specified an "opera" with Latouche. In the end, he and Latouche referred to the finished piece, *The Golden Apple,* as a "musical" rather than an opera, but an opera the work arguably remained, with Moross calling it more specifically, as his daughter recalled, "an opera for Broadway."[1]

On his side, Latouche's 1948 Guggenheim application proposed neither an opera nor a musical, but rather a "series of lyrical plays ... suitable for university and experimental, as well as professional, production." Received by the foundation in early November 1948, this proposal vented the lyricist's frustration at having had to work largely within the "restrictions" of commercial theater, which "have hampered my going as far as I would like in the evolution of new dramatic methods," although he distinguished his aims as "experimental" as opposed to "esoteric." As for the prospective new work, which would "be American in character, as distinct from 'Americana' and would employ musical and cinematic backgrounds, as well as folk poetic sources," Latouche imagined a study of American family life from Jamestown to the present day; this idea might have been suggested partly by a musical that had just opened, *Love Life* by Kurt Weill and Alan Jay Lerner, a supposition supported by the application's allusion to that show's producer, Cheryl Crawford. But in any case, on receiving his fellowship, Latouche decided to use the grant period in order to compose rather another opera with Moross, although remnants of his original proposal could be discerned in this new work nonetheless.[2]

In addition to Crawford, Latouche provided as his Guggenheim references playwright-producer Lawrence Langner, designer Oliver Smith, music critic Minna Lederman, and composer Douglas Moore. Lederman's recommendation knowingly placed Latouche in historical perspective: "He reminds one of the poets of Paris and Berlin, in the late twenties, who, working with musicians like Kurt Weill, Hindemith, and the French Group of Six, dramatized their own time and left perhaps the most lasting theatre comment that we have.... It's hard to place Latouche in any given category. Like the composer-librettist, Marc Blitzstein, he has a one-of-a kind talent." Douglas Moore's reference also warrants special notice given his later collaboration with the lyricist: "Mr. Latouche is one of the most promising talents in our lyric theater. His accomplishments to date have been substantial, particularly the *Ballet Ballads* which provided one of the most stimulating evenings in the theater I can recall. He has originality and independence but, as he points out [in his application], he manages to get his things produced."[3]

After receiving his fellowship in April 1949, Moross moved from Hollywood to an apartment in New York on West 93rd Street in order to work on the opera with Latouche. By this time, the latter already had suggested that they base the piece on Homer's classic tales, a notion the lyricist had discussed earlier in the year with Crawford, who liked the concept. Recalled Moross shortly before the opera's 1954 premiere, "John [Latouche] phoned me and said, 'We'll do the Iliad and the Odyssey as a musical.' And it was so completely fantastic all I could say was 'Why, sure.'" This idea of an opera after Homer presumably lay behind their February 1949 contract through the Dramatists Guild concerning a work provisionally entitled *Fall of Abalone*, an agreement that specified, among other things, a fifty-fifty split of all future proceeds. At any rate, having decided to set the opera in America at the turn of the century, with Olympus and Sparta jointly represented by a small town, and Troy by a large city, Latouche wrote in his journal in May 1949, "I am working with dilatory enthusiasm on Jerry [Moross]'s scenario. At the present moment I am calling it *Angel's Roost*, which is a fine name for an American version of Olympus. But the 'wicked city' name has me stuck. And the entire work, as a matter of fact, comes very slowly, almost *squeezed out* of my tubes." By June, the authors had decided to call the work *The Golden Apple* (the title, incidentally, of a 1941 musical comedy by two University of Maine students, Frank Hanson and Beatrice Besse, also inspired by Homer), with the *Times* announcing a production by Crawford in association with Bea Lawrence for the end of the year.[4]

However, by November 1949, Moross and Latouche had written only about half of the opera, and so sought additional funding to help them finish the piece, including an unsuccessful petition to the Rockefeller Foundation. Fortunately, an advance from Chappell Music for the rights to the score helped them continue their work into 1950, as did some assistance from Lawrence, who with Crawford signed a contract with the authors through the Dramatists Guild in March 1950 for some future production.[5]

By 1951, Latouche had begun hosting backer's auditions in his apartment, apparently both with and without Moross, who periodically needed to return to Hollywood for film work. In Gore Vidal's historical novel *The Golden Age* (2000), the author remembered these auditions: "Latouche's clear somewhat toneless voice could handle the wit of his own lyrics though not the emotion of the ballads of his composer, Jerry Moross, who always listened with a sad smile to what his collaborator was doing to his music." Another witness, Latouche's companion, Kenward

Elmslie, recalled that during these at-home auditions, their two pets, a black poodle and a calico cat, would time their "Mack Sennett chase scenes diabolically, to break the spell of 'Lazy Afternoon,' a luxuriantly sensuous love ballad."[6]

When Latouche and Moross actually finished the opera remains uncertain. Given that the piece, although copyrighted in 1953, remained in some flux right up to its April 20, 1954, Broadway premiere, its date of composition might be given as 1949–1954, with the understanding that the authors seem to have written most of the score in 1949 and 1950, with Moross and his assistant Hershy Kay completing the orchestrations at a much later date.

The work's long gestation period can be explained partly by the fact that despite the support of producer Cheryl Crawford and the unstinting efforts of agent Lucy Kroll, Moross and Latouche had enormous difficulty finding backers for the opera, perhaps even more so than with *Ballet Ballads* now that ANTA's defunct Experimental Theatre could no longer come to the rescue. In late 1951, exhausted from producing the musical *Paint Your Wagon*, Crawford relinquished her option on the show, leaving matters in abeyance. About this same time, Kermit Bloomgarden considered producing the work in cooperation with Oliver Smith and Herman Levin, but this too came to naught. Meanwhile, the prominent entertainment lawyer H. William Fitelson urged the heads of the Theatre Guild, which he served, and which had produced *Porgy and Bess*, *Oklahoma!*, and *Carousel*, to stage the opera: "I have read and heard at an audition at my house a musical which has distinction, humor, wonderful lyrics and wonderful music as well as a solid story.... It has great scope and if properly produced should be a great hit and the important musical of the year. It is ready to go. I understand [choreographer] Jerome Robbins would like to do it." However, the Guild declined as well, with one of its directors, Theresa Helburn, explaining to Latouche in July 1952 that the work's "appeal is somewhat too special to justify the terrific cost of the commercial theatre." Nor did Moross's petition to the Ford Foundation for funding in early 1953 yield any results.[7]

Then, as announced in early 1954, producer T. Edward Hambleton and director-designer Norris Houghton decided to include the opera as part of their initial 1953–54 season at the Phoenix Theatre off Broadway. The Phoenix had been founded by Hambleton and Houghton in 1953 as a high-minded and affordable alternative to commercial Broadway fare, with productions held at a former Yiddish theater located at Second Avenue and 12th Street in Manhattan's East Village that seated over a thousand. Scheduled to open in March 1954 on the heels of *Coriolanus* as the third of the company's first four productions, *The Golden Apple* would prove one of the most notable accomplishments in the Phoenix's thirty-year history.[8]

In his preface to the opera's published libretto, Latouche provided a brief account of how this turn of events came about, starting with his discovery in 1953 that Houghton had a Vermont home close to the one he recently had acquired: "I went over to wail on his doorstep, but he paid no mind to my woes, filled with excitement as he was about the Phoenix Theatre, which he and T. Edward Hambleton intended to inaugurate the coming season. I paused in mid-wail, and began a glowing pitch about the need for a bright new musical on their schedule. He looked interested, and I told him I happened to have the show right on me." Latouche neglected to say that Hambleton already had patronized him and Moross by helping to bring *Ballet Ballads* to Broadway in 1948. Nor did he mention that this latest development seemed to hinge on Hambleton and Houghton reaching a crucial agreement with two other producers, Roger L. Stevens and Alfred de Liagre Jr., both of whom had shown interest in the work as early as 1952, that in return for financial backing they would have the option to take the work to Broadway following its run at the Phoenix. Indeed, Stevens raised most of the approximately $80,000 (including a $5,000 investment by Kenward Elmslie) ultimately needed by the Phoenix to stage the opera, a hefty amount for an off-Broadway show, but considerably less than the $200,000 or more projected for a Broadway production. After five years, and by Latouche's estimate about seventy auditions, the opera would see the light of day.[9]

The Golden Apple parodies the story of the Trojan War, with the first act a retelling of the Judgment of Paris (a myth only alluded to by Homer), and its second act corresponding to both the war itself (the subject of the *Iliad*) and Ulysses' travels home and reunion with his wife, Penelope (the subject of the *Odyssey*).

The Judgment of Paris relates how Paris came to marry Helen, the wife of Menelaus, King of Sparta: Eris, the goddess of discord, angered that she had not been invited to an Olympian wedding feast, hurls a golden apple, inscribed "for the fairest," among the guests. Juno, Minerva, and Venus all vie for the apple, whereupon Jupiter appoints the handsome shepherd Paris—actually the son of King Priam of Troy—to choose the winner. Juno, Minerva, and Venus promise Paris wealth, fame, and the most beautiful wife, respectively. After selecting Venus, Paris sails to Greece under her protection and persuades Helen to elope with him to Troy. Because various Greek chieftains (at the suggestion of Ulysses, King of Ithaca) had sworn to defend Helen from harm, they honor their pledge by assenting to Menelaus' call that they wage war against Troy.

Intrigued by the presence of Mount Olympus in the state of Washington, and the happy coincidence of the apple as the fruit most associated with that state, Latouche, for the opera's first act, transferred this tale to a small Washington town, Angel's Roost, in the year 1900. Menelaus becomes the town's sheriff; his wife, Helen, a farmer's daughter; Juno, Mrs. Juniper, the mayor's wife (her name a conflation of Juno and Jupiter); Minerva, Miss Minerva Oliver, a school teacher; Venus, Lovey Mars, a matchmaker and the wife of Captain Mars; Eris, Mother Hare, a village psychic; and Paris, a traveling salesman from the big city of Rhododendron, the name apparently suggested by Washington's state flower. (Moross and Latouche decided to make Paris a mute role, an idea that harkened back to their earliest work together, but that also intimated the influence of Gian Carlo Menotti's 1946 opera *The Medium* and Burton Lane's 1947 musical *Finian's Rainbow*, both of which featured dancers in essentially nonspeaking principal parts.) This first act further introduces Ulysses Spelvin (his last name an in-joke allusion to the traditional pseudonym in the American theater, George Spelvin) and other surrogates for the Greek heroes of the Trojan War as hometown soldiers returning from America's war with Spain (The Heroes); and the act concludes with these same soldiers declaring war on Rhododendron and departing for the city in order to reclaim Helen.

The second act, set mostly in Rhododendron, opens with a retelling of the Trojan War, with Prince Hector now Hector Charybdis, the city's devilish mayor, and the Trojan Horse represented by civil unrest incited by The Heroes. Following the defeat of Rhododendron by way of a boxing match, Ulysses' travels occur metaphorically within the city's limits, with the nymph Calypso, Madame Calypso, a fashionable hostess (played by Mrs. Juniper); the monsters Scylla and Charybdis, two stockbrokers (played by Menelaus and Hector, respectively); the seductive Siren, a nightclub entertainer (played by Lovey Mars); a character without clear Homeric precedent, The Lady Scientist (played by Miss Minerva), but an episode that perhaps draws on Ulysses' encounter with the magic ships of the Phaeacians; and the sorceress Circe (enacted by either Mother Hare or Penelope, depending on the version)—an odyssey that climaxes with an episode reminiscent of Ulysses' trip to the underworld (with in one version Mother Hare an ostensible analogue to the blind prophet Tiresias). In the denouement, Four Suitors represent the courtiers kept at bay by Penelope, who rather than weave a tapestry, as in Homer, sews a quilt.

As indicated above, some uncertainty exists about which character doubles the part of Circe. For the work's initial production at the Phoenix Theatre and later transplant on Broadway at the Alvin Theatre, Mother Hare sang Circe's music while a dancer interpreted the role (an option, according to Moross, if Mother Hare herself does not dance the part), whereas in the published libretto, Latouche made a point of insisting that Penelope assume the part: "Circe does not suggest lurid sex in the sense that the sirens have. Here, the effect is a total one—domination over everything that has been pushing Ulysses around is offered to him. In order to secure this he must give up what is most tender and most alive in himself. That is why Penelope is used to represent Circe." Relatedly, in the original production, an offstage chorus echoed Ulysses' questions in his second-act soliloquy, whereas in the published libretto Mother Hare and the chorus respond to Ulysses in turn. Such discrepancies would seem to reflect the kinds of conflicts between composer and lyricist that plagued their collaboration.[10]

An entirely throughsung opera, *The Golden Apple* features arias, duets, and choruses connected by particularly tuneful recitative. "The sung dialogue," explained Latouche, "instead of the artificial recitative of opera, is rendered in short songs whose separate melodies become part of the major production number." The programs for the Phoenix and Alvin Theatre productions both wrestled, somewhat unsatisfactorily, with such distinctions by listing the work's "musical sequences" either with quotes, suggesting more freestanding numbers, or without quotes, suggesting more general scenes, a not entirely consistent practice adopted as well in the following synopsis of the original Phoenix production.

The action takes place in Washington State between 1900 and 1910, the first act entirely in the township of Angel's Roost on the edge of Mount Olympus.[11]

Act I, scene one. In the Orchard. In the small community of Angel's Roost, Helen, a coquettish farmer's daughter married to the town's elderly sheriff, finds the town a bore, especially with its young men away at war, but Lovey Mars, the local matchmaker; Mrs. Juniper, the mayor's wife; and Miss Minerva Oliver, the spinster schoolmarm, remind her of the town's assets ("Nothing Ever Happens in Angel's Roost," for Helen, Lovey Mars, Mrs. Juniper, and Miss Minerva). Mother Hare, the town oracle, predicts future events (Mother Hare's Seance). Penelope and Menelaus joyously announce the end of the war ("My Love Is on the Way," for Penelope).

Scene two. The Village Green. The townspeople welcome the returning soldiers (The Heroes Come Home, for the entire company), who relate their experiences fighting in Cuba and the Philippines ("It Was a Glad Adventure," for Ulysses and The Heroes). All look forward to celebrating that evening at a church social ("Come Along, Boys," for The Heroes and the ensemble). Ulysses and Penelope lovingly reunite ("It's the Going Home Together," for Ulysses and Penelope). To Ulysses' hopes and Penelope's fears, Mother Hare foresees great changes afoot (Mother Hare's Prophecy). The returning veterans look forward to dallying with Helen but, learning that she has married Menelaus, acquiesce to Ulysses' request that they take an oath to defend her honor ("Helen Is Always Willing," for The Heroes).

Scene three. The Church Social. The townspeople entertain themselves with games and dances (The Church Social, for The Heroes and the ensemble). Paris, a traveling salesman from the city of Rhododendron, descends in a hot air balloon and displays his wares ("Introducin' Mr. Paris," for Paris and the ensemble). Lovey Mars, Mrs. Juniper, and Miss Minerva compete in a bake-off, and Mother Hare, insulted at not being invited to the town social, mischievously offers a golden apple to the winner of the best cake or pie. After agreeing to allow Paris to judge the contest, Mrs. Juniper attempts to bribe him with riches, Miss Minerva with fame, and Lovey Mars with women. Paris awards the prize to Lovey Mars (The Judgment of Paris, for Lovey Mars, Mrs. Juniper, Miss Minerva, Mother Hare, and Paris).

Scene four. At Helen's House. Lovey Mars introduces Paris to Helen, who seduces him ("Lazy Afternoon," for Helen and Paris). Helen departs with Paris in his balloon, and Menelaus and the other older men pressure Ulysses and The Heroes into pursuing them. As Menelaus and The Heroes depart, Penelope and the women weep, and Mother Hare bites her thumb at the lot (The Departure for Rhododendron, for the entire company).

Act II, scene one. The Seaport of Rhododendron. Helen revels in her glamorous new life in the city of Rhododendron ("My Picture in the Papers," for Helen, Paris, and the male ensemble).

Scene two. The Main Street of Rhododendron. Ulysses schemes to conquer the city by organizing a committee and a countercommittee so as to foment conflict among the local citizenry. After pandemonium erupts, Hector Charybdis, the city's dapper mayor, suggests that Helen's future be settled by a boxing match between Menelaus and Paris; after a mishap incapacitates Menelaus, Ulysses takes his place and knocks out Paris. As Menelaus and Helen depart for home, Ulysses and his men, encouraged by Hector, decide to go on a spree in the city (The Taking of Rhododendron, for Ulysses, Hector, and Paris [and others]). Hector gleefully looks forward to having his revenge (Hector's Song, which anticipates the events to follow much as Mother Hare's Seance predicts the action of the first act).

Scene three. Back in Angel's Roost. Penelope's Home. Sewing a patchwork quilt, Penelope remembers her life with Ulysses ("When We Were Young" [retitled "Windflowers" for Broadway], for Penelope).

Scene four. The Main Street Again. Outfitted in snazzy clothes, Ulysses and The Heroes prepare for an evening on the town ("Store-bought Suit," for Ulysses [and The Heroes]).

Scene five. The Big Spree.

Madam (Madame) Calypso's Parlour. Hector introduces Ulysses and his crew to the society hostess Madame Calypso, who hails them as the toast of the town; but as The Heroes become old news, one of the men, Patroclus Whiting, desperate to remain in Calypso's circle, follows her to his doom (Calypso, for Mrs. Juniper [and others]).

The Brokerage office of Scylla and Charybdis. As Hector lures the veterans into playing the stock market, the hero Ajax Finucane loses his entire investment and jumps out of a window to his death (Scylla and Charybdis, for Menelaus and Hector [and others]).

A waterfront dive. The Heroes relax at a nightclub on Hector's advice, but as The Siren and The Sirenettes lull the men with song, some sailors shanghai most of them ("By Goona-Goona Lagoon" [retitled "Goona-Goona" for Broadway], for Lovey Mars [and others]). At Hector's arrival, one of the soldiers, Bluey Weinerwitz, runs off in fear.

The Hall of Science. Hector suggests that the remaining heroes—Ulysses, Doc MacCahan, and Achilles Akins—put their faith in science. Volunteering for a space mission, Doc departs in a rocket ship created by The Lady Scientist, who never considered how to design its return home ("Doomed, Doomed, Doomed," for Miss Minerva [and others]).

The Wrong Side of the Tracks. Hector brings Ulysses and Achilles to Circe, who offers Ulysses ultimate power in the form of a golden apple ("Circe, Circe," for Mother Hare and a dancing Circe [or just Penelope in the published libretto], along with the ensemble). Egged on by Hector, Paris attempts to stab Ulysses, but Achilles intercepts the assault and dies. Now alone, Ulysses casts the golden apple aside and seeks answers to the meaning of life (Ulysses' Soliloquy, for Ulysses and chorus [and Mother Hare in the published libretto]).

Scene six. Angel's Roost: In the Orchard ([on Broadway, Angel's Roost: In the back yard] this scene significantly shortened and revised before the Broadway premiere). Ulysses joins Four Suitors in their courtship of Penelope, who, now that she has completed her quilt, agrees to keep her word and marry one of them; blindfolded, she kisses her various suitors until Ulysses removes her blindfold and disposes of the

Four Suitors with one blow (The Sewing Bee, for Penelope, Helen, Miss Minerva, Mrs. Juniper, Lovey Mars, the Suitors, and Ulysses). Penelope angrily chastises Ulysses for his long absence (The Tirade [this title added for Broadway], for Penelope); but both agree to renew their love ("We've Just Begun," for Ulysses and Penelope).

The Golden Apple thus took its place among innumerable works of art inspired by the Homeric stories and their surrounding mythology, including two seminal modernist texts with which Latouche had some familiarity, namely, James Joyce's *Ulysses* and Ezra Pound's *Cantos*. How much Latouche might have known about musical adaptations of Homer—from Claudio Monteverdi's *The Return of Ulysses* (1639–40) and such British burlesques as *Penelope* (1728) and *The Rape of Helen* (1833), to Kurt Weill and Maxwell Anderson's aborted *Ulysses Africanus* (1938–39, a planned treatment of the *Odyssey* story set during the Civil War with the hero a black slave, and a work that in various ways prefigured *The Golden Apple*)—remains unknown, but he presumably had at the least some acquaintance with *Helen Goes to Troy* (1944), a Broadway adaption of Jacques Offenbach's operetta *La belle Hélène*, with a book co-written by Gottfried Reinhardt, Latouche's collaborator on *Polonaise* (1945). In any event, Latouche's approach to Homer proved highly original, recalling in particular his earlier efforts in adapting myth and fable for the lyric theater, especially *The Eccentricities of Davy Crockett*, which concluded the *Ballet Ballads* by portraying, through a series of vignettes, the epic life of its heroic subject.[12]

Although one scholar deemed *The Golden Apple*, as compared to Weill's abandoned *Ulysses Africanus*, a "silly farce," Latouche and Moross intended the work as no mere travesty. Discussing the opera's relation to the Homeric legends, Moross wrote to the Rockefeller Foundation, "The analogies become very interesting and, we hope, will have the effect of causing people to re-examine our national dictae [*sic*] concerning morality, justice, liberty and so in [*sic*] in the almost satiric aspects the story acquires in its new setting." Similarly, in his preface to the published libretto, Moross wrote, "On its surface the piece is a retelling of the Trojan War legend in an American fin-de-siècle setting and is constructed as a series of continuous musical-comedy production numbers. Actually, our intention is broader and encompasses a review of many aspects of the American scene and the American dream." Interviewed with Latouche shortly before the premiere, Moross went so far as to remark, "You might say that it's a philosophical musical comedy," to which Latouche groaned and said, "Oh, no, don't say that. Nobody'll come to see it." For his part, Latouche more obliquely described his aims as "no adaptation of Homeric grandeurs, but a comic reflection of classical influence on the way we think nowadays. Therefore any myths we might use were to arise out of our native songs, dances, jokes and ideas." And in early 1950, while in Boston helping Burgess Meredith prepare Donagh MacDonagh's ballad opera *Happy as Larry* for its Broadway premiere, Latouche told the *Boston Post*, "I have tried to do it [adapt Homer] in such a way that popular audiences will be pleased, and students of the classics will also be pleased."[13]

The work's more serious themes include the dislocation and change caused by war; indeed, during these years, the character of Ulysses had become a familiar emblem for the returning veteran, as evidenced by the 1948 film *Homecoming*, based on Sidney Kingsley's 1944 story, "The Homecoming of Ulysses." Among other concerns, the opera explores the disparity between war as imperialistic fantasy (as represented by the Spanish-American War) and catastrophic reality (as represented by the fight against Rhododendron). Regarding the former conflict, only Mother Hare strikes a mordant note, asking at the war's end, "Isn't anybody dead?" For the rest, the Spanish-American War seems but a "glad adventure," as The Heroes proclaim their affection for Theodore Roosevelt (by way of an anachronistic jab at critics of Franklin Roosevelt: "Oh Theodore, Oh Theodore / The Roosevelt that we adore") and Ulysses blithely recounts the resentments of native populations:

Wherever we went they loved us
They cheered when they saw us arrive
 They loved us so much
 Their affection was such
We're lucky to get home alive!

In contrast, the Rhododendron crusade, which can be seen as symbolizing the cataclysmic world wars to follow, leaves Ulysses far more chastened and wise.[14]

These opposing views of war form part of a parallel dialectic between small-town and big-city American life that unfolds in the opera's first and second acts, respectively. From the start, with Helen's lament, Latouche establishes the satirical tone with regard to rural American life that dominates the opening act as a whole:

Nothing ever happens in Angel's Roost
It nestles where the mountains brush the sky
 It has a pretty view
 But there's just three things to do
You're born and then you live and then you die.

In the course of this first act, the work continues to lampoon the foibles and provincialism of small-town America, from the chamber-of-commerce boosterism of its civic leaders to the obtuseness of its vengeful elders eager to send the young off to war for "the principle of the thing." At the same time, this parody also has, in both word and music, its affectionate side, with a high-spirited if ironic depiction of a village social and a charming ode to Helen by the sex-starved veterans.

As for the second-act vivisection of the metropole, Latouche and Moross, who likely appreciated the neat congruity of their central metaphor of a golden apple with the jazzy nickname for the city of New York, "the big apple," strategically placed the action in the first decade of the twentieth century, a ten-year period, meant to correspond to Homer's *Odyssey*, that witnessed, as Mother Hare prophesizes, enormous change. Stated Latouche shortly before the premiere, "The turn of the century is the period of our greatest energy and optimism. From 1900 to 1910 came our greatest innovations. Fashions progressed during that period. Since then there have been only improvements on basic structures." But the opera makes the point that such progress also created new threats and challenges, here dramatized as Ulysses and his men find themselves confronting a range of modern pitfalls involving fame, money, popular culture, scientific advances, and political governance.[15]

Latouche parallels these new perils with several of the ones faced by Homer's Ulysses on his travels, so that in the episode set in a waterfront dive, for instance, The Siren becomes a hoochy-koochy dancer who, accompanied by The Sirenettes, stupefies the drunken soldiers by dancing to a hypnotic song that parodies Tin Pan Alley:

By a goona goona goona
By a goona goona goona lagoon.
We will croona croona croona.
We will croona croona real jungle tune.

Upon that golden shore, kids,
We'll lie on beds of orchids
And then later
By the crater
Of the old volcano
We can promise we won't say No
A Noa

Latouche creates an additional symbolic layer by ingeniously double-casting the rural folk from Angel's Roost as the city slickers from Rhododendron, as indicated in the synopsis above—a head-spinning conflation of correspondences that not only integrates the characters of the Judgment of Paris story with those of the *Odyssey*, but in doing so, underlines how the frailties of country and city life form two sides of the same coin.

Much as *Ballet Ballads* alternates folkloric and urban styles in its separate parts, so *The Golden Apple* employs similar contrasts to distinguish its two acts, although in ways specifically aimed at conjuring the early twentieth century, with the Rhododendron sequence in particular tapping a number of popular idioms. "Each 'trap' set for Ulysses and his crew," note Deniz Cordell and Robert Edridge-Waks, "is given its own unique musical identity, each one satirizing a songwriting genre, turning it on its ear to provide a jovial and sinister subtext to each happening." "Calypso," for instance, parodies palm court music; "Scylla and Charybdis," a Gallagher and Shean vaudeville routine; "Goona-Goona," Hawaiian hula music; "Doomed, Doomed, Doomed," early jazz; and "Circe, Circe," the blues. The authors seem to have cast their nets beyond the era's popular vernacular, however. "Lazy Afternoon," for example, evokes the sensuous elegance of Satie and Debussy in its music, and, complementary enough,

Gallery 2 (captions are on pages xii–xv)

Figure 29

Figure 30

Figure 31

Figure 32

Figure 33

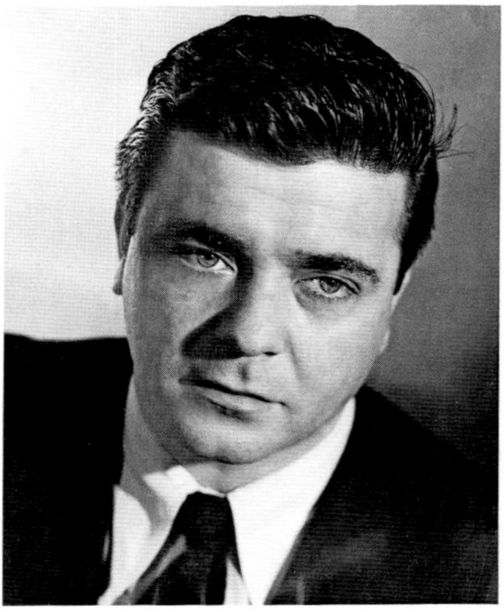

Figure 34

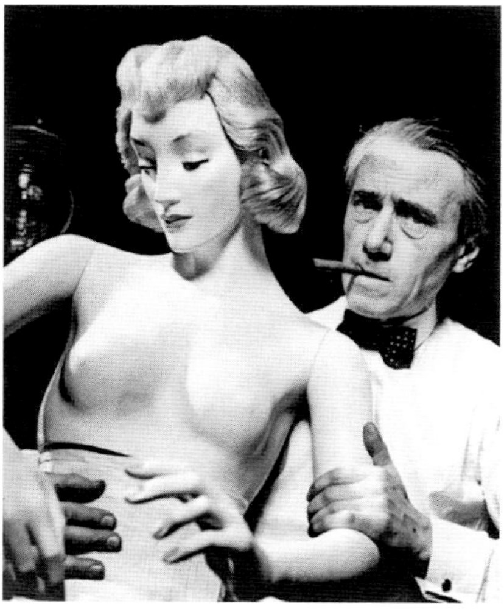

Figure 35

Figure 36

Figure 37

Figure 38

Figure 39

Figure 40

Figure 41

Figure 42

Figure 43

Figure 44

Figure 45

Figure 46

Figure 47

Figure 48

Figure 49

Figure 50

Figure 51

Figure 52

Figure 53

Figure 54

Figure 55

Figure 56

Figure 57

Figure 58

the symbolist tenor of Verlaine in its words; the music for The Sirenettes in "Goona-Goona" similarly seems to tip its hat to Debussy's "Sirènes." Latouche likewise appears to have availed himself of philosophical tracts of the period, with one early review finding an echo of William DeWitt Hyde's statement "The world we live in is a world of mingled good and evil," from *The Art of Optimism* (1900), in Mother Hare's "Good is a word that fools believe / And evil's a word that the wise achieve."[16]

At the same time, Moross and Latouche had their contemporary world in mind as well, so that the opera tends to have a tricky triple focus, parodying both early and midtwentieth-century America along with the Homeric legends. For instance, "Goona Goona" caricatures not only such turn-of-the-century hits as Bob Cole and J. Rosamond and James Weldon Johnson's "Under the Bamboo Tree," but the kinds of more contemporary film and stage South Seas exotica satirized by Marc Blitzstein in *The Cradle Will Rock* (1937) and Leonard Bernstein in *Trouble in Tahiti* (1952, and possibly composed with some knowledge of *The Golden Apple*). Similarly, while the line "And time is running out at a rather hectic pace" from The Lady Scientist's dystopian "Doomed, Doomed, Doomed" can be placed in the context of Einstein's theory of relativity, the song speaks also to the concerns of the postwar atomic age, including predictions of ecological devastation:

> Oh, our continent is crumbling and dissolving
> As our rivers wash the topsoil out to sea
> And what land we can retrieve'll
> Be devoured by pest and weevil
> And there won't be nothing left for you and me.

Latouche similarly translates dissension among the Trojans over the Trojan Horse into a spoof of contemporary American demagoguery by having Ulysses disruptively form a local committee for Helen and a countercommittee against her, with each group singing, "Mutter mutter / And grumble grumble," much as the U.S. congressmen sing "Bicker bicker bicker bicker / snap snap snap" in *The Eccentricities of Davy Crockett*. Such a critique of political action committees found parallel expression in the "Discs and Nudes" episode that Latouche had written only recently for Hans Richter's film *Dreams That Money Can Buy* (1947).

Above all, however, *The Golden Apple* addresses the subject of marriage, particularly in the context of tumultuous times, as it follows two couples—in classic tradition, a noble couple, Penelope and Ulysses, and a more comic pair, Helen and Menelaus—as they separate in act one and reunite in act two, with the opera tracing the more complex relationship, that between Penelope and Ulysses, from expectancy ("My Love Is on the Way") to bliss ("It's the Going Home Together") to conflict (The Departure for Rhododendron) to nostalgia ("Windflowers") to renewal ("We've Just Begun"). Once again, Latouche seems to have projected something of his own relationship with Theodora, not only in terms of thematic content—including the matter of a returning veteran hoping to rebuild a frayed relationship—but in the portrayals of the characters themselves, to the point that the opera even could be read as a certain wish fulfillment.

As a study of modern marriage seen through the prism of the American past, the work accordingly might be compared to Rodgers and Hammerstein's *Allegro* (1947) and Weill and Alan Jay Lerner's *Love Life* (1948). But a comparison of, say, "It's the Going Home Together" from *The Golden Apple* with "A Fellow Needs a Girl" from *Allegro* only serves to highlight the especially wide gulf between Oscar Hammerstein and Latouche, whose smart tone often suggests parody. Compare, for example, the opening lines of Hammerstein's decidedly paternalistic lyric with those of Latouche:

"A Fellow Needs a Girl"
A fellow needs a girl
To sit by his side
At the end of a weary day,
To sit by his side
And listen to him talk
And agree with the things he'll say.

"It's the Going Home Together"
It's the coming home together
When your work is through
Someone asks you How de do
    And How'd it go today?

It's the knowing someone's there
When you climb up the stair
Who always seems to know
    All the things you're gonna say.

The relationship between Penelope and Ulysses grows that much deeper by their final duet, as the latter, looking at his wife's patchwork, suggests that they likewise piece together the scraps of their past and start anew, the opera ending with an enchanting duet for husband and wife:

We've just begun
We've opened our eyes
Our new-born day
Is about to rise.

We're one not two
We finally see

That I am you
And that you are me.[17]

The newfound insight undergirding Ulysses' reconciliation with Penelope, borne out of his disillusioning experiences in Rhododendron, manifests itself earlier in the second act, when alone, his men gone, he asks himself questions about life and death, with ghostly echoes providing answers, so that, for instance, he hears the word "Life!" to the query "What is the meaning of life?" This key sequence concludes, in a vein similar to his final duet with Penelope, with Ulysses stating,

I know that I am myself
And I am also other men
And knowing this truly
I can go home again.

An apparent parallel to the Tiresias episode in Homer's *Odyssey*, this sequence falls within a literary tradition that, in Robert Rabel's words, sees Ulysses' voyage to the underworld as inaugurating "a literary trope of death and rebirth subsequently used frequently to signal major transformations of character, and, by extension, of social and political systems."[18]

As a rhymed and metered text not unlike *Ballad for Americans* or *Ballet Ballads*, but on a much grander scale, Latouche's libretto merits special attention as a tour de force. Without entirely escaping a certain childlike lilt, actually part of the work's charm, Latouche circumvents sing-song regularity through enjambment, mosaic rhymes, broken rhymes, near rhymes, and other techniques, with some of the rhyming purposefully broad and comic, such as the long list of words used to rhyme with "Scylla." Hector's description of Madame Calypso offers an example of the librettist's skill at creating a flowing narrative in dramatic verse:

Haven't you heard
Of Madame Calypso?
The nympho megalo ego dipso
Maniac who sets the pace in
Rhododendron? You've seen her face in
The social columns and front page scandals
Oh, she's the hostess who only handles
Big Names (both the Best and Worst Names)
Call[s] celebrities by their first names.

Such resourceful use of rhyme naturally makes this intricate text that much easier to grasp across the footlights.[19]

The libretto's detailed directives with respect to scenery, costume, lighting, action, and mood also deserve mention. The prize fight scene, for example, receives a full page of instructions, including the caution, "Although choreographed in the period manner, the prize fight should not be precious in style. It should convey, for instance, the vitality of [George] Bellows's *The Knock Out at Smoky Joe's* [*sic*]." This same passage also specifies that Paris, after losing the fight, be "sadly carried away by the townsfolk in a cortege reminiscent of the death exit in *Hamlet*." In his preface to the published libretto, Latouche sounded a somewhat self-congratulatory note about all this, writing, "Some critics, when *The Golden Apple* was performed, remarked on the debt it owed to its scenic and choreographic effects. This is certainly true, but as is evident from the libretto, I hope, these efforts were conceived as an integral part of the work—leaving, of course, a free hand for each creative department to contribute its unhampered best."[20]

Thanks to Jerome Moross's careful preservation of materials, several preliminary drafts of the libretto, including handwritten sketches, survive—an unusual circumstance in Latouche's case. For one of his earlier drafts, the librettist penned, possibly for the delectation of potential backers at auditions, a "Curtain Announcement" in the manner of the early modern dramatic prologue, but here brought up-to-date by discussing his and Moross's contract with Cheryl Crawford and Bea Lawrence, including these lines:

Each tiny Clause, when Underlined,
Disputed, Signed and Countersigned,
Was Borne off to the Drama Guild
Where formal Notice was Fulfilled—
Replete with Ifs and Ands and Buts—
Concerning Billing, Agents' Cuts;
The Document, now Free of Fault
Was locked in Mrs. Sillcox' Vault.

These drafts reveal that throughout the compositional process Latouche largely retained the more self-contained set pieces, but in general revised and streamlined the whole by eliminating a good deal of exposition and choral commentary, including, at one point, interjections from Ulysses' personified house. Among other things, he also omitted a wedding scene for Helen and Menelaus; a ballad about the Trojan Horse for Ulysses (with the "wooden horse decoy" explicitly associated with the seeds of "prejudice" and "hate" the hero intends to sow among the citizens of Rhododendron); an extra episode in the big spree sequence, namely, a critique of modern technology in which Mother Hare as Polly Femme—an allusion to Homer's Polyphemus (Cyclops)—lords over some machinery that crushes a few of Ulysses' men; and a passage in the underworld scene, strongly redolent of the spectral cave in *Davy Crockett*, in which Ulysses confronts the tribulations of generations of

Americans before him, an encounter reflected in this stanza cut from his Soliloquy (and that, if retained, would have given the Soliloquy a more explicit social context):

I know that out of suffering
The spirit renews itself to sing
Until the world darkened by fear
Grows clear....

Conversely, Latouche expanded a few sections; for instance, he initially thought simply to depict the final reunion of Penelope and Ulysses through pantomime, and end the work with Helen reprising "Nothing Ever Happens in Angel's Roost," only later deciding to conclude the work with Penelope and Ulysses reaffirming their love alone on stage.[21]

Jerome Moross's melodious score sprints vigorously from one tuneful idea to the next, sometimes a bit unrelentingly, but not without its subtleties, and always expressive of its similarly jam-packed text. Formally, the music, in its organicism, seems in some ways more akin to ballet or animated film than traditional opera, and even more specifically to the kind of variation structures long associated with the composer's theatrical work; its many nice touches include the return of the opening music at that moment when Helen departs with Paris, so that the overture can be seen as a forewarning of the first act's climactic turning point. Producer Norris Houghton even quoted Latouche as asserting that Moross "worked it [the piece] all out in sonata form," a claim that remains intriguing if enigmatic. At any rate, at least on formal grounds, the description of the work as a musical rather than an opera seems a fundamental misnomer, although one instituted by Latouche and Moross themselves, and that furthermore speaks to the work's distinctiveness.[22]

Moross's trademark modal harmonies provide further unity and individuality, as do the elegant orchestrations, with their prominent use of vibraphone and celesta. Indeed, notwithstanding its use of myriad popular idioms, from polka to hula song, and its echoes especially of cartoon music, the opera, like *Ballet Ballads,* largely goes its own way stylistically; if some moments evoke western film scoring of the postwar era, this has much to do with Moross's own memorable contribution to the genre with, above all, *The Big Country* (1958).

Assisted by Alfred de Liagre, the Phoenix hired an expert production staff for the opera's launching, including director Norman Lloyd and costumer Alvin Colt, both of whom had worked on previous Phoenix shows; and musical director Hugh Ross and choreographer Hanya Holm, both of whom had collaborated with Moross and Latouche on *Ballet Ballads*. In contrast, set designers William and Jean Eckart and lighting designer Klaus Holm (Hanya's son) were at the beginnings of their careers; indeed, the Eckarts would establish their reputation largely through this production. The couple had met as undergraduates at Tulane University and had pursued their studies with Donald Oenslager and Robert Edmond Jones at Yale before moving to New York, where they attended an audition of *The Golden Apple*; fascinated by the work, they snatched a script and on their own created sketches and models that in due course secured them a contract with the Phoenix. Cognizant of the opera's seamless flow, the Eckarts hung small flat panels on hemp lines in overlapping planes that could rise and fall, allowing smooth and visible transitions from scene to scene (see Figure 45). In addition, they stylistically caught the spirit of the work by incorporating, as epitomized by the show curtain, designs and graphics from turn-of-the-century America with geometric forms inspired by Mondrian.[23]

In early February 1954, de Liagre provided backer Roger Stevens with the following news: "All the principal parts, with the exception of Menelaus, are now cast. . . . The Eckarts, in general, are doing a good job although, sometimes, a little lacking in inspiration. . . . Hanya Holm has selected the dancers with taste and care. . . . Norman Lloyd is showing more understanding of the material than I dared hope. . . . LaTouche and Morass [*sic*] are still a bit inflexible but, with a little daily pressure here and there, they are becoming more amenable." At some point, management fired Norman Lloyd—allegedly because of unauthorized cuts taken in the score, although friction with Holm apparently played some part as well—a development that shattered Lloyd's longstanding friendship with Latouche; Holm duly assumed responsibility for the entire direction, although Lloyd remained credited in the program. By all accounts, including her own, Holm staged the work as something "danced from the beginning to the end," that is, as a dance-opera not unlike *Ballet Ballads*, and the Eckarts matched her conception by creating sets that "seemed to dance on and off."[24]

The leads—Priscilla Gillette (Penelope), Stephen Douglass (Ulysses), Kaye Ballard (Helen), Dean Michener (Menelaus), Jonathan Lucas (Paris), Jack Whiting (Hector), Bibi Osterwald (Lovey Mars), Geraldine Viti (Mrs. Juniper), Portia Nelson (Miss Minerva Oliver), and Nola Day (Mother Hare)—had varied backgrounds in opera, musical comedy, and nightclub entertainment. Although the cast of about forty included some seasoned professionals like Jack Whiting, most consisted of young performers with relatively modest credentials, including Kaye Ballard and, in the small role of Mayor Juniper, Jerry Stiller, two comedians then little known. Ballard had to audition numerous times before winning the part of Helen—perseverance well rewarded as the production catapulted her to stardom, to the point that during the run of the show she appeared on the covers of both *Life* magazine and the *New York Post*'s *Week-End Magazine* (a seeming case of life imitating art, considering that Helen sings at the top of the second act, "Oh it's grand to see my picture in the papers"). As with the production team, some of the cast had been involved in Blitzstein's *Regina* (1949) or would participate later in that composer's *Reuben Reuben* (1955), suggesting a certain continuum with respect to the presentation of Moross and Blitzstein during these years.[25]

The Phoenix cut corners as they could, limiting rehearsal time to four weeks, wrangling concessions from the unions with regard to salaries, and reducing the pit orchestra to under twenty players. Rehearsals took place in a building at Second Avenue and Houston Street on the Lower East Side, where Seymour Peck of the *New York Times* caught up with the composer and lyricist, reporting on the latter's love for the neighborhood (where years earlier he had learned to speak "Yiddish with a Southern accent") and on both men's admiration for the Phoenix's "enterprising spirit and its artistic determination in the face of financial limitations." In his preface to the published libretto, Latouche further expressed his delight with the cast, feelings apparently reciprocated to judge from the reminiscences of Ballard, who called him "a spectacular, wonderful person," and Shannon Bolin, who fondly deemed him "a rascal and a genius." Jerry Stiller—whom Holm had roller-skate on his left leg, his right leg raised behind him, "like a swan," at the end of the first act—similarly recalled that at rehearsals Latouche "sparkled the place up with his presence. He just sat there and listened, everyone getting tuned in to him as an ordinary guy. He didn't come off as an impresario."[26]

In his memoirs, producer Norris Houghton offered his own remembrance of this "southern charmer":

> Small, black-haired, and black-eyed, with a thin but winning smile when pleased and a childish pout when upset, he had a devastating wit, which shone through his writing and gingered his conversation. He made friends and admirers easily, and cast them off with equal ease. He abhorred clichés and was never a bore. I, alas, having a mind that is at home with the cliché, must admit to having frequently been uneasy in his company. But I admired his considerable talent and his not inconsiderable skill in getting on in the world.[27]

After three preview performances, *The Golden Apple* premiered on March 11, 1954, for a six-week run at the Phoenix Theatre. Latouche and Moross received congratulatory telegrams from an array of well wishers, including Leonard and Felicia Bernstein, Maya Deren, Coleman Dowell, Lillian Hellman, Billy Strayhorn, Gore Vidal, and composer-librettist Marc Blitzstein, who wrote to the pair, "I hope your years of work and your great talents produce a shining success." Coincidentally, the opera debuted one day after Blitzstein's own off-Broadway landmark, namely, his adaptation of Brecht and Weill's *The Threepenny Opera*, a work with which *The Golden Apple* had some close points of contact, suggesting that the time was ripe for sophisticated musical satire away from the bright lights of Broadway.[28]

On opening night, at one point in the first act, as conductor Hugh Ross dropped and then scrambled to retrieve his hastily assembled conductor's score, Kaye Ballard filled time by wiggling her brightly painted toes, an improvised shtick that so amused the audience that she regularly repeated the gag in subsequent performances. As the final curtain fell, the "smart first-night audience," reported the *Mirror*, "rocked the rafters with robust applause," the cheers continuing so long that the theater had to switch on the house lights to get the attendants to leave. Even so, Dawn Powell reported in her diary that she discovered Latouche in the theater on the night of the Phoenix premiere "weeping" amid of all the ovations. "They've ruined my second act—they've ruined it—spoiled everything!" he told her, and then added, "Come downstairs [to the cast party in the theater basement] and have champagne!" What Latouche felt "ruined" and "spoiled" remains unknown, but possibly involved certain cuts or perhaps the casting of Mother Hare, rather than Penelope, as Circe.[29]

In his depiction of the opera's opening night in *The Golden Age* (2000), Gore Vidal similarly described the librettist sobbing about his "ruined" show to Powell, a detail the author could have borrowed from Powell's published diary, although he attended the premiere himself, and added to Powell's description the detail of Latouche drunk on brandy. In Vidal's novel, three characters—Aeneas, Peter, and Diana—ponder the audience's strong emotional response to the work, which Aeneas attributes to the end of the Second World War—an interpretation greeted skeptically by Peter, who cites continued Cold War hostilities, prompting the following exchange:

> "The war," Aeneas growled, "is over on the stage of the Phoenix Theatre as of March eleventh, 1954. That's why everyone's cheering in there. That's what everyone wants. That's what we thought we had when World War Two ended. We were all ready to start up our lives again. Then, we got Korea and ..."
>
> "But," said Diana to Peter, "it's really over now. And we can," she reprised the song, "*go home at last.*"
>
> "I wouldn't count on it." But Peter could tell that there were all sorts of conflicting emotional crosscurrents at work in the American psyche, and Latouche had certainly tapped into one.

Some additional reflection about the opera reappears at the end of the novel, making the work's significance to Vidal all the clearer. The action having arrived at 2000, a much older Peter says with respect to the debut of *The Golden Apple*, "Oh, that night was unforgettable. But the golden age, if there had ever been one, was already shut down by then—1954, wasn't it?" to which Vidal, as himself, responds, "Yes. Which means that what we thought was a bright beginning was actually a last flare in the night."[30]

The critics of the day widely shared the first-night audience's euphoria, often outdoing one another with superlatives. "The best [musical] of a number of seasons," stated John McClain (*Journal-American*); "the best musical in ten years," reported George Freedley (*Morning Telegraph*); "the best thing that has happened in and to the theatre in a very long time," wrote John Chapman (*Daily News*). Not a few called the work "a milestone," particularly in terms of its organization, one comparable to *Oklahoma!* but at the same time, according to such commentators as George

Freedley, "a great advance" over that earlier show. Surprisingly, few couched such observations in the context of the operatic tradition, but rather accepted Moross and Latouche's own description of the work as a musical at face value, notwithstanding some scattered references to the piece as a "folk opera," "ballad opera," "jazz opera," and "operetta." One exception, F. M. Pugell (*Theatre Arts*), went so far as to draw analogies to Monteverdi, Verdi, and other operatic masters, writing with respect to such so-called integrated musicals as *Show Boat* and *Oklahoma!* that "*The Golden Apple* carries this integration even further, because the musical language genuinely stems from the story; it illustrates the action, the emotional content of every role and the over-all atmosphere of the production. This, after all, is the ideal toward which every conscientious composer of opera strives."

Although the reviews enthused about virtually every aspect of the work and the production, Latouche in many instances garnered the lion's share of praise. Virgil Thomson (*Herald Tribune*) thought the libretto "vivacious, sparkling, ingenious and at many moments very, very funny," and Richard Watts Jr. (*Post*) found the lyrics "not only gay, satirical, intelligent and versatile, but [they] also carry on the narrative with theatrical effectiveness." "He [Latouche] has outdone himself," opined Freedley. "I can only say that he has mastered the polysyllabic technique of Cole Porter, Ira Gershwin and Lorenz Hart. Could anyone ask for more? Mr. Latouche has added his own touch which is not as yet imitable."

Arriving relatively late in the season, the opera earned, about a month after opening, a particularly prestigious accolade: by a wide margin, the New York Drama Critics' Circle Award for best musical of the season, although admittedly against such relatively weak competition as *Can-Can* and *Kismet*. Moross and Latouche also won a Page One Award from the Newspaper Guild of New York, again for best musical, while various Donaldson Awards—soon-to-be-discontinued honors comparable to the New York Critics' Circle and Tony Awards—went to Latouche for both book and lyrics, the Eckarts for scenic design, Jonathan Lucas (who played Paris) for best male dancer, and the show as a whole for best musical. Even Eleanor Roosevelt put in a good word for the production in her "My Day" column, congratulating Latouche and Moross "for having done a clever and enjoyable play to music."[31]

But although the received wisdom holds that the opera garnered nothing but raves, several critics, including such influential voices as Brooks Atkinson (*Times*) and Virgil Thomson (*Herald Tribune*), expressed mixed feelings about the work. Negative reaction tended to target what several commentators regarded as a certain monotony in the musical flow, described by Thomson, as much as he appreciated the superiority of the orchestrations, as "insistently on the jiggy side," although Latouche similarly came under fire, at least from *Variety*, who stated that his "unevenly-metered oddly-rhyming lyrics never permit the singers or the audience to relax." Some also found the opera's whole concept somewhat pretentious or strained or, as concerned John Gassner (*Educational Theatre Journal*) later in the year, too much like a college varsity show.

Such differences of opinion prompted a number of follow-up reviews, mostly in the Sunday papers ten days after the opera opened, in which Brooks Atkinson and Virgil Thomson restated their reservations, and Richard Watts, John Chapman, and Robert Coleman reiterated their praise and countered especially the charge of pretentiousness. However, Chapman, who thought "show business should be show business, even at the Phoenix Theatre on Second Avenue," raised one objection himself, stating that the finale needed "a more rounding ending," and suggested that the piece perhaps conclude with a reprise of "Lazy Afternoon."

With such superb reviews and reasonably priced tickets compared to Broadway musicals, including a $4.80 top for Saturday evening performances, the show scored well at the box office, with sold-out houses for much of its limited six-week run. Roger Stevens and Alfred de Liagre quickly decided to transfer the production to Broadway, as they had hoped; and supplementing the Phoenix's initial investment of about $80,000 with some $38,000, they unveiled the show, in association with Hambleton and Houghton, on April 20, 1954, at the Alvin Theatre (now, the Neil Simon Theatre), a house only slightly larger than the Phoenix.[32]

Stevens and de Liagre presided over a few changes with regard to this move. Martha Larrimore already had taken over for Nola Day (Mother Hare) during the run at the Phoenix, but the producers now replaced Geraldine Viti with Shannon Bolin and eventually Charlotte Rae as Mrs. Juniper. Moross and Hershy Kay attended to the expanded orchestrations. But the most dramatic change involved a major rewrite of the work's final scene. As early as March 29, some two weeks after the opera's premiere, de Liagre had expressed discontent over the piece's ending, writing to Stevens,

> Despite your sabotaging comments that the present operatic duet ending was just dandy, I am trying to pursuade [*sic*] the boys to rewrite a better, gayer finale. Possibly Ulysses might return home paddling his weather-beaten boat all alone with the same figurehead as Act I, only now looking bedraggled and beat up. I think this could be quite funny but the chances of getting Touche and Moross to agree on *anything* strains my fanciest diplomacy.[33]

Some dissatisfaction with the opera's finale as voiced, for instance, by John Chapman, cited above, presumably prompted or reinforced such concerns. In any case, Latouche and Moross drastically abbreviated and revamped the finale, which now barely featured the Four Suitors, and which had Ulysses return with The Figurehead—after the Suitors exit—just as de Liagre suggested. These revisions included some new utterances for Ulysses, in which, "with persuasive male logic" (to quote the libretto's stage directive), he tells Penelope, "Here in your familiar eyes / Is all the wisdom of the wise"; and a reprisal of "It's the Going Home Together," first by Ulysses alone, then with Penelope, and finally with the entire cast "forming a glowing tableau as the show moves to its finale" (as also specified in the published libretto). This restructured finale not only sacrificed the intimacy and poignance of the original ending, with Ulysses and Penelope alone on stage, but imposed a certain sentimentality on what had been a more sober reconciliation. Indeed, the reprise of "It's the Going Home Together," as Erik Haagensen observes, brought Ulysses and Penelope back to where they had been early in the first act, subverting the work's principal dramatic trajectory.[34]

Given that the sewing bee music anticipated the original final duet, Moross further decided to write a new and shorter sewing bee episode so as to better prepare the return of "It's the Going Home Together," with a recollection of "Lazy Afternoon" (with new words) thrown in for good measure, and with Penelope's outburst remaining the only music from the original finale to stay essentially intact. The interweaving of earlier stated melodies in a finale accorded with traditional Broadway practice, but such cuts and pastes, devised if not necessarily staged during the production's off-Broadway run as evidenced in part by the original cast album, disturbed the opera's integrity as well as its architecture, making the whole denouement seem rather perfunctory and disjointed—changes, however, that, as Erik Haagensen suggests, seem to have been the price that the authors needed to pay in order to move uptown.[35]

The opera fared well on Broadway for a few months, with a feature article in *Life* magazine in late May providing a nice bump in ticket sales. But attendance dwindled over the course of the summer, and by early July the show had started operating at a loss, at which point Latouche and Moross, who had been earning a few hundred dollars each week from box-office revenue, had to waive their royalties by agreement. The production closed in the red on August 7, 1954, for a total of 173 performances including the 48 shows at the Phoenix. As with *Ballet Ballads*, for all the critical acclaim, the work failed to become a popular hit, although in 1981 agent Lucy Kroll, in a letter to producer Roger Stevens, imagined that had the opera not moved to Broadway, it might have "joined the ranks of *The Fantastics* [*sic*] long runs," a reference to the off-Broadway musical then some twenty years into its spectacular run of over four decades.[36]

In mid-April, while still at the Phoenix, the cast recorded portions of the score for RCA Victor, who released excerpts, alternately conducted by Hugh Ross and Ben Steinberg, on one long-playing record, with some jingly narration written by Latouche (and read by the production's Hector, Jack Whiting) to help stitch the fragmented parts together. Whereas the cover art of this release displayed the same Al Hirschfeld illustration used for the Phoenix and Alvin Theatre program books, one that depicted Ulysses surrounded by tempting sirens, when Elektra Records reissued this album a few years later, the cover art featured rather a photograph from the original production showing Helen and Paris ascending in the latter's hot air balloon. In 1997, RCA Victor reproduced the original Hirschfeld cartoon for their release of the recording on compact disc, with a booklet that confusingly provided the cast list from the Alvin Theatre production, including Charlotte Rae as Mrs.

Juniper, whereas Geraldine Viti sang the role on this recording, as intimated in the liner synopsis. Although long a treasured item by musical theater aficionados, this 1997 reissue elicited only a lukewarm response from critics David Parsons (*American Record Guide*) and Richard Traubner (*Opera News*). Fortunately, a tape of much of a live performance at the Alvin Theatre (possibly with Virginia Copeland as Penelope, Charlotte Rae as Mrs. Juniper, and Robert Zeller on the podium) also survives—an account whose zest and high spirits help explain, better than the commercial cast album, the production's enthusiastic reception.[37]

Additionally, in 1954, Random House published the libretto of the Broadway version, accompanied by prefaces by both Latouche and Moross and some photographs from the production. Latouche, who dedicated the volume to his friend Alice Bouverie, hired the young poet Frank O'Hara, then in dire financial need, to prepare the typescript; Kenward Elmslie later credited O'Hara for the publication's novel typography, specifically its mimicking of the score's melodic swoop as Paris descends in his hot air balloon:

It's a balloon
It's a bal
l
o
o
n . . .

However, in his long-hand draft, Latouche similarly attempted to replicate musical gestures in his calligraphy, suggesting that the Random House layout represented a collaboration between himself and O'Hara.[38]

Latouche's preface to the Random House publication not only discussed the opera, but offered some rare commentary with regard to the difference between poetry and lyric writing in which he argued that the "interior melody" of poetry "usually prevents it being set to music effectively," citing as an example the Shakespeare sonnets: "I have never heard them in any musical setting that did not detract from the originals. When Shakespeare intended his words to be sung, he wrote lyrics—lyrics which *are* most telling in a melodic framework." He similarly finds the "original mood" of such poets as Walt Whitman and Emily Dickinson "muted or distorted" by musical treatment. In contrast, "Lyrics are deliberately designed for music: they must adhere to a central idea, with a minimum of verbiage—except in those cases where complicated verbiage is used for a comic or violently emotional effect." All this seems partly by way of excusing, as he writes at the end of his preface, the "possible flatness of these lyrics (without the support of the ever-inventive Moross score)," and he suggests that readers who have not yet heard the music "make up your own score as you go along, and see what comes out."[39]

After closing on Broadway, *The Golden Apple* played successfully in Washington, D.C. (1954), Highland Park, Illinois (1955), and Houston (1955), but the work never established itself in any canon and enjoyed only sporadic revivals over the years, mostly by stock and amateur companies. In 1961, the nonprofit Equity Library Theatre brought the opera back to New York as part of a celebration of "great American playwrights," their selection of works made in consultation with Marc Connelly, George Freedley, and Thornton Wilder, who in 1967 told Jerome Moross that he "greatly admired" the opera. In 1962, the piece also appeared at the city's York Playhouse under the same director as that of the Equity Theatre production, Robert Turoff. Other notable revivals included those by Boston University (1974); York Theatre off Broadway (1978 and 1990); Light Opera Works/Pegasus Players in Evanston, Illinois (1995); 42nd Street Moon in San Francisco (2006); Shaw Festival in Niagara-on-the-Lake (in concert, 2006); Lyric Stage in Irving, Texas (2014); Musical Theatre Guild in Los Angeles (in concert, 2015); and Encores! at New York City Center (as a staged concert, 2017).[40]

From Jay Carmody's 1954 review for the *Washington Evening Star* to Nancy Churnin's 2014 notice in the *Dallas Morning News*, both of which thought the opera "irresistible," the work generally won a warm reception as it traveled around the country. The 1955 Houston production by Theatre, Inc., even proved something of a local sensation, occasioning an unusually thoughtful account of the score in the *Houston Post*, perhaps because written by its music critic, Hubert Roussel: "It is a score—all of one piece, conceived and executed with impressive intelligence and imagination. The rhythm, which is buoyant and anything but conventional; the harmony, which is free, modern and wide of modulation; the structural style, which bristles with impetuous counterpoint—these make up a texture which is absolutely novel and which offers the performers a singing line such as you have never heard before in this branch of the theatre."[41]

Admittedly, the York Playhouse's 1962 rendition, probably the highest-profile revival to date, received its share of negative reviews, with James Davis (*Daily News*) even wondering if the critics who gave the show the Critics' Circle Award had been "intoxicated." But the majority of critics covering even this production remained charmed, Frances Herridge (*Post*) stating that the work seemed "even more deliciously comic now than before," and Norman Nadel (*World-Telegram*) opining that at its best it deserved "more right to a place in the Met's repertoire than a couple of the operas in that institution's book." The York Theatre's 1990 revival similarly elicited good reviews from such seasoned critics as Stephen Holden (*Times*), Ken Mandelbaum (*Theater Week*), Rex Reed (*Observer*), and Michael Feingold (*Village Voice*), who pursued an intriguing comparison between the work and Gershwin's *Of Thee I Sing*, arguing that both had attempted "to make an American type of comic opera, merging the vaudeville esprit of the musical with the worldly-wise, politically aware panache of the European form. One might say the infrequency with which the works are revived is proof that they succeeded."[42]

For all this acclaim, the opera remained a novelty. Plausibly, the piece might have found a place in the American operatic repertoire, as did such more or less kindred Broadway operas as *Four Saints in Three Acts*, *Porgy and Bess*, and *Regina*; but perhaps because of its uncommon profile as, in Ken Mandelbaum's phrase, "a musical-comedy opera," *The Golden Apple* remained ignored by opera companies, indeed, hardly acknowledged as an opera at all.[43]

At the same time, "Lazy Afternoon," one of five numbers from the score published by Chappell (the others including "Goona-Goona," "It's the Going Home Together," "Store-bought Suit," and "When We Were Young"/"Windflowers"), attained widespread popularity, one of the very few operatic arias, along with several from *Porgy and Bess*, to become a jazz and cabaret standard—surprisingly so, considering that, much like "Summertime," which it vaguely resembled, the song hardly conformed to commercial expectations, even with Chappell tailoring some of the number so as to give it a more conventional shape. A song of seduction addressed by Helen to Paris, its highly poetic lyric, which after a fashion reflected Latouche's involvement with Eastern spirituality, features bucolic imagery suspended in time, all richly alliterative and assonant, as in the opening and bridge stanzas given below (note, in the first strophe, not only the soothing euphony of "[after]noon," "zoom[in]," "tu[lip]," "bloom[in]," "hu[man]," "view," and "two," and the subtle echo of "beetle bugs" and "tulip trees" in the phrase "not another," but the ingenious palindromic rhyme, "human" and "in view"):

It's a lazy afternoon
    And the beetle bugs are zoomin
    And the tulip trees are bloomin
    And there's not another human
                        In view
                        But us two....

A fat pink cloud hangs over the hill
    Unfolding like a rose
If you hold my hand and sit real still
    You can hear the grass as it grows.

Moross adeptly complemented this lush lyric with a sinuously descending vocal line supported by a static bass that hardly budges from one section to the next, although the harmonies shimmer as they alternate between suggestions of the Dorian and Mixolydian modes. Deemed by composer Vernon Duke "about as perfect an 'atmospheric' song as one can hear," the number, all in all, seems a bluesy American descendent of not only Satie and Debussy, as remarked earlier, but two classic French arias of seduction, Bizet's "Habanera" and Saint-Saëns's "Mon cœur s'ouvre à ta voix." A sampling of the legion of singers and instrumentalists who recorded the number includes Regina Belle, Tony Bennett, Jackie Cain (with Roy Kral), Marlene

Dietrich, Kenny Dorham, Joe Henderson, Shirley Horn, Hank Jones, Stan Kenton, Wynton Marsalis, Mabel Mercer, Helen Merrill, Lucy Reed (with Bill Evans), Barbra Streisand, Pat Suzuki, Cecil Taylor, and Sarah Vaughan. Marveling at the success of so "musically sophisticated" a song, critics David Jenness and Don Velsey attributed its popularity partly to its "hypnotic vocal line," but also its lyric, described as "perhaps the most purely imagistic of all classic popular songs, to be rivaled only by some of those in the singer-songwriter tradition, notably Joni Mitchell."[44]

The opera's vocal score, meanwhile, remained for many years unpublished, although available for rental through the Tams-Witmark Music Library. In preparation for an ultimately canceled concert performance of the opera at New York's Town Hall scheduled for May 1977 (in what would have been the last of a three-part series produced by Richard Grayson and John Bowab), Moross decided to reinstate the work's original concluding duet (although not the entire final scene), and revised the Tams-Witmark score accordingly, retaining the choral reprise of "It's the Going Home Together" only for the curtain call. That October, CBS aired the aborted Town Hall production on two thirty-minute episodes of the network's *Camera Three* program, with Sally Jo Anderson (Penelope) and Edward Evanko (Ulysses) performing the restored duet, and with Margaret Whiting (Lovey Mars) providing some narration. Starting the following year with the York Theatre's production at Parish Hall, stagings of the complete opera similarly adopted the original ending, typically with "It's the Going Home Together" appended for the curtain call as indicated in the revised score, although Texas's Lyric Stage chose the appealing alternative of concluding simply with the final duet.

In 2009, Alfred Music released the first commercial piano-vocal score of the complete opera. For this enterprise, underwritten by the Moross estate, Larry Moore, an expert in the restoration of Broadway musicals, conscientiously consulted the composer's manuscripts, the original orchestral parts, Hugh Ross's conducting score, and the Tams-Witmark rental score. Reconciling numerous discrepancies, the end result could be seen as incorporating aspects of both the Phoenix and the Alvin Theatre productions as well as some slight revisions made by the composer in 1977. The only outstanding textual issue remained Moross's decision to reinstitute just the very ending of the original finale as opposed to the entire scene, which arguably would provide a more musically unified and dramatically ample—although possibly too protracted—conclusion to a work whose denouement still seemed somewhat abrupt. Among other infelicities, as the finale now stood, the sewing bee episode prepared the reprise of "It's the Going Home Together" rather than the restored "We've Just Begun."

Despite the absence, until recently, of a complete recording and an available score, not to mention the dearth of professional revivals, the published libretto and the original cast album seemed enough to establish the opera as a favorite among such knowing chroniclers of the Broadway musical as Steven Suskin, Ken Mandelbaum, Ethan Mordden, Larry Stempel, and Thomas S. Hischak. Mandelbaum called the piece "perhaps the most neglected masterwork of the American musical theatre," and Stempel, "one of the most original, witty, and affecting of all American musicals." Mordden also lauded the opera for its "glowingly tuneful music" and "what may be the single most brilliant set of lyrics ever written for Broadway," an opinion with which Mandelbaum concurred. By some contrast, Mark Grant's history of the Broadway musical offered a more critical assessment, finding the work, for all its virtues, "dramatically inert, lacking narrative urgency and characterizations the audience can empathize with." But commentators more typically placed the onus on the audience for the work's limited success. "Maybe the public doesn't know its Homer well enough to appreciate Latouche's gloss on him, turning a Heroic Age into an era of entrepreneurs," wondered Mordden; and Mandelbaum concluded his study of flop musicals by writing, "Most of the shows in this book failed their audiences; it was the audience that failed *The Golden Apple*."[45]

Otherwise, critical commentary proved only occasional. In a seminal article on the opera, Erik Haagensen, among other keen observations, discerned the work's anti-imperialist subtext: "Written less than a decade after Hiroshima and Nagasaki, *The Golden Apple* employs the lightest of touches and the vocabulary of that most American art form, the musical comedy, to suggest the need for maturation of the American manifest destiny mindset." In a published guide to Moross's film score to *The Big Country*, Mariana Whitmer observed the debt of the composer's movie music to the techniques and styles cultivated in his earlier ballets and operas, including *The Golden Apple*. And in their dissertations, Pamyla Stiehl and James Rogers deemed *The Golden Apple*, like *Ballet Ballads*, a high point in the triangulation of dance, music, and word in the American theater, Stiehl focusing more on Hanya Holm's contribution, and Rogers underlining Moross's visionary aspirations, although Latouche obviously played as key a role as any with respect to this achievement.[46]

In 2015, PS Classics issued a two-CD release of the 2014 Lyric Stage production staged by Stefan Novinski and conducted by Jay Dias, with a cast of forty-three, including Christopher J. Deaton (Ulysses), Kristen Lassiter (Penelope), and Danielle Estes (Helen), and an orchestra of thirty-six. Stitching together sections of several live performances along with some studio work, this premiere release of the full-length opera held the promise of a new era of appreciation for the piece, beginning with the excellent liner notes, including an insightful essay co-written by Robert Edridge-Waks and the production's vocal director Deniz Cordell, which drew connections between the work and both ancient Greek theater and contemporary megamusicals, but that remained attuned as well to the opera's singular qualities: "It [*The Golden Apple*] is a sui generis work that exists in the past (its musical evocations of vintage song forms, its basis in ancient myth), present (its seemingly eternally trenchant social commentary—looking at matters of class, war, sex, science and the economy) and future (the collision of linear and picaresque storytelling, the holistic fusion of artistic disciplines, the purity of its design)." Cognizant of Latouche's prowess as a librettist, Cordell and Edridge-Waks noted, "Latouche provides daffy rhymes ('Oh Helen, Helen you can't betray us / You ain't gonna marry ol' Menelaus?'), bitter bromides ('Old men always do the shouting / Young men have to do the shooting'), and simple eloquence that speaks to deeper truths ('We don't get any younger / Everything ages but the heart's hunger'). To capture all of these things is a difficult enough task; to do it and rhyme so purely is downright Herculean."[47]

Whatever the recording's shortcomings, critics and listeners hailed the release as an expertly performed account of an opera widely regarded as "a lost masterpiece," although *Fanfare* magazine provided two reviews rather at odds, with Bill White deeming the work "a bit of a slog," and Barry Brenesal, "the greatest American opera ever written." But even here, among other points of accord, White and Brenesal agreed on Latouche's remarkable talent, White finding the lyrics "worthy of Lorenz Hart, Dorothy Fields, or Alan J. Lerner," Brenesal complimenting Latouche on his ability "to write simply, directly, but at times with unusually strong imagery: a kind of heightened speech that never gets in the way of the music.... These are evocative words that make one's ears sit up and pay attention."[48]

In his introduction to the 1954 published libretto, Moross himself lavished praise on Latouche, as discussed earlier in the context of *Ballet Ballads*. And yet the strife that beset their working relationship—as ticket sales to *The Golden Apple* plummeted over the summer and Latouche heard complaints about the unintelligibility of the words, he wrote in his journal, "Jerry [Moross] so obdurate about microphones!"—threw some doubt with regard to any future collaboration. Indeed, Latouche seemed relieved when in early 1955 the composer turned down the opportunity to work with him on a musical adaptation of Eugene O'Neill's *Ah, Wilderness!* For his part, Moross long had found Latouche exasperatingly "difficult." True, they had managed to reconcile differences in the wake of *Ballet Ballads*, and had Latouche not died so young—less than three years after the premiere of *The Golden Apple*—it seems possible that he and Moross might have collaborated again, although the composer's daughter believes not.[49]

Moross remembered Latouche warmly in any case. "He was my dearest friend and between 1939 and his death in 1956 we worked on many projects, two of which came to brilliant fruition," he wrote in May 1973 to Margaret Freeman Cabell, the widow of Latouche's mentor James Branch Cabell. And discussing popular music trends in April 1979 with Craig Reardon, he declaimed, "I happened, for one period of my life, to have worked with John Latouche, who was probably one of the greatest lyric writers that ever lived, and to have that kind of brilliance, you know, and now suddenly nobody knows how to write lyrics, and instead you get one phrase for a whole song sometimes. Oh, it's just too much!"[50]

19

Touche's Salon

During his final years, Latouche faced some discrimination and censure as a result of his inclusion in a 1950 handbook entitled *Red Channels: The Report of Communist Influence in Radio and Television*. Issued by the publishers of *Counterattack*, a right-wing newsletter, *Red Channels* cited 151 artists, journalists, and others, including such luminaries as Leonard Bernstein, Marc Blitzstein, Aaron Copland, Lillian Hellman, Lena Horne, Langston Hughes, Dorothy Parker, Artie Shaw, and Orson Welles, along with the alleged communist front organizations or activities with which each personage had or once had some association—information, much of it dated and misleading, and some of it simply wrong. The ten items listed under Latouche's name included his work for the Council on African Affairs, but mostly concerned either his support for Henry Wallace's 1948 presidential campaign or his defense of the civil rights of persons identified as communists or fellow travelers. In its preface, *Red Channels* disingenuously conceded that in many cases the persons profiled included unsuspecting dupes; but released in June 1950 just days before the start of the Korean War, the book stoked, as intended, fears of subversive control of the airwaves, and became a decisive factor in making it difficult if not impossible for those named to work for several years in radio, television, and film, among other negative ramifications.[1]

In later years, the publishers of *Red Channels* continued to single out Latouche in their *Counterattack* newsletter. The paper stewed, for instance, over the 1954 success of *The Golden Apple*, stating that although the show contained "no outright pro-Communist propaganda," it "does help Moscow and the Fifth Column here by its slick mockery of various aspects of American life. Moscow owes a vote of thanks to the many critics who have heaped praise on 'The Golden Apple.' "[2]

Fortunately, Latouche worked primarily in a milieu—that of Broadway—rather impervious to anticommunist hysteria, in large part due to the independence of theatrical producers, the anti-blacklist policies of Actors' Equity, and the rialto's general atmosphere of urbane tolerance. At the same time, both composer Earl Robinson and writer Gore Vidal recalled that the "much blacklisted" Latouche saw his work "kept off radio, TV and the movies." In light of his previous radio career, Latouche might well have otherwise gained a foothold especially in television. Indeed, much as he might have teased Vidal about the latter's television work—on one occasion remarking, "Whoever suspected that you would end up the [prolific Baroque Spanish playwright] Lope de Vega of television"—he thought highly enough of Vidal's teleplay *Dark Possession*, which aired on CBS's *Studio One* on February 15, 1954, to suggest that the two adapt the script as a full-length play.[3]

Latouche's inclusion in *Red Channels* surely led to increased scrutiny by the FBI, which apparently had been keeping tabs on him since at least since 1940, including recording allegations of communist party membership. (Neither *Red Channels* nor the FBI, incidentally, noted any activities on Latouche's part prior to 1940, doubtless because he came to wide public attention only with *Ballad for Americans* in late 1939.) On a trip to Washington in 1951, seated by the Potomac with his friend Harry Martin, Latouche observed "a small fat boy who plumped himself down on the shore in front of us, fishing ostensibly, but obviously vibrating his fat FBI ears in the breeze, trying to make sense of our chat concerning the creation of Adam, the indirection of Michelangelo, the significance of the Pentecostal fire, etc."[4]

As seen here, Latouche managed to keep a sense of humor about all this, but such recrimination and surveillance, in addition to curtailing work and travel opportunities, must have taken a personal toll. After lunching with Copland and Bernstein in June 1954, Latouche quoted Bernstein as saying, "I hear they've already built civilian detention camps for over a million people in Colorado," a suspicion that pointed to real fears among those targeted as communists or communist sympathizers. And for someone like Latouche, already suffering from panic attacks, mild paranoia, and other disorders, such anxiety no doubt exacerbated his fragile psychological and physical health.[5]

As in the past, Latouche sought some repose through yoga, breathing exercises, and psychotherapy, including at least consultations with Martha Jaeger, a Jungian analyst best remembered today for treating Anaïs Nin. Jaeger drew on the work of Otto Rank, the Austrian psychiatrist known especially for his studies on creativity, and in a 1954 diary entry Latouche referred, in this context, to Rank's concept, impressed on him by Jaeger, that "the artist must first use his creative concept on himself, and then the artifacts can take care of themselves." Reflected Latouche,

> Self-pity aside, I begin with such a *lack* of any nexus in me: Mother's primitive and unlettered personality my earliest slide-rule: (I leave out the psychotic tragedy of my father's personality, since it cannot be considered anything but an empty horror in anybody's language.)
>
> I shall have to painfully reconstruct that infantile vacuum in my consciousness, trying to stay pliable enough to allow it not to crystallize at the present state.

In 1951, Latouche also underwent some tests with the noted German psychiatrist Max Rinkel, under whose supervision he reportedly took mescaline, and who reassured him that a mental collapse seemed unlikely. Characteristically, Latouche became personal friends with both Jaeger and Rinkel, as he had with his doctors Max Jacobson and Andrew Salter.[6]

Assertions by Earl Robinson to the contrary, Latouche furthermore set out to clear his name by voluntarily providing information about his association with the political left to the FBI. Initially he appeared at the bureau's New York offices on April 19, 1954 (testimony summarized in a report to national headquarters), and then sent two affidavits to the FBI, the first dated January 27, 1956, the second, May 18, 1956, less than three months before his death. These documents have been cited earlier in the context of Latouche's attraction to certain aspects of communist ideology, his sympathy for Republican Spain, his involvement with the Council on African Affairs, his preoccupation with "spiritual" concerns, and his dedication to personal freedom and democratic principles; but these same materials allude to other matters as well, including his disenchantment with Wallace and the Hollywood Ten, and his many activities alleged to be inconsistent with communism, as evidenced by the negative criticism of communists, dating back to his college days, toward some of his work.[7]

Pressed in his meeting with the FBI in 1954 about the politics of Hanns Eisler and Ella Winter, both present at a party he had attended in Hollywood, Latouche stated that he assumed Winter (the wife of the exiled blacklisted writer Donald Ogden Stewart) a communist. But he essentially avoided naming names. When asked about a benefit concert held at his apartment for the Voice of Freedom Committee—a group founded in 1947 and headed by Dorothy Parker to protest the firing of progressive radio commentators—he simply said, for instance, that he had lent out his place to an acquaintance named Stella whose surname he did not know (although this might have been his friend Stella Adler, someone active in the committee whose last name he knew very well). Some two months after this encounter with the FBI, he wrote in his diary about his ongoing "attempt to get my political onus cleared up without sacrificing my integrity as a thinking human being."[8]

Although Latouche's 1954 FBI interlocutor, impressed with his "voluntary appearance" and "straightforward" demeanor, saw no need for further investigation, this particular show of cooperation might not have sufficed to win him a security clearance, given the fact that despite repeated plans to visit Europe, no such trip materialized, which suggests some difficulty in obtaining a passport, a common enough hardship for someone in his position. Perhaps this helped prompt the two 1956 affidavits. In any case, had he lived longer, he likely would have faced questioning from the House Un-American Activities Committee during their sweeping investigations into the New York theater community during 1957 and 1958; tellingly, during these later inquiries, HUAC asked producer Norris Houghton about his association with the deceased Latouche, suggesting that the latter remained associated with subversive or treasonous activities.[9]

What Latouche thought during this time about communism or, for that matter, the Soviet Union—a topic not raised in any of his FBI testimonies—remains largely undocumented. His surviving diaries rarely allude to such matters, but at no time did he ever show particular sympathy for the USSR, especially as compared to many of his leftist friends (including his partner during these years, Kenward Elmslie). In his historical novel *The Golden Age*, Gore Vidal described Latouche as a "Marxist," but in his memoirs, he more ambiguously wrote that he "pretended to be a Communist." Vidal's friend, socialite Joseph O'Donohue, similarly stated, although less affectionately, that Latouche "thought he was a Communist," saying, as if by way of explanation, that he would "go to dinner parties in a black shirt rather than in evening dress." In a privately recorded discussion with Max Jacobson from May 1949, Latouche in fact sounded distinctly critical of both the Soviet Union and Karl Marx, lauding America's "belief in the individual as a solution rather than the mass personality of, first, Germany, and then Russia," and extolling Ralph Waldo Emerson over Karl Marx, remarking, with regard to "Self-Reliance," an 1841 essay by Emerson, "It is a very interesting essay which used to be the mainspring of every young American. As a matter of fact, it is still one of my mainsprings."[10]

However Latouche regarded the Soviet Union and communism, his diaries and letters of the period plainly reveal discontent with the state of the world, his own country very much included. He spoke of Washington, D.C., as a place where "hysteria hangs grimly in the air choking one as insidiously as smog," and of "the high paranoic [*sic*] voice of Walter Winchell lauding [General Douglas] MacArthur (that dismal pro-consul), braying warnings to the nation at large calculated to sharpen its fears into incoherent frenzies." In 1950, he wrote to Vidal, "As the Hydrogen Follies unfolds, everyone babbles and rearranges patterns and falls down and hopes and develops attitudes and wreaks tiny revenges and follows miniscule aims and mediocrity is still as valuable as Tel and Tel and dear me, it's after five a.m. and I have to go to bed." The following year, he similarly told another friend, Harry Martin, "But the horror of this era becomes plainer as the atomic sunbursts light up the twilight: the interchangeable personalities thrust up their conformist banners, brazen and strident in their numbers since only in their numbers do they have any personality among them. 'Conform or die out!' The cry is tapped out in a billion typewriters by a billion bureaucratic fingers . . . 'Be ashamed of your thoughts, your destiny, your sex.' " In reference to an unpleasant phone conversation he had in June 1954 with comedian Ronnie Graham, he stated in his diary, "Emotional result of McCarthy hearings—everything private has to be necessarily aired publicly for a while. Absolutely revolting." And a month later he noted "how difficult it is even for intelligent people to concentrate in this tedious epoch." Such sentiments and concerns drew him to friends like Vidal and Martin, and, moreover, found an outlet in his work of these years, sometimes rather overtly, as in *Candide*.[11]

These extant letters and journal entries from the 1950s rarely mention concerts, movies, or shows, the few exceptions including T. S. Eliot's 1948 verse drama *The Cocktail Party*, which he saw on Broadway in 1950 ("a very great play, I stoically admit"); his friend Carson McCullers's 1950 dramatization of her novel *The Member of the Wedding*, seen both on Broadway and on tour in Boston; an all-Vivaldi recital at Town Hall in 1950 (the Italian composer "finally receiving his due after all these years"); a New York Philharmonic concert in 1950 that included Virgil Thomson's Second Symphony ("a brightly assertive excursion into personal magic"); and the 1953 movie *Money from Home* with Dean Martin and Jerry Lewis ("boring beyond any belief. The smug, debauched Martin, the frantic epicene movements of the once-talented Lewis—another Hollywood victory").[12]

On the other hand, these same writings often refer to books, from studies on religion, spirituality, sexology, anthropology, and folklore to poems, plays, biographies, and all manner of fiction, including ghost stories, detective mysteries, and pulp novels. After visiting the Old Corner Bookstore in Boston in 1951, he confessed to purchasing "a senseless jumble" of books, including among other things poetry by Whitman, Anna de Noailles, René Char, and Paul Éluard; two novels in French by Balzac; *The Devil's Share* by the Swiss cultural critic Denis de Rougemont; essays by the British philosopher Bertrand Russell; *Modern Sex Life* by Edwin Hirsch; and anthropologist Ruth Benedict's study of Native American life, *Patterns of Culture*. "If I read even one I'll surprise myself," he wrote in his diary, although a few days later, he told Harry Martin that he was reading the Whitman poems, Russell essays, and Balzac novels, saying,

> It's a shame you cant read him [Balzac] in his own language yet; although he survives very well in English, unlike Proust (who is actually clearer and far more impressive in translation than in the original, since the French language finds its truest genius in concentrated and direct sentence structures, and is resistant to the meandering style so natural to the English tradition), although de B[alzac]'s intensity as a creative source would survive rendering into Esperanto, still he (and Baudelaire and Rimbaud among the poets) employs the sounds as well as the sense of his tongue to gain his fullest affects. Oh, to hell with literature.

At the same time, Latouche generally recorded just brief reactions to only a small sampling of boundless readings, including *The Bad Seed* by William March ("appalling"); *Time Must Have a Stop* by Aldous Huxley ("cerebral and boring: not Huxley with an edge"); *The Tunnel of Love* by Peter De Vries ("trivial and rather appalling"); and a book (probably *The First and Last Freedom*) by Jiddu Krishnamurti ("compact and provocative").[13]

As indicated by some of these readings, Latouche maintained an interest in the occult, including a new friendship with the Viennese-born researcher and writer about paranormal phenomena Hans Holzer (1920–2009). Biographical information about Holzer remains sketchy, but he reportedly arrived in New York, after studies at the University of Vienna, just prior to the Anschluss of 1938, and continued his education at Columbia University. Holzer dabbled in the theater, providing sketches for the 1955 off-Broadway revue *Safari!* and writing the script and incidental music for an off-Broadway comedy, *Hotel Excelsior,* which coincidentally opened on the day of Latouche's death, August 7, 1956. But he became increasingly engrossed in especially the study of ghosts, often organizing séances with such psychics as Ethel Johnson-Meyers; and in the years after Latouche's death, he published voluminously on the subject, including well-known inquiries into the so-called Amityville Horror.[14]

Latouche and Holzer met through their mutual friend, the medium Eileen Garrett, over lunch at the Hotel St. Regis sometime in the early 1950s. Their shared interests in the theater and the occult forming a natural bond, Latouche soon after invited Holzer, along with medium Ethel Meyers and actress Future Fulton (thought "very psychic" by Holzer), to a party at his penthouse apartment, including an after-dinner séance. "Picture my surprise," recalled Holzer, "when it was John [Latouche] who went under first, showing he had trance abilities also." (On this occasion, Holzer reported, Latouche heard from an eighteenth-century ancestor, a "Breton lady" who "wanted to manifest and reassure him in his work and quest for success.") Other adventures followed: in early 1956, on the first anniversary of the gruesome murder of the Russian-born financier Serge Rubinstein, Holzer and Latouche, at the invitation of the Rubinstein family, brought Meyers to the deceased's Fifth Avenue home, where she conducted a séance in the slain man's bedroom.[15]

According to Holzer, several months after Latouche's death, Ethel Meyers, while in a trance during a "routine investigation of a haunted house," channeled greetings to him from the deceased lyricist; from that time on, Latouche's spirit regularly advised him about his career—or so he claimed—through Meyers and other psychics. Holzer further informed his readers that the lyricist had "adjusted to his sudden departure from the physical world . . . and that he was still creating works of art for the stage, Over There. . . . I don't know when the celestial Board of Directors will want to send John back to earth in his next incarnation, but for the moment at least, he seems to be a free spirit doing his thing."[16]

Ghost hunting with Holzer and Meyers seemed only one of endless social activities for Latouche, who continued to amass friends as vigorously as ever. After what appears to have been a particularly busy day, he wrote to Kenward Elmslie, "I had lunch with [writer] Lilla van Saher, dinner with [actress] Rosika [*sic*] Dolly, supper with [singer] Liz Doubleday and [conductor] Thomas Schippers, cocktails with the niece of [Irish dramatist] Lady Gregory (a tweed-covered dike), and phone calls with [painter] Mrs [Margarett] McKean, and I wish I was dead." Drinking brandy or bourbon neat (he liked the Four Roses brand), chain smoking English Ovals, Latouche frequently caroused till the early morning hours—dining out, attending parties, nightclubbing, playing bridge—after which he would sleep, in the nude as his preference, for a few hours, with perhaps a nap during the day, sometimes in his bathtub. "He would work and talk all day, and drink and talk all night," observed Lord Kinross, who came to know Latouche in 1956, "carrying along with him, irresistibly, his small court of adherents." In his biography of Vidal, Fred Kaplan similarly wrote, "Sleeplessly, from dusk to dawn, at openings, parties, dinners, bars, clubs, he [Latouche] was part of a New York nightlife that dressed for dinner, partied in tuxedos in Harlem, embraced high musical culture and the latest jazz, and for a while seemed to have revivified its own version of the high-kicking spirit of the 1920s. That Latouche was usually broke made no difference."[17]

Latouche often hosted parties and receptions himself, especially after taking up residence in his spacious penthouse on East 67th Street in 1951. He became particularly known for his annual Twelfth Night celebrations at which, as composer Jack Beeson recalled, "flush with money, or without any, he had presents for the guests." Illustrious figures in the arts, strikingly diverse in their ethnicity as well as their sexual and aesthetic orientation, often could be found at Latouche's, although so too could such future stars as Jack Kerouac, Frank O'Hara, and Larry Rivers, with some of the lyricist's newer friendships discussed below.[18]

John Bernard Myers, a frequenter of Latouche's soirées, actually discerned two distinct sets among the lyricist's friends, ostensibly actors and entertainers on the one hand and poets and painters on the other, a duality that Latouche himself embodied. "I seem to fit right into the varnished sophistication of certain evenings," wrote Myers; "luckily Latouche has a serious side and another group of friends who are gifted and dedicated. But here, too, the socializing and drinking goes on until dawn." This social network, incidentally, overlapped considerably not only with that of Leo Lerman, as stated earlier, but of composers—and companions—Samuel Barber and Gian Carlo Menotti, as the mention of Thomas Schippers above might suggest.[19]

Only a few depictions of Latouche's parties survive. In his correspondence, Carl Van Vechten, for instance, mentions a gathering at Latouche's in 1949 at which Juanita Hall, soon to win a Tony Award for her performance as Bloody Mary in *South Pacific*, performed at 2:30 a.m., after which "two of the Negro boys took off their clothes and danced marvellously." And in his history of New York cabaret life, James Gavin tells of a Latouche "party game in which guests took turns describing, in ascending order, their five best sexual experiences. Tennessee Williams detailed bondage scenes, and Carol Channing's eyes widened as she expressed her love for '*biiiiig* men, with big torsos and biceps—football players.' Kaye Ballard and Eudora Welty could be seen tiptoeing toward the door before their turns came."[20]

The most knowing description of "Touche's Salon" took the form of a poem so titled by Kenward Elmslie; commissioned for the revue *Taking a Chance on Love* and published in 2000, the poem portrays a 1954 bash at Latouche's penthouse, where, among the foie gras, quiche, Beluga caviar, and vodka, the goings-on include Ned Rorem "horny" for "top dollar hustler" Steve Reeves; Vernon Duke and Larry Rivers "making out in the john"; Gore Vidal "trashing" Truman Capote; Jane Bowles sitting on Lena Horne's lap (having "just kvetched" to Jean-Paul Sartre, "Sartre's full of crap!"); Marlene Dietrich reciting Rilke; duo-pianists Arthur Gold and Robert Fizdale playing Satie; and Virgil Thomson dancing the cha-cha with a lampshade on his head. Writes Elmslie further,

Meet Jack Kerouac. Humpy and available.
His novel *On the Road* is unreadable. And unsalable.
John Cage is sober, Tennessee [Williams] loaded.
Better not ask how his last flop show did.[21]

Latouche entertained not only at home, but on the town at restaurants like Johnny Nicholson's trendy Café Nicholson near the Queensboro Bridge, as well as at clubs and cabarets, notably, Spivy's Roof on East 59th Street (until it closed in 1951); the Bon Soir on West 8th Street in Greenwich Village; and the Blue Angel on East 55th Street, mockingly called "Juliet's tomb" by Latouche on account of its "sombre decor" and owner Herbert Jacoby's "funereal voice." This cabaret world, where several of Latouche's friends held the stage as singers and comedians, intersected with his private as well as his professional life, as such nightclub entertainers as Kaye Ballard, Carol Channing, Bibi Osterwald, and Charlotte Rae also figured prominently in his shows.[22]

Among any group, Latouche always stood center stage. "In a gathering of witty stars," recalled composer Ned Rorem, "the room never really caught fire until 'Touche' emerged." He ostensibly inherited some of his formidable gift of gab from his mother, whose "aimless and beguiling chatter" he found both exasperating and endearing, although in his case, his talk was marked by enormous wit and sophistication, and often lubricated with drugs and alcohol. In *The Golden Age*, Vidal attempted to reproduce Latouche's badinage, having him say, for example, about a life-size plaster sculpture of a llama in his apartment at the Chelsea Hotel, "I call this my llama in sheep's clothing. The sculptor does only one work every five years. Like clockwork. He rolls what he calls his worms of plaster of Paris with his own hands and then, slowly, builds up his figures. The llama took him most of the thirties to complete. As you can see, very prewar in feeling. Better than Brancusi. For me, he is the Donatello of Macon, Georgia." Latouche seems to have taken his role as wag and farceur rather seriously, rehearsing and retelling stories for maximum effect, and according to Leo Lerman, "thinking up puns" during a private hearing of Copland's *The Tender Land* prior to the opera's premiere.[23]

Not everyone found Latouche as winning as did Vidal and Rorem. The writer Patricia Highsmith, for instance, thought him "horribly, sickeningly flippant," as mentioned previously, and socialite Joseph O'Donohue similarly bristled at the way he would "try to dominate conversation." Even admirers could find him at the least taxing. An acquaintance of Vidal, for instance, wrote with regard to Latouche's discourse, "I'm not sure I could survive a long siege of it, for either my mental capacities would shrivel away (what few there are) being blanched in the reflective glory of his verbal acumen, or the constant assaults upon my ears would soon leave me deaf and dumb." And Lord Kinross similarly recalled an evening with Latouche at the Bon Soir in which "John's talk grew more vehement and his manner more challenging and his eyes more consuming. Mercilessly he nagged at me, bent on bullying me into agreement with some premise, alcoholically-inspired, on the Meaning of Life.... 'You know it,' he hammered away at his point, 'you know it. You know it.' But the mists of incoherence became such that I took in barely a word of what he was saying. We were the last to leave the restaurant." Still, however relentless his talk, cafe society and the art world widely considered him one of New York's most brilliant wits and raconteurs.[24]

A few anecdotes also speak to his sheer zaniness. Cafe proprietor Johnny Nicholson, who "adored" Latouche and thought him "one of the champion personalities," recalled, for instance, a late night at Spivy's Roof with Latouche and several others followed by an excursion to Harlem for spareribs during which, as dawn approached, Latouche began "talking about his hometown and how the dogs used to bark in the morning. Before you knew it, he was on his hands and knees like a dog, howling, showing us. It was enchanting." Ralph Weeks, the Vermont handyman who worked on Latouche's country home, similarly remembered the time Latouche invited him to stay for drinks after work and how he got "roaring drunk," eventually dancing on a table and throwing money about. Writer Phoebe Pierce Vreeland, a high school friend of Truman Capote, related perhaps the strangest incident:

> LaTouche was just marvelous. Once I met him at the Blue Angel. For some mysterious reason he had a fried egg on his hand. I said to him, "How did you get into this situation, LaTouche?" He said, "Honey, I have no idea." So I said to the waiter, "Waiter, could we have a plate, a napkin, and a fresh drink for the gentleman?" So the waiter came. He slipped the fried egg off LaTouche's hand and put it on the plate, handed him the napkin, and LaTouche said, "My, I ad-mire that." He was just a darling man.[25]

A friend, although never a lover, from 1944 to the end of Latouche's life, Ned Rorem (b. 1923) became one of the many younger artists to acquire a high regard for the lyricist, writing that "a hilarious single supper" with him (along with similarly memorable encounters with Jean Cocteau, Paul Éluard, and Pavel Tchelitchew) provided "a contact, a generosity, a participation, a heat, a curiosity, an indelibility which permit me to say I knew and know and will always know them well." As with Minna Lederman, Latouche reminded Rorem of Marc Blitzstein, describing each as "the most irresistibly quick man in the world," at least "when on his best behavior." Latouche and Blitzstein, in turn, each liked and admired Rorem, both attending a concert of his songs at the home of Alma Morgenthau in late 1952, with the three men going out for beers together afterward.[26]

Rorem's reminiscences of Latouche preserve a few examples of the latter's celebrated wit. He recalled, for instance, how the lyricist commented, on hearing that the strikingly handsome young composer copied music for Virgil Thomson, "Really? I didn't know people who looked like you ever did anything." Another time, noting the scarcity of African Americans in a Greenwich Village bar, he quipped to Rorem,

"Où sont les nègres downtown" ("Where are the downtown Negroes?"), a bilingual pun on poet François Villon's famous line "Mais où sont les neiges d'antan" ("But where are the snows of yesteryear?").[27]

Something of a rarity among Latouche's artist friends, Rorem further commented on the lyricist's work, offering this ultimately tentative assessment:

> He was one of a kind, not a chip off the old American assembly line, and, as [Oscar] Wilde said of himself, put his genius into his life and his talent into his art. The art as I saw it never quite jelled, or maybe it just wasn't my sort, being a sort of preface to Sondheim (the way Marc Blitzstein was an afterword to Weill). The theater pieces with Jerry Moross had a jazzy panache, *Ballad for Americans* was patriotic to a turn, *Cabin in the Sky* still has original lyrics, and the libretto for Douglas Moore's *Baby Doe* remains a model for today's composers to lust for. But that's not enough.... Touche (as everyone called him) mingled with the upper crust but catered to the middlebrow. That, plus hard living, sullied his craft—his point of view. Or did it?[28]

About the time that Latouche became acquainted with Rorem, he also befriended two immigrant composers who had settled in New York in 1941, namely, the Australian Peggy Glanville-Hicks (1912–1990), and her British husband, Stanley Bate (1911–1959). Glanville-Hicks and Bate had met in the early 1930s while attending London's Royal College of Music, where they studied with Ralph Vaughan Williams; both further worked with Nadia Boulanger in Paris after lessons, for Glanville-Hicks, with Egon Wellesz in Vienna, and for Bate, Paul Hindemith in Berlin. Latouche probably encountered the two expatriates through Glanville-Hicks's good friend and for a short while lover Paul Bowles, who remembered the Australian composer as "an interesting person, who had much to say about music, about most things, in fact," and her husband as "rather jealous" and "difficult." Latouche assisted Glanville-Hicks and Bate financially, including providing bail money for the latter on an arrest for disorderly conduct and homosexual solicitation; Glanville-Hicks reciprocated by assisting Latouche in mundane chores. Glanville-Hicks's diaries reveal in general a fair number of dates with Latouche both before and after her divorce from Bate in 1949, with an October 25, 1946, entry, "Touche Temper," ostensibly alluding to one of the lyricist's familiar tantrums.[29]

Meanwhile, Latouche's writer friends of this later period included playwrights Patricia Coleman and Tennessee Williams and novelists Jack Kerouac, Truman Capote, and Gore Vidal. Of these, aside from Vidal, he seemed closest with Coleman (1918–1965), a lesser author of plays and television scripts; in correspondence with his friend Harry Martin, he referred to her as "filled with her usual urgent problems," in this particular instance some apparently involving her collaborator, actress Louise Dowdney, for the letter occasioned another bilingual sally that parodied the opening of the song "Louise" ("Every little breeze seems to whisper 'Louise' / Birds in the trees seem to twitter 'Louise' ") and that alluded as well to Coleman's excessive drinking: "Every little *crise* [French: crisis] seems to whisper Louise; the rise of D.T.'s [delirium tremens] seems to spell out Louise."[30]

Latouche seems to have met Jack Kerouac (1922–1969) in 1949 through Robert Giroux, the eminent bisexual editor who knew Latouche from their years together at Columbia, and who in 1950 published Kerouac's first book, *The Town and the City*. Latouche's relationship with the dashing and sexually adventurous Kerouac, some eight years his junior, seemed very occasional, documented principally by a postcard mailed from the former to the latter in early 1950, but one, signed "affectionately," that suggests some familiarity nonetheless, and that opens in a characteristic vein: "Naturally I'm never in—this is the Hydrogen Age, and I'm trying to devastate everyone over an area of 50 miles. Not very successfully, but I've developed a kind of nuisance value that has its points." Moreover, in February 1953, Kerouac told Carolyn Cassady about an evening with Latouche (whom he knowingly and whimsically identified as the "author of lyrics of [Nat] King Cole's *Strange*, and author of *Ballad for Americans* sung by Paul Robeson, and of a few tunes of tin pan alley, and of *Cabin in the Sky* sung by Ethel Robeson Robinson Waters [*sic*]") in which his host read aloud a short story, "The Monster of Dakar," by Kerouac's friend Allen Ginsburg: "It [the Ginsburg story] sounded terrific to me but he [presumably Latouche] said it stank and I really dont know what everybody means by opinions when the facts are more interesting." And as seen above, Kerouac appears in Kenward Elmslie's remembrance of Latouche's salon circa 1954. Whether Kerouac paid any special attention to the launching of *The Golden Apple* that same year, the jazz singer Mark Murphy included the opera's "Lazy Afternoon" on a 1986 album of songs he imagined Kerouac would have enjoyed.[31]

Latouche made a pivotal contribution to the life of playwright Tennessee Williams (1911–1983) by introducing him to Frank Merlo, Williams's partner from 1948 until Merlo's death in 1963. On an excursion to see Buffie Johnson in Provincetown during the summer of 1947, Latouche and Merlo, lovers at the time, visited Williams, the recently acclaimed author of *The Glass Menagerie*, and someone new to Merlo, but presumably not to Latouche, given that he and Williams shared several close friends, including not only Buffie Johnson but Paul and Jane Bowles and Carson McCullers. "La Touche was going through some sort of nervous crisis involving his mother, I think," recalled Williams, "and he suddenly took off, leaving Frankie Merlo on the Cape," after which Williams and Merlo spent a passionate night making love on the beach. Latouche in time purchased a Buick Roadmaster from Williams, and Elmslie would jest—perhaps having heard this from Latouche—that the lyricist traded Merlo for the car, although in fact, Williams and Merlo did not become lovers until their paths crossed again in late 1948, and Latouche seems to have acquired the car still later, in the early 1950s.[32]

Latouche felt some professional rivalry with Williams, his envy over the latter's "lucky career" inspiring an "anxiety-drawing" penned in early April 1949 at five in the morning (see Figure 41); but he seems to have deeply admired his work all the same. In Vidal's *The Golden Age*, Latouche invites some friends to a performance of *A Streetcar Named Desire* soon after its December 3, 1947, opening ("Latouche is a friend of Irene Selznick, the producer," explains one of them), and while taking them to a postperformance party with Williams in attendance, he expresses excitement for what seemed "a total realignment of the sexes as demonstrated onstage at the Ethel Barrymore." In the wake of some particularly harsh reviews of Williams's *Camino Real* in 1953, Latouche, along with eleven other notables, including Vidal, the Bowleses, and Willem and Elaine de Kooning, signed a "Statement in Behalf of a Poet" urging support of a play deemed by the signatories "romantic, intensely poetic and modern." For his part, Williams reportedly liked the "Southern aspect" of Latouche and his mother, whose singing of regional songs he appreciated. But he and Latouche do not appear to have been that close, at least to judge from the fact that, among other things, Williams and Merlo did not know that *The Golden Apple* had opened "till we heard the shouting."[33]

Another distinguished writer, Truman Capote (1924–1984), who had seen *Cabin in the Sky* while in high school, mingled with the Latouche crowd as a young man, so he and the lyricist must have known each other early on. However, Latouche remains remembered in the Capote literature almost wholly on account of an anecdote concerning the writer's popular novella *Breakfast at Tiffany's*, published in 1958, two years after Latouche's death. In a 1968 interview with *Playboy* magazine, Capote stated that he based the book's heroine, Holly Golightly, on a German refugee who arrived in New York at age seventeen at the start of World War II, and who later disappeared into Africa; and that after the war, Latouche, back from his expedition to the Belgian Congo, told Capote that he had seen a "wooden head carving of Holly" in a "jungle village," Capote adding, "It's all the evidence of her existence that remains." Capote adapted this particular incident in the opening pages of *Breakfast at Tiffany's* as bartender Joe Bell shows the narrator photographs of an African carving deemed "the spit-image of Holly Golightly."[34]

Although scholars dispute the notion that Capote patterned Holly Golightly after any one person, the *Playboy* interview at least raises the question of how Latouche would have been able to recognize the putative Holly Golightly's visage in an African carving, and what this might say about the whole matter. The fact that Latouche was so deeply immersed in Europe's exiled bohemian and artistic community gives credence to the notion that some German, very possibly German-Jewish, émigré served as the prototype for Holly Golightly; certainly anyone resembling Holly would have been at home in Latouche's social circle, a circle with which Capote himself "fit in," according to a high school friend, and one that very likely helped shape his sensibilities.[35]

Latouche developed a particularly intimate relationship with Gore Vidal (born Eugene Louis Vidal, 1925–2012); according to Elmslie, the two had even been lovers early in their friendship. Adopting "Gore" from his mother's maiden name, Vidal grew up in Washington, D.C., the son of a well-connected family, his maternal grandfather a U.S. senator, and his stepfather, by a still later marriage, stepfather as well to Jacqueline Bouvier Kennedy. After Latouche's death, Vidal casually recalled knowing him "a dozen years," which would date their acquaintanceship back to 1944; but they certainly had become friendly by 1947, the year before Vidal established his reputation with *The City and the Pillar*, a novel, like Truman Capote's coeval *Other Voices, Other Rooms*, that proved a landmark in terms of its frank homosexual content.[36]

Especially close in the late 1940s and early 1950s, Vidal and Latouche admired each other enormously. "I hadnt realized how really fond of you I'd become…," wrote Latouche to Vidal in 1950, "you are developing temperament, in spite of your doubts about it—your quality is alive, and these metropolitan zombies are *so* deep down under." That same year, on purchasing a stately Georgian home, Edgewater, in Barrytown, New York, in the Hudson River valley, Vidal even designated an upstairs bedroom as Latouche's own on account of his frequent visits there. Describing Latouche, along with Dawn Powell, as "the personification of Manhattan, particularly its nightside," Vidal in later years recalled how the "short, stubby, blue-eyed, wildly witty" lyricist "talked and talked and kept everyone excited and laughing"; long after his death, Latouche appeared in Vidal's novel *The Golden Age* as an alluring "Pied Piper" who led a "train of admirers… from dark place to dark place until he arrived at the elegant door to the Blue Angel."[37]

Declaring him "probably the best lyricist in the history of the American musical," Vidal esteemed and likely drew something from Latouche's work as well; *The Golden Apple*, at least, presumably helped inspire Vidal's novel *The Judgment of Paris* (1952), making his telegram to Latouche on the occasion of the opera's premiere all the more ironic: "My lawyers are preparing a suit for your plagiarism of The Judgement [*sic*] of Paris. Yours for a clean America. Homer Vidal." The two also sought opportunities to collaborate. Mention already has been made of Latouche's interest in adapting a Vidal teleplay for the stage, and of Vidal's possible involvement in *Tamborito*, but the two furthermore entertained the notion of working together on a musical based on Max Beerbohm's romantic farce *Zuleika Dobson* (1911). In addition, they drafted a few original screen ideas, including "The Girl of the Golden East," "Love Is a Horse Named Gladys," and "The Devil May Care," this last securing them a $2,500 advance from their friend Alice Bouverie in exchange for a 10 percent share of any profits, with the ever-strapped Latouche, according to one source, pocketing the entire amount.[38]

The surviving scenarios for "The Girl of the Golden East" and "Love Is a Horse Named Gladys" combine low comedy and absurdist farce, not unlike *Tamborito*. "The Girl of the Golden East" involves a love affair between a gangster's moll and a cowboy, with their wedding ceremony temporarily interrupted by a gun battle between gangsters and cowboys. The more developed "Love Is a Horse Named Gladys," which reads like a short story, concerns the picaresque adventures of a character called, like their friend, Jane Bowles, and a retired New York police horse, Gladys, placed in her care, including an after-hours affair at the Bronx Zoo between Gladys and a zebra, and Gladys's triumphant apprehension of America's most wanted criminal. Vidal apparently submitted these or some such collaborative treatments to his literary agent Audrey Wood, who responded during the summer of 1950, "I'm very fond of each of you [Vidal and Latouche], but having read the three ideas for screen-originals you recently submitted to me, I don't think either of you are taking the picture business too seriously these days.... Each of these ideas seems very trivial, seems very forced, seems very phony to me.... Do either of you two ever go to see a motion picture?"[39]

Around 1950, Vidal introduced Latouche to his dear friend Alice Bouverie, to whom Latouche, too, subsequently grew particularly attached. "Your Mrs. Bouverie has asked me to lunch," Latouche wrote Vidal early in 1950, "which was highly agreeable, she being brightly tentative about the world.... I have enjoyed seeing Alice B. very much, as I said: that is probably... the only thing I have enjoyed the past months." Indeed, Bouverie—whom Latouche described to another friend as "a witty and profoundly vague woman who is certainly more brilliant than her tycoon-daddy was, and certainly twice as *flexible*"—became one of the most cherished friends of his later years.[40]

Thought by a historian of the Astor clan to be "probably the most genuinely wasted and tragic member of the dynasty," Ava Alice Muriel Pleydell-Bouverie, née Astor (1902–1956) belonged to one of New York's most patrician families, one whose fortune derived from trade and real estate, including ownership of such luxury hotels as the St. Regis and the Waldorf-Astoria. Bouverie's father, John Jacob Astor IV, a direct descendant of the late-eighteenth-century German immigrant who founded this dynasty, died aboard the *Titanic* in 1912, with most of his vast fortune inherited by his son Vincent (whose third wife, Brooke Astor, became a popular socialite), but with Alice nicely provided for as well. Growing up mostly in England, Alice forged an unconventional path of her own, cultivating friendships with many British artists. By the time Latouche met her, she had been married four times: to an émigré Russian prince, Serge Obolensky; to Raimund von Hofmannsthal, son of the Austrian poet Hugo von Hofmannsthal; to a British journalist, Philip Harding; and to a British architect, David Pleydell-Bouverie. She problematically often became romantically involved with homosexual men; both Harding and Bouverie were primarily homosexual, as was the British choreographer Frederick Ashton, with whom she had an extramarital affair in the 1930s and to whom she remained very devoted.[41]

Thought by Latouche to be "like a more attenuated Virginia Woolf," the tall and slender Bouverie graciously made Marienruh, the manor house that she and her first husband had built in the late 1920s on the Astor grounds in Rhinebeck, New York, available to the lyricist and many other of her friends; wrote Leo Lerman, "It's like the dream prewar English country houses—endless nannies, dogs, friendly servants, flowers everywhere, wonderful food 'created' by a great chef, such privacy, space, and fun—and so many books and beautiful things and your shoes and clothes all cleaned and pressed every day and breakfast in bed or on the terrace, which looks out over the Hudson—and scones for tea at elevenses (but nobody is down that early save I)." Marienruh became for Latouche a welcome retreat, as did the country homes of such other friends as Vidal, John Hammond, and Libby Holman.[42]

For a period, Latouche and Bouverie—who shared Latouche's nocturnal habits, one of their many bonds, like their enjoyment of games and attraction to the occult—reportedly became lovers, but at the very least fast friends. "In the city, the two of them would go from one smoky club to another...," recalled Vidal. "In one very dark club... Latouche returned from the lavatory and presented her with the chain to the toilet. She often wore this chain, usually wound around a ruby-and-emerald necklace." Assisting Latouche financially, including helping to underwrite his film company, Aries Productions, Bouverie also welcomed his boyfriends into her life, as discomfiting as that might have been, for by several accounts she hoped to marry Latouche and perhaps divorced Pleydell-Bouverie in 1952 with that intention in mind. Wrote Jane Bowles to Libby Holman in February 1951,

> He [Latouche] has been drinking like a tank lately, emptying bottle after bottle all through the night. You've seen him do it; I think that his situation with Alice [Bouverie] has been a strain. I think she would like to marry him and he is probably tempted though ashamed because of her wealth and position. Also there is his other love life [presumably Harry Martin] who would be crushed by the marriage, so Touche thinks. None of this really exists to me but I repeat it to you because you are interested in Touche. I like Alice more and more though she is tedious beyond belief. It is just so very hard to listen to her. She talks and talks and one is conscious only of the strain.

Allegedly aggrieved by Latouche's neglect, Bouverie drifted apart from him somewhat over time. As early as September 1952, the society pages reported that their "romance" had "waned." But the two remained inordinately fond of each other, and apparently only family obligations prevented Bouverie—to whom Latouche dedicated the 1954 published libretto to *The Golden Apple*—from attending the Central City premiere of *The Ballad of Baby Doe* on July 7, 1956, less than two weeks before she died of a heart attack on July 19. Latouche even set about planning a memorial service for her, a project halted by his own death on August 7.[43]

Throughout these same years, Latouche also cultivated a similarly warm friendship with the writer Doris Julian, who seems to have aided him at times as some sort of assistant. In turn, Latouche offered her guidance with respect to her work on an aborted musical, *Be My Guest*, for producer Perry Watkins—a show, about a white magazine executive and a black nightclub singer who trade places, that at one point was to feature music by Duke Ellington and Billy Strayhorn. Described by writer

Coleman Dowell as a blonde beauty, Julian also seems to have fallen for the lyricist, at least as suggested by a set of "Three Sonnets for a Miniature Lion" written in August 1955 and dedicated to Latouche, with the final lines of the first poem, "And Then You Came," implying some sexual intimacy:

> You came—warm-breathed, strange creature of the night,
> Your mouth touched neck and cheek, found once its mark,
> Paused fleetingly. But ever since, my sight
> Has pierced the ice-clad prison of the dark
> And sought you out across all distant place,
> Needing for survival, your instant grace.[44]

Latouche and the artist Margarett Sargent McKean became close during this later period as well, although he surely had known her for a number of years as Jane Bowles's friend and sometime lover. From an elite Boston family—she could claim the artist John Singer Sargent as a distant cousin—McKean (1892–1978), after studies in Florence, Boston, and New York, earned some praise as a portraitist but stopped painting in midcareer, devoting herself rather to gardening. "An old friend of John [Latouche], possessed with much of his surging energy and devouring need for people," observed Lord Kinross on meeting McKean at the premiere of *Baby Doe*, "she was a woman of passionate enthusiasms and downright ideas, with a rare sense of quality and fastidious critical values." Like Latouche a heavy drinker, she also found in the lyricist someone against whom she could match wits. "There is no doubt that her [McKean's] wit is keener than anyone's in New York," wrote Jane Bowles to Libby Holman, "but it is frightening more than it is amusing because it seems to operate only as a kind of smokescreen for an endless plot which she herself ignores."[45]

In her biography of McKean, the painter's granddaughter Honor Moore relates an anecdote that exemplifies the sort of raillery and high jinks for which McKean and Latouche became reputed. Merrily traveling by car to Bouverie's upstate home, Latouche, McKean, Bouverie, and Latouche's boyfriend Harry Martin, impeded by a snowstorm, returned to the lobby of the Gladstone Hotel in Manhattan, where they continued their carousing. Writes Moore,

> Touche began a wild monologue in which he told the story of every Christian martyr, miming the fate of each. Everyone was laughing. Margarett could not keep from laughing, laughing until tears rolled down her cheeks. "Stop! Stop!" she protested as if the next blasphemous vignette would send her to hell—she was, after all, a Catholic! Finally, drunk and laughing, she got up for another drink and fell to the floor. In a flash, Touche put his foot on her large fallen torso and raised his right arm heavenward as if holding a sword aloft. "Saint George and the Dragon," he said.[46]

Latouche apparently met and began an affair with Harry Martin, then a junior at St. John's College in Annapolis, Maryland, in the spring of 1950, falling deeply in love with the young man, as evidenced by a series of ardent letters that occasionally ran parallel to his libretto to *The Golden Apple*, as in a reference to "the you in me and the me in you." "At times," he wrote to Martin in October 1950, "everything translates itself into you: someone mentions a house—I think, will he enjoy joining me there; someone speaks of a landscape—I think, he would move so exactly in it; someone reads a passage from a book—I think, can I retain this wisdom long enough to reflect it for him? So on and so on." "Sometimes I think this spring will not be bearable without you," he wrote again in May 1951. Latouche framed his love for Martin, as for Vidal, against his melancholic dismay with the world, as in this letter from May 1950: "You seem to generate a certain freedom in me—I've always had it, rather, but you are an alternating current which makes it function truly, makes it move both of us (for we will only move equally) toward serenity, toward the world as it is, rather than the imaginary Gehenna most people are stumbling about in nowadays, each locked in his solitary darkness, peopling that darkness with a host of private phantoms." Latouche nicknamed Martin "Lion" and himself "Lamb," the two of them forming a "peaceable kingdom."[47]

Tall, handsome, and athletic, Harry Martin grew up in Queens, New York, and served as a medical orderly in the navy before attending St. John's on a basketball scholarship. An aspiring painter, he considered dropping out of college; but Latouche helped persuade him otherwise, expressing regret that he himself never completed his degree, something he still contemplated doing in the hopes that that might help structure his chaotic life. So for a while, Latouche and Martin conducted their romance long distance, with the latter frequently spending weekends in New York.[48]

After graduating in 1951, Martin moved in with Latouche, who, according to Lord Kinross, "in Socratic fashion" taught the younger man "to live and to seek human values, to discover and to develop himself. This influence, I knew also, had its destructive side, since John [Latouche] was dominating in his friendships and, moreover, lived at a turbulent pitch such as few human beings can sustain for long." After some "crazy and fun and wild" months, Martin, finding life with Latouche "impossible," decided to pursue his art studies in Paris, where Latouche continued to support him monetarily and counsel him from afar about life and art, observing in some recent drawings sent him, for instance, "an exuberant talent still with insufficient technique and restraint implicit in them." Some advice in another letter included the following:

> So please, brave Lion, draw and draw and draw the human figure; objectify it, dissect it; forsake your own image to find it; untrap your reflections from a thousand mirrors. Rembrandt was the Lincoln of the self-portrait, and find out what you look like and what everybody looks like and then

> the abstractions of *that* reality cannot be surpassed by any unformed mystique that has not made up its mind about anything except leading its own private life of the hillside you sent me than I am in Piet Mondrian's uncluttered spatial dimensions. Painting is not a form of prophecy; and our world is cluttered and cobwebbed and I want to know about all of that. In front of me is a tiny conch shell, pale brown, with wonderful black runes all over it; that shell knows more about abstraction than Kandinsky ever tickled out of his brush. I want to know what the conch shell is all about—God help me, not with MY ubiquitous ideas on what naturalism [is], but it's [*sic*] ideas. Painting is just another way of looking inside and outside at the same time; it's a mismosh [*sic*] of canvas and pigments and turpentine and Damer [read: Damar] solutions and crosshatching and chiaroscuro and whatever else that comes to hand that is not abstract, but cries out: Re-create me in another image.[49]

By the time Martin returned to New York, Latouche had a new living companion, Kenward Elmslie. But Martin, who started driving a taxi to supplement his income as an artist, remained part of Latouche's most intimate circle, establishing ties with not only Elmslie but such other close friends as Howard Griffin (1915–1975), a poet known for his probing published conversations with W. H. Auden; and Elmslie's childhood pal and Harvard schoolmate Gerrit Lansing (b. 1928), then working in publishing but eventually a respected poet in his own right. Lansing, who recalled the extremes of Latouche's "incredible generosity" and his often alcohol-induced "elemental rages," even credited the lyricist—whom he regarded as "a man of the streets" in contrast to the "rather rarified Englishness" of his Harvard background—with helping to make him a poet.[50]

Martin, in turn, introduced into Latouche's world an impoverished and obscure although later famed painter just returned from Paris, Ellsworth Kelly (1923–2015), who helped Martin paint the walls of Latouche's apartment gold. Kelly welcomed the encouragement he received from both Martin and Latouche—the antithesis of the reactions of Frank O'Hara and Robert Rauschenberg, who thought his boldly colored geometric paintings "too European"—and he additionally enjoyed their *joie de vivre*, recalling late in life some examples of Latouche's "humor" and "wonderful spirit." On one occasion, the lyricist, eyeing a mattress on the floor of his studio, said to him, "Oh God, this mattress is telling me all kinds of things. What went on on this mattress?" And at a lunch he once hosted, Latouche surprised the shy young man by saying, "Ellsworth, why don't you entertain these people? Tell them about yourself!"[51]

Latouche liked organizing excursions with these young gay artists, including out-of-town visits to the homes of wealthy friends scattered around the Eastern seaboard. A carnival photograph taken at Coney Island showing Latouche, Martin, Lansing, and Elmslie as gangsters in a getaway car, with Latouche naturally in the driver's seat, documents one such outing (see Figure 48). Latouche also arranged trips with a skeptical Martin to Richmond to behold Lady Wonder, the nationally renowned horse reputedly able to type out answers with her head, and to western New York to spend time at Lily Dale, a leading spiritualist center.[52]

Also introduced to Latouche by Martin, John Patrick Douglas Balfour, 3rd Baron Kinross—better known as Lord Kinross—provided a rare profile of this coterie in his travel account of his 1956 trip to America, *The Innocents at Home* (the title a play on Mark Twain's *The Innocents Abroad*). Having met Martin as a passenger in his taxi, Kinross and the young artist struck up a friendship to the point that the former moved out of his hotel and into Martin's fourth floor walk-up in a "slummy tenement" on York Avenue on the East Side. Of Scottish peerage and Oxford educated, the homosexual Kinross, an expert on Egyptian and Turkish history, would dedicate his travel book to Martin, for which the latter provided illustrations.[53]

Describing Martin as "a blend of disillusion and zest, of sensitivity and toughness, which I found sympathetic," Kinross distinguished him, Lansing, Griffin, and Kelly—all "relatively poor and outwardly unconcerned about money"—from "hipsters" and "the 'beat' boys" as follows:

> For their spirit of protest was positive: it was based on ideals. Gerrit [Lansing] was at heart a serious scholar. Howard [Griffin] had a deep love of literature. Harry [Martin] was seeking to find himself as a painter. Ellsworth [Kelly] had already done so. Their values were European, though, paradoxically, they hardly knew Europe. They would not conform. Yet they were not of the breed who, as Harry once put it to me, are 'beat' and declare that nothing matters and then go on to *make* nothing matter. They were neither negative nor destructive. I was contented among them.

Kinross further shed a somewhat ambiguous light on the relationship between Martin and Latouche. He recounted one incident, for example, in which Martin, while driving Latouche's car home cross-country after the premiere of *Baby Doe,* lost all his cash in a crap game, after which he wired the lyricist for more money "due to a large and unexpected outlay for car repairs," a falsehood that showed Martin capable of taking advantage of Latouche. Kinross also reported that, wearied by Latouche's harangues and diatribes, Martin facetiously would refer to him as "St. John," sarcastically alluding on one occasion, for instance, to "other revelations from the gospel according to St. John." At the same time, Martin stayed devoted to Latouche, spending the lyricist's final days with him in Vermont; indeed, he became the last person to see him alive.[54]

The circumstances surrounding Latouche's sudden death, including accusations of foul play, so unhinged Martin that, at Kinross's invitation, he left for England soon after, but he eventually returned to New York and resumed driving a cab. In 1958, John ("Jack") Hays Hammond Jr. (1888–1965), an old friend of Latouche who long had taken an interest in Martin, invited the painter to move to his castle in Gloucester, Massachusetts, where the two, according to Gerrit Lansing, discreetly conducted an affair, and where Martin became curator of the Hammond Castle Museum. (Born into a wealthy mining family, Hammond, an important inventor in the field of radio transmission, had built the castle in the late 1920s as a home, laboratory, and repository of his collection of ancient and early modern artifacts.) After Hammond's death in 1965, Martin departed the castle, but remained in Gloucester, where Lansing too had settled, and where, among other things, Martin taught English and art at a preparatory school before his death in 1984 at age fifty-seven.[55]

Kenward Elmslie (b. 1929), Latouche's principal companion for the last five years of his life, came from a prominent family; his father was the son of a British judge, and his mother, the daughter of the Hungarian-Jewish-American newspaper magnate Joseph Pulitzer, making Elmslie the beneficiary of a sizable income, something he felt, in light of his socialist convictions, guilty about; indeed, he made a point of living modestly and downplaying the Pulitzer connection. A musical theater aficionado and aspiring lyricist, he early became enamored with the work of Ira Gershwin, Oscar Hammerstein, and Lorenz Hart, but especially Brecht and Latouche, whose *Ballad for Americans, Cabin in the Sky, Beggar's Holiday* (the Boston tryout of which he attended as a freshman at Harvard), and *Ballet Ballads* (which he saw in New York) he admired for their "innovative" and "visionary" qualities. That many of Latouche's shows flopped only seemed to serve "as a vindication of sorts—John, magic survivalist, the greatest lyricist in the world."[56]

After graduating Harvard in 1950, Elmslie moved to Cleveland as an intern for the interracial Karamu House, and persuaded its director Benno Frank to produce *Susanna and the Elders* and *Willie the Weeper* from *Ballet Ballads* on a fall 1951 triple bill that, as noted earlier, also included, sandwiched in between, a new work of Elmslie's own with black composer J. Harold Brown (using his pseudonym J. Harl Bron) about the judgment of Solomon, *Song of Solomon*, later described by Elmslie as "pretty lousy ersatz Brecht-Latouche." While in Cleveland for the performance, which he attended on September 23 in the company of actress Mildred Smith, Latouche initiated an affair with the tall and bespectacled lyricist some fifteen years his junior, for whom *Ballet Ballads* represented, as he wrote Latouche, "a symbol or goal or standard, a sort of artistic ideal that at times perplexed me, but more often gave me a sense of sureness that there were boundless and bountiful frontiers that were being ignored by the other writers. And the result of this belief was the creation of a phantom personage that I gave your name to, a personage that watched over my work and tried to keep it from descending into banality, dullness, falseness, cheapness." At Latouche's invitation, the twenty-two-year-old Elmslie moved to New York in 1952 in order to live with him. "It was exciting, but scary," recalled Elmslie, "this idol falling for *me*."[57]

"A reserved young man with a quiet wit, sensitive perceptions and a promising talent," according to Kinross, "sociable, well-mannered without being mannered, with a hint of a British accent," as described by poet Ron Padgett, Elmslie found himself not wholly at ease in Latouche's world. "Touche, as his sophisticated bohemian friends called him, was a charismatic charmer with a complex love life I, silent pimply worshipful youth, was a recent addition to," remembered Elmslie. "I called him John, primly. Touche sounded too fancypants." Rather naïve about sex, and given to monogamy, Elmslie now faced a bed partner who took pleasure in light bondage and erotic games, and who, moreover, juggled various lovers simultaneously. However, Elmslie tended to keep whatever dissatisfactions he had to himself, and as with Theodora Griffis and other former partners, Latouche once again found communication with the often withdrawn young man difficult. "Ken [Elmslie] is so gifted, so developed in many ways," he wrote in his journal in 1954, "that this *trapped* quality in him is more poignant than in ordinary personalities, although God knows it's acute with such personalities as well (and they lack the capacity for expression which helps mitigate the private agonies of people like Ken—and like myself, for that matter).... Even someone as close to me as Ken (and no one is closer) could not penetrate through the distance."[58]

Latouche nurtured Elmslie's ambitions as a writer, collaborating with him on some lyrics. He also introduced him to composer Donald Fuller, with whom Elmslie wrote a musical play about a tennis match in the Caribbean, *Thirty-Love* (completed 1955), a concert rendition of which, narrated by Latouche and directed by Herbert Machiz, was given at the Martha Graham Studio in 1955. In addition, while working on *The Ballad of Baby Doe* with Douglas Moore, Latouche helped bring Elmslie together with Moore's own protégé, composer Jack Beeson, with whom Elmslie initiated a fruitful partnership with an opera about the American evangelist Aimee Semple McPherson, *The Sweet Bye and Bye* (completed 1956, and revised 1958), although their greatest success, *Lizzie Borden* (1965), lay further ahead. For his part, Elmslie aided Latouche monetarily, including investing in both Aries Productions and *The Golden Apple*.[59]

During the summer of 1953, Latouche and Elmslie purchased a country home for themselves in the small town of Calais (pronounced CAL-us) in north-central Vermont, an area somewhat familiar to Latouche through his friendship with Helvetia Perkins, a sophisticated and politically progressive divorcée who lived in nearby East Montpelier. Latouche no doubt had been acquainted with Perkins since the early 1940s through her long and sometimes intensely romantic friendship with Jane Bowles, with whom in 1943 she discovered the East Montpelier farmhouse that subsequently served not only as her home but as a vacation spot for many of her friends. In 1953, Perkins introduced Latouche to a local newspaper columnist and food writer Louise Andrews Kent (1886–1969), better known by her pen name Mrs. Appleyard, whose daughter Elizabeth ("Kenty") Kent Gay (1913–1985) helped find him his Calais home. Only several years earlier a working dairy farm, the property included a large tract of mostly wooded land, with a small farmhouse, cowshed, brook, and secluded meadow—a gorgeous parcel of forested terrain with eagles and many varieties of wild flowers; Elmslie purchased the buildings, and Latouche, some additional acreage (see Figure 50). More than three hundred miles from New York, The Eyrie, as Latouche christened the place, offered a remoter, wilder, and, relative to its size, more affordable property than the sorts of country homes in Connecticut and the Hudson River valley owned by several of the lyricist's well-to-do friends.[60]

Latouche and Elmslie set about renovating the place. A local handyman, Ralph Weeks, remodeled the farmhouse and cowshed, built a grape arbor, and partially blocked a stream in order to form a pond; Weeks's wife, Elsie, stitched patchwork curtains; and Latouche scoured the area for furnishings and planted a vegetable garden. The lyricist also characteristically took an interest in Weeks's work as a dowser, the mysterious art of locating underground materials, and he returned to New York with a divining rod himself in an attempt to find water underneath the pavement outside his home on East 67th Street. Antiquing or gardening or just gazing at the land—on Christmas Eve 1955 he wrote to his mother, "The countryside is incredibly lovely—all in white velvet, with a sheer cloudless blue sky going straight up like a backdrop behind the rolling hills"—Latouche seemed to find, at least at times, some contentment and calm at The Eyrie that eluded him elsewhere.[61]

Latouche also cultivated friendships with some of his Vermont neighbors, including the spinster folk artist Bessie Drennan and her two widowed sisters, who operated a family hotel in Woodbury; he commissioned paintings from Bessie, and invited all three sisters (although only two attended), along with Helvetia Perkins, Louise Kent, and Elizabeth Gay, to attend a performance of *The Golden Apple* in New York, purchasing a steel blue taffeta dress with a beaded bodice for Gay to wear for the occasion: "He was creating a fairy tale magic for her," remarked Gay's daughter, Olivia. Latouche reportedly also socialized in Vermont with his friend, writer Mary McCarthy, who similarly vacationed in the area, and who, stated Latouche, "moved like a cobra," at least according to the highly unreliable Coleman Dowell, who confessed at being "appalled" by the "thin-lipped and predatory" McCarthy after meeting her at The Eyrie.[62]

To judge from Louise Kent and daughter Elizabeth Gay's cookbook à clef, *The Summer Kitchen (Mrs. Appleyard's, of course)*, in which Latouche appears as Geoffrey Toussaint—and at one point as Emperor Geoffrey Toussaint the First—the lyricist enjoyed simply whiling the time in Kent's kitchen with the locals, spouting such aphorisms and wisecracks as "all old ladies look like either [Albert] Einstein or Thomas Jefferson." Kent and Gay plainly took delight in cooking for Latouche, whom they described as a "scatterer of gifts, who travels in a haze of electric frying pans, chiffon stoles, circus tickets for entire families, sets of china, books on psychic phenomena, albums of long-playing records—all wittily inscribed, all flying away from him by centrifugal force." Published in 1957, following Latouche's death, *The Summer Kitchen* bore the dedication, "for John Treville Latouche / one of his many kindnesses to the authors was reading the manuscript of this book," and included a menu prepared especially for him ("High Breakfast with a Genius") that consisted of orange-banana whip, grilled short ribs, guacamole, and tutti-frutti, the authors assuring the reader, in ostensible homage to Latouche, "All these three [*sic*] dishes are *terribly healthy*. They also taste good."[63]

After Latouche's demise, Kenward Elmslie purchased from the lyricist's mother his partner's share of the Calais property, which he renamed Poet's Corner. As he continued to divide his time between New York and Vermont, Elmslie forged his own notable career writing the words to popular songs (including the minor hit "Love-Wise," with music by Marvin Fisher), musicals (including *The Grass Harp* and *Lola*, both with music by Claibe Richardson), and operas (including Jack Beeson's *Lizzie Borden* as stated, but also Ned Rorem's *Miss Julie*, and Thomas Pasatieri's *The Seagull*, *Washington Square*, and *Three Sisters*), not to mention a spate of stories, plays, poems, and translations admired by such discriminating readers as John Ashbery, W. C. Bamberger, John Bernard Myers, Ron Padgett, and Michael Silverblatt. "Let's face it," Elmslie stated in 1990. "Creatively, I'm a floozie who plays the field."[64]

The sheer variety of Elmslie's work—of which the recorded anthologies *Ben Bagley's Kenward Elmslie Visited* (1982) and *Palais Bimbo Lounge Show* (1985) gave some indication, as did the musical revue *Lingoland* (2005)—suggested an indebtedness to Latouche, whom Elmslie always acknowledged as a mentor. "I learned how to cut from him," he once remarked. "I went through his original scripts to *The Golden Apple* to see what he had eliminated. It was my model for how to write a musical." Latouche's influence also could be seen not only in the whimsy and fantasy of Elmslie's work, but in literal borrowings, as in the use, in his song "Schlock 'n' Sleaze R & B," of the rhyme "cobra" and "no bra" ("Goona-Goona" from *The Golden Apple*). Like Latouche, too, Elmslie appreciated the "chasm between poetry and song lyrics," naming Langston Hughes, Ogden Nash, Frank O'Hara, and in the single instance of "Glitter and Be Gay" Richard Wilbur as among those relatively few poets capable of writing "a really good song lyric," and asserting that "the one time song lyrics and poetry totally combined was back in Elizabethan times, thanks to Thomas Campion."[65]

Around the time Latouche started living with Elmslie, he discovered a whole new circle of young artist friends through gallery owner John Bernard Myers (1920–1987), a habitué of Latouche's parties, as already mentioned. A native of Buffalo, New York, Myers moved to Manhattan in 1944, while still in his early twenties, in order to work for Charles Henri Ford's journal of the arts *View*, and soon came to know Latouche, on whom he developed something of a crush. In the late 1940s, Myers, a puppeteer, started his own marionette theater in cooperation with Tibor de Nagy, a recent Hungarian emigrant, and in 1950, the two, with financial support from artist Dwight Ripley, established on East 53rd Street an art gallery called Tibor de Nagy. Following the lead of such gallery owners as Kirk Askew, Peggy Guggenheim, Julien Levy, and Betty Parsons—all familiar figures to Latouche—Myers championed contemporary art, in his case mostly the work of young painters born in the 1920s, including Nell Blaine, Helen Frankenthaler, Jane Freilicher, Grace Hartigan, and

Larry Rivers. This group of artists, whatever their debts to Willem de Kooning and Jackson Pollock, whose paintings they admired, tended to work in a more playful and figurative style, often with ties to early French modernism.[66]

Gore Vidal's recollection that during this period he and Latouche would "read aloud from gallery catalogues," finding "nothing more wonderfully loony and pretentious than a painter explaining his greatness," suggests that the lyricist would have found the unpretentiousness of many of the artists sponsored by Myers refreshing. In any case, he quickly allied himself with the Tibor de Nagy gallery, attending an exhibition of Freilicher's paintings there in 1952 and purchasing at some point a sculpture by Larry Rivers for his apartment, where on March 1, 1956, he hosted a reception in conjunction with a showing at the gallery of Dwight Ripley's work. He more generally socialized with de Nagy's stable of artists both in New York and in the Hamptons, a community of villages about two and a half hours from Manhattan on eastern Long Island that served as an art colony, and where Elmslie acquired Westhampton beachfront property in 1954.[67]

In the very early 1950s, Myers further introduced Latouche to several poets also born, like most of his young painters, in the 1920s, including the close-knit group of John Ashbery, Kenneth Koch, Frank O'Hara, and James Schuyler. Myers championed these poets through both his literary serial *Semi-Colon* (1953–1956) and the establishment, with his partner, stage director Herbert Machiz, of the Artists' Theatre (also 1953–1956), which operated off Broadway and produced noncommercial theater that depicted, in the words of Machiz, "the irony with which contemporary man must view a world where everything has become incredibly difficult to understand." Discussing his decision to create a literary journal and a theater company alongside his gallery work, Myers explained that "the poetry and plays helped to enhance the climate in which we could breathe."[68]

In a brief 1962 discussion, Myers dubbed Ashbery, Koch, O'Hara, and Schuyler as constituting—along with some other poets, including by this time Kenward Elmslie—the "New York School of Poetry," largely citing as their defining attribute not much more than "a sharp distaste for literary pretentiousness," which distinguished them, argued later critics, not only from such high modernists as Pound and Eliot, but from such Beat poets as Allen Ginsburg and Gregory Corso. "Unlike the Beats," stated Mark Silverberg, for example, "the New York School poets were not interested in offering a new (more progressive, liberated, hip) culture but rather in working with American culture as they found it—exposing, playing up, and camping up its quirks, absurdities, and odd (queer) mannerisms."[69]

No doubt recognizing kindred sensibilities, Latouche took a lively interest in these poets about ten years his junior. As James Schuyler recalled, he, Ashbery, Koch, and O'Hara, all in New York by 1951, began frequenting Latouche's apartment, which led, in the summer of 1952, to the *Presenting Jane* film project with the gay members of this core group—John Ashbery, Frank O'Hara, and James Schuyler—along with painter Jane Freilicher and cameraman Harrison Starr, as discussed earlier.

Returning to New York from a weekend shooting the film in East Hampton, Ashbery and Schuyler began their comic novel *A Nest of Ninnies* (published in 1969), whose offbeat tone seems redolent of the unfinished film short. Meanwhile, O'Hara's "Day and Night in 1952," originally entitled "The Golden Apple of Juno," and written that summer in East Hampton, would seem cognizant of Latouche's *The Golden Apple*, then still awaiting its premiere.[70]

That fall, Latouche hosted a legendary soirée at which Ashbery, O'Hara, and another young poet, Barbara Guest, presented their work before a group of about forty. Guest read some short poems that reminded Schuyler of a Kurt Schwitters collage; Ashbery, a poem, "He," that put Elmslie in mind of one of Cole Porter's catalog songs; and O'Hara, a long poem, "Easter," whose "scabrous violent language" variously stunned and outraged auditors. Later that same year, at least O'Hara and Ashbery also attended a party at Latouche's in honor of editor Sonia Orwell, the widow of George Orwell, that occasioned the meeting of O'Hara and Ned Rorem. Latouche furthermore became involved in the February 25, 1953, debut of the Artists' Theatre at the Theatre de Lys in Greenwich Village—a quadruple bill consisting of Tennessee Williams's *Auto-Da-Fé*, James Schuyler's *Presenting Jane*, Frank O'Hara's *Try! Try!: A Noh Play*, and Kenneth Koch's *Red Riding Hood*, all under the direction of Herbert Machiz; *Presenting Jane* included clips from Latouche's unfinished film short of the same name, while *Try! Try!* (about a love triangle involving a returning veteran, an earlier version of which had premiered in 1951) featured music by Latouche and sets by Larry Rivers. Although the event proved too fringe to attract mainstream coverage, the critic John Gruen remembered *Try! Try!* as particularly "thrilling."[71]

Described by Ashbery as "a nice man," and by Schuyler as a "marvelous librettist, lyricist and general man of good humor," Latouche became especially close to O'Hara (1926–1966), whom he hired to prepare, as mentioned, the typescript of *The Golden Apple* for its 1954 publication. Through O'Hara, Latouche might have met the young composer Morton Feldman (1926–1987), who at any event apparently fell within the lyricist's orbit in the early 1950s, for in a sketchbook from that time Feldman started work on an operatic adaptation of André Gide's novel *Strait Is the Gate*, projected to have a libretto by O'Hara and sets by Frederick Kiesler, all to be directed by Stella Adler and "presented" by Latouche. "Such friendly daydreaming," states Ryan Dohoney about this venture, "evinces a close friendship that brought Feldman into O'Hara's circle of young poets and painters," one that "would serve as the composer's first and most enthusiastic audience," although in this instance, the particular combination of O'Hara, Kiesler, Adler, and Latouche points more specifically to Latouche's world than to O'Hara's.[72]

In his lunch-hour cityscape "A Step away from Them," written on August 16, 1956, the day after Jackson Pollock's funeral, O'Hara honored the recent and untimely deaths of not only Pollock but V. R. ("Bunny") Lang and Latouche as well—Lang of Hodgkin's lymphoma on July 29, Latouche of a heart attack on August 7, and Pollock of a car accident on August 11—in four eloquent lines:

First
Bunny died, then John Latouche,
then Jackson Pollock. But is the
earth as full of life was full, of them?

Commenting on this poem, O'Hara's friend Joe LeSueur, who described Latouche as "the kind of cosmopolitan New Yorker whom one who is new to the city dreams of meeting," drew distinctions between O'Hara's relations with each of these three deceased, especially in light of Pollock's belligerent homophobia: "Bunny [Lang] was the only one he [O'Hara] knew really well.... Frank [O'Hara] hardly knew the kind and thoughtful Touche, and Jackson Pollock he knew even less well.... It is, then, Jackson Pollock the artist who is eulogized along with Frank's great and cherished friend Bunny Lang and his new friend John Latouche." James Schuyler similarly evoked Latouche in his poem "Beautiful Funerals" (1971), in which the lyricist "hands out / his smile extending" to some imagined celestial gathering of the recently deceased Libby Holman and other departed souls. "Beautiful Funerals" and especially "A Step away from Them" keep Latouche's name alive for many readers of poetry who otherwise know nothing about him.[73]

After Latouche's death, Elmslie maintained the tradition of the former's Twelfth Night parties, the old circle of friends eventually expanded to include artist-writer Joe Brainard, Elmslie's romantic partner from 1963 until Brainard's death from AIDS in 1994, and such poets as Ron Padgett, Bill Berkson, and Ted Berrigan, as well as painters Alex Katz and Andy Warhol. And an artistic reunion of sorts occurred on October 15, 2003, with a concert, "The New York Poets," by the New York Festival of Song featuring settings of poems by Ashbery, Koch, O'Hara, Schuyler, and others, along with a number by Latouche and Vernon Duke, "Little Poppa Satan," from *Cabin in the Sky*. However, as observers like John Bernard Myers and Miles Kreuger had long recognized, the end of Latouche's salon in 1956 marked the close of an era.[74]

20

The Vamp

The Vamp—a 1955 musical starring Carol Channing that flopped on Broadway—originated as *Samson and Lila Dee,* a planned all-black retelling of the biblical Samson and Delilah story. As initially conceived, the show was to have had a score adapted from Camille Saint-Saëns's opera *Samson et Dalila* (completed 1876), a project for which in February 1953 the musical's novice producers, Martin B. Cohen (1923–2007) and Oscar S. Lerman (1919–1992), signed two African-American artists—Frederick ("Freddy") L. Lights (1922–1995) as bookwriter, and James ("Jimmy") Mundy (1907–1983) as composer, or "adaptor," as stated in his agreement—along with Latouche as lyricist, a logical choice given, among other things, his experience lyricizing classic melodies and his long association with black artists.[1]

Latouche further provided a more practiced hand than either of his principal collaborators. A recent Yale graduate, bookwriter Lights up to this point had written only student plays. And although far more seasoned, composer-arranger Mundy—who seems to have been hired on Latouche's recommendation—had had little involvement with musical theater. Born in Cincinnati, Mundy had grown up in Chicago and attended Northwestern University on an athletic scholarship, majoring in chemistry. Active as a jazz tenor saxophonist, he soon distinguished himself both as an arranger for Earl Hines, Benny Goodman, and other leading bandleaders and as a popular song composer, most notably co-writing (with lyricist Al Stillman and composer Illinois Jacquet) the 1950 hit "Don'cha Go Way Mad." During periodic gigs in Los Angeles, including film work, Mundy studied composition with the German-American composer Ernst Toch; "Everytime [*sic*] I'm in California," he stated, "I go to absorb more of his [Toch's] knowledge."[2]

Over the spring and summer of 1953, the press, which described the title characters of *Samson and Lila Dee,* set in Louisiana and Chicago, as a backwoods prizefighter and a scheming nightclub entertainer, announced a tentative launching in the fall. But perhaps because of the unavailability of possible leading ladies Lena Horne or Dorothy Dandridge, in the course of the year, the musical, renamed *Delilah* (and still later, *The Vamp*), was reimagined as a star vehicle for Carol Channing.[3]

Raised in San Francisco and educated at Bennington College, Channing (b. 1921) had made an auspicious 1941 New York stage debut as the nightclub entertainer Bobby in Marc Blitzstein's opera *No for an Answer*, and had become an overnight sensation in 1949 as Lorelei Lee in Jule Styne's musical comedy *Gentlemen Prefer Blondes*. The thought of tailoring the Samson and Delilah musical to Channing might well have originated with Latouche, for the two enjoyed a close personal and professional relationship, including collaboration on the children's animated film *The Peppermint Tree*; wrote Channing in her memoirs, "He [Latouche] was for years my dear confidant." Latouche certainly thought highly of Channing's "peculiar genius," stating, "I consider her the last of the great musical performers in the grand manner." But although intrigued by the proposed musical and happy to work with Latouche, Channing deferred making a decision about the show until she could read a finished script.[4]

During the fall of 1953, the producers hired Edward Chodorov (1904–1988) to replace a reportedly squeezed-out Lights as bookwriter. The writer and producer of numerous films, Chodorov recently had been blacklisted by Hollywood as a suspected communist (as had his brother Jerome, the co-author of the 1940 comedy *My Sister Eileen*, and its 1953 musical adaptation, *Wonderful Town*); at the moment, he had his hands full preparing his comedy *Oh, Men! Oh, Women!* for its December 17, 1953, Broadway premiere, but he planned to turn his attention to the Latouche show afterward.[5]

In February 1954, the *Times* reported that Chodorov had *Delilah* "all blocked out," but about a month later stated that the playwright needed to quit the show because of conflicting responsibilities. By this time, in addition to recruiting Channing's second husband, former professional football player Alexander Carson, as co-producer, Cohen and Lerman had handed over responsibility for the book to Latouche along with Ronny Graham (born Ronald Montcrief Stringer, 1919–1999) and Mel Brooks (born Melvin Kaminsky, 1926). Two versatile comedian-composer-lyricist-writers known for wacky satire, Graham and Brooks had co-written the sketches for the Broadway revue *New Faces of 1952*, and would continue to work together in the decades ahead, including co-writing the screenplays for *To Be or Not to Be* (1983) and *Spaceballs* (1987).[6]

Around this same time, Latouche seems to have charted a new direction for *Delilah* independently, or rather, one inspired by an after-theater conversation at the Algonquin Hotel with designer-producer Oliver Smith. "We were discussing our mutual friend Carol Channing, improvising various situations that would fit her remarkable personality," Latouche recalled shortly before *The Vamp* opened. "The idea of placing her in the giddy milieu of the East Coast studios during the early teens of this century came up. When some days later I had settled on the concept of Miss Channing as a vamp enamored of a cinematic cowboy, Oliver had been whisked away to Hollywood to toil in the Goldwyn vineyards [presumably to work on the film version of *Guys and Dolls*] and faded from the scenario." Latouche apparently had considered alternately setting the musical in Hollywood during the transition from the silents to the talkies, a topic so reminiscent of the highly popular 1952 film musical *Singin' in the Rain* as perhaps only to encourage the more novel milieu of movie making in the 1910s—a time period, incidentally, closer to that of *The Golden Apple* as well. In any case, Latouche reasoned that the period songs already composed for *Samson and Lila Dee*, set during the Depression, could be adapted easily enough to this somewhat earlier era. As for the change of racial intention, he later asked Carol Channing if the overhauled musical gave her "the feeling that it might have been written as a colored show," to which she responded, "Frankly, no. I did notice that you didn't have any G's at the end of some words, but I thought that was because you came from Virginia."[7]

Latouche and Ronny Graham worked on the musical in the spring, although not harmoniously, as Graham found Latouche too "domineering." Things deteriorated to the point that Graham requested to write the script exclusively with Mel Brooks, but producers Cohen and Lerman rallied behind Latouche's unwillingness to relinquish some control over the book, as evidenced by the lyricist's diary entry of June 12:

> They [Cohen and Lerman] were unexpectedly sympathetic about the situation with Ronnie [Graham], and agreed to follow my instinct about turning the book over to him and Mel Brooks. Brooks had nailed me down over the phone earlier, finally getting rather triumphant as he sensed my confusion, and attempting to force a situation that would rule me out utterly. I found myself equally tough inside, out of automatic response rather than intention, and shaped the situation into something rather practical for myself—I took a sub-billing on the book, but insisted on the credit 'based on a story by J.L.,' which gave me *three* mentions on the program, including my lyric credit.

However, even this compromise apparently failed to satisfy, for by mid-July Graham and Brooks had left the show and management had enlisted a new co-author, Sam Locke (1917–1998). A prolific writer also stigmatized during this period for leftist political activities, Locke in later years would become a successful television screenwriter, but his credits at this point consisted primarily of scripts and sketches for sundry radio programs and musical revues.[8]

Latouche and Locke, both of whom had worked on *Sunday Night Varieties* back in 1939, finished a preliminary draft of *Delilah* in the fall, submitting a script for copyright in early November 1954, about the time that Leonard Bernstein discharged Latouche from their work in progress, *Candide*. Channing—then with the road company of *Wonderful Town* after having replaced Rosalind Russell for the last four months of that musical's Broadway run—liked the book and agreed to star in the show once the tour concluded and a suitable director and choreographer could be found. More work needed to be done on the second act in any event, although as with Ronny Graham, the collaboration between Latouche and Locke proved problematic; and in the winter of 1955, as Latouche continued to work on the score with Mundy, he and Locke prepared two separate and competing versions of the second act.

Meanwhile, plans to hire choreographer Michael Kidd failed to materialize; nor did Latouche welcome Channing's suggestion that the show engage director Joshua Logan, whom he refused to work with "at any cost." In the early spring of 1955, the outstanding choreographer-director Jerome Robbins (whose friendly 1953 testimony before the House Un-American Activities Committee had contributed, coincidentally, to the blacklisting of the Chodorov brothers) seriously considered staging the musical, although he thought some of the material wanting, and suggested that outsiders help doctor both the book and the score. In May, however, he also extricated himself from the project, publicly citing conflicting duties with the New York City Ballet, but privately, his own inability to work with Latouche.[9]

Over the summer of 1955, management finally lined up as choreographer and production supervisor, the veteran dance director Robert ("Bob") Alton; and as director, the lesser known David Alexander, who had staged the successful 1952 Broadway revival of *Pal Joey*. Further hires included Milton Rosenstock as musical director; Raoul Pène du Bois as set and costume designer; and as the male lead, David Atkinson, the Canadian-born baritone who had created the role of Sam in Leonard Bernstein's opera *Trouble in Tahiti* (1952). In addition to Channing (Flora Weems/Delilah Modo) and Atkinson (Oliver J. Oxheart), the large cast included Jack Waldron (Myron H. Hubbard), Bibi Osterwald (Bessie Bisco), Paul Lipson (Barney Ostertag), Robert Rippy (Stanley Hubermyer/Dick Hicks, and a last-minute substitute for Danny Scholl), Patricia Hammerlee (Elsie Chelsea), Matt Mattox (Charlie), and in smaller roles, the blacklisted actor-activist Will Geer (Uncle Garvey), later a familiar television presence as Grandpa Walton on *The Waltons*, and the handsome bodybuilder-actor Steve Reeves (Muscle Man and Samson), who recently had made his Broadway debut in the musical *Kismet*. James Mundy arranged and orchestrated the score, assisted by Don Walker and others, and Jack Pfeiffer supplied incidental music.[10]

After spending part of the summer in his country home in Vermont working on various projects, Latouche returned to New York in order to help ready *Delilah* for its fall launching, providing a progress report to his companion, Kenward Elmslie, sometime after rehearsals began in August:

> The rehearsals zigzag on, with tiny dramas and intricate piecework, and that artificial esprit de corps that is transient but gratifying à the ego. The production staff on this show is probably the nicest I've ever been in harness with—it's a real relief to work with real pro's at last, after the turgid vagaries of the Phoenix [which had produced *The Golden Apple*], and the frenetic *Beggar's Holiday* outfit, which was mainly composed of sub-lugs and Yale Drama grads—a grisly and inept mixture if there ever was one.... Bob Alton is fascinating to work with—he's a product of the old Shubert-Hollywood axis, but has tremendous drive and organization with a natural feeling for this epoch since it spawned him... he has rallied Carol and me into a shaky amity which will probably save the rag-ends of the show.... Our only problem is a corny

> second act, which was pressured in by Sam Locke while I was up there in our placid green nest... it is being unravelled now because it doesnt play, but it's a tough assignment, and I end up each day in a comatose condition.

Publicly, Latouche praised the work of Channing, Locke, and Mundy, whose music, he stated, contained "some really new sounds" (this presumably fostered by having in the pit such jazz colleagues of Mundy's as drummer Jimmy Crawford and saxophonist Eddie Barfield).[11]

Delilah premiered at Detroit's Shubert Theatre on September 26, a generally well-received debut despite an overlong playing time and a star hobbled by laryngitis and memory slips. About this same time, Gilda Dahlberg, an associate producer who had been released from the show over the summer with her investment returned, sought damages and a restraining order against the musical, alleging that management had failed to honor its agreement with her—a dispute that threatened to derail the show's scheduled opening in New York. But the producers quickly resolved the issue, as with related claims made by former bookwriter Ronny Graham.[12]

After two weeks in Detroit, the musical moved to the Shubert Theatre in New Haven for the week beginning October 11, and then the National Theatre in Washington for three weeks starting October 18. In response to the apparently widely shared misperception that the piece had a biblical theme, the show opened in New Haven as *Delilah: The Vamp*, a renaming eventually shortened to *The Vamp*—two alternate titles that actually had been bandied about for some time. The musical faced still more problems during these final weeks on the road, aside from the constant rewriting common enough during a tryout period. In New Haven, production supervisor Robert Alton suffered a ruptured appendix and needed to be hospitalized, preventing him from attending the Washington debut, a performance further complicated by the fact that bad weather prevented the timely arrival of the sets, leading to a delayed curtain and an only partially furnished stage—but a premiere that met with an enthusiastic audience response nonetheless.

So far, the critics liked the show as well, especially Channing's performance, thought "an uproarious tour de force," although the "excellent" supporting cast, "outstanding" choreography, "brilliant" sets and costumes, "imaginative Dixieland-style jazz score," and "witty, literate lyrics" also elicited praise, with Jay Carmody of the *Washington Evening Star* specifically lauding Latouche for giving Mundy, as with Moross in *The Golden Apple*, "an occasion to break with the cliches of popular music." Several papers posted near raves, including the *Windsor Star*, which called the musical "a delicious dish of delightfully daffy delineations," and the *New Haven Evening Register*, which thought that the production provided "the sort of explosive evening that few people can resist." *Variety* further viewed the material as "a natural for wide-screen picture adaptation and for tv spectacularization." The only major disagreement concerned the book, thought "deftly satirical" by some, but "belabored and obvious" or at least "much too loosely bound" by others, although even the more mixed notices endorsed the musical, deemed "a must" by Richard Coe of the *Washington Post and Times-Herald*. However, despite the generally good critical and popular reception, the show consistently lost money on the road, so that the production, although budgeted at $250,000, wound up costing more than $300,000 by the time it arrived on Broadway.[13]

Meanwhile, the book underwent constant revision, Channing remembering daily script changes during tryouts, although "to no avail, because the entire show was basically not well thought out." Mundy and Latouche also tweaked the score, and before the show opened in New York, three numbers—"Mr. Right," "Who Needs Love," and "Little Miss Dracula"—had been dropped, and two others, "That's Where a Man Fits In" and "Delilah's Dilemma," added. As Steve Reeves recalled, at some point director Joshua Logan arrived to help doctor the production as well.[14]

Several extant songs never even made it to Detroit, including "Another Opening Night," "Back Home Where I Come From," "In Love with Love," "Rolling Stone," "Sultan" (adapted from Latouche's cabaret song "Oh Sultan!"), "Without You," and "You Can't Buy a Ticket to Broadway," although "Another Opening Night" surfaced in the 2000 revue *Taking a Chance on Love* (if not its cast album). This last number, an ironic gloss on such odes to show business as Irving Berlin's "There's No Business Like Show Business"; Arthur Schwartz and Howard Dietz's "That's Entertainment"; and Cole Porter's "Another Op'nin', Another Show," seems Latouche's own in its mocking depiction, by way of a commenting chorus, of a movie premiere in the early days of cinema:

> Another opening night, another pre-mi-ere,
> The star of the piece is in a funk,
> The cast is upset, the author's drunk
> Producers and their backers breathe up a silent prayer.
>
> The crowd is coming in sight, the men look so refined,
> The ladies wear mink and sable pelts
> And ev'ryone looks at ev'ryone else,
> The picture is the last thing on anybody's mind.[15]

Of the two known surviving scripts, neither corresponds exactly to the show as it opened on Broadway. The first, the 1954 draft by Latouche and Locke mentioned above, includes only a few lyrics; the more complete second version represents a reconstruction, with "additional scenes and dialogue," undertaken by Sam Locke in 1967 in the hopes of a possible revival, the author explaining to Lucy Kroll in November of that year,

> As you may know, there isn't a copy of the final version of *The Vamp* or *Delilah* as it was done in New York around. I had lots of isolated scenes and

> even a few incomplete acts... starting with versions of 1954. What I finally did was start at the beginning and reconstruct the entire musical... cannibalizing from all the different versions[,] inventing new scenes... new dialogue etc. etc. It took me more than a month but what I have finally achieved is a musical which—if we had started our rehearsals with THAT in 1955—would have made us all wealthy.

Given that the first acts of both extant scripts, aside from their final scenes, are actually quite similar, and that even their second acts bear some fair resemblance, these two texts, combined with programs and reviews, at least permit the following scenario of the musical as it more or less appeared on Broadway.[16]

The action of the play begins in New York in 1913.

Act I, scene one. Hubbard's Coliseum, Fourteenth Street. Assisted by his employee Bessie Bisco, Myron H. Hubbard, the owner of a dime museum called Hubbard's Coliseum, solicits customers ("The Spiel," for Hubbard, Bessie, and Patrons of the Coliseum). As the crowd disperses, movie director Oliver J. Oxheart, formerly of Facsimile Films, persuades Hubbard to show his latest picture, *The Honey Bunny Girl*, starring America's sweetheart, Elsie Chelsea. The movie proves a hit, and Oxheart, "a mixture of genius and windbag," talks Hubbard and Barney Ostertag, the proprietor of a lady's undergarment store, into forming with him a film company, Ostertag-Hubbard-Oxheart (OHO). When the president of Facsimile Films, the "smooth-talking" mogul Stark Clayton, arrives with the "big, strapping" policeman Stanley Hubermyer to serve an injunction against Oxheart and his associates, the irrepressible director talks the dim-witted cop into becoming a movie cowboy hero, Dick Hicks, by promising him a starring role with Elsie Chelsea. Patrons extol the movies ("The Flickers," for Ticket Girl and Patrons). After one look at Dick, Elsie agrees to leave Facsimile Films and make a western with him for OHO.

Scene two. A farm in the Bronx. The following morning. Oxheart and his makeshift team, including the company's in-house movie villain Charlie, trespass on Garvey and Hester Dill's farm in the Bronx in order to start filming the western. As the crew gets ready to shoot, Garvey, "a wizened old tyrant" of a local circuit judge; Hester, "a squalid slattern"; and Flora Weems, Hester's wholesome niece from Louisiana, prepare for the day ("Keep Your Nose to the Grindstone," for Flora, Garvey, and Hester). Flora pines for a man ("That's Where a Man Fits In," for Flora). As Uncle Garvey starts firing at the movie crew with an old musket, Dick hides by diving into a well. After rescuing Dick, an infatuated Flora dries the movie star's wet clothes. Finding Flora holding Dick's long underwear, Garvey presides over a shotgun wedding, with Dick attired in a tablecloth, while Oxheart happily instructs his cameraman Bluestone to film the entire proceedings. Although Garvey neglects to have Dick sign the wedding certificate, Flora, believing she is legally married, packs a suitcase and leaves the farm ("I've Always Loved You," for Flora and Farm Folk).

Scene three. Hubbard's Movie House. A few weeks later. Bessie, having become a movie gossip columnist, arrives to see Oxheart's new western starring Elsie and

Dick, *Love Among the Yuccas*. Elsie and Dick mock the hype of movie people ("You're Colossal," for Elsie and Dick) and desert OHO for Facsimile Films, Elsie for more money, Dick, to avoid Flora. In the hopes of winning over Dick, Flora agrees to Oxheart's proposal that she become Delilah Modo, a movie vamp. Motion picture fans leave for Grand Central Station to greet Elsie and Dick on their return from making a new film ("Fan Club Chant," for Movie Fans).

Scene four. Grand Central Station. Three months later. Oxheart introduces Delilah, a supposed Arabian princess, to an awestruck public ("Have You Met Delilah?" for Oxheart). Delilah presents herself ("Yeemy Yeemy," for Flora and Oriental Entourage). As Delilah exits, a mesmerized Dick (who does not recognize her as Flora) follows after. Under the influence of Delilah, women transform themselves into vamps and dominate men ("The Vamps," for Matt Mattox, Barbara Heath, Cathryn Damon, and Fans).

Scene five. A rooftop movie studio in Manhattan. Sometime later. Oxheart has set up a studio on a Manhattan rooftop, where he simultaneously shoots two films starring Flora. The latter broods over the paradox that as Delilah she finally has captured Dick's heart, but that as a movie siren she cannot have a romance with a popular cowboy hero. Harassed by rival Facsimile Films, Oxheart decides to move his company west ("Delilah's Dilemma," for Flora and Movie Fans).

Act II. Scene one, part 1. The northeast corner of Hollywood and Vine. Oxheart relocates to Hollywood.

Scene one, part 2. OHO Film Company. One year later. Ostertag gives a self-congratulatory speech on the occasion of the first anniversary of OHO studios. Elsie, Dick, and Bessie—now all on the West Coast as well—join Charlie in explaining how they have capitalized on their eccentricities ("Four Little Misfits," for Elsie, Bessie, Dick, and Charlie).

Scene two. Interior of OHO Film Studios. Oxheart directs a film extravaganza, *Samson and Delilah* ("Samson and Delilah," for Flora, Matt Mattox, Samson, Whip Man, High Priest, Cathryn Damon, and Movie Company), and finds himself in love with Flora ("Why Does It Have to Be You?" for Oxheart). Bessie expresses her preference for a rowdy lover over a respectable one ("Ragtime Romeo," for Bessie, Charlie, and Boys).

Scene three. Flora's dressing room. Flora ponders the allure of vamps to men ("I'm Everybody's Baby," for Flora).

Scene four. Executive office, OHO Film Company. The next day. Flora insists that she play an ingénue in her next film (reprise of "I'm Everybody's Baby," for Flora, Ostertag, and Hubbard). Oxheart reflects on the sovereignty of women ("The Impossible She," for Oxheart and OHO Boys).

Scene five. Hubbard's Movie Cathedral. Hollywood. At the premiere of her latest film, Flora, who gets stuck in cement making handprints and footprints outside the theater, chooses Oxheart as her mate ("Finale," for the ensemble).

In writing the musical, Latouche drew on his own recollections of the silent movies, which had so enraptured him as a child; but he also researched the genre's formative years in the 1910s, collecting colorful anecdotes from such friends as movie producer Jesse Lasky, film actress Mae Murray, and silent screen temptress Nita Naldi, who served the show as a sort of dramaturge and coach. For the character of Flora, Latouche, even while acknowledging such pioneer vamps as Alice Hollister and Lucille Younge, seems to have had in mind above all the silent screen's most famous femme fatale, Theodosia Goodman, whose stage name, Theda Bara, no doubt helped inspire that of Delilah Modo, and details of whose life story—although not her Jewish background—worked its way into the script. The jingly "cadence" of Florence Lawrence, a leading ingénue of the 1910s, similarly suggested the name Elsie Chelsea, although Latouche intended the latter as "a blend of all possible soubrettes," including Mary Pickford, like Elsie a shrewd businesswoman. The name Dick Hicks, meanwhile, echoed that of famous cowboy star Tom Mix. In addition, the writers ostensibly modeled Oliver Oxheart after D. W. Griffith; Bessie Bisco after Louella Parsons; Hubbard's Coliseum after Huber's Museum; and OHO after MGM. Other period references, possibly lost on audiences even in 1955, included, in "Ragtime Romeo," the mention of the Rover Boys and the Merriwell brothers, juvenile fictional heroes of the early twentieth century who contrast to the "drugstore cowboy" for whom Bessie yearns. Likewise, the numbers "The Spiel" and "The Flickers" enumerate in knowing detail the sorts of attractions found, respectively, at a dime museum and a nickelodeon in the dawning years of the twentieth century.[17]

Latouche plainly found the slapdash filmmaking of the 1910s and the ruthless rivalries among the fledgling movie studios and their superstars intriguing, including the ambiguity between the offstage and onstage personae of film celebrities as managed by fan magazines and industry marketing. In an article about the show published shortly before its Broadway premiere, he wrote,

> Ironically, the real events that occurred around the Fort Lee Studios and Edison's outfit in the Bronx were often so outrageous as to seem unbelievable on paper. Our contemporary artistic scene, with its climate of conformity, is oddly at variance with the grand manners of those lens-happy pioneers. . . . Certainly no figures in history before or since have known such world-wide adulation as was lavished on the silent screen stars. Political, religious, and literary figures were limited by lingual and/or ethnic barriers. But the basic story—simplicity imposed by the soundless films[,] the emphasis on pantomime—made these dream creatures understandable and adorable everywhere, regardless of barriers.

At the same time, Latouche discerned continuities between the nascent film industry and modern film trends: "We should not feel superior to these faded sartorial conventions; within recent memory, a platinum blonde coiffure or a pneumatic sweater were sufficient trappings to give even the most unlikely girls an unfailing allure. And at the moment, any man who fails to whistle and sway when Marilyn Monroe is mentioned is automatically suspected of pallid corpuscles. (I whistle and sway.)" Indeed, Latouche regarded the sultry vamps, manly cowboys, virginal ingénues, and dastardly villains of the silent screen "as truly Americana as anything ever celebrated in a folk song or a tall story," and even more than this, universal archetypes, to judge not only from Delilah's name, but from the number "The Impossible She," with its comparisons of the vamp to Eve, Cleopatra, and Josephine.[18]

As a kind of ironic Cinderella story, the musical further drew on, even if parodistically, a longstanding musical comedy tradition. But in contrast to many Cinderella tales, including *Annie Get Your Gun* (1946), to which critics often compared *The Vamp*, and *My Fair Lady* (1956), a smash hit on the horizon, the unassuming heroine metamorphoses not into an acquiescent princess but into a conquering goddess. "Come back here, you puppet! . . . Kiss me, my fool," Flora orders a stunned Oxheart near the end of at least the surviving early draft. In one apparently cut scene, the show even placed the emergence of the likes of Theda Bara against the background of the suffragette movement, a feminist reading of the vamp phenomenon embraced by Carol Channing herself. Elsie Chelsea's career savvy and Bessie Bisco's frank sexuality only amplify this central theme of female agency.[19]

The Vamp also differed from most contemporary musicals in its penchant for the sort of madcap humor more typical of the screwball comedies of the prewar era than of later trends, the *Washington Daily News* observing that the show possessed "a fine, crazy quality which has all but vanished from the American musical comedy during the Rodgers-Hammerstein era of sense and sentiment." Several viewers noted in particular a resemblance to the work of George S. Kaufman, who similarly enjoyed skewering baloney and hypocrisy, although the play seemed to reflect as well the sort of humor associated with Latouche's erstwhile collaborators Ronny Graham and Mel Brooks, and popularized by such comedians as Sid Caesar and Imogene Coca. Elsie, with her "little girl manner that cloaks a heart of stainless steel," provided a particularly inviting target, but all the characters prove ridiculous in one way or the other. "It's a pretty spring day," says Flora after performing a number of exhausting farm chores, "and what better pastime could a girl ask than plowin' up a pasture." "If I don't get out of this alive," cries Oxheart in retreat from Uncle Garvey on the rampage, "remember my full screen credit lasts fourteen frames and I get billing on posters and throwaways." The glamorous exoticism associated with silent screen vamps naturally allowed a good deal of spoofery as well, with Mundy and Latouche providing a number for Flora, "Yeemy Yeemy," that featured one of the lyricist's specialties, namely, concocting a nonsense language, in this case, fake Arabic. Even the show's rare romantic numbers tended toward the jokey, with Flora's "I've Always Loved You" climaxing with the phrase, "I'm so glad you came, / By the way, what's your name?" and Oxheart's "Why Does It Have to Be You?" seeming more exasperated than anything else. "There's nothing soft in the whole production, not an ounce of romance that isn't tongue-in-cheek, not a breath of friendship that doesn't hang on a profitable contract, not a moment of quiet relaxation," reported the *New Haven Evening Register* in its review of the show. "Never that!"[20]

If anything, the script's original second act as drafted by Latouche and Locke in the fall of 1954 was that much zanier, including the introduction of a character later cut from the show, Pancho, a farcical Mexican bandit who accosts the OHO company on their way to Hollywood—"Sorry. No casting today," Oxheart tells him—and each of whose two children, like their father, wears a black eye patch; later in the act, Pancho turns up as Elsie's handler Morris Pancho, now wearing a suit and a white eye patch and talking not like a hackneyed Mexican movie villain but a slick Hollywood talent agent. Such burlesquerie recalled the book for the aborted *Tamborito*.

Starting with the overture, during which the script specified a filmed close-up of Delilah Modo in elaborate headgear smiling at the audience "with sultry disdain," followed by a list of show credits "presented in the typical movie manner," the bookwriters also imagined the sporadic projection of film throughout the musical, including, in the first act's third scene, clips from the western that is shown being shot in the previous scene—with the result that, for example, the intertitle "The Old Prospector Turns Out To Be the Brains Behind the Rustlers," accompanies film images of Uncle Garvey wielding his musket. In addition, the bookwriters at times called for the use of a "flicker machine," that is, strobe lights, in order to simulate motion pictures on stage. The production employed at least some of these ideas, with surviving footage from the show housed in the film archives of the Museum of Modern Art, including the western parody. Along with the musical's extensive interlacing of mime and dance, such incorporation of film accorded with Latouche's persistent aim of making musical theater a more fully integrated art form.

Mundy provided an uneven but generally attractive score in the tradition of late Kern, Berlin, and Porter, although some of the music, especially several of the discarded songs, veer more toward folk styles, perhaps residue of the work's early origins as *Sam and Lila Dee*. However, Latouche's lyrics form the score's main attraction, representing at their best crowning achievements of his wit. "Keep Your Nose to the Grindstone," a sendup of American puritanism, alternates barnyard allegories that turn on amusing puns with long lists of old-timey saws, ingeniously rhymed, all set to music by Mundy in "hillybilly style":

Keep your neck in the harness
Keep your shoulder to the wheel
Keep your fist on the cashbox
Keep your wife beneath your heel
Keep her knees bent for scrubbin'
Keep her mind on higher things
You can have a week's vacation
When you wear a pair of wings.

In contrast, "Have You Met Delilah?" projects, though jazzy word and tone, that very different world of the movie dream factory:

She [Delilah] uses hashish and mascara,
Men who went for Theda Bara,
Now make a beeline for that feline
Harum scarum gal.

"Four Little Misfits," Latouche's favorite among these songs, shows the lyricist at his most Gilbertian, with Elsie, Bessie, Dick, and Charlie tracing their success to their quirky childhoods, Elsie explaining in her case,

I wasn't like the other girls
In my home town in Akron
I held on to my golden curls
My vocal chords were sacchrine [*sic*]
When told that I was infantile
I smiled at my attackers
Now I've parlayed that baby smile
Into a million smackers
So be happy you're a misfit
Be happy you're a freak
Who cares if you are horrible
At twenty grand a week.

For its part, "Ragtime Romeo" uses slang and flashy rhymes to underscore its essential conflation of jazz and sex, including a dizzying string of internal rhymes apparently inspired by the name "Romeo" (itself made to rhyme with "slow, oh ho!" "blow, oh ho!" and "[St. Louie,] Mo., oh ho!"), as in the line "Now this lassie's chassis fries / And her pulse emulsifies / With a snazzy jazzy Ragtime Romeo."

In the show's thematically central number, "I'm Everybody's Baby," Flora puzzles over her greater appeal as a red-hot viper than as a virginal maid, with the score's musical directives alternating between "sweetly" or "sweet" and "stomp it!" a Jekyll-and-Hyde opposition heightened in the original production by having Channing move between white and green lights:

[Sweetly]
When I am sweet and shy
The fellows pass me by,
[Stomp it!!]
But when I howl and yowl and chew the scenery,
Climb the woodwork, wreck machinery,
I'm everybody's baby.

Emblematic of Latouche's sly wit, the song's bridge section puns the expression "the girl next door" with the phrase "the ghoul next door":

> [Sweet]
> Pollyanna may be dutiful and earnest,
> But she always winds up poor.
> [Stomp it!]
> While the only girl who really feathers her nest
> Is the ghoul next door.

Called "one of the funniest songs of modern times" by Jay Carmody in his review for the *Washington Evening Star*, "I'm Everybody's Baby" proved a showstopper for Channing, as "Ragtime Romeo" did for Bibi Osterwald.[21]

Debuting on Broadway on November 10, 1955, at the Winter Garden Theatre, *The Vamp* reaped a handful of well-disposed reviews, including one in the *Daily News* by John Chapman, who thought the show "a grand extravaganza about the silent movies, with some pretty good music by James Mundy and some very good lyrics by John Latouche." Most reviews further conceded the appeal of at least some facets of the production, including the show's premise; indeed, the years ahead would witness musicals that similarly pitted a movie director and an actress against the background of the early film studio days, namely, Leroy Anderson's *Goldilocks* (1958) and Jerry Herman's *Mack & Mabel* (1974). But in contrast to the largely favorable response garnered out of town, the majority of New York critics excoriated what Thomas Dash (*Women's Wear Daily*) called "an incredibly hopeless mishmosh." Alluding to the nasty weather on opening night, Wolcott Gibbs (*New Yorker*) wrote, for instance, "The final effect of the whole disastrous enterprise might easily be to turn a vast new public to the contemplation of their television sets, where almost exactly the same sort of entertainment is available at no cost whatever and with never a thought of getting a taxi to Broadway and Fiftieth Street in the rain," a comment that at least highlighted what appears to have been the show's debt to such television entertainments as *Your Show of Shows*, which counted Mel Brooks as one of its writers. The critics especially faulted a script deemed "labored," "juiceless," "corny," and "unfunny," with several reviewers targeting as two specific weaknesses its diffuse attempt to encapsulate the entire history of early cinema and its failure to create characters as opposed to caricatures. "This is all the more surprising," wrote Richard Watts (*Post*), "since John Latouche had an important hand in it, and Mr. Latouche usually has a notable talent in such matters."[22]

Notwithstanding the occasional kind words for the "brisk and brassy" score, the reviews also lambasted the "uninspired" and "nondescript" music, in particular the "loud" and "hideous" orchestrations. The show's lyrics, along with its performances, choreography, costumes, and set designs, met with more favor, although Latouche's work encountered the occasional objection as well. Hobe Morrison (*Variety*), for instance, intended no compliment in describing the lyrics as "elaborately tricky," and Richard Watts similarly opined that the "ingenious" lyrics were "inclined to be . . . a little heavy-handed in their satire, rather in the fashion of the book."

The audience seemed no more pleased than the critics. Carol Channing recalled not hearing "a peep out of the audience" on opening night, and Walter Kerr, in his review for the *Herald Tribune*, confirmed, "The silence in the theater gets spooky after a while." Even with *Life* and *Look* magazines publishing articles about the show, with Channing as Delilah Modo making the cover of the former, ticket sales quickly flagged; and within weeks after opening night, Latouche and his collaborators by agreement had to forgo their royalties. The show finally expired on New Year's Eve 1955, after a total of sixty performances.[23]

The Vamp nonetheless managed to snag Tony Award nominations for Channing, choreographer Robert Alton, and musical director Milton Rosenstock, all of whom lost, however, to nominees from *Damn Yankees*, the Richard Adler and Jerry Ross show that swept the 1956 Tonys, including the award for outstanding musical (with Rodgers and Hammerstein's *Pipe Dream* the only other contender in this category). But despite the many accolades earned by Channing for her performance, *The Vamp* became remembered as "the show that almost ended Carol Channing's career," perhaps in part because Channing herself, aside from fondly recalling the warm solidarity among the cast members, spoke derisively about the production. At the 1975 Tony Award ceremonies in New York, wearing one of du Bois's over-the-top costumes for the show, Channing told her audience, "There were many mistakes made in *The Vamp*, but as the adage goes, the major mistake was taking the curtain up." All the same, in her memoirs, she acknowledged Latouche's talent as a lyricist, writing, "If we could have just made a concert of his songs, *The Vamp* might have been fine, or at least more tolerable."[24]

Unfortunately, no record company issued a cast album of the show. Nor did any individual songs attract much attention, even with Robbins-Wise publishing "Have You Met Delilah?" "I've Always Loved You," "Ragtime Romeo," and "Why Does It Have to Be You?" and Terri Stevens recording "I've Always Loved You" with Joe Reisman's Orchestra in 1955. The burlesque nature of the score surely militated against wide dissemination of any particular numbers. That said, in recent years, artists have taken to excavating the musical's hidden gems, with several songs appearing especially in the revue *Taking a Chance on Love* (2000) and the recital *The Broadway Musicals of 1955* (2008).[25]

In 1967, the noted producer and film noir director Robert Aldrich took an interest in obtaining the film and other rights to *The Vamp*, perhaps recognizing a kindred relation to his recent work, which included the campy thrillers *What Ever Happened to Baby Jane?* (1962) and *Hush . . . Hush, Sweet Charlotte* (1964); certainly, at least in looks, Bette Davis as Baby Jane bore some resemblance to Patricia Hammerlee as Elsie Chelsea. With this prospect in mind, Sam Locke reconstructed the script, as mentioned before, but Aldrich failed to reach an agreement with agent Lucy Kroll. In 1980, Martin Cohen, who had left Broadway for Hollywood to become the producer of such horror films as *Humanoids of the Deep*, similarly thought to revive the work for television, but nothing came of that either.[26]

Meanwhile, critical reassessments of this largely forgotten show surfaced only in such specialized histories as Ken Mandelbaum's study of Broadway musical flops, *Not Since Carrie* (1991), and Ethan Mordden's survey of the American musical in the 1950s, *Coming up Roses* (1998). Mandelbaum granted that the show had "superb lyrics," but in a caption for a still from the shotgun wedding episode that showed a joyful Flora (Carol Channing) in blond pigtails and gingham, an alarmed Dick Hicks (Robert Rippy) in a checkered table cloth, and a tearfully hammy Elsie Chelsea (Patricia Hammerlee) in ludicrously garish make-up, the author reasonably asked, "Could anything that looked as strange as this ever be a hit?" Ethan Mordden thought the story "perfect for musical comedy," but claimed that although Latouche "had done his homework... [he] didn't really have a take on the movies."[27]

As with his previous flops, Latouche appeared to take the failure of *The Vamp* in stride. But this particular fiasco pointed to two disturbing trends: an increasing difficulty in working with collaborators, and a tendency to overextend himself beyond the breaking point. Neither development augured well for the future, although during this same time period, he managed to complete with Douglas Moore one of the masterworks of the American operatic canon, *The Ballad of Baby Doe*.

Meanwhile, Latouche continued to write lyrics for independent songs, including three that made their way into print: "Co-Co-Coconut" (music by Paulo Alencar, 1950); "Strange" (music by Marvin Fisher, 1953); and "On the Waterfront" (music by Leonard Bernstein, 1954). Several other songs exist in manuscript, including "My Dream" (music by Lillian Stratton, 1952); "Beside a Peaceful River" (music by Alex Alstone, 1952); "The Song of My Love" (music by Alstone, 1953); "The Deep Blue Sea" (music by Ulpio Minucci, 1953); "You Make Up (For All I've Missed)" (lyric originally by Freeman Cohn, music by Robert Miles, 1954); "The Other Side of the Moon" (music by Dana Suesse, 1956); "After a While" (music by Minucci, copyrighted posthumously in 1961); and a handful of songs by Donald Fuller, all copyrighted in 1956, mostly after Latouche's death in August, namely, "Be Discriminating," "The Blue Countries," "At Home in Your Heart," "A Rainy Day" (also called "A Rainy Night"), and "A World of Our Own." One final song, the comedy number "A Nail in the Horseshoe" (music by John Strauss, probably circa 1955), also survives thanks to its inclusion on Charlotte Rae's 1955 solo album on the Vanguard label, *Songs I Taught My Mother*.

Typical for Latouche, his collaborators on these songs included a conspicuous number of émigrés, including Alex Alstone (born Siegfried Stein, 1903–1982), a prolific songwriter who had written several popular songs like "Place Pigalle" (words by Maurice Chevalier) in France before moving to America; Lillian Stratton (born Lillian Stignitz, 1905–1982), a student of Franz Lehár who had left her native Vienna in 1938 with her doctor-publisher husband, Henry Stratton (born Max Slovsky), for New York, where she devoted herself mostly to philanthropic activities; Paulo Alencar (born Isaac Feldman, 1913–2010), a Brazilian-American violinist and bandleader who helped popularize the bossa nova; and Ulpio Minucci (1917–2007), an Italian-born composer then residing in New York but who subsequently had a Hollywood career, including writing the original themes for the animated television series *Robotech* and its various off-shoots.

As for the native-born collaborators in this group, Dana Suesse (1909–1987), dubbed "the girl Gershwin" in the 1930s for writing both hit songs and light concert fare, had worked with Latouche earlier on the 1940 revue *Crazy with the Heat*; Marvin Fisher (1916–1993), the son of songwriter and publisher Fred Fisher, had a background as a jazz pianist and arranger that, in the estimation of David Jenness and Don Velsey, gave his songs, like his biggest hit, "When Sunny Gets Blue" (1956), "a jazz sensibility"; Robert Miles (b. 1920) adhered closely to the tradition of Kern and Berlin; and Leonard Bernstein (1918–1990), Donald Fuller (1919–1900), and John Strauss (1920–2011) all had strong contact with more serious musical currents, including study with composers Walter Piston, Darius Milhaud, and Paul Hindemith, respectively.[28]

The circumstances surrounding these songs remain largely obscure, with more known about some than others. Regarding "You Make Up," its composer, Robert Miles, met Latouche at the apartment of actress Gertrude Bryan, and suggested that the two work together, whereupon Latouche invited Miles to audition his work at his home; admiring a song Miles recently had written with lyricist Freeman Cohn, "You'll Fill My Heart," Latouche relyricized the number as "You Make Up (For All I've Missed)," a new lyric revised once again years later by Roger Schore. As Miles recalled in 2015, he actually thought the original Cohn lyric perfectly fine, but nonetheless overhauled the song on Latouche's advice: "I was in awe of him, of course," he explained. "He was a big name as far as I was concerned."[29]

Latouche, with the assistance of Kenward Elmslie, ostensibly lyricized "On the Waterfront" at the behest of Leonard Bernstein, who derived the music from his film score for the Elia Kazan picture so titled, fashioning the melody specifically from the love theme as heard as a popular dance tune in the wedding party scene. Latouche and Bernstein worked on the song on Martha's Vineyard while otherwise preoccupied with *Candide* during the summer of 1954, about the time of the movie's American release; they plainly hoped to capitalize on the growing interest in movie theme songs, with the Robbins sheet music cover duly showing the picture's romantic leads, Marlon Brando and Eva Marie Saint, in a romantic pose.[30]

With respect to "The Deep Blue Sea," composer Ulpio Minucci's wife, Catherine, remembered that her husband and Latouche composed this particular song for possible use in the New York production of British playwright Terence Rattigan's melodrama of the same name, in which case the song, although copywritten in mid-January 1953, probably dates from 1952, as the Rattigan play, a study of unrequited love comparable to the work of the American playwright William Inge, opened on

Broadway in November of that year. That the show's co-producer, Alfred de Liagre, by this time also had become interested in producing *The Golden Apple* gives further credence to the notion of some connection between the song and the Rattigan play, not to mention the number's title and the song itself, with its romantic melody and its image of a lover "condemned to always be / adrift upon the deep blue sea." Catherine Minucci further supposed that the composer-publisher Larry Spier brought her husband and Latouche together; if so, Spier also might have played some part regarding Latouche's collaborations with Alex Alstone and Dana Suesse, for the publisher had affiliations with them as well.[31]

Latouche and John Strauss wrote "A Nail in the Horseshoe" for the latter's wife, Charlotte Rae, either for her nightclub act or specifically for the *Songs I Taught My Mother* release. In any case, Latouche knew Rae (born Charlotte Rae Lubotsky, 1926), "widely considered," according to one authority, "the best singer-comedienne of the '50s," from her club appearances as well as from her performances as Mrs. Peachum in *The Threepenny Opera* and Mrs. Juniper in *The Golden Apple*. Often compared to the Canadian-British comedian Beatrice Lillie, Rae similarly specialized in ridiculing old-school gentility, with Latouche and Vernon Duke's pseudo-madrigal "Summer Is A-Comin' In" (from *The Lady Comes Across*), as sung by Rae both on *Songs I Taught My Mother* and in Ben Bagley's *The Littlest Revue*, forming a congenial part of her repertoire. Her husband since 1951, Strauss had studied at Yale with Hindemith after service in the army, and worked during these years primarily as a pianist and arranger, as in the 1955 *Songs* album on which he and his Baroque Bearcats accompanied his wife. Alcoholics who later embraced sobriety, Rae and Strauss (a closeted gay man who after his divorce from Rae in 1976 lived with a male partner) became drinking buddies with Latouche, who entertained them with "stories about all the weird people in his family and growing up in the South." In her memoirs, Rae further recalled that Latouche ("What a genius he was") and her husband planned "to collaborate on an opera" for her that "never quite came to fruition." In later years, Strauss and Rae worked primarily in film and television, including for Rae a featured role in the sitcom *Diff'rent Strokes* and its spinoff, *The Facts of Life*.[32]

In short, Latouche seems to have been motivated to write these songs out of some combination of friendly goodwill and financial incentive, although many of these numbers defied commercial expectations by finding their own middle ground between high and low art traditions, including the Fuller songs, some or all of which might have been intended for a work of musical theater that never materialized. In any case, these songs reveal a wide diversity of musical styles, from the "novelty calypso" of "Co-Co-Coconut," the operetta-like romanticism of "My Dream," the suave Latin jazziness of "Strange," and the Italianate lyricism of "The Deep Blue Sea" to the haunting bluesiness of "On the Waterfront," the old-fashioned tunefulness of "You Make Up," and the operatic pastiche of "A Nail in the Horseshoe." Perhaps no other collection of songs so amply demonstrates Latouche's ability to tailor a lyric to a particular composer's language and aesthetic, including his charming play with Caribbean patois in "Co-Co-Coconut" that somehow also makes room for the very Latouchian rhyme of "protoplasm" and "swamp that has 'm." At the same time, most of the songs speak of love—either sadly as something absent from the singer's life, or rapturously, as something consoling and unearthly.[33]

"A Rainy Day" represents not only one of the best of these songs, but one of the most personal of the lyricist's entire career, so much so that, although a man figures as the song's love object, for the revue *Taking a Chance on Love*, Erik Haagensen, who devised the show, had a male singer perform the number, an excerpt of which follows:

> Where is the guy that I was saving for a rainy day?
> His heart was sure and so secure it couldn't ricochet
> There was such a gang around I didn't concentrate
> I thought he would hang around but I got home too late.
> Where is the Romeo that I was keeping under key?
> In time of need I thought that he'd be right on tap for me
> There's a ring around the moon and that means rain they say
> So I hope he shows up soon to make the dark skies gay
> Now that the weatherman says there's a storm in sight
> Where is the guy that I was saving for a rainy, rainy night?

For its part, the lyric to "On the Waterfront," although deemed "uninspired" by film music scholar Jon Burlingame, nonetheless reveals merits similarly characteristic of its author, including some thematic unity suggested by the central image of the waterfront, and a keen sensitivity to the placement of words with respect to pitch and rhythm; at the song's conclusion, for example, the rhyming words "fate" and "straight" sound out on climactic long notes: "And hope that fate will lead you straight to me."[34]

"A Nail in the Horseshoe" deserves special comment as a late and masterful expression of that cabaret humor with which Latouche initially made his reputation. The song caricatures the kind of society dames found in the first tier of the Metropolitan Opera House, the so-called diamond horseshoe, by way of a Mozartian recitative and aria, its main theme taken from "Non più andrai" from *The Marriage of Figaro*. The recitative recounts the singer's youthful encounter with an Italian singing teacher who "went mad for my cadenza and my trill," and her subsequent forced marriage to an "old merchant prince," whereas the aria reflects on her current status as "one of the nails in the horseshoe at the opera." "Ev'ry music lover flocks, when they dust off my box," sings the inebriated patron, "when I open it the season has begun." The number satirizes, above all, the woman's insensibility to opera, as opposed to its social trappings, by, among other means, various mispronunciations of composers' names and works, including one section that also parodies a line from Victor Herbert and Harry B. Smith's "Gypsy Love Song":

And things by Massenate [Massenet]
Just simply do not fascinate
This little birdie
Not a thing by Virdie [Verdi], nor Pussini [Puccini], nor Rossini,
Not one teeny-weeny.
I can't stand Beethoven, nor Mosart [Mozart], nor Schubert,
Though I do like Victor Hubert [Herbert].
"Slumber on, my little tipsy gypsy" ["my little gypsy sweetheart"]
[spoken]: Ah, now there's a catchy tune for ya!

After enumerating everything she adores about the opera—"I love it when the baritones wear tights," and so forth—the singer asks, "But why in the hell do they have to sing?"

A florid instrumental version of "The Deep Blue Sea," arranged by Nelson Riddle and recorded in late 1953 by Riddle and His Orchestra for Capitol Records, became, along with such similar songs as Robert Maxwell's "Ebb Tide" (also 1953) and Erroll Garner's "Misty" (1954), part of the easy listening landscape of the postwar era; and Latouche's other number with Minucci, "After a While," a song about the fragility of love, also attained some currency as recorded by the Italian crooner Remo Capra in 1960 for Columbia Records. In addition, Eddie Korbich, performing in drag, provided a hilarious cover of Charlotte Rae's "A Nail in the Horseshoe" in *Taking a Chance on Love*. But of these later Latouche popular songs, only "Strange" enjoyed any real popularity; the others, including "On the Waterfront," faltered. "There's a pop tune out (horrid) called On The Waterfront," wrote Leonard Bernstein to David Diamond in August 1954, "but no dough. Fuck it."[35]

The exceptional success of "Strange" owed much to a 1952 recording of the song for Capitol by the suave African-American singer-pianist Nat King Cole, accompanied by Nelson Riddle and His Orchestra. "My juke-box hit, 'Strange' has been a god-send thanks to Nat King Cole's satin sibilances," wrote Latouche to his friend Libby Holman, "so for the time being I can coast." For the rest of Latouche's life and after, the song remained something of a Latin jazz standard, with a number of recordings by instrumentalists, but also by such vocalists as Frankie Vaughan, Jackie Paris, Roy Hamilton, Mose Allison, Sylvia De Sayles, and Freddy Cole. "Typically for Latouche," write popular song experts David Jenness and Don Velsey in their discussion of the song, "there is a lot of compound rhyme ('enjoying with me' / 'toying with me') and cross-rhyme ('hum**drum** thing'/ '**some**thing'). This is a lyricist's prerogative, and it can be delightful; for this rather slight song, it may be a bit much." As with "Co-Co-Coconut," how the song's lyric, with its depiction of love as "strange," "dangerous," and "sweet and rare," relates to a current Latin dance craze, in this case the cha-cha, deserves notice as well, including the connection between the dance's flirtatious movements and the notion of love as "a game you're enjoying with me."[36]

21

Candide

After a long and rocky journey, the operetta *Candide* opened on Broadway in December 1956. Presented by Ethel Linder Reiner in association with Lester Osterman Jr., the show had a book by Lillian Hellman, music by Leonard Bernstein, and lyrics mostly by Richard Wilbur, but also by Latouche (who had died the previous August) and Dorothy Parker as well as by Hellman and Bernstein themselves.

Lillian Hellman (1905–1984) had proposed collaborating with Bernstein, her junior by some thirteen years, as early as the spring of 1950. Raised in New Orleans and New York, and the author of such highly regarded plays as *The Children's Hour* (1934), *The Little Foxes* (1939), and *Another Part of the Forest* (1946), Hellman had little interest in musical theater, but she had advised her and Bernstein's good friend Marc Blitzstein on his operatic adaptation of her play *The Little Foxes*, which opened on Broadway as *Regina* in 1949—an experience that she apparently found satisfying enough to encourage her in this direction.[1]

A partnership with Bernstein also offered Hellman a chance to hitch her wagon to a rising star even as her own career had begun to wane. For by this time, Bernstein, the son of Jewish immigrants and a graduate of Harvard and the Curtis Institute, had distinguished himself, although still only in his early thirties, as one of the country's foremost conductors and composers, his credentials including a stunning conductorial debut with the New York Philharmonic in 1943 and the score to the 1944 hit musical *On the Town* (book and lyrics by Betty Comden and Adolph Green). On the verge of even greater glory, in the course of the 1950s, in addition to holding teaching positions at Tanglewood and Brandeis, appearing on a popular educational television program, and leading a busy international conducting career, he would complete, besides *Candide*, the one-act opera *Trouble in Tahiti* (1952, to his own libretto), the film score to *On the Waterfront* (1954), *Serenade* for solo violin and orchestra (1954), and the musicals *Wonderful Town* (1953, book by Joseph Fields and Jerome Chodorov, lyrics by Comden and Green) and *West Side Story* (1957, book by Arthur Laurents, lyrics by Stephen Sondheim)—that is to say, much of his most successful and influential music.[2]

Hellman's suggestion of a collaboration intrigued Bernstein; he regarded her as "one of our greatest playwrights," and went on record, shortly before the premiere of

Candide, as saying that he "always wanted to do a musical with a great playwright" (he had proposed as much to Tennessee Williams, who after some thought responded, "Why should a playwright split the honors with a musician?"). However, finding the right opportunity to work together proved another matter. "I've written Lillian [Hellman] to count me out," he told his sister in April 1950. "I'm banking on Adolph [Green] & Betty [Comden]." And although several months later the press reported that Bernstein and Hellman were "thinking of writing a musical together," as fall approached Hellman's preoccupation with her new play *The Autumn Garden,* which opened on Broadway in March 1951, necessitated deferring any such plans to the future.[3]

Tantalizing rumors of a Hellman–Bernstein collaboration continued to surface nonetheless. Interviewed by the *Times* in November 1951, Hellman herself referred to such a project as "temporarily cold, but not completely forgotten," and raised the prospect of working with Bernstein that winter. At the same time, this announcement seems to have come as something of a surprise to Bernstein, for he subsequently wrote to his secretary, "I know nothing about working with Lillian H., but I would of course love to. I think I'll write her."[4]

Some eight months later, in the wake of the July 26, 1952, death of Argentina's charismatic first lady Eva ("Evita") Perón, Bernstein asked Blitzstein what he thought about his writing an opera with Hellman about Evita, an idea that seems to have originated with the playwright, who in 1949 had adapted Emmanuel Roblès's recent French play about the Venezuelan war of independence, *Montserrat,* and who had developed a fascination with Argentina. Blitzstein liked the idea, as he told Bernstein, but wondered whether Hellman would be "the precisely right librettist" given the similarities between Evita and Regina Hubbard, the protagonist of *The Little Foxes* and *Another Part of the Forest*: "Once the Latin color is snagged, and the expanded picture of power-area registered, will she (L[illian]) not find herself treading well-worn paths? Then you could call the opera 'The Bigger Foxes' or 'The Same Old Part of Another Forest.'" However, nothing materialized along these lines.[5]

Then in late 1953, Hellman wrote to Bernstein, in Milan to conduct at La Scala,

> This time I think I have it. I don't know, but maybe. Voltaire's "Candide." I think it could make a really wonderful combination of opera-prose-songs. It's so obviously right that I wonder nobody has done it before, or have they? I am very excited by it, but I want to read it two or three times more, think about it, and not decide until—Anyway, please reread it quickly and let me know what you think, if you're free when you come back, etc. I think, done right, it could have real style & wit, and great importance....
>
> I wouldn't want to do the song lyrics. So if you like the idea,—and I still do by the time you write—who would be good. Maybe a good *poet*? And it would have to be written with kind of doll-like, fairy-tale scenery.

In early January 1954, Bernstein, still abroad, informed his wife, the Chilean-American actress Felicia Montealegre Cohn, that he had decided "to go along with Lillian [Hellman] on Candide—imagine, after having written her a letter saying no and tearing it up, I think it . . . will allow me to do other things as well." Two days later, he telegrammed Hellman, "Hold everything. Will do Candide. Terribly excited. Hope you are."[6]

Published pseudonymously in 1759, *Candide, or Optimism,* a satirical novella by the celebrated provocateur Voltaire (*nom de plume* for François-Marie Arouet, 1694–1778), recounts the adventures of its foolishly naïve eponymous hero, whose name implies his honest nature. The bastard nephew of the Baron of Thunder-ten-tronckh of Westphalia, Germany, Candide has been raised, along with the Baron's arrogant son and his lusty daughter, Cunégonde, under the tutelage of Professor Pangloss, a caricature of the philosopher Gottfried Leibniz, famous for arguing that God created the best of all possible worlds. On discovering Candide and Cunégonde in a compromising situation, the Baron expels Candide, who, wandering far and wide, finds trouble reconciling a Panglossian worldview with the many examples of thievery, fanaticism, lewdness, savagery, and hypocrisy he encounters virtually at every turn but in the idyllic land of Eldorado in the New World. Increasingly skeptical, Candide finds a second mentor in an ill-fated scholar, the pessimistic Martin. Meanwhile, Cunégonde, forced into a life of debauchery, acquires a protector in the resourceful Old Woman. Settling down with Cunégonde, Pangloss, Martin, the Old Woman, and others on a farm outside of Constantinople, and impressed by a Turkish family who counsel collective work as a means of preventing "boredom, vice, and poverty," Candide proposes that he and his friends set aside theorizing and "work in the garden."[7]

Although written in response to the horrors of both the Lisbon earthquake of 1755, which left tens of thousands dead and the city decimated, and the ongoing Seven Years' War (1756–1763), a worldwide conflagration that ultimately witnessed hundreds of thousands of deaths, Voltaire's caustic allegory, an enormous success from the start, proved timeless in its appeal, no less so than in the years following the Second World War. In a 1949 open letter in the *New York Times* to the U.S. Congress, former Texas congressman Maury Maverick, for example, endorsed the book as "truly essential," explaining with tongue in cheek, "The propriety of loot, the politeness of murder on a grand scale, starvation, rapine, and the usual incidents of glory are applauded in the book by Dr. Pangloss, the Great Philosopher, who proclaimed this the best of all possible worlds. It makes a Congressman appreciate the world of today, which is about the same as Candide's." A few days after this letter appeared, the *Times* also quoted V. S. Pritchett, in a review of Aldous Huxley's *Ape and Essence,* as saying, "Hiroshima is Lisbon; but where is our Voltaire?"[8]

Hellman and Bernstein thought the novella's lampooning of the Catholic Inquisition particularly germane to the current American crackdown on communists and communist sympathizers—a very personal matter, given their own subjection to anticommunist vilification, including citation, like Latouche, in the 1950 publication *Red Channels* (with Hellman's lover, detective novelist Dashiell Hammett, imprisoned for five months in 1951 for refusing to cooperate fully with government investigators). "The particular evil which impelled Lillian Hellman to choose *Candide* and present it to me as the basis for a musical stage work," Bernstein stated at a 1989 performance of the work, "was what we now so quaintly and, alas, faintly recall as McCarthyism—an 'ism' so akin to that Spanish [read: Portuguese] Inquisition we just revisited in the first act as to curdle the blood." But at the time of the work's premiere, Bernstein also claimed for the novella, which he had admired since his student days, a more general relevance for America: "The matters with which it [the novella] is concerned are as valid for us [Americans] as for any—and sometimes I think they are especially valid for us in America. Puritanical snobbery, phony moralism, inquisitorial attacks on the individual, brave-new-world optimism, essential superiority—aren't these all charges leveled against American society by our best thinkers? And they were also the charges made by Voltaire against his own society." Hellman, who similarly had loved *Candide* from a young age and who reread it "every five or six years," placed the novella in an even broader context, stating, "I thought of it [the book] as an attack on all rigid thinking, on all isms."[9]

The successful premiere of Marc Blitzstein's English adaptation of Bertolt Brecht and Kurt Weill's *The Threepenny Opera*—a work both Bernstein and Hellman considered a paragon of musical theater—on June 14, 1952, at Brandeis University, at Bernstein's invitation and under his direction, presumably helped point the way to *Candide* as well. Similarly derived from an eighteenth-century satire, namely, John Gay's 1728 ballad opera *The Beggar's Opera*, whose London premiere Voltaire might have attended, *The Threepenny Opera* generally enjoyed, as did *The Beggar's Opera* itself, heightened attention during these postwar years, as evidenced by, among other things, Latouche and Ellington's *Beggar's Holiday* and, less directly, Auden, Kallman, and Stravinsky's *The Rake's Progress*. In the end, Hellman's script for *Candide* suggested the impact of *The Threepenny Opera* (as well as Brecht's *Mother Courage and Her Children*) much as Bernstein's score showed the influence of Weill and Stravinsky. Tellingly, Robert Rounseville, who created the title role in Bernstein's *Candide* in 1956, also starred as Tom Rakewell in the 1951 world premiere of *The Rake's Progress*, and in later years Macheath in Blitzstein's adaptation of *The Threepenny Opera* as well.[10]

In February 1954, some mere weeks after Hellman initially floated the idea, the *Times* mentioned a possible *Candide* musical by the playwright and Bernstein, although the two had yet to secure a producer or a lyricist. "We're having a fling at this thing... there's nothing official about it," stated Bernstein. During the late winter and early spring, as Bernstein worked on the film *On the Waterfront* in Hollywood, he and Hellman pondered possible lyricists long distance. Hellman's first choice, approved by Bernstein, seems to have been Archibald MacLeish, which reflected her preference for a poet as opposed to a lyricist; but with MacLeish otherwise occupied,

Hellman suggested in mid-April that Bernstein, still in California, talk matters over with his regular partners, Betty Comden and Adolph Green, as well as with Ira Gershwin, while she contact Latouche—whom Bernstein long had known—in New York. "If we wait too long everybody is going to have plans for the summer," she wrote Bernstein, for at this point they had in mind a production for the 1954–55 season. However seriously Hellman might have considered working with Comden and Green (about whom she had doubts) or Ira Gershwin (a close personal friend), those lyricists would not have been available, what with Comden and Green in Hollywood, and Gershwin largely retired from lyric writing. In any case, Hellman and Bernstein came to an agreement in May with Latouche, whose abilities as a lyricist of wit and sophistication, as displayed in the recent March 1954 unveiling of *The Golden Apple*, made him a natural candidate for this venture.[11]

Around this same time, poet Richard Wilbur (b. 1921), a young Harvard Fellow who had been recommended to Hellman by her friend, Harvard professor Harry Levin, and who earlier had turned down her suggestion that he become the show's lyricist, informed the playwright that he would be interested in writing the lyrics after all; in addition, Hellman learned from writer Roald Dahl that the British poet and humorist A. P. Herbert would be willing to do likewise. In responding to both Wilbur and Dahl, Hellman explained that she and Bernstein already had entered into, as she wrote Dahl, "a moral contract" with Latouche, couching her regrets in such ways as to suggest real reservations, if not misgivings. "I am sorry that commitments have been made," she wrote to Wilbur, "and there is now no turning back from them." Even more regretfully, she told Dahl a few days later that learning about Herbert's interest had left her "absolutely broken-hearted. The news that he is immediately available has sent me into a tailspin all morning, but having talked with Lenny [Bernstein], I know now that there is no turning back from La Touche—and maybe everything will turn out for the best."[12]

Bernstein, Hellman, and Latouche spent much of the summer of 1954 working on *Candide* along with their own individual projects in Vineyard Haven on Martha's Vineyard. After arriving on the island in mid-June, Latouche wrote to composer Douglas Moore, "Vineyard Haven is fun, and Leonard B., as always, is an experience (of the irreligious variety, however)." He initially stayed with Bernstein, but after Latouche's boyfriend Kenward Elmslie arrived, the couple rented their own home, a converted school owned by psychiatrist Ruth Fox, whose furnishings seemed to Latouche "unnecessarily squalid," and where his mother soon joined them in order to keep house. "It's all very apple-cheeked and cosy," he wrote a friend, "with a copper kettle bubbling away on the stove, the roses and honeysuckle becking through the window, the inevitable bird chair working overtime outside, and a little posset of mescalin bubbling by the hearth."[13]

Latouche kept his diary on the island for about two weeks. Most of the entries registered, as usual, a good deal of malaise, in particular his inability to get work done and his personal problems with Elmslie. "Leonard Bernstein kept at me to get up and start pulling *Candide* together (lyrically, that is)," he wrote on June 30, followed by a flowchart of other pressing obligations, including work on *The Vamp* and *The Ballad of Baby Doe,* that left him "a bit frayed at the prospects of every morning." In typical fashion, he responded to these conflicting demands by talking with friends, taking naps, having sex, playing games, eating and drinking excessively, and reading a variety of books, including plunging into a study of physics. But he managed nonetheless to get some work on the show done, including the lyrics for "Candide's Lament" and "Ringaroundarosy," the latter described by Latouche as "A complicated song, a bubbling aria about the history of Pangloss's syphilis. It has taken four days to establish the tricky beats and unexpected musical stresses in L.[eonard Bernstein]'s style: the song will probably never be used, but it's been a fascinating exercise in technique."[14]

Although Latouche rarely discussed Hellman or Bernstein in his journal, some entries suggest a fair degree of conflict and tension, notwithstanding the consolation he received from Hellman on hearing the news about the imminent closing of *The Golden Apple* on Broadway. On July 9, he wrote, for example, "Lennie to me some days ago: 'You're always looking for some kind of system, some elaborate discipline to achieve . . . it's so infantile' . . . And in half an hour, he was being peevish and ill-tempered, throwing a bathing suit in my face (which enraged me), and squabbling desperately with me over anagrams. Why do I upset him? There is some projection, but it is not yet apparent." And the day after a July 10 dinner party at Hellman's with Dashiell Hammett also in attendance, Latouche reflected,

> What medium can convey the qualities of human feeling I perpetually sense in a room, unspoken of, unexpressed in movement. Felicia, Leonard's wife, like a delicate spring under pressure, about to zoom up at any moment. His brother [Burton Bernstein], a handsome lad with an air of fake shyness concealing an aggressive, rather bitchy observation. Lillian [Hellman], coruscating and capricious, but strong and sharply observant, under the pressures of social interchange. "Isolation," "loneliness," these clap-trap words . . . there's another quality at work under the personae of these not-too-well-meaning bright people.

Such thoughts led him to muse on the relevance of the 1931 novel *Hunger and Love* by the socialist writer Lionel Britton, which he might reasonably have found in Ruth Fox's home (her husband, McAlister Coleman, being a socialist writer), and whom he quoted as saying (although actually from the introduction by Bertrand Russell), "individuals are human individually by metaphor in so far as they contribute to the human in civilisation," a comment that in turn prompted his own observation, "how divisible we have all become, how lacking in totality."[15]

Latouche characteristically devoted more space in his diary to his dreams than to his professional work. In one instance, he dreamt of having an erection lying in bed in the arms of Dashiell Hammett. "My bewilderment," he wrote, "stemmed from my conscious memory of him [Hammett] as a tough, combative figure, and my sensing him here . . . as a kind and gentle force." A young child enters, watching and grinning, and refuses to go away. "I hopt out of bed to push him out, but there was an astonishing strength in the little figure. In a rage, I began to smash wildly at him, hammering him down with blows, and tearing away at his face. Awoke very distressed. And small wonder!"[16]

In September, as Bernstein left for Venice to conduct the premiere of his *Serenade*, Hellman continued working on the show's book, a draft of which she hoped to complete by October. "I think maybe *Candide* is going to be very, very good, and I feel cheerful about it," she wrote in early September to Gerald Goode, an agent for producer Sol Hurok, who had expressed interest in the show. However, a few days later, one of her own representatives from MCA Artists wrote to her, "I think we're all agreed we will do nothing about a producer until Lenny gets back from Venice and we know how we stand in the lyricist department," a comment presumably related to a late-summer rift between Latouche and his collaborators. After Bernstein returned to New York in late September, he resumed work on the piece with Hellman and Latouche, the three meeting a few times each week. Then, in mid-November, the *Times* reported, "After spending months writing the lyrics to 'Candide,' for which he had finished the first act's quota, John Latouche has asked to be excused. Mr. Latouche said the step had become mandatory because Carol Channing was waiting for the delivery of a new show, 'Delilah' [later, *The Vamp*], on which he, Sam Locke and James Mundy are in the throes of completing final revisions." This same item further named Ethel Linder Reiner, who officially became the show's producer in early 1955, as having the "inside track" on the job (Hellman and Bernstein having rejected Sol Hurok's proposed budget of around $100,000 as unacceptably paltry).[17]

Whatever the accuracy of the *Times* item regarding Latouche's departure from the show—and he indeed had other projects on the docket—Bernstein clearly precipitated this rupture; long frustrated by Latouche's slowness, he already had broken with him once before, sometime toward the end of the summer. "We've had real tsuros [Yiddish: serious aggravation] with *Candide*; we split with LaTouche, which we should have done long ere this," he wrote to composer David Diamond. "The mistake was to take him back again when I returned in September." As Bernstein further told some other friends, he felt that he and Latouche should have finished the score by summer's end, but since his return from Italy there had been

> a long stretch of trying to eke out *Candide* with Touche, and not getting much of anywhere. Then the last two weeks [in mid-November] of searching desperately for a new lyricist, in vain . . . Lil[lian Hellman] and I have decided to do what I've been screaming for since the beginning: namely to write the lyrics ourselves. It's so natural and right: what were we

> futzing with Touche for all this time? So now I feel creative and set-up again, and ready for a two-month creative dash.[18]

Although Latouche's working relationships often seemed fraught, the situation in this case appears to have been particularly so from the start. Hellman herself later recalled that although she "had a good time on *Candide* when I was working alone," the collaboration had been "stormy," so much so that it ultimately wrecked her friendship with Bernstein. According to one source, Hellman, who had a homophobic streak despite her friendships with gay men and her own homosexual inclinations, specifically "was known to express homophobic objections" about Latouche (perhaps involving what some unsympathetic acquaintances of the lyricist referred to as his "flamboyant" personality). In any case, she did not look back fondly on her time with Latouche, writing to Bernstein in 1955, "Last summer now seems to me a dream and I've even forgotten Touche."[19]

Bernstein, meanwhile, could be a high-handed collaborator, often meddling with the work of his lyricists. "Lenny Bernstein has to do everything, as you know," commented Dorothy Parker, who eventually became one of the show's lyricists, "and do it better than anybody—which he does—except for lyrics." Another of the operetta's lyricists, Richard Wilbur, so exasperated with Bernstein that he nearly quit the show, wrote to Hellman along these lines, "If you catch L.[eonard Bernstein] rewriting my lyrics, clip his piano wires." By January 1955, Hellman herself had expressed weariness over the "tiresome arguments [with Bernstein] about music requirements."[20]

In addition, Hellman and Bernstein from the beginning seemed to undervalue Latouche, as suggested by Hellman's initial reservations, and Bernstein's long-held supposition that he and Hellman could write the lyrics themselves. In August 1954, Bernstein described Hellman's work to David Diamond as "great," but Latouche's as only "fairly good (don't quote me!)." And in a letter to Dorothy Parker from early December 1954, Hellman similarly identified various Latouche lyrics as "good," "fairly good," "half good," and "very bad." "I cannot defend the lyrics [to the show]," she wrote Harry Levin about a month later, at a time when the lyrics still mostly represented Latouche's work. "I never liked them and have always known they would have to be changed and polished. But I have rather given up hope. (They do, however, sound much better with the music.) It's a low-down form of writing." Even after Latouche left the show, Hellman wanted him to revise his lyrics, writing to Bernstein sometime in 1955, "He [Latouche] told me [over the phone] that on rereading his lyrics he was very pleased. I had exactly the opposite reaction: all the lyrics seem to me to need real work."[21]

For all this, the separation seems to have been relatively amiable. Latouche came to an agreement with Bernstein and Hellman in December 1954 that he would receive, among other things, 1 percent royalties on weekly gross box-office receipts and billing equal to that of any other lyricist, a reasonable accord considering that he had written nearly all the lyrics for the first act. Moreover, he remained involved in the show—often through production associate Thomas Hammond, a friendly ally who had worked with Latouche on Lehman Engel's *Mooncalf*—virtually up to the time of his death several months before the show's Boston opening. He attended, for example, an audition held by Reiner in early 1955, later telling Bernstein's secretary Helen Coates, in ostensible reference to some songs written since his departure as lyricist, that "he had heard a lot more of the music of *Candide* and loved it. He said he didn't like 'all of the words,' but he liked some of them." Furthermore, in letters to Bernstein from early 1955, Coates and Hellman referred to Latouche as "very friendly" and "very loving," respectively, even if in such a way as to suggest that all had not been that "friendly" and "loving" in the past. And on the occasion of the November 1955 Broadway premiere of Latouche's musical *The Vamp*, Bernstein and wife, Felicia, cordially sent the lyricist a telegram signed, "All the best. Rooting for you. Affectinately [*sic*]."[22]

After breaking with Latouche, Bernstein set out to revise some of the first act, including writing the words and music for an episode that would become the "Pray for us" section in the Lisbon scene; and both he and Hellman began composing lyrics for the second act as well. But in late 1954, they further sought the assistance of two poets: James Agee (pronounced AY-jee, 1909–1955), the elegant writer familiar in musical circles for Samuel Barber's settings of his words, and for providing the inspiration for Aaron Copland's 1954 opera *The Tender Land*; and Hellman's close friend Dorothy Parker (1893–1967), a renowned wit whom Bernstein found "very sweet, very drunk, very forthcoming, very cooperative and, in sum, a dream to work with." (About this same time, Ted Geisel—better known by his pen name, Dr. Seuss—also offered to compose lyrics for the show.) Hellman and Bernstein specifically wanted, among other things, Agee or Parker to write a first-act finale intended to depict Candide's sojourn to Eldorado. "We had always planned it [this finale] as entirely opera, to be sung in verse," wrote Hellman to Parker. "Master La Touche had a try at it, but the try isn't any good. So it remains to be written." Ultimately, Hellman and Bernstein decided against any Eldorado scene whatsoever, although for the Boston tryout, the program book added "Eldorado" in parentheses alongside "Intermission," with Hellman telling the *New York Herald Tribune*, "Maybe paradise is getting a drink at the nearest bar during intermission."[23]

Both Agee and Parker contributed several items, but Bernstein set only a few of these, chiefly Parker's "The Marquise's Gavotte" (later revised by the composer and Richard Wilbur). Hellman probably had Agee in mind when she wrote to Harry Levin in January 1955 that she and Bernstein had "called in a good poet" but that "the job he did is just plain bad, and it is bad because he is a real poet." In any case, Agee died in May 1955 aware, according to Hellman, that she and Bernstein would not use any of his work, although she subsequently arranged to have an honorarium sent to his widow, Mia, in appreciation of his effort. As for Parker, she quickly excused herself from the project, citing "too many geniuses," although she too received financial compensation in the way of a tiny fraction of royalties.[24]

In early 1955, Hellman and Bernstein completed a rather finished draft of the work as documented by a fair copy in ink of the piano-vocal score submitted for copyright in February and a near complete script, two sources that include lyrics by Bernstein, Hellman, Latouche, and Parker, and that most fully preserve Latouche's work on the show. The script identified the action as taking place "any time before the middle of the eighteenth century," and specified much doubling of roles, including that of Pangloss and Martin. For the numbers named in the scenario that follows, unless otherwise indicated, Latouche wrote the lyrics, with the caveat that Bernstein might have edited them.

Act I, scene one. Westphalia, Germany. The castle of the Baron Thunder-ten-tronckh. The Baron presides over an estate that includes his wife, the Baroness; his natural children, the pretty Cunegonde and the supercilious Maximillian; his adopted son, the innocent Candide; his children's tutor, Dr. Pangloss; and his serving maid, Paquette. As the act opens, German troops rout the Bulgarian army and the seven characters mentioned above sing a "Victory Chorale" in the style of a Lutheran hymn, one stanza of which follows:

Now let the trumpet's blaring throat
Call out across our castle moat,
And o'er Westphalian hamlets float,
Proclaiming with each joyful note
Another victory.

Pangloss gives the Baron's children their daily lesson ("Lesson Song," for Pangloss, Candide, Cunegonde, Maximillian, and Paquette); drawing the Leibnizian moral, "Once one dismisses / The rest of all possible worlds, / One finds that this is / The best of all possible worlds," from tutorials in biology, philosophy, and Latin (the last involving the conjugation of the Latin verb for "to love," *amare*, as Paquette, the object of Pangloss's desire, makes her appearance), with Pangloss also providing rationales for such things as war and snakes:

PANGLOSS
'Twas Snake that tempted Mother Eve.
Because of Snake we now believe
That though depraved
We can be saved
From hellfire and damnation.
CANDIDE, CUNEGONDE, AND MAXIMILLIAN
Because of Snake's temptation.
PANGLOSS
If Snake had not
Seduced our lot

And primed us for salvation,
Jehovah could not pardon all
The sins that we call cardinal
Involving bed and bottle.
Now on to Aristotle.

The music for these explanations echoes—at a faster clip—the "Victory Chorale," underscoring the social context of Pangloss's worldview.

After Candide and Cunegonde express their intention to marry, the Baron, appalled at Candide's presumption, banishes him. The Bulgarians renew their attack, leaving Pangloss, Cunegonde, and Maximillian dead ("Battle Music," instrumental). Finding the body of his beloved, Candide mourns Cunegonde ("Candide's Lament," for Candide, with the world-weary spoken interjections for the King of Bulgaria presumably by Hellman). For this lament, Bernstein recycled a short piano piece apparently written several years earlier that he eventually published as "Ilana: The Dreamer" (one of a set of *Four Sabras* for piano, a sabra being a native-born Israeli Jew), the music's main four-note motive conveniently fitting the name, Cunegonde; the composer subsequently adapted this same music for other portions of the work, including the "Paris Waltz Scene," the "Quartet," and eventually the opening of "Make Our Garden Grow," to the point that the music became known as the Cunegonde theme.[25]

Scene 1a. Travels from Westphalia to Lisbon. Tired and hungry, Candide encounters little sympathy for a displaced foreigner.

Scene two. Market Square in Lisbon. The day of the famous earthquake of 1755. "What a day, what a day / For an auto-da-fé! / What a sunny summer sky!" sing two girls walking a dog, the start of a sequence for the ensemble, "Lisbon Opening," in which professionals, tradesmen, and prostitutes advertise their wares in a series of stanzas that employ the same seven-line *aabaccc* rhyme scheme, as in this strophe for the doctor:

Here be powders and pills
For your fevers and chills.
I've a cure safe and sure
For whatever your ills.
For a fit of migraine,
Or a pox on the brain
Here's an herb that will curb any pain!

This "Lisbon Opening" concludes with the Arab Conjurer presenting to the crowd the gin-drinking Infant Casmira, who although twenty-five years old appears to be a child, and who predicts a devastating earthquake.

Candide discovers in the crowd his old tutor, Pangloss (the characters in Voltaire's *Candide* have a way of resurrecting), who has contracted syphilis, but who takes an upbeat view of the matter ("Ringaroundarosy," for Pangloss and chorus). The music for this syphilis song corresponds to that from the "Lisbon Opening," with both numbers ridiculously ebullient for the subjects at hand, including a jazzy syncopated figure presumably related to the scene's Iberian setting; Latouche probably had such syncopation in mind when he spoke of the music's "tricky beats and unexpected musical stresses," with in the following example Scotch snaps on the words, "haunting," "never," "seafar[ing]," "certain," "[for]gotten," and "given":

Oh my darling Paquette!
She is haunting me yet
With a dear
Souvenir
I shall never forget!

'Twas a gift that she got
From a seafaring Scot
He received
(He believed)
In Shalott.

In Shalott, from his dame
Who was certain it came
With a kiss
From a Swiss.
(She'd forgotten his name).

But he told her that he
Had been given it free
By a sweet
Little cheat
In Paree.

Like "Lesson Song," this Gilbertian patter song—with its winking allusion to Alfred Tennyson's poem "The Lady of Shalott," as seen above, and elsewhere its double entendres on "stung" and "wasp" (involving the age-old use of an insect sting as a metaphor for sex, but possibly in addition, especially given the mention of an "English lord," a pun on "wasp" as a newfangled acronym for a white Anglo-Saxon Protestant)—amusingly enlarges Hellman's depiction of Pangloss as a glib academic.[26]

The scene's concluding episode, "The Inquisition," in which two inquisitors and two professors try Pangloss and Candide among other alleged heretics, provided Hellman with an opportunity to parody McCarthyite tribunals, including the testimony of friendly witnesses:

GRAND INQUISITOR: What is the charge?
FIRST PROFESSOR: The overbuying of candles for the overreading of books in subversive association with associates.
GRAND INQUISITOR: From whom did you get the books, and to whom did you give the books?
OLD MAN: Great judge, I learned to read as a very young man. I can see now that I was a tool and a fool. I was poor, I was lonely—
FIRST PROFESSOR: Who are your associates? Be quick.
OLD MAN: Yes, sir. Well, there was Emmanuel, Lillybelle, Lionel, and Dolly and Molly and Polly, of course. And my Ma and my Pa and my littlest child. A priest, deceased, and my uncle and my aunt. The president, his resident, and the sister of my wife—
GRAND INQUISITOR: All right. All right. Thank you for your splendid cooperation.

"What a lovely day, what a lovely day, / What a day for a holiday!" sing the chorus, who periodically comment on the proceedings, including this antisemitic outburst:

He don't mix meat and dairy:
He won't eat humble pie:
So sing a Miserere
And hang the bastard high!

As with "meat and dairy" and "Miserere," the chorus subsequently rhymes "lied and tricked us" and "Benedictus," "[foreign]ers like this come" and "Pax vobiscum," and "can be cheery" and "Dies Irae"—the clever sort of rhyming especially reminiscent of Latouche's cabaret work. An earthquake leaves Pangloss hanging from the gibbet.

Scene 2b. Travel scenes from Lisbon to Paris. Candide journeys to the outskirts of Paris on a talking wooden horse.

Scene three. A House in Paris. As Candide and other beggars watch from outside, two wealthy members of an international banking family, the cousins Marquis Milton de Hochheimer and Marquis Sultan de Hochheimer, who share the favors of Cunegonde, host a masked ball ("Paris Waltz Scene," instrumental with obbligatos for Cunegonde, the Old Lady, and the two Hochheimers, with both the sung and spoken dialogue presumably by Hellman). Cunegonde spots Candide and arranges a rendezvous through her duenna, the Old Lady, a shrewd woman of dubious aristocratic background. In "The Reunion Waltz" for Candide and Cunegonde that follows, both Latouche and Bernstein, taking their cue from Voltaire's satire of romantic novels at this point in the story, parody such operetta numbers as Victor Herbert's "Ah! Sweet Mystery of Life" (*Naughty Marietta*) and Rudolf Friml's "Indian Love Call" (*Rose-Marie*):

CANDIDE
Dearest lady, pray explain.
I had thought you slain;
Thought you rudely violated too.
CUNEGONDE
That is very true.
Ah, but love will find a way.
CANDIDE
Then what did you do?
CUNEGONDE
We'll go into that another day.
But now what of you?
You are looking very well.
How did you contrive to survive?
CANDIDE
I've a sorry tale to tell
I escaped half-dead, half-alive.

As Cunegonde exclaims, "Oh, what torture, oh, what pain," and Candide recalls his wanderings in "Holland, Portugal, and Spain," the duet spoofs operatic conventions further by having the two singers alternate the rhyming phrases, "Ah, what torture," and "Holland, Portu." Attacked by the two marquis, Candide kills them both, and flees with Cunegonde and the Old Lady.

Scene 3c. Travel scenes from Paris to Buenos Aires. Candide, Cunegonde, and the Old Lady join a procession of pilgrims about to board a ship to the New World ("Pilgrim's March and Hymn," for small chorus).

Scene four. Buenos Aires. The square in front of the Governor's Palace. Candide, Cunegonde, the Old Lady, and the pilgrims, set to be auctioned as slaves, arrive in Buenos Aires. The Governor's scheming servant Iago and Iago's diabolical eight-year-old son Fernando make their appearance, as does the callous Governor, who hopes to conquer the rich land of Eldorado. Disdainful of Candide's pedigree, the Baron's son Maximillian, now an officer in the Governor's service, opposes his planned marriage to Cunegonde, thereby angering Candide, who slays him and goes into hiding. The Governor, attracted to Cunegonde, sings of the transient pleasures of love ("Governor's Serenade," for the Governor):

Passion, my love
Leads me to ration my love.
Chiefly, my love,
Let us love briefly, my love.

Pleasure is sweet,
So use it discreetly.

Love me completely,
But love me fleetly, my love.

The Old Lady counsels Cunegonde to marry the Governor in order to save Candide ("Old Lady's Tango," later retitled "Tus Labios Rubi," and eventually "I Am Easily Assimilated," for the Old Lady, Cunegonde, and two Señoritas [later, Señores], lyrics by Bernstein, with the Spanish lines by his wife, Felicia). As Candide prepares to leave Buenos Aires, the Governor reprises his "Serenade" as Candide, Cunegonde, and the Old Lady reflect on their individual predicaments ("Quartet," for the Governor, Candide, Cunegonde, and the Old Lady).[27]

For an aborted fifth scene, apparently intended to be set in Eldorado and end the first act, Bernstein composed a song, "This I Know," that appears untexted in his 1955 ink score, but whose lyrics, unattributed, survive among his papers—a text depicting Candide's realization that he cannot live without Cunegonde; this same music, relyricized by Bernstein and Richard Wilbur, and alternately titled "No More Than This" and "Nothing More Than This," would resurface in revivals of *Candide* as a climactic number toward the close of the second act.

Act II, scene one. Buenos Aires. The square in front of the Governor's Palace. The people vainly await the return of the army from Eldorado ("Gloria," for Iago and chorus, lyrics unattributed). Accompanied by the pessimistic Martin, Candide arrives from Eldorado on the back of a dove with two pink sheep laden with gold and jewels ("The Ballad of Eldorado," for Candide and chorus, lyrics by Hellman). Learning that the Governor has seduced Cunegonde and sold her as a slave, Candide attempts to slay him, but before he can do so, Iago kills the Governor himself. Iago's equally treacherous son, Fernando, betrays his father and, learning the whereabouts of Eldorado from Candide, spearheads a children's crusade to travel there ("Fernando's Lullaby," also referred to as "Song to a Pure Child" or "Pure Child," for Fernando and chorus, lyrics unattributed, with spoken lines for Martin and Candide presumably by Hellman, the music composed in late 1954, and later adapted as "Sheep's Song," with words by Stephen Sondheim, for the 1973 revival of *Candide*). As Candide and Martin plan their departure for France in order to find Cunegonde, Fernando drills a fatal hole in their vessel and steals one of the sheep.

Scene 1a. Travel scenes from Buenos Aires to Paris. Adrift in the ocean on their one remaining sheep, Candide and Martin philosophize. After a shark yanks Martin to the watery depths, Candide encounters Pangloss and five dethroned kings clinging to a log; recently galley slaves on a pirate ship lost at sea, Pangloss and the Five Kings resolve to pursue the simple life under Candide's patronage.

Scene two. A House in Paris. The Marquise de Parolignac allows her friend Feron to run a fashionable gambling establishment in her home. As two scrubwomen (Cunegonde and the Old Lady) attend to their work, Feron confers with the Marquise in her boudoir. Guests move among the gaming tables ("Gambling Scene," including both the minuet from Mozart's *Don Giovanni*, and the refrain "Money, Money, Money," for Feron, Croupier, and the ensemble, lyrics unattributed, with spoken lines presumably by Hellman). The Marquise attempts to seduce and rob Candide as Pangloss enjoys his gambling winnings with the Five Kings and various ladies ("The Marquise's Gavotte," for the Marquise, Candide, and Pangloss, lyrics by Dorothy Parker). Finding Cunegonde wretched and ugly, Candide sadly perceives the depravity of the world and leaves, as Pangloss futilely waits for the Five Kings to return the gold they have stolen from him.

Scene 2b. Travel scenes from Paris to Westphalia. Candide, Cunegonde, the Old Lady, and Pangloss sit exhausted from their trek. Candide's dove arrives with news that the children's crusade sold Eldorado to an international syndicate and that its people committed mass suicide to avoid deportation. Candide breaks down.

Scene three. Westphalia. The castle of the Baron Thunder-ten-tronckh. Candide, Cunegonde, the Old Lady, and Pangloss arrive at the ruined castle to find Maximillian and a band of German soldiers waging war against the King of Bulgaria and his men. Candide urges all to undertake constructive work ("Get You Up," for Candide and the ensemble, lyrics and spoken lines apparently by Bernstein and Hellman). Candide proposes marriage to Cunegonde, and the act ends slowly and softly as the latter says, "I take you for my husband. And if I talk dinner will burn" ("Love Duet," for Candide and Cunegonde, unattributed lyrics surviving only in a pencil sketch; and "Marriage Ceremony," subtitled "Chorale Prelude on the Theme of the Love-Duet," instrumental with spoken lines for the principals presumably by Hellman, a humming chorus based on the "Love Duet" melody, and a contrapuntal accompaniment derived from "Get You Up," the whole number described by Hellman as "in the style of Bach"). As the drama concludes, the curtain rises for a "Finale Reprise," subtitled "Best of All Possible Worlds" (for the ensemble, lyrics unattributed), in which the company sings—to the music of the "Lesson Song"—the concluding moral, "Admit it is neither the best nor the worst / Of all possible, possible, possible, possible worlds!!"

Bernstein and Latouche further collaborated on some songs that never made their way into this 1955 score. In one of these, a "Complaint Song" written for the travel scenes between Paris and Buenos Aires, Cunegonde, the Old Lady, and other women (including Manon, the tragic heroine of a 1731 novel by the Abbé Prévost) relate their tales of woe. (The authors probably intended the appearance of Manon, a comic conceit omitted from later drafts, as a reminder that the operetta could be read as a burlesque of the *Manon* operas by Jules Massenet and Giacomo Puccini, much as the original Voltaire in some ways parodied Prévost's novel.) Sketches for this number among Bernstein's papers offer rare evidence of one of Latouche's working methods, namely, the compilation of possible words or phrases for use, in this case including "mayhem," "strangling," "dismembering," and "tarred and feathered." As for the music, its sniveling main theme reappeared in a comparable number later written by Bernstein and Richard Wilbur, "Quiet," which contained, as opposed to Latouche's rhyme of "merry air" and "derriere," the rhymes "black side" and "backside," and "dump" and "rump," an example of the way in which Wilbur adopted Latouche's general approach.[28]

By the time *Candide* reached Broadway, Bernstein and Hellman had discarded or revamped much of this early 1955 version, but some of these rejected sections would reemerge not only in subsequent productions of *Candide*, but in *West Side Story*. Most notably, Bernstein adapted the "Love Duet" as "One Hand, One Heart" (for Tony and Maria, lyrics by Stephen Sondheim), with Sondheim recalling that Bernstein handed him, along with the tune, a "long-since discarded" lyric that opened, "One hand, one heart / Your hand, my heart"; Sondheim credited this lyric to Latouche, although sketches suggest that Bernstein himself wrote this lyric specifically for *West Side Story* as well as another lyric to this same music ("In this moment / Time lies dreaming") for *Candide*. In addition, according to Bernstein biographer Humphrey Burton, a lost song by Bernstein and Latouche, "Where Does It Get You in the End?" morphed into "Gee, Officer Krupke" from *West Side Story*, the earlier number's punch line ostensibly fitting the same melodic phrase as Stephen Sondheim's similarly suggestive, "Deep down inside us there is good!" A surviving pencil sketch of the "Gee, Officer Krupke" tune that has, as its only text, the words, "in the end," would seem to support this story, although the specifics of Burton's anecdote—including the claim that Bernstein intended the song for the gambling scene—again throw the matter of authorship into some question, given Latouche's apparent noninvolvement in the second act.[29]

In her 1955 script—whose acidulous humor suggests a blend of Bertolt Brecht and George S. Kaufman—Hellman managed to conflate more episodes from the Voltaire novella than generally recognized, going only far afield with the Iago and Fernando subplot (which afforded her, however, an opportunity to achieve some of those objectives that drew her to the notion of an Eva Perón opera). But whereas Voltaire's book parodied the clergy and aristocracy of his time, Hellman put a Marxist spin on the tale by exposing the foolishness of romantic illusions in a modern consumer society dominated by money, sex, and power, a theme she had long explored, with Candide recalling in different ways Karen in *The Children's Hour*, Alexandra in *The Little Foxes*, David in *Watch on the Rhine*, and Sophie in *The Autumn Garden*. Meanwhile, the Westphalia scenes allowed her to ridicule military bluster; the Lisbon scene, prejudice and intolerance; the Paris scenes, upper-class venality; and the Buenos Aires scenes, demagoguery and political corruption.

As noted, Hellman and Bernstein at one point thought to conclude the first act with a scene set in Eldorado, but Hellman persuasively argued against the idea; she apparently had a harder time than Bernstein—the future composer, after all, of "Somewhere" from *West Side Story*—imagining a utopian society. Instead, she and Bernstein depicted Candide's time in Eldorado simply by way of "The Ballad of Eldorado," her lyric so fantastical ("Up a seashell mountain / Across a primrose sea") as to suggest some lovely but deluded romantic dream. Nor did Hellman engage in any heroics, as in *The Little Foxes* or *Watch on the Rhine*, whose valiant climaxes clearly bespoke the ideals of the popular front. "We are not wise nor good nor pure," states Candide in the concluding

"Marriage Ceremony," adding, "We wish no longer for what never was, / Nor now could ever be." The "attack" on "isms" that Hellman spoke of in relation to the operetta would seem to include, by this point, not only optimism and pessimism along with fascism, capitalism, and McCarthyism, but probably also communism as many pro-Soviet leftists like herself learned more about the cruel realities of Stalin's rule.[30]

Relatedly, Hellman revised Voltaire so as to have Candide take his initial leave from a war-ravaged land, specifically, a defeated Germany, thereby establishing contact with those dramas and books of the period, discussed earlier in the context of *The Golden Apple*, that explored shell-shocked veterans struggling with idealistic preconceptions in a postwar world. That Hellman's Candide sets out on an odyssey that eventually brings him back home and into a matured relationship with his beloved underlined the operetta's connection to *The Golden Apple* all the more.

In writing his lyrics, Latouche, like Hellman, took many of his cues directly from *Candide*, which he probably reviewed in the original language as well as in translation; he derived "Lesson Song" and especially "Ringaroundarosy" and "The Reunion Waltz" from passages in chapters 2, 4, and 7 of the novella, respectively. In "Ringaroundarosy," for example, he adapted Pangloss's "genealogy" of his syphilis, including implications of homosexual transmission, but with a different cast of characters; and in "The Reunion Waltz," he closely followed the parallel passage in the novella so that, for instance, Candide's "So you weren't ravished or disembowelled?" and Cunégonde's response, "I was indeed, but people don't always die of those mishaps," became Candide's "I had thought you slain, thought you rudely violated too," and Cunegonde's, "That is true. Ah, but love will find a way."[31]

More generally, Latouche evoked the world of Voltaire through the use of such expressions as "sword and lance," "serried ranks," "the noble and the commoner," "death ill-bred," "prithee," and "paramour," although viewed ironically from a contemporary perspective. The "Lisbon Opening," with its vivid evocation of the bustling harbor and its "powders and pills," "bags full of wine," "silken hose, furbelows," and "paper and quill," proved a particularly notable achievement along these lines, displaying the lyricist's ability not only to conjure an historic time and place, but to use details of mercantile life, including its frustrations, to frame a larger story, as in his comparable catalog of turn-of-the-century consumer items in "Introducin' Mr. Paris" from *The Golden Apple.*

Regarding the music, the diverse locales along with a time period described by Bernstein shortly before the work's Boston premiere as "ranging from 1750 to 1830" (although Hellman's book contradictorily specified "any time before the middle of the eighteenth century") encouraged the composer, even in this preliminary version, to mediate his trademark jazzy sound through a variety of old European styles. While working on the music in July 1954, he even wrote to Copland (who long had criticized Bernstein's eclectic tendencies), "It's [*Candide*'s] the hardest thing I ever tried, and—you won't believe this—it's very hard trying to be eclectic," adding, with reference to two early nineteenth-century French composers who wrote popular comic operas, "I am raising the unwilling ghosts of [Ferdinand] Hérold and [Daniel] Auber." Bernstein similarly wrote to David Diamond a month later, "It's [*Candide*'s] turning out to be a sort of neo-Hérold oeuvre." At the same time, Bernstein appropriated not only nineteenth-century styles, but also those of the eighteenth century, so that especially by the time the operetta reached Broadway, the chorale and gavotte rubbed shoulders with the waltz, tango, schottische, polka, and barcarolle.[32]

All this more or less placed the score in the context of contemporary neoclassicism as represented by Bernstein's composer colleagues at Brandeis—Arthur Berger, Irving Fine, and Harold Shapero, all three like himself students of Walter Piston at Harvard. Indeed, something of Stravinsky could be discerned in "Money, Money, Money"; Hindemith in "Marriage Ceremony"; Copland in the "Love Duet"; both Hindemith and Copland in "Get You Up"; Blitzstein in "This I Know" and in some of the "Paris Waltz Scene"; but perhaps above all, Prokofiev, as in the "Lisbon Opening," "Paris Waltz Scene," "The Marquise's Gavotte," and much else, including the work's general harmonic language. Bernstein's neoclassical orientation showed itself as well as in the score's formal unity, one based, as insightfully studied by John Baxindine and Helen Smith, on the trenchant use of not only recurring themes and motives, but more basically the intervals of the fourth and the seventh, the kind of cohesiveness familiar to students of *West Side Story* (with its ubiquitous use of the tritone) but rarely observed here.[33]

At the same time, the score had a character all its own, by turns brash, flippant, and romantic, one that came closer in many sections, including "The Inquisition," to Gershwin than to any severe neoclassicist. Some of the music's humor converged with popular Jewish styles, including the apparent play with shofar calls in the "Lesson Song" and "The Inquisition," the florid melismas of the Arab Conjurer in the "Lisbon Opening" (music that in later versions of the operetta appeared as underscoring for the entrance of the rich Jew, Don Issachar), the farcical kvetching in the "Complaint Song," and most obviously, the Yiddishkeit in the "Old Lady's Tango" (later, "I Am Easily Assimilated"), called in the author's manuscript "Old Lady's Jewish Tango," with its tempo jokingly marked, in reference to Hasidic Jewish culture, "Moderato Hassidicamente." A subtler Jewish connection involved the use of the piano piece "Ilana: The Dreamer" as the Cunegonde theme, suggesting a correspondence not only between the sabra Ilana and an idealized view of Cunegonde, but between the recently established state of Israel and the mythic land of Eldorado as well. All in all, Bernstein's score showed a master humorist at work, with deliciously comic depictions of the pedantry of Pangloss, wiliness of the Old Lady, hauteur of the Governor, and duplicity of Fernando.[34]

The work's use of European styles, including its light operatic vocal writing, helped mark *Candide* as more an operetta than a musical, although Bernstein and Hellman seemed of two minds, calling the piece a "musical" for its world premiere in Boston, but then a "comic operetta" for its Broadway debut. In a *New York Times* article on this subject published shortly before the Boston premiere, Bernstein referred to the piece as both "an American musical comedy" and "a kind of operetta," stating further, "Maybe it

[*Candide*] will turn out to be some sort of new form; I don't know. There seems to be no really specific precedent for it in our theatre, so time must tell." In an October 1956 *Omnibus* telecast, "American Musical Comedy," which aired about month prior to this *Times* article, Bernstein similarly concluded that popular American musical theater comprised a "new form," although he referred to all such works as "musical comedies," a term he would employ even for *West Side Story*. Concerning the alleged lack of any "specific precedent" for *Candide*, Bernstein might have at least noted, for all its uniqueness, the work's kinship to the operettas written by the Gershwin brothers with George S. Kaufman and Morrie Ryskind—*Strike Up the Band*, *Of Thee I Sing*, and *Let 'Em Eat Cake*—as suggested by his own comment in the *Omnibus* telecast, "What fascinates me about *Of Thee I Sing* is the brilliant way in which it uses operetta technique, of all things, to produce this highly original American show."[35]

Candide would have appeared even more operatic had it come forth in something closer to its 1955 draft than its 1956 presentation, notwithstanding the coloratura showstopper "Glitter and Be Gay," which eventually made its way into the score (and even that number, while parodying the likes of Verdi's "Sempre libera" and Gounod's "The Jewel Song," remained more in line with Jacques Offenbach, Arthur Sullivan, and Victor Herbert). But by March 1955, Bernstein had come to the conclusion that the show needed a major overhaul, not least because of the presence of two long and talky scenes in the second act that introduced several new characters; he also surely recognized, relatedly, the discrepancy between the first and second acts that resulted in part from the loss of Latouche, as the work moved from whimsy and satire toward melodrama and sermonizing. At any rate, he viewed the piece as uneasily perched between serious and light musical theater, and doubted, as he wrote to Hellman from abroad, "whether cutting would be the answer." "I would be happy for a postponement of a year on *Candide*...," he wrote to his wife in May. "It's wrong the way it is now.... I'm a bit sick of the whole thing."[36]

And so even as Ethel Reiner secured the services of the eminent British director Tyrone Guthrie (1900–1971) in mid-1955 for a production planned for the 1956–57 season, Bernstein and Hellman duly placed *Candide* on hold, Bernstein devoting much of his compositional attention to *West Side Story*, and Hellman adapting Jean Anouilh's *L'Alouette* as *The Lark*, which opened on Broadway, with incidental music by Bernstein, on November 17, 1955, and which enjoyed a substantial run.

By the time they resumed work on *Candide* in 1956, Hellman and Bernstein had decided that they needed a lyricist after all. Stephen Sondheim (b. 1930), Bernstein's collaborator on *West Side Story*, offered his help (although in later years, he recalled only recommending the British lyricist Michael Flanders), but Bernstein and Hellman recruited rather Richard Wilbur, by this point a professor at Wellesley College, and the author of a translation of Molière's *The Misanthrope* that had met with considerable acclaim as staged in Cambridge in 1955. Over the late spring and summer of 1956, Bernstein, Hellman, Wilbur, and Guthrie gathered at Martha's Vineyard to work on the operetta, Bernstein describing Wilbur to David Diamond in late May as "a marvelous young poet who has never written a lyric in his life, and is already doing wonders. I now have hope for *Candide*, for the first time in ages."[37]

Eventually removing the Baroness, Iago, Señora Iago, Fernando, the two sheep, the dove, and the dethroned kings (although one morphed into Prince Ivan, also called Fat Man), and transporting the second-act Paris gambling scene to Venice (and reducing the Marquise to a lesser role as the Contessa), Hellman revamped and shortened the book, especially the first scene of the second act, which rather than feature political intrigue simply had the Governor dispose of Cunegonde and the Old Lady, and then bamboozle Candide. Such changes required major modifications in the score, and leading up to the Boston premiere, Bernstein and Wilbur accordingly dropped some numbers, including "Fernando's Lullaby," "Get You Up," and "Marriage Ceremony," and added or revised others. Regarding Latouche's lyrics, Wilbur tweaked "The Reunion Waltz" as "You Were Dead, You Know" (the altered title derived from a new line of verse); reworked the "Governor's Serenade" as "My Love"; and more thoroughly rewrote the "Victory Chorale" as "Wedding Chorale," "Lesson Song" as "The Best of All Possible Worlds," "Candide's Lament" as "Lament" (although later called "Candide's Lament" as well), "Pilgrim's March" as "Pilgrim Procession," and the "Quartet" as "Quartet Finale." In addition, Bernstein greatly reduced and revised Latouche's "Lisbon Opening" (retitled "What a Day" for the Boston premiere), and, long concerned about the use of the same music in "Lisbon Opening" and "Ringaroundarosy," cut this latter item as well, collaborating rather with Wilbur on a new syphilis song, "Dear Boy," although this number never made it to Boston either. Hellman's "The Ballad of Eldorado" (now, "Eldorado") and Bernstein's "Old Lady's Tango" (for the moment, "Tus Labios Rubi") remained intact, as did, at least to some extent, Parker's "The Marquise's Gavotte" (now, "Sweet to See Two Hearts, So True," and sung by Candide, Pangloss, Cunegonde, and the Old Lady).

New songs, all with lyrics by Wilbur, included the "Proposal Duet" (later called "I Love You") for Candide and Cunegonde; "It Must Be Me" for Candide; "Glitter and Be Gay," for Cunegonde; "Quiet," for Cunegonde, the Old Lady, and the Governor; "Bon Voyage," for the Governor and chorus; "The Kings' Barcarolle," for Candide, Pangloss, and the Five Kings (a number cut prior to Boston); "Pass the Soap," for Cunegonde and the Old Lady (seemingly lost, but probably based on the previous number, as the Boston program called the number a "barcarolle"); and "Make Our Garden Grow" for the entire company. Several of these new songs derived from older music, however. "Proposal Duet"/"I Love You" contained an interlude, for instance, based on the Cunegonde theme. Bernstein further exhumed an instrumental episode, "Farce-Pantomime Music," earlier intended for the Paris gambling scene (as seen in the 1955 score) for the laughing vocalise from "Glitter and Be Gay." And part of "Quiet" recycled, as remarked, "Complaint Song," although the number's opening now featured a new passage meant to depict the boredom of Cunegonde, the Old Lady, and the Governor by way of a campy sendup of the current vogue for twelve-tone music.

Had Latouche not died in August 1956, he might well have revised some of this material himself, for he presumably enjoyed certain rights with regard to his lyrics, and he maintained some real if remote involvement in the show, one that might have intensified as the premiere neared. But in the event, Wilbur wound up writing or rewriting by his own estimate 82.5 percent of the work's lyrics, something that raised complications for the work's publicity, given that Latouche's December 1954 agreement with Hellman and Bernstein specified his billing as "equal in size, type, and prominence to that accorded any other lyricist." At one point, Hellman, Bernstein, and Latouche decided to have the credits simply read "Lyrics by Richard Wilbur, John Latouche, and Dorothy Parker," but in response to a July 20, 1956, letter from Thomas Hammond that argued for further adjustment in light of Wilbur's extensive work, Latouche permitted the following billing: "Lyrics by Richard Wilbur/Other Lyrics by John Latouche and Dorothy Parker." As suggested by the layout of this typed letter, composed a few weeks before his death, Latouche still expected his name to be of equal size and type to that of Wilbur, which posed another dilemma as the show moved into production, as management wanted to advertise Latouche and Parker in smaller type. Some extant correspondence from October seems to pertain to this issue, including a letter from Hellman to Latouche's agent, Lucy Kroll, asking her to "reconsider your decision about John's billing," adding that she and Bernstein made this request "in the belief that John would have been the last man—he was kind and just to writers—to want credit where it was not due him"; and a letter from Latouche's executor that allowed his deceased client's billing to be "of a type satisfactory to Mr. [Thomas] Hammond." In the end, the original production credited Latouche with having written "other lyrics," as he had allowed, though with his name in smaller print than he personally had sanctioned. None of this affected Latouche's royalties, which remained at 1 percent, only fractionally smaller than Wilbur's.[38]

Reiner assembled an expensive production costing more than $300,000. Max Adrian (Dr. Pangloss and Martin), the accomplished Irish thespian, arrived from abroad to headline a cast that also included Robert Rounseville (Candide), Barbara Cook (Cunegonde), Irra Petina (pronounced PEH-tin-a, Old Lady), and William Olvis (Governor of Buenos Aires). Oliver Smith designed the sets, Irene Sharaff, the costumes, and Paul Morrison, the lighting. Wallace Seibert and Anna Sokolow created the dances, Samuel Krachmalnick directed the music, and Hershy Kay assisted Bernstein with the orchestrations.

Candide opened at Boston's Colonial Theatre on October 29, 1956, with the program book acknowledging as lyricists not only Wilbur, Latouche, and Parker, but in small print at the end of the playbill, Bernstein and Hellman. The reviews thought the operetta attractively lavish—the production reportedly featured some three hundred costumes—but found the show otherwise tedious and pretentious, especially the book, although some criticized the music as overly highbrow as well. In response, Hellman, Bernstein, and Wilbur quickly undertook more revisions.

Among other changes, Hellman thoroughly rewrote the Venice scene, excising the character of the Contessa, and having the Old Lady, under the disguise of Madame Sofronia, work as a shill for Ferone (that character's name having changed from Ladrino back to Ferone, this time with a second "e"); at the scene's climax, the Old Lady and Cunegonde, both masked, assault Candide, also masked, in an attempt to rob him until their disguises get knocked off in the scuffle, leaving the lovers startled and chastened.[39]

For this newly devised Venetian scene, Bernstein and Wilbur speedily wrote "What's the Use?" for the Old Lady, Ferone, Bazzini (Prefect of Police), Prince Ivan, and chorus; and revised "Sweet to See Two Hearts" (originally "The Marquise's Gavotte") as "Gavotte" for Candide, Cunegonde, the Old Lady, and Pangloss, changing all the lyrics to the first part so that Pangloss's portion of the number remained Dorothy Parker's only contribution to the show. In addition, Bernstein and Wilbur relyricized "I Love You" as "Oh, Happy We"; replaced the "Lament" with "It Must Be So" (using the same music as "It Must Be Me" sung later in the act); further revised "What a Day" and expunged much of the "Inquisition Scene" (the entire episode now called "Lisbon Sequence," with Latouche's "What a day, what a day / For an auto-da-fé!" changed, apparently by Bernstein, to "Look at this, look at that, / What a pretty new hat!"); renamed "Tus Labios Rubi" as "I Am Easily Assimilated"; and cut "Pass the Soap." By the time the show arrived in New York, aside from most of "You Were Dead, You Know," only some of "My Love" and the "Quartet," and whatever survived from the original Lisbon scene, could be credited to Latouche.

Some have asserted that the show gutted the Inquisition episode because of political pushback, with Wilbur admitting that the "swats we took at McCarthy did alarm our producers," although he also stated contrariwise that the show simply needed to be shortened and that the scene in question ran tangential to the main story; at the same time, Wilbur claimed that the producers cut "Dear Boy" because of fears of offending patrons, and that they expressed concern as well over the phrase "a bloody North African riot" in "Quiet," and the line "Me muero, me sale una hernia!" in the "Old Lady's Tango," a Spanish idiom which translates as, "I'm dying, I'm having a hernia!" (and that Felicia Bernstein suggested to her husband, struggling to find something to rhyme with, "A long way from Rovno Gubernya"). Meanwhile, replacing Latouche's "auto-da-fé" with the phrase "pretty new hat" apparently was prompted by concerns that audiences would not understand this Portuguese expression (in English, "act of faith") for ritualized penance and punishment during the Inquisition. It might be noted, too, that the Infant Casmira episode (words mostly by Latouche), an electrifying depiction of mass hysteria retained for the Broadway run (but not included on the original cast album, and rarely presented since), constituted at least as powerful, if more elliptical, social critique as the satire of the Inquisition that it so effectively framed—to the degree that later productions, even when they restored some of the Inquisition material, lost a good deal of punch by removing or diluting this sequence.[40]

With ineffectual producers, a deferential director, and a lyricist and bookwriter inexperienced with musical theater, Bernstein took charge of the rewrites during this pre-Broadway period. Intimidated by the composer, Hellman reluctantly made changes that she subsequently regretted—a traumatic ordeal that not only led her in later years to withdraw her script for any stage presentation, but also soured her generally toward playwriting and poisoned her relations with Bernstein, although not her friendship with Guthrie, to whom she dedicated the published libretto to *Candide*; nor with Wilbur, to whom she dedicated her last original play, *Toys in the Attic*, with music by Marc Blitzstein (1960).[41]

Candide opened in New York at the Martin Beck Theatre on December 1, 1956, newly subtitled "a comic operetta based on Voltaire's satire," and with no mention of Bernstein or Hellman as lyricists despite their having one lyric apiece in the show. Critical opinion proved widely divergent. At one extreme stood Brooks Atkinson (*Times*), John Chapman (*Daily News*), and Hobe Morrison (*Variety*), who all hailed the piece as "an artistic triumph," and at the other, Walter Kerr (*Herald Tribune*), who deemed it "a really spectacular wreck," although even many of the show's advocates admitted that the operetta had its slow patches, and even its naysayers thought the music rapturous, the production stunning, and the performances enchanting. *Candide* received a Tony Award nomination for outstanding musical (along with *Bells Are Ringing*, *The Most Happy Fella*, and *My Fair Lady*, which won), as well as nominations for Irra Petina (supporting musical actress), Oliver Smith (scenic designer), Irene Sharaff (costume designer), and Samuel Krachmalnick (conductor and musical director), even if the show failed to capture a single award (although Smith won for *My Fair Lady*). Bernstein, Wilbur, Latouche, Parker, and perhaps Hellman too presumably would have landed a nomination for best original score had that category become standard by this time.[42]

Not that the score, and in particular the lyrics, entirely escaped criticism. Henry Hewes (*Saturday Review*), for example, deemed a few of the lyrics "fine," but many others "undistinguished," while Kerr thought Bernstein "trapped . . . by lyrics which have no purposeful edge and therefore cannot join him in his jests." However, most observers commended the lyrics as, in the words of Tom Donnelly (*World-Telegram*), "witty and graceful." Unlike in Boston, the New York program book did not identify the lyricists for individual songs, so critics had no way of distinguishing the work of Wilbur, Parker, and, as consistently identified, "the late John Latouche," let alone the unacknowledged Bernstein and Hellman. Significantly, however, several reviews found "You Were Dead, You Know," that rare Latouche song to remain essentially intact, especially funny, raising the question of how much more droll *Candide* might have been had Latouche been better represented.

Some criticism of Hellman's script, broadly targeted as the show's principal weakness, suggested an animus toward its author's well-known leftist politics, although the play, with its resigned conclusion and its emphasis on personal freedom, deviated considerably from her more socially proactive earlier work. In any event, the critics more generally faulted the book as not fully in the spirit of either Voltaire or Bernstein. At the same time, Harold Clurman (*Nation*), who thought the production in need of a more "sharp, polished, spare, economic 'Brechtian' treatment," pinpointed this shortcoming but without singling out Hellman: "I was not certain which of the talented people who fashioned this 'operetta' had refused to yield to the other.... The total effect of the show... is of an enormous, splendid pastry, at the center of which is a hard, bitter pit." (In later years, Stephen Sondheim remarked, "Lenny [Bernstein]'s score was pastiche, Lillian [Hellman] wrote a black comedy, Guthrie directed a wedding cake.")[43]

A good number of observers actually found much to admire in Hellman's book. John Chapman, for instance, complimented Hellman for writing "a strong, clear and humorous libretto," and Tom Donnelly, for providing "the basis for an almost continuously stimulating show." "It is worth the price of admission," wrote Marya Mannes (*Reporter*), "just to bask in the civilized climate of astringency, to make fun of common attitudes, to juggle with heresy, to rejoin an adult world after exposure to the phony beatitudes of the fools in the 'hit' musicals." "It's not for softies," concluded Robert Coleman (*Daily Mirror*), "but for the hardy who can tear the tinsel off reality and take it in stride."

The show's creators proved, ironically, among the show's harshest critics. Dorothy Parker, for instance, described the operetta as "so overproduced that you couldn't tell what was going on at all." Richard Wilbur, who identified as the work's "inherent fault" its origin in "a one-joke novel that goes on for thirty chapters," commented, "There was no single villain. Lillian Hellman doesn't really like musicals. Lenny's music got more and more pretentious and smashy—the audience forgot what was happening to the characters. Lillian's book got to be mere connective tissue. And I was inclined to be too literary and stubborn." In a letter to Hellman, Wilbur further stated, "The show should have been what Voltaire's original is: light, bright, hard. There should never have been any emotional wallowing. The finale, for example, is set in an atrociously inspirational way, when it should be quiet and rueful" (as so concludes the 1955 version). Hellman declined to go into particulars, but simply stated that the work had been "botched, and I helped to do the botching." Bernstein placed the onus squarely on Hellman, citing her lack of experience in writing a musical: "Suddenly there were five deposed kings who appeared in the show at 11:30 at night, when everybody was exhausted, just to make some ironic point, yet again about hypocrisy" (although he neglected to identify this as a tryout version that Hellman later pared extensively). Observed Gerald Weales in his 1962 survey of postwar drama, "No comment on American theater could be as acrid as this picture of a group of creative people, having chosen to do an imaginative musical, backing away from their creation in horror on discovering that the audience that made hits of *Happy Hunting* and *Li'l Abner* had failed to take their baby to its bosom."[44]

Candide folded on February 2, 1957, after a disappointing seventy-three performances. That same year, Columbia Records released an original cast album (which had been recorded a little over a week after the show opened), and Random House, the libretto; the next year, G. Schirmer issued a vocal-piano score. Despite some surprisingly negative reviews, the recording quickly acquired an avid following, prompting both a multicity tour in 1958 of a concert version of the piece prepared by Michael Stewart and starring Martyn Green, who not only played Pangloss and Martin, but narrated the recital as well; and a British production that opened at the Saville Theatre (now, the Odeon Covent Garden) on April 30, 1959, directed by Robert Lewis and featuring Denis Quilley (Candide), Mary Costa (Cunegonde), Edith Coates (Old Lady), and Laurence Naismith (Pangloss and Martin), with a revised book by Stewart under the supervision of Hellman, and a charming new duet by Bernstein, the polka "We Are Women" (lyrics by Bernstein), for Cunegonde and the Old Lady.[45]

Even as the work's splendid overture established itself as a staple of the symphonic repertoire, the operetta managed to survive as well. A successful production at UCLA directed by Gordon Davidson for the Theatre Group in 1966, with a revised script by Davidson and a refashioned score by musical director Maurice Peress, proved a milestone; Davidson devised the show so that the actor playing Pangloss and Martin (in this instance Carroll O'Connor, prior to his days as Archie Bunker in the television series *All in the Family*) also took the role of a Narrator, an idea implicit in Hellman's original book and already employed in concert versions, but one that became common practice in future stage adaptations as well. Following this, Peress and writer-director Sheldon Patinkin (a cousin of actor Mandy Patinkin) prepared similarly well-received presentations of the work, including a November 10, 1968, benefit performance in New York in honor of Bernstein's fiftieth birthday, with a particularly fine cast headed by David Watson (Candide), Madeline Kahn (Cunegonde), Irra Petina (Old Lady), and Alan Arkin (Narrator, Pangloss, and Martin). Patinkin and Peress further collaborated on a 1971 production of the work for the Los Angeles and San Francisco Civic Light Opera Associations that played in San Francisco, Los Angeles, and Washington, D.C., but not on Broadway as hoped; and that starred Frank Porretta (Candide), Mary Costa (Cunegonde), Rae Allen (Old Lady), and Douglas Campbell (Narrator, Pangloss, and Martin, replaced by comedian Robert Klein in Washington).[46]

For one or another of these productions, Peress found room not only for "We Are Women" from the London premiere, but several never-performed trunk songs, including Latouche's "Ringaroundarosy," as well as newly lyricized versions by Richard Wilbur of "Victory Chorale"/"Wedding Chorale" (now titled "Westphalia Chorale"), "This I Know" (renamed "No More Than This," and later "Nothing More Than This," and reconceived as a song of rebuke and dismay for Candide), and "The Kings' Barcarolle" (for the time being called "Barcarolle: The Simple Life," and performed by a motley group of characters). In addition, Bernstein composed a brand new song to help amplify Martin's character, a bolero called "Words, Words, Words" (subtitled "Martin's Laughing Song," lyrics by Bernstein and Wilbur). (During these later years,

Bernstein took full credit for a few lyrics that apparently contained lines or even stanzas by Wilbur, including "No More Than This" and "Words, Words, Words.")

Working with Peress, both Davidson and Patinkin retained the general outlines of Hellman's plot and honored her social concerns more than many later adaptations, but various considerations—the introduction of a narrator, the expanded score, the desire for laughs—led to considerable pruning and revision of her dialogue. Drawing on his experience as artistic director of Chicago's Second City comedy theater, Patinkin crafted a particularly playful version of the show, although at considerable sacrifice to Hellman's pointed wit and barbed absurdities.

Feeling that she had failed Bernstein, Hellman looked the other way as Davidson and Patinkin adapted her material; but in the course of the 1971 tour, she refused to allow her name to be used in connection with the work, a disaffiliation solidified two years later with the arrival on December 11, 1973, of a popular new one-act version of the piece at the Brooklyn Academy of Music (BAM) in downtown Brooklyn, directed by the famed producer-director Harold Prince (b. 1928) on commission from the nonprofit Chelsea Theater Center.[47]

Remembering the work's original 1956 production as heavy-handed and dull, Prince chose to present the operetta as a sort of sideshow at a circus. Hellman reportedly countenanced the idea—she herself had thought of the work as "a musical circus"—but she had little admiration for Prince and forbade him not only the use of her name or any of her dialogue or lyrics, but even details of the plot not found in the original Voltaire. Prince accordingly engaged the British-born American writer Hugh Wheeler (1912–1987) to create an entirely new book, and, with Richard Wilbur unavailable, Stephen Sondheim to compose lyrics as needed. (The team of Prince, Sondheim, and Wheeler had just launched the musical *A Little Night Music*, and would collaborate again later in the decade on *Pacific Overtures* and *Sweeney Todd*.) On Bernstein's recommendation, Prince further recruited conductor John Mauceri (b. 1945) as music director.[48]

Wheeler drew on the original novella to make the operetta that much more picaresque, and as in previous revivals, incorporated a narration—with the narrator now explicitly Voltaire—so as to help elucidate the action. Wheeler further deleted the character of Martin (thereby undoing the story's basic dialectic), and in general moved the show in the direction of burlesque, to the point of having the Governor sing "My Love" to Maximilian (now with one "l") disguised as a female slave, and having a cow keel over at the end of "Make Our Garden Grow" as Voltaire utters, "Ah me! The pox!" Sondheim rewrote the "Gavotte" as an opening number for Candide, Cunegonde, Maximilian, and Paquette, "Life Is Happiness Indeed"; the "Lisbon Opening"/"What a Day" as "Auto Da Fé (What a Day)," a rewrite whose grisly comedy, so different from Latouche's original conception, looked ahead to *Sweeney Todd* (compare Latouche's "Everyone in town / Is coming down / So raise the prices high!" with Sondheim's "It's a lovely day for drinking and for watching people fry!"); "Candide's Lament" as "This World," making Sondheim the third person, after

Latouche and Wilbur, to lyricize this music; and the long dormant "Fernando's Lullaby" as "Sheep's Song." The repurposed "Gavotte," along with the need to cut Hellman's one lyric, "Eldorado," removed both Dorothy Parker and Hellman from the picture entirely, with the show accordingly crediting Wilbur, Latouche, and Sondheim (but not Bernstein) for the lyrics. Having first become Bernstein's assistant for a production of *Carmen* at the Metropolitan Opera, Mauceri also adapted some music from the Bizet opera in honor of this previous association.[49]

The show's scenic and costume designers, Eugene and Franne Lee, transformed the Chelsea Theater Center's 180-seat theater on the fourth floor of the Brooklyn Academy into a maze of ramps, runways, and platforms, with a small thirteen-piece band, orchestrated by Hershy Kay, divided into four separated groups for "quadraphonic" sound, and stools, benches, and bleachers scattered throughout the house and available on a first-come, first-served basis. Patricia Birch staged the dancing and Tharon Musser designed the lights, with the principals including Mark Baker (Candide), Maureen Brennan (Cunegonde), June Gable (Old Lady), and Lewis J. Stadlen (Voltaire, Pangloss, Governor, and others). The production, with its young shaggy-haired hero, bespoke a countercultural sensibility peculiar to the times, as evidenced, too, by such works as Bernstein's *Mass*, written in collaboration with Stephen Schwartz (1971), which likewise tapped the vogue for quadraphonic sound; Schwartz's own musicals *Godspell* (1971) and *Pippin* (1972), which also evoked the circus; and Galt MacDermot's musical *Dude: The Highway Life* (1972), which similarly featured an environmental staging. "You might think that Voltaire, Bernstein, Wheeler and other collaborators, Richard Wilbur, Stephen Sondheim and John LaTouche, were precocious teen-agers on a far-out trip," wrote Richard Coe (*Washington Post*) in his review of the show.[50]

After forty-eight sold-out performances at the Academy, *Candide* moved to Broadway, opening on March 5, 1974, at the Broadway Theatre, whose 1,800 seats had been removed—as was done with MacDermot's *Dude*—so that the space could be reconfigured in order to simulate the set-up in Brooklyn, although at an investment in the neighborhood of $350,000 as opposed to the original cost of $125,000, and seating for around 800 as opposed to 180. Garnering raves by Clive Barnes and Walter Kerr in the *Times*, the production won four Tony Awards, and received in addition a special Tony for being an "outstanding contribution to the artistic development of the musical theatre," perhaps partly as compensation for its ineligibility, as a revival, for the best musical award, which otherwise the show probably would have won as well.[51]

However, despite the common notion that the 1956 premiere received nothing but criticism and the Chelsea revival nothing but praise, both productions in fact elicited a similarly mixed reception. Certainly, not everyone liked this new *Candide* as much as the *Times*, even aside from those patrons discomfited by the wooden seats and obstructed sightlines. Douglas Watt (*Daily News*), for instance, thought the show "still something of a drag and even confusing at times," and Martin Gottfried

(*Women's Wear Daily*), "a salvage job" for a piece that "still doesn't work." Jack Richardson (*Commentary*), who considered the original version "an amusing, mildly intelligent piece of theatre that knew its stylistic place," deemed this current one "a long directorial gimmick" that disguised "the paltry imagination of that ubiquitous *homme du théâtre*, Harold Prince." And if Bernstein found the production "exciting, swift, pungent, funny, and touching," and Richard Wilbur, to his surprise, "lively and pleasing," Lillian Hellman, as might be expected, proved far less sanguine, writing to her former agent in 1982,

> I was . . . horrified that night I went to sit on those hard benches to see that piece of shit that appeared. It was as if Mr. Prince had taken out his penis and waved it at a gaggle of fags and Mr. [Hugh] Wheeler stood right behind him doing the same thing. It was a trashy mess and a disgrace to be seen. . . . Lennie [Bernstein]'s description of how successful it was with people shouting and jumping up and down does not impress me. Diet books have been successful and so has Herman Wouk.

A hit indeed with audiences, the show ran for nearly two years on Broadway, with Columbia Records releasing a cast album both in stereo and quadraphonic sound.[52]

On October 13, 1982, the New York City Opera debuted an expanded rendition of this Chelsea version, one that became known as the Opera House version, but that better might be called, in light of the work's subsequent history, the City Opera version. John Mauceri, who in the interim had prepared a concert suite of the work for orchestra, vocal soloists, and chorus that he premiered in Tel Aviv in 1977, collaborated again with Prince and Wheeler, retaining in large part the book and score of their 1973 adaptation, but tempering some of the gags (no poxed cow, for instance) and enlarging the whole into a two-act entertainment, mostly by reinstating music unused in the Chelsea version, including "Dear Boy," "Quiet," "Eldorado," and "What's the Use?" For this endeavor, Richard Wilbur, back on the scene, refashioned his lyrics to "Quiet" and "What's the Use?" to accommodate new dramatic contexts, and wrote one completely new lyric, "Ballad of the New World," to replace Hellman's words to "Eldorado," still off-limits. Prince transformed his circus concept to a proscenium stage by mounting the work as a traveling show with moveable stages and an onstage audience, and with some action spilling over into the auditorium; and Mauceri arranged and supplemented the 1956 Bernstein and Hershy Kay orchestrations for a relatively large fifty-five-piece ensemble.[53]

Although this new adaptation closely resembled the Chelsea version on paper, the opera house venue, along with the expanded orchestra and the use of such City Opera company members as David Eisler (Candide), Erie Mills (Cunegonde), Muriel Costa-Greenspon (Old Lady), and John Lankston (Voltaire, Pangloss, Governor, and others), led to some reconsideration of the work's classification, with the question now not so much musical versus operetta, as musical or operetta versus opera. "Since Lenny [Bernstein] has called this the operatic version of *Candide*, I would say it's an opera," stated City Opera's general director, soprano Beverly Sills, whereas Bernstein, who continued to subtitle the work "a comic operetta," remarked, "It would be pretentious to call it an opera, but I still think and hope it belongs in an opera house." In any event, this City Opera version, recorded by New World Records (1985, a Grammy Award winner that featured several of the same leads as in 1982, but with Joyce Castle as the Old Lady), established the work's viability for opera houses as the Chelsea version had done for smaller theaters, with the City Opera alone reviving the work numerous times, most recently in 2017.[54]

Despite the success of the Chelsea and City Opera versions, Bernstein and Mauceri both felt dissatisfied with these later incarnations, and with Mauceri's appointment as musical director of the Scottish Opera in 1986, the opportunity arose to retool the piece once again for a production sponsored jointly by the Scottish Opera and London's venerable Old Vic. Bernstein especially wanted to restore some of the work's original, more serious intentions, an objective shared by the Old Vic's new director, Jonathan Miller (b. 1934), who agreed to direct the production.

After Hugh Wheeler, engaged to rewrite his book, died in July 1987, Miller and his associate John Wells (1936–1998), an actor and writer famous for his satiric portrayals of Prime Minister Margaret Thatcher's husband, Denis, adapted the show themselves; among other things, they reinstated the Paris and Venice settings (a restoration facilitated by Hellman's death in 1984 and a more yielding stance by her estate, which also permitted the use of her "Eldorado" lyric) and not only reintroduced the role of Martin, but added some of Voltaire's episodes and characters, such as Cacambo and Vanderdendur, not found in earlier versions of the piece. In addition, the production incorporated nearly all the numbers that had accrued over time (in one version of another), including both syphilis songs for Pangloss (but not the remarkable episode for the Arab Conjurer and the Infant Casmira); the show even excavated the 1955 score for the choral hymn from "Get You Up" for the chorus "Universal Good," the music for which appeared with the original words by Bernstein and Hellman near the end of the work, but also earlier in the show with new words (adapted from Alexander Pope) by Bernstein, who also wrote a new lyric for the "Westphalia Chorale." The increasingly complicated storytelling prompted even greater use of narration, with the authors deciding, at least at some point, to bring the work to an end by having Pangloss ask, before the final chords, "Any questions?" "I tried," recalled Jonathan Miller, "to some extent to restore it to Voltaire, and to make Europe at least the center of it. What had happened was that layer upon layer of rather vulgar New York vaudeville had replaced practically everything. . . . I got the impression that he [Bernstein] felt we had delivered it, finally, to him. He said: 'We've got it now.' "[55]

The Scottish Opera version premiered at Glasgow's Theatre Royale on May 17, 1988, with a cast headed by Mark Beudert (Candide), Marilyn Hill Smith (Cunegonde), Ann Howard (Old Lady), and Nickolas Grace (Voltaire, Pangloss, Cacambo, and Martin); and after traveling to Newcastle, Liverpool, and Edinburgh, arrived in London, opening at the Old Vic with a few cast changes (including Patricia Routledge replacing Ann Howard as the Old Lady) on December 6, 1988. A critical triumph, the show won the Olivier Award for musical of the year, as well as Oliviers for Routledge's performance and Richard Hudson's designs. In 1988, TER Records issued a recording (reissued with extra tracks in 1997) of the Glasgow cast under the direction of Justin Brown, who had assumed the podium from John Mauceri in the course of the run, before turning over the baton to Peter Stanger and Stephen Clarke in London.

In a valedictory gesture about a year before he died, Bernstein tweaked the Scottish Opera score into a "final revised version" that could serve both stage and concert purposes, with the Concert version debuting at London's Barbican Centre on December 12 and 13, 1989, with a narration written by Wells and Bernstein, who, in a poor state of health, led the London Symphony Orchestra and Chorus and an all-star cast featuring Jerry Hadley (Candide), June Anderson (Cunegonde), Christa Ludwig (Old Lady), Adolph Green (Pangloss and Martin), and Nicolai Gedda (Governor and other characters)—the first time the composer ever had conducted the work. In 1991, Deutsche Grammophon released both a studio recording of the production (with "Candide's Lament" misattributed in the liner notes to Latouche as opposed to Wilbur) and a video recording of the second of the two concert performances. Several critics thought Green miscast as Pangloss and found Bernstein's conducting indulgently slow, but overall lauded both the studio recording (which earned a Grammy Award) and even more so, the video recording as the best representation of the score to date. "What emerges," wrote Susan Reiter (*Musical America*) about the studio recording, "is a more profound, expansive *Candide* that blends grandeur with whimsey—a *Candide* of far greater musical coherence than before."[56]

In 1993, Bernstein's longtime business manager Harry Kraut commissioned Erik Haagensen, who the previous year had reconstructed Bernstein's flop musical *1600 Pennsylvania Avenue,* to create an official narration for the Concert version based on the one Bernstein and Wells had co-written in 1989. The San Francisco Symphony debuted this edition, billed as the American premiere of the Scottish Opera version, on April 21, 1993, with a cast featuring Tracey Welborn (Candide), Lisa Saffer (Cunegonde), Maureen Forrester (Old Lady), Jonathan Green (Pangloss and Martin), and John Lankston (Narrator and other characters) under the baton of David Zinman.

Candide maintained its popularity in the years following Bernstein's death in 1990, but despite the composer's final revisions, nothing close to a standard text circulated. On the contrary, faced with an array of materials, performances often featured different characters, plots, scripts, and songs. Many productions, such as the 1994 Chicago Lyric Opera mounting (directed by Harold Prince), the 1997 Broadway revival at the Gershwin Theatre (also directed by Prince, with a cast album issued by RCA Victor), and the 2004 New York Philharmonic staged concert at Lincoln Center (directed by Lonny Price, with a DVD released by Image Entertainment), followed along the lines of the broadly comic Chelsea and City Opera versions, although Lonny Price borrowed as well from the 1993 Concert edition. Others, such as the 1995 Los Angeles production at the Ahmanson Theatre (directed by Gordon Davidson), the 2003 staging at the Euro Mediterranean Festival in Rome (directed by Enrico Castiglione, and released on video by Kultur), and the 2006 mounting at the Théâtre du Châtelet (directed by Robert Carsen, and aired on French television), adopted the more serious approach of the Scottish Opera version, with in this last instance, Robert Carsen and Ian Burton rewriting the book to accommodate its new setting in America around the time of the Kennedy administration. In general, international productions—and the work traveled the globe—favored the Scottish and Concert versions, with the lyrics, less so the spoken dialogue and narration, often left in English, although they appeared as well in Catalan, Danish, Dutch, French, German, Japanese, Polish, Portuguese, Spanish, and Swedish. Whatever version employed, many accounts, as with stagings of Gilbert and Sullivan, incorporated topical jokes and references: in the Price production, for instance, the Grand Inquisitor appeared as Donald Trump; and in the remarkable Carsen version, which took as its premise "the loss of belief in the utopian ideal of the American Way of Life," images of ecological devastation accompanied the "Make Our Garden Grow" finale.[57]

On April 13, 1999, London's Royal National Theatre, under the artistic directorship of Trevor Nunn, presented another landmark version of the work at the Olivier Theatre, this one adapted and directed by John Caird, who had assisted Nunn on the blockbuster musical *Les Misérables* for the West End in 1985. Drawing on previous editions of the operetta as well as on the Voltaire novella, the show starred Daniel Evans (Candide), Alex Kelly (Cunegonde), Beverley Klein (Old Woman), and Simon Russell Beale (Voltaire and Pangloss), who won an Olivier Award for his performance, as did the piece itself for outstanding musical production. Its original cast album released by First Night Records, the show ran for about nine months at the Olivier and provided the template for still other productions, including one that toured the United Kingdom in the summer of 2003 produced by the Opera Group and directed by John Fulljames.

Excluding suites and other arrangements, this brought the total number of performance editions of the work to five: the City Opera, Scottish Opera, and Concert versions (the last two sharing essentially the same score), all handled by Boosey & Hawkes; and the Chelsea and Royal National Theatre versions, both licensed by Music Theatre International. Because they all derived from Hugh Wheeler's 1973 book, they featured, for all their differences, many similarities that distinguished them, often problematically, from the original 1956 show. For instance, whereas Hellman transformed Voltaire's mockery of Jewish and Christian power brokers into a stinging satire of capitalist privilege by replacing the banker Don Issachar and the Grand Inquisitor with the bankers Marquis Milton and Marquis Sultan, the Wheeler-based revivals, in their use of Voltaire's Don Issachar and the Grand Inquisitor (or if using a Paris setting, the Cardinal Archbishop), opted rather for farce, in the process divesting "Glitter and Be Gay" of its intended context. To take another example, moving "My Love" to the second act prevented the music's appearance in the first-act finale from sounding like returning material. In a 1982 *New Yorker* review of the premiere of the City Opera version, Andrew Porter noted a range of such dramatic infelicities, not all redressed by subsequent versions. Some future incorporation of Hellman's original script or scenario, perhaps with an eye to the early adaptations by Gordon Davidson and Sheldon Patinkin, might prove ameliorative in this regard.[58]

Meanwhile, Latouche generally gained a greater presence in these later versions than he had in 1956. Not only did his "The Reunion Waltz" (that is, "You Were Dead, You Know") and at least some of his lines from "Lisbon Opening," "The Inquisition," and "Governor's Serenade" (that is, "My Love") appear regularly, but beginning with the 1973 Chelsea version, productions uniformly used Latouche's "Lesson Song" in lieu of Wilbur's "The Best of All Possible Worlds" (although under Wilbur's title), providing the only virtually unadulterated example of Latouche's work encountered in practically every performance. In addition, "Ringaroundarosy," early unearthed by Davidson and Patinkin (and apparently first introduced on stage by Carroll O'Connor in the 1966 Los Angeles staging), also resurfaced in the Scottish Opera and Concert versions, both of which adopted more of Latouche's "Lisbon Opening" and "The Inquisition" than usual as well. (A 1970 publication of Hellman's original libretto by Avon Books and a 1971 edition of her *Collected Plays* by Little, Brown featured an even more complete restoration of Latouche's lyrics for the Lisbon scene, although miscredited to Bernstein on the copyright page.)[59]

Candide's complex textual history—the subject of doctoral dissertations by Karen Olsen Ganz and Leanne Pettit, who agreed that the sheer musical weight of the Scottish Opera version encumbered the work dramatically—posed a daunting challenge to critical discussion. Commentators at least had, as one more or less stable point of reference, the discarded Hellman book, sometimes dismissed as a faulty adaptation of a great classic, although as early as Gerald Weales's 1962 study, in which he declared *Candide* "not only the most sophisticated product of the American musical stage but probably the most imaginative American play to reach Broadway since the war," several thoughtful critics—including literary scholars Doris and Leonard Fleischer and Timothy Wiles and musical theater historians Lehman Engel, Ken Mandelbaum, Ethan Mordden, and John Baxindine—found Hellman's script an adroit adaptation of the original Voltaire. Some of these observers even stood the prevailing wisdom on its head by faulting Bernstein for not properly accommodating either Hellman or Voltaire, in this regard often citing—as Wilbur did himself—the seemingly extrinsic uplift of "Make Our Garden Grow," with musicologist Raymond Knapp wondering further if "the musical languages of 1956 Broadway, even augmented by Bernstein's musical sophistication and his ambitions for a truly Americanized opera, were inadequate, *fundamentally*, to the challenges posed by Voltaire's *Candide*."[60]

While commentators often targeted the discordance between the novella and the operetta, or the cross-purposes of the show's various collaborators, some located troubling inconsistencies within the score itself. Baxindine, for instance, noted that whereas certain numbers engaged a Brechtian distance, others did less so or not at all. Ethan Mordden similarly cited three "romantic" numbers—"It Must Be So," "Eldorado," "Make Our Garden Grow"—that "war with the rest of the score, which is predominantly satiric." Tellingly, all three of these "romantic" songs, like the melancholy "Lament" and the distraught "Nothing More Than This," are sung by Candide, whom Bernstein apparently wanted to portray, for all his foolishness, as in some ways a romantic hero. Had the show retained, say, either Latouche's or Wilbur's original "Lament" (with its wry spoken commentary by the King of Bulgaria) or Wilbur's "Proposal Duet," Candide's character might have assumed an ironic profile more in line with the work as a whole. But in any case, burlesque stagings of these more somber numbers, such as having a poxed cow collapse at the end of "Make Our Garden Grow" (as in the Chelsea production), or having Candide pack a long-playing recording of *West Side Story* in the course of "It Must Be So" (as in Lonny Price's account), only heightened such contradictions. On the other hand, the emotional intensity of "Nothing More Than This" provided those productions that employed this number, as Kenneth LaFave pointed out, with a more persuasive transition to the moralizing of "Make Our Garden Grow" than those that did not.[61]

Although critics of the piece widely praised the score's lyrics, they generally treated them en masse, other than sometimes to assert Wilbur's preeminence. Humphrey Burton wrote, for instance, that Wilbur "revised his predecessors' [read: Latouche's] work on the first act, often with startling improvements.... Thanks to Richard Wilbur, *Candide* is throughout impeccably versified." In correspondence with the present author, Sondheim similarly described Wilbur's work as "far superior to his [Latouche's] static, self-conscious 'poetic' writing, despite some occasionally funny lines."[62]

However, the unavailability of many of Latouche's lyrics, compounded by misattributions, made such assessments tentative. Comparing the duet "Oh, Happy We" to its earlier incarnation as "Proposal Duet," Michael H. Hutchins, the creator of an impressively encyclopedic online guide to *Candide*, deemed, for instance, Wilbur's words to the song "far superior" to Latouche's, although Wilbur seems to have written both sets of lyrics. Similarly, Kenneth LaFave credited Sondheim in 1973 with "correcting or replacing many of LaTouche's awkward-to-sing phrases and imperfect rhymes, such as the one in the song, 'The Best of All Possible Worlds' that tries to rhyme 'fonder' with 'Cunegonde,'" whereas in fact Latouche wrote the claimed corrected lyric, and Wilbur, the allegedly faulty one—the confusion arising from the reinstatement of Latouche's lyric for the Chelsea version. (Ironically, Sondheim's single alteration to the Latouche lyric in question, namely, changing the phrase, "Today's event / Makes evident," to "Philosophers make evident," although dictated by the scene's altered context, not only sacrificed one of Latouche's many melodious inner rhymes, but specifically failed to duplicate the jingle as found in the parallel spot in the previous strophe: "If Snake had not / Seduced our lot.") Quite possibly the greater reputations of Wilbur and Sondheim colored critical commentary concerning such matters.[63]

At the same time, observers found in the lyrics as a whole a comparable standard of craft and wit, which already said much in favor of Latouche, given Wilbur's skill and refinement. Wilbur himself deemed Latouche "an excellent lyricist," calling the refrain, "What a day, what a day / For an auto-da-fé!" the "best bit of lyrics ever written for the show." Indeed, Latouche seems to have served Wilbur as a helpful, even indispensable model, with the structure and content of Latouche's lyrics often echoed in his successor's work.[64]

As for distinctions, Latouche arguably took a more theatrical approach than Wilbur, with closer attention paid especially to setting, including extensive use of period language. Moreover, he revealed greater experience in writing for the musical stage. A comparison of Latouche's "The Reunion Waltz" and its subsequent revision by Wilbur as "You Were Dead, You Know" exemplifies such differences, including Latouche's more archaic language ("dearest lady," "pray explain," "rudely violated") and more assonant verse ("lady," "pray," "explain," "slain, "violated," and "you," "rudely," "too"), not to mention the lyric's allusion to rape, derived as seen from the Voltaire novella, but absent in Wilbur's version:

LATOUCHE'S VERSION
Dearest lady, pray explain.
I had thought you slain;
Thought you rudely violated too.

WILBUR'S VERSION
Dearest, how can this be so?
You were dead, you know.
You were shot and bayoneted, too.

Similarly, whatever else might be said about the show's two syphilis songs—Latouche's "Ringaroundarosy" and Wilbur's "Dear Boy"—the latter, although containing more Voltairean irony, and considered by Wilbur his best *Candide* lyric, does not project over the footlights as well as the former; observes Ethan Mordden, Wilbur's lyric "is so intelligently delineated . . . that audiences cannot follow it and it dies on stage every time."[65]

Latouche's lyrics relatedly evidenced his special sensitivity to musical rhetoric. For example, in the lines, "I had claimed thee / For my own: / Death has named thee / His alone," from "Candide's Lament," he deftly set the melody's two prominent sighing figures with an internal rhyme ("claimed thee" and "named thee") not found in the rewrites by Wilbur ("Could our young joys, just begun, / Not outlast the dying sun?") and later Sondheim ("What is kindness / But a lie? / What to live for / But to die?"); and in the same verse's rhymed opposition of Candide ("my own") and death ("his alone"), he further effected a particularly neat mirroring of the music's move from one key (A major) to another (F major).

After Latouche's death, Bernstein and Hellman took a more appreciative stance regarding the lyricist than during their troubled collaboration. In a note about "our friend Touche" to Ruth Yorck in 1958, Bernstein spoke about "his [Latouche's] very real contributions to *Candide*" as well as "the many other wonderful things he did." And in his remarks at the 1989 concert presentation of *Candide*, Bernstein stated, "We [he and Hellman] quickly set about our work with a young whiz lyricist called John La Touche, who wrote the second of the two syphilis songs ['Ringaroundarosy'] you heard in Act I. The other syphilis song you heard ['Dear Boy'], equally inspired, if somewhat more literary, was written by our second great lyricist, Richard Wilbur." Hellman similarly spoke respectfully of Latouche in later years, referring to him on one occasion in the same breath as Bernstein and Dorothy Parker. Latouche remained nonetheless the operetta's unsung hero, an artist who helped Bernstein and Hellman formulate its distinctive character and tone.[66]

22

Late Work

In 1955, while still occupied with *The Vamp*, *The Ballad of Baby Doe*, and to an extent *Candide*, Latouche started work with composer Coleman Dowell (1925–1985) on a musical adaptation of Eugene O'Neill's 1933 comedy *Ah, Wilderness!* under the auspices of producer David Merrick. However, in due course Merrick dismissed both Latouche and Dowell, and eventually engaged composer-lyricist Bob Merrill to write the score for the show, which premiered in 1959 as *Take Me Along*.

Set in "a large small-town in Connecticut" over the July Fourth holiday in 1906, *Ah, Wilderness!* concerns two eventful days in the life of Richard Miller, a recent high school graduate set to enter Yale in the fall. A romantic intellectual who has fallen under the influence of, among others, Omar Khayyám (from whose line of verse from *The Rubáiyat*, "Oh, Wilderness were Paradise enow!" O'Neill derived the play's title), Richard has grown irritable and disdainful toward his provincial family, including his father, Nat, who owns the local newspaper; his mother, Essie; his bachelor uncle, Sid (his mother's brother); his spinster aunt, Lily (his father's sister, who loves but refuses to marry the charming but alcoholic Sid); his older brother, Arthur; his younger sister, Mildred; and his kid brother, Tommy. Devastated by a letter from his girlfriend Muriel (one actually dictated by her priggish father) declaring their relationship at an end, Richard celebrates his own day of independence by getting drunk in a dive with a prostitute. But meeting with Muriel the next day, and realizing that she still loves him, he blissfully embraces the world.

Premiered by the Theatre Guild in October 1933, *Ah, Wilderness!* enjoyed a solid run, thanks in good part to songwriter George M. Cohan's winning portrayal of father Nat, and quickly established itself as a repertory staple. In 1935, MGM released a star-studded movie version directed by Clarence Brown to a watered-down adaptation by Frances Goodrich and Albert Hackett; and in 1948, the studio released a less-successful musical version produced by Arthur Freed under the title *Summer Holiday*, with a score by composer Harry Warren and lyricist Ralph Blane, which aside from the musical numbers seemed in many ways a colorized clone of the earlier black-and-white picture, and which featured another all-star lineup, including Mickey Rooney—who had been better cast as little Tommy in the 1935 film—as Richard Miller.

In early 1953, producer David Merrick (born Margulois, pronounced Mar-GUL-is, 1911–2000), then at the relative beginning of his prodigious and colorful career, acquired permission from O'Neill (who died later in the year) to present *Ah, Wilderness!* as a stage musical, an idea that had occurred to Merrick years earlier on attending the original production of the play on tour in his native St. Louis. Merrick showed a general predisposition toward adapting prewar drama, producing a musical version of Marcel Pagnol's Marseilles film trilogy (1931–36) as *Fanny* (book by S. N. Behrman and Joshua Logan, music and lyrics by Harold Rome) in 1954, and Thornton Wilder's revision of his 1938 play *The Merchant of Yonkers* as *The Matchmaker* in 1955 (which in turn formed the basis for Merrick's blockbuster 1964 musical, *Hello, Dolly!*).[1]

As early as the spring of 1953, Merrick and his producing partner, set designer Jo Mielziner, considered entrusting the music for *Ah, Wilderness!* to the young songwriter Coleman Dowell, who recalled a long tryout process in which he wrote ten songs for a "phantom book." The composer further remembered convening with S. N. Behrman, the person, according to Dowell, Merrick most wanted to write the script; but by the fall, the producer had set his sights on hiring Latouche for the book and lyrics, at least to judge from a November 1953 audition for Dowell hosted by Latouche at his apartment before a group that included Carol Channing and Merrick. (After this event, Dowell described Latouche in a letter to his parents as "a famous writer you probably are not familiar with.") Merrick possibly gravitated toward Latouche on the evidence of *The Golden Apple*, also set in a small American town at the turn of the century, and a work that he, like so many other producers, presumably had heard, at least in part, before its official March 1954 debut.[2]

Following the opening of *The Golden Apple*, Latouche still had a number of other irons in the fire, but Merrick and Mielziner seemed willing to wait for him to become available; and in January 1955, Latouche signed a contract with Merrick that included a $1,000 advance against royalties, and a promised 3.5 percent of gross box-office revenue.[3]

By his own account, Dowell made a good impression at his audition at Latouche's in 1953, and by the time of the premiere of *The Golden Apple* (which he described as "a fascinating piece of work—not high-brow, but wonderfully poetic and, on occasion, terribly funny"), he spoke of Latouche as his "collaborator-to-be," even anticipating traveling to Haiti with him to work on the show (a trip that never materialized). However, as late as 1955, Merrick and Latouche had yet to settle on a composer, with Harold Arlen, Cy Coleman, Jerome Moross, and Alex North all under consideration, though Latouche thought that he might "lose his mind" working with Arlen, and neither he nor Moross had much stomach, at least at this juncture, for working with each other again. At one point, film composer Alex North, whose songs for the unproduced musical *Queen of Sheba* both Merrick and Mielziner admired, seemed a frontrunner; but by March 1955, Merrick and Latouche had decided to go with Dowell, whose April 1 contract with Merrick specified an advance of $1,000, and 1 percent of box-office receipts.[4]

Coleman Dowell grew up in rural Kentucky—"I think everything I write grows out of Kentucky ballads," he once stated—and served two years in the military (1944–1946), during which time he attended the University of the Philippines. Largely self-taught as a musician, he pursued a career as a popular songsmith, first in his native Kentucky, and then after 1950 in his adopted home of New York, where he wrote songs for a satirical television series on the DuMont Network, *Once upon a Tune*, on which the likes of Beatrice Arthur and Elaine Stritch appeared. Forging a reputation as a promising songwriter along the lines of Noël Coward and Cole Porter, in 1953 he caught the interest of Merrick, who placed him on his payroll for fifty dollars a week. After meeting his partner, the psychiatrist Bertram Slaff, in 1954, and losing his commission for *Ah, Wilderness!* in 1957, Dowell left Merrick's sponsorship for that of Carl Van Vechten, whose 1924 novel *The Tattooed Countess* he adapted as a musical so titled. Following that show's failure off Broadway in 1961, Dowell turned increasingly to fiction, writing several experimental novels that found favor among the cognoscenti, so that the trajectory of his career roughly resembled that of the more famous Paul Bowles. In poor physical and mental health, in 1985 Dowell jumped to his death from the balcony of his fifteenth-floor apartment, leaving behind a suicide note to Slaff that read, "I can't bear the pressure anymore. I am so very sorry."[5]

Dowell spent much of the spring and summer of 1955 with Latouche at the latter's country home in Vermont working on the musical, with the composer often camped out in the living room of the main house, although when Slaff visited, the two sometimes slept in the one-room shack that Latouche had built on the premises. Dowell, at least at first, seemed pleased not only with life at The Eyrie, with its stimulating visitors and its leisure hours filled with bridge and backgammon, but with work on the show as well. He very much liked both Latouche's opening lyric, "Six Doves," which he described as "a true poem, and very beautiful," and another "wonderful lyric" that Latouche apparently had tailored to one of the composer's preexisting melodies. Wrote Dowell to Slaff on April 21,

> John [Latouche] has finished the first scene now, and has improved so over the O'Neill dialog and awkward plotting that it's a pleasure to think about. There was a reading this morning for Helvitia [sic: Helvetia Perkins] and Ken[ward Elmslie], and I sang the first song when the time came. I'm happy to report that John more than liked it, and everyone thought it was exactly right. We called David [Merrick] about casting Imogene Coca as Aunt Lily, and he was in agreement. This may seem as off-beat to you as it did to me at first, but think about it and I think you'll agree that she has a

perfect mixture of comedy and pathos called for. John wants Hiram Sherman for Uncle Sid, and again this, to me, is a good choice. Of course, none of these people can really sing, but that seems to be the latest trend in musicals.

If progress proved slower than he liked, Dowell understood that Latouche was "purely an inspirational writer and it's no good pushing him."[6]

Over the summer, on a trip to New York, Latouche told journalist Douglas Watt that he had completed the lyrics to eight songs for the show (with Watt beginning his report in the *Daily News* by writing, "A country boy named John Latouche came back to the big city the other day for a visit; and immediately, as always happens on these visits, the city began to bend a little under the strain"). And in September, Merrick likewise informed his attorney that Latouche had showed him "a very rough draft of the first act of the show," and had written ten songs with Dowell. "From what I have seen and heard of it," stated Merrick, "I would say that the project is still very promising." True, Latouche would now have to interrupt work on the show in order to help prepare *The Vamp* (set to begin out-of-town tryouts in late September), but Merrick had expected this when he originally signed Latouche, making the latter "not really very much behind his contractual schedule." However, after waiting several more months in vain for new material, Merrick decided by February 1956 to have playwright William Inge adapt the script, and Dowell write both the music and lyrics, formally severing his contract with Latouche in late March. Some of this delay involved Latouche's preoccupation with other tasks, but growing strife between himself and Dowell presumably played a part as well.[7]

Information concerning such conflicts comes almost entirely from Dowell's recollection of working with Latouche during the summer of 1955, including describing the latter in 1968 to writer Richard Lebherz as "the biggest son of a bitch I've ever known.... John was talented, yes. But a Grand Guignol horror, bloated on hunks of other people. My God, he even ate one's sleep: all the time we were writing in Vermont, from March through September, he never allowed me to go to bed before dawn.... When I think of him, I hope that Hell has real flames." Such loathing took published form posthumously by way of a reminiscence issued by *Bomb* magazine in 1985 and later reprinted in his autobiography. Calling Latouche a "well-known goniff [Yiddish: thief] of other people's ideas" who "could have qualified as a dwarf," Dowell wrote,

His [Latouche's] ego could have outfitted a Sicilian village composed of Mafia chieftains. He was talented but perhaps not commensurate with his ideas of his worth. He had a bad temper and his determination to prevail matched that of the cockroach. He broke all the rules to cheat at games.... He pushed croquet balls with his feet and behaved outrageously at bridge. He was the perfect despot and at times incomparably good

> company, thus his allure.... He insulted his friends, his guests, me. My lover is a psychoanalyst and Latouche reserved his hatred for that profession (he had sent through the mail to his own analyst a box of shit) to those times when my friend... was there. My lover is also Jewish and Latouche insulted Jews continuously.

Dowell further claimed that although Merrick had advised him "to do anything, by which he implied *anything*, to keep the temperamental Latouche content," no sexual favors seemed necessary given the entourage of young men who kept him "happily well-fixed in that department." However, Dowell still felt obliged to accommodate Latouche in other ways, including cooking, cleaning, and picking up after his host's "imperial-mannered guests." He also resented having to hide from Merrick the fact that Latouche's involvement with *The Vamp* and *The Ballad of Baby Doe* stalled progress on *Ah, Wilderness!* and that even as Merrick paid "the great Latouche" thousands of dollars for a mere two lyrics, Dowell received only a modest retainer. As he recalled, things came to a head toward the end of the summer when Latouche returned from a visit to New York with a "carload of spoiled and no doubt bone-weary sycophants," and ejected Dowell and the visiting Slaff from the house: "I had taken insults, had spent every penny of my advance money on the household, had labored, had lied to Merrick if only by omission, and slept like a slavey only when allowed. It was the end for Latouche and me and I told him so."[8]

As with Dowell's recollections generally, this account appears exaggerated to the point of sheer fabrication. Explained Dowell's friend, the writer Edmund White, "He [Dowell] was what the French call a *mythomane*. Somebody who makes up myths, not necessarily to advance his career or to hoodwink others, but because he himself believes them.... He's a very bad reporter on the facts of his own life, but if you can decipher them correctly, I suppose that you can figure that this is his version of reality and therefore interesting, too." Although Latouche could exasperate even his dearest friends, Dowell's extreme hostility to someone so generally admired indeed begs some sort of interpretation. Perhaps his venom toward Latouche—as toward Merrick—involved his dashed hopes for a Broadway success. But in addition, as an alcoholic who, in White's estimation, "alternated between grandiosity and self-hatred," Dowell perhaps discerned enough of a resemblance with Latouche (and Dowell himself admitted that they shared "that most American thing, that shamefaced longing for a nobility tagged like trees wearing their Latin names") to project his own vanity and petulance, including an antisemitism (his Jewish lover notwithstanding) far in excess of anything Latouche might have harbored. Dowell's penchant for the scatological, as seen above, similarly suggested personal obsessions. Even so, he commended "as simple and appropriate as can be" Latouche's lyrics for the arias of the "beautiful and affecting" *Ballad of Baby Doe* (if not its "lazy" sung dialogue, described as "a compendium of clichés"); and he retained warm memories of Latouche's mother, as mentioned earlier.[9]

For a while, *Ah, Wilderness!* remained in limbo. Notified of his termination, Latouche petitioned for an extension, reminding Merrick in April 1956 that he had completed a rough draft of the first act as well as ten songs, and explaining that he needed a more experienced composer than Dowell, specifically, someone who knew how to set lyrics other than his own. But Merrick remained unmoved, and in letters to both Latouche and his agent, Lucy Kroll, in early August 1956, only days before the lyricist's death, Merrick requested the return of his $1,000 advance. Meanwhile, Merrick dropped Dowell from the project as well, although for a period he kept him on payroll. "The show that I've been slaving over for three years is dead as a doornail," Dowell wrote to his sister sometime after Latouche's demise, "among other things, John Latouche died in July [*sic*] of a heart-attack. He was only thirty-nine [*sic*], and although I had grown to sincerely hate him, I didn't want him to die."[10]

Determined nonetheless to produce *Ah, Wilderness!* Merrick, even before Latouche's death, planned for composer Harold Karr and lyricist Matt Dubey (who recently had collaborated on the show *Happy Hunting*) to write the score, and for Herbert and Dorothy Fields to write the book. However, in the aftermath of *New Girl in Town*, a successful musical version of O'Neill's *Anna Christie* produced in part by Harold Prince, which premiered in May 1957, Merrick, now without Mielziner, decided to hire that show's composer-lyricist, Robert ("Bob") Merrill (1921–1998), for *Ah, Wilderness!* The result, *Take Me Along*, with a score by Merrill and a book by Robert Russell and Joseph Stein, debuted on Broadway at the Shubert Theatre on October 22, 1959, and ran for over a year, with Robert Morse (Richard Miller), Walter Pidgeon (Nat Miller), Jackie Gleason (Sid Davis), and Eileen Herlie (Lily Miller) all garnering Tony Award nominations (and a win in the case of Gleason) for their performances, and the show itself earning a nomination for best musical.[11]

As for the adaptation by Latouche and Dowell, or just Dowell on his own, the extant material seems limited to only a few lyrics: the forementioned "Six Doves," which survives among Andrew Drummond's papers (as "Ballad"); and several unattributed others housed in the Coleman collection, including "It Only Comes Once a Year," for the ensemble; "Waterbury," for Uncle Sid; "A Woman's More Well Off Alone," for Essie; and "Robespierre, Maribeau [*sic*], Marat and Me," "Why," and "April Girl," for Richard. Certain evidence suggests that Dowell rather than Latouche wrote some if not all these anonymous lyrics, but their authorship remains undetermined.[12]

"Six Doves," the one surviving lyric for *Ah, Wilderness!* unquestionably by Latouche, shows the influence of Irish folk balladry and likely W. B. Yeats as well. The lyricist conceived the text as an opening number in which the Irish maid Nora describes six turtledoves "aflying two by two," each pair symbolizing one of the play's three main couples—Richard and Muriel, Sid and Lily, and Nat and Essie—so that the lyric, as Dowell observed, "outlines the entire plot in a mystic Irish song":

The first two doves
By a dream were led,

The next two were tied
With a tangled thread
The last two were linked
With a golden chain
As they flew through the sun
and the rain.

The first two were jangled
Because they were young,
The next two were tangled,
Their song still unsung,
The last two were linked
With a chain of gold
To bind them in love
As they grew old—
As they flew through the sun
and the rain.
As they flew through the sun
and the rain.

This tender lyric belies Dowell's assertion that Latouche considered the show nothing but a "potboiler" that would help keep him afloat financially—a claim that once again might well have involved some projection on Dowell's part, for he later confessed that he had no affection for O'Neill's work, including the "coy" *Ah, Wilderness!* At any rate, Latouche and Dowell patently took their source material more seriously than did the creators of *Take Me Along,* which, presumably in deference to Jackie Gleason's star power, shifted the focus from the education of young Richard to the redemption of Uncle Sid, whose "tangled thread" with Aunt Lily gets tied up in a bow by the final curtain; certainly none of Merrill's lyrics display the poetic elegance of "Six Doves." David Merrick at least had the satisfaction of producing a hit with *Take Me Along,* including having United Airlines adopt the show's jaunty title song for a 1967 advertising campaign that attempted to sell the notion of wives traveling with their husbands on business trips.[13]

In 1966, G. Schirmer published *Six Doves,* a setting of the Latouche lyric, the words slightly tweaked, by composer-conductor John C. Sacco (1905–1987) for mixed chorus, piano, and two optional flutes. How Sacco obtained this lyric remains a mystery, but at any event, his folklike treatment of the text captured, though the mixed use of major and minor modes, its bittersweet essence, with its pairs of love birds flying "through the sun and the rain." This obscure chorus proved what seems the only tangible fruit of Latouche's association with David Merrick and Coleman Dowell.[14]

In the spring of 1956, a few months before Latouche's death, the Phoenix Theatre, the off-Broadway company that had launched *The Golden Apple* two seasons earlier, presented a revue "conceived, cast and assembled" by Ben Bagley (1933–1998), *The Littlest Revue,* which included, in addition to Latouche and Vernon Duke's "Summer Is A-Comin' In" from *The Lady Comes Across* (1942), sung here by Charlotte Rae, a new Latouche song, "Opening Number," for the ensemble, the lyric co-written with Kenward Elmslie, with music by Rae's husband, John Strauss. Latouche's Broadway career accordingly ended much as it had begun: with contributions to a revue.

By the mid-1950s, the Broadway revue had become increasingly obsolete as such television programs as the *Ed Sullivan Show* eclipsed the form, to the point of making especially more spectacular stage revues financially untenable. In 1955, Bagley, then an enterprising twenty-one-year-old, devised a viable response by producing the *Shoestring Revue* in an intimate space, the President Theatre on 48th Street, with a small but brilliant cast (including Beatrice Arthur and Chita Rivera) and a two-piano accompaniment, all for a total cost of about $15,000. The success of this show encouraged T. Edward Hambleton and Norris Houghton, the directors of the Phoenix, to engage Bagley the following year to help mount a revue with a somewhat less frugal budget of $30,000 as the final offering of their 1955–56 season.[15]

For the score, Bagley turned mostly to the team of composer Vernon Duke and lyricist Ogden Nash, who provided both old and new songs. But Bagley cast his net wide, soliciting musical numbers from Sheldon Harnick, Charles Strouse, and Lee Adams, and comedy sketches from Eudora Welty and Michael (here, "Mike") Stewart, among others. (Strouse, Adams, and Stewart subsequently would combine forces to create the 1960 musical *Bye Bye Birdie.*) Paul Lammers stage directed, Charles Weidman created the dances, Klaus Holm designed the sets and lighting, Alvin Colt fashioned the costumes, John Strauss prepared the orchestrations, and Will Irwin directed the pit band. The small cast of eight included rising stars Joel Grey, Tammy Grimes, Charlotte Rae, and Larry Storch.

The Littlest Revue proved amiably satirical, with the focus on such cultural (as opposed to political) topics as Norman Vincent Peale's *The Power of Positive Thinking* (1952), Sloan Wilson's *The Man in the Gray Flannel Suit* (novel 1955, film 1956), Marcelle Maurette's French play *Anastasia* (1952, adapted for Broadway, 1954, and Hollywood, 1956, its famous recognition scene set here in a Brooklyn candy store), Orson Welles's performance as King Lear in a wheelchair (1956), the off-Broadway stage, television censorship, and the Hotel Brevoort and the Third Avenue El, both recently demolished. Three musical numbers caricatured classical music: in the case of Sheldon Harnick's "The Shape of Things," and Duke and Latouche's "Summer Is Icumen In" (as spelled in the program), by similarly mismatching period mannerisms with a modern sensibility; and in the case of Strouse and Adams's "Spring Doth Let Her Colours Fly" by presenting a parody of Wagner as sung by one Brunhilde Benzine in a nightclub, complete with show girls and chorus boys—an undisguised jibe at opera star Helen Traubel's widely publicized two-week engagement for the grand opening of the Royal Nevada Hotel in Las Vegas. Producer Bagley clearly presumed a sophisticated audience conversant with classical music, bestselling books, contemporary theater and film, and life generally in metropolitan New York.

The extended "Opening Number" by Latouche, Elmslie, and Strauss simulated a backer's audition—Bagley renamed the number "Backer's Audition," when he rereleased the show's cast album on compact disc—in which a pitchman lays out a proposed revue to potential angels, with the ensemble singing, for example, in a shuffling song-and-dance refrain, the show's planned opening chorus:

> It's rather nice to see your not-too-shiny faces out front
> As we cut up a bit to help you relax.
> It's actually rather pleasant
> To amuse a local peasant
> As long as he pays for a ticket plus amusement tax.

The number goes on to mimic the bluesy riverboat song "Mark Twain" as written and performed by Harry Belafonte in John Murray Anderson's 1953 revue *Almanac*, and burlesque the nostalgic "Penny Candy" as written and sung by June Carroll (composer Steve Reich's mother) in another revue, *New Faces of 1952*. In the "Mark Twain" spoof, the singer, impersonated by Joel Grey, born in the Bronx and raised in Queens but "a hick at heart," learns to play the "eight-string guitar" from a "correspondence course" and now rides around Bucks County "in a brand new Jag-u-ar"; in the "Penny Candy" satire, a childlike waltz full of incongruous sexual innuendos performed mostly by Charlotte Rae, a couple recalls sharing bubblegum as children, the reminiscence concluding, "The minty flavor has gone / But love lingers on / When I chew the bubblegum you gave me long, long ago." Near its conclusion, the number becomes even more self-mocking as the singers explain, for instance,

> We cannot offer to our future fans a
> Tremendous musical extravaganza.
> Though talented and brash,
> We're rather shy of cash.
> Our budget is no Shubert Alley topic.
> It's microscopic.

Although characteristic of Latouche in various ways, this hilarious lyric, smartly set to music by Strauss, exhibits too a certain daffy charm that seems Elmslie's own. Had Latouche lived, he and Elmslie, with whom he also co-wrote "On the Waterfront," perhaps would have continued to collaborate to good effect, while the team of Latouche and Strauss, as additionally evidenced by "A Nail in the Horseshoe," held promise as well.[16]

The Littlest Revue debuted on May 22, 1956, for a four-week engagement at the Phoenix Theatre, with Latouche sending its principal authors, Vernon Duke and Ogden Nash, an opening night telegram that read, "Bravos and blessing tonight from your strongest fan." Reviewing the show, Brooks Atkinson (*Times*) thought this "harlequinade" to offer "a uniformly high standard of intelligence and humor," but many others found the production little more than mildly diverting, with Charlotte Rae's performance of "Summer Is Icumen In" often singled out as a rare high point. Such tepid response ruled out a continuation of the revue elsewhere following the end of its limited engagement at the Phoenix on June 17, 1956; but despite its short run, about a month after the show folded Epic Records released a cast album, later reissued on the Painted Smiles label.[17]

Shortly before he died, Latouche began work on a musical, *The First Time,* adapted from the three-act satiric comedy *To Tell You the Truth* by Eva Wolas, which had premiered off Broadway at the New Stages Theatre in Greenwich Village in April 1948. A graduate of Cornell and Yale, the Russian-born Wolas (1915–2003) over time pursued a career mostly as a television writer, although she remains best remembered for her adaptation of Jean-Paul Sartre's controversial one-acter *The Respectful Prostitute,* which New Stages (co-founded in 1947 by Wolas's husband, David Heilweil) had presented on a double bill earlier in 1948, and which, with a different companion piece, moved to the Cort Theatre on Broadway in March 1948 for an impressive 318 performances.

To Tell You the Truth had less success, running a mere two weeks and then falling into obscurity. Described by the *Wall Street Journal* as "a sort of fable in slang," the play reconceived the Garden of Eden story as a battle of the sexes, with Adam (played by a young Tony Randall, then billed as Anthony Randall) and Woman/Eve learning to love each other, at the price of paradise lost. The modest cast included a secondary romantic couple—Adam's guardian angel, Michael, and the lascivious fallen angel Zillah—supplemented by a chorus of three singers, with music provided by George Karlin. Directed by Ezra Stone, the play received mixed notices. George Jean Nathan (*Theatre Book*) found the comedy to contain "not the slightest wit, taste, or invention," whereas Brooks Atkinson (*Times*) thought that Wolas wrote "intelligently and imaginatively," although he too concluded that the overlong show "never really takes flight."[18]

As early as May 1956, a plan evolved to adapt *To Tell You the Truth* into a musical for possible tryout presentation toward the end of the summer season at the Bucks County Playhouse (then under the leadership of Michael Ellis) in New Hope, Pennsylvania. The creative team included Ezra Stone as director and co-bookwriter, Latouche as bookwriter-lyricist, Milton ("Milt") Rosenstock as composer and conductor, and Frederick Kiesler as set designer. As the director of the original Wolas play, and as someone with close ties to the playhouse, Stone (born

Feinstone, 1917–1994), who years earlier had made his name playing the hapless teenager Henry Aldrich on Broadway and radio, likely spearheaded and perhaps underwrote the project. The creative team seems to have constituted in any case a congenial group, with Rosenstock a former collaborator with Stone on Irving Berlin's 1942 revue *This Is the Army*, and with Latouche on *The Vamp*; and with Kiesler, one of Latouche's closest friends.[19]

An accomplished clarinetist, Rosenstock (1917–1992) studied composition and conducting at Juilliard before establishing himself as a top Broadway conductor, for some fifty years directing many leading musicals. Awarded a Tony for *Finian's Rainbow* (1947) and Tony nominations for *The Vamp* (1955) and *Gypsy* (1959), he also seems to have been something of a frustrated composer, although in 1973, he succeeded in providing the music for a Broadway show of his own, *Nash at Nine*, a revue of verse and songs based on the work of Ogden Nash that received some good reviews but managed only twenty-one performances.

A few days after Latouche's death on August 7, the *Times* stated that Stone, Rosenstock, and Kiesler, all in attendance at the lyricist's funeral, had been working with the deceased on a show called "To Prelude the Truth," apparently an alternate name for the Wolas adaptation, although Kiesler (the probable source for this news) sometimes misspoke names and the like (including referring elsewhere to this show as "Adam and Eve" and its composer as "Rosenzweig"). Several months later, *Variety* further reported that at the time of Latouche's demise, a draft of the show's first act and seven of fifteen planned songs had been completed; Kiesler similarly mentioned eight finished songs, which he described as "O.K., oh, very O.K."[20]

The lyrics of six such songs, dated July 1956, survive among Kiesler's papers: "Opening," an introductory number for Michael and the ensemble; "Two by Two," for Michael and Adam, in which the latter goes from naming animals to bemoaning his loneliness; "Zillah's Song," a seductive number, reminiscent of "Lazy Afternoon," presumably sung to Adam; "I've Got a Girl on My Mind," in which Adam dreams of his ideal mate; "Where You Are Is Paradise," for Adam and Woman, the title self-explanatory; "Etiquette," a facetious number about the advantages of social diplomacy, likely sung by Zillah to Adam; and "The First Time," in which the chorus sings of discovering love. The content and even specific phrases of these lyrics echoed Latouche's earlier work—"I've Got a Girl on My Mind," for instance, recalled "Girls Want a Hero" (*Beggar's Holiday*), "Maybe You're My Man" (*The Happy Dollar*), and "Ragtime Romeo" (*The Vamp*)—but they revealed at the same time some bold new directions the lyricist might have pursued had he lived longer. The "Opening," for example, starts with the sounds of volcanic eruptions and atomic explosions, and the ensemble singing, "In the beginning, God created Heaven and Earth," after which the archangel Michael appears suspended before the curtain, saying, ostensibly accompanied by music,

> You have just heard a fission
> Emerge from confusion

You have just heard 'Old Adam'
Emerge from an atom,
Electron, proton, neutron, meson
Shattering under cosmic pressure
Forming the Father of us all
From a small pinch of clay
And a divine dream.

And although reminiscent of "Take Love Easy" (*Beggar's Holiday*) in its hardboiled outlook and even its language, "Etiquette" displayed a new daring as well, as illustrated by this excerpt:

Push and shove
But you must always wear a velvet glove
When stealing eyeballs, do it
Oh so lightly and exclaim politely
Please excuse
What can you lose
You are a mess
But with finesse
You can succeed
And with a touch of breeding
Comes authority you won't regret
That's etiquette!

Rosenstock apparently set and recorded at least some of these numbers; but no scores or recordings seem to have survived. In any event, with *The First Time*, Latouche's career came full circle once again, with a musical that, like *Cabin in the Sky*, used emissaries of God and Satan to dramatize man's relation to good and evil and the challenges of love and marriage, although these particular topics tended to inform his oeuvre generally, as did the employment of myths and fables from around the world.[21]

Following Latouche's death, and after unsuccessfully attempting to interest Gore Vidal, William Saroyan, and Michael Myerberg in the property, Stone decided to work on the script with writer Bernard Evslin, imagining further that either Evslin or Kenward Elmslie might complete the score with Rosenstock. "I hope it will be a credit to John's memory and talent," wrote Stone to Kiesler. Stone worked on the show into 1957 with Evslin, and although nothing materialized, this unfinished venture anticipated the trend for intimate off-Broadway musicals, as represented with most commercial success by *The Fantasticks* (1960) by bookwriter-lyricist Tom Jones and composer Harvey Schmidt.[22]

23

The Ballad of Baby Doe

Latouche's career ended on a high note with the opera *The Ballad of Baby Doe*—an unlikely collaboration between himself, a bohemian Columbia University dropout, and composer Douglas Moore, a patrician Columbia professor some twenty years his senior. "They were an odd couple," remembered Moore's Columbia colleague, composer Jack Beeson, "but odd couples can make good opera!" Regarded as Moore's undisputed masterpiece, *Baby Doe* played a decisive role with respect to his reputation, taking the sixty-two-year-old from the relative margins of the new music scene to a prominent place among contemporary American composers. But the work represented one of Latouche's most impressive achievements as well, showing him to be not only a master of comedy but also of tragedy.[1]

The son of a well-to-do publisher descended from a farming family long settled on eastern Long Island, Douglas Moore (1893–1969) grew up in the Bedford-Stuyvesant section of Brooklyn—not far from the childhood home of the somewhat younger Aaron Copland—although he spent summers in Cutchogue on the north fork of Long Island, and, after a certain age, the academic year in boarding schools, including the Hotchkiss School in Lakeville, Connecticut. Playing piano, composing songs, and acting on stage, Moore developed a twin passion for music and theater; as late as the 1920s, while living in Cleveland, he trod the boards of the Cleveland Playhouse; and in still later years, after inheriting a family house, Salt Meadow, in Cutchogue, he expanded its living area with a raised stage so that he, his wife, and his two daughters, along with other family and friends, could present theatricals at home.[2]

Weaned on the music of Bach, Schubert, Brahms, and Tchaikovsky, Moore came to regard Mozart, Mussorgsky, Verdi, and Puccini as operatic paragons, as opposed to Beethoven, Wagner, and Strauss. He also acquired a love for American popular music, including folk melodies, gospel hymns, black spirituals, minstrel ballads, and parlor songs, along with the operettas of Victor Herbert and Rudolf Friml, the hit songs of Harry Von Tilzer and Irving Berlin, and the musical comedies of Jerome Kern and, in time, Cole Porter, George Gershwin, and Richard Rodgers. He could sing and play such fare at the piano for hours on end, a trait he shared with Latouche—not that either could carry a tune very well. Indeed, for all his urbanity and open-mindedness, including a high regard for such rival opera composers as

Virgil Thomson, Marc Blitzstein, and Gian Carlo Menotti—whose influences, along with that of Stravinsky's *The Rake's Progress* and Britten's *Peter Grimes*, could be discerned in *The Ballad of Baby Doe*—Moore rarely exhibited the sort of enthusiastic praise as found in a 1962 tribute to Irving Berlin, in which he lauded the songwriter for representing better than any other composer "the American people in its thoughts, its enthusiasms, its ideals, and its language," an achievement that "qualifies him, along with Stephen Foster, Walt Whitman, Vachel Lindsay, and Carl Sandburg as a great American minstrel." Moore encouraged one of his few prominent composition students, John Kander, in time the composer of *Cabaret* and *Chicago*, to pursue a career in popular theater, telling him on one occasion, "You know if I had to do it all over again, I think I'd write for Broadway."[3]

For all this, Moore had a highly pedigreed music education, including six years at Yale (1911–17), during which time he studied with David Stanley Smith and Horatio Parker, who, observed composer Otto Luening in 1943, set Moore "on the path he has consistently followed." After two years in the navy (1917–19), Moore pursued his education (as did his friend the Kentucky folklorist John Jacob Niles, as well as fellow Yalies Cole Porter and Quincy Porter) in Paris at the Schola Cantorum (1919–21), a more academic alternative to the Paris Conservatory, and one soon superseded, so far as concerned most American composers, by the American Conservatory at Fontainebleau and the Parisian atelier of Nadia Boulanger. At the Schola Cantorum, Moore studied composition under Vincent d'Indy, who helped refine his sense of form, and whose music he commended throughout his life (Jack Beeson could detect "whiffs" of d'Indy even in Moore's mature work); he also took organ lessons with both Boulanger and Charles Tournemire, whom he revered as "a man of great piety and gentleness."[4]

As organist and curator of music at the Cleveland Museum of Art (1921–25), Moore continued his composition studies with Ernst Bloch at the Cleveland Institute of Music (1921–22), where his fellow students included such future luminaries as Roger Sessions, Quincy Porter, Bernard Rogers, and Theodore Chanler. "The great thing about Bloch," recalled Moore, "was that he wanted you to be yourself. . . . He could see what you were trying to do and he would go along with you." Hearing Vachel Lindsay recite his poem "Bryan, Bryan, Bryan, Bryan" in 1923 proved similarly decisive: "It was partly through Vachel Lindsay that I discovered the glamor and excitement of American things." Moore responded immediately with his orchestral suite *The Pageant of P. T. Barnum* (1924), whose success helped establish his name. Meanwhile, he returned to Paris to complete his musical education with Nadia Boulanger, with whom he worked in early 1926, but the experience proved less than satisfactory; she allegedly had little sympathy for his music, while he could not share her enthusiasm for Fauré, Ravel, and the later Stravinsky.[5]

In the fall of 1926, Moore joined the Columbia University faculty at the invitation of composer Daniel Gregory Mason, who also had studied with d'Indy and who, although more conservative than Moore, likely viewed the younger man as an upholder of certain shared values. Moore remained on the faculty for thirty-five years, succeeding Mason as department head in 1940 and retiring in 1962. Little interested in teaching composition, Moore devoted himself rather to general music classes (he authored two music appreciation texts) and to university and professional administration, including serving as president of the National Institute of Arts and Sciences (1946–1952), the American Society of Composers, Authors and Publishers (1957–1960), and the American Academy of Arts and Sciences (1959–1962). He further supervised Columbia's Alice M. Ditson Fund, which under his watch provided a much-needed research appointment to the expatriate Hungarian composer Béla Bartók in 1941, and commissioned a series of operas, including Britten's *Paul Bunyan* (1941), Menotti's *The Medium* (1946), and Thomson's *The Mother of Us All* (1947).[6]

Residing in an apartment on Manhattan's Riverside Drive, with vacation time largely spent in Cutchogue, Moore composed mostly during the summer, finding it difficult to do more than copy or orchestrate scores during the school year; but he managed to produce a rather sizable catalog nevertheless. He drew enduring inspiration from his perception of American culture as set forth in a 1931 interview: "To begin with, we are incorrigibly sentimental as a race, and our realism in drama and literature usually turns out to be meltingly romantic in execution. . . . The best of what we accomplish is usually achieved by dint of high spirits, soft-heartedness, and a great deal of superfluous energy." Although he reportedly only occasionally quoted native folk or popular music, his own work struck many as having a distinctively American quality, including a certain directness and restraint that Copland thought akin to the music of Virgil Thomson, and utterly different from European music.[7]

Like Thomson too, Moore showed himself to best advantage in his stage work, which in the years before *Baby Doe* most notably included *The Headless Horseman* (1936, libretto by Stephen Vincent Benét), *The Devil and Daniel Webster* (1939, libretto by Benét), and *Giants in the Earth* (1950, and winner of the 1951 Pulitzer Prize, libretto by Arnold Sundgaard). Wrote Marc Blitzstein to Tennessee Williams in 1963, "He [Moore] is a rip-snorting good theatre composer, skillful and lyrically at home, who sets naturally and passionately what he feels. He works easily with a text, with or without a collaborator; he neither pulls the reins stiffly in behalf of his ego, nor gives in when the work and its new-medium demands are at stake." In selecting his operatic subjects, Moore expressed his partiality to American tales with "figures that are a bit larger than life," stating late in his career, "The notion of 'realistic' opera is nonsense. The trick is to get the audience to accept the unreality." Notwithstanding the adept pacing and shaping of larger scenes, his operas further tended to favor lyrical vocal writing—what Virgil Thomson called the composer's "abundant melody"—over symphonic development.[8]

Baby Doe started life in late 1953 as a commission from Colorado's Central City Opera for a work by Moore and playwright Paul Green about the fabled life of the Colorado mining baron Horace Tabor and his wife, Elizabeth, popularly known as

"Baby Doe." Housed in an intimate 750-seat theater (reduced to 552 after plush seating replaced old hickory chairs in 1999) built in Central City (about forty miles west of Denver) in 1878, the Central City Opera had been hosting a summer festival of operas and other works since 1932; but this would be its first commissioned piece. The received wisdom credits stage director Herbert Graf and especially set designer Donald Oenslager, both long associated with the festival, with spearheading the project in conjunction with Frank Ricketson Jr., the owner of a chain of movie theaters, and the president of the Central City Opera Association; but the commissioned librettist, Paul Green, the North Carolinian Pulitzer Prize–winning playwright who had written the book and lyrics to Kurt Weill's *Johnny Johnson* (1936) and an adaptation of Ibsen's *Peer Gynt* (1951)—two productions with sets by Oenslager—and who in addition had prepared, at Graf's request, an English version of Bizet's *Carmen* for a 1953 Central City staging, presumably played some role as well. For surely not coincidentally, Green had been a story writer for *Silver Dollar*, a 1932 First National film about Horace Tabor based on David Karsner's *Silver Dollar: The Story of the Tabors* (also 1932), and starring Edward G. Robinson, Bebe Daniels, and Aline MacMahon as (in essence, for the movie fictionalized the names) Horace, Baby Doe, and Horace's first wife, Augusta, respectively. (The popular Lux Radio Theater aired an adaptation of this film, narrated by Cecil B. DeMille, under the same name in 1939.) Moreover, beginning with *The Lost Colony*, an outdoor "symphonic drama" about the English founding of Roanoke Island that had played every summer since 1937 on North Carolina's Outer Banks, Green had made a specialty of epic pageants on American historical topics, often presented in their original environs; so he very possibly proposed the Tabor saga, which he thought Hollywood had trivialized, as a similarly appropriate vehicle for Central City.[9]

Meanwhile, Oenslager, who knew Moore from their student days at the Hotchkiss School and Yale, and who had attended performances of *The Devil and Daniel Webster* and *Giants in the Earth* (which concludes, like the Baby Doe saga, with a protagonist freezing to death in a blizzard), recommended the composer as an eminently suited partner to this venture. Oenslager possibly even knew that Moore, on reading an account of Baby Doe's death in the *New York Times* in 1935 ("Here was a woman," Moore recalled, "once famous for her beauty, who had been married to the richest man in Colorado, whose wedding had been attended by the president of the United States, found frozen to death in a miserable shack by an abandoned silver mine"), had made preliminary plans to write an opera about Baby Doe in collaboration with another of the composer's friends from Hotchkiss and Yale, poet Pierson Underwood. If so, perhaps this also factored into consideration. But whatever the circumstances behind the commission, including Denver composer Max DiJulio's claim that Central City settled on the Tabor story only after hearing about his own Baby Doe opera in progress, Green and Moore, although hardly acquainted, agreed to work together, the latter "thrilled" at the prospect of collaborating with the author of *Johnny Johnson*.[10]

First, however, Frank Ricketson had to persuade a wary Central City Opera Association to fund such an unprecedented undertaking, which he partly did by arguing that if Central City hoped "to attain important stature as a national festival," it needed to broaden its "sphere of activities" by commissioning new works, "preferably based on western history or folklore." In early 1954, the board consented to pay Green and Moore $5,000 each for an opera about Horace Tabor approximately two hours long to be presented in the summer of 1955. In addition, the board budgeted a small honorarium to Caroline Bancroft, a well-known local expert on Colorado history, to serve as an advisor to the authors.[11]

Born on a Vermont farm near the Canadian border, tall and burly Horace Tabor (1830–1899) met his first wife, the slender and comely Augusta Pierce (1833–1895), in the early 1850s while working for her father as a stonecutter in Augusta, Maine. With the assistance of an abolitionist association, Horace homesteaded a farm in the Kansas Territory, where he served in the insurrectionist antislavery Topeka legislature; and in early 1857, he returned to Maine to marry Augusta, who accompanied him back to Kansas, giving birth later in the year to a son, Nathaniel Maxey (known as Maxey or Maxcy, 1857–1929). In 1859, the Tabors joined other so-called fifty-niners in the search for gold in the sparsely populated area around Pikes Peak, still Kansas Territory, but by 1861, Colorado Territory, and by 1876, the State of Colorado. Although Horace for many years had little success as a prospector, he and Augusta, moving from one mining camp to another, modestly prospered by selling supplies, providing mail and banking services, and taking in boarders. As the gold rush gave way to a silver boom, the Tabors relocated in 1877 to a new settlement, soon to be named Leadville, where they opened a store and where Horace became the town's first mayor.[12]

The following year, in 1878, Horace grubstaked two prospectors—that is, outfitted them with provisions in return for a share of future profits—who unearthed a highly profitable silver mine, the Little Pittsburg. Suddenly wealthy, Horace not only acquired other mining property, including the even more lucrative Matchless Mine, but invested in newspapers, real estate, saloons, hotels, banks, railroads, stocks, and mahogany—investments that spanned the continent. Elected the first lieutenant governor of Colorado (1878–1884), Horace concurrently maintained residences in Leadville and the state capital, Denver, and personally helped develop both cities, including bringing various municipal services to Leadville; financing the Tabor Opera House (1879) in Leadville, and the five-story Tabor Block (1880) and the Tabor Grand Opera House (1881) in Denver; and making charitable contributions, including donating land for the frontier synagogue Temple Israel (1884) in Leadville and the U.S. Post Office (opened 1892) in Denver. Given to high living, including some consorting with prostitutes, Horace drifted apart from his more conservative wife; and after spending increasingly less time at home, he left Augusta for good in early 1881.

By this time, he had started an affair with a petite and pretty blond-haired and blue-eyed divorcée nearly twenty-five years his junior, Elizabeth ("Lizzie") Doe, commonly called "Baby Doe" after the felicitous pairing of a youthful nickname, "Baby," with her first husband's surname, Doe. Born Elizabeth Nellis McCourt, Baby Doe (1854–1935) had been raised in a devout and sometimes prosperous Irish Catholic family in the lumber boom town of Oshkosh, Wisconsin. In 1877, she married Harvey Doe, the charming only son of a prominent Protestant family, whereupon the newlyweds left Wisconsin in order to work some Doe family mining property in Central City, Colorado. As Harvey's career floundered, Baby became romantically involved with Jacob Sandelowsky (also known by his Anglicized name, Jake Sands), a young and enterprising Jewish merchant born in Poland. In March 1880, having given birth to a stillborn boy several months earlier, Baby divorced Harvey (the divorce, however, not finalized until 1886) and moved to Leadville, where Jake had opened a store. How Horace and Baby became acquainted remains unclear—several sources claim that they met in a Leadville restaurant in 1880 during the intermission of a performance at the Tabor Opera House—but it appears that by the summer of that year they had become lovers.

With Augusta unwilling to divorce him, Horace arranged a fraudulent divorce in Durango, Colorado, in early 1882 and married Baby in St. Louis later in the year; the divorce contested and overruled, in early 1883, nearing the end of a campaign for a seat in the U.S. Senate, Horace, by withholding financial support, finally pressured Augusta to grant a divorce, her settlement including their mansion and a portion of her husband's multimillion-dollar estate. Although Horace lost the senatorial election, the Colorado legislature nonetheless appointed him to a thirty-day vacancy in Congress, during which time, on March 1, 1883, he remarried Baby in a lavish wedding in Washington, D.C., attended by President Chester A. Arthur, but boycotted by many women invitees, who widely considered the marriage a disgrace.

On his return to Denver, Horace purchased a grand residence for himself and his new wife, with whom he had three more children: Elizabeth Bonduel Lillie (known as "Lily," 1884–1946); a boy who died at birth, Horace Joseph (1888); and Rosemary Echo Silver Dollar (called "Honeymaid," but best known as "Silver," 1889–1925). Denver society by and large spurned Baby as a mercenary Irish-Catholic homewrecker, a factor that likely played a part in Horace's failed attempts to become state governor in 1884, 1886, and 1888. Meanwhile, because of unwise investments and profligate spending, not to mention the rising cost of mining and the falling price of silver, Horace fell deeper and deeper into debt. The Panic of 1893 and subsequent repeal of the Sherman Silver Purchase Act helped bankrupt him entirely, driving him and his family from their mansion and into poverty, and provoking Horace, as a last glimmer of hope, to leave the Republican Party in favor of William Jennings Bryan, the free-silver 1896 Democratic presidential candidate who lost the election to William McKinley. (Having invested her money more cautiously, Augusta died a wealthy woman in California in 1895.) With his appointment as Denver postmaster in 1898, Horace made a modest financial recovery before his demise, due to complications related to appendicitis, the following year.

Not long after Horace's death, the penniless Baby moved with her two daughters into a miner's shack by the ramshackle Matchless Mine, dubiously thinking that she owned the mine and could get it operating again. The older daughter, Elizabeth, soon after left for Chicago in order to live with her mother's family, and eventually married her first cousin, which caused serious friction between her and her increasingly devout mother. Baby's younger daughter, Silver, an aspiring writer, similarly made her way to Chicago, where a dissolute lifestyle seems to have contributed to her sensational death by scalding in 1925. Meanwhile, Baby became something of a mystical hermit, living in the most abject poverty, dressing shabbily, and keeping a journal brimming with inscrutable jottings. (As Baby came to be regarded as an eccentric rather than a femme fatale, Margaret Brown, another legendary Irish-American wife of a Colorado silver king—and someone who similarly would become the subject of a work of musical theater, namely, Meredith Willson's 1960 musical *The Unsinkable Molly Brown*—came to her aid and defense.) Baby lived long enough to witness the renewed interest in her life spurred by the 1932 book and film about her and Horace, but refused to see the picture. In 1935, after thirty-five years living mostly alone at the mouth of the Matchless Mine, she froze to death at about age eighty-one in her cabin during a blizzard.[13]

With its scandalous romance, its great wealth gained and lost, and its extraordinary and unexpected coda, the Baby Doe saga proved one of the most enduring legends to come out of the Old West, as evidenced by its many historical and quasi-historical accounts, including the distinguished German-American playwright Carl Zuckmayer's *The Life of Horace A. W. Tabor*, which premiered in Zurich in 1964—an interest only intensified by the success of *The Ballad of Baby Doe*. At the heart of this fascination would seem to lie the flawed but sympathetic characters of Horace, Augusta, and Baby Doe as typically portrayed: Horace, brazen, convivial, garish, and extravagant; Augusta, stalwart, stern, nagging, and charitable; and Baby Doe, charming, bold, ambitious, and devoted—with the story's appeal similarly drawing on notions of the triumph of love over social propriety and material wealth.

Both long influenced by Brechtian concepts, Moore and Green collaborated on a nine-page scenario, completed in early 1954, that traced this epic drama through eight scenes spread over two acts (separated by interludes), with a final epilogue showing Baby Doe in her final years—a structure very much like the drama eventually realized by Moore and Latouche. Indeed, Latouche would follow this preliminary story outline closely, and not only its larger structure. For instance, the scenario's third scene—in which Baby Doe writes to her mother about Horace, confronts a haughty Augusta, tears up her letter, and vows eternal love to Horace—reads virtually like a synopsis to the completed opera's fourth scene. True, Latouche reconceived especially the first and final scenes, and instituted many other changes, for example adding, to Moore's delight, the business of Augusta discovering lace gloves bought by Horace for Baby. But to the extent that Green helped devise the story outline, he contributed significantly to the work's structure and substance, with some early commentators tellingly drawing comparisons between Green's pageants and the finished opera, apparently without even knowing about the playwright's early involvement in the project.[14]

However, by the early spring of 1954, the collaboration between Green and Moore had derailed. Sent a draft of the first scene, Moore found the text unusable, an assessment with which director Herbert Graf concurred, as did Latouche, who told Moore, "This sounds as if it were translated from a foreign language." Meanwhile, Green registered his own disappointment after hearing Moore play some of *Giants in the Earth*, informing a later interlocutor, "Moore has the modern idiom, and never does seem to climb, seems to gravel along." Realizing that they could not work together, Moore and Green gave each other permission to use their scenario as each saw fit, with the composer subsequently proposing to Central City that he perhaps collaborate with Arnold Sundgaard, his librettist for *Giants in the Earth*. But fearing legal difficulties, among other concerns, Central City decided instead to drop the whole thing.[15]

Without any firm prospects in view, in the spring of 1954 Moore nonetheless approached Latouche about collaborating on the opera. The composer had admired the latter's work for some time, writing him, as mentioned earlier, a glowing 1948 reference for a Guggenheim fellowship, a favorable impression that presumably only had deepened since the arrival of *The Golden Apple*. Moore likely recognized similarities between his proposed Tabor opera and not only *The Golden Apple*, with its turn-of-the-century setting, but *The Eccentricities of Davy Crockett* (from *Ballet Ballads*), which chronicled the frontiersman's life through a series of small vignettes. For his part, Latouche, "an ardent fan" of Moore's *The Devil and Daniel Webster*, already had suggested to the composer, on the occasion of that work's highly successful 1953 revival at the Old Sturbridge Festival in Massachusetts, that the two of them work together.[16]

Coincidentally, Latouche had been approached years earlier about developing the Tabor story with composer Jerome Kern for a musical to be produced by Billy Rose, an idea aborted, according to Latouche, by Kern's death in 1945. But now, in the spring of 1954, when Moore broached the subject of collaborating on a Tabor opera over lunch at the Columbia University faculty club, Latouche felt some reluctance about embarking on another work that might be labeled a piece of "Americana," a patronizing term, he thought, that "implies instantly a tinycraft quaintness, a precious whimsy with no continuity into the realities of the twentieth century," and that seemed particularly resistant to grand and tragic theater. "Therefore, when Douglas Moore suggested what sounded like a compendium of *all* the nostalgic elements—rags to riches, the West, a luscious round-heel with a heart of gold, a termagant of a wife, and William Jennings Bryan thrown in for good measure—I was a trifle hesitant." However, on investigating the story, which he called, "an archetype of The Tired Businessman legend," he found the material "lurid, earthy, human and deeply touching." Meanwhile, the challenge of moving beyond stereotype could be accomplished, he felt, by "the addition of the musical element, which contains its own emotional magic."[17]

As a next step, Moore needed to raise money for the work's composition. During the summer of 1953, he had received a $1,500 commission from the Serge Koussevitzky Music Foundation for an orchestral work in honor of the bicentennial of Columbia University. (Established by conductor Koussevitzky in 1942 in order to support new music, the foundation by this point had underwritten such outstanding works as Bartók's *Concerto for Orchestra*, Britten's *Peter Grimes*, Copland's Third Symphony, and Messiaen's *Turangalîla Symphony*.) Orphaned for the moment by the Central City Opera, but having decided to work with Latouche, in May 1954 Moore successfully petitioned the foundation, whose board included Koussevitzky's widow, Olga, and composers Leonard Bernstein, Aaron Copland, Howard Hanson, and William Schuman, that he compose an opera rather than an orchestral work honoring Columbia University—in later years, justifying the matter to Olga Koussevitzky by identifying Latouche as "a Columbia College man," and noting that the opera's musical director, Emerson Buckley, had been educated at Columbia as well. The specifics of Moore's financial arrangement with Latouche remain unknown, but the grant in any case allowed them to proceed with the opera.[18]

After preliminary discussions about the piece in the spring, by early June Latouche had produced enough of the planned two-act libretto for Moore to begin composing, for the latter preferred to work sequentially scene by scene rather than from a completed text. However, in mid-June, Latouche had to leave for Martha's Vineyard in order to start work on *Candide* with Bernstein and Lillian Hellman—a source of frustration for Moore, who hoped to complete the first act by the end of the summer and who wanted to work in closer proximity to his librettist. "Wont you see if you can give me some time either here or in New York?" he wrote to Latouche from Cutchogue in early August.[19]

Indeed, as work progressed, Moore, like so many before him, found Latouche difficult to pin down, reminiscing late in life,

> Latouche was always disappearing. He was always busy. He was doing something for Carol Channing [*The Vamp*] and something for Leonard Bernstein, and so I was so excited that I would go ahead and write things. Because John was always involved in so many things, it was hard to get hold of him and he would come down here [to Cutchogue] and we would imprison him and say, "Now you can't have a cocktail until you get that scene finished."

(The composer's daughter Mary Kelleher, who thought Latouche "lively" and "enchanting," as did her sister, Sarah Moore, recalled one such occasion in which the Moore family "quietly began cocktails" at home while the librettist worked in another part of the house: "We were half through when suddenly John appeared on the stage [in the living room] with a yell of a wounded animal and said, 'You started without me.'") Moore became so impatient that in the early stages of their collaboration, especially for the first few scenes, he wrote some of the dialogue and lyrics himself, including the "Willow Song" and the "Letter Song," although he at least took his cue for the former from a few lines provided by Latouche: "Willow, weeping by the river / Willow, weep for the lovers true, / Willow, etc." Among other setbacks, Latouche had to rewrite the opera's final scene after he left the script in a taxi on his way to deliver it to Moore.[20]

And yet when corralled, Latouche proved, as Moore noted, "a quick and effective worker," and the composer managed to complete the first act of the piano-vocal score by March 1955 and the second act by August of that year, with the orchestration completed on April 1, 1956. After considering such titles as *The Silver Echo* and *The Saga of Baby Doe,* Moore and Latouche decided by November 1955 to call the piece *The Ballad of Baby Doe,* which, the composer explained, "has a nice lilt and seems better than just Baby Doe." Initially, Moore and Latouche had termed the work a "music drama," but in due course settled on the more conventional "opera in two acts," with the score's inscription reading, "Commissioned in honor of the Columbia University Bicentennial by the Koussevitzky Foundation of the Library of Congress and dedicated to the memory of Serge and Natalie [Serge's wife before Olga] Koussevitzky." There had been some talk about a premiere at Tanglewood, but Moore maintained his connections with the Central City Opera, and after he auditioned the opera for the association's board in October 1955, including singing many of the parts himself, Central City decided to present the work at its 1956 summer festival in alternation with Puccini's *Tosca.*[21]

During the winter of 1955, Moore and Latouche traveled to Colorado, according to Evelyn Furman, a Leadville writer and businesswoman who, having recently acquired the Tabor Opera House, showed the historic building to the composer and librettist one cold day in March, recalling that one of the two said, after looking the place over, "I've got it. I've got it." This eureka moment presumably concerned the second act, perhaps the finale, as Moore and Latouche by this time already had completed the first act.[22]

Latouche had assorted publications to consult for his research, including David Karsner's *Silver Dollar* (1932), Lewis Cass Gandy's *The Tabors* (1934), and Caroline Bancroft's *Silver Queen* (1950, adapted from her pseudonymous five-part article for *True Story* magazine); and to judge from the libretto, he drew on these varied authorities, especially Karsner. But he publicly admitted consulting only contemporary newspaper reports and excerpts from Augusta Tabor's diary, which amazed him "by the awareness and passionate drive reflected in the beautifully written account of their [her and Horace's] difficult journey [West]."[23]

Latouche had good reasons especially to avoid crediting Bancroft, a notorious gadfly who even in the project's earliest days had proved nettlesome. Although no longer officially associated with the commission, she wrote Moore and Latouche in

April 1955, ostensibly in the spirit of good will, but patently eager for credit and royalties, and vaguely threatened legal action in the event of any perceived plagiarism; in another letter to the two from January 1956, she even claimed rights to the name Baby Doe, but demonstrated her professed generosity by requesting simply a credit line in the Central City Opera program for both her and the maker of a Baby Doe doll (a request never honored). In an article about the opera published in July 1956, Latouche pointedly expressed regret that he had read Bancroft's work "too late" for him to use (even if in a later printing of *Silver Queen*, Bancroft erroneously claimed that Latouche, in his article about the opera for *Theatre Arts*, had stated a preference for her "booklet" over "all available treatment of the Tabors"). He further tried assuaging Bancroft by informing her that he planned his next show around a story by her Denver friend Libbie Block, and by meeting with her about the script shortly before the premiere, a consultation that led to two minor changes in the text: the replacement, for various historical reasons, of a Chinese or Native American servant with a Welsh worker (the "Cousin Jack" mentioned in the libretto); and the substitution of the term "fifty-niner" with "forty-niner" as a more apt phrase for Coloradan miners. "Now it's a good script," pronounced Bancroft after their meeting, "and LaTouche has shown a wonderful understanding of what Baby Doe and Augusta were like."[24]

The libretto tells the complex Tabor story skillfully, neatly providing some background material about the principal characters before they reveal more about themselves. The finale (which seems particularly indebted to David Karsner's book and possibly its film adaptation as well) goes so far as to encapsulate, through the use of both flashbacks and, like *The Golden Apple*, flashforwards, the entire hundred-year saga from Horace's childhood in Vermont to Baby's long vigil at the Matchless Mine. Some matters, such as Horace's political career, receive marginal attention, with only the most passing references, say, to his position as lieutenant governor or his senatorial campaign. Nor does the work mention Horace and Augusta's son, Maxey (who, like his mother, remained well-to-do, and who died in 1929). But in the end, the opera covers enormous historical ground, right down to particulars about Baby Doe's sumptuous wedding gown and the Tabor Grand's luxuriant decor.[25]

Latouche only rarely quoted historical sources, however. In William Jennings Bryan's solo, "Good People of Leadville," to take a notable instance, he incorporated phrases from Bryan's speeches, including his famed "Cross of Gold" address delivered at the Democratic Party national convention in 1896, although for this same aria he also borrowed his favorite phrases "nation of nations" and "race of races" from Whitman's *Leaves of Grass*, and availed himself, like Bryan, of some biblical rhetoric as well, so that the number, as Moore observed, wound up a mixture of Bryan, the Bible, Whitman, "and the rest vintage Latouche." And for the chorus that begins "The opera house, a union grand" in the final scene, Latouche yoked together a quatrain written by journalist Eugene Field in tribute to Tabor on the occasion of the opening of the Tabor Grand Opera House and some lines from poet Charles

Kingsley's 1848 poem, "Old and New," that ornamented Elliott Daingerfield's painted drop curtain for the Tabor Grand, and that proved, as concerned Horace's fate, poignantly prophetic: "So fleet the works of man, back to the earth again. Ancient and holy things fade like a dream."[26]

Otherwise, Latouche simply but brilliantly imagined the language and manners of the story's time and place, from the salty lingo of Horace and his cronies to the grandiloquence of Augusta and her friends, to the sometimes flowery parlance of Baby Doe, with her "silver orb," "Beulah Land" (a biblical phrase popular in nineteenth-century American hymnody), and "love's bright heraldry" (this last akin to Aloysius Coll's poem "Love's Heraldry," published in *Munsey's Magazine* in 1904). Latouche even adopted the time-worn use of Baby Doe's birthplace, Oshkosh, as a joke town by having some fun with the name himself (along with that of lispy Duluth). So vivid an evocation of nineteenth-century Colorado appears all the more impressive in light of Latouche's coeval depiction of eighteenth-century Europe in *Candide* and the early American film industry in *The Vamp*, not to mention the sort of contemporary popular lyrics he consistently wrote.[27]

For his part, Moore avoided quoting or even researching period music, aside most noticeably from some brief allusions to a period ditty associated with the California gold rush, "Oh My Darling, Clementine," a tune that had figured prominently in both the *Silver Dollar* motion picture and radio drama, and that Moore uses early in the opera to accompany a taunt by the saloon girls to an elderly miner, "Git on home now to yer shack and yer darling Clementine." Rather, he relied instinctively on his familiarity with American popular music and long experience as a musical regionalist in order to conjure the frontier, with pentatonically inflected melodies helpful in this regard. Describing the composer's approach as one of "stylized realism," Lewis J. Hardee discerned nonetheless resemblances between Horace's "I Came This Way from Massachusetts" and Stephen Foster's "Oh! Susanna" and "Camptown Races"; Baby's "Willow Song" and "Oh Shenandoah"; Baby's "Letter Song" and Phoebe Knapp's "Blessed Assurance"; and Baby's "Farewell Song" and Charles Converse's "What a Friend We Have in Jesus" (although as David McKee has pointed out, this final number, for good reason nicknamed, in homage to *Tristan und Isolde*, the "Leadville Liebestod," also echoes Wagner's "Tristan chord" at the word, "love"). Not entirely unlike the work of Charles Ives, another Horatio Parker student, bits of familiar fragments appear elsewhere, as in, for example, the sly quote of the nursery tune "London Bridge" for the phrase, "[re]taliation barriers," as the Four Dandies discuss tariff policy. Moreover, for the music that accompanies Baby Doe's entrance, Moore remembered a waltz used for the American actress Maude Adams in a production of J. M. Barrie's *The Little Minister* (presumably by the Scottish composer Alexander Mackenzie, whose name Moore had forgotten), a show that the composer perhaps saw on Broadway in 1916; he further requested, in response to his recollection of Adams as a "romantic, slightly tinny figure from the past," that this "Baby Doe Waltz" be played on a sort of honky-tonk piano, so that

Baby Doe seems to appear, at least initially, through the prism of Maude Adams (as Barrie's seductively winsome Lady Babbie). "We were both fortunate in the fact of his [Moore's] having been brought up on the popular music of the turn of the century," stated Latouche. "Waltzes, polkas, patriotic marches, ragtime, formal arias introduce the characters, and shade into an increasingly personal idiom as the characters turn inward at the conclusion of the opera."[28]

Moore and Latouche also received some assistance and inspiration from other sources. Composer Jack Beeson recalled that as he and Kenward Elmslie worked on their opera, *The Sweet Bye and Bye*, in tandem with Moore and Latouche, the two composers would play "our latest passages for one another, one of us sometimes finding a careless word-setting or an unwisely judged high note in the other's sketch." The young soprano Leyna Gabriele, eventually cast as an alternate Baby Doe in the debut production, similarly aided Moore by trying out sections with the composer at the piano. Others report that Moore consulted with Richard Rodgers about the score, and that he received help on the orchestration from his German-born colleague at Columbia, conductor Rudolph Thomas. Meanwhile, Latouche took a cue for the "Silver Song" from Moore's daughter Sarah's suggestion that "Baby Doe would particularly like silver because she was a nighttime person, as opposed to a daytime person." And as the opera moved into final production, the librettist credited designer Donald Oenslager, musical director Emerson Buckley, and co-directors Hanya Holm and Edwin Levy with making suggestions that greatly benefited the work, including "the elimination of anachronisms."[29]

As mentioned, Latouche worked within the guidelines of the story outline devised by Green and Moore, an indebtedness that would have been even more pronounced had the opera retained, as in an early draft, a final scene in which an aged Baby Doe disregards a miner's warnings about an approaching storm (the opera concluding in this version not with the "Farewell Song," but with a reprise of the "Willow Song"). Although Latouche and Moore ultimately dispensed not only with this epilogue, but with the scenario's planned interludes, the composer provided some scenes with instrumental prefaces in order to enhance continuity, and in the end, discerned "no loss of momentum as the story develops."[30]

From the start, Moore hoped to include "extended arias without slowing up the action; thanks to Latouche's remarkable theater sense, this was achieved. Baby Doe has five real arias, Augusta two, Tabor two." Still other sections, such as Augusta's tirade in the first scene, might be described as ariosos. Considering the aria an operatic "ideal" in that it "allows you to express an emotional situation," Moore smoothly incorporated such solos by writing in so songful a style throughout that set pieces typically arose without any special stylistic demarcation, although they often concluded firmly enough for applause.[31]

After the opera's opening on July 7, 1956, Moore and Latouche, partly in Colorado, partly back in New York, made some revisions to the work. Most notably, the librettist replaced Horace's moody "Out of the Darkness" with the more confessional

"Warm as the Autumn Light" (with the nostalgia of Baby Doe's "Willow Song" now triggering his own), and replaced Baby Doe's jaunty "Wake, Snakes!" with the more sober "The Fine Ladies Walk"—two new arias that more fully explored the inner lives of the lovers, with the apparent intention of gaining additional sympathy for them (although "Warm as the Autumn Light" musically derived from "Out of the Darkness," effectively so as the instrumental music that followed the aria, ingeniously juxtaposing the themes for "What a Lovely Evening" and "Out of the Darkness," remained intact). In addition, Latouche wrote an opening folk chorus, "Oh You Columbine," a jovial love song for offstage men's chorus; and an entirely new scene for Horace and his Four Cronies, a so-called gambling scene that, in addition to helping offset cuts taken in the campaign sequence, further delineated Horace's growing desperation, in the process providing the character with a dramatic second aria, "Turn Tail and Run, Then!" Moore spoke of Latouche's work as completed before his death on August 7, 1956, but the lyricist's young assistant at the time, Miles Kreuger, remembers him saying that he had yet more work to do on the opera.[32]

As they revised the piece, Latouche and Moore heeded the advice of producer Michael Myerberg, who hoped to bring the opera to Broadway, and who stayed in Colorado for a week after the Central City premiere in order to consult with the composer and librettist about the work. "I was afraid at first that he would want to make it less an opera and more of a show," wrote Moore to Olga Koussevitzky, "but the changes he suggests are good and I am quite willing to make them. The contract will give me complete artistic control." On August 2, less than a week before Latouche's death, agent Lucy Kroll wrote to Myerberg, away in Europe, "John [Latouche] has never been in a more creative mood and the collaboration between John and Douglas has been absolutely brilliant. All your suggestions have been well taken and I think that you will be proud and happy when you get back and see the work that has been done." The interpolation of the gambling scene in particular pointed to Myerberg's input, not only in its enhancement of the sort of narrative continuity that he felt lacking in the work, but in its extensive use of accompanied speech, for Myerberg hoped to convert much of the work's sung recitative, which he thought "stood in the way of the dramatic development," into speech with musical accompaniment (as had been done successfully with *Porgy and Bess* in the early 1940s). Moore finished setting the revised text after Latouche's death, including a folksy setting of "Oh You Columbine" that ultimately went unpublished and—aside, it seems, from a 1957 production of the opera at Stanford University—unperformed (explaining the leap from rehearsal 7 to rehearsal 8H in the published piano-vocal score).[33]

Aside from this opening chorus, the following synopsis describes the opera so revised, with the voice ranges of the main characters and the titles of the main set pieces given in parentheses, titles never specified as such except in the case of those six numbers published by Chappell Music: "Willow Song," "Warm as the Autumn Light (Tabor's Love Song)," "Letter Song," "Silver Song," "Augusta's Aria," and "Farewell

Song." Some bracketed remarks concerning the material in the context of the historical record follow the summary of each scene.

Act I, scene one. Outside the Tabor Opera House, Leadville, 1880. A drunken Old Miner, kicked out of a saloon by its Bouncer, rejoices that Horace Tabor wants to buy his Matchless Mine. Horace (baritone) and several Cronies take a break from a gala performance at Tabor's new opera house, and amuse themselves with some dance hall girls ("I Came This Way from Massachusetts," for Horace, Cronies, Kate, Meg, and chorus). At the gala's intermission, Horace's wife, Augusta (mezzo-soprano), scolds Horace and his friends for deserting their wives and cavorting with saloon girls. As the patrons return to the theater, a stranger to Leadville, later identified as Elizabeth ("Lizzie," "Baby") Doe (lyric soprano), asks Horace for directions to the Clarendon Hotel, and Horace, after assisting her, introduces himself before rejoining Augusta ("Baby Doe Waltz," instrumental, with Baby Doe, Horace, and Augusta).[34]

[This first scene, which gives the time as 1879 in the printed libretto but 1880 in the published piano-vocal score, slightly conflates historical events: if the gala marks the opening of the "brand new" Tabor Opera House, that would indicate a date of November 1879; and if Baby Doe's arrival represents her first visit to Leadville—as distinguished from her settling there in the spring of 1880—that rather would place the action, at least according to one source, in December 1879. The name "Bushy" no doubt refers to Horace's real-life right-hand man, William Bush. The fittings of the theater as detailed by Tabor describe not the Tabor Opera House in Leadville, but the Tabor Grand Opera House in Denver, which opened in 1881; and Adelina Patti, the mentioned featured soprano at the gala, did not make her Colorado debut until 1884, although Denver's Tabor Grand, as Latouche might have known, opened in 1881 with a performance by the Emma Abbott English Grand Opera Company.][35]

Scene two. Outside the Clarendon Hotel, later that evening. Augusta, Tabor, and their friends return home after the concert ("What a Lovely Evening," for Tabor, Augusta, and chorus). Two saloon girls, Kate and Meg, in earshot of Horace, gossip about Baby Doe and her husband, Harvey Doe of Central City, after which Horace hears Baby sing a melancholy song at the piano from within the Clarendon ("Willow Song," for Baby Doe). Horace tells Baby that her singing has awakened in him forgotten dreams and yearnings ("Warm as the Autumn Light," for Horace); the two gaze tenderly at each other, and Horace kisses Baby's hand. At Augusta's call, Horace enters the hotel.

[Horace and Augusta had homes, during this period, in both Leadville and Denver, making it improbable that they would stay at the Clarendon, as conductor John Moriarty has mentioned along with other discrepancies between the libretto and historical fact. The opera never alludes, incidentally, to Baby Doe's lover, the Jewish merchant Jake Sands, as her purported reason for coming to Leadville in the first place, although Latouche adopted the name for the person who sells the Matchless Mine to Horace, so that Sands and the Old Miner seem to be one and the same; in a preliminary draft, Horace negotiates for the mine with this Jake Sands, who provides some information about Baby Doe, a function later assumed by Kate and Meg.][36]

Scene three. The Tabor apartment, several months later. While supervising a maid cleaning Horace's study, Augusta finds lace gloves accompanied by a love note to Baby from Horace, and laments the toll taken by her frontier life ("Look at My Hands!" for Augusta). On Horace's entrance, he and Augusta squabble about both his proposed purchase of the Matchless Mine and his affair with Baby Doe. Augusta threateningly exits, followed by her husband.

[Since the subsequent fourth scene at the Clarendon follows "shortly thereafter," this "Tabor apartment" would seem situated in Leadville, although by this time—apparently late 1880, before the two separated in early 1881—Horace and Augusta lived primarily in Denver. Moreover, in 1880, the Tabors would have been married twenty-three years, not twenty-seven as stated by Augusta in the libretto (a remark, incidentally, colored by a sour dissonance in the musical accompaniment, as David McKee observes); nor did the two marry in April, but rather in January. Far from "idiotic," the purchase of the Matchless proved an extraordinary bonanza, but Latouche apparently felt the need to present Augusta's opposition to the sale as a foil to Baby's later attachment to the mine, and perhaps to indicate that Horace knew something about business after all. In any case, Horace purchased the Matchless Mine in the fall of 1879, that is, about a year before the action depicted in this scene. Finally, Augusta, in her lament, speaks of "tending kids," a seeming oversight as she had only one child, although as a makeshift nurse to the mining community, she might well have attended to other children as well.][37]

Scene four. The lobby of the Clarendon Hotel, shortly thereafter. Baby plans to return to her family in Oshkosh, explaining in a letter to her mother that although she has found a rich and desirable lover, she feels obliged to leave him because he is not free to marry ("Letter Song," for Baby Doe). Augusta enters and cautions Baby Doe; although initially acquiescent, after Augusta departs, Baby—apparently appalled at Augusta's denigration of Horace—tears up the letter to her mother and resolves to remain with Horace, who rushes to her side. After expressing their love, the two climb the stair together ("All That Is Bountiful," for Horace and Baby Doe).

[The "Letter Song," the text written by Moore as noted, plainly strives to exculpate the historical Baby Doe, who in fact loved Harvey Doe, at least at first, and who, as mentioned later in the opera's wedding scene, divorced him, not the other way round (although during their marriage, Harvey periodically absented himself). Nor does any evidence suggest that Baby considered parting from Horace because of any moral scruples. The only documented meeting between Baby and Augusta took place at the wedding of Maxey Tabor in 1884, although Augusta's calling card turned up among Baby's possessions, indicating perhaps other meetings—not that a confrontation in a hotel lobby likely would have transpired.][38]

Scene five. Augusta's parlor in Denver, a year later. Augusta's friends, hoping to goad Augusta into doing something about Horace's affair with Baby Doe, relate various rumors, including word that Horace already has divorced her. Augusta vows to cause a public scandal should Horace pursue a divorce.

[Historian Duane Smith has noted that the libretto situates Horace's fraudulent divorce in nonexistent Durango County as opposed to Durango in La Plata County.][39]

Scene six. A suite in the Willard Hotel, Washington, D.C., 1883. At the reception following Horace and Baby's marriage, the bride's mother, Mama McCourt (contralto), gushes about the wedding as Four Dandies discuss politics. After Horace enters with his bride, he and the Dandies argue about the future of silver, but Baby Doe defuses the situation by proclaiming her preference for silverish things like the moon ("Silver Song," for Baby Doe). Horace presents Baby with a diamond necklace said to contain Queen Isabella's jewels. Mama McCourt disparagingly mentions Harvey Doe and Augusta to the officiating priest, Father Chappelle, who, aghast to learn that both former spouses are still living, stonily departs the reception, leaving other attendants prepared to do likewise—a potential fiasco averted by the arrival of President Chester Arthur, who along with the guests, drinks a toast to the bride and groom.

[Father P. L. Chappelle learned that he had married divorcées, in violation of his Catholic faith, the day after, not the day of, the wedding. The discussion by the Four Dandies about the administration's decision to address high tariffs, incidentally, refers to the "Mongrel" Tariff Act, passed by Congress two days after the Tabor wedding, on March 3, 1883, at the end of the legislative session.][40]

Act II, scene one. The Windsor Hotel, Denver, 1893. At a governor's ball in honor of Horace, Augusta's friends snub Baby Doe, who pities them ("The Fine Ladies Walk," for Baby Doe). Knowing of impending legislation harmful to silver, Augusta warns Baby Doe that falling silver prices and Horace's extravagance have brought him to the edge of ruin, and urges her to make Horace sell the Matchless Mine. Overhearing this, Horace rebukes Augusta, who assures him that she will not trouble him again. Baby Doe loyally offers her jewelry to Horace as her "bet on silver," and agrees always to keep the Matchless Mine.[41]

[Augusta's allusion to the repeal under President Grover Cleveland of the 1890 Sherman Silver Purchase Act, which had helped bolster the price of silver, puts the action specifically in the fall of 1893; silver might not have lost half its value over the preceding decade, as Augusta contends, but the price had declined precipitously since Tabor struck it rich in the late 1870s, and would continue to do so after the repeal. However, this scene, and the second act generally, exaggerates the role legislative action played in the tycoon's downfall, which seems to have involved largely ill-advised speculation and market forces, in particular, the Panic of 1893. Baby's protest that she has "no head for bus'ness" would seem to contradict, as has been argued, her documented involvement in various business matters, although whatever her abilities in this area, she apparently lacked the prudence that characterized Augusta. Meanwhile, Tabor's plea that Baby "hold on to the Matchless Mine," often regarded as a melodramatic fiction despite its centrality to the entire Tabor yarn, finds strong support in a statement by Baby Doe's brother Philip McCourt on the occasion of his sister's death in 1935: "Tabor used to say, 'We must keep the Matchless, Phil. There is still money in it.'... When he died he told Elizabeth to hold on to it."][42]

Scene two. A club room in Denver, 1895. Finding four of his Cronies playing poker, Horace vainly seeks their financial assistance. Outraged by his desertion of his political party in favor of presidential candidate William Jennings Bryan, the Cronies withdraw ("Turn Tail and Run, Then!" for Horace).

[Tabor's abandonment of the Republican Party—the unnamed political party in this scene—proved common enough among Coloradans during these years thanks to Republican monetary policy, as opposed to the free-silver platform of the Democratic Party, which helped Bryan carry Colorado by a large margin.]

Scene three. The Matchless Mine, 1896 (with the libretto specifying both "summer" and "a sunny afternoon"). Horace, Baby Doe, and their two young daughters attend a rally for William Jennings Bryan (bass-baritone), who christens the younger Tabor girl "Silver Dollar" ("Good People of Leadville," for Bryan).

[Bryan's christening of the younger Tabor daughter as Silver Dollar presumably derived from an anecdote, told by Karsner, about a comment made by Bryan in the Tabor nursery—"that baby's laughter has the ring of a silver dollar"—that allegedly led Horace and Baby to adopt the phrase as part of Silver's name. Tabor's support of Bryan in this and the preceding scene, like his defense of the saloon girls in the opera's first scene, pictures him as a man of the people, a notion consistent with his many public services and charitable gifts, although obviously less so with his suppression, as lieutenant governor of Colorado, of an 1880 strike among Leadville miners for an eight-hour work day and a rise in pay to four dollars a day.][43]

Scene four. Augusta's parlor, November 1896. After Bryan's defeat, Mama McCourt visits Augusta in order to obtain financial assistance for the penniless Horace, but a conflicted Augusta finds herself unwilling to help ("Augusta's Aria," also known as "Augusta! How Can You Turn Away?" for Augusta).

[Although this scene ostensibly occurs just after the November 1896 presidential election, Augusta died, as Latouche and Moore well knew, a year earlier, in 1895. Moreover, the indication "a few weeks later," as found in the score, contradicts the summer setting for the previous scene, at least as cited in the libretto. In addition, some ambiguity exists concerning the scene's locale, with the libretto specifying, in acknowledgment of Augusta's move to Pasadena, California, in 1894 for health reasons, "Augusta's home in California," whereas the score simply says "Augusta's parlor," as in the table of contents, or "Augusta's study," as in the score proper, which would perhaps suggest a Denver setting were it not for Augusta's remark, "I left Colorado to close the last door on all that had been." That Mama McCourt would seek assistance from Horace's ex-wife as opposed to one of her own wealthy family members or, for that matter, Horace's never-mentioned son—a group, by the way, who seem to have concluded that handouts to Horace and Baby meant money down the drain, but who aided them to varying degrees anyway—seems sheer dramatic contrivance. Some newspapers indeed trumpeted Republican candidate William McKinley's win as a "landslide," although hardly warranted, as maintained elsewhere, by McKinley's 51 percent of the popular vote as against Bryan's 47 percent.][44]

Scene five. The stage of the Tabor Grand Theatre, April 1899. Now a poor laborer, Horace revisits the stage of the opera house that he had built years earlier. Recalling the gold watch fob presented to him by the citizens of Denver on the occasion of the theater's opening, with its links containing symbols of his career, Horace remembers episodes of his life: his childhood in Vermont, his courtship of Augusta, his trek westward, and his ascent to power and wealth. Feeling himself a failure, Horace takes comfort in thoughts of his family, but the spirit of Augusta reveals a future in which his daughter Elizabeth will reject his name, and his daughter Silver Dollar will decline into jazz-age debauchery. On Baby's arrival to bring him home, Horace tells her that she was "the only real thing" and expires. As Baby Doe reflects on the eternal youthfulness of their love, she pulls back her hood to reveal herself elderly and white-haired as she takes her place by the Matchless Mine ("Farewell Song," also known as "Always Through the Changing," for Baby Doe).[45]

[Horace died a middle-class postmaster at home in the Windsor Hotel, not an impoverished worker on the stage of the Tabor Grand Opera House, miscalled, incidentally, the Tabor Grand Theatre in both the libretto and the score. In an early draft of this scene, Horace indeed appears as a postmaster, although with the setting of his collapse still the opera house. Like this theatrical coup, Latouche's portraiture of Horace's mother Sarah, including her supposed preference for her son Lemuel, derived from Karsner's biography, although a good deal of this scene simply seems to have been invented. Finally, the libretto states that Horace's daughter Elizabeth "will change her name so no one will call her Tabor," whereas Elizabeth really disowned her mother, stating falsely in an interview after Baby Doe's death that she was the daughter of Horace's brother John Tabor.][46]

Many commentators familiar with both the Tabor saga and *The Ballad of Baby Doe*, starting with Caroline Bancroft, and including musicologist Randie Lee Blooding, historian Duane Smith, and conductor John Moriarty, even while noting deviations from the historical record, have applauded the opera for its authenticity, both in terms of its delineation of character and its depiction of time and place. "*The Ballad of Baby Doe* recaptures an era as few other accounts have," opined Smith, who credited the opera, about which he wrote a book with Moriarty, with inspiring his lifelong study of nineteenth-century Colorado, including a 1989 biography of Horace Tabor. In contrast, singer Kari Ragan and especially literary historian Judy Nolte Temple critiqued, from a feminist perspective, the opera for perpetuating gender stereotypes, with Temple describing its authors as "another generation of ventriloquists—this time eastern males steeped in highly fictionalized materials about the Tabors" who "put their words in Baby Doe's mouth." Whereas Randie Blooding thought the identification of Augusta with Horace's mother in the last scene "an especially clever idea of Latouche's" as "Augusta was, in many ways, a mother figure to Horace," Temple considered this conceit "a plot twist characteristic of the pop-Freudian anti-momism of the 1950s," and suggested that the opera could have profited from a third act devoted to Baby Doe's later years based on her journal entries (although still inaccessible at the time Latouche wrote his libretto), including the lines, "Snow is falling ore mound & forest / Winds are wafting the flakes around us / Our blood is congealing and freezing / As the tinkle of burying bells come [*sic*] nearer." However, neither Moore nor Latouche made any pretense to literalism or factual accuracy, with the composer stating that he and Latouche "felt free to take liberties with history whenever necessary for the sake of the drama," including creating scenes "of no historical authenticity."[47]

Although they were generally of one mind regarding the characters, Moore apparently steered Latouche away from portraying Baby Doe as too much of an adventuress. In a preliminary draft, Baby, ambivalently described as "innocent in appearance," says at the end of the first scene, alone on stage after meeting Horace, "I knew what I came for, but this is surprising"; and in a section of the second scene later cut, after Jake Sands shouts "God save Tabor, the Silver King!" Baby peers out of the hotel and only afterward sings the "Willow Song," so that she ostensibly performs the number for Horace's benefit, with her subsequent remark to Horace, "I had no idea anyone was listening," presumably mere coquetry. Moore apparently found some of this problematic, writing to Latouche on August 5, 1954, "The scenario which I gave you provided for characters which I understood. . . . As it is going now Augusta is pretty much the same but Baby Doe has changed greatly and it puzzles me to write music when I dont feel I know the character. Until we can talk through the whole story and reach an understanding about her, I am very much handicapped." Tellingly, in its final form, the opera only vaguely implied some cunning on Baby's part by having her say at the end of the first scene, "Indeed we'll meet again" (and perhaps by preparing her entrance with a chorus of miners singing "Dig-digger dig"); nothing suggests that she intends to seduce Horace with her "Willow Song" aside possibly from the stage direction that she play "with a crossed-hand elegance." In discussing her character, Moore went only so far as to state on a 1962 episode of the CBS Television series *American Musical Theatre*, "I think she [Baby] was a little gold-digger at the start."[48]

In any case, in both the early draft and the completed opera, Baby evinces a quick change of heart on meeting Horace, as seen in the exchange, verbalized as well as mimed, that follows the "Willow Song." With the aria "The Fine Ladies Walk" added after the premiere, Latouche clarified this transition, pointing to Horace's kiss (ostensibly of Baby's hand at the end of the second scene) as a defining moment (the word "maybe" here more an admission of guilt than of doubt):

> Maybe when I first met Horace, Mama,
> I thought of his money and the power that was his.
> But the moment he kissed me
> All that was forgotten.
> I only knew that the other part of me
> Lost for so long

Had come home...
And that's how it always will be.

Moreover, Baby decides to remain with Horace, perhaps even to have sex with him (or so the fourth scene can be read), because of Augusta's contempt for her husband as opposed to any self-centered motive.[49]

The opera additionally sympathizes with Baby as a scorned outsider, an aspect of the work that in its own way reflected—like such contemporary operas as Copland's *The Tender Land*, Menotti's *The Saint of Bleecker Street*, Blitzstein's *Reuben Reuben*, and Carlisle Floyd's *Susannah*—the political climate of the time, so that the work wound up encapsulating two postwar theatrical trends: the social outcast drama and the troubled marriage play. That Baby finds a congenial place among the women supporters of Bryan provides an explicit political dimension to this subtext. She seems, in any case, a poetic soul, as evident from her penchant for metaphor—an aspect of her personality enhanced by the imaginative and graceful melodies that contain, as Lewis Hardee observes, "an abundance of frills and rolades, and colatours [*sic*], that is to be found in none of the other parts, in this or any of the other operas [by Moore]." Both strongly independent and, in Moore's words, "a symbol of faithfulness," she emerges as a sort of Goethean eternal feminine who administers salvation to an overly striving man, with her music becoming more somber as the drama progresses.[50]

Horace and Augusta have their own complexities. Moore, who as early as his *Overture on an American Tune* (1931), a work intended as "a defense" of the eponymous hero of Sinclair Lewis's 1922 novel *Babbitt*, had shown an interest in the American businessman as a type, presents Horace as a swaggering, impulsive, and expansive mogul who descends, like an Aristotelian hero, into tragic self-awareness as his fortunes ebb—a decline mirrored by Bryan's failed progressive campaign, so that Horace's unraveling takes on a larger national resonance. Augusta, thought by Moore "a wonderful woman," similarly evolves from a rigid and pompous termagant, to use Latouche's word, to a compassionate and self-critical woman, although some such dichotomy appears as early as the third scene with her two leitmotives in quick succession: a stately theme, derived from the rhythm of the word, "Augusta," that represents her imperiousness, and a smoother, tenderer melody that reveals her more sensitive side. Both Horace and Augusta embody, in their own ways, the tragic effects of hubris, but the work, which early in the drama paints them with a rather ironic brush, regards them with ever-increasing compassion as their world crumbles around them, although the opera's title and final aria privilege Baby's loftier vision.[51]

The libretto enriches the story through thematic correspondences of a sort analogous to some of the musical reminiscences that inform the work. The opera opens, for instance, with Horace's Leadville opera house as the embodiment of his glory and concludes with his Denver opera house as the site of his fall. Relatedly, the Matchless Mine, whose name itself sounds like a valentine, weaves its way through nearly every scene, becoming a symbol alternately of ambition, conflict, hope, and love. Similarly,

Tabor's confidently breezy account of his life in "I Came This Way from Massachusetts" in the opening scene bookends his tortured recollections in the finale, much as Baby Doe's nostalgic "Willow Song" frames the deeper pathos of her "Farewell Song." And Silver Dollar's "Come down moonshine" grotesquely echoes Baby Doe's ode to the moon in the "Silver Song," highlighting Silver's degraded state.

The individual scenes feature similar niceties, such as the way Horace's teasing of his wife in "I Came This Way from Massachusetts" anticipates his subsequent spat with her; the way the choral paean to the classical muses prepares Horace's response to Baby Doe's "Willow Song"; and the way the social rebuff of Baby Doe at the governor's ball sets the stage for Augusta's kindness to her.

Meanwhile, the work provides some comic relief through such minor characters as the Old Miner, Mr. Mulligan, and Mama McCourt, as well as through the banter of the Cronies in the opening scene and the Dandies in the wedding scene. The section in which Mama McCourt maligns Harvey and Augusta to the strains of a waltz constitutes a comedic highlight, as does the one in which the guests at the governor's ball chatter about Baby Doe to the music of a polka—episodes reminiscent of the party scene in Blitzstein's more consistently ironic *Regina*. As a whole, the opera unfolds a half-tragic, half-humorous narrative congruent with the use of the term "ballad" in its title, its comedy helping to make the ending all the more poignant.

Although Latouche and Moore thought the use of rhyme and symmetrical rhythms as employed in *The Golden Apple* inappropriate to the story at hand, the librettist nonetheless composed an enormously poetic libretto, in large part through the use of carefully calibrated meters, an aspect of the work that eluded Reinhard G. Pauly in his discussion of the opera's "rhythmically free" text. For example, Latouche cast much of the first scene in what for convenience he referred to, in a letter to Moore, as a "seven-beat rhythm," but what more precisely might be called a catalectic trochaic tetrameter (meaning four feet of alternating strong and weak beats, with the final syllable suppressed), a meter characteristic of ancient Greek drama, but of much else, including popular American song. Consider the following exchange, which except for the Old Miner's "yippee!" illustrates this particular "seven-beat" meter (with strokes demarcating the meter):

THE OLD MINER

(woozily)

What's the matter, Fogarty,/ ain't my money good enough?/ Lamp this lovely silver ore!/ Got a right to celebrate,/ found a peerless matchless mine—/I call it the Matchless Mine,/ got a right to raise some hell,/ silver oozing from the soil—yippee!

BOUNCER

Don't you fire that cannon off!/ There's a concert on next door/ in the brand new opry house./ Decent folks don't want no noise.

THE OLD MINER

Horace Tabor's opry house./ Tabor don't care what I do/ 'cause he wants to buy my mine./ Don't you try to tell me off—/ I am Tabor's little lamb,/ Tabor wants my Matchless Mine.

BOUNCER

(as the girls giggle)

Go on home and sleep it off./ This saloon is Tabor's too.

And so the meter proceeds, including the ditty sung by the girls, "Tabor owns the opry house," the Bouncer's "Girls, shut up! And you, go home," and an exit line for the Old Miner that musicologist Kenneth Nott especially liked for its use of three first-person pronouns in quick succession: "Tabor loves my mine and me."[52]

At Tabor's first entrance, the text expands into trochaic alexandrines, that is, lines of twelve syllables alternating strong and weak beats, or what the librettist, again in correspondence with Moore, called "a kind of cowhide alexandrine," a shift perhaps intended to suggest Tabor's heroic stature in imitation of Pierre Corneille and Jean Racine:

TABOR

(to his Cronies)

It's a bang up job (if I say it as shouldn't),/ smart as any opry house you're likely to see./ Chandeliers a-glitter—real imported velvet—/ brass and mahogany, tapestries from Europe./ Yessir, it's a fittin' place for art and culture./ We can use some culture here in Colorado.

At Baby Doe's appearance, the meter, by contrast, turns largely dactylic, "in case," Latouche told Moore, "you want to make it sort of waltzy or gay," an opportunity of which the composer took full advantage with his "Baby Doe Waltz."[53]

Baby Doe remains to some degree associated with such dactylic meters in the course of the opera, whereas Augusta has her own metrical profile, her confrontation with Baby Doe assuming Horace's alexandrine loftiness, although somewhat softened through the use of dactyls:

Augusta

Excuse me, but aren't you Mrs. Harvey Doe?.../ I'm Augusta Tabor. *Mrs. Horace Tabor*.../ I'll save your time and mine by telling you frankly/ I know all about you, about you and Horace./ I've come here to warn you that there will be trouble,/ *serious* trouble, if there's no end to it.

In the fifth scene, Augusta and her friends similarly express their indignation in alexandrines, as in Augusta's climactic, "I'll make him rue the day / That he was ever born," although as Horace and Augusta turn increasingly self-reflective, their lines fragment until reduced, in Horace's case, to two-syllable gasps: "Nothing. No time. No where." The drama ends, in Baby Doe's concluding aria, by circling back to a trochaic tetrameter as in the first scene, but now transformed into a rhymed rumination of love and death: "Always through the changing of / Sun and shadow, time and space / I shall walk beside my love / In a green and quiet place."[54]

Also in response to the opera's milieu, Latouche generally avoided writing anything "too flowery" or "too florid and inflated," telling Moore, "To make even Tabor too wild and wooly takes us off into the folk-hero category, and that seems the antithesis of what you were guiding me toward doing." The second scene's ode to music, with its "improbably florid *pensées*," in the words of David McKee, essayed one exception to this general principle. But the character of Baby Doe allowed particular latitude in this regard, and the librettist took wing especially in her "Silver Song" and "Farewell Song." In the former, Baby Doe mediates the controversy over bimetallism by comparing gold to the sun and silver to the moon; declaring her kinship with the moon, she further relates silver to dreams in a radiant stanza that subtly rhymes "dreaming," "gleam," and "dreams," as well as "adore," "ore," and "core":

I am a child of the moon
And always
Will adore her element
Dreaming as I watch it gleam.
I am mining heavenly ore—
Gold is the sun, but silver, silver
Lies hidden in the core of dreams—

However, only in the "Farewell Song" did Latouche allow himself more of the polysyllabic rhyming for which he was known—"alter me" and "heraldry," "joy is spent" and "transient"—although here used not for humorous effect but rather for spiritual depth.[55]

Regarding Latouche as a "true genius," Moore praised the libretto both for its structural finesse and its "marvelous" language. "Finding a libretto is almost the hardest task of a composer," he stated in 1958, "and I am profoundly thankful to have had the opportunity to compose music to such a beautiful libretto." For his part, Latouche never seems to have gone on record concerning Moore or his music, although he wrote on the occasion of the opera's premiere, "I feel that together we [Moore and himself] have animated a compelling section of American history that might have lain fallow in the newspaper morgue. Its interest for an audience, naturally, remains to be seen. But the making has been a memorable and rewarding experience."[56]

After deciding to produce *Baby Doe*, Central City apparently deferred to Moore's request that Emerson Buckley, who might have known Latouche from their overlapping time at Columbia, and who since had gained broad experience in opera and radio especially, conduct the work. Moore, Buckley, and Elmer Nagy—a Central City regular who would conduct and design the *Tosca* scheduled to alternate with *Baby Doe*—proceeded to line up a director and cast, presumably in consultation with Latouche. Central City needed in particular two sets of principal players, given especially the demands of singing at an oxygen-deprived elevation of some 8,500 feet above sea level. (During the days leading up to the July 1956 premiere, Latouche welcomed newcomers to Central City by advising them "to lie flat on our backs for the first 24 hours.")[57]

Thinking about a cast in early November 1955, Moore had imagined as one attractive possibility Patrice Munsel as Baby, Brenda Lewis as Augusta, and George London as Horace, which confirms Frances Bible's contention that the composer initially conceived Augusta as a dramatic soprano, not a mezzo, and which suggests, further, that he had a bass-baritone, or at least a low-lying baritone, in mind for Horace, as implied too by the fact that virtually all his ideal candidates for Horace included among their signature roles Mozart's Don Giovanni. In the end, however, Moore decided that Augusta would be depicted better by a mezzo, and Horace, by a baritone rather than a bass-baritone per se, voice types that also would provide more contrast with Baby Doe's lyric soprano and William Jennings Bryan's bass-baritone—with the result that the mezzo writing for Augusta sits relatively high, and the baritone writing for Horace, relatively low, presenting distinctive challenges for both parts. As for Baby Doe, Moore wanted "a top-flight lyric soprano who can do coloratura," although he seemed willing to temper some of the role's more taxing demands—in particular, its soft stratospheric notes—should a singer like Munsel have some trepidations about the part.[58]

In the end, Central City selected, for the first cast, Dolores Wilson (whose singing of "The Last Rose of Summer," a song that Moore thought "in the mood" of the "Willow Song," left him "deeply moved") as Baby Doe, Martha Lipton as Augusta, Walter Cassel as Horace, and Lawrence Davidson as Bryan; and for the second cast, Leyna Gabriele (Baby Doe), Frances Bible (Augusta), Clifford Harvuot (Horace), and Norman Treigle (Bryan), with Beatrice Krebs appearing in both casts as Mama McCourt. Aside from Gabriele, all these singers had performed at either the Metropolitan Opera or the New York City Opera.[59]

Donald Oenslager designed the picture-book sets, costumes, and lighting, but with his usual partner, stage director Herbert Graf, not feeling at home with the subject matter, Central City hired as co-directors Edwin Levy, a professor of theatre at the University of Denver known locally for his direction of operettas and musicals; and, very likely at Latouche's urging, Hanya Holm, the choreographer-director who had worked on *Ballet Ballads* and *The Golden Apple*, and whose most recent credits included the choreography for *My Fair Lady* (although as with *The Golden Apple*, Holm clashed with her *Baby Doe* co-director, and seems to have assumed rather full responsibility for the stage direction). Holm's son, Klaus, assisted on the set and lighting designs, and Patton Campbell, on the costumes, in what amounted to an expensive production for Central City, the scenery and costumes alone costing over $30,000.[60]

Rehearsals began in New York in late spring, with some runthroughs in early June for the benefit of Broadway producers whom agent Lucy Kroll hoped to interest in the work. Joined by Moore and Latouche, the principals arrived in Colorado in mid-June to continue rehearsals with the full company, which included a chorus of twenty-two and an orchestra of thirty-six. "The rehearsals are going very well," Moore wrote to Kroll on June 24. "The cast, both of them in fact are excellent and Hanya is doing lovely work. There is not a single scene which lets down and several of them are hair raising. The chorus is a student group, lively and attractive. Everyone is yeasty about the show." As rehearsals proceeded, Buckley proved snappy on occasion, Oenslager, a force for calm, and Holm, a stimulus and inspiration. "She knew how to draw every ounce of blood out of us...," recalled Walter Cassel, "and it felt like we were turning into the people we were supposed to be playing." In later years, the cast further remembered Moore as a sweet man who, after the opera opened, "wept every time he went backstage."[61]

As for Latouche, Emerson Buckley found him less easy to work with than he did Douglas Moore, recalling in particular the librettist's unwillingness to take cuts in the campaign scene. In some contrast, co-director Edwin Levy, speaking about Latouche's attendance at rehearsals, recalled, "Occasionally, he would make a suggestion about staging, but he rarely intruded upon our rehearsal plans." Claire Jones, who played one of Augusta's friends, similarly stated, "John Latouche was just a delightful man, and he was very undemanding about everything. It was very important to him that every word was distinct because he said, 'I didn't put those words down just to amuse myself.' Then he'd laugh, because he's just a fun man. He would be out square dancing with us in the streets and everything, and he was just a wonderful man." Leyna Gabriele recollected that Latouche and Dolores Wilson—both of whom, she thought, had a drinking problem—enjoyed going out to pubs together, and that she too became friendly with Latouche until he turned "nasty" and "cruel" because of an article by her booster, the *Daily Mirror* gossip columnist Lee Mortimer, that also antagonized and ruined her relationship with Wilson and Holm. Walter Cassel more simply remembered Latouche as "kind of full of gin or something," a reminiscence that echoed Horace Tabor's description of himself as "full of gin and glory."[62]

The cast admired the opera as well, although both Frances Bible and Walter Cassel stressed the elusiveness of its appeal. "I think the fact that it sort of has little snatches of this and that—folksy—turns them [the critics] off at first," commented Bible, "but you begin to realize the point of it after you've lived with it awhile, and it does pull on you, it grows on you, which is a good sign." "The more we heard it, the more we liked the opera," Cassel likewise stated. "To me it's a masterpiece, and I know it takes people time, some... more than others." On the other hand, Leyna Gabriele thought that, for all the work's stature, Moore and Latouche "missed the boat" by not revealing the more "coquettish side" of Baby Doe: "I really think that had they made Baby a much more flippant character in the beginning and revealed how she was really looking for Horace, it would have been more interesting to see the change in her." Some later productions redressed this perceived flaw by having Baby Doe consciously attempt to beguile Horace with the "Willow Song," the sort of reading congruent with Latouche's early conception, but subsequently obscured, as discussed above, whereas Gabriele, in her own direction of the scene for a college workshop, chose an alternative approach by having Baby sing the song casually while unpacking her clothes in her hotel room.[63]

On May 24, 1956, about the time the opera went into rehearsal in New York, another Baby Doe opera premiered at Denver's Loretto Heights College with a libretto and score by one of its faculty, Massimo ("Max") DiJulio (1919–2005), a Philadelphia native who had played in the Glenn Miller Orchestra and had studied composition with Darius Milhaud and Cecil Effinger. DiJulio researched and wrote the libretto, inspired by Caroline Bancroft's *Silver Queen*, during the second half of 1953, and alleged, as mentioned, that news of this project prompted Central City to commission their own Baby Doe opera. In any case, DiJulio initially conceived *Baby Doe: An Opera in Four Scenes* as an hour-long television special, and the work bore the marks of such intentions in its rhymed doggerel and unassuming music, thus warranting the label "folk opera" or "folk operetta" far more than the Moore opera, notwithstanding some similarities between the two pieces. The opera, which only alluded to Augusta, won respectful reviews in the local press, although more for its music than its libretto. A revised and expanded version of the work, retitled *Portrait of Baby Doe* and presented in 1976, again at Loretto Heights College, evoked a similar response. In a 1998 interview, DiJulio confessed some jealousy over the success of *The Ballad of Baby Doe*, whose music he thought uneven, although he felt compelled to admit, with regard to the libretto, "that guy [Latouche] *knows* how to do things."[64]

The friends and family who joined Latouche for the opera's July 7 Saturday night debut included his mother, his partner, Kenward Elmslie, and his friends Margarett McKean, Lord Kinross, and Harry Martin, who had driven Latouche's car out to Colorado for him. The premiere happily coincided with Central City's silver anniversary season, making the event all the more newsworthy, attracting television as well as press coverage. United Airlines at its own expense flew in some twenty critics from around the country, with Denver's historic Brown Palace Hotel providing them lodging and hosting a Friday eve banquet with Moore and Latouche in attendance. Along with a matinee performance of *Tosca*, which had opened June 30, the afternoon of the premiere witnessed, before record crowds of many thousands, a Pony Express race, a hard rock drilling exhibition, band performances, square dancing, and a parade, among other events. After dinner at the town's Teller House, ushers and debutantes led guests to the opera house for the 8:30 curtain, with such notables in attendance as Olga Koussevitzky, opera singer Lily Pons, movie star Kim Novak, writer Mary Chase, producer Michael Myerberg, and Colorado Gov. Edwin C. Johnson. Latouche expected a success, telling Kinross, "It's sure to go. It's about love and it's about money, and there's no combination an American audience likes more." And indeed, the opening-night audience, wrote Kinross, "laughed and cried and applauded and cheered" (even if some knowing folks in the audience felt that the story had been "sanitized"), with the final curtain greeted by a cascade of carnations and a prolonged standing ovation for Moore and Latouche, both of whom attended a post-performance champagne supper at the Teller House. "Here, for the first time," Kinross opined, "was the folklore of the American West, enshrined in a medium more elevated than the screen and the music-hall—in its composition a harmonious marriage of Western American drama with Eastern Europeanized culture."[65]

So warm a response from the audience—even down to the appreciative murmurs evoked by the historic photographs projected on the stage curtain—put some critics on their guard, especially concerning the opera's ability to travel beyond Central City. A smaller minority simply did not like the piece at all. Roger Dettmer, the prickly critic of the *Chicago American*, posted an especially damning notice, calling the music "chiefly fluff," and writing, "There is, in this story, possibly the material for a trenchant domestic drama, a fact not unobserved by Mr. Latouche. Yet he has written, sometimes banally and generally pretentiously, a kind of period pageant whose people strike poses—some satiric, some lowly comic, some attemptedly tender, some nearly human—but inevitably poses."[66]

However, the opera garnered overall very positive reviews, including raves from John Chapman (*New York Daily News*) and Tucker Keiser (*Boston Post*), who ranked the piece with *Porgy and Bess* and *The Most Happy Fella* as "a significant contribution to American opera," and who lauded not only Moore's ability to shape a melodic line according to "the natural inflections of speech," but the libretto as well: "The composer was lucky indeed to have as his librettist, John Latouche, an author whose knowledge of the theatre . . . has prevented the common opera malady, libretto muddle, from intruding itself. Mr. Latouche's story line is swift, coherent and intense. He creates gripping dramatic moments." As the country's music magazines joined the discussion, Emily Rogers (*Musical America*), William Crosten (*Musical Quarterly*), Paul Jackson (*Opera News*), and George Lynn (*Etude*) similarly hailed the work, with Rogers, for instance, complimenting Latouche's "fine feeling for the theatre." By August, *Life* magazine justifiably could report that the opera had been "warmly praised by music critics."

With its sixteen scheduled performances sold out even before the premiere, Central City managed to offer, by popular demand, a few more performances, which immediately sold out as well. Latouche happily realized that he had a hit on his hands, and according to Lord Kinross, responded "eagerly to the limelight which the composer, more modestly, shunned," and welcomed "the sweet smell of admiration and success...without inhibition." Having the time of his life, he rode a roller coaster in a local amusement park—perhaps Elitch's Gardens—and attended a party in full western regalia, including a drooping mustache à la Horace Tabor.[67]

During the course of the opera's run, Walter Cassel taped several performances as piped into his dressing room over the theater's public address system, with the idea of preserving for the soloists their work with various casts, as the production featured the principal players in different permutations. A few such recordings fortunately survive, all apparently with Leyna Gabriele, who sometimes substituted for an indisposed Dolores Wilson. Artistically satisfying, these recordings also hold interest for, among other things, their use of material later cut from the opera. In addition, the federally sponsored Voice of America radio station independently recorded the opera, which they broadcast to both sides of the Iron Curtain in ten installments in late August and early September 1956. The government even considered sending the work to the spring 1957 Paris International Theatre Festival, although later decided rather to export Eugene O'Neill's *Long Day's Journey into Night*, which had its Broadway premiere in November 1956.[68]

Meanwhile, since viewing the opera in rehearsal in New York, producer Michael Myerberg (1906–1974) had planned to launch the work on Broadway. For more than twenty years, Myerberg had staked a claim as one of New York's most adventurous managers, from presenting Charles Weidman's dance-play *Candide* on Broadway in 1933 to more recently producing a revival of Marc Blitzstein's *The Cradle Will Rock* (1947), the landmark stop-motion animated film *Hansel and Gretel* (1954), and the Broadway premiere of Samuel Beckett's *Waiting for Godot* (1956). He also owned the Mansfield Theatre (now, the Brooks Atkinson Theatre), and perhaps related to the figure of Horace Tabor as another theater owner who took risks. In any case, he considered *Baby Doe* "one of the greatest American works ever to appear in our time," in particular, the final scene, which he compared to Oedipus's self-blinding.[69]

Latouche's sudden death on August 7 did not seem to dampen Myerberg's resolve; on the contrary, he expressed determination to proceed with the production as "a monument" to the librettist's memory. Prior to a September planning meeting, he sent to his creative team a dense nine-page memorandum suggesting numerous changes to the work beyond the ones that Latouche already had made; this included the insertion of a proposed barbershop scene in the first act in which Tabor's friends would warn him against marrying Baby Doe, and Horace would respond with a "great" love song. In general, Myerberg felt the need, as mentioned earlier, for more narrative clarity, and to this end he also imagined projecting, along with the sorts of historic images used in Central City, newspaper headlines that would help elucidate the action. At the same time, he did not seem particularly concerned about who would now revise the text—he might have supposed that Moore could handle this—but in any case, he anticipated at least four weeks of tryouts before opening on Broadway.[70]

Moore quickly nixed the idea of the barbershop scene, informing Myerberg that such an addition not only would make the first act too long, but would undermine the opera's dramatic arc:

> He [Tabor] was not an "all for love" man. He had many mistresses. Baby did touch him deeply and differently and he felt the need of her. But he never expected that in marrying her he was endangering his financial or political future. He was arrogant in his wealth and he believed that the talk would die down and he could buy her a social position.... Tabor's discovery in the last scene that Baby is more real than money or success has force and drama. If he believed this in act one there would be no unfolding and deepening of his character.

How far Moore might have accommodated Myerberg in other matters went untested, as the production never materialized per se, although the *Omnibus* television airing discussed below suggests that he might have allowed the occasional replacement of sung recitative with accompanied speech.[71]

As the summer ended, Myerberg, in consultation with his music director Sylvan Levin, began tallying a production budget of around $250,000, and auditioning singers, with one dream cast including Virginia Haskins as Baby Doe, James Pease as Horace, and either Brenda Lewis or Martha Lipton as Augusta. Partly because of problems obtaining a theater, he periodically pushed back his opening date, eventually announcing extended runs in San Francisco and Los Angeles for the winter and spring of 1957, followed by a national tour and a Broadway opening during the 1957–58 season. Meanwhile, in October 1956, C. V. Whitney, the patrician businessman who had helped finance *Gone with the Wind*, expressed some interest in a motion picture version of the Baby Doe story in association with Myerberg and producer-writer Charles Martin as part of a series of western films that occupied him during these years, including *The Searchers*, although nothing came of this either.[72]

In early 1957, Myerberg reached an agreement with *Omnibus*, the ninety-minute cultural program produced by ABC Television and sponsored by the Ford Foundation, to present excerpts of the opera, with the thought that the broadcast could serve as a sort of nationwide backer's audition. *Omnibus* aired this shortened version, produced by Robert Saudek and supervised by Myerberg, on Sunday night, February 10, along with a rerun of a photo essay by Barnaby Conrad that had appeared on *Omnibus* the previous October. Featuring the original Oenslager costumes, the production starred Virginia Copeland as Baby Doe, William Johnson as Horace, and Martha Lipton as Augusta (with Margery Mayer as Mama McCourt, and the young Evelyn Lear as one of Augusta's friends), all under the stage direction of Charles S. Dubin, with Sylvan Levin leading members of the Symphony of the Air—personnel notably different, with the exception of Lipton, from those featured at Central City. The show's host, Alistair Cooke, introduced the opera's two acts, separated by a commercial from Union Carbide extolling the benefits of uranium mining in contemporary Colorado and neighboring states.

Reduced to less than an hour in length, this *Omnibus* version not only omitted the third and fourth scenes from the first act and the new gambling scene from the second act, but took cuts in all the other scenes as well. Such excisions made the opera all the more episodic, leaving some viewers wishing that, rather than repeat the Conrad photo essay, *Omnibus* had devoted the extra time to *Baby Doe*. Even so, the program received generally good reviews, although it failed to help carry Myerberg toward the goal of a Broadway production; and confronted with fellow producer Roger L. Stevens's decision, after months of deliberation, not to invest in the work, Myerberg relinquished his option on the opera in August. One additional impediment surely involved the death of William Johnson, the scheduled Horace, who had delivered a moving interpretation of the role (including introducing the aria, "Warm as the Autumn Light") on television, and who in March 1957 died suddenly of a heart attack at age forty-one, uncannily like Latouche, leaving Myerberg scrambling to replace him with the likes of Howard Keel or Alfred Drake. Meanwhile, in the course of 1957, the opera enjoyed two concert presentations with piano, narrated by the composer, and a full-fledged production at Stanford University in late May and early June.[73]

The failure of *The Ballad of Baby Doe* to make it to Broadway helped signal the end of the rialto's more-than-twenty-year reign as a preeminent showcase for new American opera, a role that the New York City Opera steadily had been assuming since its founding as a self-proclaimed people's opera in 1943, and that would become even more pronounced after the appointment of the Viennese-born American conductor Julius Rudel as the company's general director in early 1957. Indeed, the collapse of Myerberg's plans coincided with a new initiative by the City Opera, bankrolled by a $105,000 grant from the Ford Foundation, for a scheduled spring 1958 season of ten American operas composed within the preceding twenty years, enabling Rudel not only to present the New York premiere of *Baby Doe*, but to use the opera to kick off the season: "Moore's opera," he recalled, "had all the necessary attributes for a festive opening—including John LaTouche's poetic yet so-true-to-life libretto."[74]

The New York City Opera adapted the Oenslager sets and costumes—the purchased backdrops extended to accommodate its home at New York City Center, a Moorish Revival theater on West 55th Street seating three times the number of patrons as did the Central City Opera House—and engaged the Russian-American Vladimir Rosing to stage direct. Some disagreement arose about who should play the title lead; Rudel advocated for Beverly Sills (born Belle Miriam Silverman, 1929–2007), an up-and-coming twenty-eight-year-old company member, whereas Moore and Emerson Buckley, slated to conduct, reportedly thought the stout five-foot-eight soprano too large for the part. Aware of this, Sills, with characteristic chutzpah, auditioned for the role wearing stiletto heels and a white mink hat, later recalling, "I dressed up like a skyscraper to show Moore that *I*, not he, was boss of my destiny." After auditioning some arias from the opera, she won everyone over,

Moore telling her, "Miss Sills, you *are* Baby Doe." The City Opera cast further included Walter Cassel, Martha Lipton, and Beatrice Krebs, as in the original production, with company stalwart Joshua Hecht assigned the part of William Jennings Bryan.[75]

The April 3, 1958, premiere—the first of four performances—put to rest any concerns that the opera might not play well outside Colorado. "The opening night audience," reported *Variety*, "became increasingly exultant as scene followed scene, as the accumulative power of the work, and the success of the production became clear." Rudel remembered hearing "audible sobs" in the audience during the final scene and "deafening" applause at the final curtain. For the critics, the star of the evening proved not so much Sills, who received accolades commensurate with those accorded Cassel and Lipton, but the opera itself. "Hats off, ladies and gentlemen," began Miles Kastendieck's review for the *Journal-American*, "to the most authentic American opera yet produced in this country." In his front-page notice for the *Herald Tribune*, Jay S. Harrison similarly wrote, "Apart from 'Porgy and Bess' and 'The Mother of Us All,' no single American work has mirrored so clearly the way of life of an era and a people." Meanwhile, Winthrop Sargeant's review for the *New Yorker* placed the work's achievement beyond the confines of the American repertoire: "The work is, actually, a sort of declaration of independence—independence from all the fashionably highbrow fiddle-faddle and mysterious technical mumbo-jumbo that during the past forty years have tended to reduce the art of opera to a feeble caricature of itself." Although Moore naturally elicited kudos for the music, Latouche shared posthumously in the glory, his libretto deemed "lusty and poetic" by Douglas Watt (*Daily News*) and "extraordinarily vital" by Harrison (*Herald Tribune*), with, according to Sargeant (*New Yorker*), "several quite penetrating studies of human character." Although "in his grave," wrote *Variety*, Latouche "is definitely a hero of the occasion."[76]

The opera's continued success encouraged the New York City Opera to revive the work as part of its fall 1958 season; its second all-American season in 1959; its third and final all-American season and subsequent national tour in 1960; and then virtually annually throughout the 1960s—often with Sills, Cassel, and Frances Bible as the love triangle. (Discussing the inside joking that happens on the operatic stage, Sills recalled that during one of these performances, at the moment in the first-act finale when the ensemble sings with amazement, "Queen Isabella's jewels?" Jack Harrold, the comic tenor playing Chester Arthur, whirled around to her and sang, "Queen Isabella's Jewish?") Winning the 1959 New York Music Critics' Circle Award for best opera against such formidable competition as Samuel Barber's *Vanessa*, Benjamin Britten's *The Turn of the Screw*, and Robert Kurka's *The Good Soldier Schweik*, the work continued to garner excellent notices, with Eric Salzman in 1959 describing Latouche's libretto as "absolutely a mode[l] of what an opera libretto for this day and age ought to be." On the other hand, when the City Opera brought the work to Chicago in 1960, Claudia Cassidy criticized the work from top to bottom, reporting that the "extraordinarily vulgar" libretto "never seeks a fresh phrase when a cliche will serve."[77]

In 1957, Chappell Music published the work's piano-vocal score as well as six arias from the opera, as cited above; and in 1958, the Program Publishing Company issued a poorly edited libretto riddled with omissions and typos. Reviewing the score for the Music Library Association's quarterly journal *Notes*, musicologist H. Wiley Hitchcock delivered a scathing critique of the work, including the libretto, deemed "now prattling, now pseudo-poetic, now a strange mixture." Hitchcock reiterated this unfavorable assessment in his popular text *Music in the United States* (1969), setting the stage, along with Wilfrid Mellers's highly muted praise for the opera in his classic study *Music in a New Found Land* (1964), for widespread academic dismissal and neglect. At the same time, a few other historical surveys, such as those by Gilbert Chase (1966) and Kyle Gann (1997), showed keen appreciation for the work, as did, more amply, Elise Kirk's study of *American Opera* (2001), which thought Latouche "totally successful in bringing his characters to life. He was equally adept at handling a broad setting that ranged across almost a century, from Tabor's early life to Baby Doe's death."[78]

In June 1959, MGM Records, assisted by a grant from the Koussevitzky Foundation, recorded the work with the New York City Opera cast heard earlier that spring, including Beverly Sills (Baby Doe), Walter Cassel (Horace), Frances Bible (Augusta), Beatrice Krebs (Mama McCourt), and Joshua Hecht (Bryan), under the baton of Emerson Buckley. Meagerly financed, the recording took place in a hotel ballroom in a single session, with the singers paid a flat fee of a few hundred dollars, the instrumentalists, much less than that. "All of us were new to recording and frightened out of our wits," recalled Sills, at the time seven months pregnant with her first child. The album, remastered, was reissued by Heliodor in 1966; then, with a new cover, by Deutsche Grammophon in 1976; and then, on compact disc, by Deutsche Grammophon in 1999. Critics bemoaned the recording's poor sound, but generally commended both the performance and the work, with *High Fidelity* in 1959 deeming Latouche's text, whatever its flaws, "on an infinitely higher plane than that of most Broadway lyricists and contemporary librettists," and *Opera News* forty years later calling the album "an authentic masterpiece."[79]

Although the role of Baby Doe did not catapult Beverly Sills to stardom as sometimes alleged—that phenomenon followed her sensational 1966 debut as Cleopatra in Handel's *Giulio Cesare*, along with subsequent achievements that landed her on the cover of *Newsweek* (1969) and *Time* (1971), whose feature stories did not so much as mention *Baby Doe*—she viewed her debut in the Moore opera as "the first major triumph of my career," a performance that provided her with a satisfaction comparable only to her appearances as Cleopatra in the Handel opera, the title role in Massenet's *Manon*, and Queen Elizabeth in Donizetti's *Roberto Devereux*. Similarly gratified with her recording of the opera, which she judged "an extraordinary piece of singing," Sills—who also sang the "Willow Song" and discussed the opera with Moore on the forementioned 1962 television episode of *American Musical Theatre*—thought the part's greatest challenge lay not in its technical demands, which she compared to Sophie in Richard Strauss's *Der Rosenkavalier* as one of those "high, lyrical parts which demand endless breath control, arching legato lines, and sustained pianissimo singing," but in gaining sympathy for her role as the other woman; accordingly, she portrayed Baby Doe "as very reluctant to get involved with Tabor," taking a cue from, among other things, movie star Marilyn Monroe, whom she described as the type of woman "who is aware of the fact that men stop and look at her on the street and enjoys that but who's not in any way willfully evil"—an association that presumably would have intrigued Latouche, a fan of Monroe who drew a similar parallel between the actress and the title character of *The Vamp*. Sills additionally could draw on the cold treatment she experienced from some upper-crust members of Cleveland society when, as a Jew, she married the divorced scion of one of that city's most prestigious gentile families. In performance, she downplayed Baby Doe's more capricious side, and emphasized rather her warmth, recalling that she and Cassel shed tears every time he sang to her, "You were always the real thing, Baby."[80]

Even without the benefit of Sills, *The Ballad of Baby Doe* became one of the most frequently performed American operas of modern times. With its colorful cast, moving story, and melodic score, the work found a niche especially among schools, smaller companies, and summer festivals, although it appeared as well in such big houses as the Houston Grand Opera (1970), Washington National Opera (1997 and 1998), Boston Lyric Opera (1998), and San Francisco Opera (2000). On April 21, 1976, the Public Broadcasting Service, as the second offering of their new *Live from Lincoln Center* television series, aired a performance of the work by the City Opera starring Ruth Welting (Baby Doe), Richard Fredericks (Horace), Frances Bible (Augusta), Jane Shaulis (Mama McCourt), and Richard McKee (Bryan), directed by Patrick Bakman, and conducted by Judith Somogi, the company's first female conductor. Similarly, on June 25, 1995, Iowa Public Television broadcast a live performance of the opera by the Des Moines Metro Opera with Evelyn de la Rosa (Baby Doe), Richard L. Richards (Horace), Gwendolyn Jones (Augusta), Anne Larson (Mama McCourt), and Paul Geiger (Bryan) under the stage and musical direction of Robert L. Larsen. In 1997, Newport Classic released a recording of the opera conducted by John Moriarty, which featured a cast almost identical to the one appearing in Central City the previous year, including Jan Grissom (Baby Doe), Brian Steele (Horace), Dana Krueger (Augusta), Myrna Paris (Mama McCourt), and Mark Freiman (Bryan). And on July 30, 2015, the Janiec Opera Company premiered at the Brevard Music Center in Brevard, North Carolina, a reduced version of the opera with single winds and brass prepared by conductor-composer Michael Ching on commission from the Douglas Moore Fund for American Music. Some of these later performances suggested a trend toward more leisurely tempos since Emerson Buckley first conducted the piece, with David McKee observing that at such slow rates, "what is cinematic becomes episodic, and sentiment is mushed into sentimentality."[81]

The Ballad of Baby Doe enjoyed far less exposure internationally. The Santa Fe Opera, which had programmed *Baby Doe* in 1961 as part of its fifth summer season, presented the work's European premiere, under the auspices of the State Department, at the West Berlin Festival on September 26, 1961, with the open-air Santa Fe Opera House replicated on stage of the Theater des Westens, and with Laurel Hurley (Baby Doe), Robert Trehy (Horace), and Elaine Bonazzi (Augusta) under the musical direction of Robert Baustian and stage direction of Henry Butler—a production that alternated with a Stravinsky double bill, and that subsequently made its way to Belgrade, the tour's second and last stop. In 1986, fifteen years later, the Bielefeld Opera, a company devoted to little-known works, especially those in the tradition of the German *Zeitoper*, reintroduced the work to Germany, this time as *Die Ballade von Baby Doe* in a skilled German translation by a descendant of the noble family famous for patronizing Haydn, Paul Esterházy, who here faced the challenge of finding German equivalents for such phrases as "you're still a lop-eared cut-throat from a squatter's claim" (Esterházy came up with, "bist du das alte Schlitzohr vom Besiedlungsland," which roughly translates as, "you're an old sly fox from the settlement"). London's University College Opera launched the work's British premiere at the Bloomsbury Theatre on March 11, 1996, with professional leads (Regina Nathan as Baby Doe, Omar Ebrahim as Horace, and Klara Uleman as Augusta) and a student chorus; another semiprofessional rendition, with similar personnel, by the English Touring Opera followed in August 1998 at the Arts Theatre in Cambridge. On June 4, 2000, the opera returned again to Germany in the form of a concert performance by the Wuppertal Opera; in July 2005, the American Opera Studio, a touring group based in Kansas, reportedly brought the piece to St. Ulrich and Innsbruck, Austria; and on January 26, 2008, the Calgary Opera unveiled Canada's first production of the work by a professional company.[82]

At home, critical response to the work diverged along familiar lines, with admirers describing the piece as "moving," "charming," "lovable," and "lusty," detractors, "banal," "kitschy," "obvious," and "musty." *Opera News* even published side-by-side opposing views, "The Battle of Baby Doe," by opera composers Harold Blumenfeld and Lionel Lackey on the occasion of the work's return to the New York City Opera in 1969, with Lackey grouping the piece with *The Bartered Bride* and *Boris Godunov* as "epics in music embodying the personality traits, humor and temperament of their people against a musical background representative of their national idiom," and Blumenfeld finding the work to exemplify "a kind of safe, comfy, homespun Gesamtkitschwerk in which music and text, situation and character are designed to echo each another in a tedium of mutual redundancy," the sort of work whose "stranglehold" on American operatic life prevented the likes of Roger Sessions's *Montezuma* from wider exposure. Contemplating such conflicting opinions, David Kanzeg reasonably conjectured that the opera's acceptance depended on such variables as the quality of the production and the intimacy of the venue, but a wide sampling of reviews seemed to point just as well to differences of taste and perception.[83]

The work's reception abroad similarly tended to be mixed, although generally better in later years, for at the time of its European premiere in 1961 critics seemed too stunned by the work's traditional melodic writing to imagine the piece much more than an example of American provincialism. The Germans especially, who seemed focused on the work's alleged indebtedness to Puccini, began to draw distinctions with the Italian master, assisted in this matter, in Bielefeld at any rate, by director John Dew's insightful program notes, which argued that the opera did not so much replicate late-nineteenth-century styles as create, more along the lines of ballad opera, a "Zeit-Atmosphäre" ("time atmosphere") in its portrayal of a country in transition from a frontier society (represented by the Old Miner) to a global power. (Dew placed the opera rather in the tradition of Mozart and Verdi in its ability "to find for every scene, for every situation, the right musical gesture," as well as in its capacity to reach both a general and an elite public.) Covering the 1996 British premiere, some reviewers, like their American colleagues, faulted the opera as "hollow" or "wordy," although composer-journalist Malcolm Hayes (*Sunday Telegraph*), who the year earlier had published a biography of Anton Webern, thought the work to offer "just about everything that a successful opera needs: strongly characterized and not too difficult principal roles, some good minor ones, some rousing chorus scenes, and an interesting story. And the libretto is even written in something syntactically resembling English." Tom Babin's review of the 2008 Canadian premiere for the *Calgary Herald* likewise recommended the piece: "it will make you laugh; it will make you cry, and it most certainly reflects upon the nature of human relationships and the power of the one human emotion we all know to be at our centre: love."[84]

Over time, the opera attracted an ardent group of devotees, and in the late 1990s, David Kanzeg, a Cleveland radio programmer, and Derek Mills, a Seattle strategic planning consultant, formed a sort of club, the Doeheads, for likeminded enthusiasts who enjoyed attending performances of the work, its name (after Doenuts had been rejected) a play on those avid fans of the rock band the Grateful Dead, the Deadheads. At Mills's suggestion, Kanzeg also launched a website, DoeHEADS, which posted a wealth of material about the opera, including a 1998 essay by Mills, "American Opera: The Sublimation of Ordinariness," which found Latouche's use of cliché an apt complement to Moore's "uniquely Yankee *Sprechstimme*": "One of Baby Doe's greatest strengths is John Latouche's inspired libretto. Latouche, who had a remarkable ear for the American idiom, assembled here our vernacular in a manner at once poetic and natural. Whole scenes are written using collections of cleverly captured clichés and oral rhythms woven together musically; they have an ease which makes them seem more a part of a play than of an opera. It is recitative that ripples with reality." And in a piece posted in 2003, "*The Ballad of Baby Doe* and the American Spirit," Kanzeg, intimating a striking resemblance in both its scansion and musical setting between Baby

Doe's "I have a love that will keep me aglow / As the world grows gray and cold," and Maria's "I have a love, and it's all that I have. / Right or wrong, what else can I do?" from *West Side Story* (1957, lyrics by Stephen Sondheim), helpfully described *Baby Doe* as "an opera-as-musical counterpoint to Bernstein's musical-as-opera."[85]

(That both Baby and Maria state these lines in explanation of a transgressive love further suggests that the homosexual subtext sometimes attributed to *West Side Story*—a work that Moore called in 1962 "the best thing that's ever been done in the American musical theater"—would seem relevant to *Baby Doe* as well, especially given Latouche's sexual orientation. Indeed, some reading of the opera along these lines emerged, albeit tongue in cheek, by way of a 2002 mock report in *Opera News* by William Madison that satirized current directorial trends by way of a profile of one Horst Gabarit, the fictional director of an imaginary Italian language version of *Baby Doe*, "La Ballata di Baby-Doe," in which Gabarit claims to have cast a countertenor as Baby Doe "to highlight the undercurrent of homosexual passion that runs throughout this opera. When I first read the libretto, I kept thinking here's a love affair that completely scandalizes the society in which these characters live. They're shunned, ostracized, ruined because of it. This is a fundamentally homosexual experience. The story simply isn't credible in any other terms.")[86]

For admirers like Kanzeg, Mills, Rebecca Paller, and David McKee, the work's content as much as its style made *Baby Doe* the "quintessential" American opera, with Kanzeg, for instance, finding the piece to embody not only the country's "frequent myopia over what's really important," but "aspects of the American character that we lately find missing from much of our public consciousness: tolerance, love, faithfulness, reverence, forgiveness, immortality." However delicate its balance between irony and nostalgia, the work surely reaches beyond the merely "quaint," with Horace and Augusta remaining familiar archetypes—the man who "grew" with the land, the woman who has had to "manage"—and Baby Doe, a transformative agent of light and love.[87]

As with the demise of the poet Stephen Vincent Bénet (1898–1943), who also died young of a heart attack after working with Moore, Latouche's death represented not only a personal blow for the composer, but a professional one; for although he wrote three more operas after *Baby Doe* (*Gallantry*, 1957, libretto by Arnold Sundgaard; *The Wings of the Dove*, 1961, libretto by Ethan Ayer; and *Carry Nation*, 1966, libretto by W. N. Jayme) their only mildly positive welcome left commentators like Jerry McBride surmising that if Moore and Latouche had had "an opportunity to work together again, Moore's later works might have had a chance to be as successful as *Baby Doe*." Noting the lack of "vitality" in *Carry Nation* as compared to *Baby Doe*, Ethan Mordden similarly wondered if Latouche's "expert libretto made all the difference." In any event, Moore considered Latouche's death "a great loss," although he took some consolation in the fact that the librettist died knowing, "from the warmth of the reception" he had received in Colorado, "that he had been equal to the challenge of this great American story."[88]

24

The Death and Legacy of a Renaissance Man

John Latouche died at age forty-one in the early morning hours of August 7, 1956, at his summer home in Calais, Vermont. Having more or less completed revising *The Ballad of Baby Doe,* he had gone up to Vermont a few days earlier with his friend Harry Martin partly to rest, but also to continue work on the Milton Rosenstock musical in progress, *The First Time,* and perhaps to do some further revision on *Baby Doe* and *Candide.* Harry Martin, meanwhile, hoped to get some painting done.

Most accounts portray Latouche in his final days as seeming perfectly fine, although the day before leaving for Vermont, Martin wrote Lord Kinross about finding the lyricist the previous night "filled with alcohol and dire prophecies about my soul, his soul, the World soul." Whether Latouche ever saw the August 6 article in the *New York Times,* "Poet, 35, Is Named 'Candide' Lyricist," announcing Richard Wilbur as that show's "principal lyricist," remains unknown; but if so, the item—although hardly news to Latouche—can only have dejected him that much more. To the very end, he turned for consolation to spiritual writings, specifically, as Martin recalled, "an ultra-esoteric book" about George Gurdjieff and P. D. Ouspensky, perhaps Ouspensky's classic account of Gurdjieff's teaching, *In Search of the Miraculous,* which Latouche thought "relevant to my present state" when first read back in 1949.[1]

On the evening of Monday, August 6, Latouche and Martin returned home around midnight after a quiet dinner with friends; and at about 3:30 a.m., Latouche woke Martin, "complaining of a terrific chest pain," as the latter recounted to Lord Kinross soon after. Not having a telephone at the house or anyone living nearby, Martin suggested that he go find a doctor; but Latouche, not wanting to be left alone and thinking that he simply might be having "acute indigestion," preferred rather to wait things out. After taking some bicarbonate of soda, he returned to bed, a medical dictionary in hand, and appeared to fall asleep. However, Martin found him dead the next morning, with some blood on his bed linen, indicating that he had hemorrhaged overnight. According to Latouche's death certificate, the regional medical examiner determined that he had died at about 4:00 a.m. from a coronary occlusion—that is, an arterial blockage leading to a heart attack—of about two hours in duration. Claiming that Latouche, "always the autodidact," had been found dead with the medical dictionary opened on his lap, Gore Vidal later wrote, "Everyone was most impressed that the page he [Latouche] was reading was exactly the right one for someone suffering from an arterial embolism nourished by too much brandy and too many cigarettes."[2]

Hearing the news, Latouche's friend the novelist Dawn Powell immediately wrote in her diary,

> Incredible that this dynamo should unwind and I think I can guess how. Talentless but shrewd users pursued him always—he was *driven*: harnesses and bridles and wagons were always being rushed up to him to use this endless gold. I have seen him so harried by the users he burst into tears. Contracts, advances, deals, love offers were all around—trying to get him in a corner room, lock him up and get out the gold when he wanted only to talk all day and all night. He never could sleep—lights on all night—so there were sleeping pills and for the grim collaborators demanding the real work, he must have Benzedrine, Miltown tranquilizers, Nembutal, dex[edrine]. I'm sure this was a desperate, hysterical escape from Lillian Hellman and others waiting for his output to finish up "Candide." Like George Gershwin—a natural gusher that grim syndicates tried to harness for the stock exchange. Ending up now an incorrigibly sweet, indestructible little ghost.

With striking coincidence, Lord Kinross also referred to Latouche as a "dynamo" in his similar explanation for the latter's collapse:

> His own energy had consumed him. The dynamo in which, in his lust for life, he had always trusted implicitly, had proved unable to carry the load. Destroying abruptly and without warning, his seemed to me a characteristically American death... rejoicing in the stresses and extremes of America, he had chosen to live recklessly, developing to the full the best American qualities of zest and warmth and unchecked enthusiasm. Tempting the Gods, he had chosen a life too exacting, perhaps, for the human species; and now Nemesis had destroyed him.

Kinross further found it ironic that, despite Latouche's profound love for European culture (including his hope to write an opera about Robert Burns, whose poetry he recited by heart), he had never been to Europe, leaving Kinross to wonder if such exposure to "the reduced voltage of European life... might... have led him to moderation in some things, and a completeness in civilized terms," in turn forestalling his early death.[3]

Obituaries appeared throughout the country, mistakenly giving the lyricist's age as thirty-eight, as in the *Times*, or thirty-nine, as in the *Daily News*. His body was shipped to New York, where friends organized a funeral service on August 9 at the Church of the Transfiguration on East 29th Street and Fifth Avenue, an historic Episcopal parish commonly called the Little Church Around the Corner. Latouche's mother Effie, his brother Louis, and his sister-in-law Ora Lee attended the service, as did such notable friends as Frederick Kiesler, Douglas Moore, Jerome Moross, Sono Osato, Dawn Powell, and painter Lucia Wilcox, who "wept without control," as Kiesler observed. "Have never been to a more moving funeral," wrote *Musical America* editor (and sister to architect Philip Johnson) Theodate ("Theo") Johnson to composer Virgil Thomson. "Everyone, male and female, was in tears. I sent a large spray of large yellow crysanthemums [*sic*] from us both." Kiesler delivered a eulogy written by Carson McCullers, the typescript of which read in part,

> John was not like a person of this century, but a man of the Rennaissance [*sic*]. I mean by that the immense talent and the soul and the sense of life. As an artist John was unique and I have never known a man more gallant. He had theatrical defeats as all writers do from time to time and he took them courageously and always with his own high heart. His wit was known to all of us but the wittiness was never malicious. John had humanity and gaiety, there was in him a sense of communication I have known with no other. Whether it was a house servant or a guest or a king, John always communicated with sure delicacy, fantasy and understanding. I have never known a man more versatile.... I have never known a man of such faithful friendship.... In his appreciation of the works of others he was the most generous and the most perceptive person. (John was a man who died as he was approaching the peak of his greatness. We can only think with wonder and sorrow about the work he would have done. *Cabin In The Sky* and *The Golden Apple* are already classics. *The Ballad of Baby Doe* is surely one of the greatest modern operas.) One thinks of John with his prismatic talent as a man of the Rennaissance [*sic*] but now that he is no longer here we are thinking of his love and our everlasting love. Although we have lost John's radiance, the music of his life is still with us.

In consultation with some friends, Kiesler cut and edited this eulogy slightly, including perhaps changing the phrase "as he was approaching the peak of his greatness," to "at the peak of his greatness," or so the line has been cited since its initial quotation by the *New York Times*.[4]

Latouche's body was returned to Vermont for internment on August 10 in Robinson Cemetery in Calais on a lot owned by his friend Louise Kent, ostensibly a gift of the Kent family. However, Louis Latouche, noting that his brother had hemorrhaged blood—an unusual occurrence with heart attacks—and that Harry Martin had had the mattress and bed linens burned, began to suspect Martin of foul play and requested an official inquiry, which culminated in an exhumation and autopsy on September 8, and a reburial the following day. The autopsy confirmed the original medical examiner's findings and exonerated Martin, who nonetheless was left traumatized by the entire ordeal. Indeed, the spectacle of Effie and Louis spearheading a murder investigation of one of Latouche's dearest companions appalled the lyricist's friends, with Ruth Yorck commenting to Lord Kinross, "I always respected John. But I must say I do respect him twenty times more, now that I see just what he sprang from." Frederick Kiesler subsequently designed for the gravesite an obelisk headstone simply engraved with Latouche's name and dates (his birthdate given as November 13, 1915, still off by a year) and four stone markers, each representing a major accomplishment—*Cabin in the Sky*, *Ballet Ballads*, *The Golden Apple*, and *The Ballad of Baby Doe*—by way of carved illustrations of a log cabin, a ballerina, an apple, and a doe, respectively (see Figure 58).[5]

In the weeks and months after Latouche's death, newspapers and journals published encomiums and reminiscences. Leonard Lyons, who in his chatty syndicated column "The Lyons Den" frequently had reported on the lyricist's escapades, recalled the time Latouche wrestled to unconsciousness "a husky stranger" at the Copacabana nightclub who had taunted him after overhearing him refer to himself as "class poet" at Columbia: " 'In addition to being a poet at Columbia,' said Latouche, dusting his hands, 'I also was on the wrestling team' [this last boast an apparent fabrication]." Drama critic Jack Gaver observed that "the very nature of his [Latouche's] interest and type of work" prevented him from attaining the success of some of his contemporaries. As discussed earlier, poet Frank O'Hara memorialized Latouche by way of one of his most celebrated poems, "A Step Away from Them." Composer Earl Robinson, writing for the *Nation*, spoke of the lyricist's interest in "exploring new poetic paths" even while remaining "committed to reaching a wide popular audience," and offered as an example of his wit a parody of "John Brown's Body," composed for Spivy LeVoe, that featured the lines (presumably for the "Glory hallelujah" chorus), "We're the Daughters of the American Revolution. But we'll never be the mothers of another!"[6]

Another musical collaborator, Vernon Duke, in tributes in *Variety* and *Theatre Arts*, noted how Latouche's abilities as "a poet rather than a lyricist" accommodated the aims of composers as opposed to tunesmiths; and remembered how theatrical producers would balk at the idea of engaging him ("Why Latouche? He thrives on trouble—we have trouble enough without him"), prompting Duke to write, "Calamity did hold a perverse fascination for Latouche. But somehow, no one took his tantrums seriously—and, typically neither did he who knew how to disarm yesterday's adversary with warmth and genuine affection the very next day." Herbert Machiz, director of the Artists' Theatre, wrote to the *New York Times* from Rome, reminding readers not only of Latouche's involvement with "what he called a 'lyric theatre'—a theatre that would use music, dance, film and décor in new and delightful combinations," but of his support of younger artists: "Again and again he gave generously of his time and whatever money he could afford to painters, composers, poets, dancers—he was prodigal in writing letters, introducing artists to impresarios and his apartment was always the scene of artistic gatherings, auditions, activities indicating true ferment." And Virgil Thomson dedicated his 1956 orchestration of Brahms's Eleven Chorale Preludes for organ "in memory of John Latouche."[7]

Encouraged by Latouche's friends, Ruth Yorck set out soon after his death to publish an anthology, *The Ballad of John Latouche*, that would contain prose and poetry dedicated to his memory, personal recollections of the man, and a sampling of his unpublished poetry and letters; to this end, she solicited material from a number of the lyricist's associates. "I want people to dedicate something for the book," she wrote Gore Vidal, "a short story . . . a scene . . . a poem . . . not necessarily a memory directly connected with an experience they had with Touche. No eulogies. No pompous stuff. No slap one's own back stuff." James Branch Cabell offered to write about the young Latouche, and Gore Vidal, to submit a story ("He was unique," he wrote Yorck, "the best company in the world and a monster of egotism. I do miss him"), whereas Aaron Copland and Leonard Bernstein politely declined. Sadly, the volume never came to fruition.[8]

On the afternoon of May 12, 1960, Latouche's friends gathered once again for a memorial in his honor, this one organized by entertainment attorney William Fitelson. "I know that the Memorial for John touched every heart that was there," wrote the lyricist's agent, Lucy Kroll, to his mother the following day. Around this same time, the press reported that the chanteuse Anita Ellis had begun to record an album of Latouche's songs, but no such recording ever surfaced. Producer Ben Bagley similarly hoped to release, with financial backing from Kenward Elmslie, a Latouche album featuring Carol Channing, Jerry Orbach, and the young Barbra Streisand (reportedly "a tremendous fan of Latouche"), but this project also never materialized. However, in later years Streisand recorded on separate solo albums "Taking a Chance on Love" and (at the suggestion of director Francis Ford Coppola) "Lazy Afternoon," in both instances taking tempos slow enough so as to be able to caress every word.[9]

Because Latouche died intestate, his mother, Effie, inherited both his modest assets and numerous debts. Kenward Elmslie would have seemed a likely choice as literary executor, but Effie, whose relationship with her son's lover had become strained, turned for guidance rather to her attorney, Carl Blank, and to Latouche's devoted agent, Lucy Kroll, who continued to serve the deceased lyricist with tireless care. George Freedley, the longtime curator of the theater division of the New York Public Library, expressed interest in acquiring Latouche's papers as early as 1959, but these remained in Effie's hands, even after the estate finally closed in late 1962.[10]

In 1964, Effie herself died without leaving a will, making her three surviving siblings—Rosa Chandler Mimms, Abraham Seigel, and Emanuel Seigel—heirs to her son's estate, Latouche's brother, Louis, having died in 1962. After the deaths of the Seigel siblings, the estate passed to the descendants of Rosa Mimms and Emanuel Seigel, and in the case of Abraham Seigel, who had become estranged from his son, to Libby Green, the daughter of a close friend; and after Lucy Kroll retired in 1994, her associate Barbara Hogenson acquired her literary agency, which continued to represent Latouche.[11]

In 1965, Kroll wrote to Jerome Moross about some "manuscripts and medals" going to the New York Public Library, but no record of any such transaction survives; and without an executor at the helm, Latouche's effects became all that much more dispersed. Elmslie gave Pavel Tchelitchew's portrait of the lyricist to the Museum of the City of New York in 1967; Gore Vidal donated several scripts and other Latouche-related materials that apparently he had kept in storage at Edgewater to the New York Public Library in 1970; and Rosa Mimms's daughter Virginia Luck sold for $6,400 a small collection, including the lyricist's extant journals, to Columbia University's Butler Library in 1997. Some other items surfaced here and there, while still others ostensibly disappeared.[12]

In the 1970s, undeterred by the scattered dissemination of Latouche's papers, theater professor Andrew H. Drummond undertook the first and until now only biography of the lyricist, the unpublished *John Latouche*. Born on a farm in Kansas, Drummond (1929–2005), a director and theater historian, took his undergraduate studies at Grinnell College and, after serving in the army, pursued graduate work in New York, obtaining a master of fine arts from Columbia University and a doctorate in educational theater from New York University for his 1969 thesis on the librettos of American operas performed at the New York City Opera, a document later expanded into the 1973 publication *American Opera Librettos*. This scholarly work, along with directing a performance of *The Ballad of Baby Doe* for the Colorado Springs Opera Association in 1971, helped spur his interest in Latouche; and in 1973, as a member of the Kingsborough Community College faculty, he began investigating the lyricist's life and work in full. Over the next decade, he traveled near and far, collecting materials and conducting interviews with, among others, friends and family in Richmond, Virgil Thomson in New York, Harry Martin in Massachusetts, and, during a sabbatical year, Spivy LeVoe in Paris, André Cauvin in Provence, and Paul Bowles in Morocco, who reminisced about Latouche through a haze of hashish. Drummond's completed draft resembled an omnibus, with transcriptions of letters and diary entries, one likely cause for its failure to find a publisher; but for just such reasons, the manuscript, along with other materials preserved by the author's widow, Maria, constitutes an invaluable resource for Latouche scholarship.[13]

In 1984, about the time that Drummond abandoned work on *John Latouche*, the accomplished concert composer and jazz singer-pianist Richard Rodney Bennett (1936–2012) released an album on the Audiophile label entitled *Take Love Easy: The Lyrics of John Latouche*, with himself on vocals and piano, Dick Sarpola on bass, and Tony Tedesco on drums—part of a series of recordings by Bennett devoted to single songwriters. For the reissue of *Take Love Easy* on compact disc (2001), the now knighted Sir Richard took advantage of the extra playing time afforded by digital technology and included five additional Latouche songs with bassist Linc Millman.

Bennett's involvement with Latouche, about whom he entertained some unfounded gossip, dated at least as far back as 1982, when he presented a selection of the lyricist's songs at Washington's Corcoran Gallery as part of a popular Great American Songwriters series. How Bennett came to champion Latouche remains unknown, but he likely received help locating the lyricist's songs from pianist Buddy Barnes, who provided some such service with respect to Bennett's research into Harold Arlen, and who wrote the liner notes to *Take Love Easy* (in which he compared Latouche's "verbal alchemy" to Lorenz Hart, and claimed this "classy collection of songs" to contain "some of the finest lyrics ever written"). Bennett selected from the Latouche catalog sundry romantic ballads, all sung with charm and conviction in the raspy-voiced chanteur's best Americanese. The recording also revealed Latouche as an auteur in his own right, his urbane wit smoothly unifying the somewhat diverse musical styles represented by the album's seven composers.[14]

Taking a Chance on Love: The Lyrics & Life of John Latouche, a 2000 revue presented by Manhattan's York Theatre, offered a more momentous musical accounting of the lyricist's achievement. The York's artistic director, James Morgan, a longtime advocate of underappreciated musical theater, including *The Golden Apple*, pitched the idea of a Latouche revue to Kenward Elmslie, who agreed to provide monetary assistance and approved the decision to have Erik Haagensen devise the piece. A playwright, lyricist, director, and critic who held a master's degree in musical theater writing from New York University, Haagensen (b. 1954) by this time had a long list of credits, including, as previously mentioned, a commissioned narration for the Concert version of *Candide*.[15]

With the aid of his partner, Joseph McConnell, Haagensen exhaustively researched Latouche's life and work; he interviewed numerous people, parsed the lyricist's diaries and correspondence, and amassed a substantial trove of Latouchiana, including scores, scripts, articles, photographs, and recordings. Creating the piece for a cast of four, Haagensen ingeniously used more than thirty songs interspersed with spoken dialogue to paint a vivid picture of the lyricist, with some numbers representing particular events in his career, others rather illustrating aspects of his personal life. Jeffrey R. Smith arranged the music, which featured a jazzy vocal quartet style in the tradition of the Martins, and in addition performed the stylish two-piano accompaniment with David Harris. James Morgan directed and Janet Watson choreographed. Opening at the York on March 2, the cast consisted of Terry Burrell, Jerry Dixon, Donna English, and Eddie Korbich, who won a 2000 Obie Award for his performance.[16]

The revue received generally good reviews. Admitting that the name Latouche currently meant little even to Broadway musical theater mavens—a preview article in *American Theatre* magazine bore the header, "The Lyricist Nobody Knows"—the critics thought, whatever their reservations about the show, Latouche "a truly capricious and fascinating subject," and his lyrics, the "witty" and "sophisticated" work of a "sublimely gifted songwriter." The revue ran for twenty-nine performances and resulted in an original cast album, released in 2001, which contained much of the script and nearly all the songs, and which remains, notwithstanding some occasional artistic license with respect to lyrics and historical sources, a highly informed and entertaining celebration of the man and his work.[17]

Meanwhile, critical commentary about Latouche proved generally sparse and perfunctory. As one exception, in 1991, Richard Merkin (1938–2009), the artist-dandy-connoisseur best known for his drawings for the *New Yorker*, penned a lively appreciation of the lyricist in his style column for *GQ* magazine; illustrated with a portrait of Latouche in Merkin's distinctive manner, the author described his subject as "a brilliant and sophisticated redneck from Richmond, a sort of Holy Beast who was responsible for some of the most imaginative and intelligent lyrics in the body of American popular music." In contrast, several prominent overviews and anthologies of American lyricists, including Lehman Engel's *Their Words Are Music* (1975), Philip Furia's *The Poets of Tin Pan Alley* (1990), and Robert Gottlieb and Robert Kimball's *Reading Lyrics* (2000), tended to treat Latouche (if they mentioned him at all) rather equivocally, with Gottlieb and Kimball asking if *The Golden Apple* represented "a daring and revolutionary new step or a pretentious cul-de-sac." At the same time, Thomas Hischak, in his own survey, *Word Crazy* (1991), showed no hesitancy in declaring Latouche's librettos and lyrics "superb examples of quality craftsmanship, versatility and humor," adding that his early death "cut short the career of one of Broadway's finest and least recognized lyricists."[18]

To the extent that commentators had anything to say about Latouche, they often took their cue from Ned Rorem's description of him as "a sort of preface to Sondheim" (a backhanded compliment, incidentally, in more ways than one, considering Rorem's mixed feelings about Sondheim). But the two men's work, as evidenced by the lyrics that each wrote for *Candide*, differed considerably, as discussed earlier. Sondheim himself admitted, "Our [his and Latouche's] styles couldn't be more different," claiming as his progenitors rather the likes of Dorothy Fields, E. Y. Harburg, and Frank Loesser. Discussing various lyricists in *Finishing the Hat* (2010) and *Look, I Made a Hat* (2011), Sondheim had little to say about Latouche, especially in the first volume, which situated him "among the lower deities in the Pantheon" for the debatable reasons that he "didn't write steadily for the theater" and that his work, however "skillful," bore "no discernible stamp or personality"; expounding further in the second volume, Sondheim found in Latouche's work, as with Johnny Mercer, "a poetic sensibility often identified with the South," and went on to say, citing some of his musicals, "He [Latouche] had neither the earthiness nor the idiosyncratic inventiveness of Mercer, but he had a large vision of what musical theater could be."[19]

Latouche seemed a precursor more definitely of Kenward Elmslie, as also mentioned before. But in any case, his outlier status spoke to the uniqueness of his career and work. For one thing, few American lyricists pursued so wide a range of activities, including not only composing books for musicals and librettos for operas, but working extensively with cabaret; writing a book about the Congo; translating and adapting poems and plays; creating his own poems and plays; writing for and producing films; appearing on stage and screen; and championing progressive political causes—the sorts of things that prompted Ruth Yorck to speak of him as the American Jean Cocteau, and Carson McCullers, as a renaissance man.[20]

Relatedly, although he functioned primarily in the commercial realm of popular song and the Broadway musical, he showed a distinct proclivity toward elite and cutting-edge artistic trends, not only in the work that engaged him, but in the friendships he maintained and the artists he patronized, such as John Cage, Maya Deren, Ellsworth Kelly, and Frank O'Hara. Such tensions could be discerned in the work he produced; building on David Kanzeg's description of *The Ballad of Baby Doe* (or, for that matter, the operas Latouche wrote with Jerome Moross) as an "opera-as-musical" as opposed to a "musical-as-opera" like *West Side Story*, a similar differentiation might be drawn between Latouche's poetry-as-lyrics as opposed to the lyrics-as-poetry characteristic of Ira Gershwin or Lorenz Hart. Such a distinction—which naturally derived from Latouche's early decision to channel his energies from poetry to musical theater, partly because of financial necessity, but also because of his conviction that musical theater represented "an authentic reflection of American culture"—expressed itself in the kind of subtle wit and deft use of metaphor, alliteration, rhyme, and meter that characterized his best work. As such, he warranted comparison not so much with Broadway's popular lyricists, who often practiced more conversational styles, as with such poet-lyricists as Maxwell Anderson, John Hollander, Langston Hughes, Ogden Nash, Richard Wilbur, and perhaps above all, Bertolt Brecht, a formative influence; observed Ruth Yorck, "Latouche is not alone in believing and proclaiming that in our time poetry belongs in a musical. And that is where he hides it, or presents it." Given his age and background, he even could be placed in the context of such serious contemporary poets as John Berryman, Elizabeth Bishop, Robert Lowell, Theodore Roethke, and Delmore Schwartz, a generation of artists profoundly affected by the successive shocks of the Depression, World War II, and the Cold War—although in his maturity, Latouche essentially operated in a different milieu, notwithstanding his early friendship with E. E. Cummings, his eventual involvement with the New York Poets, and his own sporadic efforts as a serious poet. Even among Broadway's poet-lyricists, he forged his own voice, one alternately dreamily romantic, slyly raffish, and whimsically campy, although commentators differed as to whether he elevated the musical theater lyric to new heights of artistry or succumbed to the pitfalls of artifice.[21]

Latouche's conception of the poetic song lyric, at any rate, formed part of a renewed approach to the lyric theater generally, as suggested above by Machiz's mention of the lyricist's hopes for a "theatre that would use music, dance, film and décor in new and delightful combinations," and by Sondheim's reference to his having "a large vision of what musical theater could be." In some ways, he realized these aspirations best in those works over which he exerted most control, such as *Beggar's Holiday*, *Ballet Ballads*, *The Golden Apple*, and *The Ballad of Baby Doe*, though as with Brecht, again a principal stimulus, his goals by no means excluded but rather welcomed similarly adventurous collaborators, making popular music theater a congenial medium for such novelty and experimentation. As with previous reformers of lyric theater, Latouche found that myths, fables, and legends, although typically handled ironically or parodistically, provided good springboards for rehearsing and practicing such new ideas, with nearly all his theatrical pieces, like much of his radio and film work, involving fantastical or historical characters.

As Vernon Duke emphasized, Latouche's sort of skill and artistry naturally appealed to composers similarly equipped and disposed, that is, cultivated musicians hoping to reach the large audience for popular song and musical comedy—composers like Earl Robinson, Vernon Duke, Jerome Moross, Duke Ellington, Donald Fuller, Leonard Bernstein, and Douglas Moore. Moreover, whether or not he wrote the words first, he created lyrics wholly responsive to the special traits and sensibilities of these collaborators—to Robinson's humanity, Duke's exuberance, Moross's charm, Ellington's style, Fuller's elegance, Bernstein's vitality, and Moore's warmth. This gift—implied in Peter Davis's observation, regarding *The Ballad of Baby Doe*, that "[Douglas] Moore must have realized that he had been handed a libretto made expressly for him, because he characterizes and animates virtually every scene with lively, direct, infectious, tuneful music that comes straight from the heart"—made it possible for Latouche to write cabaret songs tailor-made for such entertainers as Spivy LeVoe, Hope Emerson, and Charlotte Rae; to find apt words for the melodies of Kreisler and Chopin; to adapt the work of Paul Verlaine, Jura Soyfer, Jean Cocteau, Bertolt Brecht, Pierre Beaumarchais, August Strindberg, Ring Lardner and George S. Kaufman, and Sidney Howard; to compose fitting ditties for film director Hans Richter; and to write suitable lyrics for such varied popular song composers as Billy Strayhorn, Walter Donaldson, Rudolph Goehr, Ulpio Minucci, and Marvin Fisher. Concomitantly, he displayed an adroit command of diverse modes and forms of expression, from biting satire and zany farce to tender romance, surreal fantasy, and high drama.[22]

Between his chaotic and overburdened life, and the need to compromise with collaborators, producers, and, in general, the exigencies of the commercial stage, including popular taste, Latouche struggled to fulfill his potential and ideals. Perhaps had he "found his proper Mozart," as Andrew Drummond suggests, he might have ascended to greater heights; had he lived beyond his forty-one years, he at least surely would have continued to produce works of daring and brilliance. But driven to succeed, in the course of his short life he managed nonetheless to move and impress many with his genius and vision, in the process significantly enriching American culture and its musical theater.[23]

NOTES

In quoting and citing sources, I have endeavored to retain the syntax, punctuation, and spelling of the original texts (without flagging errors by way of a bracketed "*sic*" regarding the frequent misspellings of Latouche as La Touche or LaTouche, or the common dropping of apostrophes from contractions like "can't" and "won't," although maintained for incorrect uses of "its" and "it's"). I also refer to several New York papers without necessarily mentioning their identifying city, including the *Amsterdam News, Daily Mirror, Daily News, Herald Tribune, Journal-American, Post, Sun, Times,* and *World-Telegram*. Note too that endnote numbers refer back to entire paragraphs.

Abbreviations

ADP	Andrew Drummond Papers, courtesy of Maria Drummond
AFL	Austrian Frederick and Lillian Kielser Private Foundation
AHD	Andrew H. Drummond, *John Latouche* (manuscript)
DMP	Douglas Moore Papers, Columbia University
EHP	Erik Haagensen Papers, courtesy of Erik Haagensen
ERP	Earl Robinson Papers, University of Washington
FBI	John Latouche, FBI file, National Archives and Records Administration
GMF	Guggenheim Memorial Foundation, New York
GVP	Gore Vidal Papers, Harvard University
KEP	Kenward Elmslie Papers, University of California, San Diego
JL	John Latouche
JLD	John Latouche Diaries, John Latouche Papers, Columbia University
JLL	John Latouche Lyrics and Scripts, Billy Rose Theatre Division, New York Public Library
JLP	John Latouche Papers, Columbia University
LBP	Leonard Bernstein Papers, Music Division, Library of Congress
LC	Library of Congress
LHP	Lillian Hellman Papers, University of Texas at Austin
LKP	Lucy Kroll Papers, Music Division, Library of Congress
MCP	Margaret Freeman Cabell Papers, Virginia Commonwealth University Libraries
n.d.	no date
n.s.	no source
NYHT	*New York Herald Tribune*
NYPL	New York Public Library

NYT	*New York Times*
RTD	*Richmond Times-Dispatch*
RYP	Ruth Yorck Papers, Boston University
VDP	Vernon Duke Papers, Music Division, Library of Congress
VTP	Virgil Thomson Papers, Yale University

Introduction

1. Ned Rorem, *Knowing When to Stop: A Memoir* (New York: Simon & Schuster, 1994), 252.
2. Ned Rorem, liner notes, *Taking a Chance on Love* (Original Cast Records, OC-4444, 2000).

1. John Latouche and His Family

1. Virginius Dabney, *Richmond: The Story of a City* (Garden City, NY: Doubleday, 1976), 356; Henry James, *Collected Travel Writings: Great Britain and America* (New York: Library of America, 1993), 663.
2. Edgar MacDonald, *James Branch Cabell and Richmond-in-Virginia* (Jackson: University Press of Mississippi, 1993), xiii.
3. Emily Clark, *Innocence Abroad* (New York: Knopf, 1931).
4. James Branch Cabell, *Let Me Lie* (New York: Farrar, Straus, 1947), 12; Marie Tyler-McGraw, *At the Falls: Richmond, Virginia and Its People* (Chapel Hill: University of North Carolina Press, 1994), 253; see also Alfred Kazin, *On Native Grounds: An Interpretation of Modern American Prose Literature* (New York: Reynal & Hitchcock, 1942); Louis D. Rubin Jr., *No Place on Earth: Ellen Glasgow, James Branch Cabell, and Richmond-in-Virginia* (Austin: University of Texas Press, 1959); Edmund Wilson, *The Bit Between My Teeth: A Literary Chronicle of 1950–1965* (New York: Farrar, Straus and Giroux, 1965), 291–325; and Ellen Glasgow, *The Woman Within: An Autobiography*, edited with an introduction by Pamela R. Matthews (Charlottesville: University Press of Virginia, 1994).
5. Ronald David Ward, "The Life and Works of John Powell (1882–1963)" (PhD diss., Catholic University of America, 1973); J. Lester Feder, "Unequal Temperament: The Somatic Acoustics of Racial Difference in the Symphonic Music of John Powell," *Black Music Research Journal* 28 (Spring 2008): 17–56; Barbara Bair, "Remapping the Black/White Body: Sexuality, Nationalism, and Biracial Antimiscegenation Activism in 1920s Virginia," in *Sex, Love, Race: Crossing Boundaries in North American History*, edited by Martha Hodes (New York: New York University Press, 1999), 399–419; Bair, "Garveyism and Contested Political Terrain in 1920s Virginia," in *Afro-Virginian History and Culture*, edited by John Saillant (New York: Garland, 1999), 227–49.
6. JL to John Powell, June 17, 1940, John Powell Papers, University of Virginia; JL to Archibald MacLeish, Aug. 2, 1940, Music Division Old Correspondence Collection, LC; JLD, Feb. 12, 1945.
7. Carson McCullers, "John Latouche—An Eulogy," LKP; Ruth Landshoff-Yorck, *Klatsch, Ruhm und kleine Feuer: Biographische Impressionen* (Berlin: Kiepenheuer & Witsch, 1963), 125, 128; Lord Kinross, *The Innocents at Home* (New York: Morrow, 1960), 163.
8. "John Treville Latouche," *Current Biography: Who's News and Why: January–June 1940* (New York: H. W. Wilson, 1940), 480–82; "*Flair Flair*: *The Idol of Paree*," *Jester* 27 (March 1935): 9; George Ross, "Broadway," *Pittsburgh Press* (Apr. 24, 1940); Kenward Elmslie, interview with author, Mar. 13, 2013; Harry King Tootle, "John Latouche at Work on Four Plays," *RTD* (Feb. 6, 1949).
9. "John Treville Latouche." See also these other seminal articles: Obed Stearns, "Sing a Song of America," *NYHT* (July 7, 1940); Luther Davis and John Cleveland, "And You Know Who I Am," *Collier's* 106 (Oct. 19, 1940): 80, 91; and Elizabeth Copeland, "John La Touche Comes Back to His Home Town for a Day," *Richmond News Leader* (Oct. 24, 1940).

10. "John Treville Latouche"; Tootle ("boy wonder").
11. "John Treville Latouche," 481; *"Flair Flair"*; Copeland (for christened name); Evelyn C. Newman (a daughter of Effie's sister Rosa) and her son Harold Newman, interview with author, Sep. 16, 2012; AHD (for noble French heritage).
12. Joseph Wheelan, *Libby Prison Breakout: The Daring Escape from the Notorious Civil War Prison* (New York: Public Affairs, 2010), 93, 173; JL to Effie Latouche, c. Oct. 1943, JLP.
13. "LaTouche Tailor Shop Traditional," *RTD* (Nov. 25, 1929).
14. JL to Effie Latouche, Feb. 13, 1940, JLP.
15. *Younger Poets: An Anthology of American Secondary School Verse*, edited by Nellie B. Sergent (New York: Appleton, 1932), 391; Elmslie; Gore Vidal, *Virgin Islands: Essays 1992–1997* (London: Deutsch, 1997), 25; Gore Vidal, *Palimpsest: A Memoir* (New York: Random House, 1995), 246; Eileen Garrett, *Many Voices: The Autobiography of a Medium* (New York: Putnam's, 1968), 147–48; Carol Channing, *Just Lucky I Guess: A Memoir of Sorts* (New York: Simon & Schuster, 2002), 74; Yorck, 123–24.
16. Newman.
17. *The Jewish South* 1 (Aug. 25, 1893); Myron Berman, *Richmond's Jewry, 1769–1976: Shabbat in Shockoe* (Charlottesville: University of Virginia Press, 1979), 253; "Glad Loeb Story Saw Light of Day," *RTD* (Dec. 31, 1910).
18. "Stabbed by Her Husband," [St. Petersburg, VA] *Daily Progress* (July 28, 1909).
19. "Twenty-Two Blissful Ones See Marriage License Man," *RTD* (Apr. 18, 1911); "Shoots Negro in Arm," *RTD* (Dec. 10, 1918); "Two Are Given Year for House-Breaking," *RTD* (Jan. 18, 1930).
20. AHD; Effie Latouche, "Biographical Notes on John Latouche," JLP.
21. Virginia ("Jenny") Chandler Luck and Josephine Jordan (two daughters of Effie's sister Rosa), interview with Erik Haagensen, c. August 1999, courtesy of Haagensen; Effie Latouche, "Biographical Notes" (John received this Bible from the Trinity Methodist Church, which he attended after his divorced mother moved to East Broad to live with his father's uncle and aunt, Frederick and Frances Latimer).
22. JL, affidavit, May 18, 1956, FBI; JLD, Jan. 21, 1944; Dec. 15, 1943; Max Jacobson and JL, untitled transcript, Apr. 14, 1949, JLL.
23. Burford Latouche to Effie Latouche, postmarked Aug. 26, 1927, AHD.
24. Burford Latouche Jr., interview with author, Sep. 15, 2012.
25. Tootle; AHD; *Hill's Richmond City Directory* (Richmond: Hill Directory, 1927), 858.
26. Effie Latouche, "Biographical Notes."
27. Miles Kreuger, interview with author, Sep. 19, 2016, recalled hearing that Louis had developed rheumatic fever as a child, which left him with the heart trouble that precipitated his death.
28. Luck; "Bus to Take Richmonders to See Musical," *RTD* (Aug. 12, 1954); Sue Dickinson Durden, "LaTouche Work Set by Choral Society," *RTD* (June 22, 1975); Barbara Shaw, "Central City's 'Ballad of Baby Doe,'" *San Francisco Examiner* (July 15, 1956).
29. Millicent Dillon, *A Little Original Sin: The Life and Work of Jane Bowles* (New York: Holt, Rinehart and Winston, 1971), 302, 305; Mary McGlone, "Opera Lode Diggin's," *Central City Weekly Register-Call* (July 6, 1956); Coleman Dowell, *A Star-Bright Lie* (Normal, IL: Dalkey Archive, 1993), 92; Lucy Kroll to Rosa Chandler Mimms, Dec. 21, 1964, LKP; Elmslie; Gerrit Lansing, interview with author, Apr. 4, 2013; AHD; Millicent Dillon, *You Are Not I: A Portrait of Paul Bowles* (Berkeley: University of California Press, 1998), 6.
30. Lansing; Dowell, 92; JL to Effie Latouche, Feb. 23, 1933; Feb. 13, 1940; June 8, 1955; Dec. 24, 1955, AHD and JLP.
31. JLD, April 1951; Libby Green, interview with author, Sep. 27, 2012; Bob Luttrell and Rose Manning Seigel (Emanuel's widow), email to author, Oct. 4, 2012.
32. Luck.
33. Latouche Jr.

2. The Young Writer

1. JLD, [Feb. 16], 1938.
2. Sue Dickinson, "$5,000 Haircut Inspired LaTouche," *RTD* (Nov. 20, 1956); Robert Francis, "Candid Close-Ups" (c. 1941), VDP; Lucy Kroll to JL, June 24, 1954, LKP.
3. AHD (ostensibly from an interview with Rosa Mimms); "*Flair Flair: The Idol of Paree*," *Jester* 27 (March 1935): 9; Jack Woodford [Josiah Pitts Woolfolk], *The Autobiography of Jack Woodford* (Garden City, NY: Doubleday, 1962), 246.
4. Woodford, 246; AHD.
5. JLD, Nov. 12–27, 1943; Woodford, 246–49; AHD.
6. JLD, Apr. 20, 1945.
7. Margaret C. Leake, *John Marshall High School: A Richmond Legend* (Richmond: Dietz, 1985); James W. Yankovich, "John Marshall High School: 'The People's University,' 1910," *Public Education in Virginia* 24/4 (1986): 11, 25, courtesy of Shelia Demetriadis; Ann Catherine Cross, "Highlights of the History of John Marshall High School," courtesy of Demetriadis.
8. AHD (for "slum child" and Engleberg anecdote); "Little Marshallites Celebrate Big Event," *Monocle* (Nov. 14, 1930); "Marshallites Seen at Beaux Arts Ball," *Monocle* (May 6, 1932); "Members of Club Hear Writer of Juvenile Fiction," *Monocle* (Feb. 27, 1931); "*Flair Flair*"; Frances Reynolds, "John Treville LaTouche," *Record* (December 1956): 5 (for Beverly anecdote, and yet another story that resembles the Engleberg anecdote); "Who's Who Fray Returns Received for Publication," *Monocle* (Feb. 27, 1931); "Winners of Who's Who Contest Tell Reporter Interesting Facts," *Monocle* (Mar. 6, 1931); "Record Makers," *Record* (March 1931): 2 ("coterie"); "Miss Florence Rhea Talley Tells of Whereabouts of Class of '31," *Monocle* (Mar. 3, 1939).
9. Treville/Trevil La Touche [JL], "The Snoop," *Monocle* (Sep. 27, 1929); "Fragments," *Monocle* (Dec. 13, 1929; Feb. 28, 1930; Dec. 5, 1930; Mar. 27, 1931; May 1, 1931; Oct. 16, 1931; Nov. 6, 1931).
10. Treville/Trevil La Touche [JL], "Fragments," *Monocle* (Feb. 28, 1930; Oct. 3, 1930; Oct. 16, 1931; Oct. 30, 1931; Dec. 18, 1931; Apr. 8, 1932).
11. "Mr. Beverly Talks to J.M. Faculty on Chinese Thinker," *Monocle* (Dec. 19, 1930); Treiville (*sic*) La Touche [Walter F. Beverly], "Fragments," *Monocle* (Oct. 17, 1930; Dec. 4, 1931).
12. Trevil La Touche [JL], "My First Day at High School," *Record* (October 1928): 17–18; untitled ["I saw a wheel"], *Record* (April 1928): 23; "On Reading a 'Mystery' Story," "Friends" (March 1929): 28–30, 35; "Traffic Lights," *Record* (May 1929): 18; "The Lamp of Beauty: A Portrait of Ann Rutledge," [uncredited], "The End of the Song," *Record* (October 1930): 24–27, 34; "Supplication," "Chant Macabre," *Record* (November 1930): 15, 27–30; "The Tree . . . ," "Three Tales," *Record* (December 1930): 20, 29–34; "Record Makers" (for "Gothic"), "Return," *Record* (March 1931): 2, 21–25; "Postlude," "Paul and the Dragon," *Record* (May 1931): 5, 18–21; "Death and the Poet," "Where No Flame Burns," *Record* (October 1931): 7, 14–15; "Nocturne," "Image," "The Blind," "Baroque," *Record* (November 1931): 5, 22, 30, 33; "No Green On the Oak," "Variations on a Theme by Blake," *Record* (December 1931): 16–21, 32; "Folk Song," *Record* (March 1932): 29; "Two Nocturnes," *Record* (April 1932): 34–35; "Fragments," *Monocle* (April 17, 1931); copies of these poems and stories courtesy of the Library of Virginia, which holds only a few of these issues, and Shelia Demetriadis, John Marshall High School; four additional stories from the *Record* survive in ADP, only one of which has a date indicated: "Black Laughter: A Fragment Torn from the Life of a Negress," *Record* (April 1930): 8–11; "The Lamp and the Lama"; "Laughter"; "The River—An Allegory."
13. *Edgar Allan Poe Letters Till Now Unpublished In the Valentine Museum, Richmond, Virginia*, edited by Mary Newton Stanard (Philadelphia: Lippincott, 1925), JLP, remained one of the lyricist's few books preserved among his papers.
14. JL, "Three Tales," "Paul and the Dragon."
15. John Kellogg to JL, Dec. 14, 1930; Jan. 4, 1931; JL to Kellogg, undated from the same time period, Papers of John Latouche, University of Virginia.

16. Treville/Trevil La Touche [JL], "Market Scene," *Monocle* (Nov. 26, 1929); "Evening Comes to Seventeenth Street," *Black Swan* (April 1930): 19.
17. "Awards Given in Tournament Contests Here," *RTD* (Apr. 15, 1931); "Trevil La Touche Wins First Prize in Tournament," *Monocle* (Apr. 17, 1931); Treville La Touche [JL], "Strange Dusk," Archive of *Pagany*, University of Delaware, courtesy of Tim Murray; "Gorgos [*sic*] Medallion Given by Memorial Won by La Touche," *Monocle* (Feb. 13, 1931); "Two John Marshall Students Praised in Recent Contest," *Monocle* (May 8, 1931); *Younger Poets: An Anthology of American Secondary School Verse*, edited by Nellie B. Sergent (New York: Appleton, 1932), 83, 175, 312 (these poems included "The End of the Song," "The Tree . . . ," and a third poem, "Bribe").
18. JL, "Three Tales" ("wild berries"); "Paul and the Dragon" ("dragon"); "No Green on the Oak" ("pink-fat"); "Fragments," *Monocle* (Apr. 1, 1930) ("One smile"); "Traffic Lights"; "Fragments," *Monocle* (Oct. 30, 1931) ("Beauty"); Vernon Duke, "Tribute to a Poet," *Theatre Arts* 41 (March 1957): 26 (Duke miscited the poem as "Death of the Poet").
19. " 'Pearls,' One-Act Play to Be Given Next Week," *Monocle* (May 24, 1929); "Little Nell Given by Class of Drama," *Monocle* (Oct. 17, 1930); "High School Pupils Are Cast in French Comedy by Moliere," *Monocle* (Mar. 6, 1931); "John Marshall Is Victorious in Tournament," *Monocle* (Apr. 24, 1931); "Songs, Plays, and Debate on Program," *Monocle* (Jan. 9, 1932); *The Marshallite: Year Book of John Marshall High School* 22 (1932).
20. Carole Kass, "Children's Theater Has Come Very Far, Now Needs Funds," *RTD* (May 10, 1979), for Latouche's claimed participation in the founding of the company (Kass gives a founding date of 1927, the received wisdom, although the first production did not take place until the fall of 1928); "More Than 100 Will Take Part in Adventure Days Pageant Here," *RTD* (Apr. 17, 1930); "Historical Pageant to Feature Adventures Day Program Today," *RTD* (May 1, 1930); "Historical Pageant at Swan Island Witnessed by 5,000," *RTD* (May 2, 1930; the earliest of these three articles states that Latouche wrote the prologue, not the epilogue).
21. AHD; the Wigglesworth Players likely performed Bruce Morrissette's dramatization of Cabell's *Simon's Hour* staged by the Children's Theatre in 1929.
22. May Weston Tucker, "About Little Theatres," *RTD* (Jan. 24, 1932), for Goldoni; Mary Weston Tucker, "About Little Theatres," *RTD* (Feb. 28, 1932); Alice Lichtenstein, "Children's Players Close Season in Play 'The Golden Dwarf,' " *RTD* (Mar. 6, 1932).
23. "Class of Drama Brings to Close Year of Successful Production," *Monocle* (May 22, 1931); "Xmas in Ix Is Name of Senior Play," *Monocle* (Dec. 18, 1931); "Christmas in Ix," *Marshallite*, 284; JL, "Christmas in Ix," ADP.
24. Duke, 24.
25. Marie Keane Dabney, *Mrs. T. N. T.* (Richmond: Dietz, 1949); Lucy Dabney, interview with author, Apr. 16, 2013; Meredith Mackay-Smith, interview with author, Apr. 22, 2013.
26. Marie Keane Dabney, 124–25.
27. Lucy Dabney; Mackay-Smith; Annette Dabney Stone, "Democracy Preferred," *RTD* (Nov. 27, 1943); JL, Military Records, National Personnel Records Center, St. Louis (Latouche describes Stone as a "cousin," but Marie Dabney makes no mention of any such relationship).
28. JL to Lilian (alternate spelling) [Loehr], c. September 1931; JL to James Branch Cabell, c. summer 1931, MCP.
29. Pryor McN. Grant to James Branch Cabell, July 5, 1932; undated letters from JL to Cabell, MCP; Georgia Tucker, *Riverdale at 100: A Living History* (Riverdale, NY: Riverdale Country School, 2007).
30. Tucker; AHD; "Riverdale Students to Present Play," [Yonkers, NY] *Herald Statesman*, Mar. 8, 1933; undated letters from JL to James Branch Cabell, MCP.
31. AHD; Obed Stearns, "Sing a Song of America," *NYHT* (July 7, 1940).
32. Undated letters from JL to James Branch Cabell; Ruth L. Yorck to Cabell, Dec. 17, 1957, MCP; J. Treville Latouche [JL], "Pastiche," *Columbia Review* 16 (Nov. 1934): 34.
33. JL, transcript, Columbia University Archives.

34. Nora Lourie Percival, interview with author, Aug. 7, 2016; Nora Lourie Percival and Herman Gund, *Silver Pages on the Lawn: A True Story of Student Love During the 1930s* (Vilas, NC: Kent Hollow, 2005, 2006), 16–17, 77, 80; Karen Christel Krahulik, *Provincetown: From Pilgrim Landing to Gay Resort* (New York: New York University Press, 2005), 123–25.
35. Percival, 83–84, 95; Woodford, 250–51; "Art Association Ball," *Provincetown Advocate* (Aug. 16, 1934); "Artists Ball Held in Town Hall," *Provincetown Advocate* (Aug. 30, 1934), this article stating that Latouche went as a "Russian poet."
36. Lily Koppel, *The Red Leather Diary: Reclaiming a Life Through the Pages of a Lost Journal* (New York: HarperCollins, 2008), 233–47, 313.
37. JL, transcript; JL, "Fellowship Application Form," acknowledged Nov. 2, 1948, JL file, GMF; on this form, in which he gave his birth year as 1916, he contended that he did not complete college "due to illness"; Percival, 127, 375.
38. "Cocteau Will Advise Philolexian Play," *Columbia Daily Spectator* (Feb. 19, 1934).
39. Treville LaTouche [JL], "Gothic," "Admonition," *Columbia Review* 15 (November 1933): 21; "Four Sonnets for Mlle. M—A—," *Columbia Review* 15 (December 1933): 12–13; "The Gull," *Columbia Review* 15 (April 1934): 30–32; "Elegy Before Dying," *Columbia Review* 15 (May 1934): 29; "The Early Spear," *Columbia Review* 15 (May 1934): 17; "Two Variations from a Night Club Suite," *Columbia Review* 16 (November 1934): 17; "Legend for a Great City," *Columbia Review* 16 (May 1935): 13–14; "The End of the Song."
40. "Two Variations"; "Legend"; Lionel Trilling, "Trilling Says Authors Show Talent in Review's New Writers' Number," *Columbia Daily Spectator* (Mar. 20, 1935).
41. "Communications," *Columbia Daily Spectator* (Apr. 30, 1934; May 7, 1934; May 10, 1934); Treville Latouche [JL], "Art and the Artisan," part of a symposium, "Art and Propaganda," *Columbia Review* 15 (May 1934): 3–12.
42. Treville Latouche [JL], "Jeffers Among the Marxists," "The Old Gray Mare," "Ivory Tower with a View," *Columbia Review* 15 (May 1934): 8–12, 35–39; review of *Make It New*, *Columbia Review* 16 (May 1935): 43.
43. [J.] Treville Latouche [JL], "Pastiche," *Columbia Review* 16 (November 1934): 32–34; *Columbia Review* 16 (January 1935): 22–24; *Columbia Review* 16 (March 1935): 34–36; Trilling.
44. "*Flair Flair*."
45. E. M. Halliday, *John Berryman and the Thirties: A Memoir* (Amherst: University of Massachusetts Press, 1987), 35; Paul Mariani, *Dream Song: The Life of John Berryman* (New York: Morrow, 1990), 43; "Ex-Show Men Wainer and Latouche Help Write 'Sing for Your Supper,'" *Columbia Daily Spectator* (May 2, 1939).
46. "*Flair Flair*"; "1200 Expected to Attend Opening of Varsity Show at Astor Tonight," *Columbia Daily Spectator* (Mar. 12, 1935); Percival, 154; see also reviews of *Flair-Flair* in the *Post*, *NYHT*, *NYT*, and *World-Telegram* (all Mar. 13, 1935).
47. "*Flair Flair*"; Millicent Dillon, *A Little Original Sin: The Life and Work of Jane Bowles* (New York: Holt, Rinehart and Winston, 1981), 158; Kenward Elmslie, interview with author, Mar. 13, 2013.
48. "*Flair Flair*."
49. Robert Francis, "He Thinks It's Privilege to Be Murdered," *Brooklyn Daily Eagle* (Mar. 31, 1941), for Manulis; "*Flair Flair*," 20.
50. "Varsity Show Takes Premiere in Stride; Ponies Wiggle and Shake to Score Hit," *Columbia Daily Spectator* (Mar. 13, 1935); reviews of *Flair-Flair*.
51. Review of *Flair-Flair*, *NYHT*; "*Flair Flair*," 9.
52. "John Treville Latouche," *Current Biography: Who's News and Why: January–June 1940* (New York: H. W. Wilson, 1940), 481.

3. *The Boy Wonder of Broadway*

1. JL to Henry Moe, Mar. 2, 1949, GMF.
2. Vernon Duke, *Passport to Paris* (Boston: Little, Brown, 1955), 77–78.

3. Duke, 224, 249; for the Duke-Dukelsky issue, see, in addition to Duke, William W. Austin, *Music in the 20th Century from Debussy through Stravinsky* (New York: Norton, 1966), 384–85; and Alec Wilder, *American Popular Song: The Great Innovators, 1900–1950* (New York: Oxford University Press, 1972, 1990), 357; David Jenness and Don Velsey, *Classic American Popular Song: The Second Half-Century, 1950–2000* (New York: Routledge, 2006), 87.
4. Duke, 314–15.
5. *Maria Marten, or The Murder in the Red Barn*, edited by Montagu Slater (London: Howe, 1928).
6. Reviews of *Murder in the Old Red Barn* in the *American, NYHT, NYT,* and *Post* (all Feb. 3, 1936); *New Yorker* (Feb. 15, 1936); and *World-Telegram* (Apr. 25, 1936).
7. "Murder's Latest Outing," *NYT* (Jan. 26, 1936).
8. Robert P. Smith, "Whispering Galleries," *Columbia Daily Spectator* (Feb. 14, 1936); "Boy at Work," *Brooklyn Eagle* (Jan. 15, 1939); AHD.
9. AHD; Erik Haagensen, email to author, Sep. 2, 1913; Richard Lewine, taped interview with Haagensen, courtesy of Haagensen.
10. Haagensen.
11. *Pepper Mill*, clipping file, NYPL; JL, "Ballet Dancers Like Soda Pop," *Richmond News Leader* (Mar. 4, 1937); Luther Davis and John Cleveland, "And You Know Who I Am," *Collier's* 106 (Oct. 19, 1940): 80, 91; Duke, 321.
12. Duke, 297, 321.
13. Duke, 321–22; Davis, 80, 91.
14. Duke, 322; JL, "Ballet Dancers"; JL to Virgil Thomson, postmarked Mar. 17, 1937, VTP, indicates that Latouche had not been traveling with the company, suggesting that he met them in Richmond perhaps just for this engagement.
15. Helga Keiser-Hayne, *Erika Mann und ihr politisches Kabarett "Die Pfeffermühle," 1933–1937: Texte, Bilder, Hintergründe* (Hamburg: Rowohlt, 1995); Andrea Weiss, *In the Shadow of the Magic Mountain: The Erika and Klaus Mann Story* (Chicago: University of Chicago Press, 2008), 62; Frederic Spotts, *Cursed Legacy: The Tragic Life of Klaus Mann* (New Haven, CT: Yale University Press), 89–91; *Pepper Mill*, clipping file.
16. Keiser-Hayne, 188, 219 ("Und mein Vater droht, es setzt Hiebe, / Und die Mutter schickt mich davon: / Denn der Jüngling, welchen ich liebe, / Ist vom alten Levy des Sohn").
17. Paul Bowles, *Without Stopping: An Autobiography* (New York: Harper Perennial, 1972, 2006), 191.
18. Reviews of *Pepper Mill* in the *American, Brooklyn Eagle* (Arthur Pollock), *Daily News, Daily Mirror, Evening Journal* (John Anderson), *NYHT, NYT, Post* (John Mason Brown), *Sun, Women's Wear Daily,* and *World-Telegram* (all Jan. 6, 1937); *Variety* (Kauf., Jan. 13, 1937); *Billboard* (Eugene Burr, Jan. 16, 1937); *Modern Music* (Virgil Thomson) 14 (January–February 1937); and Keiser-Hayne, 190–91 (for a *Neue Volkszeitung* review, Jan. 9, 1937).
19. Arthur Pollock, "Welcome Strangers," *Brooklyn Eagle* (Jan. 10, 1937); Thomson, 102.
20. Erika and Klaus Mann, *Escape to Life* (Boston: Houghton Mifflin, 1939), 324.
21. Keiser-Hayne, 189.
22. Duke, 321.
23. "Night Club Notes," *NYT* (May 25, 1935); "Real Night Life at Spivy's Roof," *New York Life* (Aug. 10, 1941) ("Russian-born"); "You'd Never Think Her Song Career Began in Church," *Palm Beach Post* (Dec. 1, 1948); Frank Rasky, "Last of the Speakeasy Chanteuses," n.s. (c. 1948), ADP; George Chauncey, *Gay New York: Gender, Urban Culture, and the Making of the Gay Male World, 1890–1940* (New York: Basic Books, 1994), 349; T.S. [Theodore Strauss], "News of Night Clubs," *NYT* (Nov. 19, 1939) ("première"); Frederick Kiesler, *Inside the Endless House: Art, People and Architecture: A Journal* (New York: Simon & Schuster, 1964), 86; Spivy's birth year is sometimes given as 1907.
24. Strauss; James Gavin, *Intimate Nights: The Golden Age of New York Cabaret* (New York: Grove Weidenfeld, 1991), 37.

25. “Real Night Life”; Irving Drutman, *Good Company: A Memoir, Mostly Theatrical* (Boston: Little, Brown, 1976), 208–11; Gavin, 38–46; “Spivy, 64, Actress and Entertainer,” *NYT* (Jan. 10, 1971).
26. JLD, Jan. 23, 1938; [Jan. 27], 1938; JL to Spivy LeVoe, postmarked Sep. 26, 1938, ADP; Rasky.
27. JL, “I’m Going on a Binge with a Dinge,” ADP; AHD.
28. JL, “Clair de Lune,” ADP; *One Hundred and One Poems by Paul Verlaine: A Bilingual Edition*, translated by Norman R. Shapiro (Chicago: University of Chicago Press, 1999), 28–29 (“Votre âme est un paysage choisi / Que vont charmant masques et bergamasques / Jouant du luth et dansant et quasi / Tristes sous leurs déguisements fantasques”).
29. JL to Spivy LeVoe, postmarked Sep. 8, 1937, ADP.
30. Discrepancies exist between the recorded and written versions of these songs, as found in ADP; Spivy, for instance, sings “sex à la Dali,” not “love à la Dali.”
31. John Bernard Myers, *Tracking the Marvelous: A Life in the New York Art World* (New York: Random House, 1981, 1983), 75–77.
32. Gavin, 25–31; JLD, [Feb. 5], 1938.
33. Jack Gould, “News and Gossip of the Night Clubs,” *NYT* (Mar. 6, 1938); Theodore Strauss, “News Notes of the Night Clubs,” *NYT* (May 14, 1939).
34. JL, “Simeon Babbit” (*sic*), ADP (the lyric differs in some details from Emerson’s recording).
35. Tony Buttitta and Barry Witham, *Uncle Sam Presents: A Memoir of the Federal Theatre, 1935–1939* (Philadelphia: University of Pennsylvania Press, 1982); Ned Lehac, “The Story of *Sing for Your Supper*: The Broadway Revue Produced by the Federal Theatre Project,” in *Musical Theatre in America: Papers and Proceedings of the Conference on the Musical Theatre in America*, edited by Glenn Loney (Westport, CT: Greenwood, 1984), 189.
36. JLD, Jan. 22, 1938.
37. JLD, [Jan. 29], 1938.
38. Eric Winship Trumbull, “Original Musicals of the Federal Theatre Project: Relief, Relevance, and Regionalism” (MA thesis, University of Maryland, 1983), 43–48 (Trumbull, apparently unaware of the December *Melodies on Parade*, presumes that the August 1938 *Melodies on Parade* used the extant Latouche script); “WPA Theatre Announces Plans for Sepia Actors,” *Amsterdam News* (July 9, 1938); “WPA Theatre Studies New Negro Scripts,” *Amsterdam News* (July 16, 1938); Hallie Flanagan, *Arena: The History of the Federal Theatre* (New York: Blom, 1940, 1965), 391; “Free Plays Offered Tonight,” *NYT* (July 24, 1937); “WPA Actors Give Old West Musical,” *Brooklyn Eagle* (Dec. 11, 1938).
39. “WPA Caravan Programs Tonight,” *NYT* (Aug. 19, 1938); “WPA Actors.”
40. John Latouche, *Melodies on Parade*, FTP Records, George Mason University and LC; some other materials catalogued under *Melodies on Parade* survive in FTP Records, including a few set designs and stills, and several arrangements for pit band; the photographs, which show an interracial cast in Gay Nineties costumes against Paul Ouzounoff’s designs, date from July 1937, so plainly depict the first of the two Caravan productions—the *Melodies on Parade* with which Latouche apparently had no involvement; the existing musicals scores similarly seem to belong, at least largely, to that earlier *Melodies on Parade*.
41. Trumbull; John A. Lomax and Alan Lomax, *American Ballads and Folk Songs* (New York: Macmillan, 1934).
42. JL, *Melodies*, I-5, I-9-11.
43. David Alan Rush, “A History and Evaluation of the ILGWU Labor Stage and Its Production of ‘Pins and Needles,’ 1937–1940” (MA thesis, University of Iowa, 1965); Trudi Ann Wright, “Labor Takes the Stage: A Musical and Social Analysis of ‘Pins and Needles’ (1937–1941)” (PhD diss., University of Colorado, 2010).
44. Rush; Wright; see also Michael Denning, *The Cultural Front: The Laboring of American Culture in the Twentieth Century* (New York: Verso, 1996); Ilka Saal, *New Deal Theater: The Vernacular Tradition in American Political Theater* (New York: Palgrave Macmillan, 2007); and Daniel Katz, *All Together Different: Yiddish Socialists, Garment Workers, and the Labor Roots of Multiculturalism* (New York: New York University Press, 2011).

45. "Two More Leave Federal Theatre," *Journal-American* (May 25, 1938); Seymour Bernstein, *Monsters and Angels: Surviving a Career in Music* (Milwaukee, WI: Leonard, 2002), 394.
46. "Boy at Work"; "J. P. D. Treville LaTouche Sings Songs of Social Significance," *Post* (Feb. 25, 1939); *Pins and Needles*, clipping file.
47. Rush, 69, 70; Katz, 225; *Pins and Needles*, clipping file, EHP; "Add Five New Numbers to 'Pins and Needles,'" *Workers Age* (Mar. 8, 1939).
48. "Boy at Work"; "J. P. D."; *Pins and Needles*, clipping files, NYPL and EHP.

4. The Little Friends

1. Virgil Thomson, *Virgil Thomson* (New York: Da Capo, 1966, 1977), 280.
2. Paul Bowles, *Without Stopping: An Autobiography* (New York: Harper Perennial, 1972, 2006); Christopher Sawyer-Lauçanno, *An Invisible Spectator: A Biography of Paul Bowles* (New York: Weidenfeld & Nicolson, 1989), 234; Norman Mailer, *Advertisements for Myself* (New York: Putnam, 1959), 468; see also Gena Dagel Caponi, *Paul Bowles: Romantic Savage* (Carbondale: Southern Illinois University Press, 1994); and Virginia Spencer Carr, *Paul Bowles: A Life* (Evanston, IL: Northwestern University Press, 2004, 2009).
3. Bowles, 169.
4. Thomson, 280.
5. Bowles, 191.
6. Thomson, 206; Sawyer-Lauçanno, 124; Langston Hughes, *I Wonder As I Wander* (New York: Hill and Wang, 1956), 333.
7. Thomson, 264; JL to Virgil Thomson, postmarked Aug. 22, 1936, VTP; JLD, Jan. 22, 1938; Ned Lehac, "The Story of *Sing for Your Supper*: The Broadway Revue Produced by the Federal Theatre Project," in *Musical Theatre in America: Papers and Proceedings of the Conference on the Musical Theatre in America*, edited by Glenn Loney (Westport, CT: Greenwood, 1984), 189; Bowles, 191, 213 ("cheap," "nomadic").
8. Martin Duberman, *The Worlds of Lincoln Kirstein* (New York: Knopf, 2007), 227–28, 650 n. 5; JLD, Jan. 23, 1938; Caponi, 58.
9. *In Touch: The Letters of Paul Bowles*, edited by Jeffrey Miller (New York: Farrar, Straus and Giroux), 89; Bowles, 191; Sawyer-Lauçanno, 136 (for Staten Island); *Out in the World: Selected Letters of Jane Bowles, 1935–1970*, edited by Millicent Dillon (Santa Barbara, CA: Black Sparrow, 1985), 45, 51; JLD, Jan. 22, 1938.
10. *In Touch*, 269; Kenneth Lisenbee, email to author, May 29, 2015; Millicent Dillon, *You Are Not I: A Portrait of Paul Bowles* (Berkeley: University of California Press, 1998), 221.
11. Harry Dunham to Virgil Thomson, Feb. 19, 1937, VTP; JLD, Jan. 23, 1938.
12. JLD, Nov. 12–27, 1943; JL to Marian Chase Dunham, c. November 1943; c. December 1943, JLP.
13. Bowles, 187–88, 215–16, 222–23.
14. Wallace S. Wharton to George Burton, stamped May 19, 1944; SAC to Director, Apr. 19, 1954, FBI; JL, affidavits, Jan. 27, 1956, and May 18, 1956, FBI.
15. Earl Robinson, "Balladier for Americans," *Nation* (Aug. 25, 1956), 161; Fred Kaplan, *Gore Vidal: A Biography* (New York: Doubleday, 1999), 376; Kenward Elmslie, interview with author, Mar. 13, 2013; Bowles, 230, 340; Max Jacobson and JL, "To Range from Preventive Illnesses to Concentration Camp Psychology," May 2, 1949, JLL.
16. Jimmy Ernst, *A Not-So-Still Life: A Memoir* (New York: St. Martin's Press, 1984), 178 (at least as reported here, Kiesler used the term "little people"); JL to Virgil Thomson, postmarked Mar. 19, 1937, VTP.
17. Millicent Dillon, *A Little Original Sin: The Life and Work of Jane Bowles* (New York: Holt, Rinehart and Winston, 1981), 32, 82; John Wakeman, editor, *World Authors 1950–1970* (New York: Wilson, 1975), 203; AHD; John Bernard Myers, *Tracking the Marvelous: A Life in the New York Art World* (New York: Random House, 1981, 1983), 75; the drinking habits

of both Jane Bowles and Latouche have suggested to commentators alcohol addiction, but for denials of alcoholism, see for Bowles, Dillon, 115, and for Latouche, Elmslie.

18. Bowles, 196; Suzanne Robinson, email to author, Oct. 9, 2016; Dillon, 63.
19. JLD, [Jan. 29], 1938.
20. Dillon, 104, 113, 275; Sawyer-Lauçanno, 223; Jane Bowles to Virgil Thomson, October (?) 1941, VTP; *My Sister's Hand in Mine: The Collected Works of Jane Bowles* (New York: Farrar, Straus and Giroux, 1966, 2005), 16, 18; Carr, 164; AHD.
21. JLD, Jan. 23, 1938; Dec. 21, 1945 (for Gertrude as a "communist"); for conflicting claims concerning Chase's sexual orientation, see Carr, 136, and Anthony Tommasini, *Virgil Thomson: Composer on the Aisle* (New York: Norton, 1997), 293; Virgil Thomson to Marian Chase, July 16, 1938; Thomson, 280.
22. The Latouches apparently divorced in 1945, although some sources say 1946.
23. Stanton Griffis, *Lying in State* (Garden City, NY: Doubleday, 1952).
24. JLD, [Feb. 5], 1938; [Feb. 6], 1938.
25. Patricia Highsmith, diaries, July 2, 1942, Swiss National Library, Bern, Switzerland.
26. JL to Harry Martin, c. 1953, JLP.
27. "Mrs. Latouche, Ex-Envoy's Kin," *NYHT* (Jan. 30, 1956); "Seaport Given $50,000," *Hartford Courant* (Feb. 16, 1956); "Memorial Plaque Dedicated," *New Canaan Advertiser* (May 23, 1957); Ruth Landshoff-Yorck, *Klatsch, Ruhm und kleine Feuer: Biographische Impressionen* (Berlin: Kiepenheuer & Witsch, 1963), 129–31; Hughes Griffis, interview with author, June 11, 2013; [Theodora Latouche to Effie Latouche], c. 1941, JLP; Stanton Griffis to Theodora Latouche, Nov. 18, 1955, Stanton Griffis Papers, Harry S. Truman Library.
28. Virgil Thomson, 280; Virgil Thomson to Marian Chase, Jan. 26, 1939; June 29, 1939, VTP.
29. JLD, Feb. 12, 1945; JL to Virgil Thomson, 1946 (?), VTP.
30. JLD, Jan. 23, 1938; [Feb. 6], 1938; JL, 1941 bankbook, Leo Lerman Papers, Columbia University; Virgil Thomson to Paul Bowles, Oct. 30, 1941, VTP; Thomson, 280; Bowles, 191.
31. Bowles, 222.
32. AHD; Aaron Copland and Vivian Perlis, *Copland: 1900 Through 1942* (Boston: Faber and Faber, 1984), 258.
33. JLD, [Feb. 5], 1938; [Feb. 6], 1938.
34. For some information regarding Latouche's art collection, see JLL.
35. Gerry Max, *Horizon Chasers: The Lives and Adventures of Richard Halliburton and Paul Mooney* (Jefferson, NC: McFarland, 2007), 59; Gerry Max, *Many Mansions* (manuscript, 1999), courtesy of Craig Holmes (which includes a facsimile of a letter from JL to William Alexander dated Apr. 29, 1942).
36. JL to Virgil Thomson, postmarked Aug. 22, 1938, VTP ("charming," "beautiful"); JLD, Jan. 22, 1938 ("pretty," "extremely," "red-headed"); [Feb. 6], 1938 ("fine"); the Brook painting is at the Butler Institute of American Art; the Tchelitchew painting, at the Museum of the City of New York; the Johnson painting, in a private collection; the Van Vechten photographs, at Yale University; the Burckhardt photographs, in JLL.
37. "Design's Bad Boy," *Architectural Forum* 86 (February 1947): 88–91, 138, 140; Lisa Phillips et al., *Frederick Kiesler* (New York: Whitney Museum of American Art, 1989), 13, 21; Michael Kimmelman, "An Architect's Dreams and What He Built," *NYT* (Jan. 27, 1989); Hans Richter, *Encounters from Dada till Today*, translated by Christopher Middleton (New York: Prestel, 2013), 84–87; Myers, 46.
38. Frederick Kiesler, *Inside the Endless House: Art, People and Architecture: A Journal* (New York: Simon & Schuster, 1964, 1966), 46–54.
39. Treville Latouche, "Pastiche," *Columbia Review* 16 (January 1935): 24; JL [to Stefanie Kiesler], c. November 1943, AFL.
40. Stefanie Kiesler, diaries, AFL; Frederick Kiesler, designs and sketches, AFL; Kiesler, 46–54.
41. Richter, 85; untitled and unattributed obituary for Stefanie Kiesler, AFL.
42. JLD, [Jan. 29], 1938.

43. John Houseman, *Run-Through: A Memoir* (New York: Simon & Schuster, 1972), 97–99; Steven Watson, *Prepare for Saints: Gertrude Stein, Virgil Thomson and the Mainstreaming of American Modernism* (Berkeley: University of California Press, 1998, 2000), 189.
44. Bowles, 220; Dillon, 35; JLD, Jan. 22, 1938.
45. Houseman, 98; Jack Gould, "News of the Night Clubs," *NYT* (Dec. 5, 1937).

5. *Ballads for Americans*

1. Malcolm Goldstein, *The Political Stage: American Drama and Theater of the Great Depression* (New York: Oxford University Press, 1974); Michael L. Greenwald, "Actors as Activists: The Theatre Arts Committee Cabaret, 1938–1941," *Theatre Research International* 20 (Spring 1995): 19–29.
2. Theodore Strauss, "News of Night Clubs," *NYT* (Nov. 27, 1938); "John Henry Hammond, Jr.," *TAC* 1 (January 1939): 3; John Latouche, "New Year's Resolutions," *TAC* 1 (January 1939): 8–9; John Latouche, "Books," *TAC* 1 (February 1939): 22.
3. "4th Cabaret TAC Show Tomorrow," *Daily Mirror* (Feb. 11, 1939).
4. "The Political Cabarets," *TAC* 1 (May 1939): 17; David Koenig, *Danny Kaye: King of Jesters* (Irvine, CA: Bonaventure, 2012), 38–41.
5. *Pins and Needles* advertisement, *TAC* 1 (Feb. 1939): 29; "Tattooed Lady" possibly had some connection to the Lewine-Latouche song, "I've Got Designs on the Tattooed Lady," discussed earlier.
6. Abel Gorham, "Wit, Song, Dance at 'Variety Night,'" *Daily Worker* (Mar. 7, 1939); Koenig, 40; review of *Sunday Night Varieties* in *Variety* (Apr. 12, 1939).
7. Reviews of *Two for Tonight* in the *Daily Mirror* and *Post* (both Dec. 29, 1939); *Village Bugle* (Jan. 4, 1940); *Billboard* (Jan. 13, 1940); and *Two for Tonight*, clipping file, NYPL; "Stage News," *Brooklyn Daily Eagle* (Nov. 27, 1939).
8. Michel Mok, "When Viennese Meets Viennese in Exile, They Turn Their Experience into a Revue," *Post* (June 14, 1939); "And Now 'From Vienna,'" *NYT* (June 18, 1939); Brooks Atkinson, "Sanctuary for the Free," *NYT* (July 2, 1939); "Musical Shows Make Broadway Hit," *Life* (July 17, 1939).
9. *The Legacy of Jura Soyfer, 1912–1939: Poems, Prose and Plays of an Austrian Antifascist*, edited and translated by Horst Jarka (Montreal: Engendra, 1977); Horst Jarka, "Jura Soyfer and the United States," in *Jura Soyfer and His Time*, edited by Donald G. Daviau (Riverside, CA: Ariadne, 1995), 22–49.
10. Jarka, "Jura."
11. Jarka, *The Legacy*; see also *Eddie Lechner's Trip to Paradise*, translated by Jarka, in *Modern International Drama* 4/2 (1971): 59–78; and "Trip to Paradise" in *"It's Up to Us!": Collected Works of Jura Soyfer*, edited, translated, and with an afterword by Horst Jarka (Riverside, CA: Ariadne, 1996), 123–66.
12. John Latouche, *Journey to Paradise*, Copyright Drama Deposits, LC; Jarka, *Legacy* ("it's all," p. 263; in *"It's Up to Us!"* Jarka translates the last phrase, "auf uns kommt's an," as "that's up to us," p. 166); Jarka, "Jura," 32–34.
13. Reviews of *From Vienna* in the *Brooklyn Eagle, Daily Mirror, Daily News, Journal-American, NYHT, NYT, Post, Sun,* and *World-Telegram* (all June 21, 1939); *Daily Worker* and *Wall Street Journal* (both June 22, 1939); *Variety* (June 28, 1939); *Billboard* (July 1, 1939); and *Nation* (July 22, 1939); Cecil Smith, *Musical Comedy in America* (New York: Theatre Arts, 1950), 293.
14. Jarka, "Jura," 33; reviews of *From Vienna.*
15. Brooks Atkinson, "'Reunion in New York' Is the Second Revue by the Kleinkunstbuehne from Vienna," *NYT* (Feb. 22, 1940); Jarka, "Jura," 46 n. 22, learned from André Singer that he accompanied Stella Adler on a performance of Latouche's "Moritat in Paradies" at the White House on President Roosevelt's birthday in either 1939 or 1940; if so, the date probably would have been Jan. 30, 1940.

16. "Satire on the WPA Backfires on Cast," *NYT* (Oct. 9, 1938); "A Revue That Was Made to Order," *Sun* (June 12, 1939); John O'Connor and Lorraine Brown, *Free, Adult, Uncensored: The Living History of the Federal Theatre Project* (Washington, DC: New Republic Books, 1978); Tony Buttitta and Barry Witham, *Uncle Sam Presents: A Memoir of the Federal Theatre, 1935–1939* (Philadelphia: University of Pennsylvania Press, 1982); Ned Lehac, "The Story of Sing for Your Supper: The Broadway Revue Produced by the Federal Theatre Project," in *Musical Theatre in America: Papers and Proceedings of the Conference on the Musical Theatre in America*, edited by Glenn Loney (Westport, CT: Greenwood, 1984), 187–97.
17. Most contemporary sources refer to this work as the "Ballad of Uncle Sam," a title that also turns up among the show's early source materials; but the Federal Theatre program used the phrase "Ballade," rather than "Ballad."
18. "It's Going to Cause a Little Confusion," *Brooklyn Eagle* (Dec. 11, 1938).
19. *Sing for Your Supper*, three scripts, Federal Theatre Project Records (George Mason University and LC).
20. "Legitimate," two pages of score, KEP.
21. Sidney B. Whipple, "Federal Theater Revue Is Opened at Last," *World-Telegram* (Apr. 25, 1939); in an earlier version, "Perspiration" concluded with composer Schnook making a call to one of the Shubert brothers with an idea for an elaborate revue with "forty-four scenes—a hundred chorus girls—big orchestra."
22. Earl Robinson with Eric A. Gordon, *Ballad of an American: The Autobiography of Earl Robinson* (Lanham, MD: Scarecrow, 1998).
23. Robinson, 76.
24. Drafts of *Ballad for Americans*, ERP.
25. JL, "Preface," *Ballad for Americans: A Modern Narrative* (New York: Robbins, 1940).
26. Buttitta, 193, recalls, "Latouche rewrote verses, got them approved or rejected by [Harold] Hecht, and passed them on to Robinson to fit them to his music."
27. Douglas Gilbert, "An American Song, at Last, Without Moon and June," *World-Telegram* (Apr. 19, 1940); JL, "Preface."
28. Reviews of *Sing for Your Supper* in the *Brooklyn Eagle, Daily News, Journal-American, NYHT* ("clumsy"), *NYT, Daily Mirror* ("dull"), *Women's Wear Daily*, and *World-Telegram* (all Apr. 25, 1939); *Wall Street Journal* and *Variety* (both Apr. 26, 1939); *Billboard* and *New Yorker* (both May 6, 1939); *Daily Worker* and *Newsweek* (both May 8, 1939); *Catholic World* 149 (June 1939): 345–46 ("raucous," "stirring"); and *Theatre Arts* 23 (June 1939): 404; descriptions of one sketch that appears to have been cut in the course of the run, Charlotte Kent's "We Didn't Know It Was Loaded," apparently adapted ideas from Jura Soyfer's *Der Lechner-Edi*, recently translated by Latouche.
29. Reviews of *Sing for Your Supper*; Hallie Flanagan, *Arena* (New York: Limelight, 1940); "'Sing for Your Supper' New WPA Box Office Hit," *Daily Worker* (May 19, 1939).
30. C. P. Trussell, "Fight Forecast on Proposal to Make Over WPA," *Sun* (June 15, 1939); Buttitta, 227; Lehac, 194.
31. "Robeson 'Hot' over the Air," *Pittsburgh Courier* (Nov. 11, 1939); Robinson, *Ballad*, 78, 95.
32. "Bravos," *Time* (Nov. 20, 1939): 56; "Robeson Is Lauded for Broadcast," *Chicago Defender* (Dec. 2, 1939); Louis Reid, "The Song That Stirred a Nation," *Sun* (July 13, 1940); Michelle A. Stephens, "'I'm the Everybody Who's Nobody': Genealogies of the New World Slave in Paul Robeson's Performances of the 1930s," in *Hemispheric American Studies*, edited by Caroline F. Levander and Robert S. Levine (New Brunswick, NJ: Rutgers University Press, 2008), 166–86.
33. Russell Sanjek, updated by David Sanjek, *Pennies from Heaven: The American Popular Music Business in the Twentieth Century* (New York: Da Capo, 1996); Vernon Duke, *Passport to Paris* (Boston: Little, Brown, 1955), 380–81, 384; an example of Robbins's oversight can be found in dictated comments made over the telephone on Feb. 21, 1949, preserved in *The Littlest Revue* file, VDP.

34. Howard Taubman, "American Music Heard in Stadium," *NYT* (June 26, 1940); "Robeson Soloist at the Stadium," *NYT* (July 12, 1942); Howard Taubman, "20,000 at Stadium Hear Robeson Sing," *NYT* (July 2, 1943); "Ovation for Paul Robeson," *Amsterdam News* (Oct. 12, 1940); Isabel Morse Jones, "Outstanding Bowl Event Lures 23,000," *Los Angeles Times* (July 24, 1940); Clarence Muse, "What's Going On in Hollywood," *Chicago Defender* (Aug. 3, 1940).
35. Earl Robinson to John Latouche, Nov. 21, 1941; Robinson to George H. Gartlan, Nov. 5, 1942; Jan. 24, 1942, ERP.
36. "First Day of Republican Convention Ends in Climax of Keynote Address," *NYT* (June 25, 1940); Eleanor Roosevelt, "My Day," *World-Telegram* (Apr. 22, 1942); "Ballad for Republicans," *New Yorker* (June 29, 1940); JL to Jerome and Hazel Moross, July 19, 1940, EHP.
37. Earl Robinson to Abraham Olman, Feb. 6, 1941, ERP; Howard Pollack, *Marc Blitzstein: His Life, His Work, His World* (New York: Oxford, 2012), 265–66; for reviews and other information about the U.S. Army Negro Chorus, see *I Can Tell The World 1943–1944*, edited by Alexander B. Jordan ([Ipswich, Suffolk?] U.S. Army Negro Chorus, 1944).
38. *I Can Tell*, 68-69; Robinson, *Ballad*, 67–68.
39. Bill Gottlieb, "Swing Sessions," *Washington Post* (Apr. 7, 1940); Archibald MacLeish to JL, July 31, 1940, Music Division Old Correspondence Collection, LC; Nat Hentoff, "An Appreciation," in *Paul Robeson: Scandalize My Name* (Classic Record Library, 30–5647, 1976); *The Rosenberg Letters: A Complete Edition of the Prison Correspondence of Julius and Ethel Rosenberg*, edited by Michael Meeropol (New York: Garland, 1994), 157.
40. Hillen Dale, "Broadway Tackle," *TAC* 2 (Mar. 15, 1940): 6; JL to Effie Latouche, Feb. 13, 1940, JLP; Jeffrey Spivak, *Buzz: The Life and Art of Busby Berkeley* (Lexington: University Press of Kentucky, 2010), 188–89; Robinson, 96; reviews of *Born to Sing* in *Variety* (Jan. 21, 1942); *Christian Science Monitor* (Apr. 2, 1942); and *Baltimore Sun* (Apr. 13, 1942).
41. JL, "Preface," 4.
42. Robinson, 280, 419; Faith Petric, "The Folk Process," *Sing Out!* 49 (Summer 2005): 82.
43. James Agee, "Pseudo-Folk," *Partisan Review* 11 (June 1944): 219–23; Robert Warshow, *The Immediate Experience: Movies, Comics, Theatre & Other Aspects of Popular Culture* (Cambridge, MA: Harvard University Press, 2001), 3–18, 47; Kevin Jack Hagopian, "'You Know Who I Am!': Paul Robeson's *Ballad for Americans* and the Paradox of the Double V in American Popular Front Culture," in *Paul Robeson: Essays on His Life and Legacy*, edited by Joseph Dorinson and William Pencak (Jefferson, NC: McFarland, 2002), 172; Annegret Fauser, *Sounds of War: Music in the United States during World War II* (New York: Oxford University Press, 2013), 240.
44. Michael Denning, *The Cultural Front: The Laboring of American Culture in the Twentieth Century* (New York: Verso, 1996), 135–36; Robert Cantwell, *When We Were Good: The Folk Revival* (Cambridge, MA: Harvard University Press, 1996); Lisa Barg, "Paul Robeson's *Ballad for Americans*: Race and the Cultural Politics of 'People's Music,'" *Journal of the Society for American Music* 2 (February 2008): 27–70; Stephens.
45. H. R. Hays, "Introduction," in Bertolt Brecht, *Selected Poems* (New York: Grove, 1947), 6.
46. Jimmy Ernst, *A Not-So-Still Life* (New York: St. Martin's, 1984), 179.

6. New Friends

1. Luther Davis and John Cleveland, "And You Know Who I Am," *Collier's* 106 (Oct. 19, 1940): 80.
2. *In Touch: The Letters of Paul Bowles*, edited by Jeffrey Miller (New York: Farrar, Straus and Giroux, 1994), 326; Ned Rorem, *Knowing When to Stop: A Memoir* (New York: Simon & Schuster, 1994), 150, 484; JL to Effie Latouche, Feb. 13, 1940, JLP; Jimmy Ernst, *A Not-So-Still Life* (New York: St. Martin's, 1984), 192.
3. "John Treville Latouche," *Current Biography: Who's News and Why: January–June 1940* (New York: H. W. Wilson, 1940), 481; Ruth Landshoff-Yorck, *Klatsch, Ruhm und kleine Feuer: Biographische Impressionen* (Berlin: Kiepenheuer & Witsch, 1963), 129–30; JL to Virgil Thomson, Feb. 13, 1940, VTP; JLD, [Feb. 5], 1938.

4. John W. Scott, *Natalie Scott: A Magnificent Life* (Gretna, LA: Pelican, 2008), 327–28; JL to Virgil Thomson, n.d., VTP.
5. Dorothy Kilgallen, "Broadway," [Mansfield, OH] *News-Journal* (Oct. 13, 1941); Theodora Latouche to Effie Latouche, c. 1941, JLP.
6. Ernst, 176–77.
7. Ernst, 192–93.
8. Sherill Tippins, *February House* (Boston: Houghton Mifflin, 2005); Oliver Smith, who eventually took over Golo Mann's attic apartment, also left for Mexico for a period, but then, unlike the Bowleses, returned to Middagh Street.
9. Tippins, 183; *Letters from a Life: The Selected Letters and Diaries of Benjamin Britten, 1913–1976*, vol. 1, edited by Donald Mitchell (Berkeley: University of California Press, 1991), 198.
10. Carson McCullers, *The Heart Is a Lonely Hunter* (Boston: Houghton Mifflin Harcourt, 1940), 23, 158; "Latouche Tribute Given at Funeral," *NYT* (Aug. 10, 1956); Carson McCullers, "John Latouche—An Eulogy," LKP; JL to Virgil Thomson, c. 1946, VTP.
11. Rorem, 425; John Geiger, *Nothing Is True, Everything Is Permitted: The Life of Brion Gysin* (St. Paul, MN: Disinformation, 2005), 55, 73; John Kruth, "Soprano Saxophonist Steve Lacy Recalls the "Multifarious' Brion Gysin," *DooBeeDooBeeDoo NY*, http://www.doobeedoobeedoo.info/2010/05/21/soprano-saxophonist-steve-lacy-recalls-the-%E2%80%9Cmultifarious%E2%80%9D-brion-gysin/.
12. Geiger, 56; Ted Morgan, *Literary Outlaw: The Life and Times of William S. Burroughs* (New York: Holt, 1988), 64; "William S. Burroughs interview on Brion Gysin" (June 13, 2011): briongysin.com/?p=994.
13. Geiger, 56–57; Barry Miles, *The Beat Hotel: Ginsberg, Burroughs, and Corso in Paris, 1958–1963* (New York: Grove, 2000), 151.
14. Geiger, 55; Carol Channing, *Just Lucky I Guess: A Memoir of Sorts* (New York: Simon & Schuster, 2002), 74.
15. Brion Gysin, interviewed by Terry Wilson, *Here to Go: Planet R-101* (San Francisco: Re/Search Publications, 1982), 4–9, 12–13; as an example of the unreliable nature of Gysin's recollections, he named the astrologer at Latouche's party as Evangeline Adams, who died in 1932.
16. Gysin, 11–12; Eileen Garrett, *Many Voices: The Autobiography of a Medium* (New York: Putnam's, 1968), 147–48.
17. Bessie Mona Lasky, *Candle in the Sun* (Los Angeles: DeVorss, 1957), 100–101; JLD, June 20, 1944.
18. Michael Morris, *Madam Valentino: The Many Lives of Natacha Rambova* (New York: Abbeville, 1991); James H. Smith and Natacha Rambova, *Technique for Living* (New York: Essential Books, 1944); Andrew Drummond, notes, Jan. 7, 1976, ADP; JLD, Aug. 16, 1943.
19. *The Grand Surprise: The Journals of Leo Lerman*, edited by Stephen Pascal (New York: Knopf, 2007), xiii; Trip Gabriel, "Leo Lerman Remembered for Buoyant Style, Wit and Elegance," *NYT* (Nov. 8, 1994).
20. *Grand Surprise*, 3, 7, 15, 16, 213; JLD, Dec. 3, 1944; Frederick Kiesler, *Inside the Endless House: Art, People and Architecture: A Journal* (New York: Simon & Schuster, 1964, 1966), 53.
21. Yorck; Thomas Blubacher, *Die vielen Leben der Ruth Landshoff-Yorck* (Berlin: Insel, 2015), 9; "Wenn Sie wüssten: Ruth Landshoff-Yorck," *Spiegel* (Sep. 25, 1963); Steven Bach, *Marlene Dietrich: Life and Legend* (New York: Morrow, 1992), 7–8.
22. "Ruth Yorck, Wrote Novels and Plays," *NYT* (Jan. 20, 1966); Diana Mantel, "Carnival and Carnivorous Plants: Gender and Humor in the Works of Ruth Landshoff-Yorck," *Gender Forum: An Internet Journal for Gender Studies* 35 (2011); John Gruen, *The New Bohemia: The Combine Generation* (New York: Shorecrest, 1966), 169; Christian Schröder, "Germany's First It Girl," *Handelsblatt* (Sep. 16, 2015); for more on Ruth Yorck's writings, see Blubacher, and Diana Mantel, *Ruth Landshoff-Yorck—Schreibende Persephone zwischen Berliner Boheme und New Yorker Underground: Analysen zum Gesamtwerk* (New York: Peter Lang, 2015).

23. *Grand Surprise*, 279–81; Gruen, 169.
24. Davis, 91; Stefanie Kielser, diaries, AFL; *Grand Surprise*, 213; this check register survives in the John Latouche folder in the Leo Lerman Papers, Columbia University; AHD.
25. JLD, Aug. 17, 1943; Feb. 12, 1944; JL to Henry G. Koppell, received Aug. 27, 1945, RYP.
26. Ruth Yorck, "The Sinister Doodles of John Latouche," n.d., RYP; Yorck, *Klatsch*, 122–38 ("Er war mir der beste amerikanische Freund, aber das kann man eigentlich gar nicht sagen, denn er war auch europäisch, wie es sonst nur Thornton Wilder ist," 122; "Er war eine Freude!" 122).
27. Salka Viertel, *The Kindness of Strangers* (New York: Holt, Rinehart and Winston, 1969), 113, 116; Thomas Blubacher, *"Gibt es etwas Schöneres als Sehnsucht?": Die Geschwister Eleonora und Francesco von Mendelssohn* ([Berlin]: Henschel, 2008); Thomas Blubacher, "Eleonora and Francesco von Mendelssohn," in Melissa Müller and Monika Tatzkow, *Lost Lives, Lost Art: Jewish Collectors, Nazi Art Theft, and the Quest for Justice* (New York: Vendome, 2010), 72–85; "Miss Mendelssohn Found Dead in Bed," *NYT* (Jan. 25, 1951); *Grand Surprise*, 328; Gottfried Reinhardt, *The Genius: A Memoir of Max Reinhardt* (New York: Knopf, 1979), 14.
28. Reinhardt, 13–14; *Grand Surprise*, 5–6; Blubacher, "Eleonora," 83; for original, see Elisabeth Bergner, *Bewundert viel und viel gescholten... Elisabeth Bergners unordentliche Erinnerungen* (Munich: Bertelsmann, 1978), 252 ("der schönste, edelste, vielbegabteste, vielgeliebteste, unglücklichste Mensch, dem ich je begegnet war").
29. *Grand Surprise*, 3, 7, 98; Blubacher, *"Gibt es etwas,"* 270, 292, 400 n. 9; JL to Eleonora Mendelssohn, c. 1942–43; Apr. 20, 1945, Eleonora von Mendelssohn Papers, NYPL; Olga Blair, "Actress Who Fled Nazi Regime at Home Here," *Christian Science Monitor* (Jan. 17, 1946); Harry King Tootle, "John Latouche at Work on Four Plays," *RTD* (Feb. 6, 1949).
30. JL [to Stefanie Kiesler], c. November 1943, AFL; for the mentioned photograph, see Blubacher, "*Gibt es etwas*," 301.
31. Rock Brynner, *Empire & Odyssey: The Brynners in Far East Russia and Beyond* (Hanover, NH: Steerforth, 2006); *Grand Surprise*, 106, 541; JLD, July 16, 1944; Feb. 8, 1945.
32. Deirdre Bair, *Anaïs Nin: A Biography* (New York: Putnam, 1995).
33. *The Diary of Anaïs Nin, 1939–1944*, edited by Gunther Stuhlman (New York: Harcourt, Brace & World, 1969), 28–29.
34. Boyce Rensberger, "Amphetamines Used by a Physician to Lift Moods of Famous Patients," *NYT* (Dec. 4, 1972); Richard A. Lertzman and William J. Birnes, *Dr. Feelgood: The Shocking Story of the Doctor Who May Have Changed History by Treating and Drugging JFK, Marilyn, Elvis, and Other Prominent Figures* (New York: Skyhorse, 2013); C. David Heymann, *A Woman Named Jackie* (New York: Carol Communications, 1989), 301–2 (for Capote).
35. Rensberger; Susan Wood, "Doctor Feelgood, Are You Sure It's All Right?" *New York* (Feb. 8, 1971); Bert E. Park, *Ailing, Aging, Addicted: Studies of Compromised Leadership* (Lexington: University Press of Kentucky, 1993), 168–86; Tennessee Williams, letter to the editor, *NYT* (Dec. 12, 1972); Dotson Rader, "The Art of Theater V: Tennessee Williams," *Paris Review* 81 (Fall 1981): 166; Doris Shapiro, *We Danced All Night: My Life Behind the Scenes with Alan Jay Lerner* (New York: William Morrow, 1990); Iver Peterson, "Regents' Vote Unanimous," *NYT* (Apr. 26, 1975).
36. Paul Bowles, *Without Stopping: An Autobiography* (New York: Harper Perennial, 1972, 2006), 242, 245.
37. Max Jacobson and JL, untitled transcript, Apr. 14, 1949, and "To Range from Preventive Illnesses to Concentration Camp Psychology," May 2, 1949, JLL.
38. Kenward Elmslie, interview with author, October 1, 2013; JLD, February 10, 1944; *Grand Surprise*, 164n45; Harold E. Doweiko, *Concepts of Chemical Dependency* (Pacific Grove, CA: Brooks/Cole, 2002), 131; Rensberger.

7. Radio and Patriotic Work, 1940–1945

1. *Variety* (Apr. 24, 1940), EHP; George W. Clarke, "Man About Boston" (c. 1941), VDP.
2. "New Shows and Gossip," *NYT* (June 23, 1940).
3. "Benedict Arnold: Portrait of a Traitor" (as "The Traitor: A Play-Portrait of Benedict Arnold"), JLL (CTR 917), and "Men with Wings, or Flight into Darkness," JLL (CTR 916).
4. Jo Ranson, "Radio Dial Log," *Brooklyn Eagle* (Aug. 17, 1940).
5. JLD, Mar. 10, 1944.
6. "Whole Nation to Join with Fairs to Pay Tribute to Broadcasting Industry," *Atlanta Daily World* (Aug. 5, 1940); Luther Davis and John Cleveland, "And You Know Who I Am," *Collier's* 106 (Oct. 19, 1940): 91.
7. JL et al., *New Walls of China* (New York: Trans-Pacific News Service, [1940]); JL, "New Walls for China," *Harper's Bazaar* (October 1942): 78–79, 139–40.
8. "World Notables Praise Roosevelt," *NYT*, and "A Radio Close-Up of America," *PM* (both Jan. 21, 1941); "Radio Program High Lights," *Indianapolis Star* (Mar. 20, 1941).
9. JL, "The Muse and the Mike," *Vogue* (Mar. 1, 1941): 64, 124–25.
10. J. Fred MacDonald, "Government Propaganda in Commercial Radio—The Case of Treasury Star Parade, 1942–1943," *Journal of Popular Culture* 12 (Fall 1978): 285–304; Albert Wertheim, *Staging the War: American Drama and World War II* (Bloomington: Indiana University Press, 2004), 191 ("impressive").
11. Vernon Duke, *Passport to Paris* (Boston: Little, Brown, 1955), 399; "War Relief Show Attended by 6,200," *NYT* (Feb. 22, 1941); reviews of *Judith Anderson in Dramatic Sketches* in the *Chicago Daily Tribune* (Apr. 1, 1944); *NYT* (Apr. 9, 1944); *Boston Globe* (May 7, 1944); and *College English* 6 (Oct. 1944): 68.
12. Lorraine M. Lees, *Yugoslav-Americans and National Security During World War II* (Urbana: University of Illinois Press, 2007), 71–72; "Air Ya Listenin?" *Mason City* [IA] *Globe-Gazette* (Nov. 5, 1942).
13. *The Treasury Star Parade*, edited by William A. Bacher (New York: Farrar & Rinehart, 1942), 33–37, 341–50; republished in *Senior Scholastic* 42 (Mar. 29–Apr. 3, 1943): 15, 21.
14. JL, *La Marseillaise*, JLL (RM 4548); Thomas Blubacher, *Die vielen Leben der Ruth Landshoff-Yorck* (Berlin: Insel, 2015), 190; Ruth Landshoff-Yorck, *Klatsch, Ruhm und kleine Feuer: Biographische Impressionen* (Berlin: Kiepenheuer & Witsch, 1963), 130; "Devotion to Allies Expressed by 5,000," *NYT* (July 15, 1942).
15. Earl Robinson with Eric A. Gordon, *Ballad of an American: The Autobiography of Earl Robinson* (Lanham, MD: Scarecrow, 1998), 129.
16. "Two Concerts Presented at Art Institute," *Detroit Free Press* (May 1, 1942); Vincent Johnson, "Music Clearance Staff Plays 'Haydn-Go-Seek' with Symphony," *Pittsburgh Post-Gazette* (Apr. 29, 1942); "WDLP Reviews World Speeches of Roosevelt," *Panama City News-Herald* (Apr. 30, 1942).
17. Reviews of the "Music for Work" concert in the *NYHT*, *NYT*, and *World-Telegram* (all May 11, 1942); and *Daily News* (May 12, 1942); Frank Rasky, "Last of the Speakeasy Chanteuses," n.s. (c. 1948), ADP.
18. Robinson, 129–30; Eleanor Roosevelt to Earl Robinson, May 26, 1942; Robinson to Roosevelt, June 16, 1942; July 2, 1942, ERP; M.K. [Marion Knoblauch], "Battle Hymn," *Music Educators Journal* 29 (April 1943): 36.
19. "Air Raid on City Feature of Show to Speed Recruiting of Defenders," *NYT* (May 30, 1943); Earl Robinson to Eleanor Roosevelt, Nov. 30, 1942, ERP.
20. Judy Dupuy, "Selected Radio Listening," *PM* (June 16, 1942); "Highlights of a Week's News in Pictures," *New Amsterdam News* (July 18, 1942).
21. JL, "Radio," *Mademoiselle* (Sep. 1942): 147, 196.
22. "Old Anthem Revived for 1942 War Song," *Cincinnati Enquirer* (Aug. 9, 1942); Richard Crawford, "Mainstreams and Backwaters in American Psalmody," in *Make a Joyful Noise*

(New World Records, NW 255, 1978), 23; "Music Notes," *NYT* (Nov. 11, 1941); "U.S. Is Seen Facing World Revolution," *NYT* (Nov. 12, 1941).

23. Ruth Jenkin, "Marching Along," *Music Educators Journal* 29 (April 1943): 36.

8. Cabin in the Sky

1. Vernon Duke, *Passport to Paris* (Boston: Little, Brown, 1955), 381.
2. Charles ("Tony") Root, interview with author, Oct. 23, 2013; Vernon Duke, "Building a New 'Cabin'" (c. January 1964), EHP.
3. George Ross, "Russian Harangue Jars Rehearsals," *World-Telegram* (Oct. 19, 1940); for a slight variant, see Duke, *Passport*, 383.
4. Duke, *Passport*, 381–384; Harold Meyerson and Ernie Harburg, *Who Put the Rainbow in* The Wizard of Oz?: *Yip Harburg, Lyricist* (Ann Arbor: University of Michigan Press, 1993), 176; untitled article, n.s. (c. November 1939), VDP (for Mercer).
5. "News of the Stage," *NYT* (Apr. 11, 1940); "News of the Stage," *NYT* (May 10, 1941); "Premiere Tonight for Ice Spectacle," *NYT* (Oct. 10, 1940); Duke, *Passport*, 336–37.
6. Duke, *Passport*, 388; Fred Fehl, William Stott, and Jane Stott, *On Broadway* (Austin: University of Texas Press, 1978), 14; Duke, "Building."
7. Ross; " 'Cabin in Sky,' Negro Show, to Be Rallying Ground for Moscow," n.s., n.d., VDP; Duke, *Passport*, 384, 388.
8. Duke, *Passport*, 384; Marjory Adams, "Composer Vernon Duke Discusses Methods During Visit Here," *Boston Globe* (Mar. 10, 1941); "Duke and Latouche Meet, Click and Gladly Stick," *Brooklyn Eagle* (Jan. 5, 1941).
9. Frank Rich with Lisa Aronson, *The Theatre Art of Boris Aronson* (New York: Knopf, 1987), 74; " 'Cabin in Sky,' Negro Show."
10. Max Wilk, *They're Playing Our Song: Conversations with America's Classic Songwriters* (New York: Da Capo, 1997), 195–98; Meyerson; JL to Vernon Duke and Ogden Nash, May 22, 1956, VDP.
11. Vernon Duke, "Tribute to a Poet," *Theatre Arts* 41 (March 1957): 26; Carmencita Romero, interview with Constance Valis Hill, "*Cabin in the Sky*: Dossier," Nov. 18, 1999, GBP; untitled article, n.s., n.d., VDP ("having").
12. "Duke and Latouche Meet" ("incongruous"); untitled article, n.s., n.d., VDP ("Hello"); Earl Wilson, "John Latouche's Feelings Are Hurt," *Post* (Sep. 25, 1941); Duke, *Passport*, 401; Grace Turner, "Ballad of Fine Food," *Milwaukee Journal* (Feb. 8, 1942).
13. Duke, *Passport*, 384, 401; Duke, "Tribute," 26, 96; Wilson; Bob Musel, "Popular Song Writers Work in Hotel Rooms," *Indianapolis Star* (Nov. 2, 1941); Benjamin Welles, "Singing of Vladimir Vernon Duke Dukelsky," *NYT* (Dec. 29, 1940).
14. Lynn Root, *Cabin in the Sky* (two typescripts of the book differing in minor details of spelling and the like survive at the NYPL, one with the call number NCOF+, the other, RM 4552, part of JLL); Allan Keller, "It Had to Be Simple with Limited Funds," n.s., n.d., VDP; in his original script, Root places the action "in the negro section of a city in the Deep South," Lynn Root, *Little Joe: An All-Negro Fantasy with Music*, Lynn Root Collection, University of Wyoming.
15. Reviews of *Cabin in the Sky* in the *Christian Science Monitor, Daily Mirror, Daily News, Journal-American, NYHT, NYT, Post, Sun,* and *World-Telegram* (all Oct. 26, 1940); *Brooklyn Eagle, Morning Telegraph,* and *PM* (all Oct. 27, 1940); *Women's Wear Daily* (Oct. 28, 1940); *Variety* (Oct. 30, 1940); *Daily Worker* (Oct. 31, 1940); *Amsterdam News, Chicago Defender,* and *New Yorker* (all Nov. 2, 1940); *Gotham Life* (Nov. 3, 1940); *Newsweek* and *Time* (both Nov. 4, 1940); *Billboard* and *Nation* (both Nov. 9, 1940); *Atlanta Daily World* and *New Republic* (both Nov. 11, 1940); and *Life* (Dec. 9, 1940). See also follow-up reviews by Richard Watts Jr., *NYHT* (Nov. 2, 1940); Brooks Atkinson, *NYT* (Nov. 3, 1940); and Dan Burley, *Amsterdam News* (Dec. 28, 1940); and specialized reviews by John Martin, *NYT* (Nov. 10, 1940); Robert Lawrence, *NYHT* (Nov. 17, 1940); and Lillian Johnson, *Baltimore Afro-American* (Nov. 30, 1940).

16. Francis Mason, *I Remember Balanchine: Recollections of the Ballet Master by Those Who Knew Him* (New York: Doubleday, 1991), 191 (for Stravinsky).
17. Susan Smith, *The Musical: Race, Gender and Performance* (New York: Wallflower, 2005); Kate Marie Weber, "Beyond Racial Stereotypes: Subversive Subtexts in *Cabin in the Sky*" (MA thesis, University of Maryland, 2008).
18. Ethan Mordden, *Beautiful Mornin': The Broadway Musical in the 1940s* (New York: Oxford University Press, 1999), 45.
19. "Latouche the Rebel," n.s. (Nov. 15, 1941), Stanton Griffis Papers, Harry S. Truman Library.
20. Leonard Harris, "Duke's 'Cabin,' With No Tom," *Telegram & Sun* (Jan. 9, 1964).
21. Vernon Duke to L. Arnold Weissberger, Sep. 9, 1954, VDP; the lyric for "It's Not So Bad to Be Good" found in the original libretto differs considerably from that found in the manuscript score, with the recording of the 1964 Greenwich Mews revival representing the latter.
22. "New Plays in Manhattan," *Time* (Nov. 4, 1940); Romero.
23. Ethel Waters with Charles Samuels, *His Eye Is on the Sparrow* (Garden City, NY: Doubleday, 1951), 255; Helen Ormsbee, "A Mirror, and Her Simplicity, Only School for Ethel Waters," *NYHT* (Nov. 10, 1940); Fehl, 14; Mason, 193.
24. Wilk, 197; Duke, *Passport*, 391.
25. Duke, *Passport*, 391.
26. "Cab Calloway Out, Ethel Waters In," *Chicago Defender* (Aug. 3, 1940); Fehl, 14.
27. Mason, 190–93; Romero; Katherine Dunham, interviews with Constance Valis Hill, Nov. 18, 1999, and Jan. 15, 2000, "*Cabin in the Sky*: Dossier," GBP; *Kaiso! Writings by and about Katherine Dunham*, edited by Vèvè A. Clark and Sara E. Johnson (Madison: University of Wisconsin Press, 2005), 141–44.
28. Mason, 190; Romero; Dunham; Zita Allen, James Hatch, and Arthur Smith, "An Interview with Talley Beatty," *Artists and Influence* (1981) ([New York]: Hatch-Billops, 1981): 1–52.
29. *Kaiso!* 128–29; Welles; Mason, 192.
30. Reviews of *Cabin in the Sky* in the *NYT* (Oct. 26 and Nov. 3, 1940); George Jean Nathan, "Laurels and Raspberries," *American Mercury* (July 1941): 104–7.
31. Reviews of *Cabin in the Sky* in *Newsweek* (Nov. 4, 1940); *NYT* (Nov. 10, 1940); *NYHT* (Nov. 17, 1940); and *Baltimore Afro-American* (Nov. 30, 1940).
32. Reviews of *Cabin in the Sky* in the *NYHT* (Nov. 17, 1940) and *Time* (Nov. 4, 1940); Nathan; Stark Young, in his review for the *New Republic*, presented a rare dissenting voice with respect to the lyrics, or at least for, ostensibly, "Love Turned the Light Out," writing, "I am so little broken in to torch songs and their parallels in general that the appalling words Miss Waters has to sing prevent my having any emotions of any kind outside of certain musical values of rhythm and tone."
33. Reviews of *Cabin in the Sky* in the *New Yorker* (Nov. 2, 1940) and *NYT* (Nov. 3, 1940).
34. Reviews of *Cabin in the Sky* in *PM* (Oct. 27, 1940); *Daily Worker* (Oct. 31, 1940); *Amsterdam News* and *Chicago Defender* (both Nov. 2, 1940); *Nation* (Nov. 9, 1940); *Atlanta Daily World* (Nov. 11, 1940); *New Masses* (Nov. 26, 1940); and *Baltimore Afro-American* (Nov. 30, 1940).
35. Reviews of *Cabin in the Sky* in the *Chicago Tribune* (May 5, 1941); *Chicago Defender* (Apr. 19, May 17, June 14, June 21, Aug. 2, 1940); and Boston newspapers, VDP; Cecil Smith, *Musical Comedy in America* (New York: Theatre Arts, 1950), 331–32; Dunham; *Kaiso!* 147.
36. JL to Edward James, Sep. 29, 1941; [JL], *Lilith, or The Deadliest Sin*, JLL.
37. Vincente Minnelli with Hector Arce, *I Remember It Well* (Garden City, NY: Doubleday, 1974), 123; "Gossip of the Rialto," *NYT* (May 24, 1942).
38. Meyerson, 176; Minnelli, 123.
39. In sum, "Happiness Is a Thing Called Joe" took the place of "Taking a Chance on Love"; "Taking a Chance," "My Old Virginia Home"; "Life's Full o' Consequence," "Love Me Tomorrow"; a reprise of "Happiness," "Love Turned the Light Out"; Ellington's music, "Lazy Steps" and "Boogy Woogy"; and a reprise of "Honey in the Honeycomb," "Savannah."
40. Reviews of *Cabin in the Sky* in *Metronome* (March 1943); *NYT* (May 28, 1943); *Wall Street Journal* (May 29, 1943); and *Amsterdam News* (June 12, 1943); Dolores Calvin, "Varied Comments on 'Cabin in the Sky,'" *Atlanta Daily World* (June 10, 1943).

41. Harris; review of *Cabin in the Sky* in the *Amsterdam News* (Aug. 1, 1953).
42. Louis Macmillan to Lynn Root, Feb. 14, 1955, VDP (for standard English).
43. L. Arnold Weissberger to Vernon Duke and Lynn Root, Sep. 15, 1954, VDP.
44. L. Arnold Weissberger to Vernon Duke and Lynn Root, Dec. 30, 1954, Root Collection.
45. Louis Macmillan to Vernon Duke, Mar. 26, 1955; Vernon Duke to Louis Macmillan, Apr. 1, 1955, VDP.
46. Lynn Root, *Cabin in the Sky: A Musical Play*, Root Collection.
47. Vernon Duke [to Arthur Whitelaw and Leo Friedman], Nov. 9, 1963, VDP; Stuart W. Little, "Auditions by Gielgud—30 Ophelias," *NYHT* (Oct. 29, 1963).
48. Effie Latouche to Vernon Duke, May 20, 1960, VDP.
49. Reviews of *Cabin in the Sky* in the *Journal-American*, *NYHT*, *NYT*, *Post*, and *World-Telegram* (all Jan. 22, 1964); *Los Angeles Times* (Jan. 24, 1964); *Variety* (Jan. 29, 1964); *Amsterdam News* (Feb. 8, 1964); and *Back Stage* (Feb. 14, 1964).
50. Reviews of *Cabin in the Sky* in *amNew York*, *Daily News*, *NYT*, *TheaterMania.com*, and *Vulture* (all Feb. 11, 2016); *Epoch Times* (Feb. 14, 2016); and *Huffington Post* (Feb. 16, 2016).

9. Banjo Eyes

1. Marion Bussang, "France's 'Cole Porter' Prefers Sad Songs," *Post* (Aug. 8, 1940); Lisa Jo Sagolla, *The Girl Who Fell Down: A Biography of Joan McCracken* (Boston: Northeastern University Press, 2003), 128–29, 143–44.
2. Bussang; reviews of *Crazy with the Heat* in the *Sun* (Aug. 4, 1940) ("sophisticated"); *Variety* (Aug. 7, 1940); *NYT* (Jan. 15, 1941); *Journal-American* and *NYT* (both Jan. 31, 1941); and *Variety* (Apr. 30, 1941).
3. John Martin, "The Dance: Ice Ballet," *NYT* (Jan. 29, 1939).
4. "The Birth of an Ice-Travaganza," *Ice-Capades of 1941 Souvenir Program*, NYPL; M. H. Orodenker, " 'Ice-Capades of 1941' Gets Under Way at A.C. in Blaze of Production," *Billboard* (Sep. 7, 1940); "Ice Capades to Feature Vaudeville," *Christian Science Monitor* (Feb. 18, 1941).
5. Orodenker.
6. "Lois Dworshak's 'Jiving on Ice' Among Features of 'Ice Capades,' " *Boston Globe* (Nov. 24, 1940).
7. Untitled articles, n.s., n.d., VDP (United China Relief).
8. Vernon Duke, *Passport to Paris* (Boston: Little, Brown, 1955), 399; Check, "Strips and Stripes," *New Yorker* (May 10, 1941); Malcolm Johnson, "Cafe Life in New York," *Sun* (c. May 1941), VDP; untitled article, n.s. (c. May 1941), VDP ("about the").
9. Gregory Koseluk, *Eddie Cantor: A Life in Show Business* (Jefferson, NC: McFarland, 1995); Herbert G. Goldman, *Banjo Eyes: Eddie Cantor and the Birth of Modern Stardom* (New York: Oxford University Press, 1997); "Warners to Bankroll Cantor's 'Banjo Eyes,' 1st on B'way, Then Pix," *Variety* (July 30, 1941).
10. Koseluk, 299.
11. Duke, 400–401.
12. Earl Wilson, "John Latouche's Feelings Are Hurt," *Post* (Sep. 25, 1941); Florence Ramon, "Duke and LaTouche Air Composer's Woes," n.s. (c. October 1941), EHP; JL to Charlotte Dieterle, Jan. 23, 1942, Marta Mierendorff Papers, University of Southern California.
13. Joseph Quillan and Irving Elinson, *Banjo Eyes*, John Cecil Holm Papers, Wisconsin Center for Film and Theater Research.
14. James Fisher, *Eddie Cantor: A Bio-Bibliography* (Westport, CT: Greenwood, 1997), 73; Barbara Seaman, *Lovely Me: The Life of Jacqueline Susann* (New York: Morrow, 1987).
15. Ramon.
16. Duke, 401; reviews of *Banjo Eyes* in the *Hartford Courant* (Nov. 8, 1941); [Boston] *Evening American*, *Herald*, *Post*, *Christian Science Monitor*, and *Variety* (all Nov. 12, 1941); varied articles, VDP.

17. "Cantor Hires Play Doctor to Work over 'Banjo Eyes,'" *Los Angeles Times* (Dec. 1, 1941); Duke, 402–3; JL to Ruth Page, postmarked Dec. 22, 1941, Ruth Page Papers, NYPL.
18. Reviews of *Banjo Eyes* in the [Philadelphia] *Daily News, Evening Public Ledger,* and *Inquirer* (all Dec. 3, 1941).
19. Reviews of *Banjo Eyes* in the *Daily News, Journal-American, NYHT, NYT, Post,* and *World-Telegram* (all Dec. 26, 1941); *Mirror* (Dec. 27, 1941); *Variety* (Dec. 31, 1941); *Billboard* and *New Yorker* (both Jan. 3, 1942); *Time* (Jan. 5, 1942); *Life* (Feb. 3, 1942); *Catholic World* 154 (March 1942): 731; and *Theatre Arts* 26 (March 1942): 155; Dan Burley, "Bill Bailey Is Dancing Star in Cantor Show 'Banjo Eyes,'" *New Amsterdam Star-News* (Feb. 21, 1942).
20. Jack Robbins to Vernon Duke, Feb. 12, 1942, VDP.
21. Stephen Sondheim, *Look, I Made a Hat: Collected Lyrics (1981–2011) with Attendant Comments, Amplifications, Dogmas, Harangues, Digressions, Anecdotes and Miscellany* (New York: Knopf, 2011), 308; varied articles, VDP.
22. Koseluk, 301–2; Goldman, 227–28; Virginia Mayo as told to LC Van Savage, *The Best Years of My Life* (Chesterfield, MO: BeachHouse, 2002), 34.
23. Koseluk, 302.
24. Goldman, 226; Ethan Mordden, *Beautiful Mornin': The Broadway Musical in the 1940s* (New York: Oxford University Press, 1999), 26; Mordden, *Open a New Window: The Broadway Musical in the 1960s* (New York: Palgrave Macmillan, 2001), 40; Albert Lewis, letter to the editor, *Variety* (Nov. 8, 1961).

10. The Lady Comes Across

1. "News of the Stage," *NYT* (Mar. 25, 1941); Vernon Duke, *Passport to Paris* (Boston: Little, Brown, 1955), 396.
2. Duke, 396; *The Diaries of Dawn Powell, 1931–1965,* edited with an introduction by Tim Page (South Royalton, VT: Steerforth, 1995).
3. Edmund Wilson, "Dawn Powell: Greenwich Village in the Fifties," *New Yorker* (Nov. 17, 1962); Gore Vidal, "Dawn Powell: The American Writer," in *At Home* (New York: Vintage, 1990), 241–71; Tim Page, *Dawn Powell: A Biography* (New York: Holt, 1998); Marcelle Smith Rice, *Dawn Powell* (New York: Twayne, 2000).
4. Dawn Powell, "The Birth of Comedy," *NYT* (Jan. 11, 1942).
5. *Diaries,* 194; Dawn Powell, "Wrote This Musical Show on the Hoof," *Boston Post* (Dec. 14, 1941).
6. Dawn Powell, "Audition," *Dawn Powell at Her Best,* edited with an introduction by Tim Page (South Royalton, VT: Steerforth, 1994), 377 (the story originally appeared in *Collier's Weekly* [May 19, 1945]); Zachary Solov, interview with Dawn Lille, Nov. 14, 2001, "*The Lady Comes Across*: Dossier," GBP.
7. Jessie Matthews as told to Muriel Burgess, *Over My Shoulder: An Autobiography* (New Rochelle, NY: Arlington Houston, 1974), 173.
8. Reviews of *The Lady Comes Across* in *Variety* (Dec. 17, 1941); [Boston] *Evening American, Globe, Herald, Post, Record,* and *Traveler,* and *Christian Science Monitor* (all Dec. 18, 1941); *Brooklyn Eagle, Daily News, Journal-American, Mirror, Morning Telegram, NYHT, NYT, PM, Post, Sun,* and *World-Telegram* (all Jan. 10, 1942); *Variety* (Jan. 14, 1942); *New Yorker* (Jan. 17, 1942); *Newsweek* (Jan. 19, 1942); *Billboard* (Jan. 24, 1942); and *Theatre Arts* 26 (March 1942): 155; untitled article, n.s., n.d., "*The Lady Comes Across*: Dossier," GBP ("satire"); Matthews, 173.
9. Marc Platt, interview with Dawn Lille, Sep. 10, 2001, "*The Lady Comes Across*: Dossier," GBP.
10. Review of *The Lady Comes Across* in the *Boston Globe* (Dec. 18, 1941).
11. Duke, 403; Charlotte Rae, *Songs I Taught My Mother* (PS Classics PS-644, 1955, 2006); *The Littlest Revue* (Painted Smiles Records, PSCD-112, 1956, 1989).
12. Michael Thornton, *Jessie Matthews: a Biography* (London: Hart-Davis, MacGibbon, 1974), 162.

13. Louis Sobol, "Cavalcade," [Harrisburg, PA] *Evening News* (Jan. 14, 1942); "Review Percentages," *Billboard* (Jan. 3, 1942); "Review Percentages," *Billboard* (Jan. 24, 1942).
14. JL to Vernon Duke, Feb. 13, 1942, VDP.
15. Eugene Barr, review of *The Lady Comes Across, Billboard* (Jan. 24, 1942); "Costly Show Ends: Opened on Friday," *NYT* (Jan. 12, 1942); Jeanne Tyler Hoyt, interview with Dawn Lille, Aug. 6, 2001, "*The Lady Comes Across*: Dossier," GBP.
16. Duke, 404; JL to Charlotte Dieterle, Jan. 23, 1942, Marta Mierendorff Papers, University of Southern California; JL to Duke, Feb. 13, 1942, VDP.
17. *Diaries*, 197, 252, 306; *Selected Letters of Dawn Powell, 1913–1965*, edited with an introduction by Tim Page (New York: Holt, 1999), 124.
18. *Diaries*, 206, 207, 231, 323.
19. JLD, Jan. 30, 1944; JL to Dawn Powell, Dec. 23, 1942; "Major Minor," Dawn Powell Papers, Columbia University.
20. *Selected Letters*, 230.
21. "Film Record Set by 'Little Foxes,'" *NYT* (Aug. 23, 1941); JL to William Dieterle, c. November 1941; JL to Charlotte Dieterle, Jan. 23, 1942, Mierendorff Papers; JL, "On the Film Front," *Modern Music* 19 (November–December 1941): 58–59.
22. James K. Lyon, *Bertolt Brecht in America* (Princeton, NJ: Princeton University Press, 1980), 101; JL to William Dieterle, c. November 1941, Mierendorff Papers; Ruth Landshoff and John Latouche, "Yes, I Live in a Dark Age," *Decision* 2 (October 1941): 74–75; Jimmy Ernst, *A Not-So-Still Life* (New York: St. Martin's, 1984), 176–77; Kenward Elmslie, interview with author, Oct. 1, 2013.
23. JL to Thomas Fisher, Jan. 16, 1941; Ruth Page to JL, Jan. 17, 1941, Ruth Page Papers, NYPL; Cecil Smith, "Ruth Page and Stone to Give 2 New Ballets," *Chicago Tribune* (Mar. 30, 1941).
24. Kurt Weill to Ruth Page, May 1, 1941; May 22, 1941, Kurt Weill Foundation; JL to Page, May 22, 1941; June 24, 1941, Page Papers.
25. Kurt Weill to Ruth Page, June 28, 1941; Aug. 18, 1941, Kurt Weill Foundation; JL to Page, Sep. 29, 1941; Dec. 22, 1941, Page Papers.
26. JL to Jerome Moross, July 27, 1944, EHP; Ruth Page, *Page by Page*, edited with an introduction by Andrew Mark Wentink (Brooklyn, NY: Dance Horizons, 1978), 103–4.
27. "Nan Kirby Comedy Due Here Tonight," *NYT* (Oct. 28, 1943).
28. Varied articles, VDP; Sam Zolotow, "Plans 'Firebrand' in Musical Form," *NYT* (Oct. 6, 1943); "Pre-Hitler German Player Sought for Broadway Show," *Los Angeles Times* (Mar. 20, 1941), for Molnár; *Diaries*, 240.
29. Sam Zolotow, "New Comedy Eyed by Celeste Holm," *NYT* (Sep. 23, 1953); Denny Beach to Vernon Duke, Nov. 12, 1953; undated letters from JL to Duke; Duke to JL, Nov. 23, 1953; Gala Ebin to Duke, Dec. 9, 1953; Beach to Duke, Dec. 9, 1953, VDP.
30. Vernon Duke, "The Late John Treville Latouche," *Variety* (Aug. 29, 1956); Duke, "Tribute to a Poet," *Theatre Arts* 41 (March 1957): 24–26, 96.

11. To the Congo and into the Navy

1. JL to Charlotte Dieterle, Jan. 23, 1942, Marta Mierendorff Papers, University of Southern California.
2. Ruth Slade, *The Belgian Congo*, 2nd ed. (New York: Oxford University Press, 1960, 1961); Roger Anstey, *King Leopold's Legacy: The Congo under Belgian Rule, 1908–1960* (New York: Oxford University Press, 1966); Jonathan E. Helmreich, *United States Relations with Belgium and the Congo, 1940–1960* (Newark: University of Delaware Press, 1998); Florence Gillet, "La 'Mission' Cauvin: La propagande coloniale du gouvernement belge aux États-Unis pendant la Seconde Guerre mondiale," *Les Cahiers d'Histoire du Temps Présent* 15 (2005): 357–83; Matthew G. Stanard, *Selling the Congo: A History of European Pro-Empire Propaganda and the Making of Belgian Imperialism* (Lincoln: University of Nebraska Press, 2012); Guy

Vanthemsche, *Belgium and the Congo, 1885–1980*, translated by Alice Cameron and Stephen Windross (New York: Cambridge University Press, 2012).

3. AHD; Rhea Talley, "John LaTouche to Join Expedition to Congo to Aid Belgian Contribution to Allied Cause," *RTD* (Aug. 17, 1942).
4. JL to Dawn Powell, Jan. 12, 1943, Dawn Powell Papers, Columbia University.
5. Gillet.
6. JL to Virgil Thomson, c. 1942–43, VTP; JL to Eleonora Mendelssohn, c. 1942–43, Eleonora von Mendelssohn Papers, NYPL; JL to Dawn Powell, Jan. 12, 1943, Powell Papers.
7. JL, "This One Weakness," *Atlanta Constitution*, *Baltimore Sun*, and *Los Angeles Times* (all Jan. 3, 1943).
8. John Latouche, "Ce temps n'est pas pour nous," translated by Yvan Goll, *La Voix de France* (Nov. 3, 1942).
9. JL, "Two Poems from Congo," *Hemispheres* 1 (Fall–Winter 1943/44): 57–58; David Perkins, email to author, July 23, 2014; JL to André Cauvin, c. March 1944, André Cauvin Papers, CEGES/SOMA, Brussels.
10. AHD (Drummond personally interviewed Cauvin, and received materials from him as well, most of which do not seem to survive in either ADP or Cauvin Papers; Drummond, who knew French, apparently translated this diary entry himself).
11. L. L. Stevenson, "Lights of New York," *Amsterdam Evening Recorder* (July 17, 1944); *The Diaries of Dawn Powell, 1931–1965*, edited with an introduction by Tim Page (South Royalton, VT: Steerforth, 1995), 208; Earl Wilson, "It Happened Last Night," *Post* (Aug. 2, 1945).
12. "Some New Shorts for the Home Front," *NYT* (Aug. 22, 1943); AHD.
13. Cauvin to JL, Mar. 31, 1944, JLP; Paul Bowles, *Without Stopping: An Autobiography* (New York: Harper Perennial, 1972), 251; Gillet.
14. JL, *Congo*, with photographs by André Cauvin (New York: Willow, White, 1945), 97, 125, 192; JL, inscription to Earle Elrick, January 1949, *Congo*, in the author's possession ("too-hastily").
15. JL, *Congo*, 11, 36, 40, 97, 185.
16. Ruth Landshoff-Yorck, *Klatsch, Ruhm und kleine Feuer: Biographische Impressionen* (Berlin: Kiepenheuer & Witsch, 1963), 132; reviews of *Congo* in the *NYT* (Du Bois, July 30, 1945); *Chicago Tribune* (Engle) and *NYT* (Cloete, both Aug. 12, 1943); *Amsterdam News* (Sep. 1, 1945); *NYHT* (Sep. 2, 1945); *Saturday Review* (Sep. 8, 1945); *Chicago Defender* (Sep. 15, 1945); *Christian Science Monitor* (Dec. 1, 1945); *Greece Press* (Jan. 31, 1946); *Big Piney* [WY] *Examiner* (Feb. 21, 1946); and *Foreign Affairs* 24 (April 1945): 563–64.
17. Sue Quinn, "The Artist and His Dream: An Interpretation of John Latouche," *Madison Quarterly* 6 (March 1946): 49–54; see also Susan Quinn, "Off the Bookshelves," *RTD* (Oct. 14, 1945); for a more recent view of *Congo*, see Charles Musser, "Presenting 'a True Idea of the African of To-day': Two Documentary Forays by Paul and Eslanda Robeson," *Film History* 18/4 (2006): 412–39, which lauds Eslanda Robeson's attempts to "demystify" Africa over Latouche's idealization of the Congo.
18. JL, "Items Called 'Ballet Ballads,'" *NYT* (June 6, 1948).
19. JL, "The Fighting French in Africa," *Saturday Review* (Feb. 17, 1945); "In Africa Before the War," *Saturday Review* (Aug. 25, 1945).
20. Hollis R. Lynch, *Black American Radicals and the Liberation of Africa: The Council on African Affairs, 1937–1955* (Ithaca, NY: Cornell University Africana Studies and Research Center, 1978); Martin Bauml Duberman, *Paul Robeson* (New York: Knopf, 1989); Penny M. Von Eschen, *Race Against Empire: Black Americans and Anticolonialism, 1937–1957* (Ithaca, NY: Cornell University Press, 1997); David Henry Anthony III, *Max Yergan: Race Man, Internationalist, Cold Warrior* (New York: New York University Press, 2006).
21. "John Latouche Explains Reason for Penning Pageant for Council on African Affairs," *New York Age* (Apr. 26, 1947); "5,000 Greet Paul Robeson at Council on African Affairs Rally," *Norfolk Journal and Guide* (May 17, 1947).

22. JL, Mary Church Terrell, and Henry Arthur Callis, letter to Paul Robeson, May 15, 1948, W. E. B. Du Bois Papers, University of Massachusetts Amherst.
23. JL, affidavits, Jan. 27, 1956, and May 18, 1956, FBI.
24. *Selected Letters of Dawn Powell, 1913–1965*, edited with an introduction by Tim Page (New York: Holt, 1999), 117–18.
25. *Selected Letters*, 118; JLD, Aug. 16, 1943; Aug. 17, 1943; Sep. 14, 1943; Oct. 9, 1943.
26. JLD, Aug. 16, 1943; Aug. 18, 1943; Aug. 20, 1943; Oct. 7, 1943 (for *Oklahoma!*).
27. JL, Military Records, National Personnel Records Center, St. Louis (his paper work also reported an average monthly salary of $600); JLD, Oct. 9, 1943; "John LaTouche Finds the Congo Is Like Pittsburgh," *RTD* (July 7, 1944).
28. JL to Effie Latouche, c. October 1943, JLP; JL to Frederick Kiesler, postmarked Oct. 23, 1943, AFL; JL to André Cauvin, n.d., Cauvin Papers.
29. JLD, Nov. 12–27, 1943.
30. JLD, Nov. 12–27, 1943; Dec. 2, 1943; Dec. 5, 1943; Dec. 21, 1943; JL to André Cauvin, Dec. 14, 1943, Cauvin Papers.
31. JLD, Feb. 11, 1944; Mar. 24, 1944; JL to André Cauvin, received Feb. 7, 1944, Cauvin Papers; see also JL, Military Records.
32. JL to Marian Dunham, c. February 1944, JLP; JLD, Dec. 8, 1943; Jan. 21, 1944; c. Mar. 3, 1944; Mar. 13, 1944; Mar. 18, 1944.
33. JL to Marian Dunham, c. February 1944, JLP.
34. JLD, c. March 1944; JL, *The Golden Apple* (New York: Random House, 1954), 23.
35. JL, letters to Virgil Thomson, c. January 1944; c. February 1944, VTP; JLD, Mar. 26, 1944 ("vain"); July 16, 1945 ("alcoherent").
36. JLD, Jan. 1, 1944; Jan. 15, 1944.
37. JLD, Dec. 21, 1943; Feb. 4, 1944.
38. JLD, June 20, 1944.
39. Richard Condon, *The Manchurian Candidate* (New York: Four Walls Eight Windows, 1959, 2003), xii; Gerald Davison, "Andrew Salter (1914–1996), Founding Behavior Therapist," *American Psychological Society Observer* 9 (November 1996): 30–31.
40. JLD, June 20, 1944; JL and Andrew Salter, *The Wax Flower*, courtesy of Erik Haagensen; this typescript, housed in the manuscript division of the Library of Congress and copyrighted May 17, 1945, lacks a first scene, possibly the remaining scene referred to by Latouche in his journals, JLD, Apr. 20, 1945; Latouche and Salter likely completed the play in preparation for an attempted tryout at the Montowese Playhouse in 1946; JLD, June 30, 1954 (JL refers to ongoing work on "Trilby" by himself and Salter "with a collab. from Ken[ward Elmslie]").
41. "Montowese Playhouse to Have Summer Season," *Brooklyn Eagle* (May 29, 1946); "To Try New Script," *Branford Review* (June 27, 1946); S. B., "Man in White Coat Stands by Montowese," *Branford Review* (Aug. 1, 1946); Vernon Rice, "Whiting and LaTouche Have Fun with 'Figaro,'" *Post* (Aug. 1, 1946); see also "Figaro," *Variety* (Aug. 7, 1946).
42. "Garde, Donald Set on WMRC," *Greenville* [SC] *News* (July 23, 1944); "Over the Local Skyways," *Poughkeepsie* [NY] *Journal* (Sep. 1, 1944); John Dunning, *On the Air: The Encyclopedia of Old-Time Radio* (New York: Oxford University Press, 1998), 96–97.
43. JLD, Aug. 24, 1944.

12. Rhapsody

1. JLD, Aug. 18, 1943.
2. Edward Kennedy Ellington, *Music Is My Mistress* (Garden City, NY: Doubleday, 1973), 156–62; James Lincoln Collier, *Duke Ellington* (New York: Oxford University Press, 1987), 272–73; Irving Townsend, "When Duke Records," in *The Duke Ellington Reader*, edited by Mark Tucker (New York: Oxford University Press, 1993), 321; John Edward Hasse, *Beyond Category: The Life and Genius of Duke Ellington* (New York: Simon & Schuster, 1993); David Hajdu, *Lush*

Life: A Biography of Billy Strayhorn (New York: Farrar, Straus and Giroux, 1996); Walter van de Leur, *Something to Live For: The Music of Billy Strayhorn* (New York: Oxford University Press, 2002).

3. Van de Leur, 27, 209–10; Hajdu; Ned Rorem, *Knowing When to Stop: A Memoir* (New York: Simon & Schuster, 1994), 252; John Franceschina, *Duke Ellington's Music for the Theatre* (Jefferson, NC: McFarland, 2001), 211 n. 10.
4. Van de Leur, 8, 29–30.
5. Van de Leur, 152.
6. Alec Wilder, *American Popular Song: The Great Innovators, 1900–1950* (New York: Oxford University Press, 1990); Allen Forte, *The American Popular Ballad of the Golden Era, 1924–1950* (Princeton, NJ: Princeton University Press, 1995).
7. Ellen Donaldson, interview with author, Feb. 17, 2014.
8. JL to Frederick Kiesler, postmarked Oct. 23, 1943, AFL; JL, "A Gallant Lady," *Free World* 11 (February 1946): 76–77.
9. Ben Bagley, liner notes, *Ben Bagley's Leonard Bernstein Revisited* (Jackson Heights, NY: Painted Smiles Records, PS 1377, 1981); Bagley gives the song's date as 1944, but an extant lyric sheet indicates a date of 1942, "It's Gotta Be Bad to Be Good," EHP; Carol Oja, *Bernstein Meets Broadway: Collaborative Art in a Time of War* (New York: Oxford University Press, 2014), 278; Adolph Green, Betty Comden, Jerome Robbins, and Leonard Bernstein, pre-production script to *On the Town*, Jerome Robbins Papers, NYPL.
10. *The Leonard Bernstein Letters*, edited by Nigel Simeone (New Haven, CT: Yale University Press, 2013), 135; *The Diaries of Dawn Powell, 1931–1965*, edited with an introduction by Tim Page (South Royalton, VT: Steerforth, 1995), 240; "Young Talents Map Broadway Musical," *Variety* (June 7, 1944); "News of the Sun," *Sun* (July 3, 1944); Leonard Lyons, "The Lyons Den," *Post* (July 8, 1944); "Top Stem Season This Fall," *Billboard* (Sep. 9, 1944); JLD, July 16, 1944; Oja, 91–92; Humphrey Burton, *Leonard Bernstein* (New York: Doubleday, 1994), 129; Vernon Duke, "Tribute to a Poet," *Theatre Arts* 41 (March 1957): 96.
11. Oja, 277–78; Leonard Bernstein, "It's Gotta Be Bad to Be Good," LBP.
12. Gerald Bordman, *American Operetta: From* H.M.S. Pinafore *to* Sweeney Todd (New York: Oxford University Press, 1981); Cecil Smith, *Musical Comedy in America* (New York: Theatre Arts, 1950), 328; Steven Beller, *Vienna and the Jews, 1867–1938: A Cultural History* (New York: Cambridge University Press, 1989); Camille Crittenden, *Johann Strauss and Vienna: Operetta and the Politics of Popular Culture* (New York: Cambridge University Press, 2000).
13. "'Rhap(ed)sody' in 400G Brodie," *Variety* (Dec. 6, 1944).
14. Louis P. Lochner, *Fritz Kreisler* (New York: Macmillan, 1950); Amy Biancolli, *Fritz Kreisler: Love's Sorrow, Love's Joy* (Portland, OR: Amadeus, 1998).
15. "Mrs. Dresselhuys Backs 'Rhapsody,' New Operetta," *Variety* (Aug. 30, 1944).
16. Blevins Davis to Alois Nagler, May 29, 1944, Alois M. Nagler Papers, Yale University.
17. "Dr. Alois M. Nagler, Refugee Editor, to Be Vassar's Guest," *Vassar Miscellany News* (Apr. 15, 1939); stories and synopses for *Rhapsody*, Nagler Papers.
18. JLD, Sep. 14, 1943.
19. "B'way Spotty," *Variety* (Nov. 29, 1944); Sam Zolotow, "Kreisler Operetta Forced to Suspend," *NYT* (Dec. 5, 1944); "'Rhap(ed)sody' in 400G Brodie."
20. Sam Zolotow, "News of the Stage," *NYT* (Nov. 7, 1944); Blevins Davis to George [Freedley], note to *Rhapsody*, n.d., Script Collection, NYPL (another copy of this script can be found, along with other materials related to *Rhapsody*, in the Blevins Davis Papers, University of Missouri); Arnold Sundgaard to Alois Nagler, Nov. 14, 1944, Nagler Papers.
21. The surviving script apparently lacks the final portion of the last scene.
22. Robert H. Keyserlingk, *Austria in World War II: An Anglo-American Dilemma* (Kingston, Ont.: McGill-Queen's University Press, 1988).
23. This list of songs attributed to Latouche, all housed in the copyright division of the Library of Congress, presumes that "To Horse" and the extant "Snipe Hunt" are one and the same;

these songs, incidentally, variously attribute the music to Kreisler, Bennett, and both Kreisler and Bennett.

24. Reviews of *Rhapsody* in the *Daily News*, *NYHT*, *NYT*, and *PM* (all Nov. 23, 1944); *Daily Mirror*, *Journal-American*, *Post*, *Sun*, and *World-Telegram* (all Nov. 24, 1944); *Wall Street Journal* (Nov. 24, 1944); *Variety* (Nov. 29, 1944); *Cue* (Dec. 2, 1944); *Billboard* (Dec. 9, 1944); and George Jean Nathan, *The Theatre Book of the Year, 1944–1945: A Record and an Interpretation* (New York: Knopf, 1945), 164–70.
25. Lochner, 323–24.
26. Zolotow, "Kreisler Operetta"; "'Rhapsody' Properties Are Given to City Center," *NYHT*, n.d., *Rhapsody*, clipping file, NYPL; Blevins Davis to friends, Dec. 23, 1944, Nagler Papers.
27. "Inside Stuff—Orchestras—Music," *Variety* (November 8, 1944).

13. Polonaise

1. JLD, Apr. 20, 1945; May 24, 1945; Aug. 7, 1945.
2. JLD, Jan. 27, 1945; Apr. 3, 1945 ("big work"); c. July 1945 (for Vauvenargues).
3. JLD, Jan. 25, 1945.
4. JL, letter to Marian Dunham, c. February 1944, JLP; *The Selected Letters of John Cage*, edited by Laura Kuhn (Middletown, CT: Wesleyan University Press, 2016), 63–64.
5. *Selected Letters*, 380; JLD, Jan. 21, 1945; Jan. 24, 1945; Jan. 25, 1945; Dec. 21, 1945.
6. "David Broekman, a Composer, 55 [*sic*]," *NYT* (Apr. 2, 1958); H.C.S. [Harold C. Schonberg], "Broekman Opera Has Concert Bow," *NYT* (Dec. 27, 1954).
7. Claire R. Reis, *Composers in America: Biographical Sketches of Contemporary Composers with a Record of Their Works* (New York: Macmillan, 1947), 132; *A History of the Class of 1940* (1940), *Yale 1940 Class Directory* (1960), *Yale 1940, Fortieth Reunion* (1979), Manuscripts and Archives Division, Yale University.
8. Minna Lederman, *The Life and Death of a Small Magazine (Modern Music, 1924–1946)* (New York: Institute for Studies in American Music, 1983), 178.
9. Ned Rorem, *Knowing When to Stop: A Memoir* (New York: Simon & Schuster, 1994); Kenward Elmslie, interview with author, Mar. 13, 2013; Ned Rorem, *The Nantucket Diary of Ned Rorem: 1973–1985* (San Francisco: North Point, 1987), 275.
10. AHD.
11. "Schmidlapp Plans New Show in Fall," *NYT* (Jan. 29, 1945); "'Parlor Foxhole' Arrives Tonight," *NYT* (May 23, 1945).
12. "News and Gossip of the Rialto," *NYT* (July 15, 1945).
13. Ivan Raykoff, "Hollywood's Embattled Icon," in *Piano Roles: Three Hundred Years of Life with the Piano*, edited by James Parakilas (New Haven, CT: Yale University Press, 1999), 274, 277; Lawrence Morton, "Chopin's New Audience," *Hollywood Quarterly* 1 (October 1945): 31–33.
14. Alex Storozynski, *The Peasant Prince: Thaddeus Kosciuszko and the Age of Revolution* (New York: St. Martin's, 2009); Halina Filipowicz, "Taming a Transgressive National Hero: Tadeusz Kościuszko and Nineteenth-Century Polish Drama," in *The Great Tradition and Its Legacy: The Evolution of Dramatic and Musical Theater in Austria and Central Europe*, edited by Michael Cherlin, Halina Filipowicz, and Richard L. Rudolph (New York: Berghahn, 2003), 33–34; see also Monica M. Gardner, *Kościuszko: A Biography* (New York: Scribner's, 1920), 111.
15. Marjan Kiepura, liner notes, *Jan Kiepura*, vol. 1 (Pearl Pavilion, GEMM-9976, 1992); Anne Midgette, "Heard for Eight Decades, Her Voice Doesn't Waver," *NYT* (Aug. 10, 2005); "Jan Kiepura Dies; Popular Tenor, 62," *NYT* (Aug. 16, 1966); Edwin Schallert, "Radio 'Find' Will Star in Columbia Musicals," *Los Angeles Times* (May 15, 1945).
16. JLD, Apr. 3, 1945; May 25, 1945.
17. JLD, July 15, 1945; July 16, 1945; July 24, 1945.
18. JLD, Sep. 11, 1945; reviews of *Polonaise* in the *Hartford Courant* (Sep. 14, 1945); *Baltimore Sun* (Sep. 18, 1945); *Variety* (Sep. 19, 1945); *Billboard* (Sep. 22, 1945); and *Washington Post* (Sep. 26, 1945).

19. The Alvin program cites "Gavotte," one of the few numbers from the show that do not survive, as adapted from a nonexistent Chopin work, *Variations on a French Air,* but this probably represents a renamed *Variations on a National German Air,* the title presumably tweaked due to wartime sentiment.
20. In his review of *Polonaise* for the *World-Telegram* (Oct. 8, 1945), Burton Rascoe claimed that this battle sequence, the music for which does not survive, actually used Chopin polonaises and a prelude, not etudes (although another lost piece, one that periodically came and went, "An Imperial Conference," employed by name the "Black Key" Etude).
21. Gottfried Reinhardt and Anthony Veiller, *Polonaise* (1-7-7), Manuscript Division, LC.
22. Reviews of *Polonaise* in the *Brooklyn Eagle, Daily News, Journal-American, NYHT, NYT, PM, Post, Sun,* and *World-Telegram* (all Oct. 8, 1945); *Variety* (Oct. 10, 1945); *Billboard* and *New Yorker* (both Oct. 13, 1945); *Newsweek* and *Time* (both Oct. 15, 1945); *Catholic World* 162 (November 1945): 167–68; *Theatre Arts* 29 (December 1945): 687; and George Jean Nathan, *The Theatre Book of the Year, 1944–1945: A Record and an Interpretation* (New York: Knopf, 1945), 115–23.
23. Erik Haagensen, email to author, Apr. 7, 2014.
24. Sam Zolotow, " 'Secret Room' Due at Royale Tonight," *NYT* (Nov. 7, 1945); Zolotow, "Jelin Wins Fight on Belasco Lease," *NYT* (Dec. 17, 1945), reporting the closing date, mentioned a total of 103 performances, but this seems a slip.
25. Winthrop P. Tryon, "Kiepura and Miss Eggerth Head Cast in Operetta," *Christian Science Monitor* (Jan. 29, 1946); " 'Polonaise' Egg May Hatch Okay in Chi," *Billboard* (May 2, 1946); Sam Zolotow, "News of the Stage," *NYT* (Dec. 3, 1945); "Sherman Seeks Hike in 'Polonaise' Award," *Variety* (Aug. 28, 1946).
26. Claudia Cassidy, "On the Aisle," *Chicago Tribune* (Mar. 6, 1946).

14. Beggar's Holiday

1. For general historical information regarding *Beggar's Holiday,* see especially John Houseman, *Front and Center* (New York: Simon & Schuster, 1979); Daniel C. Caine, "A Crooked Thing: A Chronicle of 'Beggar's Holiday,' " *The New Renaissance* 7 (Spring 1987): 75–100; John Houseman, *Unfinished Business: Memoirs, 1902–1988* (New York: Applause, 1989); Bernard Eisenschitz, *Nicholas Ray: An American Journey,* translated by Tom Milne (Boston: Faber and Faber, 1990, 1993); David Hajdu, *Lush Life: A Biography of Billy Strayhorn* (New York: Farrar, Straus and Giroux, 1996); and John Franceschina, *Duke Ellington's Music for the Theatre* (Jefferson, NC: McFarland, 2001).
2. Lillian Scott, "Perry Watkins Is Proof Hard Work Will Bring Success in New Fields," *Chicago Defender* (Aug. 9, 1947); press release, Jan. 22, 1946, EHP.
3. Perry Watkins, taped public discussion, New York Chapter of the Duke Ellington Society, Mar. 28, 1966, NYPL (not entirely accurately recorded by Hajdu, 101).
4. Henry Whiston, "Reminiscing in Tempo," *Jazz Journal* 20 (February 1967): 4–7; Edward Kennedy Ellington, *Music Is My Mistress* (Garden City, NY: Doubleday, 1973), 185.
5. Hajdu, 101.
6. Sam Zolotow, "Starring Role Set for Judith Evelyn," *NYT* (Sep. 21, 1945).
7. Allen Woll, *Black Musical Theatre: From* Coontown *to* Dreamgirls (Baton Rouge: Louisiana State University Press, 1989); *Speak Low (When You Speak Love): The Letters of Kurt Weill and Lotte Lenya,* edited and translated by Lys Symonette and Kim H. Kowalke (Berkeley: University of California Press, 1996), 306–8, 320.
8. William Eben Schultz, *Gay's Beggar's Opera: Its Content, History & Influence* (New Haven, CT: Yale University Press, 1923), 269; JL, marginalia in Schultz, JLP.
9. Dianne Dugaw, *"Deep Play": John Gay and the Invention of Modernity* (Newark: University of Delaware Press, 2001), 50, 278 n. 1.
10. JL, undated outlines and notes, Duke Ellington Collection, Smithsonian Museum; and Dale Wasserman Papers, NYPL.

11. JL, outlines; Schultz, 271.
12. JL, outlines.
13. JL, "Letter to John Gay," *NYT* (Feb. 9, 1947).
14. Houseman, *Front and Center*, 189.
15. Press release, January 1946, EHP; "Duke Writing Jazz Opera," *Down Beat* (Feb. 11, 1946); Mix [Mike Levin], "'Beggars' Show Opulent Affair But Misses Hit," *Down Beat* (Jan. 15, 1947); Houseman, *Front and Center*, 189; Danton Walker, "Broadway," *Philadelphia Inquirer* (May 11, 1946).
16. Houseman, *Unfinished Business*, 277; Houseman, *Front and Center*, 191–92; JL to William Alexander, Sep. 17, 1946, courtesy of Gerald Max; Eisenschitz, 85; Hajdu, 102.
17. Caine, 86; JL, undated first draft, interim script, and late script, Duke Ellington Collection, Smithsonian Museum; see also JLL (RM 4553).
18. Ellington, 185–86.
19. Luther Henderson, interview with Valerie Archer, July 7, 1981, Oral History of American Music, Yale University; Watkins. Hajdu, 101, writes, "Latouche found it nearly impossible to collaborate with Ellington and threatened to quit, complaining that he needed to talk to him—Ellington was the composer. 'I can't work like this,' said Watkins [read: Latouche]"; however, in the 1966 taped conversation that appears to be Hajdu's source, Watkins says nothing about Latouche quitting, only that Latouche said, about Ellington's unavailability, "I can't work like this. He's the composer. I need him, I need to talk with him," at which point Watkins arranged for Latouche to join Ellington on tour.
20. Henderson.
21. Hajdu, 104; Walter van de Leur, *Something to Live For: The Music of Billy Strayhorn* (New York: Oxford University Press, 2002), 99; for more on Strayhorn's work on *Beggar's Holiday*, see van de Leur, 98, 300 n. 20, 301 n. 21; public access to the Strayhorn papers, currently in private hands and highly restricted, might help clarify some of these issues.
22. JL, undated outlines.
23. JL, scripts.
24. JL, outlines; JL, scripts. As discussed in Chapter 16, "I've Got Me" had an even more complex history, in that the song as found in *Willie* originated in a work Jerome Moross wrote with Lynn Riggs and Ramon Naya, *A Cow in a Trailer*, with Moross keeping the music and Latouche changing the lyric, so that the song's evolution could be summarized as (1) music by Moross and lyric by Riggs and Naya, (2) same music adapted by Moross and new words by Latouche, and then (3) new music by Ellington and same lyric adapted by Latouche.
25. Franceschina, 66.
26. James Ryan O'Leary, "Broadway Highbrow: Discourse and Politics of the American Musical, 1943–1946" (PhD diss., Yale University, 2012), 173.
27. The lyrics in the late script and those in the published music do not always agree. Compare the opening stanza of "Tomorrow Mountain" as found in the former ("Just across tomorrow mountain / There's a happy city they say / Where the suckers are glad / When they are had / And it's Christmas ev'ry day") with that in the latter ("Just across tomorrow mountain / There's a happy city they say / Where the people are grand / And time is planned / So it's Christmas ev'ry day").
28. "Lena Natural for 'Beggars,'" *Down Beat* (Dec. 15, 1945); "Lena Horne Slated for Broadway Opera," *Philadelphia Tribune* (June 18, 1946).
29. Jon Bradshaw, *Dreams That Money Can Buy: The Tragic Life of Libby Holman* (New York: Morrow, 1985).
30. Bradshaw, 202–3, 259; Jack Cavanaugh, "Treetops: An Aura of Glamour, a Trail of Tragedies," *NYT* (May 18, 1997); Paul Bowles, *Without Stopping: An Autobiography* (New York: Harper Perennial, 1972, 2006), 272; Millicent Dillon, *A Little Original Sin: The Life and Work of Jane Bowles* (New York: Holt, Rinehart and Winston, 1981), 223.
31. Houseman, *Front and Center*, 192; John Martin, "The Dance: Our Unsung Grass-Roots Ballet," *NYT* (Feb. 2, 1947).

32. Houseman, *Front and Center*, 192–93; Lillian Scott, "Perry Watkins Is Proof Hard Work Will Bring Success in New Fields," *Chicago Defender* (Apr. 9, 1947); "Broadway News," *Christian Science Monitor* (Oct. 19, 1946); "'Holiday' May Be Toothache to Dental Scion Backing Show for Total of 250G," *Billboard* (Jan. 11, 1947); "Wasserman Backs Out of 'Beggar's Opera,'" *Pittsburgh Courier* (Nov. 16, 1946).
33. Houseman, *Front and Center*, 194.
34. Reviews of *Twilight Alley* in *Variety* (Nov. 27, 1946) and the *Hartford Courant* (Nov. 28, 1946).
35. Houseman, *Front and Center*, 194; reviews of *Twilight Alley* in the [Boston] *Evening American, Globe, Herald, Post,* and *Traveler*, and *Christian Science Monitor* (all Dec. 4, 1946); and *Billboard* (Dec. 14, 1946).
36. Houseman, *Front and Center*, 194–95; Houseman, *Unfinished Business*, 279.
37. Reviews of *Beggar's Holiday* in the *Brooklyn Eagle, Daily News, Journal-American, Newark Daily News, NYHT, NYT, PM, Post, Sun,* and *World-Telegram* (all Dec. 27, 1946); *Los Angeles Times* (Dec. 28, 1946); *Wall Street Journal* (Dec. 30, 1946); *Variety* (Jan. 1, 1947); *Amsterdam News, Baltimore Afro-American, Billboard, Cue, New Yorker,* and *Pittsburgh Courier* (all Jan. 4, 1947); *Newsweek* and *Time* (both Jan. 6, 1947); *Down Beat* (Jan. 15, 1947); *Commonweal* (Jan. 17, 1947); *Life* (Feb. 24, 1947); *Catholic World* 164 (February 1947): 455–56; *Metronome* 63 (February 1947): 36–37; *Theatre Arts* 31 (March 1947): 12–18, 22–27; *School and Society* 65 (Apr. 5, 1947): 252; and George Jean Nathan, *The Theatre Book of the Year, 1946–1947: A Record and an Interpretation* (New York: Knopf, 1947), 255–57.
38. Douglas Watt, "'Holiday' End Seen Mar. 29 or Sooner; Millenium on B'way," *Daily News* (Mar. 7, 1947); Ellington, 186.
39. Reviews of *Beggar's Holiday*; Brooks Atkinson, "Formula Is Broken," *NYT* (Jan. 26, 1947); Martin.
40. Reviews of *Beggar's Holiday*; Eric Bentley, "Broadway and Its Intelligentsia," *Harper's* 194 (March 1947): 211–21.
41. Houseman, *Front and Center*, 195; Houseman, *Unfinished Business*, 279; George Abbott, *Mister Abbott* (New York: Random House, 1963), 217; Henderson; Ellington, 185; Whiston, 5; Mildred Smith, interview with author, June 21, 2014.
42. Erik Haagensen, email to author, May 22, 2014; reviews of *Beggar's Holiday*.
43. Reviews of *Beggar's Holiday* in the *Chicago Tribune* (Apr. 7, 1947) and *Chicago Defender* (Apr. 12, 1947).
44. Klaus Stratemann, *Duke Ellington, Day by Day and Film by Film* (Copenhagen: JazzMedia, 1992), 281; Mercer Ellington, Richard E. Carney, and Perry Watkins to Tom Shepard, June 19, 1964, EHP.
45. Caine, 98–100.
46. "Karamu Plans Stage Fare for Coming Season," *Cleveland Call and Post* (Aug. 30, 1952); Russell Jelliffe to JL, May 27, 1953, Karamu House Records, Western Reserve Historical Society; Watkins; "'Beggar's Holiday' to Be Revived," *Back Stage* (July 2, 1971); Dwight Blocker Bowers, "And Now for Something Completely Different: Reconstructing Duke Ellington's *Beggar's Holiday* for Presentation in a Museum Setting," in *Exhibiting Dilemmas: Issues of Representation at the Smithsonian*, edited by Amy Henderson and Adrienne L. Kaeppler (Washington, DC: Smithsonian, 1997), 262–72; Richard Harrington, "Duke Ellington's Long-Lost 'Holiday,'" *Washington Post* (Feb. 1, 1992); Harrington, "A Winning 'Beggar,'" *Washington Post* (Feb. 4, 1992).
47. Bowers; "Duke Done Deal," *Variety* (Mar. 29, 1993); Thomas Walsh, "Duke's 'Holiday' Resurrected by Wasserman Search," *Back Stage* (Mar. 19, 1993); Dale Wasserman, *Beggar's Holiday*, Wasserman Papers.
48. Richard Christiansen, "Pegasus Puts Down Duke," *Chicago Tribune* (Oct. 14, 1994).
49. James Lincoln Collier, *Duke Ellington* (New York: Oxford University Press, 1987), 266; Harvey G. Cohen, *Duke Ellington's America* (Chicago: University of Chicago Press, 2010), 273–75; Terry Teachout, *Duke: A Life of Duke Ellington* (New York: Gotham, 2013), 258–61.
50. Cecil Smith, *Musical Comedy in America* (New York: Theatre Arts, 1950), 332–33; Lehman Engel, *Words with Music* (New York: Macmillan, 1972), 127–28; Ethan Mordden, *Beautiful Mornin': The Broadway Musical in the 1940s* (New York: Oxford University Press, 1999),

189–90; Gerald Bordman, *American Musical Theatre: A Chronicle*, 3rd ed. (New York: Oxford University Press, 2001), 608–9.

51. Caine, 83–97.
52. Franceschina, 66; O'Leary, 164–65; see also Calhoun Winton, "*The Beggar's Opera*: A Case Study," in *The Cambridge History of British Theatre, Volume 2: 1660 to 1895*, edited by Joseph Donahue (New York: Cambridge University Press, 2004), 143–44, for a brief appreciation.

15. Film Work

1. JL, "On the Film Front," *Modern Music* 19 (November–December 1941): 58–59.
2. Hans Richter, *Hans Richter*, edited by Cleve Gray (New York: Holt, Rinehart and Winston, 1971), 37; see also Cecile Starr, "Notes on Hans Richter in the U.S.A.," *Film Culture* 79 (Winter 1996): 17–26; and Timothy O. Benson, editor, *Hans Richter: Encounters* (New York: DelMonico, 2013).
3. Richter, 152–54; Stephen C. Foster, editor, *Hans Richter: Activism, Modernism, and the Avant-Garde* (Cambridge, MA: MIT Press, 1998); Malte Hagener, *Moving Forward, Looking Back: The European Avant-garde and the Invention of Film Culture, 1919–1939* ([Amsterdam]: Amsterdam University Press, 2007).
4. Richter, 51; Starr, 20 (for a slightly different account); *Dreams That Money Can Buy*, promotional material and program book, clipping file, NYPL.
5. Richter, 53; Milly Heyd, "Hans Richter: Universalism vis-à-vis Particularism," *Ars Judaica* 7 (April 2011): 105–22.
6. Willard Bohn, "Apollinaire and De Chirico: The Making of the Mannequins," *Comparative Literature* 27 (Spring 1975): 153–65.
7. *Dreams That Money Can Buy*, program book; Latouche's lyric as preserved in written form differs somewhat from that heard in the film's current release, which omits, most notably, a section about the wedding of the two mannequins; however, the movie's souvenir program book contains a still from this selfsame marriage episode, indicating that the section had been filmed and at some later point excised.
8. Ezra Goodman, "Musical Fantasy Filmed in Manhattan Loft," *NYT* (Apr. 11, 1948).
9. Paul Bowles, *Without Stopping: An Autobiography* (New York: Harper Perennial, 1972, 2006), 272; *Dreams That Money Can Buy*, program book.
10. Richter, 51; Louise Levitas, "Dreams That Money Can Buy," *PM* (Sep. 15, 1946); Goodman; Starr, 21; Walter Pitman, *Louis Applebaum: A Passion for Culture* (Toronto: Dundurn Group, 2002), 96; contemporaneous sources put the film length at about one hundred minutes, although current versions of the film run about eighty minutes, suggesting a cut at some point of about twenty minutes.
11. Levitas; Hans Richter, "Films Should Be Made for a Limited Public, Too," *PM* (May 24, 1948); JL, "On the Film Front"; Parker Tyler, "Movie Letter," *Kenyon Review* 11 (Winter 1949): 141–44.
12. Review of *Dreams That Money Can Buy* in *Variety* (Apr. 28, 1948); the Cinema 16 preview had been scheduled for April 14, but took place on April 22. See also Jacob Deschin, "Originality in Movies," *NYT* (Apr. 4, 1948); and Scott MacDonald, *Cinema 16: Documents Toward a History of the Film Society* (Philadelphia: Temple University Press, 2002), 43, 102.
13. Reviews of *Dreams That Money Can Buy* in *Cue*, *Daily News*, *Journal-American*, *NYHT*, *NYT*, and *Post* (all Apr. 24, 1948); *Variety* (Apr. 28, 1948); *Worker* (May 2, 1948); and *Musical Digest* 30 (May 1948): 20 ("fascinating"); see also a follow-up review by Bosley Crowther, *NYT* (May 9, 1948).
14. Reviews of *Dreams That Money Can Buy* in the *Los Angeles Times* (July 17, 1948); *Washington Post* (Oct. 14, 1948); and *Boston Globe* and *Christian Science Monitor* (both Oct. 23, 1948); A. H. Weiler, "Notes About People and Pictures," *NYT* (Sep. 26, 1948); Richter, *Richter*, 51.
15. Benson, 152; Starr, 21; Hava Aldouby, *Federico Fellini: Painting in Film, Painting on Film* (Toronto: University of Toronto Press, 2013), 48–49; David Lynch, interviewed in *Ruth, Roses*

and Revolver, directed by Helen Gallacher (BBC Arena, 1987); A. L. Rees, *A History of Experimental Film and Video: From the Canonical Avant-Garde to Contemporary British Practice* (London: BFI, 1999). 55.

16. Stephen Coates, "The Stuff of Dreams," *Guardian* (Aug. 18, 2006); Stephen Coates, emails to author, June 2014.
17. Richter, *Richter*, 147–51; Hans Richter, *Encounters from Dada till Today*, translated by Christopher Middleton (Los Angeles: DelMonico, 2013), 51.
18. Richter, *Richter*, 54.
19. Bosley Crowther, "All for the Kids," *NYT* (Mar. 3, 1957); "Film Censors Approve Blurred View of Nude," *NYT* (Mar. 12, 1957); reviews of *8 x 8* in the *Daily News*, *Journal-American*, *NYT*, and *Post* (all Mar. 16, 1957); JL, "Mock Madrigal," *Folder* 4 (1956): 6–7 (song section).
20. Press release, January 26, 1950, Press Release Archives, Museum of Modern Art.
21. A. H. Weiler, "Random Observations on Pictures and People," *NYT* (Feb. 24, 1952); "Latouche Sets up Co. in New York to Make Specialized Shorts," *Variety* (Apr. 30, 1952); JL to Libby Holman, c. August 1953, Libby Holman Papers, Boston University.
22. Vèvè A. Clark, Millicent Hodson, and Catrina Neiman, *The Legend of Maya Deren: A Documentary Biography and Collected Works*, vol. 1, Part One (New York: Anthology Film Archives/Film Culture, 1985); Stan Brakhage, *Film at Wit's End: Eight Avant-Garde Filmmakers* (Kingston, NY: McPherson, 1989); Bill Nichols, editor, *Maya Deren and the American Avant-Garde* (Berkeley: University of California Press, 2001).
23. *The Grand Surprise: The Journals of Leo Lerman*, edited by Stephen Pascal (New York: Knopf, 2007), 17, 130.
24. Correspondence, notes, and other materials in the Maya Deren Collection, Boston University; Howard Thompson, "Recent Arrivals on the 16-MM Screen Scene," *NYT* (Feb. 22, 1959); see Sarah Keller, *Maya Deren: Incomplete Control* (New York: Columbia University Press, 2015), 204–24, for more on the filmmaker's "complex imbroglio" with Aries Productions.
25. Brakhage, 107; Maya Deren to JL, Sep. 30, 1953; June 9, 1956, Deren Collection.
26. *Grand Surprise*, 244 n. 49; Keller, 206.
27. JL, "The Peppermint Tree," *Tomorrow* (March 1950); *Good Housekeeping* (December 1954): 53–54. JL apparently read the poem to the Kieslers on Dec. 27, 1949, Stefanie Kiesler, diaries, AFL.
28. Dante Alighieri, *Inferno*, translated by Michael Palma (New York: Norton, 2002), 163; JL, marginalia, "The Peppermint Tree," LKP.
29. Lucy Key Miller, "Front Views & Profiles," *Chicago Tribune* (Nov. 8, 1951); [Leonard Lyons], " 'Modern Art'? No, It's GOP Election Map," *Salt Lake Tribune* (Mar. 8, 1952).
30. Willis Pyle, interviews with author, Jan. 5, 2013, and June 23, 2014.
31. JL to Libby Holman; Pyle.
32. "Children's Theater Group to Perform at Library," *Westfield Leader* (Apr. 3, 1986).
33. James Schuyler, in conversation with Peter Schjeldahl, January 1977, courtesy of Nathan Kernan.
34. *Oral History Initiative: On "Presenting Jane,"* HFA (Harvard Film Archive) 32882 (including rushes and outtakes as well as May 9, 2014, interviews with John Ashbery, Jane Freilicher, and Harrison Starr), courtesy of Christina Davis; Gooch, 222–23.
35. Schuyler; Harrison Starr, interview with author, July 6, 2016 ("flamboyant"); David K. Kermani, *John Ashbery: A Comprehensive Bibliography* (New York: Garland, 1976), 189–90; Brad Gooch, *City Poet: The Life and Times of Frank O'Hara* (New York: Harper Perennial, 1994), 222–23; Terence Diggory, *Encyclopedia of the New York School Poets* (New York: Facts on File, 2009), 30; Mark Silverberg, *The New York School Poets and the Neo Avant-Garde: Between Radical Art and Radical Chic* (Burlington, VT: Ashgate, 2010), 247; *Oral History Initiative* ("To put it"); program for the Artists' Theatre February 25, 1953, premiere, courtesy of Nathan Kernan.
36. *Presenting Jane*; Holland Cotter, "Generosity of Everyday Surrealism," *NYT* (December 14, 2014).

16. Ballet Ballads

1. Paul Snook, unpublished interview with Jerome Moross, WRVR Radio, 1970, courtesy of Charles Turner; Noah Andre Trudeau, unpublished interview with Moross, September 1975, courtesy of Turner; Craig Reardon, unpublished interview with Moross, Apr. 16, 1979, courtesy of Turner (also posted on http://vimeo.com/87641531); Jane Coppock and Arthur Berger, "A Conversation with Arthur Berger," *Perspectives of New Music* 17 (Autumn–Winter 1978): 40–67; John Caps, "An Interview with Jerome Moross, Part I" and "An Interview with Jerome Moross, Part II," *The Cue Sheet* 5 (1988): 73–80, 99–108; David Ewen, *American Composers: A Biographical Dictionary* (New York: Putnam's, 1982), 467–69; Mariana Whitmer, *Jerome Moross's* The Big Country*: A Film Score Guide* (Lanham, MD: Scarecrow, 2012).
2. Arthur V. Berger, "The Young Composers' Group," *Trend* 2 (April–May–June 1933): 26–28; Lehman Engel, *This Bright Day: An Autobiography* (New York: Macmillan, 1974); Reardon ("Benny could," "diminished"); Caps ("idiocy," "madness"); Oscar Levant, *A Smattering of Ignorance* (New York: Doubleday, Doran, 1940), 238.
3. Henry Cowell, editor, *American Composers on American Music: A Symposium* (New York: Ungar, 1933), 10; Jerome Moross, "New Musical Revues for Old," *New Theatre* 2 (October 1935): 12–13, 33.
4. Snook ("in the midst"); Aaron Copland, "Our Younger Generation—Ten Years Later," *Modern Music* 13 (May–June 1936): 9; Ewen, 488 ("The composer").
5. Christopher Palmer, "From the Big Country with Big Style," *Gramophone* 71 (October 1993): 18.
6. "Thanks to 'Golden Apple,' He Becomes Ex-Mr. Guggenheim," *Brooklyn Daily Eagle* (Aug. 18, 1954); Isabel Morse Jones, "Little-Known Works of Music Given Expression," *Los Angeles Times* (Mar. 10, 1941); John Martin, "The Dance: An Exhibition," *NYT* (Nov. 26, 1939); Jerome Moross, "Introduction," *The Golden Apple: A Musical in Two Acts* (New York: Random House, 1953, 1954), xix.
7. JL, "Curtain Speech," *The Golden Apple*, xii–xiii; Jerome Moross, "Introduction," xx.
8. JL, "Items Called 'Ballet Ballads,'" *NYT* (June 6, 1948); "Benton's Nudes People the Ozarks," *Life* (Feb. 20, 1939); JL, "Pastiche," *Columbia Review* 16 (November 1934): 34.
9. Albert Goldberg, "The Sounding Board," *Los Angeles Times* (Oct. 1, 1950).
10. Howard Taubman, "American Music Heard in Concert," *NYT* (Mar. 9, 1940); Jones; Jerome Moross, "Hollywood Music without Movies," *Modern Music* 18 (May–June 1941): 262–63.
11. Jerome Moross to JL, Dec. 29, 1943, JLL; Moross to JL, Jan. 17, 1944; Jan. 22, 1944; JL to Moross, Jan. 22, 1944; Jan. 23, 1944, JMP.
12. Moross to JL, Feb. 14, 1944, courtesy of Susanna Moross Tarjan; JLD, Apr. 14, 1944; Apr. 26, 1944; Apr. 27, 1944; Moross to JL, Feb. 16, 1947, JMP; Lucy Kroll to JL, Apr. 7, 1947, LKP.
13. JL, *Volpone* sketches, JLL (RM 5863).
14. JL and Jerome Moross, "Great Lucifer," JLL (RM 5864).
15. JL and Jerome Moross, "A Note on Production," *Ballet Ballads* (New York: Chappell, 1949); JL, "Items."
16. Jerome Moross to JL, Aug. 10, 1944, JMP; Moross to Aaron Copland, Oct. 5, 1944, courtesy of Susanna Moross Tarjan.
17. JL's script, *Four in Hand: An Evening of Ballet Ballads*, LKP, also contains subtitles for the individual acts that, with the exception of *Riding Hood*, never appeared in published scores or programs, namely, *Susanna and the Elders: A Campmeeting Cantata*; *Willie the Weeper: A City Fable*; *Riding Hood Revisited: A Silly Symphony in E-flat Major*; and *The Eccentricities of Davy Crockett: A Tall Tale* (this last-named subtitle also found in Moross's manuscript score); the current discussion often avails itself of this script rather than the published scores for some details of spelling, punctuation, and capitalization.

18. JL and Moross, "A Note"; Goldberg; Caps, 75; Snook; JL, "Items"; see also JL, "Synopsis," LKP.
19. JL, "Items"; JL, *Four in Hand*; Latouche adapted the "liefer—reefer" line from an early cabaret song for Spivy, "I'm Going on a Binge with a Dinge."
20. Carl Sandburg, *The American Songbag* (New York: Harcourt Brace Jovanovich, 1927, 1990), 205–6; Leonard Lyons, "The Lyons Den," *Pittsburgh Post-Gazette* (Sep. 18, 1953).
21. Charles Turner, "Jerome Moross: An Introduction and Annotated Worklist," *Notes* 61 (March 2005): 659–727.
22. *Sketches and Eccentricities of Col. David Crockett of West Tennessee* (New York: Arno, 1833, 1974); Michael A. Lofaro, editor, *Davy Crockett: The Man, The Legend, The Legacy 1786–1986* (Knoxville: University of Tennessee Press, 1985); Michael A. Lofaro and Joe Cummings, editors, *Crockett at Two Hundred: New Perspectives on the Man and the Myth* (Knoxville: University of Tennessee Press, 1989); Paul Andrew Hutton, " 'Going to Congress and making allmynacks is my trade': David Crockett, His Almanacs, and the Evolution of a Frontier Legend," *Journal of the West* 37 (April 1998): 10–22; Julia L. Mickenberg, *Learning from the Left: Children's Literature, the Cold War, and Radical Politics in the United States* (New York: Oxford, 2006).
23. Hutton, 11.
24. *Sketches*, 144.
25. In the consecration chorus in the published score, the phrase "turbulent, unfettered" should read "turbulent, unlettered."
26. Moross apparently told Albert Goldberg that *Davy Crockett* encompassed "a four-movement symphony," although he never explained this enigmatic and possibly misreported claim, made even more confusing by the composer's assertion in the same article that all four dance-operas form a symphony.
27. Craig S. Womack, *Art as Performance, Story as Criticism: Reflections on Native Literary Aesthetics* (Norman: University of Oklahoma Press, 2009).
28. Lynn Riggs and Ramon Naya, *A Cow in a Trailer*, JMP; with regard to his Symphony, Moross adapted a dance for Bessie as that work's first movement, and a conversation between Bessie and Miss Spot as the work's second-movement scherzo.
29. Wolfgang Saxon, "Lucy Kroll, 87, Talent Agent for a Who's Who in the Arts," *NYT* (Mar. 19, 1997); JL to Lee Falk and William Friml, Mar. 3, 1955, LKP.
30. Lucy Kroll to JL, Nov. 28, 1947; Kroll to Mary Baker, June 4, 1946; June 25, 1946, LKP; Lewis B. Funke, "News and Gossip of the Rialto," *NYT* (Jan. 20, 1946).
31. Jerome Moross, "Ballet Ballads Revisited" (c. 1960), JMP; JL, "Items"; Lucy Kroll to JL, Sep. 11, 1946, LKP.
32. Cheryl Crawford, "Explaining the Experimental Theatre's Policy," *NYT* (Dec. 7, 1947); Crawford, *One Naked Individual: My Fifty Years in the Theatre* (New York: Bobbs-Merrill, 1977), 158.
33. Jerome Moross to Lucy Kroll, Sep. 3, 1946, LKP; Sharry Underwood, "Ballet Ballads," *Dance Chronicle* 9 (1986): 279–327; "ET's $19,300 Budget for 'Ballet Ballads' Stirs Sharp Protests," *Variety* (Mar. 31, 1948).
34. JL, "Items"; Underwood.
35. Underwood, 298.
36. Underwood, 303, 310.
37. Walter Sorell, *Hanya Holm: The Biography of an Artist* (Middletown, CT: Wesleyan University Press, 1969); Claudia Gitelman, *Dancing with Principle: Hanya Holm in Colorado, 1841–1983* (Boulder: University Press of Colorado, 2001).
38. Andrew Drummond, interview with Hanya Holm, May 20, 1973, ADP; Sorell, 109; Underwood; for JL's stage directions, see drafts of *Ballet Ballads*, JLL (RM 4553) and LKP.
39. Underwood, 314; Jerome Moross to Lucy Kroll, Oct. 23, 1958, LKP.
40. Underwood, 281, 286, 314; Drummond.
41. Reviews of *Ballet Ballads* (at the Maxine Elliott's) in the *Daily News*, *Journal-American*, *NYHT*, *NYT*, *Post*, *Sun*, and *World-Telegram* (all May 10, 1948); *Brooklyn Eagle*, *Morning*

Telegraph, and *PM* (all May 11, 1948); *Variety* (May 12, 1948); *Billboard* (May 22, 1948); and *Theatre Arts* 32 (June–July 1948): 10–11; Crawford, 158.

42. Follow-up or secondary reviews in the *News*, *NYHT*, and *NYT* (all May 16, 1948); John Martin to Nathan Kroll, May 11, 1948, LKP.
43. Reviews of *Ballet Ballads* (at the Music Box) in the *Hollywood Reporter*, *Journal-American*, and *Sun* (all May 19, 1948); *Daily News* (May 20, 1948, "flashy"); *Boston Globe* (May 23, 1948); *Time* (May 24, 1948); *Los Angeles News* (May 25, 1948); *Variety* (May 26, 1948); *New Yorker* (May 29, 1948); *New Republic* (May 31, 1948); *Saturday Review* (June 5, 1948); *NYHT* (June 20, 1948); *School and Society* 67 (June 26, 1948): 475–78; *Musical Courier* 138 (July 1948): 20; and George Jean Nathan, *The Theatre Book of the Year, 1948–1949* (New York: Knopf, 1949), 27–29.
44. "Lead N. Y. Legit Critics' Poll," *Variety* (May 26, 1948); Bert McCord, "News of the Theater," *NYHT* (May 27, 1948); Randall Thompson to Jerome Moross, June 18, 1948, JMP.
45. Review of *Ballet Ballads* in *Variety*.
46. Bert McCord, "News of the Theater," *NYHT* (June 11, 1948); Lewis Funke, "News and Gossip of the Rialto," *NYT* (May 30, 1948); "Broadway Report," *PM* (June 1, 1948).
47. Douglas Watt, "'Ballet Ballads,' with 40 Kids Going for It; Nears Hit Class," *Daily News* (June 8, 1948); Lucy Kroll to Mary Hunter, June 4, 1948, LKP; "'Ballads' Gets Fresh Bankroll," *Variety* (July 7, 1948); Louis Calta, "'Ballet Ballads' Ends Run Tonight," *NYT* (July 10, 1948); Underwood, 291; see also Sono Osato, *Distant Dances* (New York: Knopf, 1980), 258–60.
48. "'Ballet Ballads' May Go It Again," *Billboard* (Oct. 16, 1948); Albert Sirmay to Jerome Moross, May 17, 1948, JMP; Stuart W. Little, "'Off-Broadway' Shows Get Foothold Elsewhere, Philadelphia Starts Trend," *NYHT* (Jan. 28, 1959); JL, *Ballet Ballads*, production script prepared by Richard Grayson, NYPL (JNF 88–133).
49. Jerome Moross to Lucy Kroll, Oct. 13, 1946; Kroll to Moross, June 24, 1948; Moross to Kroll, June 28, 1948, LKP.
50. Jerome Moross to Lucy Kroll, Oct. 23, 1958, JKP; reviews of *Ballet Ballads* in the *Hollywood Citizen-News*, [Los Angeles] *Daily News*, *Examiner*, *Herald Express*, *Mirror*, and *Times* (all Oct. 11, 1950); Sidney Skolsky, "Hollywood Is My Beat," *Hollywood Citizen-News* (Nov. 7, 1950); Snook.
51. Lewis Funke, "News and Gossip of the Rialto," *NYT* (June 26, 1960); Moross, "Ballet Ballads."
52. Lewis Funke, "News and Gossip of the Rialto," *NYT* (June 27, 1954); archival material with respect to the 1954 Berlin production, including Lucy Kroll, memorandum, Apr. 27, 1954, LKP; Andrew DeShong, *The Theatrical Designs of George Grosz* (Ann Arbor, MI: UMI Research Press, 1970, 1982), 111–16.
53. Reviews of *Bilderbogen aus Amerika* in the [Berlin] *Abend*, *Kurier*, *Nacht-Depesche*, and *Telegraf* (all Sep. 9, 1954) ("weil es uns am amerikanischesten erscheint"); see also DeShong, 113–16.
54. Don Ross, "The Show They Never Forgot," *NYHT* (Jan. 1, 1961).
55. Reviews of *Ballet Ballads* in the *Daily News*, *Journal-American*, *NYHT*, *NYT*, *Post*, and *Times* (all Jan. 4, 1961); *Wall Street Journal* (Jan. 5, 1961); *Cue* and *New Yorker* (both Jan. 14, 1961); and *Variety* (Feb. 1, 1961); Walter Terry, "2 Arts Wrestle and Both Lose," *NYHT* (c. February 1961), LKP.
56. Lucy Kroll to Dorothy Olin, Jan. 13, 1961; Jerome Moross to Kroll, Feb. 2, 1961, LKP.
57. Turner, 701; Snook.
58. Winifred Kahn, "Envisaging a Lyric Theatre," *Educational Theatre Journal* 2 (March 1950): 52–57; Ethan Mordden, *Beautiful Mornin': The Broadway Musical in the 1940s* (New York: Oxford University Press, 1999); Mark N. Grant, *The Rise and Fall of the Broadway Musical* (Boston: Northeastern University Press, 2004), 107–9; Pamyla Alayne Stiehl, "The 'Dansical': American Musical Theatre Reconfigured as a Choreographer's Expression and Domain" (PhD diss., University of Colorado, 2008); James Bradley Rogers, "Integration and the American Musical: From Musical Theatre to Performance Studies" (PhD diss., University of California, 2010).
59. Mordden, 218; Snook.

17. More Fables

1. *The Grand Surprise: The Journals of Leo Lerman*, edited by Stephen Pascal (New York: Knopf, 2007), 143.
2. JLD, June 22, 1948 (first mention of "Walter Stayne" [sic?], presumably not only the "Walter" mentioned subsequently, but specifically the dancer Walter Stane); Sep. 4, 1949; June 29, 1949; Dec. 4, 1949.
3. JLD, June 9, 1949; June 30, 1954; JL to Gore Vidal, Feb. 14, 1950, GVP.
4. JLD, June 14, 1949.
5. JLD, May 11, 1948; June 23, 1948; June 27, 1948; Apr. 3, 1949; July 19, 1949.
6. " 'Jack Armstrong' Marks Birthday, A Children's Hero Since 1932," *Montreal Gazette* (Aug. 2, 1946); Mary Little, "Airglances," *Des Moines Register* (Aug. 6, 1946); "Radio Reviews," *Variety* (Aug. 14, 1946); "Six Actors Join Operation Housing," *Ogdensburg* [NY] *Journal* (Feb. 18, 1947); [Walter] Winchell, "Man About Town Hears Churchill Memoirs Disappoint Time & Life," *Akron* [OH] *Beacon Journal* (May 25, 1948); "We Are for Wallace," *Los Angeles Times* (Oct. 26, 1948); Danton Walker, "Broadway," *Cumberland* [MD] *News* (Aug. 8, 1948).
7. Andrew Johnstone, "Americans Disunited: Americans United for World Organization and the Triumph of Internationalism," *Journal of American Studies* 44 (2010): 1–18; "Radio Reviews," *Variety* (Aug. 14, 1946).
8. "Radio Reviews."
9. Jackson J. Benson, *The True Adventures of John Steinbeck, Writer* (New York: Viking, 1984), 588–89, 594, 597; Burgess Meredith, *So Far, So Good: A Memoir* (New York: Little, Brown, 1994), 124, 127–29; Jay Parini, *John Steinbeck: A Biography* (New York: Holt, 1995), 303, 311; Brian Railsback and Michael J. Meyer, *A John Steinbeck Encyclopedia* (Westport, CT: Greenwood, 2006), 204–5; John Steinbeck, *The Last Joan*, JLL.
10. A. H. Weiler, "By Way of Report," *NYT* (July 18, 1948); Burgess Meredith to JL, June 10, 1948, JLL.
11. Lydia Goehr, *The Quest for Voice: On Music, Politics, and the Limits of Philosophy* (Berkeley: University of California Press, 1998), 176–78.
12. Sam Staggs, *All About "All About Eve": The Complete Behind-the-Scenes Story of the Bitchiest Film Ever Made* (New York: St. Martin's, 2000).
13. "A Revolting Play," *NYT* (Apr. 29, 1913).
14. Helen Eager, review of *Miss Julie* in the *Boston Traveler* (Feb. 4, 1947), either slightly misquoted the line as "When the upper classes unbend, they bend over backwards," or the line itself had changed; August Strindberg, *Miss Julie* [adapted by JL], Theodore Komisarjevsky Papers, Harvard University; August Strindberg, *Pre-Inferno Plays*, translated by Walter Johnson (Seattle: University of Washington Press, 1970), 98; for English versions before Latouche, see those by Arthur Swan (1911), Edwin Björkman (1912), Edith and Warner Oland (1912), Charles Recht (1912), Horace B. Samuel (1914), and C. D. Locock (1930); see also Margareta Mattsson, "Strindberg's 'Miss Julie' in English: The Value of Literalness in Translation," *Scandinavica* 13/2 (1974): 131–36; Barry Jacobs, "Translating for the Stage: The Case of Strindberg," *TijdSchrift voor Skandinavistiek* 19/1 (1998): 75–101; and Michael Robinson, "Miss Julie," *Encyclopedia of Literary Translation into English*, vol. 2 (Chicago: Fitzroy Dearborn, 2000), 1347–49.
15. Reviews of *Miss Julie* in *Variety* (Jan. 29, 1947); *Washington Post* (Feb. 3, 1947); [Boston] *Evening American, Globe, Herald, Post, Traveler*, and *Christian Science Monitor* (all Feb. 4, 1947); and *Billboard* (Feb. 15, 1947); Louis Calta, "2 Bergner Plays, Recast, Resumed," *NYT* (Feb. 25, 1947); Harold V. Cohen, "The Drama Desk," *Pittsburgh Post-Gazette* (Feb. 26, 1947).
16. JLD, c. Nov. 9, 1948; Luigi Pirandello, *Trovarsi: Find Yourself*, translated by Jane Hinton, JLL (RM 4549); "Rialto Gossip," *NYT* (Aug. 27, 1939).
17. JL to Lilian (alternate spelling) [Loehr], c. September 1931, MCP.
18. Ring Lardner and George S. Kaufman, *June Moon* (New York: French, 1929, 1931); Lardner and Kaufman, *June Moon*, adapted by JL (4th rev., Mar. 15, 1949; final rehearsal, Mar. 26, 1949), JLL (CTR 915 and 915A).

19. Sidney Howard, *Alien Corn* (New York: Scribner's, 1933).
20. Sidney Howard, *Alien Corn,* adapted by JL ("First Revise," Mar. 1, 1949), JLL (CTR 925A; for an earlier draft, see also CTR 925), 58; JL, *The Ballad of Baby Doe* (New York: Program, 1956, 1958), 20, 23–24.
21. John Crosby, "Writers Take Dead Aim at Schools," *Washington Post,* May 1, 1949.
22. Hugh Dixon, "Hollywood," *Pittsburgh Post-Gazette* (Sep. 10, 1947); Harold V. Cohen, "The Drama Desk," *Pittsburgh Post-Gazette* (Mar. 12, 1949); Sam Zolotow, "'Two Blind Mice' Will Bow Tonight," *NYT* (Mar. 2, 1949); Sam Zolotow, "Producers Launch Drive on 'Scalping,'" *NYT* (June 10, 1949).
23. Sam Zolotow, "Play Critics Alter System of Voting," *NYT* (Sep. 24, 1947); Paul Knepler and Géza Herczeg, *Empress Josephine,* and Edward Eager, *Poor Josephine!* JLL (RM 4546 and 4550).
24. [Milton Gropper?], *Tamborito,* JLL (RM 4547); Gloria Castiel Jacobson, "The Life and Music of Ernesto Lecuona" (PhD diss., University of Florida, 1982); Ned Sublette, *Cuba and Its Music: From the First Drums to the Mambo* (Chicago: Chicago Review, 2004), 381–83.
25. Zolotow, "Play Critics"; "Lecuona to Do Legiter," *Billboard* (Dec. 13, 1947); Sam Zolotow, "Pemberton Ready for Second Show," *NYT* (Dec. 23, 1949).
26. Fred Kaplan, *Gore Vidal: A Biography* (New York: Doubleday, 1999), 299–99, 371–72.
27. Lehman Engel, *This Bright Day: An Autobiography* (New York: Macmillan, 1974), 166.
28. Engel; Aaron Copland, *Copland on Music* (New York: Norton, 1963), 162–63; Lehman Engel, *The American Musical Theater: A Consideration* (New York: Macmillan, 1967, 1975); Engel, *Words with Music* (New York: Macmillan, 1972); Engel, *The Making of a Musical* (New York: Macmillan, 1977).
29. Louis Calta, "'Hilarities' Starts in Adelphi Tonight," *NYT* (Sep. 9, 1948); Lucy Kroll to William Fitelson, Feb. 15, 1949, LKP; Louis Calta, "Webster to Tour Straw-Hat Circuit," *NYT* (Mar. 22, 1949).
30. Sam Zolotow, "'Autumn Garden' to Open Tonight," *NYT* (Mar. 7, 1951); *Golden Ladder* materials, Karamu House Records, Western Reserve Historical Society, including Lehman Engel to Benno Frank, Mar. 2, 1953; Engel to Rowena Jelliffe, Apr. 4, 1953; Joanna Roos to Jelliffe, May 9, 1953.
31. Reviews of *Golden Ladder* in the *Cleveland Plain Dealer* (May 29, 1953) and *Cleveland Call and Post* (June 27, 1953); Joanna Roos to Lehman Engel, Oct. 17, 1980; Engel to Roos, Aug. 22, 1981, Lehman Engel Papers, Yale University.
32. Martin Kieran [Alexander King?], *Mooncalf;* Joanna Roos and JL, *Mooncalf;* Roos, King, and Lewis Allan [Abel Meeropol], *Mooncalf,* Engel Papers.
33. Lewis Funke, "Gossip of the Rialto," *NYT* (Oct. 19, 1947); Lewis Funke, "News and Gossip Gathered on the Rialto," *NYT* (Oct. 26, 1947); Vernon Duke, "The Late John Treville Latouche," *Variety* (Aug. 29, 1956); Vernon Duke, "Tribute to a Poet," *Theatre Arts* 41 (March 1957): 24.
34. Duke, "The Late"; Gordon Parks, *Camera Portraits: The Techniques and Principles of Documentary Portraiture* (New York: Watts, 1948), 52; William Friml Jr., email to author, Aug. 29, 2014.
35. George Currie, "Theater," *Brooklyn Eagle* (Feb. 28, 1948); George Currie, "Theater," *Brooklyn Eagle* (June 23, 1948); "Theater Notes," *Brooklyn Eagle* (Sep. 24, 1948); Sam Zolotow, "Jed Harris to Buy M'Laughlins' Play," *NYT* (Nov. 12, 1948); Dorothy Kilgallen, "Voice of Broadway," *Schenectady Gazette* (Dec. 13, 1948); Zolotow, "Van Druten Work Has Bow Tonight," *NYT* (Dec. 22, 1948); Lewis Funke, "News and Gossip Gathered on the Rialto," *NYT* (Jan. 23, 1949); Zolotow, "Producers Launch"; Lewis Funke, "News and Gossip Gathered on the Rialto," *NYT* (Sep. 25, 1949); see also *The Happy Dollar,* clipping file, NYPL.
36. The earliest extant script survives in JLL; the second, at the LC and in the private collection of Erik Haagensen; and the third script, "adapted by Dick Ott," in the author's possession, courtesy of Anne Melville; as concerns the plot, the first script differs from the later ones in not having Stacky Lee's father Ike reappear in the Hero Hill scene; this first script also has some additional numbers, included in the author's synopsis.

37. B. A. Botkin, editor, *A Treasury of American Folklore: Stories, Ballads, and Traditions of the People* (New York: Crown, 1944); John W. Roberts, "Stackolee and the Development of a Black Heroic Idea," *Western Folklore* 42 (July 1983): 179–90; Cecil Brown, *Stagolee Shot Billy* (Cambridge, MA: Harvard University Press, 2003); Katherine Reed, "Stagger Lee's Come out on Top: The Ballad of Stagger Lee," https://www.youtube.com/watch?v=WTEU0rlR2yM&t=82s.
38. Arie Kaplan, *From Krakow to Krypton: Jews and Comic Books* (Philadelphia: Jewish Publication Society, 2008); Harry Brod, *Superman Is Jewish? How Comic Book Superheroes Came to Serve Truth, Justice and the Jewish-American Way* (New York: Free, 2012).
39. CD and DVD transfers of *The Happy Dollar*, courtesy of Anne Melville.
40. Sue Dauphin, *Houston by Stages: A History of Theatre in Houston* (Burnet, TX: Eakin, 1981), 304–7, 326; Anne Melville, interview with author, Sep. 29, 2014.
41. Reviews of *The Happy Dollar* in the [Houston] *Chronicle* (Ann Holmes on Apr. 21, 1954; Ray Wood on May 2, 1954 ["extremely"]) and *Post* (Apr. 21, 1954); *Variety* (May 19, 1954).
42. Review of *The Happy Dollar* in the *Dallas Morning News* (Mar. 10, 1955); JL to Lee Falk and William Friml, Mar. 3, 1955, LKP.
43. " 'Happy Dollar' Glums up the Works in Coast Foldo," *Variety* (Aug. 15, 1956); Duke, "Tribute."
44. Reviews of *The Happy Dollar* in the [Los Angeles] *Mirror-News* and *Times* (both July 10, 1956); and *Los Angeles Examiner, Hollywood Reporter*, and *Variety* (all July 11, 1956); T. Edward Hambleton to Vernon Duke, Aug. 17, 1956; Hambleton to Duke, Oct. 10, 1956, VDP.

18. The Golden Apple

1. Jerome Moross to Harry Allen Moe, Sep. 30, 1948, Jerome Moross file, GMF; JL and Moross, *The Golden Apple: A Musical in Two Acts* (New York: Random House, 1953, 1954); Jon Burlingame, "An Opera for Broadway," liner notes, *The Golden Apple* (PS Classics, PS-1528, 2015).
2. JL, "Fellowship Application Form," acknowledged Nov. 2, 1948, JL file, GMF.
3. Minna Lederman, "Confidential Report," Dec. 8, 1948; Douglas Moore, "Confidential Report," received Dec. 30, 1948, JL file.
4. JLD, Feb. 6, 1949; May 7, 1949; June 9, 1949; Seymour Peck, " 'Apple' among Bagels," *NYT* (Mar. 7, 1954); Sam Zolotow, "Producers Launch Drive on 'Scalping,' " *NYT* (June 10, 1949).
5. Jerome Moross to John Marshall, Nov. 19, 1949; Marshall to Moross, Mar. 2, 1950, Moross file; JLD, Feb. 22, 1950.
6. Gore Vidal, *The Golden Age* (New York: Vintage International, 2000), 410; William C. Bamberger, *Kenward Elmslie: A Biographical Profile* (Flint, MI: Bamberger, 1993), 5–6.
7. Louis Calta, " 'Faithfully Yours' Departs Saturday," *NYT* (Dec. 11, 1951); Sam Zolotow, " 'Venus Observed' in Debut Tonight," *NYT* (Feb. 13, 1952); H. William Fitelson to LL [Lawrence Langer], TH [Theresa Helburn], and AM [Armina Marshall], Theatre Guild Archive, Yale University; Jerome Moross to the Ford Foundation, n.d., Moross file.
8. Louis Calta, "Play to Lampoon New York Major," *NYT* (Jan. 21, 1954); Norris Houghton, "The Phoenix Rises," *NYT* (Nov. 29, 1953); Howard Taubman, "To Do Good Plays Well," *NYT* (Nov. 27, 1967); Jesse McKinley, "T. Edward Hambleton, Theatrical Producer, Dies at 94," *NYT* (Dec. 19, 2005).
9. JL, "Curtain Speech," in JL and Moross, xi–xviii; "John Latouche," *The Golden Apple*, souvenir program book, EHP; see also JL, " 'The Golden Apple': American Musical on Greek Legend," *NYHT* (Mar. 7, 1954).
10. JL and Moross; Susanna Moross Tarjan, interview with author, Oct. 25, 2014.
11. JL, "Curtain Speech," xv–xvi.
12. Robert J. Rabel, "Odysseus Almost Makes It to Broadway: The *Ulysses Africanus* of Kurt Weill and Maxwell Anderson," *International Journal of the Classical Tradition* 13 (Spring 2007): 550–70; Alberto Manguel, *Homer's* The Iliad *and* The Odyssey: *A Biography* (London: Atlantic Books, 2007); Edith Hall, *The Return of Ulysses: A Cultural History of Homer's* Odyssey (Baltimore: John Hopkins University Press, 2008).

13. Rabel, 570; Jerome Moross to John Marshall; Moross, "Introduction," in JL and Moross, xx; Peck; Elliot Norton, "Epic Poems Made Theme of Musical," *Boston Post* (Jan. 3, 1950).
14. Unless otherwise indicated, all the quotations of the libretto in this chapter found, including the typology, in JL and Moross (except for this one line about Theodore Roosevelt, which appears, however, in many drafts of the script as well as in the score and on the original cast album); Jonathan Shay, *Odysseus in America: Combat Trauma and the Trials of Homecoming* (New York: Scribner, 2002).
15. Vernon Rice, " 'Golden Apple' Set in Our Golden Era," *Post* (Mar. 10, 1954).
16. Deniz Cordell and Robert Edridge-Waks, " 'The World That's on the Way': Moross and Latouche's *The Golden Apple*," liner notes, *The Golden Apple* (PS Classics); William DeWitt Hyde, *The Art of Optimism As Taught by Robert Browning* (New York: Crowell, 1900), 3 (this observation suggested by Bernd Becher in the *Columbia Daily Spectator* [Mar. 25, 1954], who refers to Latouche's use of a "poem" entitled "The World We Live In").
17. Richard Rodgers and Oscar Hammerstein II, *Allegro* (New York: Knopf, 1948), 32; the typescript and musical manuscript sources for this final duet contain some discrepancies with regard to the use of first-person singular versus plural pronouns, although in these final stanzas, they are in agreement.
18. Rabel, 560.
19. The Random House edition misprints "calls" as "call."
20. JL, "Curtain Speech," xiv.
21. *The Golden Apple*, various scripts and sketches, JMP and LKP; see also [JL], "Ulysses in the Underworld," JLL (Rm 5865).
22. Norris Houghton, *Entrances & Exits: A Life in and out of the Theatre* (New York: Limelight, 1991), 229–30.
23. Houghton, 229–30; Andrew B. Harris, *The Performing Set: The Broadway Designs of William and Jean Eckart* (Denton: University of North Texas Press, 2006); Norman Lloyd, interview with author, Nov. 15, 2014.
24. Alfred de Liagre Jr. to Roger L. Stevens, Feb. 4, 1954, Playwrights' Company Records, Wisconsin Center for Film and Theater Research; Harris, 26–39 (35 for Lloyd's firing); Andrew Drummond, interview with Hanya Holm, May 20, 1973, ADP; Walter Sorell, *Hanya Holm: The Biography of an Artist* (Middletown, CT: Wesleyan University Press, 1969), 131–33.
25. Kaye Ballard with Jim Hesselman, *How I Lost 10 Pounds in 53 Years: A Memoir* (New York: Back Stage, 2006), 75–78; Ward Morehouse, "Kay [*sic*] Ballard Finds Life's So Crowded," *World-Telegram* (May 11, 1954; according to this earlier source, Ballard auditioned four times, not seven as stated in her memoirs). See also Kaye Ballard, "Mink Parade Helped Kaye Land Role in 'Golden Apple' ", *Des Moines Register* (June 12, 1954).
26. Peck; JL, "Curtain Speech"; Kaye Ballard, interview with author, Jan. 21, 2013; Shannon Bolin, interview with author, Jan. 22, 2013; Jerry Stiller, interview with author, Jan. 24, 2015.
27. Houghton, 228–29.
28. Marc Blitzstein to JL, Mar. 11, 1954, and other telegrams, JLP.
29. Reviews of *The Golden Apple* in the *Brooklyn Eagle, Daily Mirror, Daily News, Journal-American, Morning Telegraph* (George Freedley), *NYHT* (Virgil Thomson), *NYT, Post, Women's Wear Daily, World Telegram*, and *Variety* (all Mar. 12, 1954); *Morning Telegraph* (Whitney Bolton, Mar. 13, 1954); *Wall Street Journal* (Mar. 15, 1954); *Hollywood Reporter* (Mar. 16, 1954); *Christian Science Monitor* (Mar. 20, 1954); *Time* (Mar. 22, 1954); *Columbia Spectator* (Mar. 25, 1954); *NYHT* (Walter Kerr, Mar. 28, 1954); *Theatre Arts* 38 (August 1954): 22–25; and *Educational Theatre Journal* 6 (October 1954): 254–59; follow-up reviews in the *Daily Mirror, Daily News, NYHT* (Virgil Thomson), and *NYT* (all Mar. 21, 1954), and *Post* (May 16, 1954); dance reviews in the *NYHT* (Walter Terry, Mar. 21, 1954) and *NYT* (John Martin, May 2, 1954); *The Diaries of Dawn Powell, 1931–1965*, edited with an introduction by Tim Page (South Royalton, VT: Steerforth, 1995), 337.

30. Gore Vidal, *Virgin Islands: A Dependency of United States: Essays, 1992–1997* (London: Deutsch, 1997), 26; *The Golden Age*, 417–20 (in this excerpt, Vidal perhaps had in mind Ulysses' climactic outburst, "I can go home again," but the opera has no song or even phrase, "go home at last"), 463.
31. Eleanor Roosevelt, "My Day," *St. Louis Post-Dispatch* (Apr. 2, 1954).
32. "Show Finances," *Variety* (June 30, 1954).
33. Alfred de Liagre Jr. to Roger L. Stevens, Mar. 29, 1954, Playwrights' Company Records.
34. Erik Haagensen, "Getting to the Core of *The Golden Apple*," *Show Music* 11 (Fall 1995): 33–36, 66–67.
35. Haagensen, 36.
36. "Broadway Goes Fancy Free," *Life* (May 24, 1954); Lucy Kroll to Jerome Moross and JL, July 2, 1954, JMP; Kroll to Roger L. Stevens, May 7, 1981, LKP.
37. Reviews of *The Golden Apple* in the *American Record Guide* 61 (March/April 1998): 296; and *Opera News* 63 (August 1998): 38.
38. JL and Moross; Brad Gooch, *City Poet: The Life and Times of Frank O'Hara* (New York: Harper Perennial, 1993), 199; Kenward Elmslie, "I Remembers of [*sic*] Frank O'Hara," in *Blast from the Past* (Austin, TX: Skanky Possum, 2000), 14–15.
39. JL, "Curtain Speech."
40. *The Golden Apple*, Equity Library Theatre, program book, LKP; Thornton Wilder to Jerome Moross, Sep. 28, 1967.
41. Reviews of *The Golden Apple* in the *Washington Evening Star* (Aug. 10, 1954); *Houston Post* (Aug. 19, 1955); *Dallas Morning News* (Oct. 27, 2014); for other reviews, see the *Golden Apple* files in both JMP and LKP, as well as *Jerome Moross, American Composer (1913–2013)*, www.jeromemoross.com.
42. Reviews of *The Golden Apple* in the *Daily News*, *Mirror*, *Post*, *NYHT*, *NYT*, and *World-Telegram* (all Feb. 13, 1962); *Variety* (Mar. 7, 1962); *NYT* (Mar. 30, 1990); *Observer* (Apr. 9, 1990); *Village Voice* (Apr. 10, 1990); and *Theater Week* (Apr. 16, 1990).
43. Ken Mandelbaum, *Not Since Carrie: Forty Years of Broadway Musical Flops* (New York: St. Martin's, 1991), 344.
44. Vernon Duke, "The Late John Treville Latouche," *Variety* (Aug. 29, 1956); David Jenness and Don Velsey, *Classic American Popular Song: The Second Half-Century, 1950–2000* (New York: Routledge, 2006), 188–89.
45. Mandelbaum, 341–45; Steven Suskin, *Opening Night on Broadway* (New York: Schirmer, 1990), p. 262; Ethan Mordden, *Coming up Roses: The Broadway Musical in the 1950s* (New York: Oxford University Press, 1998), 103–6; Mark N. Grant, *The Rise and Fall of the Broadway Musical* (Boston: Northeastern University Press, 2004), 109–10; Larry Stempel, *Showtime: A History of the Broadway Musical Theater* (New York: Norton, 2010), 489–91; Thomas S. Hischak, *Off-Broadway Musicals Since 1919: From* Greenwich Village Follies *to* The Toxic Avenger (Lanham, MD: Scarecrow, 2011), 31.
46. Haagensen, 34; Mariana Whitmer, *Jerome Moross's* The Big Country: *A Film Score Guide* (Lanham, MD: Scarecrow, 2012), 34–39; Pamyla Alayne Stiehl, "The 'Dansical': American Musical Theatre Reconfigured as a Choreographer's Expression and Domain" (PhD diss., University of Colorado, 2008), 161–66; James Bradley Rogers, "Integration and the American Musical: From Musical Theatre to Performance Studies" (PhD diss., University of California, 2010), 86–91.
47. Philip Chaffin, email to author, Nov. 20, 2015; Cordell.
48. Reviews of *The Golden Apple* in the *Bay Area Reporter* (June 18, 2015); *Playbill* (June 20, 2015); *Drama Queen* (June 25, 2015); *CastAlbums.org* (July 2015); *Fresh Air* (NPR) (Sep. 24, 2015); *Fanfare* 39 (November–December 2015): 390–94; *Stage and Screen* (Mar. 26, 2016); and listeners' reviews on Amazon.com.
49. Jerome Moross, "Introduction," xx; JLD, June 30, 1954; Lucy Kroll, memorandum, Jan. 5, 1955; Moross to Kroll, Oct. 13, 1946, LKP; Tarjan.

50. Jerome Moross to Margaret Freeman Cabell, May 21, 1973, MCP; Craig Reardon, unpublished interview with Moross, Apr. 16, 1979, courtesy of Charles Turner (also posted on http://vimeo.com/87641531).

19. Touche's Salon

1. *Red Channels: The Report of Communist Influence in Radio and Television* (New York: American Business Consultants, 1950); David Everitt, *A Shadow of Red: Communism and the Blacklist in Radio and Television* (Chicago: Dee, 2007).
2. "'The Golden Apple' Has a Rosy Hue," *The New Counterattack* (Apr. 9, 1954).
3. Earl Robinson, "Balladier for Americans," *Nation* (Aug. 25, 1956): 161; Gore Vidal, *Palimpsest: A Memoir* (New York: Random House, 1995), 246; Vidal, *Virgin Islands: A Dependency of United States*: *Essays, 1992–1997* (London: Deutsch, 1997), 26; JL to Vidal, Feb. 15, 1954, GVP.
4. JLD, Apr. 15, 1951.
5. JLD, June 8, 1954.
6. JLD, June 12, 1954; July 12, 1954; Kenward Elmslie, interview with author, Mar. 13, 2013.
7. Robinson; SAC to Director, Apr. 19, 1954; JL, affidavits, Jan. 27, 1956, and May 18, 1956, FBI.
8. JLD, June 12, 1954.
9. Norris Houghton, *Entrances & Exits: A Life in and out of the Theatre* (New York: Limelight, 1991), 258.
10. William C. Bamberger, *Kenward Elmslie: A Biographical Profile* (Flint, MI: Bamberger Books, 1993), 119; Gore Vidal, *The Golden Age* (New York: Doubleday, 2000), 280; Vidal, *Palimpsest*, 246; Fred Kaplan, *Gore Vidal: A Biography* (New York: Doubleday, 1999), 299; Max Jacobson and JL, "To Range from Preventive Illnesses to Concentration Camp Psychology," May 2, 1949, JLL.
11. JL to Harry Martin, Feb. 8, 1951, JLP; JL to Gore Vidal, Feb. 14, 1950, GVP; JLD, Apr. 19, 1951; June 10, 1954; July 11, 1954.
12. JL to Gore Vidal, c. 1950, GVP (for Eliot); JL to Harry Martin, postmarked Dec. 3, 1950 (for Thomson); April [May] 11, 1950 (for Vivaldi), AHD; JLD, July 9, 1954 (for *Money*).
13. JLD, Apr. 19, 1951; June 12, 1954; June 30, 1954; July 9, 1954; JL to Harry Martin, postmarked Apr. 22, 1951, AHD.
14. William Grimes, "Hans Holzer, Ghost Hunter, Dies at 89," *NYT* (Apr. 30, 2009); "Off Broadway," *NYT* (May 8, 1955); "Comedy Opens Tonight," *NYT* (Aug. 7, 1956).
15. Hans Holzer, *The Ghost Hunter's Favorite Cases* (New York: Dorset, 2003), 20–21; Holzer, *Ghost Hunter* (New York: Bobbs-Merrill, 1963), 199–210.
16. Holzer, *Ghost Hunter's*, 22–23.
17. JL to Kenward Elmslie, n.d., JLP; Lord Kinross, *The Innocents at Home* (New York: Morrow, 1960), 46; Kaplan, 298.
18. Miles Kreuger, interview with author, Jan. 13, 2013; Peter Filichia, "Ben Bagley Meets Eudora Welty," courtesy of the author (posted on broadwaystars.com on July 25, 2001); Jack Beeson, *How Operas Are Created by Composers and Librettists: The Life of Jack Beeson, American Opera Composer* (Lewiston, NY: Mellen, 2008), 218.
19. John Bernard Myers, *Tracking the Marvelous: A Life in the New York Art World* (New York: Random House, 1981, 1983), 78.
20. *Letters of Carl Van Vechten*, edited by Bruce Kellner (New Haven, CT: Yale University Press, 1987), 239, James Gavin, *Intimate Nights: The Golden Age of New York Cabaret* (New York: Grove Weidenfeld, 1991), 100.
21. Kenward Elmslie, *Blast from the Past* (Austin, TX: Skanky Possum, 2000), 1–3.
22. Johnny Nicholson, interview with Fred Kaplan, July 4, 1997, courtesy of Kaplan; Gavin, 100; Virginia M. Dortch, editor, *Peggy Guggenheim and Her Friends* (Milan: Berenice, 1994), 147.

23. Ned Rorem, liner notes, *Taking a Chance on Love* (Original Cast Records, OC-4444, 2000); JLD, June 8, 1954; Vidal, *Golden Age*, 281; *The Grand Surprise: The Journals of Leo Lerman*, edited by Stephen Pascal (New York: Knopf, 2007), 161.
24. Patricia Highsmith, diaries, July 2, 1942, Swiss National Library, Bern, Switzerland; Kaplan, 299, 355; Kinross, 47.
25. Nicholson; Kaplan, 299; Ron Padgett, interview with author, Mar. 3, 2015; George Plimpton, *Truman Capote: In Which Various Friends, Enemies, Acquaintances, and Detractors Recall His Turbulent Career* (New York: Doubleday, 1997), 46.
26. Ned Rorem, interview with John Grimmett, Oct. 14, 2011, courtesy of Grimmett; Rorem, *The Final Diary, 1961–1972* (New York: Holt, Rinehart and Winston, 1974), 71, 419; Rorem, *Knowing When to Stop: A Memoir* (New York: Simon & Schuster, 1994), 252, 319.
27. Rorem, *Setting the Tone: Essays and a Diary* (New York: Coward-McCann, 1983), 33, 176.
28. Rorem, *Knowing*, 252.
29. James Murdoch, *Peggy Glanville-Hicks: A Transposed Life* (Hillsdale, NY: Pendragon, 2002), 46; Suzanne Robinson, "'A Ping, Qualified by a Thud': Music Criticism in Manhattan and the Case of Cage (1943–58)," *Journal of the Society for American Music* 1 (February 2007): 111; "Paul Bowles," unpublished essay, courtesy of Robinson; Peggy Glanville-Hicks, diaries, Oct. 25, 1946, National Library of Australia, Canberra, courtesy of Robinson.
30. JL to Harry Martin, c. 1953, JLP.
31. JL to Jack Kerouac, postmarked Feb. 4, 1950, Jack Kerouac Papers, NYPL; Jack Kerouac, "On the Road Again," *New Yorker* (June 22, 1998): 46–59; Jack Kerouac, *Dear Carolyn*, edited by Arthur and Kit Knight (California, PA: [Knight], 1983), 10.
32. Lerman, 142; John Lahr, *Tennessee Williams: Mad Pilgrimage of the Flesh* (New York: Norton, 2014), 164–67; Philip C. Kolin, editor, *The Tennessee Williams Encyclopedia* (Westport, CT: Greenwood, 2004), 143; Tennessee Williams, *Memoirs* (New York: Bantam, 1976); Erik Haagensen, email to author, Mar. 19, 2015; *The Selected Letters of Tennessee Williams*, vol. 2: 1945–1957, edited by Albert J. Devlin (Sewanee, TN: University of the South, 2004), 391.
33. Elmslie, interview; JLD, Apr. 3, 1949; Lahr, 275; Vidal, *Golden Age*, 317; Frank Merlo and Tennessee Williams to JL, Mar. 13, 1954, JLP.
34. Plimpton, 46; Truman Capote, *Conversations*, edited by M. Thomas Inge (Jackson: University Press of Mississippi, 1987), 142; Truman Capote, *Three by Truman Capote* (New York: Random House, 1985), 137.
35. Plimpton, 46.
36. Elmslie, interview; Gore Vidal to Ruth Yorck, July 24, 1957, RYP.
37. JL to Gore Vidal, Feb. 14, 1950, GVP; Kaplan, 334; Vidal, *Virgin Islands*, 25; Dortch, 148; Vidal, *Golden Age*, 285–86.
38. Dortch, 148; Gore Vidal to JL, Mar. 11, 1954, JLP; Alice Bouverie, contract with JL and Vidal, June 12, 1950, GVP; Kaplan, 349.
39. JL and Vidal, "The Girl of the Golden East" and "Love Is a Horse Named Gladys," GVP; Kaplan, 371.
40. JL to Gore Vidal, Feb. 14, 1950, AHD; JL to Harry Martin, postmarked May 9, 1950, AHD.
41. David Sinclair, *Dynasty: The Astors and Their Times* (New York: Beaufort, 1984), 364; Derek Wilson, *The Astors, 1763–1992: Landscape with Millionaires* (New York: St. Martin's Press, 1993); Julie Kavanagh, *Secret Muses: The Life of Frederick Ashton* (New York: Faber and Faber, 1996).
42. JL to Harry Martin, postmarked May 9, 1950, AHD; Lerman, 101.
43. Kaplan, 334, 401, 403; Gore Vidal, "How I Survived the Fifties," *New Yorker* (Oct. 2, 1995): 65; *Out in the World: Selected Letters of Jane Bowles* 1935–1970, edited by Millicent Dillon (Santa Barbara, CA: Black Sparrow, 1985), 168; "Cholly Knickerbocker," *Palm Beach* [FL] *Post* (Sep. 12, 1952); Kinross, 64–65, 140; Lerman, 3–4.
44. Franceschina, 80–85; Louis Calta, "Stage Producers Sue Fox on Title," *NYT* (Nov. 25, 1952); Coleman Dowell, *A Star-Bright Lie* (Normal, IL: Dalkey, 1993), 101, 102; Doris Julian, "Three Sonnets for a Miniature Lion," JLP.

45. Honor Moore, *The White Blackbird: A Life of the Painter Margarett Sargent by Her Granddaughter* (New York: Viking, 1966); Kinross, 140; *Out in the World*, 168.
46. Moore, 297.
47. JL to Harry Martin, May 24, 1950; postmarked Oct. 15, 1950; May 1, 1951, AHD.
48. Harry Martin, interview with Gregory Gibson, 1978, transcript, Sawyer Free Library, Gloucester MA, courtesy of Helen Freeman; "Artist Harry Martin, 57," *Gloucester Daily Times* (Nov. 8, 1984); AHD.
49. Kinross, 46; JL to Harry Martin, Aug. 1, 1953, and undated letters, AHD; JL to Martin, c. 1953, JLP.
50. Gerrit Lansing, interviews with author, Apr. 4, 2013, and Mar. 3, 2015.
51. Ellsworth Kelly, interview with author, Oct. 25, 2012.
52. Gerrit Lansing, interview with author, June 22, 2015.
53. Kinross, 23.
54. Kinross, 24, 22–29, 160–61.
55. Lansing; John Dandola, *Living in the Past, Looking to the Future: The Biography of John Hays Hammond, Jr.* (Glen Ridge, NJ: Quincannon, 2004); "Artist Harry Martin."
56. Denis Brian, *Pulitzer: A Life* (New York: Wiley, 2001); Bamberger, 100; Elmslie, *Blast*, 5, 7.
57. "Latouche to See His Own 'Ballet Ballads,'" *Cleveland Plain Dealer* (Sep. 23, 1951); Kenward Elmslie to JL, c. 1951, JLP; Bamberger, 111.
58. Kinross, 134; Padgett; Elmslie, *Blast*, 7; Elmslie, interview; JLD, July 12, 1954.
59. John J. D. Sheehan, "American Voice," *Opera News* 73 (August 2008): 32; Beeson, 256.
60. Louise Andrews Kent, *Mrs. Appleyard and I* (Boston: Houghton Mifflin, 1968); Brad Gooch, "Poet's Corner," *House & Garden* 158 (November 1986): 176–81; information provided by Donna Fitch, Calais Town Clerk, courtesy of Ron Padgett, email to author, June 22, 2015.
61. Gooch; Kent; JL to Effie Latouche, Dec. 24, 1955, JLP.
62. Olivia Gay, email to author, May 31, 2015; Dowell, 92; Coleman Dowell, diaries, Jan. 10, [1978?], courtesy of Eugene Hayworth ("thin-lipped," and for Dowell's meeting McCarthy at Latouche's, contradicted in *A Star-Bright Lie*).
63. Louise Andrews Kent and Elizabeth Kent Gay, *The Summer Kitchen (Mrs. Appleyard's, of course)* (Boston: Houghton Mifflin, 1957), 29, 63–66, 184.
64. Michael Silverblatt, "A Tribute to Kenward Elmslie," *Barney* 4 (August 1984): 79–81; John Bernard Myers, editor, *The Poets of the New York School* (Philadelphia: Falcon, 1969), 25–26; Padgett; Bamberger, 114–15.
65. Elmslie, *Blast*, 16; Kenward Elmslie and Mary Kite, *Spilled Beans: A Conversation* (Austin, TX: Skanky Possum, 2001), 9–10; Elmslie, *Routine Disruptions: Selected Poems & Lyrics, 1960–1998* (Minneapolis: Coffee House, 1998), 177–80.
66. Myers, *Tracking*; Jenni Quilter, *New York School Painters & Poets: Neon in Daylight* (New York: Rizzoli, 2014).
67. Dortch, 148; *The Diaries of Judith Malina, 1947–1957* (New York: Grove, 1984), 396; "Deeds," *East Hampton Star* (Mar. 25, 1954).
68. *Artists' Theatre: Four Plays*, edited by Herbert Machiz (New York: Grove, 1960), 9; Myers, *Tracking*, 167.
69. John Bernard Myers, "In Regards to This Selection of Verse, Or Every Painter Should Have His Poet," *Nomad* 10–11 (Autumn 1962): 30; Mark Silverberg, *The New York School Poets and the Neo-Avant-Garde: Between Radical Art and Radical Chic* (Burlington, VT: Ashgate, 2010), 135.
70. John Ashbery and James Schuyler, *A Nest of Ninnies* (Norman, IL: Dalkey, 1969, 2008); *The Collected Poems of Frank O'Hara*, edited by Donald Allen (Berkeley: University of California Press, 1995), 525.
71. Gooch, 226–27; Carl Little, "An Interview with James Schuyler," *Agni* 37 (1993): 159; Elmslie, *Blast*, 14–18; *Collected Poems*, 526; *The Later Diaries of Ned Rorem: 1961–1972* (San Francisco: North Point, 1983), 188–89; *Artists' Theatre*; program for the Artists' Theatre

Feb. 25, 1953, premiere, courtesy of Nathan Kernan; John Gruen, *The Party's Over Now: Reminiscences of the Fifties—New York's Artists, Writers, Musicians, and Their Friends* (Wainscott, NY: Pushcart, 1967), 90.

72. John Ashbery, email to author, Oct. 17, 2011; James Schuyler, in conversation with Peter Schjeldahl, January 1977, courtesy of Nathan Kernan; Ryan Dohoney, "Mourning Coterie: Morton Feldman's Posthumous Collaborations with Frank O'Hara," in *New York School Collaborations: The Color of Vowels*, edited by Mark Silverberg (New York: Palgrave Macmillan, 2013), 184–85; Brett Boutwell, email to author, Mar. 1, 2015, including portions of Boutwell's unpublished American Musicological Society 2008 conference paper, "Feldman, Guston, and the Emergence of the Figure."
73. Joe LeSueur, *Digressions on Some Poems by Frank O'Hara* (New York: Farrar, Straus and Giroux, 2003), 109–11; James Schuyler, *Selected Poems* (New York: Farrar, Straus and Giroux, 1988), 103–7.
74. *Tracking*, 192; Kreuger; Ron Padgett, *Joe: A Memoir of Joe Brainard* (Minneapolis: Coffee House, 2004).

20. The Vamp

1. *The Vamp*, contracts, LKP.
2. "'The Vamp' with Music by Jim Munday [*sic*], Is Tops," *Chicago Defender* (Nov. 5, 1955); Charles Edward Smith, liner notes, *On a Mundy Flight* (Epic, LN 3475, 1958); Bernard L. Peterson, *Profiles of African American Stage Performers and Theatre People, 1816–1960* (Westport, CT: Greenwood, 2001), 167. Kenward Elmslie remembered Mundy as a closeted homosexual, interview with author, Mar. 13, 2013.
3. Louis Calta, "Curtain Is Falling on Drama Season," *NYT* (Apr. 9, 1953); "'Samson and Lila Dee' Wants Actors, Angels," *Pittsburgh Courier* (May 16, 1953); "Seek $130,000 for All-Negro Broadway Musical," *Jet* (July 23, 1953); *The Vamp*, clipping files, NYPL and EHP.
4. Carol Channing, *Just Lucky I Guess: A Memoir of Sorts* (New York: Simon & Schuster, 2002), 74; Sue Dickinson, "$5,000 Haircut Inspired LaTouche," *RTD* (Nov. 20, 1956).
5. Lewis Funke, "Gossip of the Rialto," *NYT* (Nov. 8, 1953); "Negro Playwright Regains Rights to Musical," *Jet* (Aug. 14, 1954).
6. Lewis Funke, "Rialto Gossip," *NYT* (Feb. 14, 1954); Louis Calta, "Premiere Tonight of 'Golden Apple,'" *NYT* (Mar. 11, 1954); *The Vamp*, contract amended Feb. 27, 1954, LKP.
7. JL, "'Vamp's' Background," *NYT* (Nov. 6, 1955); Douglas Watt, "'Delilah' Goes H'wood; Boom in Cricket Cages," *Daily News* (May 26, 1954); Leonard Lyons, "The Lyons Den," *Post* (Jan. 13, 1955); *The Vamp*, clipping file, NYPL.
8. Lucy Kroll, memoranda, *The Vamp*; *The Vamp*, contract with Sam Locke, July 12, 1954, LKP; JLD, June 12, 1954; Douglas Martin, "Sam Locke, Writer for Radio, TV and Theater, Is Dead at 81," *NYT* (Sep. 29, 1998).
9. JLD, June 12, 1954; Lucy Kroll, memoranda, *The Vamp*, LKP; Lewis Funke, "News and Gossip Gathered on the Rialto," *NYT* (May 22, 1955).
10. Steven Suskin, *The Sound of Broadway Music: A Book of Orchestrators and Orchestrations* (New York: Oxford University Press, 2009), 568–69.
11. JL to K[enward Elmslie], c. August 1955, JLP; "Films Even More Fantastic Than in 'Delilah,' Author Says," *New Haven Journal-Courier* (Oct. 13, 1955); "Jimmy Mundy's Talent Shines in New Revue," *New York Age* (Nov. 5, 1955).
12. Sam Zolotow, "Joyce Grenfell Opens Bid Tonight," *NYT* (Oct. 10, 1955); Louis Calta, "'Carefree Tree' Opening Tonight," *NYT* (Oct. 11, 1955); Lucy Kroll, memoranda, *The Vamp*, LKP; JLD, June 30, 1955.
13. Reviews of *Delilah*/*The Vamp* in the *Windsor Star*, and the [Detroit] *Free Press*, *News*, and *Times* (all Sep. 27, 1955); *Variety* (Sep. 28, 1955); [New Haven] *Evening Register* and *Journal-Courier* (both Oct. 12, 1955); [Washington] *Daily News* and *Evening Star* (both Oct. 19, 1955); *Post and Times-Herald* (Oct. 20, 1955); and *Sun* (Oct. 23, 1955).

14. Channing, 110; [George Helmer], "Taking a Bite of the Big Apple," *Steve Reeves International Society Newsletter* 4/3 (1998, accessed online); see also Chris LeClaire, *Steve Reeves: Worlds to Conquer* ([Chatham, MA]: Monomoy, 1999), 162.
15. Two additional lyrics apparently written for *The Vamp*, "Learning to Live Like a Lady" and "You Gotta Give the Public What It Wants," survive among Sam Locke's papers along with other materials related to the show, Sam Locke Papers, University of Wyoming.
16. JL and Locke, *Delilah*, EHP; JL and Locke, *The Vamp*, EHP; Locke to Lucy Kroll, Nov. 13, 1967, LKP.
17. JL, "'Vamp's' Background"; "Films Even More Fantastic"; Gay J. Talese, "Then and Now," *NYT* (Oct. 16, 1955).
18. JL, "'Vamp's' Background."
19. Ryan Water, "A Vamp There Is," *Cue* (Oct. 29, 1955).
20. JL and Sam Locke, *Delilah* and *The Vamp*; reviews of *Delilah/The Vamp*.
21. The printed edition of "Ragtime Romeo" mistakenly spells "lassie's" "lasie's"; Dickinson; reviews of *Delilah/The Vamp*.
22. Reviews of *The Vamp* in the *Daily Mirror, Daily News, Hollywood Reporter, Journal- American, NYHT, NYT, Post, Wall Street Journal, Women's Wear Daily,* and *World-Telegram* (all Nov. 11, 1955); *Variety* (Nov. 16, 1955); *New Yorker* (Nov. 19, 1955); *Newsweek* and *Time* (both Nov. 21, 1955); *Saturday Review* (Nov. 26, 1955); *Life* (Nov. 28, 1955); *Look* (Nov. 29, 1955); *Commonweal* (Dec. 16, 1955); *Catholic World* 182 (January 1956): 310; and *Theatre Arts* 40 (January 1956): 20–21.
23. Channing, 111.
24. Ethan Mordden, *One More Kiss: The Broadway Musical in the 1970s* (New York: Palgrave Macmillan, 2003), 62; Channing, 74.
25. Ethan Mordden, *Coming up Roses: The Broadway Musical in the 1950s* (New York: Oxford University Press, 1998), 150.
26. Lucy Kroll, memoranda, LKP; "Martin Cohen Sets Sequels to 'Piranha,' 'Humanoids of Deep,'" *Variety* (May 28, 1980).
27. Ken Mandelbaum, *Not Since Carrie: Forty Years of Broadway Musical Flops* (New York: St. Martin's, 1991), 59–60; Mordden, *Coming*, 130.
28. David Jenness and Don Velsey, *Classic American Popular Song: The Second Half-Century, 1950–2000* (New York: Routledge, 2006), 252; Robert Miles, *First and Last Love: Thoughts and Memories About Music* (Santa Fe, NM: Sunstone, 2014).
29. Roger Schore to Erik Haagensen, Apr. 23, 2000, EHP; Robert Miles, interview with author, Jan. 14, 2015.
30. Joanna E. Rapf, editor, *On the Waterfront* (New York: Cambridge University Press, 2003), 143.
31. Catherine Minucci, emails to author, Jan. 9, 2015; Jan. 17, 2015.
32. James Gavin, *Intimate Nights: The Golden Age of New York Cabaret* (New York: Grove Weidenfeld, 1991), 112; Charlotte Rae, email to author, Mar. 13, 2013; Charlotte Rae and Larry Strauss, *The Facts of My Life* (Albany, GA: BearManor, 2015), 62–63.
33. Erik Haagensen, email to author, Jan. 12, 2015, based on recollections of discussions with Kenward Elmslie (for Fuller).
34. Rapf, 143.
35. Leonard Bernstein to David Diamond, Aug. 17, 1954, David Diamond Papers, LC.
36. JL to Libby Holman, c. August 1953, Libby Holman Papers, Boston University; Jenness, 252.

21. Candide

1. Joan Peyser, *Bernstein: A Biography* (New York: Beech Tree, 1987), 247, claims that Bernstein and Hellman met through Blitzstein in 1949, although it seems possible that they had met earlier than this; see also Jackson R. Bryer, *Conversations with Lillian Hellman* (Jackson: University Press of Mississippi, 1986); Carl Rollyson, *Lillian Hellman: Her Legend and Her Legacy* (New York: St. Martin's Press, 1988); Joan Mellen, *Hellman and Hammett: The*

Legendary Passion of Lillian Hellman and Dashiell Hammett (New York: HarperCollins, 1996); Deborah Martinson, *Lillian Hellman: A Life with Foxes and Scoundrels* (New York: Counterpoint, 2005); and Alice Kessler-Harris, *A Difficult Woman: The Challenging Life and Times of Lillian Hellman* (New York: Bloomsbury, 2012).

2. John Briggs, *Leonard Bernstein: The Man, His Work, and His World* (New York: World, 1961); Humphrey Burton, *Leonard Bernstein* (New York: Doubleday, 1994); Meryle Secrest, *Leonard Bernstein: A Life* (New York: Knopf, 1994); Burton Bernstein and Barbara B. Haws, *Leonard Bernstein, American Original: How a Modern Renaissance Man Transformed Music and the World During His New York Philharmonic Years, 1943–1976* (New York: Collins, 2008); *The Leonard Bernstein Letters*, edited by Nigel Simeone (New Haven, CT: Yale University Press, 2013); Allen Shawn, *Leonard Bernstein: An American Musician* (New Haven, CT: Yale University Press, 2014).
3. Leonard Bernstein, "Colloquy in Boston," *NYT* (Nov. 18, 1956); Don Ross, "Voltaire's 'Candide' Is Set to Music," *NYHT* (Nov. 25, 1956); Bernstein to Shirley Bernstein, Apr. 17, 1950, LBP; Louis Calta, "Odets Play Gets Kelly and Hagen," *NYT* (July 29, 1950); "Hellman, Bernstein Mull New Musical," *Variety* (July 26, 1950); Louis Calta, "Comedy by Critic to Arrive Tonight," *NYT* (Sep. 28, 1950).
4. Louis Calta, "New Ingenue Lead for Estelle Loring," *NYT* (Nov. 3, 1951); Lewis Funke, "Gossip of the Rialto," *NYT* (Nov. 11, 1951); Leonard Bernstein to Helen Coates, Nov. 15, 1951, LBP.
5. Marc Blitzstein to Leonard Bernstein, Aug. 15, 1952, Marc Blitzstein Papers, Wisconsin Historical Society.
6. Lillian Hellman to Leonard Bernstein, c. late 1953; Bernstein to Felicia Bernstein, Jan. 5, 1954; Bernstein to Hellman, Jan. 7, 1954, LBP.
7. Voltaire, *Candide: or, Optimism*, translated by John Butt (New York: Penguin Books, 1947, 1986), a version found among Bernstein's papers; see also, as another possible source in English, F. A. M. De Voltaire, *Candide, or, The Optimist*, translated by Henry Morley (New York: Dutton, [1922]).
8. Theodore Besterman, *Voltaire* (Chicago: University of Chicago Press, 1969); Haydn Trevor Mason, *Voltaire: A Biography* (Baltimore: Johns Hopkins University Press, 1981); Philip Stewart, "Candide," in *The Cambridge Companion to Voltaire*, edited by Nicholas Cronk (New York: Cambridge University Press, 2009); Ian Davidson, *Voltaire: A Life* (New York: Pegasus, 2010); Maury Maverick, "Books and Congressmen," *NYT* (Mar. 13, 1949); V. S. Pritchett, "Schools of Satire," *NYT* (Mar. 20, 1949).
9. Brooks Peters, "Making Your Garden Growl: Lillian Hellman and Candide," *Opera News* 65 (July 1, 2000): 38; Burton, 259; Bernstein and Haws, 42–43; Briggs, 195; Leonard Bernstein, "Leonard Bernstein Talks about 'Candide,'" *Bernstein Conducts Candide* (Deutsche Grammophon, 449-656-2, 1991; see also *Candide*, DVD video, Deutsche Grammophon, B0006905-09, 2006); Bernstein, "Colloquy"; Ross; Richard G. Stern, "Lillian Hellman on Her Plays," *Contact* 3 (1959): 119; Lillian Hellman, *Scoundrel Time* (New York: Bantam, 1976), 38, 148.
10. Howard Pollack, *Marc Blitzstein: His Life, His Work, His World* (New York: Oxford University Press, 2012); Davidson; Anthony Netboy, "Voltaire's English Years (1726–1728)," *Virginia Quarterly Review* 53 (Spring 1977): 341; Leanne Pettit, "An Analysis of the Effectiveness of Individual Dramatic and Musical Elements in the 1956, 1973 and 1988 Versions of Leonard Bernstein's *Candide*" (DMA thesis, Louisiana State University, 2009), 121; Helen Smith, *There's a Place for Us: The Musical Theatre Works of Leonard Bernstein* (Burlington, VT: Ashgate, 2011), 121.
11. Burt McCord, "Hellman, Bernstein Toying with 'Candide' Put to Music," *NYHT* (Feb. 12, 1954); Lillian Hellman to Theodore [no last name], Jan. 14, 1954; Archibald MacLeish to Hellman, Apr. 12, [1954]; Apr. 21, 1954; Hellman to Leonard Bernstein, Apr. 16, 1954; Hellman to MacLeish, May 7, 1954, LHP.
12. Lillian Hellman to Richard Wilbur, May 28, 1954; Hellman to Roald Dahl, May 31, 1954; Wilbur to Hellman, June 17, 1954, LHP.

13. JL to Douglas Moore, c. June 1954, DMP; JLD, June 30, 1954; JL to Jack Dempsey, postmarked July 2, 1954, EHP.
14. JLD, June 30, 1954; July 9, 1954.
15. JLD, July 9, 1954; July 11, 1954.
16. JLD, July 9, 1954.
17. Lillian Hellman to Gerald Goode, Sep. 3, 1954; October 1954; Goode to Hellman, Oct. 15, 1954; C. David Hocker to Hellman, Sep. 7, 1954, LHP; Sam Zolotow, "'One Eye Closed' to Open No More," *NYT* (Nov. 26, 1954).
18. Leonard Bernstein to David Diamond, Nov. 25, 1954, David Diamond Papers, LC; Simeone, 322–23.
19. Bryer, 59; Mellen, 316; Wright, 267; Lillian Hellman to Leonard Bernstein, c. 1955, LBP; Willis Pyle, interview with author, Jan. 5, 2013, and June 23, 2014; Harrison Starr, interview with author, July 6, 2016 ("flamboyant").
20. John Keats, *You Might as Well Live: The Life and Times of Dorothy Parker* (New York: Simon & Schuster, 1970), 269; Marion Meade, *Dorothy Parker: What Fresh Hell Is This?* (New York: Penguin, 1988, 1989), 361; Burton, 271–72; Karen Olsen Ganz, "The Metamorphosis of Leonard Bernstein's *Candide*" (DMA thesis, New England Conservatory, 2004), 14; Richard Wilbur to John W. Baxindine, Jan. 27, 2000, appended to John W. Baxindine, "'The Trouble with *Candide*': Analysis of an Operetta" (BA thesis, Harvard University, 2000); Lillian Hellman to Harry Levin, Jan. 31, 1955, LHP; see also Stephen Sondheim, *Finishing the Hat: Collected Lyrics (1954–1981) with Attendant Comments, Principles, Heresies, Grudges, Whines and Anecdotes* (New York: Knopf, 2010), 26–30.
21. Leonard Bernstein to David Diamond, Aug. 17, 1954, Diamond Papers; Lillian Hellman to Dorothy Parker, Dec. 2, 1954; Hellman to Harry Levin, Jan. 11, 1955, LHP; Hellman to Bernstein, c. 1955, LBP.
22. JL to Lillian Hellman and Leonard Bernstein, notarized Dec. 13, 1954; Helen Coates to Bernstein, Feb. 7, 1955; Apr. 20, 1955, LBP; Hellman to Bernstein, c. February 1955, LBP; Leonard and Felicia Bernstein to JL, Nov. 10, 1955, JLP.
23. Keats; Meade, 361; *Letters of James Agee to Father Flye*, edited by James Harold Flye (New York: Braziller, 1962); *The Collected Poems of James Agee*, edited with an introduction by Robert Fitzgerald (Boston: Houghton Mifflin, 1968); Ted Geisel to Katherine ("Kay") Brown, Dec. 2, 1954; Lillian Hellman to Dorothy Parker, Dec. 2, 1954, LHP; Ross.
24. Meade, 361; Lillian Hellman to Harry Levin, Jan. 31, 1955; Hellman to Leonard Bernstein, Oct. 6, 1955, LHP; Keats, 269.
25. Jack Gottlieb, *Working with Bernstein: A Memoir* (New York: Amadeus, 2010), 274; Smith, 116.
26. Fred Shapiro, "The First WASP?" *NYT* (Mar. 14, 2012), dates the acronym "wasp" only as far back as 1948.
27. Leonard Bernstein, commentary, *Candide*, DVD.
28. C. J. Betts, "Echoes of *Manon Lescaut* in *Candide*," *French Studies Bulletin* 8 (Autumn 1988): 14–16.
29. Sondheim, 44, 51; Burton, 269.
30. Lillian Hellman to Harry Levin, Jan. 31, 1955, LHP; see also Elizabeth B. Crist, "Mutual Responses in the Midst of an Era: Aaron Copland's *The Tender Land* and Leonard Bernstein's *Candide*," *Journal of Musicology* 23 (Fall 2006): 485–527; and Crist, "The Best of All Possible Worlds: The Eldorado Episode in Leonard Bernstein's 'Candide,'" *Cambridge Opera Journal* 19 (November 2007): 223–48.
31. Butt, 21, 29–30, 39–40; see also Morley, 2, 13–14, 25.
32. Howard Pollack, *Aaron Copland: The Life and Work of an Uncommon Man* (New York: Holt, 1999), 194, 196; Simeone, 319; Leonard Bernstein to David Diamond, Aug. 17, 1954, Diamond Papers; see also Smith; Paul Laird, "The Best of All Possible Legacies: A Critical Look at Bernstein, His Eclecticism, and *Candide*," *Ars Musica Denver* 4 (1991): 30–39; and Michael Schwarte, "Parodie und Entlehnung in Leonard Bernsteins *Candide*: Bemerkungen

zu einem musikgeschichtlichen Gattungs-Chamäleon," in *Festschrift Klaus Hortschansky zum 60. Geburtstag*, edited by Axel Beer and Laurenz Lütteken (Tutzing: Schneider, 1995), 567–80.

33. Baxindine; Smith.
34. Jack Gottlieb, *Funny, It Doesn't Sound Jewish: How Yiddish Songs and Synagogue Melodies Influenced Tin Pan Alley, Broadway, and Hollywood* (Albany: State University of New York in association with the Library of Congress, 2004), 179.
35. Bernstein, "Colloquy"; Leonard Bernstein, *The Joy of Music* (New York: Simon & Schuster, 1959), 152–79.
36. Leonard Bernstein to Lillian Hellman, Mar. 27, 1955, LHP; Simeone, 334.
37. Simeone, 350, 352, 359; Stephen Sondheim, *Look, I Made a Hat: Collected Lyrics (1981–2011) with Attendant Comments, Amplifications, Dogmas, Harangues, Digressions, Anecdotes and Miscellany* (New York: Knopf, 2011), 319; Burton, 258; Rollyson, 362; "Richard Wilbur: Poet," *Web of Stories*, https://www.webofstories.com/play/richard.wilbur/26.
38. Sunil Iyengar, "A Conversation with Richard Wilbur," *Contemporary Poetry Review*, http://www.cprw.com/Iyengar/wilbur.htm; Craig Lambert, "Poetic Patriarch," *Harvard Magazine* 111 (November–December 2008): 36–41; JL to Lillian Hellman, n.d.; JL to Thomas Hammond, n.d.; July 20, 1956; Hammond to JL, July 20, 1956; Hellman to Lucy Kroll, Oct. 12, 1956; Richard T. Harriss to Hellman, Bernstein, and Hammond, Oct. 17, 1956, LHP.
39. Reviews of *Candide* in the [Boston] *Globe* and *Herald* (both Oct. 30, 1956); *Variety* (October 31, 1956); and [Boston] *Evening American, Globe*, and *Herald* (all Nov. 4, 1956).
40. Secrest, 205; Baxindine, "Appendix"; Iyengar; Bernstein, commentary; DeRoss.
41. Lillian Hellman, *Pentimento: A Book of Portraits* (New York: Signet, 1973), 167–68; Bryer, 65, 279; Martinson, 278–79; [Leslie Bennetts], unpublished interview with Hellman for the *NYT*, October 1983, LHP.
42. Reviews of *Candide* in the *Daily Mirror, Daily News, Journal-American, Post, NYHT, NYT*, and *World-Telegram* (all Dec. 3, 1956); *Variety* (Dec. 5, 1956); *Time* (Dec. 10, 1956); *London Times* (Dec. 12, 1956); *Nation* and *New Yorker* (both Dec. 15, 1956); *Washington Post and Times Herald* (Dec. 16, 1956); *New Republic* (Dec. 17, 1956); *Saturday Review* (Dec. 22, 1956); *Commonweal* (Dec. 28, 1956); *Reporter* (Jan. 24, 1957); *Christian Century* (Feb. 6, 1957); *Catholic World* 184 (February 1957): 384–85; *Theatre Arts* 41 (February 1957): 17–18; and *Educational Theater Journal* 9 (March 1957): 42–43; Ken Mandelbaum, *Not Since Carrie: Forty Years of Broadway Musical Flops* (New York: St. Martin's Press, 1991).
43. Foster Hirsch, *Harold Prince and the American Musical Theatre*, revised and expanded (New York: Applause Theatre and Cinema, 2005).
44. Meade, 361; Secrest, 206; Briggs, 196; William Westbrook Burton, *Conversations About Bernstein* (New York: Oxford University Press, 1995), 88; Richard Wilbur to Lillian Hellman, Jan. 30, 1971, LHP; Bryer, 58; David Patrick Stearns, "Candide Redux," *Opera News* 56 (August 1991): 12–14; Gerald Weales, *American Drama Since World War II* (New York: Harcourt, Brace, 1962), 151–52.
45. Lillian Hellman et al., *Candide: A Comic Operetta Based on Voltaire's Satire* (New York: Random House, 1957); reviews of *Candide* (Columbia Records cast album) in the *NYT* (Feb. 17, 1957) and *Saturday Review* (Feb. 23, 1957).
46. Maurice Peress, *Dvořák to Duke Ellington: A Conductor Explores America's Music and Its African American Roots* (New York: Oxford University Press, 2004), 139–41; Maurice Peress, interview with author, Sep. 21, 2015; Gordon Davidson, interview with author, Sep. 22, 2015; much information about these and other productions, including program content and critical commentary, can be found in Michael H. Hutchins, *Guide to Leonard Bernstein's Candide*," http://www.sondheimguide.com/Candide/contents.html.
47. Lillian Hellman to Robert Lantz, Dec. 9, 1982, LBP.
48. Robert Berkvist, "'Candide,' or a Very Moving Story," *NYT* (Feb. 24, 1974); Lillian Hellman, "Audition Precis," LHP; Hal Prince, *Contradictions: Notes on Twenty-six Years in the Theatre*

(New York: Dodd, Mead, 1974), 190–215; Harold Prince, "Foreword," *Candide* (New York: Schirmer, 1976); Hellman to Leonard Bernstein, Nov. 18, 1982; Hirsch.

49. Sondheim, *Look*, 319–22; John Mauceri, liner notes, *Candide* (New World Records, NW 340/341-2, 1985); Mauceri, email to author, Oct. 29, 2015.
50. Berkvist; Richard Coe, review of *Candide* in the *Washington Post* (Mar. 13, 1974).
51. Prince, *Contradictions*; John Madden, " 'Candide' Netting 9.4 G AWeek [*sic*], Has 463.5G to Recoup," *Variety* (June 26, 1974); reviews of *Candide* in the *New York Theatre Critics' Reviews 1973* (New York: Critics' Theatre Reviews, 1973), 138–40; reviews of *Candide* in the *New York Theatre Critics' Reviews 1974* (New York: Critics' Theatre Reviews, 1974), 337–40; *Opera News* 38 (Feb. 9, 1974); *New Republic* (Mar. 30, 1974); *America* (Apr. 6, 1974); and *Commentary* 57 (June 1974).
52. Reviews of *Candide* (ibid.); Craig Zadan, *Sondheim & Co.*, 2nd ed. (New York: Harper & Row, 1974, 1986), 163; Ganz, 53 n. 151; Lillian Hellman to Robert Lantz, Dec. 9, 1982, LBP.
53. John Rockwell, "Will 'Candide' Thrive in the Opera House?" *NYT* (Oct. 10, 1982); Theodore S. Chapin, liner notes, *Candide* (New World Records); Mauceri; Hirsch; Donal Henahan, "City Opera: Candide," *NYT* (Oct. 14, 1982).
54. Rockwell.
55. John Mauceri, liner notes, *Candide* (Jay Records, CDJAY 1257, 1997); Secrest, 210–11; Burton, *Conversations*, 107–8; as opposed to the score and the *Candide* DVD, the *Bernstein Conducts Candide* recording credits John Wells as co-lyricist with Bernstein of the revised "Westphalia Chorale" and "Universal Good."
56. Richard Wilbur to Leonard Bernstein, n.d., LBP (for Wilbur's drafts of lyrics); Hutchins, "Candide: 1989 Bernstein Recording: Selected Writings," *Guide*.
57. Marie Carter, email to author, May 9, 2016 (for languages); Robert Carsen, email to author, Apr. 11, 2016; see also Carsen, "Candide Camera," *Prelude, Fugue & Riffs* (Fall/Winter 2006/2007): 1–3.
58. Andrew Porter, "Musical Events," *New Yorker* (Nov. 1, 1982): 152–53.
59. Lillian Hellman et al., *Candide: A Comic Operetta Based on Voltaire's Satire* (New York: Avon, 1970); Hellman, *The Collected Plays* (Boston: Little, Brown, 1971); "unadulterated," that is, aside from an error that dates back to the 1955 score (corrected in some recent productions) in which the response to Pangloss's "There is a reason / For everything under the sun" reads as a simple echo, as opposed to "There is a season / For everything under the sun"; and the slight change, instituted in 1973, of Latouche's "Today's event makes evident" to Sondheim's "Philosophers make evident," as mentioned below.
60. Ganz; Pettit; Weales, 153; Mandelbaum; Baxindine; Lehman Engel, *Words with Music* (New York: Macmillan, 1972); Richard Moody, *Lillian Hellman: Playwright* (New York: Pegasus, 1972); Doris Fleischer and Leonard Fleischer, "The Dramatic Adaptations of Lillian Hellman," and Timothy J. Wiles, "Lillian Hellman's American Political Theater: The Thirties and Beyond," in *Critical Essays on Lillian Hellman*, edited by Mark W. Estrin (Boston: Hall, 1989), 55–64, 90–112; Ethan Mordden, *Coming Up Roses: The Broadway Musical in the 1950s* (New York: Oxford University Press, 1998); Raymond Knapp, *The American Musical and the Performance of Personal Identity* (Princeton, NJ: Princeton University Press, 2006), 331; Larry Stempel, *Showtime: A History of the Broadway Musical Theater* (New York: Norton, 2010).
61. Mordden, 179; Kenneth LaFave, *Experiencing Leonard Bernstein: A Listener's Companion* (Lanham, MD: Rowman & Littlefield, 2015), 101.
62. Burton, *Leonard Bernstein*, 257, 259; Stephen Sondheim, email to author, Apr. 29, 2016.
63. Hutchins, "Candide: The Songs," *Guide*; various materials, including lists of credited songs in the LHP and the world premiere program, confirm the lyric of "Proposal Duet"/"I Love You" as the work of Wilbur (the 2000 revue *Taking a Chance on Love* similarly misattributed the lyrics of the duet—here called "Plain Words"—to Wilbur); see also LaFave, 100, 103.
64. Briggs, 196; Baxindine, "Appendix"; Iyengar; Hutchins, "Candide: The Songs"; Richard Wilbur, interview with author, October 2011.

65. "Richard Wilbur: Poet"; Mordden, 184.
66. Bryer, 182; Leonard Bernstein to Ruth Yorck, Feb. 18, 1958, RYP; Bernstein, "Leonard Bernstein."

22. Late Work

1. Howard Kissel, *David Merrick: The Abominable Showman* (New York: Applause, 1993), 44, 173; Sam Zolotow, "Shylock to Tread Boards at Center," *NYT* (Mar. 4, 1953).
2. Coleman Dowell, *A Star-Bright Lie* (Normal, IL: Dalkey, 1993), 86–88; Jo Mielziner to Dowell, Apr. 1, 1953, Coleman Dowell Papers, New York University; Eugene Hayworth, *Fever Vision: The Life and Works of Coleman Dowell* (Champaign, IL: Dalkey, 2007), 35–47.
3. Hayworth, 35; Sam Zolotow, "Whitehead Eyes an Active Season," *NYT* (Apr. 30, 1954); Lucy Kroll, memoranda, various dates, 1954 and 1955; JL, contract with David Merrick, Jan. 27, 1955, LKP.
4. Hayworth, 35, 39; Lucy Kroll, memoranda, early 1955, LKP; Hayworth, 39; Coleman Dowell, contract with David Merrick, Apr. 1, 1955, David Merrick Papers, Wisconsin Historical Society.
5. John Kuehl and Linda Kandel Kuehl, "An Interview with Coleman Dowell," *Contemporary Literature* 22 (Summer 1981): 280; Hayworth, 5, 186.
6. Hayworth, 42–45.
7. Douglas Watt, "Busy Stranger in Town You Can't Fool Mom," *Ah, Wilderness!* clipping file, NYPL; David Merrick to Benjamin Aslan, Sep. 1, 1955; Merrick and Jo Mielziner to JL, Mar. 28, 1956, Merrick Papers; "Inge Will Adapt 'Ah, Wilderness!' " *NYT* (Feb. 17, 1956).
8. Dowell, 89–95; Coleman Dowell to Richard Lebherz, Apr. 3, 1968, Dowell Papers, courtesy of Eugene Hayworth; Dowell, "A Handful of Anomalies," *Bomb* 13 (Fall 1985): 56–61.
9. Gene [Eugene] Hayworth, "A Conversation with Edmond White," http://www.dalkeyarchive.com/a-conversation-with-edmond-white-by-gene-hayworth; Hayworth, *Fever Vision*, xii, 46; Dowell, *Star-Bright*, 91, 97, 127.
10. Lucy Kroll, memoranda, Jan. 8, 1956; Feb. 22, 1956; Apr. 13, 1956; David Merrick to Kroll, Aug. 6, 1956; Merrick to JL, Aug. 6, 1956, LKP; Merrick to JL, Aug. 3, 1956; Merrick to JL, Aug. 6, 1956; Merrick to Kroll, Aug. 6, 1956, Merrick Papers; Kissel; Hayworth, *Fever Vision*, 45; Coleman Dowell to Martha Cline, n.d., Dowell Papers, courtesy of Eugene Hayworth.
11. Sam Zolotow, "Brandt, Stoddard Will Put on Plays," *NYT* (July 4, 1956); Lewis Funke, "Gossip of the Rialto," *NYT* (Jan. 6, 1957); Benjamin Aslan to Jane Rubin, Merrick Papers; Sam Zolotow, "Gregory Plans 1959 Production," *NYT* (Oct. 29, 1958).
12. JL, "Ballad," ADP; Dowell, *Star-Bright*, 95.
13. Dowell, *Star-Bright*, 87, 90; " 'Along' Takes Flight Again," *Billboard* (Oct. 7, 1967).
14. John Sacco, *Six Doves* (New York: Schirmer, 1966).
15. Gerald Bordman, *American Musical Revue: From the Passing Show to Sugar Babies* (New York: Oxford University Press, 1985); Lee Davis, *Scandals and Follies: The Rise and Fall of the Great Broadway Revue* (New York: Limelight Editions, 2000); Walter Winchell, "The Broadway Line," n.s., n.d., VDP.
16. Ben Bagley, liner notes, *The Littlest Revue* (Painted Smiles Records, PSCD-112, 1956, 1989).
17. JL to Vernon Duke and Ogden Nash, May 22, 1956, VDP; reviews of *The Littlest Revue* in the *Daily Mirror, Daily News, Journal-American, NYHT, NYT, Post*, and *World Telegram and Sun* (all May 23, 1956); *Variety* (May 30, 1956); *New Yorker* (June 2, 1956); *Time* (June 4, 1956); *Nation* and *Saturday Review* (both June 9, 1956); *America* (June 16, 1956); *Catholic World* 183 (July 1956): 113; and *Theatre Arts* 80 (August 1956): 73; "Col. Revives Okeh Label as R&B Outlet," *Billboard* (July 14, 1956).
18. Reviews of *To Tell You the Truth* in the *NYT* (Apr. 19, 1948); *Wall Street Journal* (Apr. 20, 1948); *Billboard* (May 1, 1948); and George Jean Nathan, *Theatre Book of the Year, 1947–1948: A Record and an Interpretation* (New York: Knopf, 1947), 351–53.
19. Lucy Kroll, memoranda, May 11, 1956; May 16, 1956; Michael Ellis to Kroll, June 8, 1956, LKP; "Latouche-Stone Musical May Get Summer Tryout," *NYHT* (June 19, 1956).

20. "Latouche Tribute Given at Funeral," *NYT* (Aug. 10, 1956); Frederick Kiesler, *Inside the Endless House: Art, People and Architecture: A Journal* (New York: Simon & Schuster, 1964, 1966), 47–49.
21. JL, "The First Time" (July 1956); Ezra Stone to Frederick Kiesler, Sep. 23, 1956, AFL.
22. Ezra Stone to Frederick Kiesler, Sep. 23, 1956; Jan. 11, 1957, AFL; "Stone-Evslin Doing 'First Time' Musical," *Variety* (Nov. 7, 1956).

23. The Ballad of Baby Doe

1. Duane A. Smith, with John Moriarty, *The Ballad of Baby Doe: "I Shall Walk Beside My Love"* (Boulder: University Press of Colorado, 2002), 7–8.
2. Jerry L. McBride, *Douglas Moore: A Bio-Bibliography* (Middleton, WI: A-R Editions, 2011), 7–8; for more biographical information about Douglas Moore, see Lewis J. Hardee Jr., "The Musical Theatre of Douglas Moore" (MA thesis, University of North Carolina, 1970); Harold Weitzel, "A Melodic Analysis of Selected Vocal Solos in the Operas of Douglas Moore" (PhD diss., New York University, 1971); Donald Joseph Reagan, "Douglas Moore and His Orchestral Works" (PhD diss., Catholic University, 1972); Jack Beeson, "Da Ponte, MacDowell, Moore and Lang: Four Biographical Essays," *Columbia Magazine* (Summer 2000): 26–35.
3. Douglas Moore, "Our Lyric Theatre," *Modern Music* 18 (November–December 1940): 3–7; Moore, "Opera by American Composers of Today," *Pan Pipes* 59 (January 1967): 12–14; Moore, "Music by Irving Berlin," *Glamour* (November 1962): 143, 179–80, 182–83, 186–87, 223; Frank J. Oteri, "John Kander: Passing Through Curtains," *NewMusicBox* (May 1, 2010): http://www.newmusicbox.org/articles/john-kander-passing-through-curtains.
4. Otto Luening, "American Composers, XX: Douglas Moore," *Modern Music* 20 (May–June 1943): 248; Douglas Moore, "Tournemire, Composer, Improviser; Tribute from an American Pupil," *Diapason* 31 (Mar. 1, 1940): 10; Beeson, 32.
5. Weitzel, 27; Hardee, 27–28.
6. Douglas Moore, *Listening to Music* (New York: Norton, 1932); Moore, *From Madrigal to Modern Music: A Guide to Musical Styles* (New York: Norton, 1942, rev. 1962).
7. Lawrence Gilman, "A New American Symphony," *NYHT*, May 17, 1931; Aaron Copland, *Music and Imagination* (Cambridge, MA: Harvard University Press, 1952, 1980), 94.
8. Howard Pollack, *Marc Blitzstein: His Life, His Work, His World* (New York: Oxford University Press, 2012), 241; Moore in turn admired Blitzstein (see Pollack, 241), although he once apparently jokingly referred to him as "Mendelssohn with wrong notes," Hardee, 43; Michael Brozen, "Douglas Moore: The Good Life," *Musical America* 83 (August 1963): 26; Weitzel, 37; Virgil Thomson, *American Music Since 1910* (New York: Holt, Rinehart and Winston, 1970, 1971), 162.
9. J. E. Smyth, *Reconstructing American Historical Cinema: From Cimarron to Citizen Kane* (Lexington: University Press of Kentucky, 2006), 53; for more on Green, see Vincent S. Kenny, *Paul Green* (New York: Twayne, 1971); for information concerning Central City Opera and the commissioning of *Baby Doe*, see Hardee; Weitzel; McBride; Smith; Charles A. Johnson, *Opera in the Rockies: The History of the Central City Opera House Association, 1932–1992* ([Denver]: Central City Opera House Association, 1992); Allen Young, *Opera in Central City* (Denver: Spectrographics, 1993); *Theatre of Dreams: The Glorious Central City Opera—Celebrating 75 Years* (Denver: Central City Opera House Association, 2007); and Minutes, Central City Opera Association Records, University of Denver, including Nov. 23, 1953; Dec. 28, 1953; Jan. 11, 1954.
10. Douglas Moore, "How 'The Ballad of Baby Doe' Was Written," *The Ballad of Baby Doe* (Heliodor H/HS 2503503, 1959, 1966); Max DiJulio, interview with David Kanzeg (July 7, 1998), courtesy of Kanzeg; Hardee, 75.
11. Minutes, Dec. 28, 1953; *Theatre of Dreams*, 113.
12. For the Horace Tabor legend, see David Karsner, *Silver Dollar: The Story of the Tabors* (New York: Bonanza, 1932); Lewis Cass Gandy, *The Tabors: A Footnote of Western History*

(New York: Press of the Pioneers, 1934); L. A. Chapin, "Baby Doe Tabor Freezes to Death While on Guard at Matchless Mine," and related articles, *Denver Post* (Mar. 8, 1935); L. A. Chapin, "Tabor and Baby Doe to Live Together in Denver Grave," and Ralph Radetsky, "Brother Weeps and Is Proud of Baby Doe Tabor," *Denver Post* (both Mar. 10, 1935); [Caroline Bancroft], "Silver Queen: Baby Doe Tabor's Life Story as Told to Sue Bonnie," *True Story* 37 (January 1938): 30–33, 90–91; 38 (February 1938): 34–37, 86–92; 38 (March 1938): 48–50, 127–33; 38 (April 1938): 40–42, 54–59; 38 (May 1938): 40–42, 67–72; Caroline Bancroft, *Silver Queen: The Fabulous Story of Baby Doe Tabor* (Boulder, CO: Johnson, 1950, 1955, 1989); Gordon Langley Hall [Dawn Langley Simmons], *The Two Lives of Baby Doe* (Philadelphia: Macrae Smith, 1962); John Burke [Richard O'Connor], *The Legend of Baby Doe: The Life and Times of the Silver Queen of the West* (Lincoln: University of Nebraska Press, 1974, 1989); Randie Lee Blooding, "Douglas Moore's 'The Ballad of Baby Doe': An Investigation of Its Historical Accuracy and the Feasibility of a Historical Production in the Tabor Opera House" (DMA thesis, Ohio State University, 1979); Duane A. Smith, *Horace Tabor: His Life and the Legend* (Boulder: University Press of Colorado, 1989); Evelyn E. Livingston Furman, *My Search for Augusta Pierce Tabor, Leadville's First Lady* (Denver: Quality, 1993); *Leadville's Story of Baby Doe* [four videotapes], script by David and Jane Wright et al. (Buena Vista, CO: Universal Systems, 2000–01); Kari Ragan Hoffmann, "*The Ballad of Baby Doe*: Historical Accuracy and Gender Ideology in the Characterization of Augusta and Baby Doe" (DMA thesis, University of Washington, 2005); Judy Nolte Temple, *Baby Doe Tabor: The Madwoman in the Cabin* (Norman: University of Oklahoma Press, 2007); James I. Metz, *Lizzie McCourt: Baby Doe's Legend Begins* ([Oshkosh, WI]: Polemics, 2013); and Marvin Brooks, *Researching the Baby Doe Tabor Legend* ([La Vergne, TN]: IngramSpark, 2015).

13. Temple; Kristen Iversen, *Molly Brown: Unraveling the Myth* (Boulder, CO: Johnson, 1999), 54, 98.
14. "Story Outline—Baby Doe (as Approved January 21 by [Paul] Green, [Douglas] Moore, Gray [Herbert Graf?], and Denslazer [Donald Oenslager?])," EHP; Hardee, 80; "Local Histories, Americana Making Return to Opera, Drama Pageantry," *Lansing State Journal* (July 8, 1956); Roger Dettmer, "Opera Mouse in Colorado," *Chicago American* (July 9, 1956).
15. Hardee, 75–77; Young, 37; McBride, 5–7; "Memorandum," Apr. 12, 1954, Central City Records.
16. Douglas Moore, "Confidential Report," received Dec. 30, 1948, JL file, GMF; JL, "About the Ballad of Baby Doe," *Theatre Arts* 40 (July 1956): 80–83; Moore, untitled statement about *The Ballad of Baby Doe*, June 2, 1958, DMP.
17. JL, "About the Ballad."
18. Harold Spivacke to Douglas Moore, Aug. 19, 1953; Moore to Olga Koussevitzky, Nov. 22, 1955; May 16, 1956; Minutes of the Board of Directors, July 4, 1953; May 8, 1954; May 27, 1954, Serge Koussevitzky Music Foundation Collection, LC.
19. Douglas Moore to JL, Aug. 5, 1954, EHP.
20. Hardee, 79–80; Smith, *The Ballad*, 95–96.
21. Moore, untitled statement; Douglas Watt, "Busy Stranger in Town; You Can't Fool Mom," n.s. (c. summer 1955), EHP; McBride, 9–10; Douglas Moore to Frank Ricketson Jr., Nov. 22, 1955, DMP.
22. Evelyn Furman, interview with David Kanzeg (August 1966), DoeHEADS (http://www.babydoe.org/index.php); contradicting Furman's story, the article "Composers to Attend 'Baby Doe' Rehearsal," *Denver Post* (June 12, 1956), claimed that Latouche's arrival in Colorado for the premiere of *Baby Doe* represented his first visit to the state.
23. JL, "About the Ballad."
24. Bancroft, 80; Caroline Bancroft to Douglas Moore and JL, Apr. 10, 1955; Jan. 18, 1956; Moore to Bancroft, May 20, 1955; Moore to Frank Ricketson Jr., Nov. 22, 1955, DMP; Alex Murphree, "Author, Historian Settle 'Doe' Score," n. s. (c. July 1956), Central City Opera Association Papers, University of Denver.
25. JL, *The Ballad of Baby Doe* (New York: Program Publishing, 1956, 1958), 10, 14, 25.

26. Walt Whitman, *Leaves of Grass, 1860*, edited by Jason Stacy (Iowa City: University of Iowa Press, 2009), 111; Douglas Moore, "Something About Librettos," *Opera News* 26 (Sep. 30, 1961): 11; JL, *The Ballad*, 39, 45 (the curtain misquoted, as common, Kingsley's phrase, "their earth," as "the earth").
27. Aloysius Coll, "Love's Heraldry," *Munsey's Magazine* 30 (Mar. 1904): 847; "Beulah Land," which alludes to God's marriage to the land ("Beulah" means "marriage" in Hebrew), here would seem to evoke both Baby Doe's love for Horace and her attachment to sacred ground.
28. Hardee, 117–18, 150; David McKee, "You've Come a Long Way, Baby Doe," *Opera News* 61 (Jan. 11, 1997): 43; Latouche, "About the Ballad," 83.
29. Jack Beeson, *How Operas Are Created by Composers and Librettists: The Life of Jack Beeson, American Opera Composer* (Lewiston, NY: Edwin Mellen, 2008), 257; Leyna Gabriele, unpublished memoir, courtesy of Rebecca Paller; Smith, *The Ballad*, 93–96; John Moriarty, interview with author, Mar. 22, 2016; JL, "About the Ballad," 83.
30. Moore, "Something," 11.
31. Moore, "Something," 11; Weitzel, 35; Hardee, 114.
32. Douglas Moore, "Foreword," JL, *Ballad*; Miles Kreuger, interview with author, May 24, 2016.
33. Hardee, 77; Douglas Moore to Olga Koussevitzky, July 23, [1956], Koussevitzky Collection; Lucy Kroll to Michael Myerberg, Aug. 2, 1956, LKP; Myerberg, "Production Notes: 'The Ballad of Baby Doe' " (accompanying Myerberg to Moore, Sep. 6, 1956), LKP ("Production Notes" also in DMP).
34. JL, *The Ballad*, 10–11, contains only two of the four stanzas of "I Came This Way from Massachusetts" found in the work's piano-vocal score.
35. Smith, *Horace Tabor*, 107; Bancroft, 32 (for December visit); "Social Matters," *Leadville Weekly Herald* (Nov. 29, 1879); John Frederick Cone, *Adelina Patti: Queen of Hearts* (Portland, OR: Amadeus, 1993), 364.
36. Smith, *The Ballad*, 56–57.
37. JL, *The Ballad*, 15; McKee, 43.
38. Gandy, 249.
39. Smith, *The Ballad*, 61.
40. "Senator Tabor's Marriage," *NYT* (Mar. 4, 1883).
41. JL, *The Ballad*, 33.
42. "The Silver Situation," *Bankers Statistics Corporation* (Nov. 30, 1920); JL, *The Ballad*, 33; Ralph Radetsky, "Brother Weeps and Is Proud of Baby Doe Tabor," *Denver Post* (Mar. 10, 1935).
43. Karsner, 245.
44. JL, *The Ballad*, 40, 41; "It Was a Landslide," *Boston Globe* (Nov. 4, 1896); "Not Much of a Landslide," *Washington Post* (Nov. 17, 1896).
45. JL, *The Ballad*, 46.
46. Karsner, 3–4; JL, *The Ballad*, 43, 45; Burke, 225; Hall, 24, states that Sarah actually favored her son John.
47. Murphree; Blooding, 33, 35; Smith, *The Ballad*, x, 74; Smith, *Horace Tabor*; Hoffmann; Temple, 62, 124; Moore, "True Tale of West," *NYT* (July 1, 1956).
48. "Sketches for libretto of 'Baby Doe,' " Koussevitzky Collection; Douglas Moore to JL; "Profile of Douglas Moore," *American Musical Theater Workshop* (WCBS-TV, videotaped Feb. 24, 1962; telecast Mar. 4, 1962); JL, *The Ballad*, 11–14.
49. JL, *The Ballad*, 20, 31.
50. Hardee, 200.
51. Reagan, 115; "Profile."
52. Reinhard J. Pauly, *Music and the Theater: An Introduction to Opera* (Englewood Cliffs, NJ: Prentice-Hall, 1970), 379; JL to Douglas Moore, c. June 1955, DMP; JL, "About the Ballad"; Moore, "Something"; JL, *The Ballad*, 9; Kenneth Nott, interview with author, Nov. 11, 2015.
53. JL to Douglas Moore; JL, *The Ballad*, 10.
54. JL, *The Ballad*, 20, 24, 46, 47.
55. JL to Douglas Moore; McKee, 27; JL, *The Ballad*, 27, 47.

56. Hardee, 77, 80; James Lyons, "'Baby Doe Ballad' Real Grand Opera," n.s. (c. July 1956), DMP; Douglas Moore, "How"; Moore, untitled statement; JL, "About the Ballad."
57. Don Short, "Opera Season in the Rockies," *Journal-American* (July 15, 1956).
58. Douglas Moore to Patrice Munsell (*sic*), Nov. 2, 1955; Moore to Frank Ricketson, Nov. 16, 1955; Moore to Ricketson, Nov. 17, 1955, DMP; Frances Bible, interview with David Kanzeg (fall 1973), DoeHEADS.
59. Douglas Moore to Frank Ricketson, Nov. 22, 1956, DMP.
60. "Colorful Sets and Costumes Make 'Baby Doe' Outstanding," *Rocky Mountain News* (July 6, 1956); Young, 40, put the cost of entire production at $112,674, a figure questioned by John Moriarty as dubiously high, especially given the author's purported unreliability; for similar reasons, Moriarty doubted Young's claim (38) that Ricketson personally advanced Moore and Latouche $40,000 for the opera, Moriarty, interview.
61. Lucy Kroll to Robert Lantz, June 8, 1956; Douglas Moore to Kroll, June 24, 1956, LKP; Walter Cassel, interview with David Kanzeg (April 1994), DoeHEADS; Smith, *The Ballad*, 13, 101; Young, 39.
62. Bruce Duffie, "Conversation Piece: Emerson Buckley," *Opera Journal* 24 (June 1991): 55; Smith, *The Ballad*, 13, 101; Gabriele; Cassel; the Lee Mortimer item in question might have been the article "No Ghost in This Ghost Town," which appeared, among other places, in the *Lebanon Daily News* on July 23, 1956, and which in discussing the "sensational success" of the opera mentioned only Gabriele by name; or it might have been something along the lines of the article "Death of 'Baby Doe' Writer Shocker for Soprano," n.s. (Aug. 15, 1956), Central City Records, which claimed that Gabriele "'stole' the show" from Wilson.
63. Smith, *The Ballad*, 99, 100; Gabriele; Gabriele, interview with author, Sep. 7, 2012; Gabriele, interview with John Grimmett, Oct. 3, 2012, courtesy of Grimmett.
64. DiJulio; "New Folk Opera to Be Premiered Here," *Denver Post* (May 22, 1956); reviews of DiJulio's *Baby Doe* in the *Denver Post* (May 25, 1956); *Rocky Mountain Journal* (May 31, 1956); and *Musical America* 76 (August 1956): 3; reviews of *Portrait of Baby Doe* in the *Denver Post* (Nov. 18, 1976) and *Rocky Mountain News* (Nov. 19, 1976); all material courtesy of David Kanzeg.
65. Lord Kinross, *The Innocents at Home* (New York: Morrow, 1960), 135–40.
66. Reviews of *The Ballad of Baby Doe* in the *Denver Post* and *Rocky Mountain News* (both July 8, 1956); *Chicago American*, *Daily News*, *NYT*, and *Pittsburgh Post-Gazette* (all July 9, 1959); *Pittsburgh Post-Gazette* (July 10, 1956); *Variety* (July 11, 1956); *Christian Science Monitor* (July 14, 1956); *Los Angeles Times*, *NYT*, and *NYHT* (all July 15, 1956); *Time* (July 16, 1956); *San Francisco Chronicle* (July 29, 1956); *Dallas Morning News* (Aug. 1, 1956); *Boston Post* (Aug. 5, 1956); *Musical America* 76 (August 1956): 3; William L. Crosten, *Musical Quarterly* 42 (October 1956): 527–29; Paul Jackson, *Opera News* 21 (Nov. 5, 1956); and *Etude* 74 (November 1956): 12, 52–53; see also "Baby Doe and Her Silver King," *Life* (Aug. 6, 1956).
67. Kinross, 139.
68. David Kanzeg, interview with author, Mar. 25, 2016; "'Voice' Broadcasts U. S. Opera," *NYT* (Aug. 28, 1956); Louis Calta, "'Baby Doe' May Go to Paris Festival," *NYT* (Aug. 25, 1956).
69. Arthur Gelb, "Folk Music Play May Be Done Here," *NYT* (June 18, 1956); "'Ballad of Baby Doe' is sellout hit, to be produced in New York this fall," n.s., n.d., Central City Records; Myerberg.
70. John Chapman, "Last Work by Latouche," *Daily News* (Aug. 19, 1956); Myerberg; correspondence and contracts related to *Baby Doe*, Michael Myerberg Papers, Wisconsin Historical Society.
71. Douglas Moore to Michael Myerberg, Sep. 14, 1956.
72. Douglas Moore to Olga Koussevitzky, July 23, [1956], Koussevitzky Collection; Sam Zolotow, "New Comedy Role for Don Ameche," *NYT* (Aug. 19, 1956); Louis Calta, "Top Role in Revue for Martha Raye," *NYT* (Aug. 20, 1956); Michael Myerberg to Arnold Weissberger, Oct. 29, 1956, and other correspondence and contracts related to *Baby Doe*, Myerberg Papers; A. H. Weiler, "By Way of Report," *NYT* (Oct. 28, 1956).

73. Reviews of *The Ballad of Baby Doe* in the *NYT* and *Washington Post and Times Herald* (both Feb. 11, 1957); *Variety* (Feb. 13, 1957); and other reviews in LKP; Michael Myerberg to Lucy Kroll, Apr. 11, 1957; Kroll to Douglas Moore, July 15, 1957, LKP.
74. Julius Rudel and Rebecca Paller, *First and Lasting Impressions: Julius Rudel Looks Back on a Life in Music* (Rochester, NY: University of Rochester Press, 2013), 78.
75. Beverly Sills, *Bubbles: A Self-Portrait* (New York: Bobbs-Merrill, 1976), 84; Sills and Lawrence Linderman, *Beverly: An Autobiography* (New York: Bantam, 1987), 115; Ralph Blumenthal, "You've Come a Long Way, Baby Doe," *NYT* (Mar. 24, 2001); David McKee, "The Great American Opera?" *San Francisco Opera Magazine* 78/3 (2000–01): 10–18, writes (11), "Moore insisted on replacing Dolores Wilson," but Rudel, 109–10, suggests otherwise; see also McKee, "You've Come," 43.
76. Reviews of *The Ballad of Baby Doe* in the *Daily News, Journal-American, NYHT, NYT, Post,* and *World-Telegram* (all Apr. 4, 1958); *Billboard* (Apr. 7, 1958); *Variety* (Apr. 9, 1958); *New Yorker* (Apr. 12, 1958); *Newsweek* (Apr. 14, 1958); and *Nation* (May 3, 1958).
77. Sills, *Beverly,* 243; reviews of *The Ballad of Baby Doe* in the *NYT* (Apr. 4, 1959) and *Chicago Tribune* (Mar. 6, 1960).
78. H. Wiley Hitchcock, review of *The Ballad of Baby Doe* in *Notes* 17 (December 1959): 140–41; Hitchcock, *Music in the United States: A Historical Introduction,* 3rd ed. (Englewood Cliffs, NJ: Prentice Hall, 1969, 1988), 228; Wilfrid Mellers, *Music in a New Found Land: Themes and Developments in the History of American Music* (New York: Knopf, 1964), 31–32; Gilbert Chase, *America's Music: From the Pilgrims to the Present* (Urbana: University of Illinois Press, 1955, 1966, 1987), 646 (1966 ed.), 555 (1987 ed.); Kyle Gann, *American Music in the Twentieth Century* (New York: Schirmer, 1997), 68; Elise K. Kirk, *American Opera* (Urbana: University of Illinois Press, 2001), 277–83; in contrast, most histories of American music, including those by Irving Sablosky (1969), Barbara A. Zuck (1978, 1980), Daniel Klingman (1979), Charles Hamm (1983), John Warthen Struble (1995), Richard Crawford (2001), and Edith Borroff (2003), had virtually nothing to say about Moore or the opera, with most—including *The Cambridge History of American Music,* edited by David Nicholls (New York: Cambridge University Press, 1998)—making no mention of the piece at all.
79. Rebecca Paller, "Whatever Happened to Baby Doe?" *Opera News* 63 (October 1998): 40; Sills, *Beverly,* 121–22; "2-for-1 Pkg. by Heliodor," *Billboard* (Oct. 29, 1966); reviews of *The Ballad of Baby Doe* (recording) in *High Fidelity* 9 (October 1959): 91; *NYT* (Nov. 8, 1959); *HiFi/Stereo Review* 4 (February 1960): 78; *Opera News* 64 (August 1999): 52; and *Fanfare* (September–October 1999): 288–89.
80. Hardee, 73; "La Sills at the Summit," *Newsweek* (Apr. 21, 1969); "Beverly Sills: The Fastest Voice Alive," *Time* (Nov. 22, 1971); Sills, *Beverly,* 117, 118, 120, 122; Sills, *Bubbles,* 84–85; Smith, *The Ballad,* 104; Beverly Sills, interview with David Kanzeg (1973), DoeHEADS; Blumenthal.
81. McKee, "You've Come," 51.
82. Eleanor Scott, *The First Twenty Years of the Santa Fe Opera* (Santa Fe, NM: Sunstone, 1976), 39–43; Craig A. Smith, *A Vision of Voices: John Crosby and the Santa Fe Opera* (Albuquerque: University of New Mexico Press, 2015), 87–88; Heiner Bruns to David Kanzeg, Jan. 21, 2001, courtesy of Kanzeg.
83. McBride, 349–406; reviews of *The Ballad of Baby Doe,* LKP; Harold Blumenfeld and Lionel Lackey, "The Battle of Baby Doe," *Opera News* 33 (Mar. 9, 1969): 8–10; David Kanzeg, "*The Ballad of Baby Doe* and the American Spirit" (January 2003), DoeHEADS.
84. Reviews of the *Ballad of Baby Doe* in the [Berlin] *Tagesspiegel* and *Telegraf* (both Sep. 28, 1961); *Zvuk* 51 (1961): 113–15; *Opernwelt* (June 6, 1986); *Neue Zeitschrift für Musik* 7–8 (July–August 1986): 57–58; *Opera* 37 (October 1986): 1182–83; *Oper und Konzert* 24/6 (1986): 5; *Independent* and *London Times* (both Mar. 13, 1996); *London Financial Times* (Mar. 14, 1996); *London Telegraph* (Mar. 17, 1996); *Opera* 47 (June 1996): 714–16; *Spectator* (Aug. 21, 1998); *Westdeutsche Zeitung* (June 6, 2000); *Wuppertaler Rundschau* (June 14, 2000); and *Calgary Herald* (Jan. 27, 2008); see also John Dew, "Option für einen

Weg," program book, *Die Ballade von Baby Doe*, Bielefeld Opera (May 1, 1986) ("für jede Szene, für jeden Situation den richtigen musicalischen Gestus gefunden").

85. Dana Bisbee, "Social Scene Faithful Doeheads Sing the Praises of 'Ballad,' " *Boston Herald* (Jan. 18, 1998); David Kanzeg, "The Original DoeHEAD" (March 1998, according to Kanzeg), DoeHEADS; Lackey; Derek M. Mills, "American Opera: The Sublimation of Ordinariness" (Feb. 9, 1998), DoeHEADS; Kanzeg, "*The Ballad*."
86. "Profile"; William V. Madison, "Lettera da Ronkonkoma," *Opera News* 66 (February 2002): 100.
87. Kanzeg, "The Ballad"; Mills; Rebecca Paller, "I Can't Live without... Baby Doe," *Opera News* 52 (April 1988): 512–14; McKee, "You've Come"; McKee, "The Great"; for "commonplace" and "quaint," see Martin Bernheimer, reviews of *The Ballad of Baby Doe* in the *Los Angeles Times* (Dec. 3, 1969; May 11, 1987).
88. Hardee, 77; Moore, "How"; McBride, 51; Ethan Mordden, *A Guide to Opera Recordings* (New York: Oxford University Press, 1987), 285

24. The Death and Legacy of a Renaissance Man

1. Denny Beach to Vernon Duke, Aug. 23, 1956, VDP; Effie Latouche to André Cauvin, received Sep. 1, 1956, André Cauvin Papers, CEGES/SOMA, Brussels; Lord Kinross, *The Innocents at Home* (New York: Morrow, 1960), 162, 172; Louis Calta, "Poet, 35, Is Named 'Candide' Lyricist," *NYT* (Aug. 6, 1956); JLD, Nov. 29, 1949.
2. Kinross, 162; Harry Martin, interview with Gregory Gibson, 1978, transcript, Sawyer Free Library, Gloucester MA, courtesy of Helen Freeman; Gore Vidal, *Palimpsest: A Memoir* (New York: Random House, 1995), 254.
3. *The Diaries of Dawn Powell, 1931–1965*, edited with an introduction by Tim Page (South Royalton, VT: Steerforth, 1995), 361; Kinross, 162–63.
4. "John T. Latouche, Stage Lyricist, 38," *NYT* (Aug. 8, 1956); "John Latouche Is Dead at 39," *Daily News* (Aug. 8, 1956); "Latouche Tribute Given at Funeral," *NYT* (Aug. 10, 1956); [Theodate Johnson] to Virgil Thomson [Aug. 9, 1956], VTP; two versions of Carson McCullers's eulogy exist: "John Latouche—An Eulogy," LKP (with the lines crossed out in pencil possibly the work of Kiesler), and a shorter "A Euology [*sic*] by Carson McCullers," AFL, both identical except for some omitted lines, and with both using the phase "as he was approaching the peak," rather than "at the peak"; Frederick Kiesler, *Inside the Endless House: Art, People and Architecture: A Journal* (New York: Simon & Schuster, 1964, 1966), 52–43 (Kiesler claimed just the opposite, that he changed "died at the height" to "died approaching the height").
5. Burial transit permits, Department of Public Health, State of Vermont, courtesy of Mary Skinner; Kinross, 213.
6. Jack Lyons, "The Lyons Den," *Long Beach* [CA] *Independent* (Aug. 11, 1956); Jack Gaver, "Legacy of Latouche," *Kentucky Post* (Aug. 14, 1956); Earl Robinson, "Balladier for Americans," *Nation* (Aug. 25, 1956): 161.
7. Vernon Duke, "The Late John Treville Latouche," *Variety* (Aug. 29, 1956); Duke, "Tribute to a Poet," *Theatre Arts* 41 (March 1957): 24–26, 96; "Drama Mailbag," *NYT* (Sep. 2, 1956); see also "Offstage: Passing of a Pioneer," *Theatre Arts* 40 (October 1956): 14.
8. Ruth Yorck, various prospectuses; Yorck to Gore Vidal (c. summer 1957); Vidal to Yorck (July 24, 1957; Aug. 2, 1957); James Branch Cabell to Yorck (Dec. 28, 1957); Aaron Copland to Yorck (Jan. 14, 1958); Leonard Bernstein to Yorck (Feb. 18, 1958), RYP.
9. Lucy Kroll to Effie Latouche, May 13, 1960, LKP; Leonard Lyons, "Lyons Den," *Pittsburgh Press* (Aug. 11, 1959); James Gavin, *Intimate Nights: The Golden Age of New York Cabaret* (New York: Grove Weidenfeld, 1991), 250–51; Anne Edwards, *Streisand: A Biography* (Boston: Little, Brown, 1997), 143–44; Streisand's press agent Richard Guttman, email to author, Apr. 21, 2016, reported that Streisand had no recollection of any such project; Barbra Streisand, liner notes, *Lazy Afternoon* (Columbia PC 33815, 1975).

10. George Freedley to Lucy Kroll, Apr. 8, 1959, LKP.
11. Libby Green, interview with author, Apr. 18, 2016.
12. Lucy Kroll to Jerome Moross, Feb. 19, 1965, LKP; Jennifer Lee, email to author, Apr. 13, 2016.
13. Andrew H. Drummond, *American Opera Librettos* (Metuchen, NJ: Scarecrow, 1973); Maria ("Molly") Drummond, email to author, Mar. 3, 2013; ADP; AHD.
14. Anthony Meredith with Paul Harris, *Richard Rodney Bennett: The Complete Musician* (New York: Omnibus, 2010), 296, 510; "Critics' Picks," *Washington Post* (Nov. 7, 1982); Buddy Barnes, liner notes, *Take Love Easy: The Lyrics of John Latouche* (Audiophile, ACD-206, 1984, 2001).
15. Erik Haagensen, emails to author, Apr. 23, 2016; Apr. 24, 2016; Seth A. Goldstein, "*Taking a Chance on Love* Study Guide," courtesy of Haagensen.
16. *Taking a Chance on Love: The Lyrics & Life of John Latouche* (Original Cast, OC-4444, 2000); *Taking a Chance*, script and score, courtesy of Erik Haagensen.
17. Mark Wood, "The Lyricist Nobody Knows," *American Theatre* 17 (February 2000): 28–29; reviews of *Taking a Chance on Love* in the *NYT* (Mar. 3, 2000); *New Jersey Star-Ledger* (Mar. 6, 2010); *Village Voice* (Mar. 7, 2000); *Back Stage* and *Chicago Sun-Times* (both Mar. 10, 2000); *New York* and *Observer* (both Mar. 20, 2000); *Show Music* 16 (Winter 2000–01): 5–6; and other reviews, courtesy of Erik Haagensen.
18. Richard Merkin, "The Holy Beast of Song," *GQ* 61 (January 1991): 36–38; Lehman Engel, *Their Words Are Music: The Great Theatre Lyricists and Their Lyrics* (New York: Crown, 1975), 200, 204; Philip Furia, *The Poets of Tin Pan Alley: A History of America's Great Lyricists* (New York: Oxford University Press, 1990); *Reading Lyrics*, edited by Robert Gottlieb and Robert Kimball (New York: Pantheon, 2000), 517–22; Thomas S. Hischak, *Word Crazy: Broadway Lyricists from Cohan to Sondheim* (New York: Praeger, 1991), 155–56.
19. Ned Rorem, *Knowing When to Stop: A Memoir* (New York: Simon & Schuster, 1994), 252; Stephen Sondheim, *Finishing the Hat: Collected Lyrics (1954–1981) with Attendant Comments, Principles, Heresies, Grudges, Whines and Anecdotes* (New York: Knopf, 2010), 14, 17; *Look, I Made a Hat: Collected Lyrics (1981–2011) with Attendant Comments, Amplifications, Dogmas, Harangues, Digressions, Anecdotes and Miscellany* (New York: Knopf, 2011), 308.
20. Vernon Duke, *Passport to Paris* (Boston: Little, Brown, 1955), 400; McCullers, "John Latouche."
21. JL to Henry Moe, Mar. 2, 1949, GMG; Ruth Yorck, "The Sinister Doodles of John Latouche," n.d., RYP.
22. Peter G. Davis, "Pure Gold" *New York* (Oct. 17, 1988).
23. AHD.

CREDITS

"BALLAD FOR AMERICANS" by Earl Robinson and John Latouche. © 1939 (Renewed) Sony/ATV Music Publishing LLC and EMI Robbins Catalog, Inc. All Rights Reserved. Reprinted by Permission of Hal Leonard Corporation.

"BALLAD FOR AMERICANS" by Earl Robinson and John Latouche. © 1939, 1940 (Renewed) EMI Robbins Catalog Inc. and Music Sales Corp. All Rights Reserved. Used by Permission of Alfred Music.

"BALLAD OF BABY DOE" by Douglas Moore and John Latouche. © 1958 (Renewed) Chappell & Co., Inc. All Rights Reserved. Used by Permission of Alfred Music.

"CALYPSO," "DOOMED, DOOMED, DOOMED," "GOONA-GOONA," "IT'S THE GOING HOME TOGETHER," "IT WAS A GLAD ADVENTURE," "LAZY AFTERNOON," "NOTHING EVER HAPPENS IN ANGEL'S ROOST," "WE'VE JUST BEGUN" (from "The Golden Apple") by Jerome Moross and John Latouche. © 1954 (Renewed) by Jerome Moross and John Latouche. Publication and Allied Rights Assigned to Chappell & Co. and Sony Tunes, Inc. All Rights Reserved. Used by Permission of Alfred Music.

"CALYPSO," "DOOMED, DOOMED, DOOMED," "GOONA-GOONA," "IT'S THE GOING HOME TOGETHER," "NOTHING EVER HAPPENS IN ANGEL'S ROOST," "WE'VE JUST BEGUN" (from "The Golden Apple") by Jerome Moross and John Latouche. © 1954 (Renewed) Sony/ATV Music Publishing LLC and Jerome Moross. All Rights Reserved. Reprinted by Permission of Hal Leonard Corporation.

"CANDIDE" by Leonard Bernstein, Stephen Sondheim, Richard Wilbur, John Latouche, Dorothy Parker, and Lillian Hellman. © Copyright 1994 by Amberson Holdings LLC. Copyright Renewed. Reprinted by Permission of Boosey & Hawkes, Inc.

"DAY DREAM" by Duke Ellington, Billy Strayhorn, and John Latouche. © 1940, 1941 (Copyrights Renewed) Reservoir Media Management, Inc., Billy Strayhorn Songs, EMI Robbins Catalog, Inc., and Sony/ATV Music Publishing LLC. All Rights Reserved. Reprinted by Permission of Hal Leonard Corporation.

"DAY DREAM" by Duke Ellington, Billy Strayhorn, and John Latouche. © 1940, 1941 (Copyrights Renewed) Reservoir Media Management, Inc., Billy Strayhorn Songs, EMI Robbins Catalog, Inc., and Sony/ATV Music Publishing LLC. All Rights Reserved. Used by Permission of Alfred Music.

"THE ECCENTRICITIES OF DAVY CROCKETT," "RED RIDING HOOD REVISITED," "WILLIE THE WEEPER" by Jerome Moross and John Latouche. © 1949 (Renewed) Chappell & Co. & Sony Tunes, Inc. All Rights Reserved. Used by Permission of Alfred Music.

"THE FINE LADIES WALK" (from "The Ballad of Baby Doe") by Douglas Moore and John Latouche. © 1958 (Renewed) Chappell & Co., Inc. All Rights Reserved. Used by Permission of Alfred Music.

"IN BETWEEN," "LULLABY FOR JUNIOR," "MAYBE I SHOULD CHANGE MY WAYS" (from "Beggar's Holiday") by Duke Ellington and John Latouche. © 1947 (Renewed) Chappell & Co., Inc., and Sony/ATV Music Publishing LLC. All Rights Reserved. Reprinted by Permission of Hal Leonard Corporation.

"IN BETWEEN," "LULLABY FOR JUNIOR," "MAYBE I SHOULD CHANGE MY WAYS," "TOOTH AND CLAW" (from "Beggar's Holiday") by Duke Ellington and John Latouche. © 1947 (Renewed) Chappell & Co., Inc. Red Fisher Music Co. Inc., and Duke Ellington Music. All Rights Reserved. Used by Permission of Alfred Music.

"JUST FOR TONIGHT" (from "Polonaise") by Bronislaw Kaper and John Latouche. © 1945 Chappell & Co., Inc. All Rights Reserved. Used by Permission of Alfred Music.

"THE NEXT TIME I CARE (I'LL BE CAREFUL)" by Bronislaw Kaper and John Latouche. © 1945 Chappell Co., Inc. All Rights Reserved. Used by Permission of Alfred Music.

"A NICKEL TO MY NAME" (from "Banjo Eyes") by Vernon Duke and John Latouche. © 1941 EMI Robbins Catalog Inc. All Rights Administered by Sony/ATV Music Publishing LLC. All Rights Reserved. Used by Permission of Alfred Music.

"SILVER SONG" by Douglas Moore and John Latouche. © 1956 (Renewed) Chappell & Co., Inc. All Rights Reserved. Used by Permission of Alfred Music.

"SUMMER IS A COMIN' IN," "THIS IS WHERE I CAME IN" (from "The Lady Comes Across") by Vernon Duke and John Latouche. © 1942 EMI Miller Catalog inc. All Rights Administered by Sony/ATV Music Publishing LLC. All Rights Reserved. Used by Permission of Alfred Music.

"TAKING A CHANCE ON LOVE" by Vernon Duke, John Latouche, and Ted Fetter. © 1940 (Renewed) EMI Miller Catalog Inc. and Taking a Chance on Love Music. All Rights Reserved. Used by Permission of Alfred Music.

INDEX

Note: The abbreviation "JL" indicates John Latouche